MW00527333

HANDBOOK
of
MORAL THEOLOGY

HANDBOOK
of
MORAL THEOLOGY

by

DOMINIC M. PRÜMMER, O.P.

translated from the Latin by
Reverend Gerald W. Shelton, S. T. L.

BENEDICTUS BOOKS
Manchester, NH

BENEDICTUS
BOOKS

Prümmer's *Handbook of Moral Theology* was first published in 1921 by Herder & Co., Freiburg, and in English in 1956 by The Mercier Press Ltd., Cork. The present *Centenary Edition* by Benedictus Books® prefers fidelity to the superb translation of 1956 over modernized diction, and so contains only minimal formatting and editorial changes that do not affect the original content or style. Citations have been added or amended where necessary.

Approbations from the original:
Nihil obstat: Revmus D. Thomas E. Bird, S. T. D., Ph. D., Censor Librorum
Imprimatur: Franciscus, Archiepiscopus Birmingamiensis
Birmingham, December 2, 1955

Scripture quotations are the author's original translations from the Vulgate, with citations included from the Challoner version of the Douay-Rheims Bible, per the imprint of John Murphy Company (Baltimore, 1899).

Printed in the United States of America. All rights reserved.
Front cover art: Cloister of San Marco.
Sermon on the Mount, by Fra Angelico (ca. 1440).
Cover design by Perceptions Studio

Benedictus Books
Box 5284, Manchester, NH 03108
1-800-888-9344
www.PrayBenedictus.com

ISBN 978-1-64413-610-2
eBook ISBN 978-1-64413-611-9
Library of Congress Control Number: 2022935408

first edition

CONTENTS

FOREWORD

In surveying the current climate both within and outside the Church, one is struck with a vision of the collapse of basic moral principle and reasoning. Outside the Church, relativism appears to reign supreme; one only has to view the mainstream media, the decisions of courts around the world, the behavior of governments, and the implosion of basic cultural norms in virtually all nations. Inside the Church, even in long-standing academic institutions, the natural law and the principles upon which moral systems were based appear to have very little influence on the reasoning process and the conclusions reached. Among members of the living Magisterium and within the Church at large, there is a growing consequentialism which appears to be negating the long-standing moral tradition of the Church. The confusion and disagreement among the various members of the hierarchy regarding moral topics as varied as the liceity of different medical injections and the sacramental blessing of same-sex partnerships harkens to the painful reality that, as predicted by Our Lady of Akita, it is now "bishop against bishop and cardinal against cardinal." Furthermore, it seems that many members of the Magisterium do not wish to contradict the wishes or commands of civil authorities, deepening the already serious degree of complicity and apparent compromise of the Church's unchanging doctrine, in exchange for some manner of temporal benefit. This is partially due to the general loss of virtue within the culture and the concomitant intellectual darkening resulting therefrom, leaving many ill-equipped to follow classical lines of reasoning; all of which leads to a consequentialist ethic in which the ends justify the means, and any action is considered good if the outcome is desirable.

At every turn, there appears to be widespread loss of the proper understanding of the three fonts of the moral act, and the necessity that all three must be good in order for the action to be rendered morally good and praiseworthy. The denigration of this principle of the integral good is seen in a variety of areas within the theological science today: some of note would include *communicatio in sacris* with non-Catholics, the use of aborted fetal tissue in the development of healthcare products, the permissibility of those in the state of mortal sin to receive Holy Communion, especially by pro-abortion politicians (and the lack of public correction of those politicians on the part of their pastors), violations of the sixth commandment in relationship to widespread cohabitation among unmarried Catholics, the growing acceptance of same-sex "marriage" and the liturgical blessing of such arrangements, the endorsement of Communism as a morally acceptable form of civil governance, and the emerging phenomena of so-called "transgenderism" and even "transhumanism." By any integrally Catholic standard and generally within the history of humanity, prior generations would have considered all of this to indicate a serious moral collapse within society and within the Church.

Studying the classical sources of morality within Catholic Tradition is the principal means by which to avoid the confusion that is currently plaguing modern society. Fr. Dominic Prümmer's classic *Handbook of Moral Theology* covers the key areas in this discipline, such as the fonts of the human act, the nature of free will, the different kinds of conscience and characteristics of sin, the theological and moral virtues as well as those sins contrary to them, the seven Sacraments and indulgences, and other pertinent considerations as well. Prümmer's text provides a foundation in perennial moral principles and their application in a manner that is generally accessible to most of the lay faithful, rendering it useful even as a "layman's guide" for proper Christian action in the world.

As a professor of theology in the University of Fribourg at the beginning of the twentieth century, Fr. Prümmer's faithfulness to the Thomistic moral tradition sets his work apart as one of the theological handbooks that may still be recommended without reservation. As Modernism slowly crept into the life of the Church over the last century, certain moral manuals began deviating from scholastic principles in the years leading up to the Second Vatican Council, especially in certain areas of the natural law, and instead began to assert practical conclusions which ran contrary to the broader Catholic tradition. As a Dominican theologian and canonist, Prümmer's was one of those manuals which remained faithful to sound Thomistic principles, as well as to the definitive teachings of the Church on every point. His writings—usually the more extensive theological texts in Latin—were used worldwide in seminary training, to such an extent that one might hear before any final exam: "Did you check your answers in Prümmer?" His work was often cited in formal theological discourse, and became a reference for the general moral conversation among priests and academics alike. In sum, Prümmer's *Handbook of Moral Theology* was among the very best within the manual tradition.

While it is true that many Modernists complained about this manual tradition, asserting that it failed to serve adequately in the formation of clergy in the past, this was not the general experience of the faithful, myself being one of them. Having grown up around priests who studied under the manual tradition, those who embraced their intellectual formation always provided great spiritual and moral direction for the faithful. While they may not have had the same degree of depth as the scholars who had done further studies beyond their seminary formation of the individual sources from which the manuals took their principles, these priests did have an overview which provided them with the proper conclusions and basic reasoning in relationship to the application of moral principles. Having been a seminary professor, I can testify to the reality of the limited time that professors very often have in order to cover a tremendous amount of material and information. Most professors would simply either write their own text for the class, which is a form of a manual, or they would choose specific works—often the moral manuals themselves—in order to cover adequately, in the limited time that they had, those things which a priest must know in order to direct the faithful and provide adequate advice within the confines of the confessional.

Making this text available once again will prove to be of great service to the Church, as it not only reclaims a text from our tradition which is greatly beneficial to those who read it, but also increases the wider awareness of such manuals, which itself is necessary today when a majority of Catholics are only aware of those things that have been printed or published in the last fifty years. It is my hope that this Centenary Edition will once again allow Prümmer's *Handbook of Moral Theology* to serve as a source for the faithful and for seminarians, as well as academics who seek a common framework from which to discuss the various moral issues of our day.

Fr. Chad Ripperger, Ph.D.

PREFACE

As a priest and theologian of the first rank, the author of the *Handbook of Moral Theology*, here republished in its Centenary Edition, requires no introduction. Fr. Dominic Prümmer's classic manual first appeared in Latin (Herder: 1921) as a compilation of his copious teaching notes, and the fact that it still remains one of the most incisive and coherent overviews of Catholic moral doctrine ever printed is perhaps best evidenced by its continued circulation, long after its several early editions entered the public domain.

This newly typeset and expanded edition offers a faithful reproduction of Fr. Prümmer's masterful original, taken from Fr. Shelton's approved English translation of 1956, with a few helpful modifications. Cosmetic changes have been made to the layout in order to make the text division clearer and render it more useful to students and instructors. Only the most minimal edits have been made to the body text, including an update to the typography and capitalization standard, relocation of non-Scriptural references to footnotes, and the specification of the author's extensive and multivalent use of "i.e."

Worthy of special attention is our expansion of the critical scholarly apparatus. Among the many hundreds of references made in the *Handbook*, previous English editions were found to contain several annotation errors that had been overlooked. As appropriate for this Centenary Edition, considerable time has therefore been devoted to reviewing every citation, carefully rectifying those that were mismarked or missing, and expanding references accordingly. Citations of Denzinger's *Sources of Catholic Dogma* and the Council of Trent's *Roman Catechism* have been added or amended where necessary or desirable (although without changing the author's original translations), thus enabling contemporary reference to specific page or paragraph numbers from editions currently in print. Finally, the topical Index has been enlarged to include a number of more current terms and moral considerations. The goal of these cautious and painstaking measures has been to allow Fr. Prümmer's original text to shine forth with still greater splendor in this new edition, and we are confident that the author would approve of the result.

A number of moral considerations face us today that could scarcely have been imagined in the 1920s. Nevertheless, good and evil have not changed, and the principles used to discern them remain as clear and timeless as ever. It is hoped that this expanded edition of Fr. Prümmer's classic *Handbook of Moral Theology* will endear him to yet another generation of clergy and laity, in service of our high calling in Christ Jesus.

HOW TO USE THIS HANDBOOK

Particularly for those new to the study of the sacred sciences, a word regarding the efficient use of this manual may be beneficial.

Although certainly readable from beginning to end, Fr. Prummer's *Handbook* is chiefly intended as a theological reference text. As such, readers may prefer to study the work as a systematic course in moral theology by following the Table of Contents, or topically by searching the Index for particular moral subjects.

As a technical work, this edition features a corrected system of running paragraph numeration in the side margin, which designates smaller sections of the body text throughout. While the Table of Contents refers to page numbers in this book, the expanded Alphabetical Index refers to these paragraph numbers for greater precision, and may be employed for rapid reference to specific topics. The author's intratext references (indicated by the designation "no."), whether made in the body text or footnotes, also refer to these paragraph numbers.

PREFACE TO THE

FIRST EDITION

In the sphere of the practical sciences summaries are extremely useful, for it is characteristic of man that no matter how great his diligence in completing his studies he gradually forgets the knowledge he has labored to acquire. Consequently, repetition is so necessary that we may rightly regard it as the mother of his studies. However, the standard manuals which are usually so diffuse are not very suitable for this purpose, which is more easily achieved by summaries whose clarity and brevity prevent such works from being either obscure or verbose. Thus, there exists an eager demand for summaries of moral theology already published. I, myself, have received many and earnest requests to produce a summary of my own manual of moral theology. It is in deference to such requests that I am now publishing this small book written some time ago which, by following the same method, presents in a nutshell the teaching contained in the larger work. It would seem unnecessary to state explicitly what is abundantly clear to everyone already—namely, that no cleric can acquire a sufficient knowledge of moral theology from this summary alone. For even when considering important questions, I have been obliged by the claim of brevity to treat of them less fully by omitting the various proofs, arguments, and examples. My sole intention has been to produce an acceptable *vade mecum* which might prove a faithful companion for the young cleric and help him to prepare easily for the necessary examinations, and which at the same time might provide a refresher course for the older priest—especially the confessor—in the doctrine studied in the schools in his earlier days and so essential for his everyday requirements.

With filial reverence I dedicate this work with all its virtues and failings to our Father, St. Dominic, who seven hundred years ago, entered into the glory of Heaven after a life of apostolic labor.

Author
Fribourg, Switzerland, August 4, the feast of St. Dominic, 1921

SECOND EDITION

Within the space of barely one year, five thousand copies of our *vade mecum* have been sold, ample evidence of the pleasure which it gave and continues to give to many clerics. This is all the more noteworthy in view of the fact that there existed already many excellent works of a similar character written by men of outstanding repute. In this second edition, numbering ten thousand copies, I have tried to expand the teaching without increasing the overall size of the book. In the appendix will be found two recent documents from the Roman Curia which seem useful for the priest's ministry in the confessional. May God again favor the publication of our *vade mecum* with His protection, and may it prove a faithful guide to clerics both in learning and applying their moral theology.

Author
Fribourg, Switzerland, January 6, 1923

PREFACE TO THE
FIFTH EDITION

In this fifth edition I have added the more important replies and declarations of recent date. Some of these could not be inserted in the text by reason of technical difficulties[1]; hence their present position in the appendix. May God grant that this fifth edition redound to His glory and be of benefit to its readers.

Fr. Englebert M. Münch, O.P.
Berlin, October 27, the feast of Christ the King, 1940

---

[1] In the present translation, all these replies and declarations have been incorporated in the text.

INTRODUCTION TO MORAL THEOLOGY

1. DEFINITION OF MORAL THEOLOGY. The words *moral theology* mean nothing more than the theological consideration of human behavior, but as a science it may be defined: *that part of theology which by a series of practical judgments directs human acts toward their supernatural end under the guidance of revelation.*

Moral theology is a genuine *science*, because it derives its conclusions from principles of faith and reason; it is a science which *directs* and not merely describes human acts. This direction is completely objective and is based on the formation of practical judgments; it is therefore to be distinguished from the subjective guidance of conscience. It has for its purpose the attainment by man of his supernatural end.

2. METHOD. Three methods are used in this science: 1) the *scholastic* or *speculative* method, which considers carefully the various moral truths, proving and defending them against their adversaries but without ignoring completely their practical application; 2) the *casuistic* method, which is chiefly concerned with passing judgment on individual moral cases; 3) the *ascetical* method, which has for its chief subject the practice of the virtues as the means of achieving Christian perfection. The best method is one which makes use of all three without sacrificing either clarity or brevity.

3. DIVISION. It is the duty of the moral theologian: 1) to pass judgment on all human acts in relation to man's supernatural end; 2) to discuss the external means required for the attainment of this end. These means are the graces of God bountifully bestowed on us chiefly through the Sacraments. Hence moral theology may be divided conveniently into two parts: 1) the morality of human acts; 2) the Sacraments. Accordingly, the following represents a brief survey of this division of moral theology:

PART ONE

1. Man's Ultimate End and His Happiness.
2. Human Acts and the Passions.
3. Law.
4. Conscience.
5. Sin in General.
6. Virtue in General.
7. Faith and Contrary Vices.
8. Hope and Contrary Vices.
9. Charity and Contrary Vices.
10. Prudence and Contrary Vices.
11. Justice and Contrary Vices. An Additional Treatise on Contracts.
12. Fortitude and Contrary Vices.
13. Temperance and Contrary Vices.

PART TWO

1. The Sacraments in General and the Sacramentals.
2. Baptism.
3. Confirmation.
4. Holy Eucharist.
5. Penance, and an Additional Treatise on Censures and Indulgences.
6. Extreme Unction.
7. Holy Orders.
8. Marriage.

PART ONE

The End and Moral Acts of Man

TREATISE I
THE ULTIMATE END OF MAN

4. **DEFINITION AND KINDS OF ENDS.** An end is *"that for the sake of which anything is done,"*[2] or, *that to which the agent's activity is directed.*

The more important kinds are the following:

1. The end *of an action* (the intrinsic and objective end) is that to which the action tends of its very nature directly and immediately: for example, the natural end of an act of almsgiving is the relief of the neighbor's need. The end *of the agent* (the extrinsic and subjective end) is that which the agent himself chooses as the primary or secondary end of his own action. This may but does not necessarily coincide with the end of the action itself. Thus, for example, if by giving alms the agent intends to relieve poverty, both ends are the same; but if the agent performs the act through vanity or the desire to seduce the poor, then the two ends differ. The end of the action is known also as the moral object of the action, and the end of the agent is correspondingly termed the moral motive (end) of the action.

2. The *principal* (or primary) end is that which is chiefly intended by the agent and more than anything else moves him to action; the *secondary* (or accessory) end is that which is not desired for itself alone but impels the agent to act only in conjunction with some other principal end.

3. The *ultimate* end is one which is desired in such a way as not to be referred to any other; the *intermediate* (or proximate) end is one which is desired for its own sake but in dependence on and in reference to a higher end.

Some theologians assert that an intermediate end is not an end in the proper and strict sense of the word but only a means toward an end. This would appear to be a question of terminology.

There seems no reason to deny that an intermediate end possesses the strict character of an end, provided that it be desired for its own sake and not as a mere instrument.

5. **NOTE.** *a)* The principal end *may* be also the ultimate end, but not necessarily; e.g., the ultimate end of all the actions of the upright man is God, but the principal end of one of his actions could be a created thing.

b) The end and the good are *materially* the same but *formally* different, insofar as the good is something desirable or suited to man's appetites, whereas an end is something to be attained through the use of means.

6. **FIRST PROPOSITION.** *The ultimate end of man is God Himself, so that in all his actions man must direct himself toward God and give Him glory.*

Presupposing the existence of God as a Person and the Creator of the world, it is easy to prove the above statement. Man in common with the rest of creation

---

[2] Aristotle, *Physics,* bk. 2, pt. 3.

must have as his ultimate end the same as that intended by God in His act of Creation. Now the end which God had in view when creating the world could not have been other than Himself; He must be His own end, otherwise He would no longer be infinitely perfect. Therefore, God is the end of all His creation, and all creatures must tend toward this end—namely, they must give glory to God. Irrational creatures glorify God necessarily, rational creatures freely.

Man is bound to give glory to God in all his actions by service and obedience, by love and reverence. Hence the advice of St. Paul: "In eating, in drinking, in all that you do, do everything as for God's glory" (1 Cor 10:31).[3] It is not necessary that man expressly and explicitly intend the glory of God in all his actions; it is sufficient that he elicit an act of charity sometimes and thus virtually direct his actions toward God.

7. SECOND PROPOSITION. *a) Man finds his happiness in the attainment of his ultimate end; b) the more perfect his attainment of this end, the greater his happiness; c) man does not and could not find happiness in anything else.*

Proof. a) Happiness may be aptly defined as *the permanent (namely, indefinite) possession of perfect good which completely satisfies all man's desires.* Now this possession of perfect good is realized in the attainment of man's ultimate end, i.e. God. Therefore, human happiness consists in the attainment of the ultimate end. Let us consider the major of this argument. Perfect happiness requires: *i)* a permanent or *indefinite* possession of goodness, since happiness ceases once the good is lost or could be lost; *ii)* the possession of *perfect* good which satisfies completely all man's desires, because the object of his desires is universal goodness and therefore any imperfect good is bound to leave man dissatisfied. The minor of the argument should be evident from the following: God is man's ultimate end, as proved already; He is infinitely perfect, and once united to Him man can never be separated from Him. This union with God as man's ultimate end is effected through knowledge and love.

b) The second part of the proposition is easily proved. The more perfect man's union with God Who is both infinitely perfect and happy, the more perfect and happy does he himself become, in the same way that the nearer one approaches to a warm and blazing fire, so much the greater heat and light does one receive. And thus it follows that the blessed in Heaven do not enjoy the same amount of happiness. "There are many dwelling places in My Father's house" (Jn 14:2). Therefore, although all the blessed see God, the perfection of their vision varies.

c) The third part of the proposition is denied by rationalists both past and present who place man's happiness in pleasure (Epicureans), or in virtue and the resigned acceptance of pain (Stoics), or in other forms of created things. No useful purpose would be served in listing all these false opinions concerning man's final

---

[3] Editor's note: Scripture references offered throughout this book are the translator's original renderings from the Latin Vulgate. Citations correspond to the Douay-Rheims Bible numeration.

happiness, since there is no created good which is perfect in every respect and which endures forever. Therefore, such things cannot constitute the true happiness of man, as is evident from the definition of happiness. St. Bernard has said wisely: "The rational soul, while it may occupy itself with other things, cannot be satisfied by them."

8. **THIRD PROPOSITION.** *The ultimate end of man (viz. perfect happiness) cannot be attained without supernatural grace which is given in sufficient degree to every man through the Redemption of Christ.*

Proof. The ultimate end of man is found in his intimate union with God—i.e., in man's vision of the divine essence. But no created intellect by its own powers and without the aid of supernatural grace can see the essence of God.

The second part of the proposition is evident from the fact that God has implanted in every soul an inescapable longing for true and perfect happiness. Therefore, it would not be fitting for God to refuse sufficient means for the satisfaction of this desire in the attainment of happiness. It must also be remembered that Christ died for everyone and merited grace for all so that they might be saved.

TREATISE II
HUMAN ACTS

NATURE AND KINDS OF HUMAN ACTS

9. **DEFINITION.** Three definitions which do not differ essentially from each other are usually given: *a human act is one which proceeds from the deliberate will of man*; or, *an act which proceeds from the knowledge of the intellect and the impulse of the will*; or, *an act of which man himself is the master.*

Therefore, the following acts are not human:

1. Acts *which proceed from the vegetative faculty* in man, such as nutrition, the pulse of the heart, and so on. For man is not the master of such acts, since they do not proceed from his intellect and will.

2. Acts elicited by *those who are completely mad, by drunkards, by children without the use of their reason, by those under hypnotic influence.* Such acts are not directed by a deliberate will.

3. The so-called *actus primo-primi* which occur so quickly that they precede the use of the reason and will, such as those sudden feelings of anger which arise from an unexpected insult. On the other hand, those acts which are called *secundo-primi* and *secundo-secundi* are human acts, although the former are not so perfect as the latter through lack of complete attention.

4. *Forced* acts which are performed under the influence of external violence. Man is not the master of such acts.

10. NOTE. Although moral acts and human acts are materially the same, they are formally different. An act is human if it proceeds from the deliberate volition of man, whereas it is regarded as a moral act insofar as it does or does not conform to some standard of morality.

11. KINDS.

1. Human acts are either *elicited* or *commanded*, insofar as they proceed directly and immediately from a faculty, or from one faculty under the influence of another faculty or habit. Consequently, every human act is an elicited act, but not always commanded. Thus, belief is an act elicited by the habit of faith, but to believe through love of God is an act commanded by charity.

One must here guard against confusion since authors do not explain these terms in the same way.

2. Human acts are either *internal* or *external*, depending on whether they are completed in the soul of man or are manifested externally. Faith is an internal act; the profession of faith by word or deed is an external act.

Other authors confine internal acts to those acts elicited by the will and regard as external all acts commanded by the will.

3. Human acts are either *good, bad,* or *indifferent*, insofar as they conform or do not conform or are indifferent to right reason. Indifferent acts exist in the abstract but not in the concrete, as will be discussed more fully in no. 55.

4. Human acts are either *natural* or *supernatural*, depending on whether they are elicited by man's natural powers alone (e.g., thinking, speaking) or with the aid of supernatural grace (e.g., an act of contrition).

5. Human acts are either *valid* or *invalid*, according as they possess or lack the conditions required by positive law for producing a certain effect. Baptism with water may be a valid act, but Baptism with wine is always invalid.

INTERNAL PRINCIPLES OF THE HUMAN ACT

The internal principles or efficient causes of the human act are the intellect and the will—or, rather, the act of knowing and the act of willing. Each must be considered in turn.

Art. 1. Knowledge Required for Human Acts

12. KNOWLEDGE—the first efficient cause of a human act—is concerned both with the act itself and with its morality. *Actual* knowledge or attention is required.

To avoid confusion the question will be treated as follows: 1) attention; 2) its contrary, namely, ignorance; 3) the influence of ignorance or inadvertence on human acts.

§ 1. Attention

13. KINDS. Attention may be:

1. *complete* or *incomplete*, according as man attends perfectly or imperfectly to what he is doing. Actions performed when one is sleepy are usually accompanied by incomplete attention.

2. *distinct* or *confused*, depending on whether man recognizes the act and its morality clearly and distinctly, or whether he realizes only in a superficial manner that he is doing good or evil without distinguishing clearly the morality of his act.

3. *actual* or *virtual*, according as man adverts at the moment both to the act and its morality, or adverts incompletely while having the power and the moral obligation to attend to the action. Virtual attention is in fact *physical* inattention since the individual is not attending to his present action, but *morally speaking* the attention and actual intention which he gave to the action on a previous occasion influence the act when it is performed and cause it. Therefore, virtual attention is sufficient for: *a)* the commission of venial sin at least; *b)* the valid administration of the Sacraments; *c)* prayer and the recitation of the Divine Office. Each of these points will be considered more fully later.

§ 2. Definition and Kinds of Ignorance

14. DEFINITION. Ignorance is opposed to knowledge and may be defined as *the lack of necessary knowledge*. It must not be confused with:

1) a *mere lack of knowledge* which the individual has no obligation to possess, or 2) *error* which is the act of judgment proceeding from the habit of ignorance.

15. KINDS.

1. In relation to its *object*, ignorance may be ignorance *of a fact*, or ignorance *of a law*, according as man is ignorant either of some fact (e.g., this person is a heretic), or of some law (e.g., it is unlawful to take part in heretical religious functions). Under ignorance of a law must be included ignorance of the punishment inflicted on transgressors of the law. Such punishment is a sanction attached to the law and thus an integral part of it; consequently, to be ignorant of the punishment is to be partially ignorant of the law itself.

2. In relation to its *subject*, ignorance is either *vincible* or *invincible*, depending on whether it can or cannot be removed by reasonable care such as would be employed by prudent and upright men in similar circumstances.

According to the degree of carelessness, vincible ignorance is either simply vincible, crass, or studied. Ignorance is *simply vincible* when there is some slight lack of care; it is *crass* or *supine* when the carelessness is grave and hardly any attempt is made to remove the ignorance. Such ignorance is either gravely or slightly culpable depending on the gravity of the matter of which one is ignorant; consequently, crass ignorance and gravely culpable ignorance are not always the same. Ignorance is *studied* (*affected*) when it is deliberately fostered by the agent as a means of being excused from sin or of not avoiding some sin.

3. In relation to *the will*, ignorance is either *antecedent* or *consequent*. It is antecedent if it exists prior to the act of the will and is therefore completely involuntary. Ignorance is consequent if it is the direct or indirect result of an act of the will which desires this state. Although consequent and vincible ignorance are in reality one and the same thing, they differ in their meaning: ignorance is regarded as consequent when it is the result of an act of the will, but it is vincible insofar as the will could overcome it.

It is customary to include *concomitant* ignorance which insofar as it exists prior to any act of the will is not desired and therefore, like antecedent ignorance, is invincible; but unlike antecedent ignorance it is not *the cause of the act* done in ignorance. It exists in a man who is of such a frame of mind that even if he possessed the knowledge which at present he lacks he would continue with the action, like a man who having a desire to kill his enemy does so accidentally while actually intending to kill a deer.

§ 3. The Influence of Ignorance and Inadvertence on Human Acts

INTRODUCTORY. Under ignorance we include also inadvertence and forgetfulness. If these are complete they are equivalent to invincible ignorance; if incomplete, they have the same influence on the morality of acts as vincible ignorance. Consequently, the following principles are equally valid for ignorance and for inadvertence.

16. FIRST PRINCIPLE. *Actions which proceed from invincible (antecedent) ignorance are neither voluntary nor imputable.*

The reason for this is that nothing can be willed unless it is previously known. Alexander VIII condemned the following proposition: "Although there is such a thing as invincible ignorance of the law of nature, this, in the state of fallen nature, does not excuse from formal sin anyone acting out of ignorance."[4]

17. SECOND PRINCIPLE. *Vincible ignorance: a) does not destroy the voluntariness of an act, b) but it does diminish the voluntariness, c) unless the ignorance is affected.*

The reason for the first part of the statement is that since vincible ignorance itself is voluntary, so also are the effects which result from it. The proof for the second part is derived from the fact that since at the moment when the act is performed perfect knowledge is lacking the act cannot be perfectly voluntary. Therefore, for example, a confessor giving wrong advice through vincible ignorance sins less gravely than if he were to give the same advice with full knowledge.

---

[4] Henry Denzinger, *The Sources of Catholic Dogma*, 30th ed., trans. Roy J. Deferrari [hereafter DZ] (Boonville: Preserving Christian Publications, 2009), 1292. See also the 1917 Code of Canon Law [hereafter CCL], Can. 2202.

The third part is evident from the fact that affected ignorance usually arises from an evil will inducing this state in order to give itself greater freedom to commit sin.

18. SCHOLIUM 1. THE INADVERTENCE OF THOSE WHO HAVE CONTRACTED HABITS OF SIN. Certain habits, such as those of blasphemy or lying, can become almost second nature to a man so that he performs the acts without adverting to them. In such cases the following distinction must be made: if the person sincerely intends through contrition to abandon his evil habit, then the acts he performs through inadvertence are involuntary and therefore blameless; if the evil habit is not revoked, guilt must be attached to each of the actions since they proceed from a habit which the individual has freely allowed to become deep-rooted. However, in the confessional such habitual sinners should not be tormented by too many questions in an attempt to discover the exact number of individual acts performed. It is quite sufficient for the confessor to inquire how long the penitent has possessed this habit and approximately how many acts were committed each day.

19. SCHOLIUM 2. IGNORANCE OF THE LAWS AND PENALTIES OF THE CHURCH. Although no form of ignorance can excuse from invalidating and incapacitating laws (such as matrimonial impediments or irregularities), unless the contrary is expressly stated,[5] nevertheless the violation of a law of which one is ignorant *through no fault of one's own* is not imputable. The degree of imputability attached to the transgression of a law depends on the culpability of the ignorance.[6] As often as ignorance excuses from *serious fault* a person who transgresses the law, he does not incur any ecclesiastical penalty.[7] The following principles apply to ignorance of ecclesiastical penalties: *a)* ignorance of the penalty alone diminishes but does not destroy the imputability of the delinquency;[8] *b)* studied ignorance does not excuse from any penalty; crass or supine ignorance excuses from the penalties themselves if the law contains the words: *shall have presumed, or dared or acted knowingly, temerariously, of set purpose*, or similar terms; *c)* other forms of ignorance excuse from medicinal penalties (censures) but not from those that are vindictive.[9]

Art. 2. Voluntary Acts

The subject is treated in the following order: 1) nature and kinds of voluntary acts; 2) indirectly voluntary acts; 3) obstacles to the voluntary act.

[5] See CCL, Can. 16, § 1.
[6] See CCL, Can. 2202.
[7] See CCL, Can. 2218, § 2.
[8] See CCL, Can. 2202, § 2.
[9] See CCL, Can. 2229.

§ 1. Nature and Kinds of Voluntary Acts

20. DEFINITION. *A voluntary act or its effect is that which proceeds from an internal source of action accompanied by knowledge of the end sought.*[10]

EXPLANATION. A voluntary act proceeds from an internal source of action—that is to say, from the appetitive faculty of man. Consequently, a voluntary act is not to be confused with: 1) *an act which man is forced to perform* since this proceeds from an external cause of action; 2) *the object willed*, for although the appetitive faculty tends toward this object, it does not produce it. Thus, although rain may be desired by the farmer it is not a voluntary act.

A voluntary act is accompanied by knowledge of the end sought. If the knowledge is intellectual the voluntary act is perfect; if it is sense-knowledge the voluntary act is imperfect. Through lack of knowledge *natural* acts (sleeping, digesting) and *spontaneous* acts (*actus primo-primi*) are not voluntary acts.

21. KINDS. Voluntary acts are classified as follows:

1. Voluntary acts are *necessary* or *free*, according as they are produced by the will freely or necessarily. The desire for happiness and the Beatific Vision are necessary voluntary acts.

2. Voluntary acts are *perfectly* or *imperfectly voluntary*. Acts are perfectly voluntary if they proceed from perfect, intellectual knowledge; they are imperfectly voluntary if they proceed from sense-knowledge. These latter acts are to be found also in brute animals; thus the swallow in building its nest performs an imperfectly voluntary act.

3. Voluntary acts are *absolutely* or *relatively voluntary*, depending on the absence or presence of a certain reluctance while the act is performed; thus, to take unpleasant medicine is a relatively voluntary act.

NOTE. Even this relatively voluntary act is genuinely voluntary in the individual circumstances in which it is performed and therefore is a perfectly moral act. Consequently, when compared with an involuntary act it is usually described as an absolutely voluntary act which is relatively involuntary. Thus, in the example quoted above, an invalid taking bitter medicine performs an absolutely voluntary act which is relatively involuntary.

4. Voluntary acts are willed either *directly* (willed in themselves) or *indirectly* (willed in their cause). An act is directly voluntary if it is an immediate object of the will and desired *in itself*; e.g., a thief directly intends his stealing. An act is indirectly voluntary if the will intends some object necessarily connected with an immediate object. Thus, the act of throwing cargo overboard in order to avoid shipwreck is indirectly voluntary; it is not desired in itself but detested; however, since it is the only means of saving life it is performed.[11]

---

[10] See Thomas Aquinas, *Summa Theologiæ* [hereafter ST], I-II, q. 6, a. 1.

[11] The divisions of voluntary acts as given under no. 21.2–4 are not explained in the same way by everyone. Therefore, care must be taken to avoid confusion.

5. Voluntary acts are either *positively* or *negatively voluntary*, according as acts are performed or acts which ought to be performed are omitted.

22. SCHOLIUM. INVOLUNTARY ACTS. Distinguish carefully between involuntary acts which occur contrary to one's intention, and those acts which are not voluntary insofar as they occur without the agent willing them. Actions which are done in concomitant ignorance are not voluntary, and yet they are not involuntary.

§ 2. Indirectly Voluntary Acts

23. PRINCIPLE. *It is lawful to perform an act in spite of a foreseen evil effect, provided that:*

1. *the act is good in itself or at least indifferent;*

2. *its immediate effect is good;*

3. *the intention of the agent is good;*

4. *the agent has a proportionately grave reason for acting.*

The same principle may be expressed in this way: *four conditions have to be verified before the agent is permitted to allow an indirectly voluntary act which is evil: 1) the cause of the evil act is in itself good or indifferent; 2) the immediate effect is good; 3) the agent's purpose is good; 4) there exists a proportionately grave reason.*

EXPLANATION. 1. First and foremost it is essential that the act which produces the evil effect be good in itself or at least indifferent. Thus, one is never allowed to do acts which are themselves evil (lying, blasphemy, fornication) even though an excellent result is expected to follow from them. In practice it is possible to decide whether an act is good in itself or indifferent by asking *whether the agent has the right (absolutely speaking) to perform such an act.* For example, an innkeeper has the right (absolutely speaking) to offer wine for sale; consequently, this act is good or at least indifferent even though it happens to be connected with the sin of drunkenness; on the other hand, no one has the right to kill directly an innocent person, and therefore the action of a doctor in directly procuring an abortion is intrinsically evil.

2. It is also necessary that *the immediate effect of the act be good*—that is to say, the evil effect must come after and not before the good effect. Let us not do evil that good may come (see Rom 3:8). This condition does not differ greatly from the first. For if the immediate effect of the act is evil, the act itself must also be evil.

3. *The agent must have a good intention.* Although a good intention does not justify the use of evil means, nevertheless an evil intention debases everything, including the means taken to achieve it.

4. *The agent must have a proportionately grave reason for acting and permitting the evil effect,* which though not intended by the agent remains a *material* sin and frequently engenders a grave risk of formal sin. Material sin or the danger of formal sin cannot be permitted without a proportionately grave reason. In this matter the following should be taken as the general rule:

24. 1. the greater the evil that is indirectly willed,

    2. the closer the union between the act and its evil effect,

    3. the greater the certainty that the evil effect will ensue,

    4. the greater the agent's obligation by reason of his position to prevent the evil effect,

so much the more serious must be his reason for permitting the evil effect.

§ 3. Obstacles to the Voluntary Act

25. INTRODUCTORY. As will be evident from previous paragraphs, the voluntary act has two internal causes: intellectual knowledge and voluntary impulse. Therefore, whatever destroys or diminishes either of these destroys or diminishes the voluntariness of man's acts. These so-called obstacles to the voluntary act are six in number—ignorance, violence, fear, passion, habit, certain pathological states of the body. Each will be considered in turn, with the exception of ignorance about which enough has been said already.[12]

1. Violence

26. DEFINITION. *Violence (coercion, force) is that which proceeds from some agent extrinsic to the sufferer whose will is totally opposed to it.* Thus, two things are required for violence: 1) an external agent, and 2) resistance on the part of the sufferer. Consequently, no one can inflict violence on himself since he cannot be an external agent in reference to himself.

27. PRINCIPLE. *Violence can affect external acts only, not the internal acts of the will.* If it were possible to force an internal act from the will, such an act would both proceed and not proceed from the will; it would be voluntary insofar as it was elicited by the will, and not voluntary insofar as the violence was being resisted by the will with all its strength.

External acts, such as walking or touch, can be forced since they are performed by external organs.

COROLLARY. Internal acts are morally imputable no matter how much violence man has to endure; external acts performed under the influence of violence are not imputed, provided that the individual withhold his consent internally.[13]

2. Fear

28. DEFINITION. Fear is defined as *the shrinking of the mind from some impending or future evil.* The evil which produces this state of mental fear is not yet present but is threatening or foreseen in the future and is troublesome; present evil causes sorrow, not fear.

---

[12] See nos. 16–19.
[13] See CCL, Can. 2205.

29. KINDS. Among the many classifications of fear the following seem the more important.

1. Fear is *intrinsic* when its cause is internal to man or is some natural agent, e.g., sickness, plague, storm, and so on. Fear is said to be *extrinsic* when its cause is a free agent distinct from the sufferer, e.g., another human being, the devil. Some authors prefer to regard all fear as extrinsic, even when it results from natural causes, such as fear caused by a storm.

2. Fear is *grave* or *slight*, according as the impending danger is grave or slight. Grave fear requires the presence of an evil which is grave, closely imminent, and difficult to avoid. If only one of these conditions is not verified, the fear is said to be slight. Grave fear is either absolutely grave, namely, grave for all men, or relatively grave, grave for a certain individual. *Reverential* fear in a subject who stands in fear of the displeasure and anger of his superior is usually regarded as slight fear. However, if the subject feared the infliction of grave punishment as the result of his superior's displeasure this reverential fear could become grave.

3. Fear is *just* if it is inflicted in a fitting manner by a person with lawful authority; otherwise it is *unjust*.

4. *Antecedent* fear is that which exists prior to an act and causes it. *Concomitant* fear is that which accompanies an act and, far from causing it, would rather prevent it, if this were possible. *Through* antecedent fear the traveler hands over his money to the highwayman, who accepts the money *in* concomitant fear since he is afraid of being captured and punished.

The Influence of Fear on Human Acts

30. FIRST PRINCIPLE. *Fear which is not sufficiently grave to deprive a person of the use of his reason diminishes but does not destroy the voluntariness of his acts.*

Fear which deprives a person of the use of his reason clearly destroys the voluntariness of any act performed under its influence; no other form of fear has the same effect since the two causes of a voluntary act—knowledge and free will—are unimpaired. However, the act is less voluntary since it would not be performed if the fear were absent.

31. SECOND PRINCIPLE. *Grave fear or, as is commonly said, grave inconvenience excuse a man from compliance with positive law (whether human or divine).*

The reason is that legislators are presumed to be unwilling to oblige their subjects to comply with these laws in such great difficulties. Sometimes, however, even grave inconvenience does not excuse a man from complying with positive law, when the common good or the interests of religion would otherwise be endangered; thus, for example, a soldier must remain at his post even though he fears death.

32. **THIRD PRINCIPLE.** *a) The unjust use of grave fear does not of itself invalidate contracts made under its influence; b) such contracts can be rescinded. c) However, positive law declares that certain contracts (or acts) made under the influence of grave fear are of their nature invalid.*[14]

The reason for the first part of the principle is that since fear does not vitiate a voluntary act, it does not prevent the consent necessary for the validity of a contract.

With regard to the second part, it is evident that a person who makes a contract while under the influence of grave fear unjustly inflicted is suffering an injury from which he is free to escape by rescission of the contract.[15]

For sufficient reasons certain contracts or acts resulting from the unjust infliction of grave fear are rendered invalid by positive law, such as entrance or admission into a novitiate, religious profession, betrothal, marriage, vows, election of a prelate, absolution from censures, renunciation of benefices and ecclesiastical offices.

3. Passion or Concupiscence

33. **DEFINITION AND KINDS.** Among the many meanings given to the term *passion* those to be found in the works of Aristotle and Plato are outstanding.

According to Aristotle, *passion is a movement in the sense appetite caused by the imaginative awareness of the presence of good or evil and productive of some change in the body.*

Aristotle speaks of *a movement,* namely, some action or operation. It is a movement *in the sense appetite,* because neither the intellect nor the will but the sense appetite (either the concupiscible or the irascible appetite) elicits these acts. This movement is caused *by the imaginative awareness of good or evil,* since passions are produced by the imagination's vivid realization of the presence of good or evil. Passions *produce some change in the body* since they have a strong reaction on the bodily organism—for example, by increasing the heartbeat, by making the face flushed or pale, and so on.

Passions in the Aristotelian sense of the word are entirely sense operations, neither good nor bad, and are to be found in every man, even in Christ Himself.

According to Plato, the Stoics, and many modern writers *the passions are inordinate acts or habits of the sense appetite.* They are therefore regarded as diseases of the mind and incline man toward sin. It would be preferable to call such passions vices.

34. *Concupiscence* may be understood in one of three ways: 1) As identical with the passions in general; 2) as one form of passion, namely *desire;* 3) as an evil inclination of the lower or higher appetite in man vitiated by original sin.

Following Aristotle, St. Thomas distinguished eleven different kinds of passion in man—six belonging to the concupiscible appetite, five to the irascible appetite:[16]

---

[14] See CCL, Can. 103, § 2.

[15] See CCL, Can. 1684.

[16] See ST, I-II, q. 25.

IN THE CONCUPISCIBLE APPETITE

in reference to good	in reference to evil
love	hatred
desire	aversion
joy	sorrow

IN THE IRASCIBLE APPETITE

in reference to good	in reference to evil
hope	courage
despair	fear
	anger

The Influence of the Passions on Voluntary Acts

35. **INTRODUCTORY.** The passions may exist *before* or *after* the operation of the will and intellect. Antecedent passion arises from causes that are independent of the human will, e.g., from the state of the body, from a sudden and unexpected disturbance. Consequent passion is caused in one of two ways: either the desire of the will for some object is so strong that it excites corresponding movements in the sense appetite, or the will may deliberately decide to excite within man some passion which it uses in order to act more promptly and vigorously.

36. **FIRST PRINCIPLE.** *Antecedent passion diminishes the voluntariness of acts performed under its influence; if it is sufficiently violent to prevent the use of reason, the acts are completely involuntary.*

The reason for the first part of the principle is that this form of passion clouds the human intellect to some extent and provides a powerful impulse toward the act—as is evident, for example, in those acts committed as the result of the inordinate passions of anger, love, and so on. Sins committed under the influence of antecedent passion are called *sins of human frailty*. The second part of the principle is self-evident.

37. **SECOND PRINCIPLE.** *Consequent passion which is deliberately fostered by the will increases the voluntary character of any act performed under its influence; consequent passion which results from the vehemence of the will's desire for some object does not increase the voluntariness of an act but is a sign of greater power in the will.*

In reference to the first part of the principle it must be noted that a man who acts as the result of such passion not only wills the act perfectly but also encourages the sense appetite to help it in its action through means of some passion.

With regard to the second part of the principle, if the will has sufficient strength not merely to move the soul but also to overflow into the sense appetite, evidently it must be extremely powerful.

38. **SCHOLIUM. THE INFLUENCE OF HABIT ON A VOLUNTARY ACT.** What has been said about the influence of the passions on a voluntary act is almost equally applicable to the

influence of human habits. A habit is nothing more than a constant inclination produced by repeated acts toward the performance of similar acts. A *voluntary* habit, that is, one which is not deliberately checked, increases voluntariness since it is a most effective help for the performance of an act; it has the same influence on a voluntary act as any consequent passion which is deliberately fostered by the will. An *involuntary* habit either diminishes or destroys voluntariness, for it exerts the same influence on an act as antecedent passion.

4. Certain Pathological States of the Body

INTRODUCTORY. Certain morbid conditions of the body diminish or even destroy knowledge and volition. Here we shall not discuss complete insanity, but only so-called fixed ideas and hysteria which exercise a powerful influence on human acts.

39. FIXED OR COMPULSORY IDEAS (phobias) inflict severe torment on many individuals and may center on an almost indefinite number of objects. Their origin is still completely unknown. Such fixed ideas greatly diminish the voluntariness of acts performed under their influence so that their victims are almost incapable of committing mortal sin. At most there may be venial sin; often there is no sin at all. There is no more effective weapon against such fixed ideas than (apart from prudent care for bodily health) strict obedience to a confessor or director who is prudent, firm, and—above all—patient.

40. HYSTERIA is a special form of nervous disease to be found more frequently in women, although it is sometimes rife in men. The exact nature of this disease is not yet known, although it seems to be *a morbid state of auto-suggestion*. It is of the first importance to remember that this disease is in no way a cause for reproach and that it does not always arise from lust. Consequently, it sometimes happens that even the most pious people suffer from this disease. *The confessor must exercise extreme care and prudence* in dealing with such persons, otherwise both he and they may easily suffer great harm.

41. CHARACTERISTIC SIGNS OR SYMPTOMS OF HYSTERIA:
   a) an exaggerated and unhealthy form of *egotism*;
   b) *excessive fickleness* in the emotions (of happiness and sorrow, love and hatred);
   c) *lack of truth* (systematic lying born of a deluded imagination)—hysterics are liars who are not always conscious of their lies;
   d) *sins against the virtue of temperance* (excessive drinking or impurity).

42. MORALITY OF THE ACTIONS OF HYSTERICS. Although hysteria greatly diminishes voluntariness, normally it does not destroy it. Therefore, hysterics cannot be excused from all blame for their evil acts; sometimes, however, their sins are not mortal, even if contrary to the sixth commandment. Therefore, the confessor must be extremely prudent and cautious in judging their actions.

CURE FOR HYSTERIA. In addition to bodily treatment, hysterics must show perfect obedience toward their confessor or director, and attack with all their strength their abnormal egotism by performing works of charity and by ceasing to think too much about themselves.

MORALITY OF HUMAN ACTS

This chapter is divided into three sections: 1) nature and kinds of morality; 2) the principles or sources of morality; 3) the extent of morality.

Art. 1. Nature and Kinds of Morality

43. THE NATURE OF MORALITY consists in the real relationship existing between human acts and a standard of morality. But there is a wide divergence of opinion regarding the character of this standard.

   Several *non-Catholic* writers have identified the standard of morality with utility, a theory which has appeared under two forms: individual utilitarianism,[17] and social utilitarianism.[18] Others have identified it with right reason so that a man must live in accord with right reason without any regard for personal happiness.[19] A third group maintains that there is no such thing as an objective or fixed standard of morality; each man must use *his own private judgment* (subjectivism, skepticism, moral nihilism).

   Some *Catholics* used to regard as the standard of morality *the free will of God* Who was and still is able to establish a moral code different from that which we now possess;[20] others regarded morality as a purely extrinsic title, or as something identical with freedom or with the intellect's advertence to the goodness of the act.

   Rejecting these different views we maintain that the morality of an act consists in its relationship to a standard of morality, the *ultimate* objective standard being *the eternal law*, and the *proximate* objective standard, human reason. The *subjective* standard is the conscience of the individual.

44. KINDS OF MORALITY. There exist three types of morality: *goodness, evil,* and *moral indifference*. Goodness consists in agreement with the eternal law, evil in divergence from it. Moral indifference is to be found in those acts which considered in themselves and *in the abstract* neither possess nor lack conformity with the eternal law, such as the act of walking. *In the concrete*, however, such indifferent acts do not exist since the circumstances and purpose of a human act will always make it either good or evil, as we shall see more fully in no. 55.

Art. 2. Principles or Sources of Morality

45. INTRODUCTORY. After discussing in the previous section the general character of morality, we must now consider the morality of acts in the concrete; that is to say, we must determine the elements which in any human act are responsible for one type of morality in preference to another. These elements are known as

---

[17] Epicurus, Diderot, Feuerbach.
[18] Francis Bacon, A. Comte, Stuart Mill.
[19] Stoics, Kant.
[20] Occam, Gerson.

the *principles* or *sources* of morality, since in practice they determine the specific moral character of a human act. St. Thomas[21] lists the following as principles or sources of morality:

1) the object; 2) the circumstances of the act; 3) its purpose.

§ 1. The Object

46. DEFINITION. The object under consideration here is not the physical but the moral object and is defined as: that to which the action tends of its very nature *primarily* and *necessarily*. For example, a thief steals five pounds from a church in order to indulge his passion of lust. The moral object of this act is the property of another that is unjustly taken; the circumstances of the act are the commission of theft in a sacred place; its purpose is the satisfaction of the thief's evil passion. The moral object considered in itself is *good* if it is in accord with reason and the eternal law; it is *evil* if it diverges from these standards; it is *indifferent* if it is neither in agreement with nor divergent from these standards, e.g., putting on a white or black garment.

The moral object may be considered in one of two ways: *materially*, when its own relationship to the eternal law is considered; *formally*, insofar as its morality is recognized by the conscience of the agent. An object that is materially evil constitutes material sin; an object that is formally evil constitutes formal sin.

47. PRINCIPLE. *The primary and essential morality of a human act is derived from the object considered in its moral aspect.*

The primary and essential morality of a human act is that which acts as the invariable basis of any additional morality. Now it is the moral object which provides such a foundation. This will be clear from an example. The moral object of adultery is the transgression of another's marriage rights. This moral object remains the invariable basis of the moral character of the act, no matter what further circumstances or motives accompany the act. It cannot be objected that in human acts the first consideration should be given to the motive rather than to the object of the act. For this motive is either the objective purpose of the act itself which is identical with the moral object, or the subjective purpose (the end of the agent) which presupposes moral goodness or evil in the object.

§ 2. The Circumstances

48. DEFINITION. Moral circumstances are those moral conditions which are added to and modify the already existing moral substance of the act, such as the added circumstance of consanguinity in fornication. From the earliest times it has been customary to list seven circumstances contained in the following verse: "Quis, quid, ubi, quibus auxiliis, cur, quomodo, quando."

---

[21] See ST, I-II, q. 18.

49. FIRST PRINCIPLE. *Human acts derive some morality from their circumstances.*

This is admitted by everyone. For just as the value of a physical object is diminished or increased by its attendant circumstances, so the morality of a human act is affected by its circumstances. Furthermore, the Council of Trent in commanding that those circumstances which change the specific character of a sin must be confessed in the Sacrament of Penance clearly presupposes that circumstances do affect the morality of an act.[22]

In order that these circumstances influence the moral character of an act it is necessary: *a)* that they themselves be *morally good or bad,* that is to say that they be in conformity with or lack conformity with human reason; *b)* that their moral character be recognized and intended at least to some extent by the agent.

50. SECOND PRINCIPLE. *Some circumstances alter the morality of an act completely, others affect merely the degree of morality.*

The first part of this principle rests on the fact that some circumstances have a distinctive and specific morality of their own. Thus, the circumstance of the sacred character of stolen goods has in the act of theft its own species of evil, since it is a grievous violation of the virtue of religion, whereas the act of theft itself is a sin against justice.

The reason for the second part of the principle is that some circumstances do not possess a moral character different from that of the object; for example, taking away something belonging to another is an act of theft which possesses its own evil character, and the amount stolen is a circumstance which aggravates the evil but does not offend against any other virtue apart from justice.

51. KINDS OF MORAL CIRCUMSTANCES.

1. Circumstances are distinguished into those which alter the morality of an act and those which do not.

2. Circumstances which alter the morality of an act are further subdivided into those which change the *moral species* of the act by offending against different virtues, and those which change the *theological species* of the act by converting what was venially sinful into something grievously sinful; e.g., a light theft is a venial sin, a great theft is a mortal sin.

3. Circumstances which do not alter the (moral) species of an act either *aggravate* or *diminish* the degree of morality, insofar as they increase or diminish the moral evil of an act. Aggravating circumstances are further divided into those which *a)* *slightly, b) notably,* or *c) indefinitely* aggravate the morality of an act. The latter are those which change venial sin into mortal sin, and thus are identical with those which change the theological species of an act.

---

[22] See also "The Qualities of Confession" in the *Catechism of the Council of Trent.* Citations from its English critical edition are included herein from the *Tradivox Catholic Catechism Index* [hereafter TCCI] (Manchester: Sophia Institute Press, 2022).

§ 3. The End or Motive

Our discussion is confined to the subjective end or end intended by the agent; we shall not consider the end of the act itself since this is identical with the moral object already discussed in no. 46ff.

52. **FIRST PRINCIPLE.** *The moral character of an act depends also on the motive of the agent (the subjective end).*

The reason for this is that the end or motive of the agent may have its own moral character in reference to the eternal law and right reason, by being opposed or conformed to them.

53. **SECOND PRINCIPLE.** *The motive of the agent a) may change an indifferent act in the abstract into a good or evil act; b) may increase or diminish the goodness of an act, and even make it evil; c) may increase or diminish the evil of an act; d) but it is never able to make an evil act good.*

With regard to *a)*: walking if viewed in the abstract is morally indifferent, but if performed for a good motive, e.g., from obedience, it is morally good, whereas if it is done from an evil motive, e.g., from a desire to satisfy a blameworthy curiosity, it becomes morally evil.

With regard to *b)*: the object of the act of almsgiving is good and its goodness is increased if the act is done in fulfillment of a vow. If vanity enters as a partial motive, the act loses some of its goodness, whereas if vanity becomes the chief motive, the act is evil. Some theologians used to teach that an evil motive always vitiated the entire goodness of an act, but today it is generally admitted that if the evil motive is a partial and incomplete motive, it is certainly evil in itself but nevertheless there remains some goodness in an act whose object is good. For if a slight evil in the motive were sufficient to destroy completely the goodness of an act which was good in other respects, could we ever perform a good act? Therefore, it must be admitted that one and the same act may be good under one aspect, bad under another—that is to say, good by reason of its object, bad by reason of its circumstances or motive, provided however that the evil motive is not the adequate cause of the act.

With regard to *c)*: the man who steals to obtain sufficient money to get drunk sins more grievously than if he were only to steal, whereas the man who steals in order to be able to give alms sins less grievously, although the sin remains because of the evil in the act arising from the evil nature of the moral object.

With regard to *d)*: a good motive can never justify the use of evil means. And thus St. Paul gives the warning: Let us not do evil that there may come good (see Rom 3:8). The intrinsic reason for this is that the evil character of the act arising from the object is so opposed to right reason that it cannot be altered by any external motive.

54. **THIRD PRINCIPLE.** *In all his actions man must put before himself some good motive which is related to God at least implicitly; under no circumstances may he act for pleasure alone.*

In this principle lies the answer to the question: What sort of intention does the agent require in order that his acts may be good? The doctrine proposed steers a middle course between two extremes, one of which demands from man an *actual* or at least *virtual* reference of his acts to God,[23] the other maintaining that for an act to be good all that is necessary is that nothing be done contrary to right reason, without any other intention being necessary. That at least an implicit reference of human acts to God is necessary follows from those condemned propositions in which it is asserted that it is perfectly lawful to act for pleasure alone: "There is no sin in eating and drinking to excess merely for the sake of pleasure, provided that there is no injury to health, since it is lawful for the natural appetite to take enjoyment in its own acts."[24] St. Thomas had already taught: "Pleasure exists for the sake of action and not vice-versa."[25] There is certainly nothing wrong in experiencing pleasure while acting but it is never good to act for pleasure alone. An actual or virtual reference of human acts to God cannot be required since nowhere is there to be found such a rigid precept.

In practice men should be advised to refer their acts to God as frequently as possible, but those who follow right reason in all their acts must be considered to possess a right intention.

Art. 3. The Extent of Morality

After considering the indifference of human acts we shall turn to the morality of external acts and their effects.

§ 1. Indifferent Acts

INTRODUCTORY. We intend to consider human acts and not those acts which, although performed by men, are not human, in order to determine their morality but not their supernatural merit.

55. PRINCIPLE. *Some human acts when viewed in the abstract are indifferent, but in the concrete such acts are never indifferent.*

Human acts viewed in the abstract derive their moral character from the object alone. But many of those objects are completely indifferent, such as walking, painting, eating.

The second part of the principle derives its truth from the fact that human acts in the concrete are always done for a motive. If this motive is good (presupposing that the object of the act is good) then the act is good; if the motive is bad, so also is the act.

56. SCHOLIUM. THE EFFECT OF THIS TEACHING ON THE ASCETICAL LIFE. The principle that every deliberate act is either good or bad should prove a *comfort* and a *spur* to men of good will. For if no act is morally indifferent, then a man who follows right reason even in the smallest matters is performing good acts, which are also meritorious if he is in the state of sanctifying grace — a most consoling doctrine.

[23] Du Bay, Jansen.
[24] DZ 1158.
[25] Thomas Aquinas, *Summa Contra Gentiles*, bk. 3, chap. 26.

And thus are excluded those so-called imperfections which are neither good nor bad. In this matter special attention is usually given to voluntary omissions of a good act, such as neglecting to hear Mass on weekdays. If such omissions have a sufficient reason, they are good acts; otherwise, they are bad. In itself, therefore, non-attendance at such Masses without sufficient reason would constitute sufficient matter for confession, but since in practice it is difficult to decide whether there was sufficient reason or not, modern theologians rightly and commonly teach that so-called imperfections are not sufficient matter for absolution. However, it would act as a spur to the performance of good acts if these imperfections were frequently thought of as being truly sinful, even though of a venial character.

§ 2. The Morality of External Acts and Their Effects

57. PRINCIPLE. *An external act increases the goodness or evil of the internal act in an accidental manner.*

An external act of itself does not add to the moral goodness or evil of the internal act, since it does not possess its own distinct freedom but derives all the freedom it possesses from the internal act of the will of which it is the completion. Therefore, the external act considered by itself does not have any moral character of its own and consequently cannot of itself increase or diminish the morality of the internal act. Thus, in Scripture a perfect act of willing is praised or condemned just as much as if it had been completed externally, so that Abraham received the same reward for being ready to sacrifice his son as he would have done if he had completed the sacrifice.

But an external act increases the goodness or evil of the internal act accidentally, because of the many circumstances which are added to the internal act. Thus, for instance, due to the influence of the external act the will may desire the object with greater *intensity* and over a *longer period of time*. The external act may give rise to scandal, encouragement to sin, excommunication, the obligation to restitution, and so on. Since this is so, the external act of sinning must be made known in confession, for even though of itself it does not increase the malice of the sin the confessor is unable to pass a balanced judgment on the state and obligations of the penitent unless he knows whether the sin was only internal or also external.

58. ANY EFFECT of a voluntary act that is foreseen and to some extent intended increases the goodness or evil of the act (whether the effect follows necessarily or accidentally). For the greater the goodness or evil of the will from which the act proceeds, so much the greater is the goodness or evil of the act itself. Now the will of a man who performs an act foreseeing and intending the good or evil effects of that act is better or worse than if he had not foreseen and intended such effects. For this added degree of morality, it is not necessary that the effects be directly intended; it is sufficient if they are indirectly intended, that is to say, if they could

and ought to be foreseen. In this connection one should recall what has been said already in no. 23 concerning acts that are indirectly voluntary.

MERIT IN HUMAN ACTS

59. DEFINITION. *Merit* understood in its strict sense is *that property of a good act which makes it deserving of reward*; in the concrete *it is the good act itself as deserving reward*.

KINDS. 1. Merit is twofold—*condign* and *congruous*. Condign merit is found in those good acts for which a reward is due in justice or at least because of some previous promise. Congruous merit is based on a certain equity or suitability; e.g., a faithful servant has a strict claim in justice to a fixed salary (condign merit), but it is only fitting that he receive certain gifts from his master (congruous merit).

2. Both forms of merit already mentioned can exist in a perfect and less perfect form. *Perfect* condign merit, or that which is based on strict justice, is an act which is equivalent to the reward obtained which therefore cannot be withheld without a manifest violation of justice. Such merit exists in the case of a just salary agreed upon as due to the conscientious worker. In the supernatural order, only the actions of the God-Man possessed this form of condign merit. Condign merit *in its less perfect form* is an act which to some extent is equivalent to the reward received. It is in this way that man merits eternal life because there does exist a certain equality between eternal life and acts based on supernatural grace. *Perfect* congruous merit rests on a genuine equity between the act and its reward; it is thus that a man in the state of grace who is a friend of God can merit the conversion of another. *In its less perfect form* congruous merit is a form of request; thus, a man can merit or rather request the grace of final perseverance.

60. SIX CONDITIONS MUST BE VERIFIED FOR THE EXISTENCE OF SUPERNATURAL MERIT:

1. The work or act performed must be free.

2. The work must be morally good.

3. The work must be done from a desire to please the reward-giver, i.e. God; that is to say, there must be at least some influence of charity.

4. The agent must be a wayfarer in this life.

5. The agent must be in the state of sanctifying grace.

6. There must exist a divine promise.

61. THE OBJECT of merit is that which can be merited in the sight of God by man's acts.

1. A man in the state of grace can perform acts that possess *condign merit* in reference to: *a)* eternal life, and *b)* an increase of grace and glory.[26] A man in the state of mortal sin cannot perform any act that possesses condign merit or perfect congruous merit.

2. Understanding merit as *congruous merit in its less perfect form*, a man *in the state of grace* can merit: *a)* final perseverance, *b)* restoration to divine friendship after a

---

[26] See Council of Trent, Session 6, Can. 32. See also TCCI 7:325ff.

mortal sin that may be committed in the future. Understanding merit *as congruous merit in its perfect form*, man is able to merit: *a*) temporal goods, *b*) actual graces, and the conversion of others.

3. The saying: "God does not deny grace to anyone doing as much as lies in his own power" must be understood in a limited sense of a person doing what is within his power with the help of actual grace.

TREATISE III
LAW

INTRODUCTORY. After the consideration of human acts, we must turn our attention to the standards that determine their moral character. These standards are the eternal law and other just laws together with the individual conscience which applies them. Consequently, we must first consider law, then conscience. This treatise on law which has the same importance in moral theology as in ecclesiastical and civil law is divided into three chapters: 1) Definition and Kinds of Law in General; 2) Divine Law; 3) Human Law.

DEFINITIONS AND KINDS OF LAW

62. DEFINITION. *Law is an ordinance of reason for the common good promulgated by the person who has care of the community.*

Ordinance of reason: whereby is signified the proper cause of law, that is, the practical reason. Notice, however, that not every ordinance of reason is a law, for even a precept[27] and a counsel may be termed ordinances of reason. For such an ordinance to be a law it is required (in addition to the points mentioned below): *a*) that it be efficacious and binding; *b*) that it be firm, stable, and enduring.

For the common good: this is the necessary purpose of any law. Therefore, the precepts of tyrants which are not directed to the welfare of society cannot be regarded as genuine laws. The common good may be promoted by law either *directly*—by ensuring that the citizens live together in peace—or *indirectly*, insofar as certain laws (or privileges) have as their first result the welfare of the individual and promote the well-being of society through the welfare of the individual.

By the person who has care of the community: these words indicate the author of law or the legislator who is no other than he who has care of a society and this a *perfect* society. Accordingly, the father of a family, for example, has no power to make laws in the strict sense of the word. *Promulgated*: because no ordinance of a superior can *actually* oblige his subjects unless it is sufficiently revealed to them.

---

[27] Even though a precept may impose as grave an obligation as law itself, nevertheless there are many differences between the two: *a*) the lawgiver must possess jurisdiction over his subjects, but this is not necessary for imposing precepts; *b*) the law has the common good as its motive, whereas a precept is frequently directed to the good of the individual; *c*) a law of its very nature is permanent, a precept temporary.

According to the more probable opinion, promulgation is not part of the essence of law but is required for its integrity.

63. KINDS. Space does not permit a complete catalogue of the different forms of law, but the more important divisions are the following:

1. In respect of its *author*, law is either *divine* or *human* depending on whether it is instituted by God or by man. Divine law is further subdivided into *eternal*, *natural*, and *positive* law: the eternal law is identical with the eternal plan of the divine wisdom, natural law is that which has been imprinted on rational creatures, and positive divine law is that law which has been promulgated explicitly by God in the Old and New Testaments.

2. In respect of its *object*, law is either *affirmative* or *negative*, insofar as it either enjoins or forbids some action: thus, "honor thy parents" is an affirmative law; "thou shalt not steal" is a negative law. *Affirmative laws are always obligatory but they do not bind to continuous fulfillment,* i.e., they do not oblige their subjects to perform the prescribed acts every moment of the day; *negative laws are likewise always binding but in addition they never cease to bind,* i.e., they oblige their subjects to refrain from forbidden acts on all occasions.

DIVINE LAW

Divine law is threefold in character: eternal, natural, and positive. Each must be considered in turn.

Art. 1. The Eternal Law

64. DEFINITION. Two definitions of the eternal law are usually given, those of St. Augustine and of St. Thomas. The definition proposed by St. Augustine reads: "*The eternal law is the divine reason or (and) the will of God commanding the preservation of the natural law and forbidding its disturbance.*"[28] St. Thomas defines the same law as follows: "*The eternal law ... is the plan flowing from God's wisdom directing all acts and movements.*"[29]

The eternal law embraces both the physical and the moral orders of the universe, but it is chiefly concerned with the moral order. It is the fount of all laws which cease to be laws once they contradict the eternal law.

Art. 2. Natural Law

65. DEFINITION. Of all the various definitions given of natural (moral) law the best seems to be that proposed by St. Thomas: "*natural law is nothing else than the rational creature's participation in the eternal law.*"[30] This participation as produced by God is natural law *objectively* considered; as known by man it is natural law *subjectively*

---

[28] Augustine, *Contra Faustum*, bk. 22, no. 27.
[29] ST, I-II, q. 93, a. 1, c.
[30] ST, I-II, q. 91, a. 2, c.

received. It is termed *natural* law because: *a)* man is subject to it from the moment of his birth; *b)* it contains only those precepts which are derived *from the very nature of man*; *c)* it can be grasped by the natural light of man's reason without the aid of divine or human authority.

66. THE EXISTENCE of a natural law is denied not only by all atheists but also by those who refuse to admit the existence of any supreme objective norm of morality; there are also many modern jurists who regard positive law as the only form of law properly so-called. Nevertheless the existence of natural law is absolutely certain: 1) from Sacred Scripture: As for the gentiles, though they have no (Mosaic) law to guide them, there are times when they carry out the precepts of the law unbidden, finding in their own natures a rule to guide them in default of any other rule; and this shows that the obligations of the law are written in their hearts (see Rom 2:14–15); 2) from the words of Leo XIII: "Such is the supreme law of all, the natural law which is imprinted and engraved on the hearts of all men";[31] 3) from the inner testimony of one's own conscience; 4) from the testimony of all races.

67. THE SUBJECTS of natural law are all men, no matter when or where they live. Therefore, even children and the insane are subject to the natural law, and in consequence it is wrong to entice them to transgress it, e.g., by telling lies, even though their transgression is not formal sin since they lack the use of reason.

68. THE OBJECT of the natural law is *the moral order as known by human reason and which has to be observed by man*. There are, however, three types of precepts in the natural law:

a) Primary precepts—the most universal precepts—such as good must be done.

b) Secondary precepts, which are easily recognized by all men, such as the precepts of the Decalogue.

c) Remote conclusions, which are deduced by man's reason with varying degrees of difficulty from the primary and secondary precepts, e.g., direct abortion is always forbidden.

69. THE PROPERTIES of the natural law are: *a)* its *universality*, insofar as it binds all men without exception; *b)* its *immutability*, inasmuch as it cannot be changed within itself; *c)* its *indispensability*, since it does not allow either dispensation in the strict sense of the word or *epikeia* (equity). Scotus and others held that some dispensation from natural law was possible, but such an opinion must be rejected since the natural law is based on the essential character of man's nature which cannot change. Instances brought forward of alleged dispensations in natural law are not dispensations *in the strict sense*. Thus, for example, when God ordered Abraham to kill his son Isaac, He did not dispense him from observing the fifth commandment; on the contrary, the supreme Lord of life at Whose bidding many thousands of men die each day arranged for the

---

[31] Encyclical *Libertas Praestantissimum* (June 20, 1888), no. 8.

cessation of Isaac's life. A fortiori no created authority—neither the Supreme Pontiff nor any civil ruler—can dispense in natural law.[32]

Similarly, epikeia (equity) in the strict sense of the word has no place in the natural law. Epikeia is a favorable interpretation of the mind of the legislator where the law is in some way deficient. But since the natural law has been instituted by the most provident of all legislators it could never be deficient.

70. IGNORANCE of the natural law. a) In respect of the *primary precepts*, ignorance is impossible in any man who has complete use of his reason, since these principles are abundantly clear. b) In respect of the *remote conclusions*, ignorance is possible not only in uneducated persons but also in the learned, so that it is possible to be ignorant that natural law forbids the dissolution of all true marriages. c) In respect of the *secondary precepts*, ignorance is possible *for a time*. St. Augustine thought that a certain woman at Antioch could believe that she ought to commit adultery in order to save her own husband from death.[33] It is also evident from experience that many youths may be ignorant for a time of the evil nature of pollution. Such ignorance, however, cannot persist forever because the secondary precepts of the natural law (and particularly the precepts of the Decalogue) are so easily known that in the act of transgression man's reason soon begins to rebel or at least to doubt. This again is evident from experience.

Art. 3. Divine Positive Law

71. ITS NECESSITY. In addition to divine natural law there is also required divine positive law, 1) because the (secondary) precepts of the natural law can be obscured by evil passion, custom, and example, as is only too manifest from the history of pagan peoples; 2) because the human race is destined for a happiness that is not merely natural but also supernatural, and it is impossible to attain to supernatural happiness without observing supernatural laws made known by God.

THE DIVINE POSITIVE PRECEPTS of the Old Law fell into three classes: a) moral; b) judicial; c) ceremonial: those of the New Law relate to morals (the exercise of the virtues) and especially to the offering of sacrifice and to the reception of the Sacraments.

72. THE SUBJECTS of divine law in the Old Testament were the Jews and their proselytes. In the New Testament all men whether baptized or unbaptized are included under its authority.

A DISPENSATION in divine law can be granted only by the pope when the law is based on a free human act. Thus, it is possible to dispense from a ratified marriage as this is based on the free consent of the parties.

---

[32] How one explains the papal power of dispensing in ratified marriages which do not permit of dissolution by natural law is discussed in the author's *Manuale Theologiæ Moralis* [hereafter MTM], vol. 1, no. 155.

[33] See Augustine, *On the Sermon on the Mount*, bk. 1, chap. 16, no. 50.

HUMAN LAW

This lengthy chapter is divided into nine articles with the following titles:

1) The Author of Human Law; 2) Its Content; 3) Its Subjects; 4) The Promulgation and Acceptance of Human Law; 5) Its Obligation; 6) The Fulfillment of Law; 7) Interpretation of Human Law; 8) Its Cessation (including dispensations, privileges, and customs); 9) Civil Law and Its Consequent Moral Obligation.

Art. 1. The Author of Human Law

73. 1. THE POPE can make laws for the whole Church and for each part of it, and this he can do even independently of bishops or an ecumenical council.

At the present time the pope usually exercises his legislative power through the various Roman Congregations which number eleven: 1) the Holy Office, 2) the Consistorial Congregation, 3) the Congregation of the Discipline of the Sacraments, 4) the Congregation of the Council, 5) the Congregation of Religious, 6) the Congregation for the Propagation of the Faith, 7) the Congregation of Sacred Rites, 8) the Congregation for Ceremonial, 9) the Congregation for Extraordinary Ecclesiastical Affairs, 10) the Congregation of Seminaries and Universities of Study, 11) the Congregation for the Eastern Church.

74. 2. ECUMENICAL COUNCILS enjoy the most extensive power of making laws. Bishops gathered in an ecumenical council are not merely counselors of the pope but are legislators in the true sense of the word, and thus each one of them usually gives his signature to the acts of the council in the form: — "definiens subscripsi." The decrees of the ecumenical council are not laws unless approved by the pope who has the power to change the approved decrees of any ecumenical council, since his power is greater than that of the council. Thus, Pius X altered the Decree *Tametsi* passed by the Council of Trent.

75. 3. BISHOPS can make laws for their own diocese either by themselves, or through plenary or provincial synods, or through diocesan synods. Bishops have been placed by the Holy Spirit "to rule God's Church" (Acts 20:28). In a diocesan synod, the power to make laws belongs to the bishop alone and not to parish priests and other members of the synod; in provincial and plenary synods, the legislative power resides in the body of bishops. A bishop can dispense on his own authority in the statutes of a diocesan synod but not in decrees of provincial and plenary synods, except in individual cases and for a just cause.[34]

The same legislative power is enjoyed by an apostolic administrator permanently appointed,[35] an apostolic vicar and prefect,[36] and by abbots and prelates nullius who are in charge of at least three parishes.[37]

---

[34] See CCL, Can. 291, § 2.
[35] See CCL, Can. 315, § 1.
[36] See CCL, Can. 294, § 1.
[37] See CCL, Can. 319 and 323 § 1.

4. There is little point in mentioning other ecclesiastical legislators since this question belongs to ecclesiastical law rather than to moral theology. However, it is useful to note that an abbess or any other superioress of nuns cannot make laws in the strict sense of the word since they have no ecclesiastical jurisdiction; however, they can issue precepts and orders.

76. LEGISLATIVE POWER POSSESSED BY CIVIL AUTHORITY. Since civil society is a perfect society and independent in its own sphere, it must possess legislative power. This power is today usually exercised by parliaments—at least in those countries which are either republics or constitutional monarchies.

Art. 2. The Content of Human Law

77. THE CONTENT of human law must fulfill three conditions according to St. Thomas: 1) it must be *consistent with religion*, that is, it must not contain anything contrary to divine law; 2) it must be *consistent with discipline*, which is to say that it must conform to natural law; 3) it must *promote human welfare*, that is, it must promote the good of society.[38]

All other conditions mentioned by various authors can easily be reduced to these three, such as that the content of the law must be good, just, possible, useful to the community, suitable to time and place, and so on. There is one important question to be considered—whether human law can control: *a)* internal acts; *b)* heroic acts.

78. INTERNAL ACTS are either: *a) completely internal*, existing in the intellect and will and accompanied by external acts only *accidentally* or not at all, such as meditation, application of Mass, and so on; or *b) partly internal*, insofar as they proceed from the intellect and will but are directed to the production of an external act either of their nature or because of some moral law, such as attention in mental prayer, contrition in the Sacrament of Penance, internal dispositions for the worthy reception of the Easter Communion. Concerning these internal acts there is universal agreement on two points, but one question remains in dispute.

1. It is agreed that acts which are *partly internal* can be commanded by both ecclesiastical and civil law, since it is within the power of human law to decide that acts be performed in a human manner and without deceiving one's neighbor. Now there are certain external acts prescribed by law which could be performed mechanically and in such a way as to deceive others if the internal intention of the agent were lacking. Thus, for example, if a witness compelled by law to take an oath were to withhold the internal intention of taking the oath, he would be acting after the manner of a machine and in such a way as to deceive others.

2. It is also agreed that *civil authority* cannot command acts that are *completely internal* since they make little contribution directly to the end of civil society, which is its temporal welfare.

[38] See ST, I-II, q. 95, a. 3, c.

But it is fiercely disputed whether the Church has the power to command acts that are *completely internal*. St. Thomas seems to deny the existence of such power, and it is certainly denied by Suarez, Schmalzgrueber, Billuart, and Benedict XIV, and St. Alphonsus calls the opinion denying this power the more probable one. In support of the possession of this power we may quote Sylvius, Elbel, Concina, Noldin, Bouquillon, and many other modern theologians.

The negative view rests on the following argument: The Church has the power to command anything which she can judge and punish. But she is incapable of judging and punishing acts which are completely internal since she is not aware of their existence. Therefore ...

On the other hand, the affirmative view is founded on two arguments:

a) the Church has the power to command everything that is necessary for the attainment of its own spiritual end. Now even those acts which are completely internal are necessary for this purpose. Therefore ...

b) in practice the Church does command certain of these acts; thus, she orders parish priests to offer Mass for the people, she ordains the act of contrition for the gaining of indulgences. But is it conceivable that the Church would command something outside her competence? Nowadays, in practice, it is widely admitted by theologians that wholly internal acts can be commanded:

1. by the confessor in the internal forum;

2. when the Church determines or explains divine law, such as in the reception of Easter Communion;

3. when religious superiors impose lawful commands on their subjects bound by the vow of obedience; thus, for example, a religious superior may order a priest who is subject to him to offer Mass for a definite intention.[39]

79. HEROIC ACTS cannot be commanded by human law in the normal course of events since they are far too difficult and for most people almost impossible. Any law which ordinarily ordains excessively difficult or even impossible acts is no longer a useful law and thus ceases to be a law. Nevertheless, there are two occasions when heroic acts may be commanded: 1) if the common good certainly requires such acts, e.g., fighting for one's country; 2) if someone freely obliges himself to perform even heroic acts, such as nursing sisters who freely tend the sick even though they endanger their own lives.

Art. 3. Subjects of Human Law

INTRODUCTORY. It has been pointed out previously that every man is subject to divine natural and positive law, whereas only those lawfully designated by their own legislator are subject to civil law. In the following paragraphs our sole concern is to determine the subjects of ecclesiastical law.

[39] See Sacred Congregation of Religious, May 3, 1914.

80. PRINCIPLE. All *baptized persons—and these alone—who enjoy the habitual use of reason after completing their seventh year are subject to purely ecclesiastical laws.*

1. *All* baptized persons. This is evident from the Council of Trent in the definition on Baptism: "If anyone says that baptized persons are exempt from the written or traditional precepts of the Church so that they are not obliged to observe them unless they freely decide to do so, *anathema sit.*"[40] Consequently, even heretics and schismatics who are validly baptized are subject to the laws of the Catholic Church, and thus are subject to the matrimonial impediments arising from ecclesiastical law. However, in certain circumstances they are exempted either explicitly or tacitly from observing such laws. Thus, for example, in the *Ne Temere* Decree, Pius X expressly exempts heretics from the obligation of contracting marriage in the presence of their parish priest, insofar as this affects the validity of the Sacrament. In the opinion of several theologians the Church *tacitly* exempts heretics and schismatics born and educated outside the Catholic Church from the laws of fasting, from assistance at Mass, and so on, and from other precepts *relating to the sanctification of the individual.*

2. *Only* baptized persons … because those unbaptized cannot be subject to purely ecclesiastical laws since they are not members of the Church. But they may be subjected *incidentally* through contracting a relationship with a baptized person; thus, for example, a pagan marrying a Catholic must observe the ecclesiastical law regarding the impediment of disparity of worship.

3. *Enjoying the habitual use of reason* … Consequently, lunatics and children are not subjects of ecclesiastical law and thus, for example, may lawfully eat meat on Friday. Sometimes in addition to the mere use of reason there is required a further development in man, as, for example, in the law of fasting.

4. *After completing their seventh year* … So even if a child attains to the use of reason before the age of seven it would not be obliged by purely ecclesiastical laws, as will be discussed later.

Because of peculiar difficulties special consideration must be given to the position of children and of those below the age of puberty, of the legislator himself, of strangers, and those of no fixed abode.

§ 1. Children and Those below the Age of Puberty

DEFINITIONS. Before the completion of his seventh year man is *an infant* or child; from the age of seven until he attains to legal puberty—for boys, the completion of their fourteenth year; for girls, the completion of their twelfth year—he is called in canonical language *impuber*; until the completion of his twenty-first year he is in his *minority* and afterward attains his *majority*.

---

[40] Council of Trent, Session 7, "On Baptism," Can. 8. See also CCL, Can. 12, and TCCI 7:131ff.

81. **FIRST PRINCIPLE.** *Children are not subject to purely human laws, even though they have already attained to the use of their reason.*

Today this opinion is regarded as certain and is found in the Code: "Such persons are not subject to purely ecclesiastical laws ... who have not yet completed their seventh year even though they enjoy the use of reason, unless the law expressly states otherwise."[41] The reason is that "the legislator has regard for what is normal and happens in the majority of cases."[42] Consequently if in one instance a child attains to the use of reason before the age of seven, the legislator does not intend (generally speaking) to subject such a child to his laws.

NOTE. Precepts commanding the confession of mortal sin and the reception of Holy Communion are divine precepts and not merely ecclesiastical. Consequently, a child who is certainly conscious of having committed mortal sin is bound to confess it even before the age of seven.

82. **SECOND PRINCIPLE.** *Persons below the age of puberty are subject to those human laws suited to their condition, provided they are not granted a special exemption by customary or written law.*

Such persons are considered to possess sufficient habitual use of their reason. However, there are certain ecclesiastical and civil laws to which they are not subject—e.g., the law of fasting. Furthermore, it is laid down in the Code: "Persons below the age of puberty are excused from penalties that are incurred ipso facto, and they should be punished with disciplinary chastisement rather than by censures and other more severe vindictive penalties."[43]

§ 2. The Legislator as Subject to His Own Law

83. INTRODUCTORY. Two distinctions must first be noted:

1. Law has a twofold power: preceptive insofar as it urges man to observe the law, and coactive insofar as it punishes transgressors.

2. The legislator is either an *individual*, such as the pope or a bishop, or a *legislative assembly*, such as a provincial synod or a parliament.

FIRST PRINCIPLE. *Each member of a legislative assembly is bound by its own laws.*

Thus, for example, the members of a parliament are subject to the laws that it passes; bishops are bound by the laws made by the provincial synod, although they retain the power to dispense themselves in individual cases.

SECOND PRINCIPLE. *A legislator acting in an individual capacity is obliged indirectly by the preceptive power of his laws but not by their coactive power.*

St. Thomas, when discussing this point says: "A ruler is not bound by the coactive power of his laws, for no one can be compelled in the strict sense of the word by

---

[41] CCL, Can. 12.
[42] ST, I-II, q. 96, a. 6, c.
[43] CCL, Can. 2230.

himself and it is the power of the ruler that is the source of the compelling force of law.... But so far as the directive force of law is concerned the ruler is subject to law by his own will.... Therefore, regarding the judgment of God (in the sphere of conscience) a ruler is not exempt from law in relation to its directive power."[44] If the ruler himself did not respect his own laws, his subjects would easily be scandalized and the power of discipline shattered.

§ 3. Strangers and Persons of No Fixed Abode as Subject to Local Law

84. DEFINITIONS. A person acquires a *domicile*; *a)* as soon as he settles in a place with the firm intention of remaining there permanently or at least indefinitely; *b)* by living in a place for ten years even though he has no intention of remaining there permanently.[45]

A *quasi-domicile* is acquired: *a)* when a person dwells in a place with the intention of remaining there for the greater part of a year provided that nothing calls him away; *b)* when he has actually dwelt in a place for the greater part of a year (i.e., for six months and a day).

In canonical terms one who is living in his domicile is an *incola*, whereas a person living in his quasi-domicile is an *advena*.

A *stranger* is one who is absent from the place where he possesses a domicile or a quasi-domicile.

A *person of no fixed abode* (*vagus*) is one who possesses neither a domicile nor a quasi-domicile.

85. FIRST PRINCIPLE. *Strangers are not bound by laws that are strictly territorial whether they apply 1) to the place of their domicile or quasi-domicile, or 2) to the places in which they are staying, except in three instances:*

    a) when otherwise scandal or some harm would be inflicted on the inhabitants,
    b) when making contracts,
    c) when incurring penalties for the commission of some delinquency.[46]

The first part of the principle follows from the fact that purely territorial laws are binding only on those who have a domicile or quasi-domicile in the territory concerned. This does not apply to *personal* laws.

With regard to the second part, it must be remembered that a stranger is not a subject of the legislator of the place where he is staying. However, exceptions must be made in the three instances quoted above where it is the natural law rather than local positive law which gives rise to the obligation. The natural law forbids strangers from causing scandal or injury to others, which would result especially if they did not observe the laws relating to contracts and to penalties inflicted for the commission of delinquency.

---

44 ST, I-II, q. 96, a. 5, rep. 3.
45 See CCL, Can. 92.
46 See CCL, Can. 14 and 1566.

86. **SECOND PRINCIPLE.** *Strangers are obliged to obey those common laws which are observed in the place where they are actually staying, even though in the place of their domicile or quasi-domicile these laws have been legally abolished or suspended.*[47]

The reason is that a dispensation granted to a particular territory does not extend beyond that territory. Thus, a German travelling to Rome in Holy Week cannot avail himself of the dispensations granted to Germans.

87. **THIRD PRINCIPLE.** *Strangers are entitled to use the privileges and indults of the territory where they are staying.*

Such privileges and indults are considered as being granted to everyone in that territory, not merely to the residents but also to its visitors.[48]

88. **FOURTH PRINCIPLE.** *Persons of no fixed abode are bound by all the laws of the place where they actually reside.*[49]

Otherwise, such persons would be better placed than anyone else, which is absurd. In some matters, especially with regard to the celebration of marriage, special laws have been laid down for persons of no fixed abode.

Art. 4. Promulgation and Acceptance of Law

89. **DEFINITION.** The promulgation of law is the authentic publication of law by the legislator. Therefore, promulgation differs both from the general publication of the law and from its recognition by others, since these are private matters and not authentic.

THE NECESSITY OF PROMULGATION. Properly speaking, promulgation does not belong to the essence of law, and yet no human law is binding on its subjects until it is authentically promulgated. Thus, the Code states: "Laws begin to exist when they are promulgated."[50] It is not required that the law be declared to each individual or that it be actually known by everyone; it is sufficient that the subjects be *capable of obtaining knowledge of the law.*

According to present discipline the laws of the Holy Father are promulgated in the periodical *Acta Apostolicae Sedis*, and such laws begin to bind on the completion of three months from the date attached to the copy of the *Acta* in which they appear.[51]

THE ACCEPTANCE of law by the people is not required for the existence of obligation, so far as human laws are concerned.

Consequently, Alexander VII condemned the following proposition: "A people does not commit sin even if for no reason at all it refuses to accept a law promulgated by its ruler."[52]

---

[47] See CCL, Can. 14, § 1, no. 3.
[48] See CCL, Can. 881, § 1, and 927.
[49] See CCL, Can. 14, § 2.
[50] CCL, Can. 8, § 1.
[51] See CCL, Can. 9.
[52] DZ 1128.

The reason is that the legislative power of a lawful *ruler* does not depend on the people.

Ecclesiastical laws do not require ratification *by civil authority* since the Church is a perfect society, autonomous and completely independent of civil government. And thus the so-called royal assent is not required for either the promulgation or the acceptance of ecclesiastical law. But sometimes in a concordat the Church does freely grant to civil government some right of intervention in ecclesiastical affairs.

Art. 5. The Obligation of Human Law

90. EXISTENCE OF OBLIGATION. It is certain that every just human law—both ecclesiastical and civil—imposes an obligation in conscience. St. Paul says: "He who resists authority resists the command of God. But they who resist in this way merit condemnation for themselves.... Therefore, of necessity be obedient not merely because of anger but also for the sake of conscience" (Rom 13:1–5).

91. NATURE OF THE OBLIGATION. The obligation of human law is:

1) grave or slight, 2) direct or indirect—that is to say, caused by the law itself or by circumstances attached to the law. Whether the obligation of individual laws is grave or slight depends on their content and purpose, and also, to some extent, on the intention of the legislator who may decide that a law relating to some matter, which in itself is grave, should be binding only under a light obligation. However, no legislator has the power to attach a grave obligation to a law relating to some matter which is in every respect of slight importance, since this would be to impose an intolerable burden on his subjects and such a law would not be of genuine benefit to society. In practice the gravity of the obligation is to be assessed from:

a) the words used in the law;

b) the gravity of the punishment with which transgressors are threatened;

c) the interpretation of learned men and the practice of the subjects.

92. SCHOLIUM. FORMAL CONTEMPT OF THE LAW. If anyone transgresses a law (even if in itself it binds only under slight obligation) through formal contempt, he commits grave sin, because such contempt implies a serious revolt against lawful authority. Formal contempt is not to be imputed: *a)* if the law is broken through passion or weakness or temptation; *b)* if anyone treats with contempt or as of little value something that is commanded but not precisely because it is commanded; *c)* if the transgressor lacks respect for his superior not in his position of authority but as a private individual, e.g., because of his worthlessness or other failings. In practice, formal contempt rarely exists.

93. THE EXTENT OF OBLIGATION. The obligation of law extends to:

1) *knowledge of the law,* so that the subjects are obliged to possess sufficient knowledge of positive laws in proportion to their position and ability; 2) *the use of ordinary means* which are *proximately* necessary for the observance of the law.

The obligation extends to the use of *ordinary* and *proximately* necessary means, not to the use of extraordinary and remote means. This obligation includes the obligation of avoiding the *proximate obstacles* to the fulfillment of law. Consequently, no one is permitted to do anything which would prevent the *proximate* fulfillment of law without a proportionate reason; thus, unless there existed a proportionate reason, one would not be justified in undertaking on a fast day some form of heavy work which would prevent the observance of the fast.

Law is sometimes indirectly binding in conscience, as happens *a)* in penal law; *b)* in invalidating laws; *c)* in laws based on a false presumption. Each of these must be considered separately.

§ 1. Penal Laws

94. **DEFINITION AND KINDS.** *Penal law is a form of law which directly and immediately binds under pain of punishment and not under pain of incurring a moral fault.*

The rules of the majority of religious institutes are considered to be penal laws which do not oblige directly under pain of either mortal or venial sin; the same is true of many of the ordinances of civil government. It is customary to distinguish between laws that are *entirely* penal and laws of a *mixed* character.

Authors do not concur in their explanation of laws that are *entirely penal.* D'Annibale and others maintain that such a law is one which contains a precept and a punishment in a *disjunctive* proposition, so that one is free either to observe what is commanded or undergo the punishment attached; for instance, recent excise laws forbid the entry of tobacco into France, otherwise one must pay a certain sum of money. Therefore, a man is free either to refrain from bringing in tobacco or to pay the duty.—Billuart, Koch, and others propose what appears to be the more correct view: a purely penal law is one which commands that something be done or omitted and imposes on transgressors a penalty but no theological fault; that is to say, the fault which is determined and punished is of a *juridical* character.

A law which is *not entirely penal* imposes at the same time an obligation which is truly and directly of a moral character and also a temporal punishment on transgressors, e.g., clerics holding benefices are bound to say the Divine Office, and if they neglect this duty they not only commit sin but also lose the fruits of the benefice.—In addition to penal laws there are also other human laws which are *purely preceptive*, which impose a moral obligation without any accompanying temporal punishment, such as the law of hearing Mass on Sundays and on holy days of obligation.

95. **THE EXISTENCE** of laws that are purely penal in character is denied by some authors, but the contrary view is the one most commonly held by theologians and by the general consent of the people who regard many civil laws as having no direct obligation in conscience, since the legislator can make sufficient provision for the common good by means of purely penal laws without directly binding the consciences of his subjects.

THE TRANSGRESSION of a penal law is an *indirect* cause of moral fault, *a)* if it was due to culpable neglect or inordinate passion or formal contempt; *b)* if the transgressor refused to accept the punishment justly imposed.—Penalties ferendae sententiae are not incurred prior to a special sentence of the competent judge; penalties incurred ipso facto, if they are negative or privative in character, must be endured normally speaking without any further declaratory sentence of the judge, but if *positive* they are not incurred unless the judge has previously determined this in explicit terms.

NOTE. The Code states: "Circumstances which excuse from every form of imputability, and also those excusing from grave sin, similarly excuse from incurring any penalty whether latae or ferendae sententiae even in the external forum, provided that the excuse is valid in that forum."[53] Consequently as often as a delinquent does not commit grave sin, e.g., because of inculpable ignorance, fear, surge of passion, he does not incur any ecclesiastical penalty attached to such an offense. But nothing prevents small penances being imposed on the delinquent.

§ 2. Invalidating Laws

INTRODUCTORY. Our discussion must be limited to human law and does not include those precepts of natural and divine law which render acts invalid; thus, for instance, the diriment impediments of consanguinity in the direct line and of an existing marriage bond always produce their effect of invalidity and no human authority is capable of dispensing from them.

96. DEFINITION. *An invalidating law is one which renders an act void or at least declares (expressly or equivalently) that the act can be rescinded because of some defect in the act.*[54]

Consequently, an invalidating law differs from a prohibitory law; the latter renders acts contrary to the law unlawful, whereas the former renders such acts void or deserving of invalidity.—An invalidating law renders an act void, 1) either *by the law itself,* and then the act is null and void from the beginning, or 2) *after sentence by a judge,* when the act remains valid until the judge passes sentence.

97. *The effects of an invalidating law in the external forum* are not avoided by ignorance, good faith, or fear on the part of the agent.[55] Thus, for example, diriment impediments which exist in fact invalidate a marriage even when the parties are in good faith.

The effects of an invalidating law in the internal forum do not seem to be incurred prior to the sentence of the judge if one considers *civil* law. The reason is that although the civil legislator certainly possesses the power to invalidate certain acts of his subjects in the internal forum, yet he is rightly presumed not to impose such an obligation since the purpose of the law can be achieved by the civil pronouncement of invalidity in the external forum. However, once the judge has passed

---

[53] CCL, Can. 2218, § 2.
[54] See CCL, Can. 11.
[55] See CCL, Can. 16.

sentence such laws are binding in the internal forum also. *Ecclesiastical* invalidating laws render the act invalid or capable of being rescinded in the internal forum even before sentence by the judge. Therefore, in brief: an ecclesiastical law which invalidates an act through the law itself destroys all the value and obligation of the act both in the external and internal fora. Thus, for example, betrothals which do not observe the form prescribed by law have no binding force either in the external forum or in the internal forum.[56]

§ 3. Laws Based on False Presumption

98. **DEFINITION AND KINDS.** In the present context *presumption means a conjecture derived from reasonable signs.*

Presumption may be of *common danger* or of a *definite fact.* In the first instance, the legislator presumes the existence of some common danger in certain circumstances; thus a legislator presumes that there is the danger of perversion in the reading of evil books and so prohibits the reading of such books. The second type of presumption is present when a legislator or judge presumes from certain indications the existence of a fact which cannot be proved in the strict sense of the word.[57]

99. **FIRST PRINCIPLE.** *A law based on the presumption of common danger always obliges even though in an individual instance the danger is absent.*[58] *The reason is twofold: a)* even though the purpose of a law is not verified in a particular instance, the law itself does not cease, as we shall discuss at greater length in a later paragraph; *b)* if a law based on presumed danger ceased to bind, the way would be open for many dangerous illusions. Hence the law prohibiting the reading of evil books still holds even for a person who considers himself free from the danger of perversion in reading such books.

SECOND PRINCIPLE. *a) A law based on the presumption of a fact obliges in the external forum until the fact is proved false; b) such a law does not oblige in conscience if the fact is falsely presumed.*

The first part of the principle is based on the truth that a presumption must be taken for granted in the external forum until it is proved to be false.

The second part of the principle is an adaptation of the common axiom: presumption must yield to truth.

Art. 6. Fulfillment of Law

The following statements are easily understood:

100. 1. *More is required in order to obey the law than not to transgress it,* since, in order not to transgress the law, one must simply refrain from doing anything contrary to the law, whereas to obey the law there is required an act that is both human and moral.

---

[56] See CCL, Can. 1017, § 1.
[57] A further division of presumption is discussed in MTM.
[58] See CCL, Can. 21.

2. To fulfill the law it is not necessary that what is prescribed should be performed under the inspiration of charity or of any other virtue; *the substance of the act and not its virtuous performances is sufficient.*

3. To fulfill the law it is not necessary that one have the intention of fulfilling it, but one must have at least the implicit intention of doing what the law commands—or, more briefly: *material and not formal obedience is demanded for the fulfillment of law.*

4. *Several laws which are not formally but only materially different can be fulfilled by one and the same act.* Precepts relating to the same matter are formally different when their motives are mutually exclusive; otherwise, they are materially different.

5. *Several laws relating to different matters can be fulfilled by one and the same act, a) if their content is not mutually exclusive, and b) if the legislator has not forbidden this method of fulfillment.*

101. SCHOLIUM. TIME FOR THE FULFILLMENT OF AN OBLIGATION. Since a law usually determines not only what is to be done but also when it is to be done, the following rules are to be observed:

1. If a time limit was imposed on the understanding that with the passing of time *the obligation would also cease,* then the law must not and cannot be fulfilled outside of this time (i.e., neither before nor after this time).

2. If the time limit was imposed *in order to urge the fulfillment of the obligation,* then even though the time has passed, the obligation to fulfill the law as quickly as possible still remains. Thus, for instance, a man who does not receive Holy Communion during Easter (whether this is due to his own fault or not) is still bound to receive it afterward as soon as possible.

3. If the legal time has *already commenced* and one foresees that later on he will be prevented from fulfilling the law, he is bound to fulfill the law before the hindrance occurs. Thus, for example, if a priest foresees in the morning that he will be unable to recite his Office after dinner, he must recite the entire Office in the morning, since the time for the observance of this law has already commenced. On the other hand, a priest who foresees that he will not be able to recite Matins and Lauds on the following day is not strictly bound to anticipate, since the time for the observance of the law has not yet commenced and no priest is obliged to avail himself of the privilege of anticipating.

Art. 7. Interpretation of Law

Interpretation of law is necessary for two reasons: 1) law is sometimes obscure; 2) doubts may arise whether the law extends to some extraordinary case. In the first instance, one makes use of interpretation in the normal sense of the word; to meet the needs of extraordinary cases equity (epikeia) is used.

§ 1. Ordinary Interpretation

102. **Definition and Kinds.** *Interpretation is defined as the genuine explanation of a law.*

In respect of its *author*, interpretation of law is either *authoritative, customary*, or *doctrinal*, according as it is given by competent juridical authority,[59] or by custom lawfully introduced amongst the people, or by learned and skilled persons. Similar to customary interpretation of law is *judicial* interpretation or jurisprudence—that is to say, an authoritative explanation derived from cases judged in a similar way, as happens in law-courts.

In respect of the *character* of the interpretation, it is either *comprehensive, extensive*, or *restrictive*, depending on whether it explains the actual content of the law, or extends it beyond its present limits, or restricts the law more closely than has been customary up to the present.

103. **Principle.** *a) Authoritative interpretation given in the form of law has the force of law and consequently imposes a similar obligation; b) customary and doctrinal interpretation must be accepted and observed if they are allowed in practice without any protest from the legislator who could easily revoke such an interpretation if he so desired.*

The reason for the first part of the principle is that an authoritative interpretation proceeds from a competent authority who has the power to impose even a new obligation.[60]

The second part is based on the well-known principle: "custom is the best interpreter of laws,"[61] and learned conscientious men are specially equipped to grasp the meaning of law.

104. **Rules to be followed in doctrinal interpretation:**

1. Special attention must be given to the immediate purpose of the law and to the mind of the legislator.

2. The words of the law are to be understood in their natural sense having regard for the context and their position in the text,[62] unless this gives rise to something which is rightly presumed to be contrary to the intention of the legislator.

3. Unfavorable laws are to be restricted, whereas favorable laws should be extended as far as possible.

4. Where obscurity exists, only the minimum is required to satisfy the law.

[59] See CCL, Can. 17, § 1.
[60] On this matter the Code states: "Authoritative interpretation given in the form of law has the same force as the law itself; and if it merely declares the meaning of the words of law that are certain, it does not require a new promulgation and reacts on past actions; if the interpretation restricts or extends the law or explains a doubtful law, it does not react on past actions and it must be promulgated. An interpretation given by way of judicial sentence or by rescript in some special case does not have the force of law and binds only the persons and affects only those matters for which it was issued" (Can. 17, § 2 and 3).
[61] See CCL, Can. 29.
[62] See CCL, Can. 18.

5. A later particular law abrogates a previous general law, but the reverse is not true: a later general law does not abrogate an earlier particular law, unless this is made quite clear in a particular instance.

§ 2. Epikeia or Equity

105. DEFINITION. *Epikeia* (or equity) *is a favorable and just interpretation not of the law itself but of the mind of the legislator*, who is presumed to be unwilling to bind his subjects in extraordinary cases where the observance of his law would cause injury or impose too severe a burden. Equity (which is an act of legal justice and belongs to that part of prudence which is called "gnome") differs from ordinary interpretation, *a)* in that the latter is intended to remove obscurity from the law, whereas the former excuses from the observance of a law that is not obscure on the presumption that such is the legislator's intention, and *b)* in that ordinary interpretation takes into account every instance of the application of the law, whereas equity applies to an individual case only.

106. RULES FOR THE USE OF EPIKEIA:

1. Epikeia applies only in those cases where the law would become harmful or excessively burdensome and difficult to observe.[63]

2. Epikeia cannot be used lawfully:

a) if the superior with power to dispense from the law can be approached without difficulty;

b) in matters concerning an evident *precept of natural law*, as also in questions relating to an invalidating law of the Church—this latter being the more probable opinion.

Art. 8. Cessation of Law

107. INTRODUCTORY. Either the entire law ceases or else the obligation of law may cease for a time. The obligation attached to law may cease for a time in one of three ways: *a)* its subjects may be incapable of observing it; *b)* the superior may grant a dispensation; *c)* there may exist a contrary privilege. The law itself ceases, *a)* through revocation, *b)* through failure of its purpose, *c)* through contrary custom. We must now consider each of these points in turn.

§ 1. Cessation of Obligation through Impossibility

108. DEFINITIONS. Impossibility is either *absolute* or *moral* depending on whether a person finds it completely impossible to observe a law or can only do so with difficulty.

PRINCIPLE. *a) Absolute impossibility excuses from the observance of any law; b) moral impossibility does not excuse from the observance of natural law, c) but it usually excuses from positive law* (with the exception of invalidating laws).

---

[63] See Alphonsus Liguori, *Theologia Moralis* [hereafter TM], bk. 1, no. 201.

The first part of the principle rests on the axiom: "no one is obliged to do the impossible."

The reason for the second part is the intrinsic evil of every offense against the natural law, and all persons are bound to do all in their power to avoid whatever is intrinsically evil. Thus, for example, it is never lawful even in extreme need to tell a lie or procure an abortion directly. If an occasion arises where there is a conflict between two precepts of the natural law, such as might arise between the prohibition against theft and the obligation to protect oneself in extreme need, then the higher law takes precedence over the lower.

The third part of the principle derives its truth from the fact that moral impossibility makes an act so difficult that the majority of men would never or only very rarely perform such an act which in itself is not of obligation. Therefore, if the legislator continues to impose an obligation on his subjects who are morally incapable of observing the law in spite of the fact that he foresees that his law will be frequently ignored, the law becomes detrimental to the common good and thus ceases to be law. This is embodied in the well-known principle: "No positive law obliges where there is grave inconvenience." This applies also to *divine positive law*. Therefore, for example, a penitent is excused from the divine law requiring integrity in confession if there is some grave external inconvenience.

ACCIDENTALLY (especially if it is closely related to natural law) a positive law may sometimes oblige even when there is the greatest inconvenience, supposing that the violation of that law would result in hatred of religion or in serious injury to the community, as is evident in the case of Eleazar refusing to eat the meat he was offered (see 2 Mc 6:18ff).

109. QUERY. *Is it permissible deliberately to make oneself incapable of fulfilling some law?* One must here use the rules that apply to acts that are indirectly voluntary. But generally speaking, it is permissible to produce situations that *excuse* from the observance of law—that is to say, a person is allowed to withdraw himself from the jurisdiction of human law. Thus, for instance, it is lawful to leave one territory in order to avoid the particular laws of that place, or one may go into another diocese to confess a reserved sin.

§ 2. Cessation of Obligation through Dispensation

110. DEFINITION AND KINDS. *A dispensation is a relaxation of the law or of the obligation of law in particular cases granted by competent authority for a special and sufficient reason.*[64]

Dispensations may be:

1. *valid* or *invalid*, depending on whether they produce the effect intended or not;

2. *lawful* or *unlawful*, according as they verify all the conditions (both essential and accidental) demanded by law or lack certain accidentals;

---

[64] See CCL, Can. 80.

3. *subrepticia* or *obrepticia*, depending on whether in the request for the dispensation some *truth* is concealed *which ought to be revealed*, or some *false* declaration is made. Certain authors identify these two kinds of dispensation.

111. THE AUTHOR OF A DISPENSATION is the legislator himself or his delegate or his successor or his superior.[65]

1. *The pope* may dispense: *a)* in all ecclesiastical laws; *b)* in the divine law in those cases where the law is based to some extent on the human will, as in the case of vows, promissory oaths, ratified marriages.

2. *Bishops* have the power to dispense: *a)* in all the laws and special statutes of their own diocese, unless they have been *enacted in detail* by the pope for a particular territory; in individual cases and for a just cause they may dispense from decrees of provincial synods;[66] *b)* in the general laws of the Church provided *i)* the case is urgent, or *ii)* the case is of frequent occurrence and concerns some matter which is not of such great importance, e.g., the law of abstinence, or *iii)* the law is doubtful and the doubt is one of fact, and the law is one in which the pope usually dispenses,[67] as in doubts regarding bodily fitness for ordination; *c)* from certain general laws where the bishop has the right to dispense from law, as he has in granting dispensations from certain irregularities, from the banns of marriage.[68]—By *delegated authority* bishops usually possess wider powers of dispensation.

3. *Religious superiors* have in virtue of their ordinary authority the power to dispense *a)* from laws and statutes of their own institute, unless they are specially prevented from doing so in some of the statutes; *b)* from general laws for their own subjects, in the same way as bishops, since religious superiors (of clerical exempt institutes) possess a jurisdiction similar to that possessed by bishops over their subjects.[69]

4. *Parish priests* cannot dispense, generally speaking, in virtue of their ordinary power in ecclesiastical law;[70] but they have the power to dispense in some special cases, e.g., from the general law of fasting and abstinence, from the observance of feast days.[71]

5. *Religious confessors* possessing the privileges of mendicants have the power to dispense:

a) from all vows, with the exception of *i)* public vows, *ii)* vows made in favor of a third party, *iii)* two reserved private vows, namely, those of perfect chastity and of entering a religious order in which solemn vows are taken, if they are made unconditionally and after the completion of the eighteenth year of age;[72]

b) from a promissory oath;

---

[65] Ibid.
[66] See CCL, Can. 291, § 2.
[67] See CCL, Can. 15.
[68] See CCL, Can. 82.
[69] See CCL, Can. 990 and 1245.
[70] See CCL, Can. 83.
[71] See CCL, Can. 1245, § 1.
[72] See CCL, Can. 1309.

c) from all irregularities in which bishops have the *ordinary power* to dispense;

d) from a private vow of chastity, when either of the parties to a marriage makes known this vow in confession immediately before the marriage and there is no time to seek a dispensation from the competent authority.

112. 6. *All confessors* in virtue of common law have the power of dispensing in urgent secret cases when it is impossible to approach the bishop and there is imminent danger of grave injury or defamation,

a) from all irregularities arising *from delinquency,* with the exception of *i)* any irregularity arising from voluntary murder and abortion, *ii)* any irregularity brought before a court of law. — This dispensation may be granted in order that the penitent may lawfully *exercise* those sacred Orders already received but it cannot be granted to those about to receive Orders;[73]

b) from the infliction of punitive penalties,[74] at the same time enjoining the obligation to have recourse to the competent superior within a month; if this recourse is morally impossible, the confessor may grant an unconditional dispensation;

c) from all marriage impediments arising from ecclesiastical law, with two exceptions, namely, the impediments that arise from the priesthood and from affinity in the direct line if this affinity has arisen from a consummated marriage.[75]

113. PERSONS TO WHOM DISPENSATIONS MAY BE GRANTED are those who in some way are subject to the jurisdiction of the individual granting the dispensation, since the act of dispensing is an act of jurisdiction which cannot be exercised in respect of those who are not subject. N. B. — *In some way* subject: consequently, according to the present discipline of the Church, dispensations can sometimes be granted to strangers and to exempt religious by the diocesan bishop or by a confessor.

114. THREE CONDITIONS FOR THE GRANTING OF DISPENSATIONS were laid down by the Council of Trent: 1) there must be a sufficient reason; 2) this reason must be known; 3) the dispensation must be granted free of charge.[76]

1. There must exist a *sufficient reason.* The reasons for granting a dispensation are: *a) internal* (the difficulty of observing the law) or *external* (the common good); *b) canonical,* which by themselves are sufficient for granting a dispensation, or *impelling,* which by themselves are insufficient but support other reasons.

115. PRINCIPLE. *Any dispensation granted without a sufficient reason is: a) always unlawful, no matter by whom it is granted; b) invalid, if it was granted in virtue of delegated authority.*[77]

The reason for the first part of the principle is that a dispensation is an injury to the law which cannot be inflicted without sufficient reason. In relation to

---

[73] See CCL, Can. 990.
[74] See CCL, Can. 2290.
[75] See CCL, Can. 1045.
[76] See Council of Trent, Session 25, "Decree on Reformation," chap. 18.
[77] See CCL, Can. 84, § 1.

the second part, it must be noted that a delegated person exceeds the sphere of his delegation in granting a dispensation from the law of his superior without sufficient reason.

When it is doubtful whether the reason for a dispensation is sufficient, the individual is allowed to ask for the dispensation and the superior may validly and lawfully grant it.[78]

2. In order that the dispensation be lawfully granted *the reason for the dispensation must be known.* So something more is required than the mere existence of a sufficient reason; the person granting the dispensation must know its character, otherwise he would be acting irrationally. Rules are laid down for the amount of knowledge required in the external forum, but no such directions exist in respect of the internal forum.

3. *The gratuitous granting of dispensations* is necessary so as to avoid all suggestion of simony. Nevertheless, some remuneration can be demanded to meet chancellery expenses. Ordinaries and their officials who ask for a fee on the occasion of granting a dispensation are bound to restitution.[79]

116. DEFECTS IN THE GRANTING OF DISPENSATIONS can be reduced to three: 1) *lack of jurisdiction* (requisite authority is lacking); 2) *lack of justice* (absence of sufficient reason); 3) *some defect of freedom in the will* of the legislator through error or fear. We have spoken already of the first two defects; something must now be said about error and fear.

1. *Error* or deception may arise in the mind of the legislator in the granting of dispensations in one of two ways: either he is told something false (*dispensatio obrepticia*), or else some truth which he ought to know is concealed from him (*dispensatio subrepticia*). — This error in the mind of the legislator invalidates the dispensation unless *a)* the dispensation was given in the form of a motu proprio, or *b)* the error was concerned with purely accidental circumstances.

2. *Fear* does not invalidate a dispensation unless it is grave and inflicted unjustly. Some authors hold the more correct view that no form of fear can invalidate a dispensation since all acts performed through grave fear even when it has been inflicted unjustly are valid acts, unless the law expressly states otherwise.[80]

117. CESSATION OF DISPENSATIONS, granted for a definite period, may be effected *a)* by the legislator himself, *b)* by the person dispensed, *c)* by the cessation of the purpose of the dispensation.

1. *On the part of the legislator,* a dispensation ceases *a)* through lawful revocation, *b)* through the death (physical or moral) of the legislator, if the dispensation contained the clause, *ad beneplacitum nostrum,* or something similar.[81]

---

[78] See CCL, Can. 84, § 2.
[79] See CCL, Can. 1056.
[80] See CCL, Can. 103, § 2.
[81] See CCL, Can. 73 and 86.

2. *On the part of the person dispensed,* a dispensation ceases by legitimate renunciation. In order that this renunciation be lawful it is necessary *a)* that it should not harm the rights of the community or those of a third party, *b)* that the grantor accept the renunciation.—Dispensation does not lapse through *failure to use it,* provided it is not a burden to others; if its non-use is prejudicial to others, it can cease through lawful prescription against it.

3. *On the part of the purpose of the dispensation,* the dispensation ceases only when its *sole motive cause* has completely ceased. It is difficult to lay down any general rule regarding this form of cessation, since in dispensations relating to vows or fasting or marriage impediments, and so on, dispensations do not cease in the same way once their purpose ceases to exist; for example, if Bertha was dispensed from her vow of chastity in order that she might marry for the sole purpose of making her child legitimate, the dispensation ceases if the child dies before the marriage.

118. INTERPRETATION OF DISPENSATIONS: 1. The faculty to dispense generally is to be interpreted *widely* since it is a favor. But the faculty to dispense *in a particular case* must be interpreted in its strictest sense.[82]

2. Dispensations themselves are normally to be interpreted in a *strict* sense, since a dispensation represents an injury to the law.[83] However, wider interpretations can be given to dispensations given by motu proprio, or in the interest of the common good or for the entire community, or if the dispensation has been granted by the law itself and has been inserted in the Code of Canon Law.

§ 3. Cessation of Obligation through Privilege

119. DEFINITION. Privileges may be understood *objectively* or *subjectively,* and each of these may be taken in a wide or strict sense.

A privilege considered *objectively* and *in its wide sense* is any particular law. In this sense of the word the laws of bishops and of parish priests, and so on, are called privileges.

A privilege considered *objectively* and *in the strict meaning* of the term is a *private law granting a special favor which is contrary to or superadded to a general law*—or more briefly: *a private favorable law.*

A privilege *viewed subjectively* is nothing other than the power of acting in accordance with a privilege understood in its objective sense (either widely or strictly considered).

120. KINDS. Among the many divisions listed by authors the following seem the more important.

1. *In regard to its subject* a privilege is either *personal* or *real* depending on whether it primarily concerns a person or a thing (e.g., a place, an office, a confraternity, and

---

[82] See CCL, Can. 85.
[83] Ibid.

so on). Similar to such privileges are the faculties normally delegated to bishops, religious superiors, and so on. Consequently, these faculties do not cease with the death or removal of the person so privileged.[84]

2. *In regard to its object*, a privilege may be *favorable* or *unfavorable* depending on whether it grants a favor which prejudices no one else or whether at the same time it imposes a burden on others. An example of an unfavorable privilege would be an exemption from the payment of income tax which would necessitate a more severe tax on others.

3. *In regard to its motive*, a privilege may be either *gratuitous* or *remunerative* insofar as it is granted either out of pure generosity on the part of the grantor or as a reward for the merits of the individual.

4. *In regard to the manner in which it is granted*, a privilege may be given *motu proprio* or *ad instantiam*, depending on whether it is granted as a very special favor to be interpreted widely or in answer to a previous request.

121. PRIVILEGES MAY BE ACQUIRED by direct grant, communication, prescription, or custom.[85]

Only those who have the power to make laws are able to grant privileges *directly*, since privileges are private laws.

By communication are acquired privileges granted to one moral person by another moral person to whom has been granted by pontifical indult the power of communicating privileges to the former. There used to exist such communication of privileges between different religious orders, but this power has now been removed for the future.[86]

Privileges may also be acquired by *prescription* or by *custom* which are likewise means of abrogating laws.[87]

122. THE INTERPRETATION OF PRIVILEGES is most difficult. What has been said already in reference to the interpretation of law can be applied more or less to the interpretation of privileges. Generally speaking, favorable privileges are to be interpreted widely, whereas unfavorable privileges are to be interpreted in their strict sense.[88]

FAILURE TO USE PRIVILEGES. *Favorable* privileges granted for the *personal* benefit of an individual need not be used and can be freely renounced, because favors must not be restricted. But privileges affecting the welfare of the entire community or of some State cannot be renounced and must be used. Thus, for example, a cleric could not renounce the privilege safeguarding him from personal injury (*privilegium canonis*).

[84] See CCL, Can. 66, § 2.
[85] See CCL, Can. 63.
[86] See CCL, Can. 63, § 1.
[87] See no. 127.
[88] See CCL, Can. 68.

§ 4. Cessation of Law Itself

123. The law itself can cease in the following ways: 1) through revocation by lawful authority; 2) through the cessation of its purpose; 3) through contrary custom. A special paragraph will be devoted to custom and its influence on law.

A LAW MAY BE REVOKED completely or partially in the following ways:

a) the law may be completely revoked: *abrogation*;

b) the law may be partially revoked by competent authority: *derogation*;

c) an addition may be made to a law already in existence: *subrogation*;

d) one law may be replaced by a contrary law: *obrogation*.

The power to revoke a law completely or partially is invested in those having the power to make that law. The general practice to be followed in this matter is the following:

A general law revokes completely or partially all previous contrary general legislation, but it does not revoke particular laws unless this is explicitly stated.

The first part of the principle is evident from the fact that contraries exclude each other.

The reason for the second part is that since a particular law was intended from the moment of its promulgation to be an exception to some general law, it is considered to endure as long as it is not clearly and undoubtedly revoked.[89]

124. WITH THE COMPLETE DESTRUCTION OF THE LAW'S PURPOSE or adequate motive the law itself ceases to exist. Thus, for example, if a bishop orders prayers for the recovery of the pope who is sick, once the pope dies the prayers cease. If, however, the purpose of the law ceases to be verified in a particular case or for an individual, the law itself continues to bind, unless the observance of the law would cause great inconvenience.

§ 5. Custom

125. DEFINITION. *Custom* (as understood here) *is a right or law introduced by the repeated behavior of a community with the consent of the legislator.* In the treatise on Penance we shall be considering custom in its material form, that is, as a habit acquired by the repetition of acts. In this section, custom is considered as interpreting, abrogating, or creating law. Custom is not the same as prescription.[90]

KINDS. 1. In relation to their *purpose* or effect, customs are either *in accordance with law* if they confirm or explain some law, or *an addition to law* if they extend it, or *contrary to law* if they destroy it.

---

[89] See CCL, Can. 6, nos. 1 and 22.
[90] The distinction between them (*custom* and *prescription*) is further to be found explained in MTM.

2. In relation to their *extent*, customs are either universal, general, particular, or individual, according as they prevail either in the whole Church, or in some province, or in a city, or in a private community. This latter type of custom hardly deserves the name, as it is rather an indult or statute.

3. In relation to their *form*, customs are either *judicial* (jurisprudence, legal usage) or *extrajudicial*, according as they exist within or outside courts.

126. THE CONDITIONS REQUIRED FOR LAWFUL CUSTOM are the following:

1) its content must be suitable; 2) it must be introduced by a competent subject; 3) the legislator must consent to the custom.

1. A custom must have for its *content* a reasonable manner of acting that is public and fully deliberate and has existed for forty years uninterruptedly.

Consequently, whatever is contrary to natural or divine law or to right reason cannot attain the force of law through custom. Moreover, a custom now in existence which is expressly forbidden by law is no longer reasonable.[91] Twenty-one such customs were withdrawn by the new Code.

2. The only *subject capable* of introducing a custom is a public community on whom law understood in its strict sense can be imposed.

Hence, for example, a diocese, a religious congregation, and so on, have the power to introduce customs, but not private families. Furthermore, it is required that the custom be introduced, *a)* by the majority of the members of the community, *b)* by frequent and spontaneous acts, *c)* with the intention either of accepting or of rejecting some obligation. According to the more probable opinion it is not required in the beginning that the custom be introduced in *good faith* provided that all the other conditions are satisfied.[92]

3. *The consent of the legislator* is absolutely necessary to give the customs of any community the force of law.[93]

The consent may be *explicit* when the competent superior expressly approves the custom introduced, or *legal* (*juridical*) when the law itself allows the introduction of customs, or *tacit* when the superior remains silent even though he could easily object to the introduction of the custom. Each of these types of consent is sufficient.

127. THE EFFECTS OF LAWFUL CUSTOM are threefold according to St. Thomas: "Custom has the force of law, abrogates law, and interprets law."[94] Nothing further remains to be said about custom as interpreting law; what has been said in no. 105ff about the customary interpretation of law applies here.

[91] See CCL, Can. 27, § 2.
[92] See TM, bk. 1, no. 107.
[93] See CCL, Can. 25.
[94] ST, I-II, q. 97, a. 3, c.

1. Customs that impose an *obligation* or create a new law are today extremely rare, but in days previous this form of custom seems to have been responsible for introducing the clerical obligation of reciting the Divine Office privately and the matrimonial impediment of disparity of worship.

2. Customs that *abrogate* law, provided they satisfy all the necessary conditions, can revoke *any* human law, as is evident from the Decretals.[95] And thus many of the disciplinary decrees of the Council of Trent have been abrogated by custom.

128. CUSTOM WITH THE FORCE OF LAW CEASES in the same way as law itself; consequently, we need only recall what has been said already in no. 123. But generally speaking—that is, when nothing is said expressly to the contrary—it must be remembered that a) a law cannot revoke customs which have existed for a hundred years or from time immemorial, b) a general law cannot destroy particular customs.[96]

Art. 9. Civil Law and Its Obligations

129. THE OBLIGATION OF CIVIL LAWS.

There is no possibility of doubting that Christians are obliged to observe civil laws even though they are made by pagan rulers, provided that they are not opposed to Christian religion or to the moral teaching of the Gospel; and the apostle himself has left no room for doubt when without making any distinction between lawful superiors he says: "Every soul must be submissive to its lawful superiors; authority comes from God only...." (Rom 13:1ff). From this most evident statement it is clear that those in the highest authority in civil government can make laws for their subjects which are binding in conscience. This is also suggested by the need of public safety, that is to say, of warding off from civil society the monster of anarchy which is worse than any dog or serpent; and there are also the outstanding examples of the early Christians who obeyed the laws of their pagan rulers so long as they were able to do so without injury to their faith and good morals.

Thus writes the Sacred Congregation for the Propagation of the Faith in its instruction to the vicar apostolic of Siam in answer to his query whether the civil law prohibiting traffic in opium was binding in conscience. Accordingly, the opinion proposed that all modern civil laws are purely penal laws is utterly false. The following rules may be used to determine the nature of the obligation attached to such laws:

130. *First Rule.* Civil laws which determine rights or *transfer ownership* normally oblige in conscience on the basis of commutative justice. Such laws are just determinations of natural law, and their non-observance would injure the

---

[95] See Gregory IX, *Liber Extra*, bk. 1, tit. 4, chap. 11.
[96] See CCL, Can. 30.

welfare of society and prevent the citizens from living in peace with each other. Thus, for example, civil laws which grant the use and enjoyment of property belonging to minors, or which set aside a legitimate part of an inheritance for children oblige in conscience.

Second Rule. Civil laws which render acts invalid oblige in conscience after judicial sentence.

This is by far the more probable opinion. Consequently, if a judge has declared invalid some will which was not drawn up in the proper form, it must be held invalid in the sphere of conscience also.[97]

Third Rule. When in doubt concerning the moral obligation of a civil law, the citizens do not directly commit any sin by acting contrary to that law.

Fourth Rule. Unless there is an evident transgression of natural, divine, or ecclesiastical law the citizens *can* always follow in conscience the precepts of the civil law. This is self-evident.

131. CIVIL LAW RELATING TO TAXES. A tax is any sum of money exacted from the citizens by civil law in order to meet the public expenses of the State.

Although duty is often understood as synonymous with tax, the word would be better reserved for that money which has to be paid for goods introduced into a kingdom or town.

Today there exists an almost unlimited number of taxes, but for the sake of convenience they can be reduced to two types: *direct* and *indirect* taxes. *Direct* taxes are those which must be paid at stated intervals by an *individual* designated by name, that is to say, those which are imposed immediately on the person because of his possessions or profession or business. *Indirect* taxes are those which are directly imposed on *things*, e.g., by reason of the exchange of rights through the contract of sale or by succession or by conveyance, and so on. Duty is a form of indirect taxation.

The payment of taxes is binding in conscience.

This is the teaching of all Catholic theologians and is clearly based on Scripture: "Render therefore to Caesar the things that are Caesar's, and to God the things that are God's" (Mt 22:21). This was the answer given by Christ to the question: "Is it lawful to give tribute to Caesar or not?" (Mt 22:17). "Pay every man, then, his dues; taxes, if it be taxes, customs, if it be customs" (Rom 13:7).

But there is no obligation in conscience to pay taxes that are unjust. In order that they be just three conditions must be verified: 1) *lawful authority*, i.e., they must be imposed by those who have lawful care of the community; 2) *a just cause*, i.e., provision for the common good; 3) *a due proportion* in the imposition of taxes in accordance with the means of individual citizens.

---

[97] See CCL, Can. 1513.

132. OPINIONS REGARDING THE NATURE OF THE OBLIGATION TO PAY TAXES.

First Opinion. All just taxes oblige *in commutative justice.* St. Alphonsus regards this opinion as the most common and the more probable, quoting twenty-three authors in support. The reasons given are, *a)* that the citizens by reason of an implicit contract are bound to meet the expenses which are necessary for the common good, and this they do by the payment of taxes, *b)* that just civil taxes oblige in exactly the same way as just ecclesiastical taxes, e.g., tithes. Now it is the most common opinion amongst theologians that the latter form of taxes oblige in commutative justice.

Second Opinion. All just taxes oblige in *legal justice* only. This is the view held by many modern theologians who place the payment of taxes on the same footing as other civil laws which oblige in legal justice.

Third Opinion. All just taxes have the binding force of *merely penal laws.* This view is shared by a few modern theologians who propose as their reasons: *a)* the common opinion of the people regard tax laws as purely penal laws; *b)* modern legislators have no intention of imposing a moral obligation on the conscience of their people; *c)* otherwise good citizens who pay their taxes would be worse off than others who use every means to evade taxes.

Fourth Opinion. Direct taxes oblige in conscience, indirect taxes are purely penal laws. This is the view held by the majority of modern theologians following Ballerini who allege as the chief reason for their view the common opinion prevailing amongst the people.

133. PRACTICAL DIRECTIONS. 1. Since in modern states many of the taxes are unjust, the faithful who evade taxes on a small scale should not be disturbed; however, in general, they should be urged to pay just taxes.

2. Those who evade *indirect* taxation should be treated more leniently in general than those who evade direct taxation, since today it is widely held that laws relating to indirect taxes are merely penal laws, at least so long as such evasion does not become a lucrative trade.

3. *Official tax-collectors* sin grievously and are bound to restitution if they knowingly lend their support to the evasion of taxes, since they commit a grave injury to the contract they have made of fulfilling their office faithfully.

4. Those who deliberately and in the form of a business evade indirect taxation usually commit grave sin, *a)* because they leave themselves open to the most serious dangers, and *b)* because they usually avail themselves of means which are most unlawful. It seems that they are bound to make restitution if by continued evasion they have caused serious damage to other traders.

134. CIVIL LAWS RELATING TO MILITARY SERVICE are in themselves binding in conscience since this service is required for the defense of one's country. It is simply one form of a *personal* tax. It may happen incidentally that this law ceases to oblige, *a)* if it is unjust, such as when exempt clerics are forced to fight with arms, *b)* if soldiers are forced to fight in a war that is manifestly unjust. There is a sufficiently common opinion amongst modern theologians that the civil law regarding military service is binding in *legal justice*. But there are three cases when this law binds in commutative justice: 1) if anyone freely and by contract enlists in the fighting services; 2) if a person by deceitful evasion of his service has been the cause of another designated citizen being compelled to fight; 3) if he offers money to doctors or other officials to bribe them into declaring him unfit for military service.

TREATISE IV
CONSCIENCE

This subject will be considered under the following headings: 1) Definition and Kinds of Conscience; 2) The True Conscience and the False Conscience; 3) The Lax Conscience; 4) The Perplexed Conscience and the Scrupulous Conscience; 5) The Certain Conscience and the Doubting Conscience; 6) Various Moral Systems; 7) The Education of Conscience.

DEFINITION AND KINDS OF CONSCIENCE

135. DEFINITION. Leaving on one side other meanings of the word, conscience is here understood for *the judgment or dictate of the practical intellect deciding from general principles the goodness or evil of some act which is to be done here and now or has been done in the past.*

1. Conscience is a *judgment or dictate of the practical intellect*, since it is not a power or a habit but an *act*, that is, the application of knowledge to an individual fact, and this application is a judgment or dictate of the practical intellect. Therefore, conscience is not an act of the speculative intellect or of the will.

2. Conscience derives its judgment *from general principles*, since it presupposes as true the general principles of faith and of natural reason, and applies these to an individual case. Therefore, conscience does not pass judgment on the truths of faith and of reason but decides whether the act to be done (or which has been done) is in conformity with existing just law.

3. Conscience decides *the goodness or evil of some act which is to be done here and now (or has been done)*. Conscience is the subjective standard of morality and therefore an act is subjectively good or bad according to the judgment of conscience. The proper and primary function of conscience is to pass judgment on an act *which is to be done*, but it may also pass judgment on acts which have been performed already.

136. SCHOLIUM. DIFFERENCE BETWEEN CONSCIENCE, MORAL HABIT (SYNDERESIS), MORAL SCIENCE, PRUDENCE, NATURAL LAW.

1. *Moral habit* (synderesis) is the habitual practical knowledge of the first principles whose proper act is to decide *in a general way* that good must be done and evil

avoided, whereas conscience decides *in an individual case* what is to be done or omitted. The moral habit of man never errs; conscience may do so.

2. *Moral science* deduces *objective* conclusions from the first principles, whereas conscience is something *subjective* which may or may not agree with moral science.

3. *Prudence* is a virtue and therefore a habit; conscience on the other hand is an act. Sometimes, however, an act of prudence coincides with conscience.

4. *Natural law* embraces the *objective* principles of morality, whereas conscience uses these principles to decide whether an act should be performed or whether it should be omitted.

137. **KINDS.** 1. *In regard to the act* considered by conscience, conscience is either *antecedent* if it precedes the act to be performed, or *consequent* if it passes judgment on acts already performed. Antecedent conscience either commands, or forbids, or counsels, or permits the performance of an act; consequent conscience either approves of the act performed, causing spiritual joy, or disapproves of the act, thus causing remorse.

2. *In regard to its conformity with the eternal law*, conscience is *true* (correct) when it deduces correctly from true principles that some act is lawful; it is *false* (erroneous) when it decides from false principles *considered as true* that something is lawful which in fact is unlawful. An erroneous conscience is further distinguished into: *a)* a *scrupulous* conscience, which for useless and almost ridiculous reasons judges or, rather, fears that an act is evil when in fact it is not; *b)* a *perplexed* conscience, which sees sin both in the performance and in the omission of some act; *c)* a lax conscience, which judges on insufficient grounds that there is no sin in the act, or that the sin is not so grave as it is in fact; the worst form of this type of conscience is the *hardened* conscience, which as the result of a long-established habit of sinning regards all — or at least some — sins to be of little importance; *d)* a *pharisaic* conscience, which minimizes grave sins but magnifies matters of little importance in the same way as the Pharisees behaved.

3. *In regard to the act of assent*, conscience is either *certain*, when without any prudent fear of error it firmly decides that some act is either lawful or unlawful, or *probable*, when it judges that some act is probably lawful or unlawful, or *doubting*, when it hesitates to pass judgment on the moral character of the act.

A doubting conscience understood in this latter sense is really a contradiction in terms. Conscience is defined as essentially a judgment or dictate of the intellect, whereas doubt signifies a suspension or denial of judgment. Therefore, it would be preferable to cease speaking of a doubting conscience and to substitute the resolution of moral doubt. Some modern authors identify a doubting conscience with a probable conscience.

THE TRUE CONSCIENCE AND
THE FALSE CONSCIENCE

138. **FIRST PRINCIPLE.** *Everyone is obliged to use serious care to possess on all occasions a true conscience.*

The reason is obvious: conscience is the proximate norm of morality which must act as the guide for the whole of man's moral life. Now it is of supreme importance that his moral life be guided by a correct and not by a false standard. — The means to be used for obtaining a true conscience are: *a)* a careful knowledge of the laws which govern our moral life; *b)* taking wise counsel; *c)* prayer to the Father of light; *d)* removal of obstacles to a true conscience, chief amongst which is the obscurity resulting from unforgiven sin.

139. **SECOND PRINCIPLE.** *Everyone is obliged to follow his conscience whether it commands or forbids some action, not only when it is true but also when it is in invincible error.*

There is a reason for the use of the two words *commands* and *forbids*, for if conscience permits or merely counsels some line of action there is no strict obligation to follow it. It is patently obvious why we must obey a *true* conscience, and the reason for man's obligation to follow an invincibly erroneous conscience is that failure to do so would mean that he was acting contrary to the subjective norm of morality and was therefore committing sin. Thus, for example, a person who is convinced that he ought to tell a lie in order to save his friend from some danger is bound to tell the lie; in so doing he does not commit formal sin. Anyone who thinks that today is a fast day, although as a matter of fact it is not, and in spite of his conviction does not observe the fast, commits formal sin.

140. **THIRD PRINCIPLE.** *It is not permissible to follow conscience when it is in vincible error no matter whether it commands or forbids some action; on the other hand, one cannot act contrary to such a conscience; the error must be corrected before any action is taken.*

As will be proved later, a certain conscience alone is the lawful guide of morality. A vincibly erroneous conscience is not a certain conscience and consequently a man who acts while his conscience is in that state exposes himself to the danger of sin. — If a man's conscience is in error through his own fault, then he must correct that error by taking suitable means to discover the truth; if his efforts fail he must refrain from action, but if even this is impossible then he must choose what appears to be the safer course.

THE LAX CONSCIENCE

141. **THE CAUSES** of a lax conscience are numerous: 1) *bad education and evil company* — all too evident from daily experience; 2) *violent disorderly passions,* which usually cloud the intellect and prevent it from making a correct judgment; 3) *a life of vice,* which causes spiritual blindness or at least shortsightedness.

142. **The remedies** for a lax conscience are: 1) devout and assiduous *prayer* to God, the Father of light; 2) *sacramental Confession* where the penitent receives grace and correct instruction; 3) *removal of the causes* of laxity.

THE PERPLEXED CONSCIENCE AND THE SCRUPULOUS CONSCIENCE

143. 1. **A perplexed conscience** is one which fears sin both in the performance and in the omission of some action. For example, a sensitive person whose duty it is to care for a sick person thinks that it is sinful not to assist at Mass on a feast day, and yet fears that he sins against charity by leaving the sick person alone in the house.

Rule to be followed. If the person suffering from a perplexed conscience is able to suspend action or to seek advice, then that without doubt is the course to be followed; if on the other hand this is morally impossible, then he should choose that which seems to him the less of two evils; if he is not able to decide which is the less evil, he is free to decide either to act or to refrain from action since no one is obliged by the impossible and no one commits sin when under the influence of force.

If the state of perplexity arises through previous negligence, e.g., if a confessor through culpable lack of knowledge does not know whether to absolve a penitent or not, what has been said already in no. 17 in reference to vincible and culpable ignorance applies here.

144. 2. **A scrupulous conscience** is a state of groundless fear rather than the judgment of a healthy mind. Such a conscience is a torment both to the penitent and to the confessor. Great care must be exercised in distinguishing it from a *tender conscience* which carefully avoids all sin, even the smallest. Therefore, it is essential to be familiar with the signs of a scrupulous conscience.

Signs of a scrupulous conscience: *a)* excessive anxiety about previous confessions; *b)* protracted accusations of irrelevant details; *c)* stubbornness which refuses to accept the decisions of the confessor.

The causes of a scrupulous conscience are sometimes (although rarely) *supernatural*, namely, God or the devil; more frequently they are *natural* and are either *moral*, such as the excessive avoidance of human company, conversation with timorous persons, hidden pride, and so on, or *physical*, namely, a pathological condition of the brain or heart or nerves or intestines.

The remedies for scruples are: *a) the removal of their causes*, for which the aid of an experienced doctor is often necessary;

b) perfect obedience to a wise director;

c) healthy recreation and manual or spiritual work to distract the mind from the scrupulous thoughts;

d) fervent and assiduous prayer to God, the Father of light and the source of peace.

THE CERTAIN CONSCIENCE AND THE DOUBTING CONSCIENCE

We shall consider: 1) the certain conscience; 2) the doubting conscience, or rather, the course of action to be followed in a state of moral doubt.

Art. 1. The Certain Conscience

145. KINDS. As stated already, a certain conscience judges without any prudent fear of error that an act is either lawful or unlawful.

Moral certainty—and this is the type of certainty to be considered here—is divided as follows: *a)* it is said to be *perfect* (*strict*) when it excludes prudent doubt, and *imperfect* (*wide*) when some slight reasons militate against the truth of a decision which is founded on serious motives.

b) Moral certainty is *speculative* when the intellect considers the truth of some matter in an objective manner without any direct reference to a practical case; it is *practical* when it is concerned with an act to be done here and now.

c) Direct moral certainty is based on intrinsic principles which clearly reveal the moral character of the act; *indirect* moral certainty is derived from what are called reflex principles, which we shall discuss later.

146. PRINCIPLE. *a) Only a certain conscience (whether the certainty is direct or indirect) is a correct guide to moral behavior, and b) to act lawfully imperfect certainty is ordinarily sufficient.*

The reason for the first part of the principle is that the man who acts without being morally certain that his act is lawful commits sin by exposing himself unnecessarily to the proximate danger of formally offending God.

The second part rests on the fact that sometimes it is impossible to obtain anything more than *imperfect* certainty regarding our actions, and no one is bound to do the impossible. The same truth is evident from the third proposition condemned by Alexander VIII: "It is not permitted to follow a (probable) opinion or among the probables the most probable."[98] Even the most probable opinion is not absolutely certain but is certain only in the wide sense of the term. Therefore, if one is permitted to follow a most probable opinion, absolute certainty is not always required, and certainty in the wide sense is sufficient.

Art. 2. The Doubting Conscience, or, Moral Doubt

147. KINDS. Doubt understood in the strict sense is the suspension of the intellect's assent and judgment in reference to a proposition, and consequently it is opposed not only to certainty but also to suspicion and opinion in which there exists a genuine intellectual assent, although imperfect and accompanied by the fear of error. When in doubt, the mind is like the arm of a balance which remains horizontal, inclining neither to one side nor to the other.—Together

[98] DZ 1293.

with St. Thomas[99] earlier authors used to distinguish three steps leading to the firm assent of the intellect: 1) the state of doubt where no assent exists; 2) the states of opinion and suspicion in which the intellect gives an imperfect assent; 3) science and faith where there exists a firm assent, without any fear of error. — Recent authors usually prefer to speak of only two stages: a certain assent without any fear of error (certainty) and uncertain assent accompanied by the fear of error (doubt).

KINDS OF DOUBT. 1. The mind may be doubtful about the existence of some *law* (*dubium juris*) or of some particular *fact* (*dubium facti*).

2. Doubt is said to be *positive* when the fear of error is based on grave reasons; it is *negative* when the fear of error rests on slight reasons.

3. Doubt is either *speculative* or *practical*. The first turns on the objective morality of a human act irrespective of its present performance or omission. Such speculative doubt exists in controversial questions when moralists argue on either side, e.g., whether an irregular will binds in conscience or not. Practical doubt is concerned with the morality of an act about to be performed here and now — for example, whether it is lawful to read this dangerous book.

148. **PRINCIPLE**. *No one is allowed to perform an act while in a state of positive practical doubt.*

The reason should be evident from what has been said already. For if certainty in the wide sense of the word is required for lawful action, it is not lawful to act while in a state of positive practical doubt, since by so doing one exposes oneself to the immediate danger of committing formal sin. If, therefore, a man doubts the lawfulness of some action he must either refrain from acting or remove his practical doubt. There are two possible ways of removing the doubt, one direct, the other indirect. The *direct* method consists in diligently searching after the truth until at length certainty is attained. If this direct method is impossible, then the doubt may be removed *indirectly* by so-called reflex principles.

149. **REFLEX OR INDIRECT PRINCIPLES** are general directions which directly and of themselves do not prove the truth of the matter under investigation but nevertheless reflect, so to speak, their own clear light on the obscure practical doubt and dispel the darkness of that doubt while the act is being performed. The more important reflex principles are the following:

    1. A doubtful law has no binding force.

    2. In doubt one must stand by presumption.

    3. In doubt possession is nine-tenths of the law.

1. *A doubtful law has no binding force* whenever the doubt concerns the lawfulness of an act and not its validity. Whatever may be said about the truth of this principle which is fiercely attacked by some theologians, all modern theologians are agreed that it cannot be applied in the following cases:

[99] See ST, II-II, q. 2, a. 1.

a) when the doubt concerns the validity of the Sacraments;

b) when the doubt concerns something which is absolutely necessary for salvation; so, for example, when there is risk of losing eternal life, the safer opinion must be followed;

c) when the question involves an established right of a third party. Thus, for example, a judge would not be justified in giving judgment on the basis of a probable opinion while refusing to follow what is certainly the more probable opinion.

2. *When in doubt one must stand by presumption.* This seems the most useful of all the principles and was already to be found expressed in the Decretals of Gregory IX. All other reflex principles rest on this and when rightly used it seems sufficient for solving all practical doubt.

3. *In doubt possession is nine-tenths of the law.* This principle forms the basis for the theory of Equiprobabilism and is known in brief as the principle of possession. In its application to matters of *commutative justice* the principle is most certain and is found in the Decretals of Gregory IX, but it has also been extended to other matters, although its practical application is not devoid of difficulty and is frequently misused.

VARIOUS MORAL SYSTEMS

150. DEFINITION. A moral system is *a method of arriving at moral certainty from a state of practical doubt.* There are seven such systems:

1. RIGORISM, or Absolute Tutiorism, maintains that the safer course must always be followed even though the opinion in favor of liberty is most probable. This was the opinion of Joannes Sinnichius, Doctor of Louvain (d. 1666) and of the Jansenists. The system was condemned by Alexander VIII who censured the following proposition on Dec. 7, 1690: "It is not lawful to follow even the most probable of probable opinions."

151. 2. MODERATE TUTIORISM teaches that the less safe opinion which favors liberty can be followed provided that it is most probable. This was the system proposed by certain doctors at Louvain[100] and by other authors, e.g., Henry of St. Ignatius, Gerdil. Although this system has not been condemned by the Church, nowadays it is rightly rejected by everyone as too severe and impossible to follow in practice.

152. 3. PROBABILIORISM asserts that one may follow the opinion that favors liberty so long as it is clearly more probable than the opinion in favor of the law. Before the days of Medina this system was the one most commonly taught, but today it finds few supporters owing to its great practical difficulties.

153. 4. EQUIPROBABILISM is summed up in the following statement: "When there are conflicting opinions which are equally or almost equally probable, it is lawful to follow the opinion in favor of liberty when the doubt relates to the *existence* of

---

[100] Steyart, Opstraet.

law, but if the doubt concerns the *cessation* of law, the law continues to bind."[101] To some extent this system resembles the previous system of Probabiliorism, insofar as it maintains that it is permissible to follow the opinion in favor of liberty when it is certainly more probable, but he *must* follow the opinion in favor of the law if this is certainly more probable. The principal exponent of this system is St. Alphonsus who was preceded by Eusebius Amort, Rassler, and others; all Redemptorists and many others follow the same view.

154. 5. PURE PROBABILISM maintains that in cases of doubt relating to the lawfulness of acts and not to their validity it is always lawful to follow the opinion in favor of liberty if the opinion is certainly probable, even though the opinion in favor of the law is much more probable.

There are various kinds of probability.

1) Probability is either intrinsic or extrinsic. Probability is said to be *intrinsic* when it is founded on reasons taken from the nature of the matter to prove its truth; it is *extrinsic* when based on the authority of learned men. An opinion is considered to be extrinsically probable when there are five or six noteworthy authorities in its favor or at least one outstanding doctor like St. Thomas or St. Alphonsus.

2) An opinion may be either *certainly*, or *doubtfully*, or *slightly* probable, according as the opinion rests on solid and firm arguments, or on doubtful or slight arguments.

3) Probability is *absolute* when the arguments in favor of an opinion considered by themselves, namely, independently of any opposing arguments, appear to be valid; probability is *relative* if the arguments in favor of an opinion retain their value only when compared with the arguments supporting the contrary opinion. The first theologian to lend his support to this theory was Bartholomew Medina, O.P., who has been followed by an almost innumerable number of theologians down to the present day.

155. 6. LAX PROBABILISM or Laxism taught that it is lawful to follow an opinion that is not only certainly probable—as Probabilism maintains—but even when the opinion is doubtfully or slightly probable. This was the teaching of Thomas Tamburinus, Caramuel, Bauny, Moya, and others. Nowadays, this theory has ceased to exist and seems to have been condemned by Innocent IX in proscribing this third proposition: "In general, when we do something confidently according to probability whether intrinsic or extrinsic, however slight, provided there is no departure from the bounds of probability, we always act prudently."[102]

156. 7. COMPENSATIONISM OR THE SYSTEM OF SUFFICIENT CAUSE maintains that one may follow a certainly probable opinion in favor of liberty while abandoning a more probable opinion in favor of the law, but when there is danger of sin there is required a sufficient reason (compensation) for acting in favor of liberty. If this

---

[101] Joseph Aertnys, C.SS.R.
[102] DZ 1153.

sufficient reason is lacking, one must follow the more probable opinion. This opinion is held by Potton, Manier, Laloux, and other more recent authors.

PRACTICAL CONCLUSION. Apart from Rigorism and Laxism, each of the above systems is tolerated by the Church, and in consequence the confessor is not entitled to force his own system on the penitent or to demand something from his penitent to which the latter is not obliged according to the principles of one or other of the systems. Therefore, the confessor may prudently advise the safer and more probable opinion, but he is not justified in imposing such on the penitent. In practice, let him choose those opinions which, taking everything into consideration, promise to be the more beneficial for the spiritual welfare of his penitent.

THE EDUCATION OF CONSCIENCE

157. It is of the utmost importance that the conscience of man be free from error and embrace the truth. For it is a true conscience that bears the best fruit, and nothing but the most grievous harm can result from a false conscience. The education of conscience has a vital part to play in enabling man to avoid error, and there are both natural and supernatural means to be used to achieve this purpose.

The *natural* means are: *a)* a good education from the beginning of childhood; *b)* a perfect sincerity in man with himself by a faithful, continual, and candid examination of his own conscience.

The *supernatural* means are: *a)* fervent prayer to God, the Father of light; *b)* a strenuous fight against man's disordered passions with the aid of divine grace; *c)* sacramental Confession and obedience to one's spiritual director.

TREATISE V
SIN IN GENERAL

In this treatise we shall consider: 1) The Nature of Sin; 2) The Various Kinds of Sin; 3) The Species of Sins; 4) The Numerical Distinction of Sins; 5) The Causes of Sin; 6) The Effects of Sin; 7) Internal Sins; 8) The Capital Sins.

THE NATURE OF SIN

Various words are used in Sacred Scripture to describe sin, e.g., disobedience, contempt of God, iniquity, impiety, prevarication, foolishness, an offense against God. It is this last phrase which best describes the malice of sin.

158. REAL DEFINITION. *Sin is a prevarication of the divine law;*[103] or, *sin is any word, deed, or desire contrary to God's eternal law.*[104]

Since every sin is a human and a moral act, it requires the advertence of the intellect and the consent of the will. If either of these is lacking, the act cannot

[103] Ambrose, *On Paradise*, chap. 8, no. 39.
[104] Augustine, *Contra Faustum*, bk. 22, no. 27.

be a formal sin. Every sin is a genuine offense against God, and there is no such thing as a purely *philosophical* sin which offends against right reason but does not give rise to a theological fault.

KINDS OF SIN

159. *Original* sin is that privation of original justice inherited at birth; *personal* sin is an offense against God committed by the deliberate will of the individual.

Personal sin is either *actual* or *habitual* sin, according as it is a transitory act (or omission) or a permanent habit. Actual sins are of various kinds:

1. Sins of *commission* are acts contrary to a negative precept, such as theft; sins of *omission* are transgressions of a positive precept, such as missing Mass.

2. Actual sins are either sins of *thought*, *word*, or *deed*, according as they are committed by the mind alone or by word of mouth or by some external action.

3. Sins of *ignorance* proceed from lack of knowledge; sins of *weakness* are the result of passion which makes the act less voluntary; sins of *malice* proceed from an evil will.

4. There are sins *against the Holy Ghost*, sins which *cry to Heaven for vengeance*, and the *capital sins*. These sins are essentially different from each other. A *sin against the Holy Ghost* is committed by the deliberate contempt of some grace withdrawing man from sin. Such sins are usually named: presumption, despair, resisting the known truth of Christianity, envy of the grace possessed by one's neighbor, obstinacy, impenitence. — *Sins crying to Heaven for vengeance* are such sins whose malice cries out to Heaven, so to speak, because of the grievous injury done to the social order; these are four in number: murder, sodomy, oppression of orphans and widows, defrauding workers of their just wage. — *The capital sins* are those which are, so to speak, the roots from which other sins spring; there are seven: pride, envy, covetousness, anger, lust, gluttony, sloth.

5. *Formal* sin is a voluntary and free transgression of the law; *material* sin is an involuntary transgression.

6. *Mortal* sin is that sin which destroys sanctifying grace and causes the death of the soul; *venial* sin is an offense against God which merely lessens the fervor of charity. This division is of supreme importance and consequently requires a more detailed explanation.

160. THE NATURE OF MORTAL SIN implies: 1) an aversion from God; 2) an adherence to creatures which is seriously inordinate; 3) grave injury to the rational nature of man and to the social order.

Three conditions must be verified for mortal sin:

1. There must be *grave matter* which is determined by the object and circumstances of the act (or omission) and which is made known to us as such in the first place through the teaching authority of the Church and her theologians. There are some sins which do not admit of slight matter and these are mortal sins *ex toto*

genere suo (e.g., lust, blasphemy, and so on); in other sins the matter is not always grave (e.g., in theft, or fasting), and thus the sin may be venial. These are mortal sins *ex genere suo*.

2. *Full advertence* to the moral nature of the act is required. Therefore, where such advertence is defective, sins are always venial (or there may be no sin at all) because of the act's imperfection.

3. *Full consent* is also necessary, and this is always presumed to be present where there is full advertence and no external violence. Therefore, fear and passion certainly diminish consent but do not destroy it, and they do not prevent mortal sin unless full advertence is lacking.

In practice, there is often reasonable doubt whether all these three conditions were verified or not in a particular case. In such instances, if the confessor fails to reach a conclusion after prudent inquiry he must leave the matter to God's judgment but warn the penitent against future dangers of sinning. If the penitent is in doubt about one or other of the requisite conditions, he should candidly reveal his doubts to the confessor and submit to his judgment.

In the following instances *advertence and consent are imperfect*:

1. when an act is committed while half asleep or half drunk;

2. when the penitent is not in complete possession of himself, e.g., because of a sudden and most vehement surge of passion;

3. when a person is suffering from pathological states or feelings, e.g., hysteria, mania, phobia;

4. when the penitent can truthfully and certainly assert that he would never have acted in that way if he had thought about it seriously beforehand;

5. when the penitent in the face of temptation is immediately agitated and sorry because of the devout state of his conscience.

161. THE ESSENCE OF VENIAL SIN consists in a certain disorder, but does not imply complete aversion from man's final end; it is therefore an illness of the soul, so to speak, and not its death.

Venial sins are distinguished as follows:

1) There are sins which *of their nature* are venial, since their moral object implies a slight disorder, such as a jocose lie; 2) other sins are venial *because of parvity of matter*, i.e. sins which in themselves are grave but because of slight matter become slight disorders, such as the theft of a shilling; 3) sins may be venial *through imperfection in the act* when there is wanting full advertence or full consent, e.g., semi-deliberate impure thoughts.

Although the frequent commission of venial sins of itself never changes venial into mortal sin, sometimes venial sin becomes grave sin, e.g., through an erroneous conscience, through the malicious intent of the sinner, through the accumulation of matter—as in theft.

In order to distinguish between venial and mortal sins one must consult the authority *a)* of Sacred Scripture, *b)* of the Church, *c)* of the Doctors.

SPECIES OF SINS

162. Since the Council of Trent teaches that both the species and the number of mortal sins must be revealed in confession,[105] it is necessary that the confessor make himself acquainted with the rules for distinguishing the species and number of sins.

St. Thomas bases the specific distinction of sin from sin on the *formal distinction between their moral object*; Scotus derives the distinction *from their opposition to different virtues*; whereas Vasquez prefers their *opposition to different precepts*.

These three criteria differ from each other only in appearance and not in fact, and are usually expressed in the following verse:

Objectum, virtus, diversa praecepta modusque
Dant speciem peccatis diversumque reatum.

In practice, sins are said to be specifically distinct from each other:

1. if they are opposed *to different virtues*—e.g., a sin against the virtue of justice is a different sin from one against the virtue of temperance;

2. if they are opposed to the same virtue but *in different ways*, e.g., by excess and by defect, and so on. Thus, theft is specifically distinct from calumny, even though both sins are opposed to the same virtue of justice;

3. if they are opposed to laws which are *formally distinct*. Laws are considered to be formally distinct if they were made for different internal reasons. Thus, for example, theft which is forbidden both by natural, divine, and civil law is nevertheless only one sin since these three laws forbid theft for the same internal reason; on the other hand, a priest who sins against chastity commits two specifically distinct sins since he transgresses two laws that are formally distinct—namely, laws with two formally distinct motives, the motive of temperance and the motive of religion.

NUMERICAL DISTINCTION OF SINS

163. In this matter it is essential to consider the prudent estimation of men, since it is morally impossible on many occasions to discover the exact number of sins committed. The following general rules may be used:

1. *Sins that are specifically distinct are also distinct numerically.*

Thus, for example, a man who commits adultery commits two sins which are not only specifically distinct but also numerically distinct.

2. *There are as many sins as there are moral interruptions in the act of the will.*

[105] See Council of Trent, Session 14, "On the Most Holy Sacrament of Penance," Can. 7. See also TCCI 7:312.

The continuity of human acts is broken by revocation or by deliberate cessation which is an implicit revocation of the act. If, however, one is compelled to cease from the act through the call of other necessary occupations, then a distinction has to be made between internal acts, external acts, and those which are partly internal and partly external. *Purely internal* acts, such as impure thoughts (unaccompanied by desires), are interrupted by physical cessation. However, in practice it is often impossible to determine the exact number of such thoughts, and so it is sufficient to confess: I have had impure thoughts for such or such a period of time.

Acts that are *partly internal* and *partly external* (such as evil desires) do not seem to be interrupted by an involuntary cessation, at least when they are directed to obtaining one and the same object. Thus, for example, a man who desires to steal a hundred pounds and yet through fear of capture steals the money in small amounts over a period of time, would seem to commit only one sin.

In the same way *external* acts do not seem to be interrupted by any involuntary cessation, provided that the cessation does not last for long and the acts are not in themselves morally complete.[106] Consequently, a group of youths engaged in obscene conversation commit only one sin even if through the intervention of some superior they are forced to cease from their talk for half an hour, whereas a man who commits pollution and then repeats the act half an hour later commits two sins, because he has performed two acts which are in themselves morally complete and entire.

3. There are as many sins as there are morally complete objects, even though these objects are attained by one and the same act of the will and by the same external act.

Objects are considered to be morally complete if they are complete in themselves and have no moral connection with each other like means with an end. Even though this rule is not universally admitted, nevertheless it appears to be true since an object that is morally entire and complete is sought by an act of will that is complete and limited to that object. Thus, a man who intends to kill ten men in one explosion commits ten murders; a person who desires to seduce five young people through one immoral conversation commits five sins. On the other hand, a man who intends to have sexual intercourse with a woman and either immediately before or after the act is immodest in his speech or looks or touch commits one sin, since these acts are parts of one entire object.

THE CAUSES OF SIN

164. PRINCIPLE. *Neither God nor the devil nor anything else other than the evil will of the sinner himself is the adequate efficient cause of sin.*

It is of faith that God is not the cause of sin, this having been defined in the Council of Trent.[107]

---

[106] See no. 163.3.
[107] See Council of Trent, Session 6, Can. 6.

That neither the devil nor any other cause can infallibly incite man to sin is evident from the fact that no one can destroy the internal freedom of man. Therefore, man always has the power to resist temptations to sin.

Although *temptations* do not produce sin infallibly, they are powerful incitements to sin. Temptations arise from three sources: evil concupiscence, the devil, and the world. To consent to temptation is to commit sin, as is abundantly evident; therefore, it is essential to resist temptation or at least not to consent to it.

The remedies to be used against temptations are vigilance, humility, confidence in God, frequent use of the Sacraments, and so on.

EFFECTS OF SIN[108]

165. 1. These are the *effects of mortal sin*:

   a) loss of sanctifying grace;

   b) loss of the infused virtues (with the exception of faith and hope) and of the gifts of the Holy Ghost;

   c) loss of all merit;

   d) a foul disfigurement of the soul;

   e) remorse of conscience;

   f) right to eternal punishment.

166. 2. These are the *effects of venial sin*:

   a) some loss of beauty of soul;

   b) difficulty in practicing the virtues;

   c) withdrawal of many graces;

   d) an inclination to mortal sin;

   e) right to temporal punishment.

INTERNAL SIN

167. DEFINITION. Internal sins are those which are completed within the heart of man without being revealed externally. They are three in number: deliberate pleasure, sinful joy, evil desire.

168. DELIBERATE PLEASURE *is the sinful complacency taken in an evil object presented to man by his imagination but which is not accompanied by any desire for the object.*

   a) A *deliberate* pleasure. In Latin the adjective *morosa* is used, not because of the length of time (*mora*) required for this complacency but because the will freely lingers in this evil complacency even though it is only momentary.

---

[108] A fuller explanation of these effects is to be found in MTM, vol. 1, no. 392ff.

b) It is complacency *in an evil object presented by the imagination* ... and thus the object of the complacency is not an external object but a representation proceeding from the imagination.

c) A complacency *unaccompanied by desire* ... because if desire is also present, then the complacency assumes an additional moral evil. There are four objects in which man may take pleasure: 1) *the external act itself* such as an act of fornication; 2) *the external act as portrayed by the imagination*, e.g., not an act of fornication that has taken place already or one which is about to take place but the representation of the act existing in the imagination; 3) the subtle and skillful *way* in which the evil act is performed (e.g., picking pockets); 4) *the knowledge that man possesses of evil acts*, e.g., a moralist may take pleasure in being able to show the intrinsic evil of fornication.

The first form of pleasure is the sin itself present in the external act. The second form of pleasure is the deliberate pleasure of which we are speaking and is of the same evil character as the act which forms its object, since no one would take pleasure in such imagination unless his will were inclined toward the evil act itself, although he may be unwilling to complete the act externally. The third form of pleasure is not of itself evil, although it is often dangerous. The fourth form is lawful, in fact praiseworthy if done for a right intention.

PRINCIPLE. *To take deliberate pleasure in an object of the imagination which is gravely sinful is itself a mortal sin whose species is determined by the object itself and its circumstances.*

The reason is that an evil imagination and its evil object possess from the moral aspect the same essential wickedness, since the external act does not increase morality.

Thus, a person who takes deliberate pleasure in adultery sins in a different way than if he were to take delight in incest. However, in practice, it is normally sufficient for the penitent to confess that he had so many thoughts against chastity without mentioning the other circumstances. For such thoughts (*which are not accompanied by an evil desire*) do not present their object clearly with all its circumstances; they usually pass quickly through the mind making it morally impossible—especially after a long time—to reveal in confession all their circumstances.

169. SINFUL JOY *is a deliberate complacency in something evil done by oneself or by others.*

It consists in some form of approval of a sin already committed and therefore has the same malice as the sin itself. Similar to this joy is pride in the commission of sin and sadness in the non-fulfillment of some evil act.

170. EVIL DESIRE *is a deliberate complacence in some sin not yet committed*, or, the longing to do something morally evil.

This desire is *efficacious* if it represents a firm and genuine resolve to commit sin, or *inefficacious* if it is a wish unaccompanied by a firm resolve.

1. An *efficacious* desire to commit an evil act is a sin of the same species and malice as the external act which forms its object. This is clear from the fact that the entire

malice of a human act is based on the evil will of man, and the external act itself does not add any new morality. And thus, Christ Himself said: "He who shall look on a woman to lust after her has already committed adultery with her in his heart" (Mt 5:28).

2. An *inefficacious* or conditional desire to commit some evil is always detestable and therefore dangerous, since the imagination is incited by it and time is wasted. What is the value of such desires? However, it is not in itself sinful, if the condition attached takes away the malice of the act—e.g., I might desire to eat meat if it were not Friday. It is sinful if it contains some disorder in spite of the condition attached. Thus, for example, it is a sin to say: I would commit fornication if there were no hell.

PRACTICAL NOTES. Should the penitent confess in a general way: I have had bad thoughts, the confessor will first inquire: Were they voluntary or involuntary? If the penitent replies that they were voluntary, he will next ask: Were there any evil desires accompanying the thoughts? If the penitent replies in the negative, it only remains to discover the approximate number of these evil thoughts, without discussing the moral species of their objects—e.g., whether the thoughts concerned adultery, fornication, and so on—as is evident from what has been said in no. 168. But if the penitent replies that he had evil desires in addition to the thoughts, then he must make known the different moral species of their objects, e.g., whether he desired adultery, or fornication, and so on. However, it sometimes happens that uninstructed penitents cannot distinguish deliberate pleasure from evil desire, in which case the confessor is not obliged to inquire about the objects of such acts.

THE CAPITAL SINS

171. DEFINITION. *A capital sin (or, preferably, vice) is one which is the source, so to speak, of other sins and vices.* The Angelic Doctor prefers to use the word *vice* in place of *sin*, in order to emphasize that here we are considering *habits* or evil inclinations which have arisen through repetition of acts.[109] And thus, for instance, a man who is drunk on one occasion has not yet acquired the vice of intemperance.

NUMBER. Following St. Gregory the Great,[110] it has become customary to distinguish seven capital vices or sins: 1) vainglory; 2) avarice; 3) lust; 4) envy; 5) gluttony; 6) anger; 7) sloth.

THE MALICE of these capital sins is not always greater than that of other sins, and not every act proceeding from a capital vice is a mortal sin—e.g., acts of envy, of anger, of sloth are frequently venial sins. However, a man who knowingly and willingly fosters these capital vices or evil inclinations without resolutely resisting them is nearly always in a state of mortal sin.

---

[109] See ST, I-II, q. 71.
[110] See Gregory the Great, *Moralia in Job*, bk. 31, chap. 45, no. 87.

St. Thomas does not include pride among the capital vices, preferring to call it the queen and source of all sins without exception.[111] However, since pride and vainglory are closely allied, we shall consider them together.

172. 1. PRIDE AND VAINGLORY.

Pride is an inordinate desire for one's own excellence.[112]

Pride is said to be complete when a man extols himself to such an extent that he is unwilling to admit subjection to God and His laws through fear that such subjection would be harmful to his own excellence. Such pride is a mortal sin, because it is a contempt of God or of those who stand in His place. Pride is *imperfect* when a man thinks of himself too highly without rejecting his subjection to God and his superiors. Such pride is in itself venially sinful since it does not imply a serious disorder. But every form of pride is an extremely dangerous vice, *a)* because it insinuates its way into all good deeds so as to destroy their merit; *b)* because nothing so quickly grows in us and so slowly dies; *c)* because it is not easily recognized.

Sins to which pride leads are: presumption, ambition, vainglory, boasting, hypocrisy, strife, disobedience.

Remedies for pride are: a sincere knowledge of oneself, consideration of Christ's humility, the practice of humility.

Vainglory is an inordinate desire to manifest one's own excellence. Therefore, while pride in its general form is an inordinate desire for one's own excellence, vainglory is primarily a desire to *manifest* one's personal excellence; it is an inordinate desire to receive praise from men.

173. 2. AVARICE.

Avarice is the inordinate love of having possessions or riches.

Avarice which offends against *justice* is a mortal sin which admits of slight matter; that which offends against the virtue of liberality only is in itself a venial sin.

Sins which ordinarily spring from avarice are: hardness of heart, unrest or disordered anxiety regarding the things of this world, the use of violence in acquiring possessions, lying and deceit.

Remedies: consideration of the vanity of this world's goods, meditation on the example of Christ.

174. 3. LUST.

Lust is the inordinate desire for sexual pleasure.

It is a mortal sin which admits of no slight matter.

---

[111] See ST, I-II, q. 84, a. 4, rep. 4.
[112] See ST, I-II, q. 84, a. 2.

Sins which result from lust are: mental blindness, precipitancy, inconstancy, self-love and hatred of God, affection for the present life and fear of the future.

Remedies: humble and frequent prayer, frequent reception of the Sacraments, avoidance of idleness, practice of temperance, avoidance of the occasions of sin.

We shall return to the consideration of this vice in the treatise on the vices contrary to temperance.

175. **4. ENVY.**

Envy is sadness on account of the goods possessed by another which are regarded as harmful to oneself since they diminish one's own excellence or renown.

Envy is a mortal sin which admits of slight matter and is directly opposed to charity.

Sins which normally result from envy are: hatred, murmuring, detraction, resentment at the neighbor's prosperity and joy in his adversity.

Remedies: practice of brotherly love, practice of humility, consideration of the evils which normally result from envy.

176. **5. GLUTTONY.**

Gluttony is an inordinate desire for food and drink.

It is of its nature a venial sin since it does not imply a serious moral disorder; however, it often becomes grievously sinful by reason of its most evil effects.

Sins which ordinarily result from gluttony are: mental dullness, excessive talking and buffoonery, immoderate hilarity, uncleanness of every kind.

Remedies: consideration of the evil consequences of this vice, practice of temperance, avoidance of the occasions of sin, especially if they involve intoxicating drink.

Further consideration will be given to gluttony and especially to drunkenness in no. 501ff.

177. **6. ANGER.**

Anger is the inordinate desire for revenge.

Anger considered in itself as a disorderly passion is a venial sin, since it involves only a slight disorder, but insofar as it is an inordinate desire for revenge it is a mortal sin which allows of parvity of matter, since such a desire offends against charity and sometimes against justice. Anger considered in its effects is a grave or venial sin depending on whether those effects ought to have been foreseen and whether they are contrary to right reason in a serious or slight manner.

St. Thomas lists six *effects* of this vice: indignation, mental disturbance, noisy speech, blasphemy, abuse, quarrels.[113]

Remedies against this vice: to foresee its causes, resistance to the movements of anger immediately and vigorously, consideration of Christ's example.

---

[113] See ST, II-II, q. 158, a. 7.

178. 7. SLOTH.

Sloth is defined either as sorrow in the face of spiritual good inasmuch as it is God's good,[114] or as sorrow regarding the means of salvation conferred on us and prescribed by God.

Sloth is a mortal sin which admits of slight matter, and is opposed to the love of God.

Sins which result from sloth: tepidity toward the divine precepts, wandering toward what is forbidden, faint-heartedness, despair of salvation.

Remedies: consideration of the evil results of this vice, meditation on man's eternal reward.

TREATISE VI
VIRTUE IN GENERAL

This treatise is divided into three chapters: 1) Nature and Kinds of Virtue; 2) The Acquired Moral Virtues; 3) The Infused Virtues.

NATURE AND KINDS OF VIRTUE

179. DEFINITION. *Virtue is that which confers goodness on its owner and makes his acts good.*[115] *This definition is primarily true of the moral virtues which make both man himself and his acts good. Another definition is that given by St. Augustine, referring to the infused virtues: virtue is a good quality of the soul enabling man to live well, which no one can use for evil, produced in man by God without man's assistance.*[116] *The nature of virtue is understood more clearly by comparing it with the gifts and fruits of the Holy Ghost and with the beatitudes.*

180. THE GIFTS OF THE HOLY GHOST *are habits accompanying sanctifying grace whereby a man is well disposed to receive the inspirations and movements of the Holy Ghost.* In the gifts, therefore, it is the Holy Ghost Himself Who inspires man toward goodness; in the virtues man is moved by right reason aided by grace. The gifts of the Holy Ghost are seven in number: wisdom, understanding, knowledge, counsel, piety, fortitude, fear.

The gift of *wisdom* (corresponding to the virtue of *charity*) is a habit infused by God which makes the soul responsive to the Holy Ghost in the contemplation of divine things and in the use of *God's ideas* to judge both created and divine matters. — The first effect of wisdom is a filial fear of God, but its supreme effect is a welcome peace in the heart of man.

The gift of *understanding* is a supernatural enlightenment given to man in the form of a habit whereby he *grasps* revealed truths easily and intimately.

---

[114] See ST, II-II, q. 35, a. 2, c.
[115] See Aristotle, *Nichomachean Ethics*, bk. 2, chap. 6.
[116] See Augustine, *On Free Will*, bk. 2, chap. 18; see also ST, I-II, q. 55, a. 4.

The gift of *knowledge* (the science of the saints) enables man through some form of spiritual relish and warmth of charity to judge everything in its relationship to his supernatural end by means of *inferior causes.*—The gifts of understanding and of knowledge aid and perfect the virtue of *faith.*

The gift of *counsel* (which aids and perfects the virtue of *prudence*) enables man to judge and command individual acts.

The gift of *piety* (which aids and perfects the virtue of *justice*) enables man to show reverence both for God as a most loving *Father* and for men as the *sons of God.*

The gift of *fortitude* (which aids and perfects the virtue of *fortitude*) gives the soul a singular strength in resisting evil and attaining to everlasting life.

The gift of *fear* (which aids and perfects the virtue of *hope*) impels man to a profound respect for the majesty of God.

181. THE FRUITS OF THE HOLY GHOST which St. Paul lists as twelve in number (charity, joy, peace, patience, benignity, goodness, longanimity, mildness, faith, modesty, continence, chastity)[117] are *human acts which result from the gifts of the Holy Ghost and refresh man with holy and sincere joy.*

The *beatitudes* (of which St. Matthew lists eight, St. Luke four)[118] are *external acts of the virtues and gifts which in their own special way lead man to happiness both on earth and especially in Heaven.*

182. KINDS OF VIRTUE.

1. In relation to their *origin*, virtues are either *acquired* or *infused*, according as man acquires them by his own acts or God infuses them together with sanctifying grace.

2. In relation to their *object*, virtues are either *intellectual, moral,* or *theological*. The intellectual virtues perfect man in his understanding of truth (whether speculative or practical), and of these there are five: understanding, wisdom, knowledge, prudence, art. The moral virtues perfect the powers of man to enable him to use correctly and well the means to his supernatural end; these can be reduced to four as being more fundamental than the rest and are known as the cardinal virtues: prudence, fortitude, justice, temperance.—The theological virtues have God as their immediate object and are given and revealed by God alone; these are three in number: faith, hope, and charity.

THE ACQUIRED MORAL VIRTUES

183. THE EXISTENCE of acquired moral virtues is as certain as the existence of man's ability to perform good acts by his own natural powers. It is by the repetition of such acts that good habits or virtues are formed. Moral virtues acquired without the aid of grace and charity are genuine virtues although imperfect, since they do not make man perfectly good.

---

[117] See Gal 5:22–23.
[118] See Mt 5:3–12; and Lk 6:20–23.

184. THE PROPERTIES of the acquired virtues are four in number: 1) they avoid extremes; 2) they are interconnected; 3) they are unequal; 4) they endure after this life.

1. A *moral virtue avoids extremes*, i.e., it does not offend against right reason either by excess or by defect. This mean of the virtues is either a *rational mean* insofar as they incline man to observe a due proportion in his acts, or an *objective mean* which in addition determines that there should be an equality between man's acts and his neighbor's due. Only the virtue of justice possesses an objective mean.

2. *The moral virtues are interconnected* to this extent that if one moral virtue is possessed in its *perfect* form then all the others must be present, whereas if one is lacking, all the others are wanting in perfection. The bond of union between the *supernatural* virtues is charity, whereas the moral virtues are united together by *prudence*. Neither the intellectual virtues nor the theological virtues are connected in this way; one may exist without the other. It is possible for a man to possess inclinations toward the moral virtues even though he is completely wanting in one of those virtues.

3. *The moral virtues are unequal* both from the point of view of their objects and from the point of view of man himself. It is quite clear that varying degrees of virtues may be found in different persons. A similar inequality exists in the intellectual and theological virtues.

4. *The moral virtues endure after this life*, at least in their *formal* element, namely, the right order of reason existing in them. As regards their material acts, those virtues which control our inordinate passions will not be found in Heaven where such passions no longer exist.

THE INFUSED VIRTUES

185. THE EXISTENCE of infused virtues—all of which the soul receives together with sanctifying grace—is today generally admitted. Therefore, even baptized infants possess all the infused virtues.[119] The infused moral virtues are of a distinct species from the corresponding acquired moral virtues, since, in the latter, reason takes the place of faith as the standard of moderation.

THREE SPECIAL PROPERTIES are to be found in the infused virtues: *a)* they increase within themselves as often as sanctifying grace increases, e.g., by the performance of meritorious acts; *b)* all of them, with the exception of faith and hope, are lost by mortal sin; *c)* they can be diminished only indirectly.

---

[119] See Council of Vienna, Decree 1 (Jan. 13, 1313).

TREATISE VII
THEOLOGICAL FAITH AND CONTRARY VICES

This treatise is divided into three chapters: 1) The Nature of Faith; 2) The Necessity of Faith; 3) Vices Contrary to Faith.

NATURE OF THEOLOGICAL FAITH

186. DEFINITION. St. Paul defines faith in the following terms: *"It is that which gives substance to our hopes, which convinces us of things that we cannot see"* (Heb 11:1). The Vatican Council defined it in this way: *"Faith is the supernatural virtue whereby under the inspiration and help of God's grace we believe that what He has revealed is true not because of the intrinsic truth of the matters grasped by the natural light of reason but because of the authority of God Himself revealing, Who can neither deceive nor be deceived."*[120]

In order to explain these two definitions more carefully it is necessary to consider separately the act and the virtue of faith.

Art. 1. The Act of Faith

187. The *immediate* SUBJECT of the act of faith is the *intellect*, since the act of faith is an assent and not a mere confidence in the divine mercy, as taught by Protestants. Although the act of faith is formally and immediately an act of the intellect, the will also has an important role to play since it has to command the assent in the act of faith. The objects of faith—the truths accepted on faith—are not evident in themselves but are obscure, and therefore they do not compel the assent of the intellect in the same way as natural truths. Consequently, the will under the influence of grace commands the assent of the intellect.

The remote subject of the act of faith, that is, the persons capable of making the act, are: *a)* all men alive on earth, with the exception of formal unbelievers; *b)* souls in purgatory, since they do not yet enjoy the Beatific Vision. Neither the angels and the blessed in Heaven who gaze on God's essence nor the damned in hell who lack grace possess faith in the strict sense of the word.

188. THE FORMAL OBJECT of faith (*objectum attributionis*) is the primary and essential Truth, the divine essence, which is primarily and principally attained by faith; everything else is believed in reference to that divine essence.

The internal motive of belief (*objectum formale quo*) is the authority of God revealing—the primary truth in speech. For if any Christian is asked why he believes, he immediately replies that it is because the articles of faith have been revealed by God.

---

[120] First Vatican Council, Session 3, chap. 3, no. 2.

The *material object* of faith is that which is formally and certainly revealed by God. Consequently, the Vatican Council has stated: "By faith which is both divine and catholic everything must be believed that is contained in the Word of God, whether written or handed down, and also that which the Church through her solemn or ordinary judgment and universal Magisterium proposes for belief as a truth revealed by God."[121]

189. **THE PROPERTIES OF FAITH.** Faith is supernatural, free, infallible, and certain.

1. The act of faith is *supernatural, a)* in its object (the truths believed), *b)* in its motive (revelation by God), *c)* in its principle (sanctifying grace), since no one can make an act of faith without the help of divine grace. Hence the Council of Trent has defined: "If anyone shall say that it is possible for man to believe as he ought without the prevenient inspiration of the Holy Ghost and His help, ... *anathema sit.*"[122]

2. The act of faith is *free*, since the intellect gives its assent to truths which are obscure and not evident in themselves. Thus, the Vatican Council has declared: "If anyone shall say that the assent given to the Christian Faith is not free but necessarily results from arguments of human reason, ... *anathema sit.*"[123]

3. The act of faith is *infallible*, since it rests on the revelation of God and on the teaching authority of the Church, both of which are infallible.

4. The act of faith is *certain* and *constant*—that is to say, no reason at all permits man to doubt and deny its truth.

Art. 2. The Virtue of Faith

190. **ITS EXISTENCE.** The virtue of faith exists in everyone possessing sanctifying grace and also in the sinner, provided he has not committed a grave sin of disbelief.

This sin of disbelief will be discussed later. The Council of Trent has declared that faith certainly remains in the sinner: "If anyone says that faith is always destroyed at the same time as grace is lost through sin, or that the faith which remains is not genuine faith even though it is not a living faith, or that a person who possesses faith without charity is not a Christian, *anathema sit.*"[124] The faith possessed by the sinner is called *deformed faith*.

191. **INCREASE AND LOSS OF FAITH.** Faith is increased at the same time as sanctifying grace and in no other way; it is lost by the act of disbelief only (*formal* heresy).

The reason is that a person who steadfastly denies even one of the articles of faith denies also the infallible revelation of God and the infallible teaching authority of the Church, and consequently destroys within himself the very foundation of faith.

---

[121] First Vatican Council, Session 3, chap. 3, no. 8.
[122] Council of Trent, Session 6, Can. 3. See also TCCI 7:63, 326.
[123] First Vatican Council, Session 3, "On Faith," Can. 5.
[124] Council of Trent, Session 6, Can. 28. See also TCCI 7:131ff, 142ff.

NECESSITY OF THEOLOGICAL FAITH

192. **DEFINITIONS.** Both the habit and the act of faith are necessary both as means of salvation and by precept. A necessary *means* of salvation is an absolute condition without which it is impossible to attain to eternal life. A *precept* makes something obligatory for salvation when a special command is made by a legitimate superior who imposes something as a condition of salvation but not in such an absolute fashion that salvation could not be obtained otherwise. Therefore, no excuse is permissible when there is question of a necessary means; on the other hand, moral impossibility is usually taken to excuse from things that are necessary from precept.

This chapter is divided into two articles: 1) the necessity of faith as a means of salvation; 2) the necessity of faith from precept.

Art. 1. Necessity of Faith as a Means of Salvation

PRINCIPLE. *The habit of faith is a necessary means of salvation for all men; so is the act of faith for all adults.*

The reason for the first part of the principle is that faith has been established by God as the substance, that is, the primary foundation of things to be hoped for, i.e., eternal happiness. The Vatican Council made the following declaration: "Since without faith it is impossible to please God and to attain to fellowship of His sons, consequently no one can attain to justification without it; neither can anyone attain to everlasting life without persevering in faith."[125] The second part of the principle rests on Christ's words: "He who does not believe will be condemned" (Mk 16:16). Furthermore, how could an adult merit eternal life unless he first believed in its existence and in the means necessary to attain to it?

In an adult, neither the desire for faith nor faith in the wide sense of the word are sufficient, as some theologians have thought; there is required explicit faith and faith in the strict sense of the word.

193. **TRUTHS TO BE BELIEVED.**

1. With at least *implicit* faith one must believe everything revealed to man by God and which the Church proposes for belief.

2. With *explicit* faith one must believe that God exists and that He rewards the good and punishes the wicked. For St. Paul says: "Nobody reaches God's presence until he has learned to believe that God exists, and that He rewards those who try to find Him" (Heb 11:6).

Theologians are not agreed whether there are other truths which should be accepted with explicit faith as necessary means of salvation. There is a probable opinion which must be followed in practice that explicit faith in Christ as Redeemer and in the Blessed Trinity is necessary for salvation. Therefore, one cannot baptize or absolve anyone who does not give explicit belief to those four

---

[125] First Vatican Council, Session 3, chap. 3, no. 9.

truths.[126] It is sufficient for the uneducated to accept with divine faith these mysteries, even though their grasp of them may be imperfect.

Art. 2. Necessity of Faith from Precept

In relation to faith, two things are commanded: 1) the internal act of faith; 2) the external manifestation or profession of faith.

§ 1. Obligation to Elicit the Interior Act of Faith

194. PRINCIPLE. There exists a divine precept commanding internal explicit acts of faith regarding at least the chief articles of faith.

The existence of such a precept is presupposed by St. John when he writes: "What He commands is, that we should have faith in the name of His Son Jesus Christ" (1 Jn 3:23). The following proposition was condemned by Innocent XI: "Faith is not considered to fall under a special precept and by itself."[127]

This precept *extends* to all men and embraces at least the following four things: the Apostles' Creed, the Lord's Prayer, the Ten Commandments, the Sacraments which are necessary for all. Many theologians maintain that the faithful should commit to memory the Apostles' Creed, the Lord's Prayer, and the Ten Commandments, but there is no agreement on the existence of a strict obligation. — The faithful should endeavor to have a good knowledge of matters belonging to the Catholic religion, and parish priests are bound to instruct the faithful carefully in matters of faith and morals.

195. *The time of the obligation.* The precept of eliciting an act of faith obliges *of itself* — that is to say, independently of every other obligation:

1. *when God's revelation has been sufficiently proposed to man.* So far as Catholics are concerned this occurs when they attain the perfect use of their reason, but for heretics and pagans the time arrives when they realize the truth of the Catholic religion. Therefore, such heretics and pagans are obliged to be converted immediately in their heart to the true religion, even though their *public* conversion may be deferred for just reasons to a more opportune moment.

2. *when a new dogma of faith is proposed by the Church.*

3. *frequently during life.* And therefore, Innocent XI condemned this proposition: "It is enough to utter an act of faith once during life."[128] It is not possible to determine the exact number of times that the act of faith should be made, but men living a Christian life satisfy this precept abundantly in performing their various religious duties.

---

[126] See Holy Office, Jan. 25, 1703.
[127] DZ 1166.
[128] DZ 1167.

4. *probably at the hour of death*, because at that moment, most of all, man is obliged to believe that God is a merciful and just rewarder. There is an *incidental* obligation to make the act of faith: *a)* when this is necessary in order to fulfill some obligation which presupposes faith, such as in the reception of the Sacraments; *b)* during serious temptations against some virtue which cannot be overcome without faith.

§ 2. External Profession of Faith

Both God and the Church command the external profession of faith.

196. THE DIVINE PRECEPT to profess one's faith externally is easily gathered from the words of St. Paul: "The heart has only to believe, if we are to be justified; the lips have only to make confession, if we are to be saved" (Rom 10:10), and it follows from the very nature of man himself who must worship God not only with his mind but also with his body.

This precept is both affirmative and negative in character. Its *negative* aspect forbids man to deny his faith externally, which he may do either *directly*—by *formal* infidelity—or *indirectly*, by some action which externally gives a clear indication of denial of faith even though the agent himself has no intention of denying his faith. Thus, for example, a person indirectly denies his faith by partaking of the Protestant communion even though in his own mind he does not believe that Christ is present in that communion. *It is never permissible to deny one's faith either directly or indirectly*, because every denial of faith is a grave insult to God since it undermines the authority of God and the reverence due to Him. Hence Christ's threat: "Whoever disowns Me before men, before My Father in Heaven I too will disown him" (Mt 10:33). But although it is never lawful to deny one's faith, occasions do arise when it is permissible to conceal or dissemble one's faith, as will be explained later.

According to St. Thomas,[129] the divine precept obliges man to make an external profession of his faith when failure to do so would detract from the honor due to God or cause injury to the spiritual welfare of one's neighbor.[130]

1. *The honor due to God* demands an external profession of faith: *a)* when a man is questioned *by public authority* (not by private persons) about his faith; *b)* when a person is provoked even by private individuals through hatred of religion to a denial of his faith in word or deed.

2. *The spiritual welfare of our neighbor* requires an external profession of faith when grave scandal would ensue from its omission.[131]

---

[129] See ST, II-II, q. 3, a. 2.

[130] The Code of Canon Law expresses the precept in the following manner: "Christ's faithful are obliged to profess their faith publicly whenever their silence, subterfuge, or manner of acting imply an implicit denial of faith, a contempt of religion, or an insult to God, or scandal to the neighbor" (Can. 1325, § 1).

[131] E.g., Libellatici amongst the early Christians.

197. THE ECCLESIASTICAL PRECEPT demanding the external profession of faith obliges the following, according to the existing discipline of the Church:[132]

1. those about to be baptized,

2. persons returning to the fold of the Church,

3. subdeacons elect,

4. all who have the right to be present at a provincial council or diocesan synod,

5. confessors and preachers before they are granted their faculties,

6. all beneficiaries, such as parish priests and canons,

7. officials in episcopal curias and ecclesiastical courts,

8. officials in the Roman Congregations and courts,

9. all professors in seminaries and religious institutes, and all who receive university degrees,

10. all religious superiors in clerical religious orders.

198. CONCEALMENT AND PRETENSE OF FAITH. It is permissible to conceal or dissemble one's faith provided there is sufficient reason and it does not entail either a direct or indirect denial of faith. Thus, for example, a heretic (or pagan) who cannot return in public to the Church without involving himself in serious temporal inconvenience may do so secretly; a priest while passing through dangerous places inhabited by unbelievers may wear lay attire.[133]

VICES CONTRARY TO FAITH

199. Sins against faith are those of commission and those of omission.

1. SINS OF OMISSION contrary to faith are: *a)* the non-fulfillment of those precepts which enjoin internal and external acts of faith;[134] *b)* deliberate ignorance of the truths of faith which ought to be known.

2. BY COMMISSION a person sins against faith either by excess or by defect.

Sins of excess contrary to faith are rash credulity and superstition. A man commits the sin of rash credulity when he believes as part of faith truths which in fact are not, such as a man who gives credence to private revelations too easily. Superstition, which is a form of profession of disbelief through an external act, is contrary both to faith and to the virtue of religion.[135]

Sins of defect contrary to faith are committed by *infidelity* whether negative or positive. *Negative* (material, involuntary) infidelity is the lack of faith in a person to whom the Faith has never been sufficiently declared. *Positive* infidelity (formal) is the culpable lack of faith in a person who does not

---

[132] See CCL, Can. 1406.

[133] Many other examples are given in MTM, vol. 1, no. 507.

[134] See no. 194ff.

[135] See no. 430.

want to believe. Paganism, Judaism, and heresy are three types of positive infidelity. *Apostasy* which is a complete lack of faith in a person who previously possessed the Faith is a form of heresy. Schism is distinct from *heresy*, inasmuch as there exists a stubborn refusal to be obedient to the pope. Therefore schism, although not directly contrary to faith, is nearly always conjoined to heresy, because schismatics not only refuse obedience to the pope but also deny his primacy.

In this chapter we shall consider separately: 1) Paganism and Judaism; 2) Heresy and Apostasy; 3) Dangers to Faith.

Art. 1. Paganism and Judaism

200. FIRST PROPOSITION. *Negative infidelity is not sinful; positive infidelity is an extremely grave sin.*

Negative infidelity is the result of invincible ignorance and therefore is not blameworthy. Consequently, the following proposition of du Bay was condemned: "Purely negative infidelity in those among whom Christ has not been preached, is a sin."[136]

The reason for the second part of the proposition is that positive infidelity reveals: *a)* a serious contempt for the authority of God revealing; *b)* a rejection of a necessary means of salvation. Therefore, Christ issued this solemn warning: "He who does not believe will be condemned" (Mk 16:16).

SECOND PROPOSITION. *a) Although pagans and Jews must not be forced to embrace the Catholic Faith, yet they should be compelled to refrain from placing obstacles in the way of Catholic worship and from offering insults; b) their rites and worship may be tolerated by Christian rulers for grave reasons.*

The first part of the proposition derives its truth from the fact that no one can be compelled to believe, since the act of faith is a free act; at the same time no one can legitimately attack the Catholic Faith.

The reason for the second part is that even God Himself tolerates many sins in order to avoid greater evils.

Art. 2. Apostasy and Heresy

201. APOSTASY *is the complete repudiation of Christian belief after it has been accepted freely.*[137]

Therefore, apostasy consists in the voluntary rejection of the Catholic Faith by a person who previously professed it. We are not speaking here of apostasy from Holy Orders and from religion. Apostasy to the Masonic sect is very often equivalent to apostasy from the Faith.

---

[136] DZ 1068.
[137] See CCL, Can. 1325, § 2.

202. **HERESY**, considered objectively, is a proposition that contradicts an article of faith; in its subjective and formal aspect heresy is *the pertinacious error of a Christian who repudiates some truth of the Catholic Faith.*

Therefore, for formal heresy there is required error in the intellect and pertinacity in the will; consequently, the following are not formal heretics:

a) those who from fear or some other motive make an external denial of faith while inwardly preserving their consent to it;

b) those who make some error in their faith through ignorance even though vincible, since the error is not pertinacious;

c) those who deny a truth held as revealed but which the Church herself has not yet proposed as revealed.

If the error is not pertinacious the heretic is a *material heretic,* such as Protestants who have been instructed in heresy since their infancy.

THE EVIL OF APOSTASY AND HERESY. *Material* heresy is not sinful since it is not voluntary; *formal* heresy is a grave sin which admits of no slight matter since it implies a formal contempt of the truthfulness and authority of God. Apostasy is not specifically distinct from heresy, but is simply a circumstance that greatly aggravates the guilt.

ECCLESIASTICAL PENALTIES. Formal heretics and apostates who profess their heresy publicly incur:

1. *Excommunication* latae sententiae specially reserved to the Holy See in the internal forum. However, should the offense of heresy or apostasy be brought before the external court, absolution may be granted by the local ordinary.[138]

2. *Irregularity* both because of the delinquency,[139] and because of the defect, if they have adhered in public to some non-Catholic sect because of infamy in law;[140] the children of non-Catholic parents are debarred from receiving Orders so long as their parents continue in their error,[141] but not after their death — a probable opinion.

3. If they do not repent after due warning, they are deprived of benefice, dignity, pension, office, and any other office which they may possess in the Church; they shall be declared infamous and, if clerics, after admonition a second time they shall be deposed.

4. *Refusal of church burial*[142] and *notoriety,*[143] if they have publicly adhered to a non-Catholic sect.

---

[138] See CCL, Can. 2314, § 1–2.
[139] See CCL, Can. 985, no. 1.
[140] See CCL, Can. 984, no. 5.
[141] See CCL, Can. 987, no. 1.
[142] See CCL, Can. 1240, § 1, no. 1.
[143] See CCL, Can. 2314, § 1, no. 3.

203. SCHOLIUM. DOUBTS AGAINST FAITH. Since faith is most certain, any voluntary doubt against faith is gravely sinful. The following points should be borne in mind:

a) A Catholic who has a *positive* doubt concerning some article of faith is a heretic, since he has undermined the infallibility of God revealing. Hence the saying: "Dubius in fide infidelis est."

b) A Catholic who suspends his assent regarding an article of faith (*negative* doubt) is bound to fight such doubts vigorously; otherwise he sins.

c) A Protestant who *positively* doubts the truth of his sect is bound to inquire diligently into its truth; otherwise he sins, without becoming a formal heretic since his error is free of pertinacity.

Art. 3. Dangers to Faith

204. Dangers to faith arise either *from within*, e.g., from pride, greed, immoral life, and so on, *or from outside*, e.g., from cooperation with heretics, from mixed marriages. Here we shall consider external dangers to faith.

§ 1. Cooperation with Pagans and Heretics

205. DEFINITIONS. 1. Cooperation with heretics and pagans is either *civil* in matters concerning man's civil life, or *religious* in matters pertaining to worship and religion.

2. Religious cooperation is either *active* or *passive*, depending on whether a Catholic takes part in unorthodox worship or a non-Catholic cooperates in Catholic worship. Active cooperation is either *formal* or *material*; it is *formal* when a Catholic takes part in unorthodox worship with the express intention of worshipping God; it is *material* when a Catholic assists at non-Catholic worship *externally* without the internal desire to cooperate.

FIRST RULE. *Civil* cooperation between Catholics and non-Catholics is not now forbidden by the law of the Church, but very often it has to be discouraged owing to the dangers involved. It is frequently the source of doubts against faith, indifferentism, and sometimes complete defection from the Faith.

SECOND RULE. *Passive* religious cooperation with heretics (but not with excommunicated persons who are to be avoided) is lawful, as a general rule.

Therefore, non-Catholics may be present at Catholic services, but they cannot publicly participate in the Sacraments, sacramentals, indulgences, and so on.

THIRD RULE. *Active* and *formal* religious cooperation is always forbidden.[144]

Such cooperation is simply a denial of Catholic Faith and a recognition of an unorthodox form of worship. Thus, for example, a Catholic cannot be a godparent at a heretical Baptism.

[144] See CCL, Can. 1258, § 1.

FOURTH RULE. *Active* and *material* religious cooperation is sometimes permitted for a sufficient reason.[145]

The reason is that such cooperation in itself is not intrinsically evil, provided there is no danger of scandal or perversion. Thus, for instance, it is permissible to attend non-Catholic funerals as a mark of courtesy, to enter non-Catholic churches in order to listen to music, and so on.

§ 2. Attendance at Non-Catholic Schools

206. Non-Catholic schools are either *positively* non-Catholic, where non-Catholic doctrine is openly and deliberately taught, or *neutral* (lay, mixed) from which all positive religion is excluded and exclusive attention given to secular instruction.

PRINCIPLE. *It is never permissible to attend non-Catholic schools, unless it is possible to remove the proximate danger of perversion.*

The reason is obvious—one can never expose oneself to the proximate danger of perversion.

Means that may be used to remove this proximate danger are: 1) the exercise of diligent care that Catholic pupils suffer no harm from bad books, from their fellow pupils, or from their teachers; 2) the provision from another source of sufficient instruction of Catholic pupils in their religion and in good conduct; 3) the encouragement of Catholic pupils to persevere in a holy and religious manner of life.

The Code lays down the following admirable directive: "Catholic children shall not attend non-Catholic, indifferent schools that are mixed, that is to say, schools open to Catholics and non-Catholics alike. It rests with the local ordinary alone to decide in harmony with the instructions of the Holy See under what circumstances and with what safeguards to prevent loss of faith it may be tolerated that Catholic children attend such schools."[146]

§ 3. Reading Heretical Books

207. There is almost nothing so harmful to a man's religious life as the reading of bad books. Consequently, the Church throughout the ages has taken care that Catholics should not suffer harm from the reading and printing of evil books. The present discipline in this matter was outlined by Leo XIII in his Constitution *Officiorum et Munerum*, (Jan. 25, 1896), and has been amplified further in the Code.[147]

---

[145] See CCL, Can. 1258, § 2.

[146] CCL, Can. 1374. See also DZ 2219ff.

[147] See CCL, bk. 3, tit. 23; see also the author's *Manuale Iuris Canonici* [hereafter MIC], q. 414ff.

§ 4. Mixed Marriages

208. Another baneful danger of perversion is mixed marriages, of which the Church has always expressed her disapproval and which she only tolerates with special precautions to be discussed later in the treatise on marriage. Therefore, a Catholic who contracts a mixed marriage without observing these precautions commits grave sin, and incurs excommunication if the ceremony was performed in the presence of a non-Catholic minister.

TREATISE VIII
THEOLOGICAL HOPE AND
CONTRARY VICES

This treatise is divided into three chapters: 1) The Nature of Theological Hope; 2) Its Necessity; 3) Vices Contrary to Hope.

NATURE OF THEOLOGICAL HOPE

209. DEFINITION. *Theological hope is a habit divinely infused and residing in the will which enables man with perfect confidence based on God's almighty help to await and obtain eternal happiness and the means necessary for obtaining it.*

In order to explain this definition better we must discover the object, subject, and properties of hope.

The primary *material object* of hope is eternal happiness; its secondary material object is the means leading to that happiness.

The formal object of hope is God Himself attained in everlasting happiness, since hope, as one of the theological virtues, has God for its immediate object.

The motive of hope is the almighty power of God providing help to His creatures. This is the view expressed by St. Thomas.[148] Other theologians[149] teach that the motive of hope is the goodness of God; others consider it to be the fidelity of God, and yet another school think it to be the omnipotence, goodness, and fidelity of God combined.

The proximate SUBJECT of hope is man's will; the *remote* subject comprises:

a) all believers, including sinners (with the sole exception of those who have fallen into formal heresy or presumption or despair); *b)* the souls in purgatory.

The virtue of hope in the sinner is true hope, although *deformed*. Hope is destroyed: 1) by formal heresy which destroys faith, the foundation of hope; 2) by presumption and despair, since these vices are directly contrary to hope.

---

[148] See ST, II-II, q. 17.
[149] The Scotists, Suarez.

210. THE PROPERTIES of hope are: its *supernatural* character and its *steadfastness*.

a) Hope is *supernatural*, since it is a theological virtue that has for its material and formal object and for its motive something supernatural. *b)* Hope is *steadfast*, insofar as it is based on the help of God; there is, however, some fear and uncertainty in the virtue inasmuch as it supposes our own cooperation. It is evident from the words of the Council of Trent that hope is completely steadfast: "Everyone must place and put the most steadfast hope in the help of God."[150]

However, Sacred Scripture points to the uncertainty and fear present in hope because of man's uncertain cooperation: "Man does not know whether he is deserving of love or of hatred" (Eccles 9:1).

NECESSITY OF THEOLOGICAL HOPE

211. PRINCIPLE. *a) The habit of hope is a necessary means of salvation for everyone; b) the act of hope is a necessary means of salvation and is commanded by God for all who have come to the use of reason.*

The reason for the first part of the principle is that no one can be saved without sanctifying grace, and the virtue of hope is infused at the same time as grace.

The reason for the second part of the principle is that all who come to the use of their reason must obtain everlasting life through their deeds. But no one will make the necessary effort to strive for something if he lacks a genuine hope of attaining it. Therefore, we are commanded in Sacred Scripture: "Israelites one and all, put your confidence in God" (Ps 61:9).

The divine precept of hope obliges *of its very nature*:

1. at the outset of man's moral life;

2. at the hour of death;

3. frequently in life.

The same precept obliges man *incidentally*:

1. when he is oppressed by a serious temptation which he cannot overcome without an act of hope;

2. when he is bound to fulfill some precept which presupposes hope, such as the precept of receiving the Sacrament of Penance.

CONTRARY VICES AND SINS

Sins are committed against the virtue of hope, 1) by omitting the act of hope, 2) by despair, 3) by presumption.

212. 1. THE OMISSION OF AN ACT OF HOPE WHICH ONE OUGHT TO ELICIT is sinful, as is evident from the preceding chapter. Such an omission exists in an *excessive affection*

---

[150] Council of Trent, Session 6, "Decree on Justification," chap. 13. See also TCCI 7:167.

for things of earth whereby one shows so great a preference for temporal possessions over eternal joys that one desires to live on earth forever.

213. 2. DESPAIR is a sin against hope by defect. Despair is either *privative* (imperfect) or *positive* (perfect). The first consists in a certain pusillanimity of soul in which state, as the result of a diabolical temptation or melancholy or some other morbid emotion, a person oppresses and tortures his soul excessively with the fear of losing eternal salvation. Positive despair is a voluntary apathy toward obtaining happiness—or better: it is a withdrawal of the will away from eternal happiness which is judged to be impossible of attainment.

Privative despair, in the form in which it most frequently occurs, is not a sin but a temptation or a form of scrupulosity; positive despair is a mortal sin which admits of no slight matter.

It is evident that privative despair is not a sin since it is involuntary, whereas positive despair implies a serious injury to God since it denies or calls into question the mercy of God.

The causes of despair are usually: 1) lust and other long-established evil desires; 2) sloth; 3) lack of faith; 4) melancholy.

The remedy for despair is the removal of its causes.

214. 3. PRESUMPTION is a sin against hope by excess for it is a *rash confidence of obtaining eternal happiness by means other than those determined by God.* Often it goes hand in hand with *tempting God* or even with formal heresy.

The presumption *of the heretic* is a mortal sin allowing no parvity of matter because it is not only contrary to faith and hope but also entails a serious injury to the justice of God.

Ordinary presumption is a mortal sin which admits of slight matter, since it violates the virtue of hope and causes grave damage to man. *The causes* of presumption are, in addition to errors in faith: pride and vainglory.

Remedies for presumption are all those mentioned in no. 172 as remedies for pride.

TREATISE IX
THEOLOGICAL CHARITY
AND CONTRARY VICES

This treatise is divided into three chapters: 1) Charity toward God; 2) Charity to Self; 3) Charity to the Neighbor.

CHARITY TOWARD GOD

In this chapter we shall consider: 1) The Nature and Properties of charity; 2) The Necessity of Charity; 3) Vices Contrary to Charity.

Art. 1. Nature and Properties of Charity

215. DEFINITION. *Charity is a virtue infused by God enabling man to love God for His own sake as the supreme good, and himself and his neighbor for God's sake.*

The formal object of charity is the divine goodness.

The *material* object of charity are all men and angels, but not the damned and the devil since they are incapable of divine friendship. The *motive* of charity is God Who is so lovable in Himself and for His own sake. Theological charity is a perfect love of benevolence and of *friendship* for God.

THE EFFICACY of charity follows from its very nature as friendship with God. Consequently, charity destroys mortal sin and confers justification on the sinner. But it is God's will in instituting the Sacraments of the dead for the remission of sin that the sinner, when eliciting an act of perfect charity through the help of actual grace, must have at least an implicit desire of receiving these Sacraments.

216. THE PROPERTIES OF CHARITY. Charity must be supernatural, efficacious, and appreciate God above everything.

1. Charity is *supernatural* in every respect, both in its object and in its source—supernatural grace.

2. Charity must be *effective*, and therefore the mere affection of charity (affective charity) is not sufficient. Thus, we are warned: "Let us show our love by the true test of action, not by taking phrases on our lips" (1 Jn 3:18).

3. Charity must show the *highest appreciation* for God (not necessarily the highest intensity)—that is to say, we must prize God more highly than all creatures, so that we are prepared to lose the whole world rather than the friendship of God.

217. SCHOLIUM. THE EXCELLENCE OF CHARITY. Charity excels all the other virtues and the gifts: 1) charity alone remits all mortal sins; 2) charity alone establishes true friendship between God and man; 3) charity alone is the form of all the virtues—all the virtues are subservient to charity, and their acts are meritorious because they have their origin in charity.

Art. 2. Necessity of Charity

218. FIRST PRINCIPLE. *The habit of charity is a necessary means of salvation for all men, the act of charity for all who have come to the use of reason.*

The habit of charity is necessary, since no one can be saved without sanctifying grace and friendship with God which cannot be separated from charity.

Since everyone who has come to the use of reason must strive for union with God and it is charity which unites man to God, therefore such persons are bound to elicit the act of charity.

SECOND PRINCIPLE. *Both from the nature of charity and incidentally for other reasons all men enjoying the use of reason are obliged by divine precept to elicit an act of charity.*

The divine precept of charity is called by Christ "the greatest of the commandments and the first" (Mt 22:38). The following proposition was condemned by Innocent XI, 1679: "It is probable that the precept of love for God is of itself not of grave obligation even once every five years."[151]

OF ITS VERY NATURE an act of charity must be elicited:

1. at the outset of man's moral life;

2. at the hour of death;

3. sometimes during life (at least more frequently than every five years).

INCIDENTALLY the obligation arises:

1. in danger of sin when temptation cannot otherwise be removed except by making an act of charity;

2. whenever a person who is in the state of mortal sin and unable to obtain confession must recover the state of grace.

Art. 3. Vices Contrary to Charity toward God

219. In a general way every mortal sin is contrary to the virtue of charity toward God inasmuch as they destroy the soul's friendship with God, but sins particularly opposed to charity are: *a)* the omission of an act of charity which ought to be made (sins of *omission*), see the preceding article; *b)* hatred of God and sloth (sins of *commission*).

220. HATRED OF GOD is a mortal sin; if it is the hatred of enmity, then it is the most grievous of all sins which nevertheless allows of slight matter. Hatred of God exists in one of two forms. There is the hatred *of disgust* whereby a person detests God inasmuch as He punishes sinners, and this type of hatred, since it is contrary to the justice of God, is a mortal sin which admits of parvity of matter. Another form of hatred is that *of enmity* whereby man wishes evil to God. Such hatred is of its nature diabolical and is the most grievous of all sins since no other sin so grievously offends God.

221. SLOTH is a state of weariness and dejection because of the difficulty experienced in obtaining and using the means of salvation. It is thus opposed to charity which *delights* in the means of union with God.[152]

CHARITY TO SELF

222. THE OBLIGATION to possess a true love for ourselves is presupposed in the precept commanding us to love our neighbor *as ourselves*. Furthermore, charity must include all those capable of attaining eternal glory, and not only our soul but also our body was created for this purpose.

---

[151] DZ 1156.
[152] See no. 178.

Sins opposed to charity to self are all the injuries which we deliberately inflict on our soul or body, such as mortal sin which causes the death of the soul, the dangers to which we expose body and soul, suicide, and so on. —Inordinate self-love, the root of many sins, is contrary to this form of charity.

CHARITY TO THE NEIGHBOR

This chapter is divided into three articles: 1) Existence, Extent, and Order of the Precept of Charity to the Neighbor; 2) External Acts of Charity; 3) Sins Contrary to This Virtue.

Art. 1. Existence, Extent, and Order of the Precept of Charity to the Neighbor

This article contains two paragraphs: 1) Existence and Extent of the Precept of Charity to the Neighbor; 2) The Order of Charity.

§ 1. Existence and Extent of This Precept of Charity

223. 1. THE EXISTENCE of a special precept of loving our neighbor with a supernatural love which is both affective and effective is evident:

a) from Sacred Scripture: "And the second (commandment), its like, is this, Thou shalt love thy neighbor as thyself" (Mt 22:39).

b) from the propositions condemned by Innocent XI: "We are not bound to love our neighbor by an internal and formal act. We can satisfy the precept of loving neighbor by external acts only."[153]

c) from reason, since even our neighbor is capable of eternal glory. *Internal* acts of charity to the neighbor are: 1) delight at his prosperity, sorrow in his adversity; 2) a sincere desire for his good.

External acts of charity are those acts of beneficence which we show to our neighbor in the performance of the seven spiritual and corporal works of mercy.

2. ITS EXTENT. The precept of charity extends to all men (capable of eternal happiness) and even to our *enemies.* We are bound to love our enemies not as enemies but as men. Thus, by divine positive precept which is founded on natural law Christ commands: "Love your enemies, do good to those who hate you, pray for those who persecute and insult you" (Mt 5:44). But we are not obliged to love our enemies *because* they are our enemies but *in spite of* their enmity. Therefore, we must:

1. avoid the hatred of enmity and all desire of revenge;

2. offer our enemy at least the ordinary signs of love;[154]

3. seek reconciliation insofar as that is within our power.

---

[153] DZ 1160, 1161.

[154] The ordinary signs of affection are those which we usually use for all men in similar circumstances.

§ 2. The Order of Charity

224. There is an order to be observed in the practice of charity: 1) between the persons loved; 2) between the goods which are loved in them.

1. *In our love of persons* the order to be observed is the following:

a) We are bound to love God above all else, then ourselves, and our neighbor in the third place.

That God must be loved above all else is evident from the fact that our love of Him must reveal the highest appreciation. That a man must love himself more than his neighbor follows from Christ's precept commanding us to love our neighbor *as ourselves* (see Mk 12:31). Therefore, true love of self is the standard and measure of the love of our neighbor.

b) We are not bound to love our neighbors equally but in proportion to their proximity to God and to ourselves.

Charity derives from two sources—God and ourselves. The nearer anything is to either of these principles, so much the greater must be our love of it. Thus, those who are better and more perfect in the sight of God are deserving of greater love than those who are less perfect, since they are more like to God. This refers to our *reverence* for and *appreciation* of such persons, not necessarily to our *feelings* toward them. Thus, a son must have a greater regard for a saintly person than for his own wicked father, but it is not necessary that he possess greater feelings of love for that person. In our charity toward our relatives and friends the order to be observed—in normal circumstances—is the following: wife (or husband), children, parents, brothers and sisters, other relatives, friends and benefactors. This order may be changed for a sufficient reason.

2. *Between the objects loved* the following order exists: *a)* one's own spiritual welfare; *b)* the spiritual welfare of our neighbor; *c)* one's own bodily welfare; *d)* bodily welfare of the neighbor; *e)* external goods.

FIRST RULE. In another's *extreme spiritual necessity*[155] we are obliged to help him even at grave risk to our own bodily life, provided that there is a reasonable hope of saving him and no serious public harm results. Our neighbor's everlasting life is a far more excellent good than the life of our own body.

SECOND RULE. Except when another is in extreme spiritual necessity there is no strict obligation of helping him at the risk of serious bodily harm.

---

[155] It is customary to speak of three types of necessity: extreme, grave, common. A person is said to be in extreme necessity when he is in immediate danger of losing either his bodily or spiritual life. In the first instance, e.g., in danger of drowning, the extreme necessity is temporal; in the second he is in extreme spiritual necessity. He is in grave necessity when he is unable to avoid grave harm to body or soul without the help of another. Common or slight necessity is said to exist when a person is in difficulties but is able to help himself.

This follows from the fact that we are not obliged to safeguard even our own life where there is risk of serious harm.

THIRD RULE. In another's *grave need* (whether spiritual or temporal) we must help him if we can do so without serious inconvenience, unless justice, piety, or our office make greater claims on us.

FOURTH RULE. In common or slight necessity, we must be prepared to suffer some slight inconvenience in helping our neighbor.

Art. 2. External Acts of Charity to the Neighbor

225. It is customary to distinguish external acts of charity into seven spiritual and seven corporal works of mercy. The seven *spiritual* works of mercy are to convert the sinner, to instruct the ignorant, to advise the doubtful, to comfort the sorrowful, to bear wrongs patiently, to forgive injuries, to pray for all. The seven *corporal* works of mercy are to feed the hungry, to give drink to the thirsty, to clothe the naked, to harbor the harborless, to visit the sick, to visit the imprisoned, and to bury the dead. For the sake of brevity only the two principal acts of charity are considered here: almsgiving and fraternal correction.

§ 1. Almsgiving

226. DEFINITION. *Almsgiving is a work of mercy whereby we give something to the needy for the sake of God.*

Therefore, almsgiving in its strict sense does not refer to the thing given but to the *action of giving* which is elicited by mercy and commanded by charity.

FIRST PRINCIPLE. *The giving of alms to the poor is commanded by natural law and divine positive law.*

The natural law ordains that we should show not merely affective love but also effective love for our neighbor. But it is impossible to show such effective love for the poor without giving alms to them. Moreover, the natural law requires the preservation of peace in society which would undoubtedly be disturbed if the poor were denied alms. Therefore, almsgiving is demanded both by charity and by legal justice, not, however, by *commutative* justice so that the poor who are denied alms cannot claim occult compensation.

SECOND PRINCIPLE. *In individual cases the duty of almsgiving must be determined: a) by the neighbor's need, b) by the donor's resources.* Consequently, the greater the need of the neighbor and the more abundant the resources of the donor, so much the greater is the latter's obligation of giving alms. On the other hand, the less severe the neighbor's need and the smaller the resources of the donor, so much the less urgent is the latter's obligation. Therefore, in common need—the state of the ordinary poor—there is a grave obligation of giving alms on some occasions from one's superfluous wealth, but there is no obligation of giving alms to any individual poor person.

The *amount* of alms cannot be accurately determined. According to St. Alphonsus, it is sufficient to give each year two percent of one's superfluous wealth.

227. SCHOLIUM. THE FRAUDULENT POOR. Persons who are not in genuine need and yet obtain alms by feigning great hardship commit sin in three ways: *a)* against *truth*, since their mode of behavior is a detestable deceit; *b)* against *charity*, because they deprive other poor persons of alms which they would otherwise have received; *c)* against *commutative justice*, since they deceive by guile those who are naturally displeased at being forcibly despoiled of these alms. Therefore, these frauds are bound to restore the alms they have obtained in this way. However, in practice such restitution is often impossible since such frauds quickly dispose of the money they obtain and thus have nothing left to make restitution.

§ 2. Fraternal Correction

228. DEFINITION. *Fraternal correction is a private admonition given to another out of charity in an endeavor to withdraw him from sin or from danger of sin.*

THE OBLIGATION of such correction arises both from natural law and from divine positive law: *a) from divine positive law:* "Confront thy friend with his fault; it may be that he knows nothing of the matter, and can clear himself; if not, there is hope he will amend" (Ecclus 19:13); *b) from natural law,* since fraternal correction is a spiritual form of almsgiving which is commanded by natural law, as already stated.

Two CONDITIONS must be verified before there exists an obligation to correct another — that is to say, there is no grave obligation to give fraternal correction unless *a)* one is certain of the grave spiritual need of another from which it does not seem he can be rescued except by such correction; *b)* this correction can be given without serious inconvenience to him who corrects.

There is a METHOD to be observed in giving fraternal correction; the correction must be guided by kindness and love, and, if given to persons enjoying some authority, by reverence and humility. Moreover, Christ commands that it be first given *secretly:* "Go at once and tax him with it (the wrong), as a private matter between thee and him" (Mt 18:15). If private correction is of no avail, one should have recourse to two or three witnesses, and finally, if the culprit is not yet won over, he must be denounced to the legitimate superior. There are occasions when private correction can and should be omitted and the culprit denounced immediately to the superior, namely, if: *a)* the sin of another is publicly known; *b)* the sin is likely to cause harm to others and it is impossible to make sufficient safeguard against such harm without denunciation; *c)* the culprit has renounced his right to private correction.

Art. 3. Sins against Charity to the Neighbor

229. INTRODUCTORY. Since the precept of charity to the neighbor is both positive (inasmuch as it commands certain acts to be done) and negative (inasmuch as it

forbids other acts), it is possible to sin against this precept either by omitting the prescribed acts (of which we have already spoken in the previous article) or by committing other acts, such as acts of hatred, enmity, envy, dissension, quarrelling, scandal, cooperation in sin. Enough has been said already about the majority of these acts, so we limit our attention to scandal and cooperation.

§ 1. Scandal

230. DEFINITION. *Scandal is some word or deed (whether of omission or commission) that is itself evil or has the appearance of evil and provides an occasion of sin to another.*

KINDS. 1. *Active scandal* is the act itself which is the occasion of sin for another; *passive scandal* is the sin occasioned by another's act.

2. Active scandal is *direct* if the sin of another is intended; it is *indirect* if the sin is not intended but is foreseen.

3. Direct scandal is *diabolical* (or *formal*) if through hatred of God or the neighbor the sin of another is intended precisely as sin; it is *simply direct* when the neighbor's sin is intended for some other purpose, such as pleasure or revenge, and so on.

4. Passive scandal is *given* when it is actually produced by the evil action of another; it is *taken* when it results not from an evil action but from a good action which is accepted by another either through ignorance (scandal of the weak) or through malice (pharisaic scandal) as an occasion of sin.

231. THE SINFULNESS OF SCANDAL: *a) Direct scandal is a mortal sin both against charity and against that virtue which the neighbor is encouraged to violate, but it admits of slight matter; b) indirect scandal is a sin, probably against charity only.*

a) That all scandal is grievously sinful is evident from the severe words used by Christ in His threat: "It must needs be that such hurt should come, but woe to the man through whom it comes" (Mt 18:7). It is clear that direct scandal is a sin against charity and against the virtue which the neighbor is encouraged to transgress, since it is intended that the neighbor should suffer harm and that a definite virtue should be violated. Thus, for instance, if a man speaks immodestly to a girl in order to seduce her, he commits three mortal sins if the girl consents to listen: *i)* he himself commits a grave sin against chastity; *ii)* he intends that the girl also should sin against chastity; *iii)* he intends the spiritual harm of the girl. Direct scandal is a venial sin if the act is imperfect or if the matter is slight.

b) Since in indirect scandal the violation of a virtue by the person taking scandal is foreseen but not desired, it is more probable that the sin is contrary to charity only and not to the virtue whose violation is not desired. There are some, however, who maintain the contrary view, e.g., St. Alphonsus.

PRACTICAL DIRECTION. The gravity of the sinfulness of scandal *increases, a)* the more one desires the sin of another; *b)* the greater the influence which the action exercises on the sin of another; *c)* the more serious the sin committed by the neighbor.

On the other hand, the gravity of the sin *decreases, a)* the less perfect the deliberation; *b)* the less influence exerted by the action on the sin of another; *c)* the less serious the sin which the neighbor is induced to commit.

232. THE OBLIGATION OF AVOIDING SCANDAL.

1. There is no obligation to avoid *pharisaic* scandal, provided there is some reasonable cause for the action causing it.

This follows from the fact that pharisaic scandal is caused by the malice of the person taking scandal.

2. Scandal *of the weak* must be avoided, if this can be done without grave inconvenience.

Charity demands that we prevent an innocent neighbor suffering harm, so far as this is morally possible. Thus, for example, a priest who inadvertently has taken food or drink may nevertheless say Mass, if otherwise great scandal would arise amongst his people.

3. For a just cause, it is lawful to permit and even to provide *the occasion of another's sin.*

In such circumstances the neighbor's sin is not intended, and even God Himself permits the occasions of sin.

REPARATION FOR SCANDAL given is necessary since it is frequently an offense against the public good and not merely against charity; commutative justice is also affected if the neighbor is induced to sin by threats, force, deceit, and so on.—Reparation is made either publicly or secretly according as the scandal was public or secret.

§ 2. Cooperation in Evil

233. DEFINITION AND KINDS. *Cooperation in evil is concurrence in another's sinful act.* Consequently cooperation differs from scandal insofar as the latter *causes* the evil will of the sinner (by advice, command, or example), whereas cooperation *presupposes* the evil will of the sinner and is a means of bringing this evil will to completion in an external act.

1. Cooperation is *immediate* if it is cooperation in the actual sinful act of another (as in the practice of onanism); it is *mediate* if it provides other acts or objects which are not so intimately connected with the sin of the agent.

Mediate cooperation is *proximate* if the help given is immediately connected with the sin of another, such as selling poison to a murderer; it is *remote* when the help is not so immediately connected with the other's act, such as selling a field to a Jew who may build a synagogue in it.

2. Cooperation is *formal* if help is given to another to commit sin as a sin; it is *material* if one cooperates in the physical action only. Consequently formal cooperation is an act which is evil in itself both because of its object and because of the intention of the agent. Material cooperation is in itself a good act which is abused by another in order to commit sin.

234. PRINCIPLE. *Formal cooperation in the sin of another is always sinful; material cooperation is sometimes permitted.*

Formal cooperation includes consent to another's sin. Accordingly, it is an offense not only against charity but also against the virtue violated by the sin in which one cooperates.

The second part of the principle is derived from the fact that material cooperation is in itself a good act which is abused by another through his own malice. Therefore, everything which has been said about acts that are indirectly voluntary in no. 23 can be applied here and is used to solve cases that frequently arise on different matters relating to the cooperation of servants, workers, shopkeepers, traders, and so on.[156]

TREATISE X
THE VIRTUE OF PRUDENCE
AND CONTRARY VICES

This short treatise is divided into two chapters: 1) The Virtue of Prudence; 2) Its Contrary Vices.

THE VIRTUE OF PRUDENCE

235. DEFINITION. St. Thomas and Aristotle define prudence as *correct knowledge concerning things to be done.*[157]

Others define prudence as the knowledge of things which ought to be desired and of those things which ought to be avoided; or, the intellectual virtue whereby man recognizes in any matter to hand what is good and what is evil. Prudence resides in the practical intellect and is either acquired by one's own acts or infused at the same time as sanctifying grace.

THE MATERIAL OBJECTS of prudence are all human and moral acts (called by Aristotle *agibilia*[158]). *The motive* of prudence is the property of practical truth and goodness which is discovered in human acts.

THE ACTS of the virtue of prudence are three in number: to take counsel carefully, to judge correctly, to direct. These acts of direction are the principal and proper acts of the virtue.

236. THE PARTS of prudence—as of any other cardinal virtue—are threefold: *a)* integral, *b)* subjective, *c)* potential.

---

[156] See MTM, vol. 1, nos. 620–621.
[157] See ST, II-II, q. 47, a. 2, s.c.; and Aristotle, *Nichomachean Ethics*, bk. 6, chap. 5.
[158] See *Nichomachean Ethics*, bk. 6.

a) The integral parts of any cardinal virtue are those things which are required for a perfect act of the virtue. For an act of prudence to be perfect St. Thomas[159] lists the following eight prerequisites:

1. memory, i.e., the recalling of the past;

2. intellect, i.e., a clear knowledge of the present;

3. docility, i.e., a readiness to learn;

4. shrewdness, i.e., a quick conjecture regarding the means to be used;

5. reason, i.e., a readiness to infer one thing from another;

6. providence, i.e., a consideration of future events;

7. circumspection, i.e., a careful consideration of circumstances;

8. caution, i.e., care in avoiding evil and obstacles.

b) The subjective parts of a cardinal virtue are the species of that general virtue. The chief species of prudence are: *personal* prudence whereby one guides oneself, and *political* prudence whereby one guides a multitude. Political prudence used to be further subdivided into military, economic, and legislative prudence, and so on.

c) The potential parts of a cardinal virtue are annexed virtues which are concerned with secondary acts or secondary matters. The following represent the potential parts of prudence:

1. eubulia—the habit of seeking right counsel;

2. synesis—the virtue of judging aright according to ordinary rules;

3. gnome—the virtue of judging aright from the higher principles. The act which proceeds from this virtue is epikeia in the interpretation of law.

CONTRARY VICES

237. Sins *by defect* against prudence are:

1. precipitancy, which acts before due consideration has been given;

2. want of thought, which neglects to take due consideration of the circumstances;

3. inconstancy, which changes resolutions too quickly;

4. negligence, which does not take sufficient care of the operation of the intellect.

Sins *by excess* against prudence are:

1. prudence of the flesh which eagerly seeks means of living according to the flesh, that is, according to the corrupt nature of man;

2. astuteness, deceit, fraud, which devise and use evil means to obtain their purpose;

3. solicitude for things of this world and for the future which prevent man from attaining to the true purpose of his life.

---

[159] See ST, II-II, q. 49.

St. Thomas notes wisely that the vices opposed to prudence by defect usually arise from *lust*, those which are opposed to the virtue by excess usually take their origin from *avarice*.[160]

TREATISE XI
THE VIRTUE OF JUSTICE
AND CONTRARY VICES

Since this treatise is extremely long it is divided for the sake of clarity into two sections:

Section I. Rights and the Virtue of Justice.

Section II. Potential Parts of the Virtue of Justice.

SECTION I
RIGHTS AND THE VIRTUE OF JUSTICE

This section is further divided into four questions:

1. Rights.

2. The Virtue of Justice Considered in Itself.

3. Injustice and Restitution.

4. Contracts.

QUESTION I
RIGHTS

This question is to be considered in four separate chapters:

1. Definition and Kinds of Rights.

2. Objects of Ownership.

3. Subjects of Ownership.

4. Titles to Ownership.

DEFINITION AND KINDS OF RIGHTS

238. DEFINITION. The Latin word *jus*—translated here as "right"—has at least four meanings:

1. the sentence of a judge (*jus dicere*);

2. law or objective right (*jus canonicum*);

3. the just thing due to another (a passive right);

---

[160] See ST, II-II, q. 53, a. 6; and q. 55, a. 8.

4. *the moral power to do or omit something or to exact something from another*, and so on (right actively considered).

RIGHT taken both in its active and passive senses constitutes a subjective right. Thus:

Objective right = laws

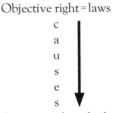

c
a
u
s
e
s

Subjective right, which is

| a *passive right*, i.e., the just thing due to another | and: an *active right*, i.e., the moral power of exacting something, and so on. |

239. KINDS. The more important kinds of right are the following:

1. In respect of their *origin* rights are either *natural* if they arise from the very foundations of nature itself (the right of self-defense), or *divine* if they arise from a positive command of God (the right to receive the Sacraments), or *human* if they take their origin from human law whether ecclesiastical (ecclesiastical rights) or civil (civil rights).

2. In respect of their *effects* rights are either *strict* if their violation is an injustice properly so-called (the right to property), or *not strict* if it is merely fitting to a greater or less degree that such rights be respected (the right to receive certain honors).

It is customary to distinguish strict rights into rights *in a thing* (ownership) and rights *to a thing* (*jura quaesita*) which a person possesses to enable him to possess as his own things which are not already in his possession.

240. OWNERSHIP which is the legitimate power to dispose of something as one's own is divided as follows:

a) Ownership is *perfect* when one has complete power to dispose both of the thing itself and of its fruits; it is *imperfect* when the power of disposal extends only to the thing itself (direct or radical ownership) or to its fruits (indirect or useful ownership). This disposal of the fruits of a thing is either unlimited (usufruct) or limited to the enjoyment of the fruits for oneself (mere use).

b) The right of eminent domain is the form of ownership possessed by the supreme civil or ecclesiastical authority which has the right of disposing of the goods of individuals for the welfare of the community when there exists a grave reason (the right of expropriation); *personal and private ownership* is that which belongs to individuals in the State and is the legitimate power of disposing of something as one's own.

241. ORIGIN AND LAWFULNESS OF PRIVATE OWNERSHIP.

Authors are not agreed regarding the origin of private ownership. Some[161] maintain that it arose from some social agreement, others[162] from civil law, others (modern Socialists) from occupation by force. According to the true opinion, private ownership is a right which follows as a conclusion from the principles of natural law, since it is exceedingly useful both for peace and for the orderly administration of property.

The opponents of private ownership are the Apostolici, Manichaeans, Waldensians, Socialists, and Communists.

OBJECTS OF OWNERSHIP

242. 1. Man has *indirect* ownership (or the use only) of those goods which form intrinsic parts of his body and soul, since he is God's steward over these things.

2. Man has a strict right (although qualified) to his reputation.

3. Man has perfect ownership of the products of his own skill and industry to the extent determined by particular civil laws. Consequently, a man who injures the rights of an author as determined by civil law is bound to restitution.

4. Men may have indirect ownership of each other. Consequently, slavery is not forbidden by natural law, although it is at present forbidden by positive law.

243. SCHOLIUM. VARIOUS TYPES OF GOODS. *a) Movable* and *immovable* property, as determined by individual laws. *b) Fungible* goods which may take the place of others in payment of debts and which are usually consumed in their first use, such as money; *non-fungible* goods which do not permit of substitution in the course of trade and must be replaced by their equivalent in kind if they have been taken away. *c)* Goods which are *consumed in their first use* (food, money), and goods which are *not so consumed* (clothing, books).

SUBJECTS OF OWNERSHIP

244. PRINCIPLE. *Neither irrational nor inanimate creatures but rational creatures only are capable of ownership*, since this is a *moral* power which can exist in rational persons alone.

1. Since animals have no rights, they cannot suffer injury in the strict sense of the word. Nevertheless, cruelty to animals (without grave cause) is sinful insofar as it is contrary to right reason.

2. Even imbeciles, and children before attaining the use of reason, and in fact any living person immediately after conception are capable of ownership, since they are rational creatures.

3. In addition to physical persons, moral or juridical bodies are capable of ownership.

[161] Grosstest, Puffendorf.
[162] Hobbes, Montesquieu, Bentham.

Art. 1. Property Rights of the Married

Here are set forth only the general principles of natural law and the statutes of ancient Roman law.[163]

245. GENERAL PRINCIPLES. Husband and wife have entered upon an undivided way of life of which man is the head. Each party is bound to provide for the reasonable maintenance of the other and of their children. The reasonable and decent maintenance of each other includes food, clothing, reasonable recreation, the ability to give alms to the poor, and to give such gifts as are proper to their state of life. Thus, a wife would not sin against *justice* by doing all these things without the knowledge of her husband or even without his consent. However, circumstances could arise where such behavior would be contrary to the virtue of prudence.

The *administration* of common property (and sometimes even of the personal property of the wife) is the right of the husband in his capacity as head of the family.

ANCIENT ROMAN LAW recognized the following different kinds of goods belonging to the wife: *a) bona paraphernalia*, of which the wife had perfect ownership and administration. (In modern codes of law these are referred to as free goods); *b) bona dotalia* (the dowry), which the wife handed over to her husband for the maintenance of the family; the wife retained the direct ownership of this property but its administration and indirect ownership passed to the husband; *c) bona communia* (common possessions), which were acquired during married life by the industry of either party; the administration and indirect ownership of these goods and the direct ownership of half of them belonged to the husband, while the other half came under the direct ownership of the wife.

The question of a wife's petty thefts will be discussed later.

Art. 2. Property Rights of Children

246. DEFINITIONS. It is customary to distinguish between *children* who have not yet completed their seventh year (infants), *children below the age of legal puberty* — for boys the age of fourteen, for girls the age of twelve — *minors* who have not yet attained their majority as determined by civil law (normally the age of twenty-one), *persons who have attained their majority*, and *emancipated minors* who enjoy by privilege the rights of those attaining their majority.

NOTE. The following principles apply to legitimate children and to children who have been made legitimate, but not to illegitimate children.

KINDS OF PROPERTY. Ancient Roman law made the following distinctions in referring to the property of children: *a) bona castrensia*; *b) quasi-castrensia*; *c) adventitia*; *d) profectitia*. These distinctions are now obsolete and have been replaced by the following: goods which are *free* and goods which are *not free*.

---

[163] For a fuller treatment of this question, see MTM.

247. **GENERAL RULES.** 1. No *injustice* is committed if a person *on attaining his majority* (or after his emancipation) retains for himself everything that he has acquired lawfully, after deducting whatever his parents require for his maintenance. This is the common opinion.

2. A *minor* living *away* from the home of his parents does not sin against *justice* by retaining his own salary. This is usually stated in modern codes of law.

3. It is not contrary to *justice* for a minor living *under* the parental roof but receiving a salary *for work performed outside that home* to keep for himself what remains after paying the expenses of his maintenance. This is valid, unless the civil law declares that his salary belongs to his parents.

4. A minor living and working *at* home seems to offend against *justice* if he steals from the household goods anything which is not required for his own reasonable maintenance.

5. A sin against the virtue of *piety* is committed by any children of a family who cause undue suffering to their parents through withholding some of their possessions.

Art. 3. Property Rights of Clerics

248. **KINDS.** Clerical ownership extends to patrimonial property, quasi-patrimonial property, revenue from benefice, savings.

1. A cleric's *patrimony* includes everything which a cleric receives outside the exercise of his ministry and distinct from the fruits of an ecclesiastical benefice (legacies, gifts, salary received for work apart from the priestly ministry); in a word, everything which the cleric receives *as a man*.

2. *Quasi-patrimonial* property consists of those goods which the priest receives in virtue of a spiritual title and not in virtue of a benefice (Mass stipends, and so on); in a word, everything received by the cleric *as a cleric*.

3. *The revenue of a benefice* consists of those goods which are intended to provide suitable maintenance for the beneficiary—namely, that property which the cleric receives *as a beneficiary*. According to present discipline, the revenue of a benefice includes: 1) pensions or salaries granted to clerics by the State; 2) contributions of the faithful—levied in the form of a tax—corresponding to former tithes; 3) foundation Mass stipends attached to the benefice; 4) stole fees received by beneficiaries; 5) the distributions made to canons for choral recitation of the Office.[164]

4. *Personal savings* are the goods accumulated by a cleric from the revenue of his *benefice* as the result of his economical way of living.

249. **PRINCIPLE.** *Clerics who are not religious are free to dispose of all their property, with the exception of the residue from the revenues of a benefice, which he is under a grave obligation to give to the poor or to pious purposes without being bound to make restitution.*[165]

[164] See CCL, Can. 1410.
[165] See CCL, Can. 1473.

Some authors are of the opinion that a cleric is bound in justice to make restitution for any superfluous income from the benefice which he does not use for the poor or for pious purposes, but since there is no universal agreement on this point the obligation cannot be urged.[166]—Although it is generally agreed that a cleric is under a *grave* obligation to give to the poor or to pious purposes that part of the revenue of his benefice which is not required for his fitting maintenance, it is difficult to decide the amount which constitutes grave matter in the violation of this precept. It seems that it would have to be much greater than the amount necessary for a grave sin of theft, since the cleric is not depriving another of his possessions but is failing to put to good use his own personal property. One must take into consideration the different circumstances affecting both the cleric and his gift.

Cardinals have special privileges with regard to the revenue from their benefices.[167]

TITLES TO OWNERSHIP

250. INTRODUCTORY. Ways of acquiring ownership are founded either on law (natural or positive) which are usually known as *legal* titles, or on agreement freely contracted between men which are termed *conventional* titles. There are four legal titles: occupancy, finding lost property, accession, prescription. Conventional titles include all the various forms of contracts, amongst which may be included the receiving of legacies.[168]

Art. 1. Occupancy

We shall consider: 1) occupancy in general; 2) appropriation of animals; 3) treasure trove; 4) war loot.

251. 1. OCCUPANCY IN GENERAL is the taking possession of a thing belonging to no one else with the intention of making it one's own. The following conditions must be verified in order that occupancy may constitute a lawful title to ownership.

a) The object seized must not in fact belong to anyone else (that is to say, they must be goods which have been abandoned or which have no owner).

b) The act of seizure must be real and physical; a mere intention is insufficient.

c) One must intend to make the thing one's own, so that the intention of taking care of an object for the benefit of its true owner would not be sufficient.

252. 2. ANIMALS MAY BE APPROPRIATED by hunting, fishing, or fowling.

a) Wild animals are such as naturally avoid the company of human beings, e.g., hare, deer, fish; *b) tame* animals are those which normally avoid man's company

---

[166] See ST, II-II, q. 185, a. 7; see also TM, bk. 3, no. 492.
[167] See CCL, Can. 239, § 1, no. 19.
[168] Some authors speak of work as a means of acquiring ownership, but work is better considered as a contract of lease (labor-contract) if it concerns the property of another, and as accession if it concerns one's own property.

but which are brought under his control by his skill and industry, such as pigeons in a dovecote, fish in a small pond; *c) domestic* animals are those which of their nature are accustomed to the society of men (sheep, hens, dogs). Animals which were previously tamed and have since *regained their freedom* and now avoid human company are in the same category as wild animals.

PRINCIPLE. *From natural law* wild animals and those which have regained their previous liberty belong to their first occupant; tame and domestic animals remain the property of their owner unless the former regain their liberty.

HUNTING AND FISHING.

253. PRINCIPLE. The ruling authority has the right to prohibit by law hunting, fishing, and fowling, and to reserve these for itself not only within the confines of its own property but also in other open spaces. Such laws are just and most beneficial to the community. Therefore, generally speaking, they cannot be regarded as mere *penal* laws. Consequently, those who transgress such laws commit sin unless they have some excuse.

Grave sin is committed by those who habitually hunt illegally with *lethal weapons*, such as poachers, since they constitute a grave danger even to their own lives, they foster strong passions, and cause grave damage to others. Similarly, those who cause grave damage to the lawful owner of game commit grave sin. The amount of damage caused is determined not merely by the value of the animals which have been captured illegally but rather *by the degree of hope* which the owner himself had of capturing the game.

PRACTICAL RULES. 1. Older theologians who consider the pursuit of hunting must be read carefully since the present situation is vastly different.

2. Special regard must be had for common opinion regarding illegal forms of hunting which are viewed with varying degrees of severity in different places.

3. It is rare that the illegal hunter has a grave obligation of making restitution since the lawful owner does not incur grave loss in the majority of cases, and furthermore many modern theologians regard laws forbidding hunting as merely penal.

254. 3. TREASURE TROVE.

DEFINITION. *Treasure trove* is defined in Roman law as *goods which have lay hidden so long that they have been forgotten and thus do not possess any owner.*

The term *goods* is here limited to the *products of man's skill* and does not include natural things. Such things as coal, metals, precious stones existing in their natural state in the ground are not considered treasure trove but the natural produce of the earth.

OWNERSHIP OF TREASURE TROVE. 1. From natural law alone treasure trove belongs in its entirety to the finder. Since it has no owner, it becomes the property of the first occupant.

2. Civil law usually determines that treasure found on one's own land belongs to the finder; if it is found on someone else's land, then the treasure must be divided between the finder and the owner of the land. This provision of civil law seems to be binding in conscience.[169]

255. 4. WAR LOOT. Ancient Roman law regarded enemy possessions as having no owner and thus capable of being acquired by occupancy. Canon law adopts the same view while limiting it to a *just* war. Modern international law, *which appears to be binding in conscience*, lays down the following rules:

a) Private property is inviolable unless there exists urgent need.

b) Everything necessary for the waging of a just war can be seized from the enemy, such as weapons, clothing, food.

c) Soldiers driven by hunger or want to deprive the enemy of necessary food and clothing without the explicit authority of their official superior are not bound to restitution since they do not violate commutative justice, even though they are acting contrary to military discipline. On the other hand, soldiers who seize other goods of great value from their enemy without legitimate authority are held to restitution.

Art. 2. Finding Lost Property

256. DEFINITION. Finding lost property is not a form of occupancy in the strict sense of the word since the object of occupancy is a thing which never had an owner, whereas lost property does have an owner, although unknown.

PRINCIPLES OF NATURAL LAW.

1. A private individual has no obligation in strict justice to take into his own safe keeping another person's property which he happens to find, but in ordinary circumstances there is at least a light obligation *in charity* to do so.

2. The finder who takes possession of a lost article is bound in justice to take care of it and to find its rightful owner.

This follows from the fact that the finder by taking the article into his possession tacitly makes a contract (*rerum gestio*[170]).

3. *If after using due care the finder has no reasonable hope of discovering the true owner, he may keep the article, although it would be more praiseworthy to give it to the poor or to some pious purpose. This is the more common and probable opinion, which may be safely followed in practice.*

4. *Although the finder may keep the article once there is no further prudent hope of finding its rightful owner, the act of finding considered in itself would not seem to constitute a sufficient title to ownership; there is also required the title of prescription as determined by*

---

[169] Translator's note: In English law, treasure trove belongs to the Crown until the true owner is found.

[170] See no. 338.

the laws of each country. This is the probable opinion which is not admitted by some authors who maintain that the finder acquires ownership of the article not by prescription but by occupancy.

Art. 3. Accession

257. DEFINITION. *Accession is a lawful title to acquiring ownership of an increment added to one's lawful possessions.*

Accession is *natural* if the increment results from natural forces alone (by birth, by fruitage, by alluvion); it is *artificial* if the improvement is made by man's unaided skill (by commixture, by building, and so on); it is of a *mixed* character if the increment is due to human skill in conjunction with natural forces.

PRINCIPLES OF NATURAL LAW.

1. If the things joined together can be separated with no great loss, each should be restored to their lawful owners.

2. If separation is impossible, "it is fitting that the increment conform to the nature of the principal object,"[171] but a suitable price should be paid for the accessory object acquired in this way.

NOTE. In the confessional one must observe the civil laws relating to accession.

Art. 4. Prescription

258. DEFINITION. *Prescription is a means of acquiring ownership in consequence of uninterrupted possession of goods during a fixed period of time determined by law.*

Prescription may be acquisitive or liberative. It is *acquisitive*—usucaption—when it confers a new right on an individual, such as the right of walking through another's field; it is *liberative* when it frees one person or his property from some burden or subjection to another, such as the burden of paying a debt.

PRESCRIPTION IS EFFECTIVE both in conscience and in the external forum. Otherwise, *a)* possessions would frequently be the object of uncertainty and subject to legal disputes; *b)* some owners would be in no hurry to justify their own rights.[172]

Prescription once it is legally completed transfers ownership of the property and its fruits *from the very moment of acquiring possession.*

259. FIVE CONDITIONS are required for lawful prescription: the object must be capable of prescription, there must be good faith, a title, actual possession, and the legitimate time must be observed.

1. OBJECTS ARE CAPABLE of being prescribed if they can become objects of perfect ownership. Therefore, the following things are not open to prescription: rights

---

[171] Regula Juris 28, in *Liber Sextus.*
[172] See CCL, Can. 1508.

of natural and divine law; goods declared exempt from prescription by civil or ecclesiastical law—such as sacred things.

2. GOOD FAITH is a prudent conviction that the thing possessed is one's own. It must exist during the entire period of prescription.[173] In *liberative* prescription *negative* good faith would seem sufficient, i.e., the absence of deceit—in other words, prescription is valid if the debtor has done nothing unlawful to prevent another vindicating his rights.

3. A TITLE is the reason on account of which a person assumes possession of a thing—or, the reason which convinces a person that what he possesses is his own. Any title which is either plausible or supposed or presumed is sufficient for prescription. A *plausible* title is an action which would certainly transfer ownership if it were not laboring under some hidden defect, such as buying stolen property in good faith. A *supposed* title (*titulus existimatus*) exists if a person is hindered from actually acquiring ownership through another's fault. A *presumed* title is one which the law supposes to have come into existence in consequence of possession over a considerable period of time.

4. ACTUAL POSSESSION is the actual retention of a thing or the exercise of a right. For lawful prescription possession must be continuous, open (not concealed), peaceable (not contended), and certain.

5. The period of time required for prescription is determined by ecclesiastical and civil law. Ecclesiastical law normally requires thirty years for the prescription of those ecclesiastical goods which do not belong to the Holy See.[174]

QUESTION II
THE VIRTUE OF JUSTICE IN ITSELF

This question is discussed in two chapters: 1) Definition of Justice; 2) The Parts of Justice.

DEFINITION OF JUSTICE

260. DEFINITION. *The virtue of justice is the constant and permanent determination to give to everyone his due.*

This is the definition given by Ulpianus, St. Thomas,[175] and almost all authors. Sometimes in Sacred Scripture justice is understood in other ways, e.g., for every virtue (see Mt 5:6), for justification (see Rom 4:3), and so on. Taken in its strict sense as a cardinal virtue, it is distinct from all other virtues by reason of the subject in which it resides and by reason of its object. The *subject* of justice is the will, whereas the subject of prudence is the intellect, the subject of temperance and fortitude is the sense appetite. The *object* of justice is the good or right due to

---

[173] See CCL, Can. 1512.
[174] See CCL, Can. 1511.
[175] See ST, II-II, q. 58, a. 1.

another; on the other hand, the object of prudence is practical truth, the objects of temperance and fortitude are the passions which have to be regulated. Special attention must be given to the difference between justice and charity to the neighbor. Each virtue is concerned with our neighbor but in different ways: charity is based on the *union* existing between the lover and the loved, and regards the neighbor as another self; justice, on the other hand, is founded on the *distinction* between a man and his neighbor. Thus, a man can display charity toward himself but not justice in the strict sense of that term, and while he can offend against charity toward himself he cannot be strictly unjust to himself.

Since the object of justice consists in rendering to each person what is his due, scholastics are correct in their view that in the practice of justice there must be observed a true *objective mean*, that is, a strict equality between one thing and another.

THE PARTS OF JUSTICE

261. 1. THE SUBJECTIVE PARTS OF JUSTICE (i.e., THE SPECIES of the general virtue) are said by some authors to be three in number—legal justice, distributive justice, commutative justice, insofar as justice regulates the parts of society in relation to the whole, the whole in relation to the parts, and the parts in relation to each other. Strictly speaking, however, virtues are to be distinguished not by their objects which they regulate, but by their *formal objects* to which they are directed primarily and essentially. Now the virtue of justice possesses a twofold formal object: the welfare of the *community* directly intended (legal justice) and the welfare of the *individual* (commutative and distributive justice). Therefore, it is better to follow the distinction given by St. Thomas[176] into *legal* (general) justice, which is the constant and permanent determination to render to society what is its due, and *particular* justice, which is the constant and permanent determination to render to individuals (whether physical or moral) what is their due. Particular justice is then further subdivided into *commutative* justice, which operates in exchanges by preserving a strict equality between the thing given and the thing received, and *distributive* justice, which inclines the ruler of a community to distribute rewards, honors, and burdens to his subjects in proportion to their merits and capabilities. Mention must also be made of *vindictive* justice which inclines the supreme authority to inflict suitable punishment on those who transgress the law. This form of justice is regarded by some authors as belonging to legal justice, by others as part of distributive justice, by others as belonging to commutative justice.

2. THE INTEGRAL PARTS of justice are listed by St. Thomas as twofold: doing good and refraining from evil—not in their wider aspects but as referring to what is *due to another*.[177]

---

[176] See ST, II-II, q. 58ff.
[177] See ST, II-II, q. 79, a. 1.

3. THE POTENTIAL PARTS of justice are nine in number according to St. Thomas: religion, piety, respect, truthfulness, gratitude, protection of others, liberality, affability, equity.[178]

The first three of these virtues are called potential parts of justice or annexed virtues because they do not preserve the *equality between one thing and another* as perfectly as justice itself does; the other six virtues differ from perfect justice insofar as they do not refer to a strict *debt* in the same way as justice itself does. All these virtues will be given separate treatment later.

QUESTION III
INJUSTICE AND RESTITUTION

This question is divided into four chapters: 1) Injustice in General; 2) Injustice Committed by Taking the Property of Another; 3) Injustice Committed by Unjust Damage to Another; 4) Reparation of Injustice—Restitution.

INJUSTICE IN GENERAL

262. FIRST PRINCIPLE. *In its essence injustice is a grave sin, but it may become a venial sin through parvity of matter or through some imperfection in the act.*

This principle is clear from Sacred Scripture where thieves and other offenders against justice are threatened with exclusion from the kingdom of Heaven.

Rule for determining the gravity of the sin. Injustice is a serious sin as often as the sufferer or the ruler of the community has due cause for being most unwilling to bear the injustice.

SECOND PRINCIPLE. *Although every form of injustice is contrary to the same virtue, they involve specifically distinct sins because their formal objects are distinct.*

Thus, for example, calumny and theft are specifically distinct sins even though opposed to the same virtue of justice, and yet it is possible for the same virtue to be violated by different vices.

TAKING THE PROPERTY OF ANOTHER

INTRODUCTORY. The unjust removal of another's property is said to be either *simple* or *qualified*: in the first sense it is identified with theft, in the second sense some new circumstance is added which changes its species, such as the sacred character of the goods taken (sacrilege) or the violence used in taking the goods (rapine). Here the discussion is confined to theft as a violation of the virtue of justice, and the chapter is divided into three articles: 1) Nature and Gravity of Theft in General; 2) Particular Forms of Theft; 3) Taking Not Theft.

Art. 1. Nature and Gravity of Theft in General

DEFINITION. *Theft is the secret removal of another's goods against the owner's reasonable will.*

---

[178] See ST, II-II, q. 80.

263. THE GRAVITY OF THE MATTER involved in theft is either *absolute* or *relative*.
Absolutely grave matter is measured only by the value of the thing stolen without taking into account the condition of the person robbed. This absolute sum is thought to be about fifty francs, gold standard.[179] Relatively grave matter is measured by the living conditions of the person robbed. Thus, it may be thought that one franc constitutes relatively grave matter for the poor, five or six francs for the middle classes, twenty francs for the rich, and fifty francs for the very rich.[180] In determining relatively grave matter, one must also take into account the *incidental* damage suffered by the injured party. Thus, for instance, it would be considered a serious sin to deprive a poor tailor of his needle and thus prevent him working for several hours, since he would thus incur a notable loss.

Art. 2. Particular Forms of Theft

The rules already given regarding the gravity of matter in theft have to be qualified to some extent if there are long intervals between petty thefts, or if the lawful owner was not entirely reluctant, or if the thing stolen does not belong in its entirety to another.

264. 1. PETTY THEFTS IN GENERAL. The term is used for rather frequent thefts of small amounts. In themselves such thefts are venial sins but they become serious sins: *a)* if one has the *evil intention* of eventually acquiring a large sum; *b)* if they are so *frequently repeated* that the intervals between each theft are short (less than a month) and there is no revocation of the thief's intention to steal, and the total amount of all the thefts is grave. However, it is the common teaching of theologians that the amount required for grave sin in petty thefts inflicted on the *same* person is *half* as much again as that required for grave sin when stealing the whole amount at one and the same time, whereas when the petty thefts are inflicted on several owners *twice* that amount is required for grave sin.

265. 2. When considering the PETTY THEFTS OF DOMESTIC SERVANTS, the following rules apply:

a) Servants rarely commit grave sin by their pilferage of ordinary food and drink for their own consumption.

Their master or mistress who has a duty to feed all his or her servants is opposed not so much to the actual loss of this food and drink as to the practice of stealth. — This rule does not apply to *unusual* and expensive food and drink nor to food and drink given to *outsiders*.

---

[179] Fr. Davis, S.J., put the absolute sum for England in the year 1934 at £3 (see *Moral and Pastoral Theology*, vol. 2, 3rd ed., p. 303).

[180] Fr. Davis proposed the following amounts as constituting the relative standard in England in 1933: one shilling in the case of the very poor; six to eight shillings in the case of day laborers; eight to ten shillings in the case of skilled workmen, artisans, or tradesmen; twenty shillings in the case of the moderately rich (see *Moral and Pastoral Theology*, vol. 2, p. 302).

266. *b) Wives are rarely obliged to make restitution for their petty thefts.* The wife is the companion and not the servant of her husband and therefore has a certain liberty in disposing of small amounts of their common possessions. Moreover, the husband is considered to be unwilling to give his consent not so much to the actual loss of money as to the stealthy behavior of his wife.

c) Children who commit petty thefts in the home are obliged to make restitution if when taking all circumstances into consideration their parents must be regarded as seriously opposed not only to the manner but also to the substance of the theft.

Since in practice children are rarely in a position to make restitution, the confessor should prudently advise them to seek forgiveness from their parents.

d) Wives and children should be treated more leniently than servants who indulge in petty thefts in the home.

The reason is that in such circumstances one can more easily presume the consent of the lawful owner.

267. 3. IN THE THEFT OF PUBLIC PROPERTY one must pay particular attention to public opinion. Thus, if in one country such thefts are regarded as transgressions of merely *penal* laws, there is no obligation of restitution; otherwise, the principles given in no. 264.1 regarding petty thefts in general will apply.

Art. 3. Taking Not Theft

There are two reasons which permit persons to take the property of another: extreme need, and justifiable occult compensation.

268. 1. *In extreme need a person may take so much of the goods of another as will free him from his present necessity.* This is agreed by all.

In such need the goods of the earth are common property. — Merely grave or common need does not justify such action. Proximate danger of death constitutes extreme need, whereas grave want constitutes grave need.

269. 2. *Occult compensation under certain conditions is justified, but recourse to it should be rare and even more rarely should the confessor advise it.*

a) Occult compensation is justifiable under the following conditions: 1) the debt must be one's due in justice; 2) the debt cannot be recovered in any other way; 3) every precaution must be taken to prevent harm to the debtor or to any third party. In these circumstances no harm is being done either to the social order or to the rights of a third person. In a word: such compensation is nothing more than justified defense against injury inflicted by another.

b) Recourse to occult compensation should not be frequent since it is wide open to the dangers of illusion and disorder.

c) The confessor should advise recourse to occult compensation even less frequently, since he is liable to become the victim of unfavorable comment and runs the risk of punishment in the civil courts.

UNJUST DAMAGE

This chapter is divided into four articles: 1) Unjust Damage in General; 2) Cooperation in Unjust Damage; 3) Physical Injury; 4) Verbal Injury.

Art. 1. Unjust Damage in General

270. **DEFINITION AND KINDS.** *Unjust damage* (in its strict meaning) *is any action which inflicts harm on another without material benefit to the person inflicting the injury*, such as burning down the house of one's enemy.

Unjust damage may be caused *with or without the cooperation of another*. It is *formal* if a theological fault is incurred at the same time; otherwise, it is *material*. A *theological* fault is a transgression of the divine law and, in the present instance, a sin against commutative justice; a *juridical* fault is a mere transgression of human law which through lack of knowledge or consent does not involve a theological fault. But it is rare that anyone commits a mere juridical fault—at least on those occasions when his act is genuinely human, since even positive law does not suppose the existence of juridical fault where all moral blame is lacking.

271. **FIRST PRINCIPLE.** *Unjust damage is a grave sin which admits of slight matter and also imposes the obligation of restitution when the act of damage was a) unjust in the strict sense, b) formally sinful, and c) the effectual cause of the damage.*

It is evident that unjust damage must be seriously sinful admitting of slight matter, since it is a form of injustice which, as already proved, is itself a grave sin which admits of slight matter. The act of damage is said to be: *a) unjust in the strict sense* of the word, when it violates the strict right of another; *b) the effectual cause* of the damage, when it is the real cause of damage that actually ensued and not merely the occasion or an essential condition or the accidental cause of the damage; *c) formally sinful*, when the act involves a theological fault and not merely a juridical fault. When the act of damage fulfills these conditions it is a formal violation of commutative justice, and it is precisely this formal violation which is responsible for the obligation of restitution that ensues, as will be explained more fully below.

PRACTICAL CASES. 1. A person who by entreaty or persuasion induces an uncle to exclude some stranger from his will is not bound to make restitution since he is not injuring the strict right of another; the situation would be altered if he had recourse to calumny.

2. An innkeeper serving drinks to a drunkard foreseeing the harm that will follow is not bound to restitution since he is the occasion and not the effectual cause of the damage.

3. A doctor who errs through no fault of his own is not obliged to make restitution since he has not incurred any theological fault.

THE GRAVITY OF THIS OBLIGATION OF RESTITUTION. All are agreed that grave damage which involves the commission of *grave* sin is responsible for a grave obligation to make restitution. If *venial* sin is committed, there is a light obligation to make restitution. This is the most common opinion, provided that the harm done was only *slight*; where *serious* harm results from an act which was venially sinful, many theologians absolve the person causing damage from any obligation of restitution since there is no proportion between the venial fault and the restitution to be made for the serious harm caused. But it is more probable that there does exist a real, although slight, obligation to make restitution for all the damage, since otherwise the injured party would incur an unjust burden and the person inflicting the damage would be undeservedly reprieved.

272. SECOND PRINCIPLE. *No obligation of restitution arises from damage which is materially unjust unless: 1) a judge orders restitution to be made, 2) or it is voluntarily agreed that restitution be made.*

In the first instance, the judge's verdict is just and must be observed. In the second case, such agreements are entirely lawful and therefore binding in conscience.

Art. 2. Cooperation in Unjust Damage

273. *Positive* cooperation may be given by command, counsel, consent, flattery, defense, participation; *negative* cooperation by silence, by failure to prevent the harm, by concealment.

GENERAL RULE. *The same two principles set forth in the preceding article regarding unjust damage inflicted by an individual also apply to cooperation.* —Since there is some difficulty involved in the application of these principles to practical cases, the following points are to be noted:

1. Whoever ORDERS or commands another to commit injustice and thus effectually and formally violates commutative justice is bound to make restitution both to the injured person and in certain circumstances to the person so commanded.

The reason for the first part of this statement is self-evident, since such commands are responsible for the violation of a strict right of the person on whom the damage is inflicted. Furthermore, restitution must be made to the person commanded for any harm he himself incurs in the execution of the command, if he was induced to commit the damage by deceit or force or abuse of authority.

2. The COUNSELOR who by persuasion is the moral cause of another inflicting harm on a third party is bound to repair the harm which he foresaw would follow from his evil counsel.

Counsel is said to be *theoretical* in character when it is sufficient to convince the reason that some action is not forbidden, or that taking all the circumstances into consideration the action must be done, or that these are suitable means for accomplishing the action; it is termed *impelling* if entreaties, exhortation, or promises are used to influence the will. —A person who earnestly retracts his evil counsel before the damage is inflicted is not bound to make restitution if the counsel given was merely impelling; if, however, it was of a theoretical nature, mere recovation is insufficient and the counselor must do all in his power to prevent harm to the third party.—Normally, the counselor is not obliged to make restitution to the *person who actually inflicts the harm* unless he has used guile, deceit, or lies, or has the duty of giving correct counsel by reason of his office.

3. One who CONSENTS to an act of damage by external approval, by his vote or judgment, cooperates effectually and unjustly in causing injury to his neighbor and is therefore bound to repair the harm caused. Those who vote in favor of unjust laws are consenting to an act of unjust damage. If such persons by mutual agreement or secret ballot or other means are the effectual causes of unjust laws, such as laws commanding the seizure of Church property, they are obliged to make restitution. But since such restitution is often impossible, recourse must be had to the decrees of the Sacred Penitentiary which have been specially drawn up for this contingency.

4. THE FLATTERER who by praise or disparagement induces another to commit injustice is practically an evil counselor.

5. Anyone who SHELTERS or defends an evil-doer or thief *as such* (and not merely as a friend) in order to protect him more securely against his pursuers or to provide him with a place to deposit his stolen property is bound to restitution, if he has cooperated effectively in causing harm to another.

6. A person PARTICIPATES in unjust damage either by *receiving* part of what has been stolen or by *helping* another in his unjust action. In the first instance, he must restore all that he has received; if he took part in doing harm to another, he must repair all the harm of which he was the effectual cause by his action and for which he incurred theological fault.

274. 7. NEGATIVE COOPERATION exists: 1) when *prior* to an act of injustice a person remains silent and does not warn the victim, even though his office obliges him to do so; 2) when a person does not prevent the harm while it is being inflicted, even though he is bound in justice to do so; 3) when *after* the harm has been inflicted a person does not denounce the evil-doer to the injured party or to his superior when there is a duty to do so. All such persons are bound to repair the harm inflicted, if they could have prevented it without grave inconvenience to themselves.

Art. 3. Physical Injury

The question will be discussed in the following order: 1) Physical Injury to Self; 2) Physical Injury to Another; 3) Injury Arising from Rape and Adultery.

§ 1. Physical Injury to Self

INTRODUCTION. No one has complete ownership of his body but the use only, since man is God's steward, so to speak; if he abuses or destroys his own body he inflicts an injury on God, but he does not inflict an injury (strictly so-called) on himself since injury is always concerned with the rights of others.

275. FIRST PRINCIPLE. *The direct killing of oneself on one's own authority is a most grievous sin against divine, natural, and ecclesiastical law.*

a) Against divine law: "Thou shalt not kill";

b) Against natural law, since it injures the welfare of society and violates the virtue of charity to self;

c) Against ecclesiastical law which deprives the suicide of ecclesiastical burial and prayers, unless the suicide was entirely secret or doubtful or committed while the person was of unsound mind or unless he manifested signs of repentance prior to death.[181]

SECOND PRINCIPLE. *Indirect suicide is forbidden unless there is a proportionately grave reason.*

Suicide is *direct* when it is directly intended and results from an action voluntarily performed and directly causing death; it is *indirect* when not intended but foreseen as the effect of a physical act which does not cause death directly but gives rise to a most serious danger of death. Among the reasons which suffice for permitting indirect suicide are the common good (soldiers fighting for their country) and the welfare of the soul (a priest administering the Sacraments to those suffering from contagious disease).

Those who expose their life to grave danger or who shorten their life without sufficient reason commit grave sin.

SCHOLIUM. A DESIRE FOR DEATH may be lawful, unlawful, or an imperfection.

a) It is *lawful* to desire death when it is inspired by a good motive, such as the desire for union with God in Heaven.

b) It is *unlawful* when inspired by an evil motive, such as tiredness with life. However, such a desire is rarely grievously sinful.

c) It is an *imperfection* when through impatience one prefers to lose one's life rather than endure a life full of severe hardship.

276. SELF-MUTILATION. *It is forbidden to mutilate oneself or to remove part of one's body unless this is necessary to save bodily life.*

Man possesses only indirect ownership of his bodily members which he must use in dependence on God's will. Thus, it is forbidden to mutilate oneself in order to escape military service or to preserve the virtue of chastity.

§ 2. Physical Injury to Another

Under this heading will be considered: 1) Capital Punishment; 2) Killing the Unjust Aggressor; 3) Dueling; 4) War; 5) Killing the Innocent; 6) Craniotomy; 7) Abortion.

[181] See CCL, Can. 1240.

1. Capital Punishment

277. PRINCIPLE. *Only the State has the right to put to death those who have committed most serious crimes.*

The State has this right since the penalty of death is sometimes necessary for safeguarding the common weal and only the State has the duty of safeguarding society. Capital punishment must be reserved for the most serious crimes and these must be fully proven.

SCHOLIUM. MUTILATION AND FLOGGING. Since the State has the power to put the criminal to death, so it has the power for a sufficient reason to mutilate the criminal (e.g., by cutting off his hand) or to flog him. But in modern times, neither of these forms of punishment is common. No one else is permitted to mutilate another without the latter's legitimate consent. Consequently, not even a surgeon can perform an operation without first obtaining the explicit and lawful consent of his patient. When the patient is a child who has not yet attained the use of reason the necessary consent can be supplied by a lawful superior. — A just flogging of one's neighbor can be performed by a legitimate superior but not by a private individual except in defense of himself or his property.

2. Killing the Unjust Aggressor

278. PRINCIPLE. *One may defend oneself against an unjust aggressor even to the point of killing him, provided that one does not injure him more than is absolutely necessary to ensure self-protection.*

Every man has a strict right to protect himself and his property against unjust aggression. On the part of the assailant, aggression that is at least materially unjust would be sufficient to justify self-defense. Accordingly, one retains the right to kill even a madman who tries to inflict grave injury. — In the act of defending oneself, it is not permitted to kill the assailant unless this is absolutely necessary to safeguard one's own life or goods of great value. Therefore, one is not allowed to kill the aggressor, *a)* if his attack is not presently but only remotely imminent,[182] *b)* if the attack is directed against goods not yet possessed[183] or of little value,[184] *c)* if the attack is directed against one's honor or good name.[185] On the other hand, we are justified in killing a man who desires to kill or mutilate us, or to injure us in our virtue of chastity (a probable opinion), or in temporal goods of great value.

3. Dueling

279. DEFINITION. *A duel is a contest between two or a few individuals waged by agreement as to time, place, and weapons which are lethal (or at least adapted to inflict serious injury).*

---

[182] See DZ 1118.
[183] See DZ 1182.
[184] See DZ 1181.
[185] See DZ 1180.

PRINCIPLE. *Dueling undertaken by private authority is gravely sinful and incurs grave ecclesiastical penalties.*

Dueling is gravely sinful since the contestants expose themselves to serious danger of death and injury without sufficient reason. The usual excuse given for a duel is the vindication of honor which is rarely achieved by dueling.

ECCLESIASTICAL PENALTIES for dueling.

1. *Excommunication* reserved simply to the Holy See incurred not only by the duelists themselves but also by those who (seriously) challenge or who accept a challenge to a duel or who offer help to them or who are deliberately present at a duel.[186]

2. *Ecclesiastical burial is denied* to those who die in consequence of a wound received in a duel unless they show signs of repentance before death.[187]

3. *Infamy in law* is incurred by the duelists and their seconds.[188]

4. *Irregularity* arising from infamy of law and from the crime of murder for the person who has wounded or killed another, from infamy of law only for all others.[189]

NOTE. Anyone who uses moral force to compel a person who is unwilling to accept a challenge to a duel and causes him serious material harm is bound to make restitution, for he is the cause of unjust damage.

4. War

280. DEFINITION. *War is an armed conflict between two opposing armies.* It therefore differs from a duel, a quarrel, or an insurrection. War is either *offensive* when it is fought to obtain satisfaction for injury, or *defensive* when it is intended as a means of warding off unjust aggression from another ruler or State. Sometimes it is far from easy to distinguish an offensive war from a defensive war, since it does not always follow that the army which opens the war is conducting an offensive war.

PRINCIPLE. *A supreme authority, a just cause, and a right intention are required to justify the declaration of war. To wage war legitimately, all the statutes of international law must be observed.*

The first condition required for the declaration of war is self-evident. The second condition—a just cause—is best explained in the words of Francis de Vittoria: "There is only one just cause for entering upon war—*violated rights.*" Therefore, one would not be justified in waging war for the purpose of self-aggrandizement or winning renown or in order to convert the pagan.

The third condition is also immediately evident.

---

[186] See CCL, Can. 2351, § 1.
[187] See CCL, Can. 1240, § 4.
[188] See CCL, Can. 2351, § 2.
[189] See Council of Trent, Session 25, "Decree on Reformation," chap. 19; see also CCL, Can. 2351, § 2.

Once war has broken out, it is necessary to observe the statutes of international law of which the most important is: war is not waged against individuals but against an entire nation as a public person. Generally speaking, one is permitted to use everything necessary for crushing the resistance of the enemy. Soldiers commit grave sin if in the course of a just war they desert or cross over to the enemy lines.

5. Killing the Innocent

281. PRINCIPLE. *a) No one is ever allowed to kill an innocent person directly; b) indirect killing is sometimes permissible—that is to say, it is not sinful on those occasions when one has an adequately grave reason to do or omit some action which, in itself indifferent, results in the death of an innocent person although this is not intended.*

The first part of the principle is evident from the words of Sacred Scripture: "Do not bring death on an innocent man that has justice on his side" (Ex 23:7). The killing of an innocent person is a sin crying to Heaven for vengeance (see Gn 4:10).

For the second part of the principle, refer to no. 23 where we discussed the indirectly voluntary act. Indirect killing often takes place in indirect abortion.

6. Craniotomy

282. DEFINITION. *Craniotomy is a surgical operation whereby a viable foetus is crushed in the mother's womb and then extracted in parts.*

PRINCIPLE. *Craniotomy and other surgical operations which directly cause the death of a child are entirely forbidden.*

Craniotomy is the direct killing of an innocent person which is always forbidden, as is evident from previous paragraphs. Thus, the Sacred Office[190] gave the following reply: *It cannot be safely taught* that craniotomy is permissible. Not only can it not be safely taught but it is also completely unlawful, as is evident from the more recent reply of the Holy Office.[191]

In practice one may sometimes leave in good faith those doctors who have recourse to craniotomy as the only means of saving the life of the mother. In such circumstances, it would be difficult to convince them that such an operation is unlawful.—Other means which can be used to save the mother and the child on such occasions are: caesarean section, symphysiotomy, pubiotomy.

7. Abortion

283. DEFINITION. *Abortion is the expulsion of a living inviable foetus from the womb.* It is therefore distinct from: 1) craniotomy which consists in killing a viable foetus in the womb, whereas abortion is the killing of an inviable foetus; 2) from the induction of premature labor when a viable foetus (i.e., after the twenty-eighth week) is expelled from the uterus by artificial means.

Abortion is *spontaneous* if it takes place by chance without any deliberate intention; it is induced or *artificial* when procured by intentional interference. Induced

[190] May 24, 1884 and Aug. 19, 1889.
[191] July 24, 1895.

abortion is procured either *directly* if the means used kill or expel the foetus immediately and of their very nature, or *indirectly* if the means used have as their immediate and direct effect the health of the mother, although it is foreseen that afterward they will cause the expulsion of the foetus.

FIRST PRINCIPLE. *The induction of premature labor and indirect abortion are permissible for sufficiently grave reasons.*

That the expulsion of a viable foetus by artificial means is permissible for grave reasons is evident from the explicit reply of the Holy Office, May 4, 1898, and from the fact that although premature labor is dangerous for mother and child, it is not intrinsically evil.

That indirect abortion is permissible for grave reasons is evident from the previous discussion of indirect voluntary acts and of indirect killing of innocent persons.

SECOND PRINCIPLE. *Direct abortion of a living foetus is grievously sinful and punished by positive laws.*

Proof. a) Anyone who procures a direct abortion of a living foetus is directly killing an innocent person, and this is never permitted. *b)* Not only the body but also the soul is being forcibly deprived of life, since the foetus is frequently unbaptized. *c)* The Holy Office[192] condemned any surgical operation which is the direct cause of killing a foetus.

284. PENALTIES INFLICTED ON THOSE PROCURING ABORTION.

1. *Excommunication reserved to the ordinary.*[193] The mother herself who procures an abortion is not excused from this censure, neither are those who order the abortion; those who cooperate are excused.

2. *Criminal irregularity.*[194] Dispensation from this irregularity is reserved to the Holy See, but in urgent need the confessor may use epikeia and give absolution, at the same time imposing the obligation of having recourse within a month to the Sacred Penitentiary.[195]

3. *Clerics are to be deposed.* This penalty must be inflicted by explicit pronouncement.[196]

Other penalties may be inflicted by *particular* ecclesiastical laws. The civil law also punishes those who procure abortion.

§ 3. Injury Arising from Rape and Adultery

285. FIRST PRINCIPLE. *There is no obligation to make restitution for the mere physical act of fornication even when obtained by force, unless there follows a legal judgment to that effect or material loss is incurred as a result of the act.*

---

[192] Aug. 14, 1889.
[193] See CCL, Can. 2350, § 1.
[194] See CCL, Can. 985, no. 4.
[195] See Holy Office, Mar. 28, 1906 and Sept. 6, 1909; see also CCL, Can. 2290.
[196] See CCL, Can. 2350, § 1.

It is impossible for private authority to estimate such a physical act in terms of money. However, a legal judge may impose a just compensation for the act. If material harm ensues from the act, then in certain circumstances restitution must be made, as will be stated in the following principles.

SECOND PRINCIPLE. *Anyone using force, grave fear, or deceit to induce a woman (whether married or not) to consent to sexual intercourse is bound to make reparation for all the harm which the woman, her offspring, her parents, or her husband suffer in consequence.*

In such circumstances the man is inflicting unjust damage.

THIRD PRINCIPLE. *A man who has sexual intercourse with a woman (whether married or not) who is a willing partner has no obligation of restitution to her, but he is bound equally with the woman to bear all the material consequences of their act.*

The reason for the first part of the principle is that no injury can be inflicted on a person who knows and freely consents to what is being done.

The reason for the second part is that both accomplices are equally blameworthy. The consequences of their action may be *a) children*, in which case each accomplice in default of the other is bound to meet in full all the expenses which ensue from the birth and education of the child; *b) a reduction in the inheritance* of other legitimate children. Great prudence must be shown in determining the means and amount of restitution in such cases.[197]

Art. 4. Verbal Injury

INTRODUCTORY. Following the method of St. Thomas,[198] we shall consider: 1) Verbal Injury in Court; 2) Verbal Injury outside Court. In the first question a brief summary will be given of the duties and sins of judges, plaintiffs and prosecutors, witnesses, advocates, defendants; in the second question will be included lies, mental restriction, the violation of secrets, injury to honor and good name, rash judgment.

1. Verbal Injury in Court
§ 1. Duties and Sins of Judges

286. FIRST PRINCIPLE. *In order to exercise his office lawfully a judge must be equipped with sufficient knowledge and pass judgment in accordance with just laws.*

Therefore, a judge would commit sin if he were not sufficiently acquainted with legal science, if he did not investigate carefully the case to be tried, if he passed sentence at variance with just laws. On the other hand, a judge cannot base his opinion on such positive laws as are in evident conflict with natural or divine law. Whether a judge is permitted from grave necessity to pronounce a decree of divorce in valid Christian marriages will be considered in the treatise on marriage.

[197] See MTM, vol. 2, no. 152.
[198] See ST, II-II, q. 67–71.

SECOND PRINCIPLE. *A judge's sentence which is manifestly unjust does not bind in conscience except incidentally—that is to say, in order to avoid public scandal or public disorder.*

Such unjust sentences are similar to unjust positive laws which are not binding when in conflict with natural or divine law but nevertheless have to be observed in certain circumstances in order to avoid greater evil.

THIRD PRINCIPLE. *In doubtful matters the judge must base his opinion on the greater probability; when the defendant's guilt is not proved, the judge must set him free.*

The first part of the principle is evident from the second proposition condemned by Innocent XI: "I think that probably a judge can pass judgment according to opinion, even the less probable."[199] The second part is based on the Regula Juris 49: "In the infliction of punishment the more favorable interpretation must be followed." For no one is presumed guilty unless this is proved.

§ 2. Duties and Sins of Plaintiff and Prosecutor

287. DEFINITIONS. A person who accuses another in court before a judge is termed the *plaintiff* in a civil case, the *prosecutor* in a criminal trial. Therefore, in general terms a prosecution is a charge brought against one accused of some crime so that he may receive public punishment, made by a person who undertakes to prove that crime. He who prosecutes another is obliged to prove the crime, otherwise he receives heavy punishment. To prosecute is not the same as to *denounce* a criminal, whereby a crime is brought to the knowledge of a superior so that he may inquire into it and punish it, but in this instance, there is no strict obligation to prove the crime. Denunciation is either *judicial* when it is undertaken for the purpose of punishing the crime, or *evangelical* when the crime is brought to the notice of a superior in his capacity as a kind father, not that of a severe judge.

PRINCIPLE. Officials in virtue of their office are obliged to make known to the legitimate superior all crimes which they detect; private persons have no strict obligation in this matter unless denunciation is demanded by: *a)* positive law (denouncing a confessor guilty of solicitation); *b)* the common good (denouncing those who are responsible for counterfeit money); *c)* the need to avert grave harm to the neighbor.

All parts of this principle are clear and require no further proof.

§ 3. Duties and Sins of Witnesses

288. THE OBLIGATION to give evidence may result from: *a) charity,* (e.g., in order to prevent the neighbor suffering injury); *b) commutative justice,* if a person is bound to testify in virtue of his office; *c) legal justice* or obedience, when a judge lawfully commands a person to testify.

THE FOLLOWING REASONS EXCUSE a person from giving evidence: *a) the seal of Confession; b) a professional secret*—at least in most cases; *c) serious damage* which

---

[199] DZ 1152.

would result for the witness or his relatives in consequence of the evidence given;[200] *d) if a judge is not entitled to ask the question proposed; e) if the witness has obtained his knowledge by inflicting injury on another.*[201]

SINS AND DUTIES OF FALSE WITNESSES. False witness involves the commission of three sins: perjury, injustice, lying. The person responsible is bound to repair all the material damage which follows unjustly. This obligation is serious. However, it is rare that a false witness is obliged to reveal his perjury, since no one is bound to damage his own good name.

§ 4. Duties and Sins of Advocates

289. THE CHIEF DUTIES of an advocate are: *a)* to possess sufficient knowledge of the law and of the case to be tried; *b)* to defend just causes by all lawful means; *c)* not to demand exorbitant fees.

An advocate commits SIN by ignoring any of these duties, or by attending to the cases he undertakes in a negligent manner, or by not honestly revealing to his client the dangers of his lawsuit.

§ 5. Duties and Sins of Defendants

290. In order to avoid confusion, we must distinguish the duties which exist prior to the judge's sentence from those which exist after it. *Before sentence* is passed the defendant *a)* is not bound to admit his crime; *b)* may defend himself by all lawful means. — Modern legal practice has changed in reference to the confession of crime. The principle formerly proposed by theologians — "when the judge proposes lawful questions to the accused which accord with justice, the defendant is bound to admit the truth" — is still true today, but the judge is no longer considered to be within his rights by forcing the accused to admit his crime.[202]

After sentence has been passed, the criminal who has been justly condemned cannot offer positive resistance to his guards in order to prevent the infliction of his punishment, but he may escape from prison if he can. It is self-evident that a prisoner is within his rights to escape an unjust punishment.

2. Verbal Injury outside Court
§ 1. Lies

291. DEFINITION AND KINDS. *A lie is a voluntary utterance contrary to intellectual conviction.*

1. A lie is said to be *profitable* if it is spoken to benefit a person, although no harm is intended.

2. It is said to be *harmful* (or pernicious) if it causes special injury to another.

---

200 See CCL, Can. 1755.
201 See MIC, q. 496.
202 See CCL, Can. 1743–1744.

3. A lie is said to be *jocose* if it is spoken for the sake of giving amusement or pleasure.

Belonging to the same category are: *boasting*, whereby one makes oneself out to be greater than one is; *irony*, whereby one lowers oneself unjustly; *insincerity*, which consists in being false not in word but in deed; *hypocrisy*, whereby one pretends to be virtuous or holy.

292. **MALICE OF LYING.** 1. *A lie is intrinsically evil, so that no reason whatsoever can justify its use.*

Sacred Scripture forbids all forms of lying without distinction: "Keep clear of untruth" (Ex 23:7); "Do not tell lies at another's expense" (Col 3:9). The intrinsic reason for the evil character of lying is that it is opposed to: *a)* the natural purpose of speech which is given to man to reveal what is in his mind; *b)* natural human intercourse which is disturbed by lying; *c)* the good of the listener who is deceived by the lie; *d)* the welfare of the speaker himself who, although he may obtain some temporary advantage from the lie, will suffer greater evils in consequence.

2. *As contrary to the virtue of truthfulness, lying is a venial sin, but it may become grievously sinful if contrary to other virtues, such as justice, religion, and so on.*

The reason for the first part is that lying, as contrary to truthfulness, is an abuse of speech which does not involve a serious disorder.

The reason for the second part is that violations of these virtues are grave sins which admit of slight matter.

§ 2. Mental Reservation and Amphibology

293. **DEFINITIONS.** M*ental reservation* is an act of the mind whereby in the course of conversation we restrict the sense of the words used to a meaning different from their obvious meaning. If a prudent man could gather the intended meaning from the surrounding circumstances, then it is *broad* mental restriction; otherwise, it is *strict*.

Amphibology is a statement with several meanings (Peter is staying at home=he is actually at home or he dines at home).

PRINCIPLE. *Strict mental reservation is never permitted, but when there is need or a reasonable cause one may have recourse to broad mental reservation or to amphibology.*

Strict mental reservation is an odious lie, whereas broad mental restriction and amphibology are a concealment of truth which in certain circumstances is not only permitted but even necessary and was used by Christ Himself (see Jn 7:8; and Mk 13:22). Generally speaking, however, mental restriction should be used as little as possible in the course of conversation.

§ 3. The Violation of Secrets

294. **DEFINITION AND KINDS OF SECRET.** In its objective sense a secret is something hidden; in its subjective sense it is the knowledge of a hidden fact and the obligation not

to reveal this fact. We are here considering the word in its subjective sense. There are three kinds of secrets: natural, promised, and entrusted secrets.

1. A *natural* secret is so called because the obligation not to reveal the hidden fact arises from natural law, such as when one discovers another's secret and shameful sin.

2. A *promised* secret is one which a person has promised to keep *after* the secret has been received.

3. An *entrusted* (rigorous) secret is one which was obtained only *after an explicit or tacit agreement* had been made that secrecy would be observed. To this category belong: professional secrets (such as those of doctors and midwives) and the sacramental secret or seal of Confession which is the most binding of all secrets.

PRINCIPLE. *Of their very nature, natural secrets bind under grave sin; likewise entrusted secrets; promised secrets are in themselves binding under venial sin in ordinary circumstances.*

The reason is that the violation of either natural or entrusted secrets is a sin against justice either because of the very nature of the secret itself or because of the agreement made, and such a sin is a mortal sin which admits of slight matter. On the other hand, when a promised secret is not kept it is the virtue of *fidelity* which is violated and this virtue does not of itself and in normal circumstances bind under grave sin, since its violation is nothing other than a lie. In practice, however, the transgression of even a promised secret is frequently a serious offense because it results in grievous harm to the neighbor, or because such promised secrets are at the same time natural secrets.

295. A REASONABLE CAUSE FOR REVEALING A SECRET is the urgent necessity of either the public or private good.

In such necessity the neighbor would be unreasonable in not consenting to the revelation of the secret—that is to say, it is permissible to think that he forgoes his right of having his secret kept hid. Since the public good must have precedence over the good of the individual, it is evident that the individual's secret must be sacrificed if the public good requires it. The good of the individual may refer either to the person who is aware of the secret, or to the person who benefits from the continued preservation of the secret, or to some third party. Where there exists a need, it is permissible to reveal a secret (apart from the confessional secret) for the benefit of any of those three persons.

296. READING ANOTHER'S LETTERS. It is grievously sinful to read the *secret* letters or writings of another without the consent of either the sender or recipient or without legitimate authority or without just cause, because in so doing a person is deprived of secrets which he has a perfect right to preserve. Just as theft is committed by secretly removing the goods of another, so it is theft to pry into secrets contained in letters. In practice, however, grievous sin is often not committed either because such letters contain nothing that is secret, or because their readers are acting with an erroneous conscience, since many people think that no grave sin is involved in reading another's letters.

§ 4. Contumely

297. **DEFINITIONS.** *Honor consists in the external recognition of a person's excellence.* This recognition may be conveyed in words (e.g., by praise), in deeds (e.g., a bow of reverence), or in external objects (e.g., by the conferment of a dignity).

Honor is principally violated by *contumely* which may be defined as *unjustly dishonoring another in his presence.*

THE MALICE OF CONTUMELY. *Contumely is a grave sin of injustice which allows parvity of matter.*

Contumely is a violation of a person's honor, which is a good of great value to which every man has a strict right. Other sins frequently accompany contumely, such as sins contrary to religion, lack of respect, blasphemy, scandal.—Contumely becomes venially sinful, *a)* if there is some imperfection in the act itself, or *b)* if the person did not intend any serious injury to another's honor, or *c)* if only slight injury resulted due to the state of the speaker and his hearer.

RESTITUTION must be made for any insult offered to a person's honor in the same way as restitution is necessary for material goods taken away unjustly.—The *method* of restitution must be determined by the status of the person who offered the insult and that of the person offended.

§ 5. Defamation of Character

298. **DEFINITIONS.** *Good esteem is the opinion which men express in words regarding the excellence of another.*

This esteem is violated by defamation whereby one *secretly blackens the good name of another.* Modern theologians usually distinguish defamation into *detraction* and *calumny.* Detraction is the unjust revelation of another's genuine but hidden fault; calumny is the untruthful imputation of some fault not actually committed. Older theologians spoke of calumny, detraction, and defamation, without making any distinction between them so far as their morality was concerned.

In this category must also be included *tale-bearing* which is a form of detraction that sows discord between friends.

299. **MALICE OF DEFAMATION.** *Unjust defamation (whether it be simple detraction or calumny) is a grave sin contrary to justice and charity which admits of slight matter.*

This is evident from the words of St. Thomas: "It is a serious matter to take away the good esteem of another, because amongst man's temporal possessions nothing is more precious than his good name; if he lacks this he is prevented from doing many good things. Therefore it is said: 'Take care of your good name; for this will be a more lasting possession of yours than a thousand valuable and precious treasures' (Ecclus 41:15). And therefore, detraction considered in itself is grievously sinful."[203]

---

[203] ST, II-II, q. 73, a. 2, c.

It is evident that calumny is a violation of strict justice since it is an *unjust* lie. On the other hand, the harm caused by detraction derives from the fact that the secret sinner still retains the good esteem of others and he cannot be dispossessed of this without a *just title*. Now the detractor does not possess such a just title for revealing his neighbor's secret sin; otherwise, it would cease to be detraction and become a justifiable revelation of a secret sin. —Moreover, detraction is the cause of harm to the *welfare of society* since it normally gives rise to quarrels, disputes, excessive hatred, all of which are contrary to *charity*; accordingly, detraction (and calumny, a fortiori) violates not only justice but also charity.

Defamation does not assume a different *species* of sinfulness, *a)* from the fact that it is calumny or detraction, since the effects of both are the same; *b)* from the fact that it is this or that sin of the neighbor which is unjustly disclosed; *c)* from the fact that it takes place in the presence of a few persons or of several. However, in all these cases there are *aggravating* circumstances, and the sin of calumny must be mentioned by name in confession, otherwise the confessor will not possess sufficient knowledge to judge of the gravity of the sin and of the restitution that must be made.

THE GRAVITY OF DEFAMATION. To decide in practice how grave is defamation one must consider:

1. the *person who speaks*, who, if he is a prudent man of some importance, will cause more harm than an unreliable, talkative character;

2. the *persons who listen*; if numerous, loquacious, and even influential, grave injury more easily ensues than if they were few, discreet, and unimportant;

3. the *person injured*; if his dignity is high and his good name intact, he is more likely to suffer grave injury than if he were a worthless character;

4. the *motive* which inspires a person to reveal another's faults. Granted that no motive is sufficient to justify calumny, yet there are reasons which justify or at least make less sinful the manifestation of another's secret.[204]

NOTE. Even the dead retain their right to their good name, and therefore it is forbidden to reveal and make known their sins and vices without sufficient reason.

300. RESTITUTION OF VIOLATED GOOD ESTEEM. A person who defames another unjustly is obliged in justice to repair: 1) the loss of good esteem; 2) all the material losses which are foreseen at least confusedly as resulting from his defamation. The first obligation is *personal*, the second *real* and therefore passes to a man's heirs; but in some circumstances it may be wiser to leave the latter in good faith if it is foreseen that the warning will cause more harm than good.

In making restitution, the calumniator will not employ the same method as the detractor. The calumniator is bound to make a public declaration of the falsity of his previous assertion, whereas the detractor must use all the lawful means he can to excuse the faults which he has unjustly revealed.

[204] See no. 295.

REASONS WHICH EXCUSE FROM RESTITUTION FOR THE LOSS OF GOOD ESTEEM ARE:

1. if the defamation has been forgotten through passing of time;

2. if the defamed has lawfully condoned reparation either expressly or tacitly. Sometimes compensation may be regarded as a form of condonation—that is to say, when the person defamed has himself dishonored the good name of the other and neither is willing to repair the loss of good name of the other.—If the defamation injured not only the person defamed but also his state of life and other persons, it is impossible to condone reparation;

3. if reparation is impossible; e.g., if those who heard the defamation are unknown or cannot be traced, or if the reparation could not be made without suffering *much greater* harm.

§ 6. Rash Judgment

301. DEFINITION AND MALICE. *Rash judgment is the firm assent of the mind (whether manifested externally or not) to the existence of sin in another without sufficient reason.*

Rash judgment in its strict sense is a grave sin of injustice which admits of slight matter.

This is so, since it violates the perfect right which each man has to the good esteem of men until the contrary is proved. Three conditions must be verified for rash judgment to be grievously sinful: 1) it must be fully deliberate; 2) it must be completely rash—i.e., it is known that there are insufficient grounds to support the allegation of sin; 3) it must concern another's grave sin. Only rarely are all these conditions fulfilled, and therefore rash judgment is rarely a grave sin.

RESTITUTION; OR, REPARATION OF VIOLATED RIGHTS

The question will be discussed in the following order: 1) The Obligation of Restitution in General; 2) Grounds of Restitution; 3) The Manner and Circumstances of Restitution; 4) Reasons Which Excuse from Restitution.

Art. 1. The Obligation of Restitution in General

302. DEFINITION. Restitution may be understood in a *wide* sense when it signifies the return of anything received and this is the meaning given to the term in the contract of deposit and in the contract for consumption; or it may be understood in its *strict* sense as *compensation for injury inflicted on another.* Restitution may be necessary whether one is or is not to blame for the injury caused.

PRINCIPLE. *The obligation of restitution arises from the transgression of commutative justice only, not from the violation of either legal or distributive justice.*

The reason is that restitution effects a strict equality between one thing and another, and such equality exists in commutative justice only, namely, between what is given and what is received, between the injury and the compensation. In legal and distributive justice, the equality is one of *proportion*.[205] But on many occasions a violation of legal or distributive justice also includes a violation of commutative justice, and this incidentally gives rise to the obligation of restitution.

NOTE. The violation of commutative justice does not cause an obligation of restitution unless some *material* damage is caused. Theologians are not agreed whether merely *personal* harm, such as a wound, pain, contumely, rape, and so on make a man liable to restitution. The affirmative view seems the more correct in theory, but in practice a strict obligation to repair the harm cannot be imposed unless a judge's sentence intervenes.

303. THE NECESSITY OF RESTITUTION. *It is necessary for salvation to make restitution either in fact or at least in intention for any notable harm inflicted on another.*

The reason is evident. One cannot attain to salvation without observing justice. But whosoever refuses to make restitution when he is able to do so, either *a)* for something that he has unjustly removed, or *b)* for something that he possesses unjustly, or *c)* for unjust damage inflicted on another is violating justice. Therefore, restitution is necessary for salvation. Hence the brief statement in Regula Juris 4 in *Liber Sextus*: "Sin is not forgiven unless one restores what has been taken away."

If actual restitution is impossible, then the intention to make restitution is both necessary and sufficient, namely, a firm resolution to repair the harm as soon as this is feasible.

Art. 2. Grounds of Restitution

304. INTRODUCTORY. St. Thomas and older theologians, understanding restitution in its wider meaning, used to propose two grounds of restitution, stating that a man was bound to restitution either 1) because of *the article received*, or 2) because of the *manner in which the article was received*. Because of the article received, the possessor of another's property is bound to restitution whether he is in good faith or in bad faith; because of the manner in which the article was received, an obligation of restitution ensues: *a)* from every formal crime which causes real damage to the neighbor, whether it be theft or unjust damage; *b)* from certain contracts, such as the contracts of loan and deposit. — More recent theologians, taking restitution in its stricter meaning, usually propose the following grounds of restitution: 1) *possession* of another's property; 2) *damage* to another's property. Since we intend to devote a special section to the obligation arising from contracts, for the present we shall confine the discussion to the two grounds of restitution understood in its strict sense. — Other theologians speak of cooperation as a separate ground of restitution, but this is without foundation since it may be included under either of the two grounds already mentioned — unjust possession or unjust damage.

[205] See ST, II-II, q. 61, a. 2.

§ 1. Possession of the Property of Another

305. **Definition.** A man may possess or retain the goods of another in good, bad, or doubtful faith. Therefore, the duties resulting from each form of possession must be considered separately.

The products of goods are:

1. *natural* products if they result from things with practically no assistance from man, such as the grass in the fields;

2. products which are acquired chiefly through the *industry of man*, such as profit made in the course of trading;

3. products which are the result of *equal efforts by man and nature*, e.g., butter;

4. products which *result from lease (fructus civiles)*.

Expenses are:

1. *necessary* for the preservation of goods;

2. *useful* for their improvement;

3. *superfluous*, if incurred in the mere embellishment of goods.

1. Possession in Good Faith

306. **General Principles.**

1. *The unjust possessor of another's goods is bound to restore them to their owner who alone has the right to the natural products of these goods, and if the goods perish, the owner is the loser. Furthermore, no one has the right to be enriched at the expense or harm of another.*

This is the teaching of all theologians in accord with the principles of ancient Roman law. However, recent laws have introduced certain modifications which may be used even in the forum of conscience, such as laws relating to the products obtained from another's property.

2. *When doubt exists, the person in possession has the better title.*

This is demanded by the welfare of the State and its citizens, otherwise the social order would soon be disturbed.

Rights and obligations.

The possessor in good faith has the following obligations and rights.

a) When he knows for certain that he possesses property belonging to another he must restore it to the lawful owner.

b) If the property perishes, he is absolved from further obligation.

c) He acquires genuine ownership of another's property after lawful prescription.

d) According to modern law, he usually retains all the products which he has acquired in good faith from the goods possessed.

e) He may demand compensation for all useful and necessary expenses, after deducting the value of the products received from the goods.

FOR PRACTICAL GUIDANCE in cases of conscience one must pay particular attention to the civil laws of each country. Since in doubtful cases possession is nine-tenths of the law, one must favor the possessor in good faith. Finally in each instance one must try to determine whether the possessor has a just title for acquiring the chattel, its equivalent, and its products.

2. Possession in Bad Faith

307. PRINCIPLE. *The unjust possessor of another's goods in bad faith is bound to repair all the foreseen damage caused to the lawful owner.*

Therefore: *a)* he must restore the thing itself if it still exists; if it has perished, he must restore its equivalent value.

b) He must restore to the owner all the natural products of his property together with any profit obtained by leasing the goods and also the increase in value which the legitimate owner would have obtained, even though the unjust possessor himself did not obtain it.

c) Generally speaking, he must recompense the owner for all ensuing loss and for the loss of profit which the owner would have obtained if the property had been in his possession and which the present owner foresaw at least vaguely.

d) He is allowed to deduct all necessary and really useful expenses.

3. Possession in Doubtful Faith

308. The possessor in doubtful faith is one who has grave reason for positively doubting whether the thing he possesses belongs to himself or to someone else. The doubt may exist before or after his possession of the thing.

OBLIGATIONS. 1. When the doubt arises *after* taking possession of the thing, the possessor must undertake a careful investigation in order to resolve his doubt; should the doubt persist after investigation he may keep the thing, since possession is nine-tenths of the law. But if he is morally certain that he is in wrongful possession of another's property, he incurs all the rights and obligations of a *possessor in good faith* already indicated.

2. When the doubt exists *prior* to possession, he is bound to restore the thing he has acquired to the original owner since he has no sufficient title to the possession of the thing. Unless he acquired the property from a possessor in doubtful faith by a *legitimate* title (by purchase, by inheritance, and so on), then he is under an obligation to try to find the rightful owner and restore the article once he is found. But if the doubt persists, he must make restitution *in proportion to his doubts* or else give to the poor or to pious causes the article in doubt.

§ 2. Unjust Damage

309. **INTRODUCTORY.** Since we have already discussed sufficiently[206] the circumstances in which the obligation of restitution arises from unjust damage, it only remains to say a few words about the restitution which must be made by those who co-operate unjustly in such damage. For the difficulty may be raised, to what extent and in what order must these unjust cooperators make restitution? The extent of their obligation may take one of three forms: 1) an *absolute obligation of complete restitution*—that is to say, an obligation binding each cooperator to repair the entire damage without having recourse to other cooperators; 2) a *conditional obligation of complete restitution*—that is to say, an obligation affecting each cooperator to repair the entire damage in default of his fellow cooperators meeting their share of the restitution. Once he has repaired the damage he may demand suitable compensation from the defaulters; 3) an *obligation of restitution pro rata*, that is, an obligation to repair his share of the damage.

310. **FIRST PRINCIPLE.** *a) In cases of cooperation, the principal cause has an absolute obligation to make complete restitution; b) in the case of several co-equal causes, each has a conditional obligation of complete restitution; c) partial causes of unjust damage are bound to make restitution in proportion to their individual share of the harm caused.*

The reason for the first part of the principle is that the principal cause of unjust damage uses the other cooperators as mere instruments, and it is only just that the principal cause (and not the instruments) should meet the entire restitution.

Concerning the second part, it must be noticed that the action of each cooperator exercises an influence on the *entire* damage, and therefore each of them is bound to repair the entire damage if the others cannot repair their part of the damage or refuse to do so.

The reason for the third part is that the cooperator in this instance is responsible for only *part* of the damage, and it is this part for which he must make restitution.

SECOND PRINCIPLE. *If several cooperators inflicted the same degree of damage in exactly the same way, all are equally bound to make restitution; otherwise, the order in making restitution is this: 1) the person who is now in possession; 2) the one who commanded the injustice; 3) he who executed the command; 4) all other positive cooperators; 5) all negative cooperators.*

This principle requires no further explanation or proof.

Art. 3. The Manner and Circumstances of Restitution

Here we consider: 1) to whom, 2) at what time, 3) in what place, 4) in what way is restitution to be made.

---

[206] See no. 271–272.

311. 1. To whom must restitution be made? The question is answered in the following distinction:

a) If the victim of the injustice is *known for certain*, then in ordinary circumstances restitution must be made to him or to his heir.

Notice: in ordinary circumstances, because in certain circumstances one is permitted to give the amount to be restored to the poor or to some pious purpose, e.g., when restitution has to be made to some society which is thoroughly immoral, or to the State, or to certain insurance companies.[207]

b) If the victim of the injustice is *not known* even after careful inquiry, the possessor in good faith may retain the property in his possession, but the possessor in bad faith and anyone who has inflicted unjust damage must make restitution to the poor or to some pious purpose.

c) If after careful inquiry there still remains some *doubt* regarding the legitimate owner of lost property, the chattel must be divided as well as possible amongst the few probable owners; if there are many probable owners, making a reasonable division of the property impossible, it should be given to the poor or to some charitable cause.

Thus, a shop-keeper who has harmed several of his customers who cannot now be traced, e.g., by adulterating the goods sold or by selling under weight or measure, may make restitution by increasing the weight or measure of the goods he sells or by lowering his prices if he knows that *practically the same customers* still patronize his business; otherwise, he must make restitution to the poor or to pious purposes.

312. 2. When is restitution to be made?

As soon as possible, morally speaking. Thus, a person commits grave sin if without sufficient reason he postpones for an appreciable length of time the reparation of grave injury; moreover, he will be obliged to make good the damage caused to the lawful owner by his culpable postponement of restitution.

3. Where is restitution to be made?

a) The possessor in good faith fulfills his obligation of making restitution for the thing that has come into his possession by error if he leaves it *in the place where it is* and allows the lawful owner to dispose of it at will.

b) The possessor in bad faith and the author of unjust damage must at their own expense restore the article to the place where the owner would have kept it if it had not been unjustly removed. Should this prove morally impossible, the property may be given to the poor or to pious purposes.

Should the article to be restored be destroyed by chance or through the fault of a third party while in transit, the possessor in good faith is quit of all obligation since the owner must bear the loss when the article perishes (*res perit domino*). The possessor in bad faith and the author of unjust damage must again do all in

---

[207] These exceptions are more fully considered in MTM, vol. 2, no. 229ff.

their power to repair all harm incurred by the owner, and this seems to remain true even if restitution had been attempted through the agency of a confessor.

4. How is restitution to be made?

Only one thing is necessary—that restitution be made in such a way that the equality of justice which had been disturbed should be fully restored. Therefore, restitution may be made secretly, or in the form of a gift, or through some other person, and so on.

Art. 4. Causes Excusing from Restitution

Causes which absolve completely from restitution must be distinguished from those which merely postpone the obligation.

§ 1. Causes which Absolve from Restitution

313. There are five causes which completely absolve from restitution: condonation, compensation, prescription, composition, extreme need.

1. CONDONATION or the remission of debt excuses from restitution, whether it is expressed, tacit, or reasonably presumed, provided that *a)* condonation is completely *voluntary*, that is, free from error, deceit, force, fear; and *b)* is made by someone who has the power to condone the debt in accord with natural and positive law.

2. COMPENSATION is the mutual destruction of two equal and certain debts; for example, A owes B £100; B owes A an article valued at £100; in such circumstances the debts could be remitted by compensation.

3. PRESCRIPTION after the specified period of time destroys only those debts incurred by a possessor in *good faith*; see no. 259 regarding the requisites for lawful prescription.

4. COMPOSITION, which is the remission of debt by the Holy See, applies only to ecclesiastical property and goods due to unknown creditors. In Spain and Portugal, special faculties exist for granting this form of remission in virtue of the Bull *Cruzada*.

5. EXTREME NEED (OR ITS EQUIVALENT) does not make a person quit of all obligation of restitution unless there is no reasonable hope of terminating this need. Otherwise, it merely postpones the obligation.

§ 2. Causes which Postpone Restitution

314. The two chief causes of postponement are: temporary incapacity and surrender of property to creditors.

1. TEMPORARY IMPOSSIBILITY of making restitution may be either physical or moral: it is *physical* when the debtor possesses nothing wherewith to make restitution; it is *moral* when restitution would cause grave harm to the debtor or to some other

person. While physical or moral impossibility endures, the obligation of restitution is postponed since no one is obliged to the impossible.

315. 2. When a debtor is no longer able to discharge his debts, he then SURRENDERS HIS PROPERTY so that his creditors may receive at least a proportionate amount of the money due to them. This surrender of property does not of itself free the debtor in conscience from restitution; it merely postpones the obligation until such time as he is able to meet his previous debts. However, in some countries the civil law seems to grant a complete discharge from all obligation of making restitution, when the surrender of effects is transacted in court. The just statutes of civil law can and in certain cases must be observed in the internal forum, when they determine the rights and duties of a debtor who surrenders his effects.

QUESTION IV
CONTRACTS

This question is discussed in two chapters: 1) Contracts in General; 2) Particular Contracts.

CONTRACTS IN GENERAL

In this chapter are considered: 1) The Definition and Kinds of Contract; 2) The Requisites for Contract; 3) The Obligation of Contract.

Art. 1. Definition and Kinds of Contract

316. DEFINITION. *A contract is the consent of two or more persons to the same resolution.*

This is the definition taken from Roman law. Thus, two things are required for a contract: an act of the intellect, that is, the practical proposition to which the parties agree, and an act of the will, namely, the consent, which is the proper efficient and formal cause of the contract.

KINDS. Among the many divisions given, the following seem the more necessary for use in the confessional.

1. A *formal* (or *explicit*) contract is one made in words or writing which formally manifests the consent of the contracting parties; a *virtual* (or *implicit*) contract is one contained implicitly in the acceptance of some office, such as that of doctor. This latter is sometimes referred to as a *quasi-contract*.

2. A contract is *unilateral* when it creates an obligation in only one of the parties, as in a gratuitous contract; it is *bilateral* when it imposes an obligation on both parties, as in the contract of buying and selling.

3. Contracts may concern things which are quite *definite*, such as buying an article at this or that price, or they may concern *fortuitous* and future events (*aleatory* contracts) such as assurance and betting.

4. A *gratuitous* contract confers a benefit on one of the parties only, as in a gift; an *onerous* contract imposes a burden on both parties, as in the contract of lease.—Every bilateral contract is to some extent an onerous contract.

317. SCHOLIUM. THE POWER OF THE CIVIL LAW OVER CONTRACTS. Civil laws can render certain contracts void both in the external forum and in the internal forum. Such power is required for the effective control of society. Whether invalidating civil laws do in fact destroy a contract in its entirety, or whether it declares that it can be rescinded, is a question of fact which must be determined in the various cases which arise.

Generally speaking, unless the contrary is obvious, contracts which are rendered null and void by civil law can also be considered void in conscience.[208]

Canon law recognizes the prescriptions of civil law in each country relating to contracts, unless there is anything contrary to natural or ecclesiastical law in those prescriptions.

Art. 2. Requisites for Contract

318. Four essential elements are required for a contract: 1) a suitable object; 2) a competent person; 3) legitimate consent; 4) a suitable form.

1. AN OBJECT SUITABLE for a contract must possess several qualities:

a) it must be *possible*, both physically and morally;

b) it must *exist*, actually or potentially;

c) it must *belong to the contracting party*;

d) it must be *capable of being valued* at a price;

e) it must be *morally good and lawful*.

Spiritual objects cannot be valued at a price and therefore, if sold, the contract is simoniacal and completely void.[209]

If the object of a contract is morally evil the *base contract* can and in fact must be rescinded *before* the evil is committed. But if the immoral act has already been performed it is not wrong to pay the agreed price. Accordingly, it is probable that an evil contract is valid *post factum*. However, since there are many theologians who hold that an evil contract is completely null and void, in practice it is better to act on the principle: "The person in possession has the better title"—that is to say, the price received for an immoral deed may be retained, but it is also permissible to refuse to pay the agreed sum in such circumstances.

2. A COMPETENT PERSON for making contracts is anyone who has the use of reason and is not specifically forbidden by positive law. Because they lack the use of reason, imbeciles, children, and the perfectly intoxicated are debarred from

---

[208] See no. 320.
[209] See CCL, Can. 729.

making contracts. Through the intervention of positive law, the following are usually forbidden (at least partially) from entering into contracts: minors, married women, solemnly professed religious, and so on.

319. 3. THE CONSENT required for contract must possess certain characteristics and may be vitiated in different ways.

The consent must be:

a) genuine or internal,

b) free and deliberate,

c) manifested externally,

d) mutual.

The consent may be vitiated by:

a) error and fraud which deceive the intellect,

b) duress and fear whereby the freedom of the will is impaired.

A *substantial error* relating to the subject-matter of the contract or to a condition without which the contract would not have been made renders the contract void. The requisite consent is then lacking. An *accidental* error which concerns incidentals does not of itself void the contract, but it often leaves the contract open to rescission. Accidental error does not destroy but only diminishes the consent and therefore positive law is justified in stating that certain of these contracts may be rescinded, especially if the error was the result of fraud.

What has been said about error applies equally well to fraud, which is present when one person uses deceits and lies to persuade another to enter into contract.

Violence renders a contract invalid since it destroys freedom.

Fear does not invalidate a contract unless it disturbs the use of reason. This follows from natural law, and the reason is that the freedom required for making contracts still remains. By positive law certain contracts, such as those of marriage and religious profession, are declared invalid if made under the influence of grave fear. Nearly all contracts are *capable of being rescinded* if fear played a part in their making—see the previous discussion of fear in no. 32.

320. 4. A DEFINITE EXTERNAL FORM is not prescribed for making contracts. It is sufficient that the consent of the parties be clearly manifested. This is all that natural law requires, but sometimes positive law demands some definite formula under pain of invalidating the contract, as in the sale of immovable goods.

Are contracts valid in conscience when made without the legal form?

a) If the legal form was demanded *by ecclesiastical law* as an essential part of the contract, then the contract is invalid both in conscience and in the external forum. Thus, the contract of betrothal made without the form prescribed by law[210] is absolutely invalid in either forum.

[210] See CCL, Can. 1017.

b) If the form required *by civil law* is not observed, then theologians are not unanimous; some maintain that the contract is binding in conscience, while others hold that it is invalid, and yet a third school affirm that preference should be shown to the possessor until he is obliged to make restitution by judicial sentence. This final opinion seems the one to be followed in practice.

Art. 3. The Effect or Obligation of Contract

321. The obligation attached to contract is threefold: a *natural* obligation, binding in conscience only in consequence of the nature of a contract; a *civil* obligation, arising from civil law and binding in the civil forum only; a *mixed* obligation, binding in conscience and in the civil forum.

The gravity of the obligation is normally determined by the gravity of the subject-matter of the contract, but special consideration must be reserved for clauses attached to the contract and which *qualify the contract*.

The chief forms of such qualified contracts are:

a) *Conditional contracts.* Leaving on one side those conditions which refer to something past or present and which render the contract valid or invalid according as the conditions are verified or not, a *condition referring to the future* either suspends a future obligation or relaxes an existent one. An *immoral condition* attached to a contract normally renders it void since it has an immoral object and thus is morally impossible. But in certain circumstances, such a condition is considered not to be part of the contract, as in the contract of marriage.

b) *Modal contracts* (sub modo) are those which stipulate the use or purpose of the object of the contract; e.g., I give you this sum of money for the purchase of books. Such a contract is not rendered void if the object is not used in the way prescribed. In practice, it is sometimes difficult to distinguish a modal contract from a conditional one.

c) *Delayed contracts* are those which postpone the fulfillment of the agreement until a determined date. Such a contract is binding immediately although it is not intended for immediate execution.

322. d) *Contracts made under oath.* General rule: a contract made under oath is not thereby changed in its character as a contract, and thus if it is invalid in itself, it is not validated by the oath. A twofold obligation ensues from a valid contract made under oath: an obligation of justice and an obligation of religion. — A promissory oath obtained under duress or grave fear is valid but may be relaxed by an ecclesiastical superior.[211]

PARTICULAR CONTRACTS

This chapter is divided into three articles: 1) Gratuitous Contracts; 2) Onerous Contracts Relating to Certain Events; 3) Aleatory Contracts.

[211] See CCL, Can. 1317, § 2.

Art. 1. Gratuitous Contracts

INTRODUCTORY. Gratuitous contracts are either unilateral—such as promises or gifts—or bilateral—such as loans for use, deposit of chattels, stake, agency, loans for consumption, usury.

§ 1. Promise

323. DEFINITION. *A gratuitous promise is a contract whereby a person freely and spontaneously obliges himself to give something to another or to omit something.* Therefore, three things are required for a gratuitous promise:

1) the intention to bind oneself; 2) a spontaneous desire free from all duress, fear, and error; 3) the manifestation and acceptance of the promise.

Since the promise is binding by reason of the virtues of truthfulness and fidelity, the *obligation* would seem to be *in itself light.* This is an opinion which is certainly probable, although contradicted by some who regard the violation of a promise that has been accepted as grievously sinful, provided that it relates to grave matter which is *four times* the amount required for a grave sin of theft.

Accidentally the obligation involved in promises may be grave if, for instance, grave damage results for the promise by the violation of the promise, or if the promisor intends to put himself under a grave obligation. Such an intention would seem to be present, *a)* if the person making the promise confirms it by oath, *b)* if his promise concerns grave matter, *c)* if he makes his promise in the presence of a notary, *d)* if he says: I intend to bind myself as far as I possibly can.

THE OBLIGATION OF A PROMISE CEASES, according to St. Thomas,[212] 1) when the matter promised is unlawful, 2) when the object promised or the circumstances of either the object or the person undergo a notable change. Modern theologians add two further reasons: if the promisee voluntarily condones the promise; if one of the parties does not stand by his promise after a mutual promise had been made.

§ 2. Gift

324. DEFINITION AND KINDS. *A gift is the generous offer of part of one's possessions to another who accepts it.*

1. *Liberal* gifts—gifts in the strict sense of the word—presuppose the existence of no obligation in the donor to make the gift; *remunerative* gifts are those which suppose an obligation of gratitude in the donor.

2. Gifts *inter vivos* are delivered with the intention of transferring ownership of at least the substance of the gift *actually and irrevocably* to the recipient. Gifts *mortis causa* transfer ownership, but the gifts themselves are *revocable* until the death of the donor; thus, I give you this sum of £1,000 to be delivered to you after my death, unless in the meantime I have need of it for other reasons. *Gifts made in the*

---

[212] See ST, II-II, q. 110, a. 3, rep. 5.

form of a will do not transfer ownership immediately but only *at some future date,* such as the death of the donor.

1. Gifts in General

325. CERTAIN CONDITIONS ARE REQUIRED to be fulfilled in order that a gift be lawful: *a)* the donor must be competent to make the gift; *b)* the donee must be competent to receive it; *c)* the thing given must be suitable; *d)* the prescribed form must be observed; *e)* the donee must accept the gift.

a) A person is competent to make a gift if he has the ownership and free disposal of the thing which he gives. Ecclesiastical and civil positive laws determine in detail those who are not competent to make gifts. Generally speaking, the following are more or less incapable of making gifts: minors, imbeciles, prodigals, wives, religious, and so on.

b) A person is competent to receive gifts if he is capable of ownership. Therefore, a child who has been conceived (but not yet born) is capable of receiving gifts. In certain circumstances, civil law excludes some people from receiving gifts: e.g., according to Gallic law, doctors are debarred from receiving gifts in the strict sense of the word from their patients.[213]

c) A thing is judged suitable for forming the object of a gift if it is at the free disposal of the donor.

d) Frequently positive law requires the observance of certain *formalities* in handing over gifts (e.g., the presence of a notary). Normally, illegal gifts—i.e., those made without observing the legal form—may be considered as binding in conscience until a legitimate judge rescinds the contract made.

e) The acceptance of the gift (at least presumed acceptance) is required for all forms of gifts.

Revocation of the contract of gift is sometimes permitted by positive law as, for example, when the gift injures the obligations of piety by depriving the donor's children of their lawful share of his goods, when another child is born unexpectedly, when the beneficiary is grossly ungrateful to the donor.

2. Gifts *inter vivos* and Gifts *mortis causa*

326. 1. All the previous principles regarding gifts in general apply also to gifts *inter vivos.*

2. Gifts *mortis causa* confer a conditional right to the property given; they differ little from legacies bequeathed in wills. In many countries, gifts *mortis causa* as distinct from legacies have been suppressed by civil law.

3. Last Will and Testament

327. INTRODUCTORY NOTIONS. Although hereditary succession is not a contract in the strict sense of the word since the consent of the person conferring the inheritance

[213] See art. 909.

and the consent of the inheritor do not exist at the same time, nevertheless one is justified in regarding it as a type of contract of gift, because by it—and especially by a will—ownership is transferred to others gratuitously.

Hereditary succession is either *legal* (or *intestate*) when the right of succession arises from the prescription of law without the expressed will of the dead person; it is *testamentary* when the right of succession derives from the last will of the testator.

The *estate* of a dead person comprises the sum total of the dead person's possessions. The *heir* or he who receives the property of the dead person is either the *sole* heir if he receives all the property, or a *joint* heir if he receives a part of the estate. An *essential* heir is one who in virtue of positive law cannot be excluded from the inheritance, except in specified cases; an *arbitrary* heir is one who shares in the inheritance through the free choice of the testator.

The *legitimate part* of an inheritance is that portion of the estate which must be left to the essential heirs in virtue of positive law to that effect. A *will* is the final and complete disposal of goods made by the dead person.

A *codicil* is an addition made to a completed will which either explains or changes something in the will.

A *legacy* is that specific part of the total inheritance which the testator decides must be given to a particular person.

328. THE FORM OF A WILL is usually determined by positive law and must be observed under penalty of invalidity. The chief forms are these:

a) an *ordinary* will, which is completed in normal circumstances according to the legal form; an *extraordinary* will, which is recognized in *extraordinary* circumstances as legal by reason of a privilege (and consequently is sometimes referred to as a privileged will), such as the will made by soldiers on active service;

b) a will *in writing* which is drawn up by a notary in strict legal form, and a *nuncupative* will (verbally declared) which is made by the testator in his own words in the presence of witnesses, and a *holograph* will which is made in the handwriting of the testator and signed by himself.

329. THE VALIDITY OF AN IRREGULAR WILL, namely, a will made without observing the legal form, cannot be denied if the intention of the testator is known. This is so by reason of natural law and before any judicial sentence declaring such a will to be void. *After legal judgment* the will ceases to be binding even in conscience, if it concerns legacies for *secular purposes*. Such a sentence is just and must be observed in conscience. If the will relates to legacies in favor of pious purposes, it remains good and valid notwithstanding the judgment of the civil court to the contrary, because such pious purposes should not be made to suffer loss through the dispositions of State law. Can. 1513, § 2 states the following rule: "In last wills made in favor of the Church all the formalities of the civil law should be complied with, if possible; if they were omitted, the heirs should be admonished to fulfill the will of the testator."

The words *should be admonished* are a command and not a mere exhortation: this was made clear by the Pontifical Commission, February 17, 1930.[214]

ACCEPTANCE OF WILLS. No one can be forced to accept a will from which he himself benefits, since a will is in the form of a gift which may always be refused. The heir may accept the inheritance "under benefit of inventory," so that he is not obliged to pay the debts of the testator beyond the amount of the inheritance.

330. REVOCATION OF WILLS. The testator is always at liberty to revoke or change his will, except in case of joint wills. After the death of the testator the State has the power to commute the will, since it possesses the right of eminent domain over all the property of its subjects. Wills made in favor of pious purposes are equivalent to vows and oaths and therefore may be commuted by the Holy See. But the interpretation of such wills falls within the province of the ordinary also, who is their executor in accordance with the statutes of canon law.[215]

4. Intestate Succession

331. DUTIES OF THE TESTATOR. *a)* In accordance with natural law, the testator is bound to leave a reasonable part of his property to his children, his wife, and to other relatives who are *in need.* This is demanded both by the virtue of piety and by the virtue of charity.

b) Any just cause—such as the immoral life led by the heir—and not merely the reasons set forth in the various codes of State law is sufficient for withholding from essential heirs their legitimate share in the estate.

c) It is probable that the testator is not bound to make restitution for depriving the essential heirs of their legitimate share and using the latter for gifts or even squandering it. This opinion is based on the fact that no harm is done to commutative justice since the heirs have no strict right to the inheritance.

332. DUTIES OF THE HEIRS. *a)* The essential heirs of an estate cannot resort to occult compensation in order to remedy any diminution in their legitimate share of the estate, but they are at liberty to go to court to obtain their due portion.

b) Essential heirs must include in the dead person's estate all the goods (which were not entirely gratuitous) which they have already received during the lifetime of the testator.

§ 3. Loans for Use, Deposit of Chattels, Stakes, Agency

333. 1. THE LOAN FOR USE is a gratuitous loan of a non-fungible thing to be used for a definite purpose and for a specified time. If money is demanded in return for the loan, the contract becomes an onerous one, namely, a contract of lease.

[214] See *Acta Apostolicæ Sedis* [hereafter AAS] 20, 196; see also CCL, Can. 2348.
[215] See Can. 1515 and 1517.

334. 2. Such loans are sometimes made on the understanding that the lender may demand the return of the object loaned at any time (*precarium*).[216]

335. 3. A CONTRACT OF DEPOSIT is one in which some movable good is placed in the custody of a person on condition that it is returned when the depositor demands it.

336. 4. STAKES are a form of deposit; the object *to be contested for* is deposited with a third party (the stakeholder) on the understanding that once the matter is settled the object will be handed to the winner. The Code of Canon Law states: "The stakeholder should be as diligent in guarding, preserving, and caring for the deposit as he is over his own possessions, and afterward he is bound with good reason to return it to whomsoever the judge decides it should be restored. — The judge should determine a suitable reward if the stakeholder asks for one."[217]

337. 5. AGENCY is a contract whereby one party undertakes to conduct some action or business on behalf of another.

338. 6. AGENCY PRESUMED. Sometimes a contract of agency is presumed (*negotiorum gestio*), and is then a tacit contract (quasi-contract) whereby one person manages the affairs of another not by express command but from his presumed desire; thus, for instance, a man who takes into his possession an article which he has found is bound in the meantime to take the place of the proprietor and act in his name. NOTE. In all the above-mentioned contracts it is essential to attend to positive law which frequently regards them not as gratuitous but as onerous contracts.

§ 4. Loans for Consumption and Usury

339. DEFINITIONS. A LOAN FOR CONSUMPTION is a contract whereby the ownership of a fungible good which is also consumed in its first use is given to another who incurs the obligation of restoring its equivalent in kind at some future date. The object of such a loan is something fungible which is consumed in its first use; nowadays it is usually *money*. Usury is "the acceptance of money for something that has been loaned for consumption."[218] *Interest*, although the word itself does not differ in meaning from usury, is usually understood to refer to profit lawfully acquired for legitimate reasons from a loan for consumption.

PRINCIPLE. *Usury in its strict sense is contrary to divine positive law, to ecclesiastical law, and to natural law.*

a) Divine law commands: "Lend to them [your enemies] without any hope of return" (Lk 6:35; see Ex 22:25; Lv 25:35–37; and Ez 18:8, 13).

b) Ecclesiastical law has severely forbidden usury in five ecumenical councils[219] and in several condemned propositions.[220]

---

[216] See L. I Dig. 43, 26.
[217] CCL, Can. 1675, § 2 and 3.
[218] ST, II-II, q. 78.
[219] Lateran III, IV, V; Lyons II; Vienna.
[220] See CCL, Can. 1543.

c) *Natural law* forbids selling the same thing twice. But in fungible goods which are also consumed at their first use, the goods themselves and their use are morally the same—that is to say, they do not possess separate prices. Therefore, a person who demands a price both for the thing he loans and for its use is selling the same thing twice and thus offends against natural law. Accordingly, St. Leo the Great well says: "Foenus pecuniae funus est animae."[221]

340. EXTRINSIC REASONS WHICH MAKE INTEREST LAWFUL.

1. *The risk involved* when the lender is reasonably afraid that he will never recover his loan;

2. *the statutory penalty*, which takes the form of money to be paid to the lender when the borrower through culpable delay postpones the return of the loan beyond the specified time;

3. *loss of profitable investment*, when the lender forgoes the *immediate* hope of gain which he would certainly have obtained if he had put the money lent to some other use;

4. *resultant loss*, which the lender suffers because of the contract of loan;

5. *legal reward*, which is a title for taking interest instituted by State law in order to encourage trade. This title is recognized by ecclesiastical law also, provided that the legal reward or profit is not excessive. In fact, it is permissible to stipulate for more than the legal rate of interest if there is a just and proportionate title to justify this.[222] Under modern conditions there are nearly always some extrinsic titles (especially, loss of profitable investment and resultant losses) to justify the taking of reasonable interest for money lent. What amount of interest is reasonable cannot be determined with mathematical precision but must be decided from considering the risk involved, the loss of profit, and so on.

341. SCHOLIUM. Nothing further need be said regarding *pawnshops*, *savings-banks*, and *banks*, which have been established for receiving a moderate rate of interest; one must apply to them the general principles of justice and contracts.[223]

Art. 2. Onerous Contracts

§ 1. Buying and Selling in General

342. DEFINITION. Buying and selling are two correlative contracts which are parts of the single contract of buying and selling, which may be defined as *an onerous contract whereby some commodity is given for a price and a price for a commodity.*

---

[221] *Sermon 17.*
[222] See CCL, Can. 1543.
[223] See MTM, vol. 2, no. 289.

1. The Commodity and the Obligations of the Seller

343. THE COMMODITY or object of a sale may be anything which can be valued at a price and which belongs to the seller, unless specifically forbidden by positive law. If the commodity is not valued at a price, then there is no sale in the strict sense of the word, but *barter*, such as purchasing ten sheep for a cow, or *exchange*, such as Swiss money for German money. Positive law forbids the sale of certain goods except under special precautions, e.g., poison, weapons.

THE OBLIGATIONS OF THE SELLER.

a) He must demand a just price. What this just price is will be discussed in a moment.

b) He is bound to reveal to the buyer any *substantial* defects in the commodity sold, for if the buyer is unaware of such defects the contract of buying is non-existent owing to the presence of substantial error. Defects in the article sold are regarded as substantial if they render it notably useless for the primary and known purpose which the buyer has in mind. If the buyer asks, he must also be informed of any accidental defects. However, the seller may refuse to answer this question and say simply: I am selling the thing as it is.

c) He is bound to hand over a commodity which is physically or at least morally the same as the buyer intends to purchase. Thus, for instance, anyone who sells artificial wine in the place of natural wine which the buyer intended to purchase is guilty of injustice.

d) He is bound to deliver to the buyer the commodity in the same condition as it was at the time of the sale. One must attend to State law regarding this matter.

2. The Price and the Obligations of the Buyer

344. THE BUYER MUST OBSERVE all the just conditions agreed upon in the contract, such as the time and manner of receiving the commodity, of paying the price, and so on. The buyer has a special obligation to pay a *just* price.

DEFINITION AND QUALITY OF THE JUST PRICE. *The price of an article is its value expressed in terms of money.* But it is far from easy to decide how this value is to be measured, whether by social valuation or by its utility to the buyer or seller. St. Thomas and St. Alphonsus were of the opinion that the value and therefore the just price of a thing must be based on:

1. the intrinsic value of the thing;

2. the resultant loss and loss of profitable investment which the seller suffers by reason of his sale.

345. KINDS OF PRICE. There are three kinds of price: the legal price, the market (or common) price, and the price agreed upon by the contracting parties themselves.

1. *The legal price* is fixed by public authority or by law, such as the price of railway tickets and of chemist's drugs, and so on.

Commutative justice requires the observance of this price unless it is manifestly unjust, since this price has been lawfully determined for the common good by public authority which has supreme ownership over the goods of its subjects. Therefore, this price is perfectly just and departure from it is unjust. Therefore, any notable departure from the legal price normally obliges a person to restitution—with a few exceptions.

2. *The market price* is that which is fixed by *common* estimation based on the varying circumstances of time and place. There is no single market price, and therefore there are the highest, lowest, and mean market prices. If no legal price has been determined one is obliged to observe the market price, so that selling above the highest price and buying below the lowest price are violations of commutative justice, since the market price is fixed by social valuation which is presumed to be just.

There are many extrinsic titles which permit one to exceed the limits of the market price. Thus, for instance, it is permissible *to sell* at a higher price: *a)* because of the loss of investment-opportunity or extrinsic losses which the seller incurs by the sale; *b)* because the seller has a special attachment to the thing he sells, although it is probably unlawful to charge more simply because the buyer has a special attachment to the thing, since this does not belong to the seller; *c)* because of the character of the sale, e.g., when a commodity in short supply must be sold in small quantities.—Likewise it is permissible *to buy* an article at less than the market price for many external reasons: *a)* because the buyer loses an opportunity of profitable investment or suffers loss as the result of his buying the article; *b)* because the article for sale is being offered free of charge; *c)* because of the character of the sale, e.g., when a commodity is being bought in large quantity.

3. *The price agreed upon* by the parties themselves is that which is freely decided between the buyer and the seller. Such a price is just, provided *a)* the article has no legal or market price attached to it, and *b)* no deceit or fear is used in the sale.

346. SCHOLIUM. COUNTERFEIT MONEY. Not only the forger himself—together with his confederates—of coins and paper money but also all who knowingly use such money in payment for goods bought are bound to restitution, since counterfeit money is not *a just price* for the article purchased. Neither is a man who spends such money excused from restitution on the grounds that he received it in good faith. The fact that he has been deceived with consequent loss to himself does not give him any right to deceive an innocent third party.—Restitution must be made to whomsoever the counterfeit money was given. If the latter suffered no loss since he in his turn succeeded in disposing of the money, restitution must be made to the person who actually suffers damage. If this person cannot be traced, then the value of the money must be given to the poor or to pious purposes.

§ 2. Particular Forms of Buying and Selling

347. 1. AUCTION SALES. These are held either voluntarily *at the owner's request* or *by direction of a judge*. In such sales a just price is that which is offered by the final bidder without recourse to unfair means and accepted by the seller. This is the practice commonly in use among the people to which the legislator consents.

348. 2. MONOPOLY is an exclusive right granted to one or a few persons of selling certain commodities. Such monopolies are usually controlled by State law (State monopolies). Where such laws are insufficient private monopolies are frequently instituted to demand excessive and unjust prices. But in general, a monopoly in itself is not unjust.

349. 3. FOR SELLING THROUGH MIDDLEMEN (agents) one must use the general principles regarding contracts and cooperation in unjust damage.

§ 3. Lease and Labor Contract

DEFINITIONS AND KINDS. Lease is an onerous contract whereby one person (the lessor) allows another (the lessee) the use or usufruct of real property or promises him certain services or work in return for a specified price. There are three types of lease:

350. 1. A LEASE OF REAL PROPERTY is one whereby the lessee is granted the use or usufruct of some thing—such as a house or a room—and is similar to the contract of buying and selling, and thus the same principles apply.

2. A LEASE OF UNDERTAKING SOME WORK—understood in its strict meaning—differs in no way from a contract of buying and selling. An agreed price is paid in return for some work which is undertaken, such as building a house, making a dress (contract work). Since this contract is to a certain extent an aleatory contract, the contractor is bound to fulfill all the conditions agreed upon, even in a case where he may suffer loss as a result. However, if unforeseen incidents occur unexpectedly, e.g., an epidemic or a thunder-bolt, then the original agreement should be modified in accordance with the statutes of civil law.

351. 3. LEASE OF SERVICE is more usually known as A LABOR CONTRACT. The object of this form of contract is the work of the individual—or rather the ability to work—which one person hires out to another for a definite period of time. This contract exists primarily between an employer and his employees.

352. THE DUTIES OF AN EMPLOYER are founded partly on justice, partly on charity.

By justice he is obliged:

a) to pay a just salary at the stated time; *b)* to grant sufficient time to his employees in order that they may fulfill their religious and domestic duties; *c)* not to impose work beyond the strength of his employees.

By charity he is obliged:

a) to show kindness to his workers and to help them in their needs; *b)* to support any laws or decrees which justly improve the conditions of the workers.

353. THE DUTIES OF EMPLOYEES are well set forth in Leo XIII's Encyclical *Rerum Novarum*, May 15, 1891:

a) "to fulfill honestly and fairly all equitable agreements freely entered into";

b) "never to injure the property of their employer";

c) "never to violate the person of their employer," e.g., by insults, or calumny, and so on;

d) "never to resort to violence in defending their own cause, nor to engage in riot, and to have nothing to do with men of evil principles." These words forbid *unjust* strikes, such as ceasing from work when a just labor contract has not yet been completed, or by demanding an excessive salary or other unreasonable conditions. But one must not conclude from this that all strikes are intrinsically evil.

354. THE MORAL CHARACTER OF STRIKES. A strike is an organized cessation from work on the part of many men in order to obtain certain benefits from their employers. A strike may be inspired by one of two reasons: either the desire to remove unjust oppression by the employer—*defensive* strikes—or by the desire to receive higher wages or shorter and easier work, even though the salary so far received has not been absolutely insufficient nor has the work been excessive. The defensive strike is lawful provided no other means are to hand for lawful defense against the injustice of the employer. The other form of strike is not intrinsically unlawful, provided 1) it does not take place before the termination of their contract with the employer, 2) that there is a proportionately grave reason, 3) that the means used in the strike are just. Nevertheless, it is most rare that recourse to strike action is expedient since it is frequently the cause of grave harm, both physical and moral, either for the workers themselves or for their employers or for the general public. Therefore, all possible means must be used to effect a peaceful settlement of differences between employers and their operatives.

355. THE JUST WAGE. A *personal* wage is one which is sufficient for the proper maintenance of the worker himself; a *family* wage is one which is sufficient for the support of the worker and his family.

A PERSONAL WAGE IS DUE TO THE WORKER IN COMMUTATIVE JUSTICE. Every worker has a strict right to sufficient maintenance in accordance with the principle: "the laborer is worthy of his hire" (1 Tm 5:18); neither is he obliged to beg for it. There are two exceptions: 1) if the price of food rises sharply and work becomes more scarce; 2) if the worker suffers from illness or old age. In such cases the employer has no strict obligation in justice—although sometimes there is an obligation in charity—to pay a perfect personal wage, since that would be an intolerable burden. It is then that the State must come to the rescue of the workers.

A personal wage is due to the worker in commutative justice.

A *family wage* must also be granted to a healthy worker when industry is normal. It is said—*when industry is normal*, because when industry and trade are in a disturbed state, then even the workers themselves must bear their share of the burden. Also—*to a healthy worker*: for there is no strict obligation to pay a sick worker even a personal wage, as indicated already. The reason why the worker has a right, ordinarily speaking, to a family wage is because he has a right to marry, and once he is married, he has to support the members of his family by his own work.

Art. 3. Aleatory Contracts

356. DEFINITION. Aleatory contracts (so called from the Latin word *alea* meaning hazard or chance) are those in which a sum of money is paid in order to gain an uncertain profit or to avoid an uncertain loss.

GENERAL PRINCIPLE. *Such contracts are lawful, provided that:*

1. *the risk is morally equal for both parties;*

2. *no deceit is practiced;*

3. *there is no scandal and no just prohibition of positive law.*

§ 1. Insurance

357. DEFINITION. *Insurance is a contract by which one person (the insurer) in return for a fixed sum of money undertakes to pay compensation for any damage which another (the insured) may suffer by involuntary chance.* Therefore, the object of such a contract is the danger which may befall in varying circumstances, such as the danger from fire, storm, death. In certain forms of life insurance an annual sum of money is paid not because of any danger which is likely to happen but in order to receive a stated sum of money at a definite time.

REQUISITES FOR JUST INSURANCE. The contract of insurance is just:

1. if the annual premium corresponds to the gravity of the danger to which the thing insured is exposed;

2. if the insured declares truthfully the value of the thing and the dangers to which it is exposed, and does not himself expose it to danger through negligence which is gravely culpable;

3. if everything required by positive law and by particular agreement justly entered upon is faithfully observed.

358. LIFE INSURANCE deserves special mention amongst the various forms of insurance both because of its frequency and because of the difficult cases of conscience which may arise. These difficulties are caused by the fact that the insured may have used deceit in taking out policies or if the doctor has been excessively lenient in describing the health of the insured. In practice, however, when the fraud is not most patent and grave, the confessor must not lightly oblige the insured to make restitution, because *a)* insurance companies exercise the utmost care and are rarely

led into grave error; *b)* civil laws favor the validity of contracts unless the fraud was substantial and manifest; *c)* it is often most difficult to decide what disease was responsible for death. How restitution is to be made to insurance companies which have suffered unjust damage has already been described in no. 311.

§ 2. Betting

359. DEFINITION. *Betting is a contract in which two or more persons disputing the truth of some event lay down a sum of money to be given to the person who was right.* Therefore, in normal circumstances such a contract is both onerous and bilateral, although occasions occur in which only one of the contracting parties puts himself under an obligation—for example: I wager I can finish the course inside an hour, otherwise I will give ten francs to the poor.

LAWFULNESS OF BETTING. Bets are lawful, provided *a)* they are made for a morally good purpose, and *b)* are laid on a suitable object—i.e., something lawful and uncertain for both parties.

Civil laws today, as a result of the many abuses which can easily arise, prohibit betting either completely or partially or declare it void. They therefore state: *a)* that no obligation to payment arises from the original wager; *b)* that anyone who gains by betting is not bound to make restitution. These statutes seem to be legitimate and, ordinarily speaking, may be followed in conscience.

§ 3. Gaming

360. DEFINITION AND KINDS. *Gaming is an aleatory contract whereby a reward is given to the winner of a contest undertaken as a pastime.* Therefore, the purpose of gaming must be lawful recreation. If its primary purpose is other than this, either the game is unlawful or the stakes must be regarded as a salary in return for work done.

a) Games of skill are those in which the result of the game depends largely on the skill of the players themselves, such as football; *b) games of chance* depend on fortune and practically no skill is used, as in dice games; *c) games of a mixed character* depend partly on skill, partly on chance, e.g., many card games.

PRINCIPLE. Games played for stakes are lawful, provided the following conditions are verified:

1. the players must be free to dispose of the stakes for which they gamble;

2. the gamble is undertaken with full knowledge and consent;

3. the players must have a morally equal chance of winning;

4. all fraud must be excluded;

5. gain must not be the chief motive of the game neither must it be sought after too eagerly.

NOTE. Since games played for stakes are most dangerous because of the serious disorders which often ensue, the confessor should prudently censure them.

§ 4. Lottery

361. DEFINITION. *A lottery is an aleatory contract whereby on payment of a certain sum of money the right is acquired of obtaining some prize, if fortune favors that person.* Since a lottery is no different from a game of chance, the same principles apply as for gaming.[224]

SECTION II
POTENTIAL PARTS OF THE VIRTUE OF JUSTICE

362. ORDER OF TREATMENT. Following the order proposed by St. Thomas,[225] after discussing the general virtue of justice we next consider the virtues annexed to the cardinal virtue. Either nine or ten potential parts of justice are proposed: 1) religion; 2) piety; 3) respect; 4) obedience; 5) gratitude; 6) friendship; 7) truthfulness; 8) affability; 9) liberality; 10) epikeia. The treatise on the virtue of religion embraces almost everything contained in the first three commandments of the Decalogue; the treatise on the virtues of piety, respect, and obedience includes what is ordained by the fourth commandment. Therefore, this section may be conveniently divided as follows into three questions:

1. The Virtue of Religion—The First Three Commandments of the Decalogue;

2. The Virtues of Piety, Reverence, and Obedience—The Fourth Commandment;

3. The Remaining Potential Parts of Justice.

QUESTION I
THE VIRTUE OF RELIGION—THE FIRST THREE COMMANDMENTS OF THE DECALOGUE

We shall consider: 1) The Nature of Religion; 2) The Different Acts of Religion; 3) The Vices Contrary to Religion.

THE NATURE OF RELIGION

363. ETYMOLOGY. Four explanations are given of the etymology of this word. It is said to be derived either from *relegere*[226]—to meditate; from *reeligere*[227]—to choose again; from *religare*[228]—to bind oneself again; or from *relinquere*[229]—to leave behind.

REAL DEFINITIONS. Religion is understood in various ways by different people. *Non-Catholics* take religion as signifying either the feeling of subjection to God

---

[224] *Speculations on the exchange*—a frequent form of aleatory contract in these times—cannot be more briefly discussed than in MTM, vol. 2, no. 231, to which the reader is referred.

[225] See ST, II-II, q. 80.

[226] See Cicero, *De Natura Deorum*, bk. 2, chap. 28, no. 72.

[227] See Augustine, *City of God*, bk. 10, chap. 3.

[228] See Lactantius, *Divine Institutes*, bk. 4, chap. 28.

[229] Attributed to Masurius Sabinus, see Aulus Gellius, *Noctes Atticæ*, bk. 4, chap. 9, no. 8.

(the more common view), or for natural morality, or in other senses which space does not permit us to list. *Catholics* understand religion: 1) in its *objective* sense, to signify an established manner of belief in God or worship of Him (the Christian religion, Jewish religion, the Mohammedan religion); 2) to signify the *entire moral life of man* (see Jas 1:27); 3) to signify *a particular state of man* (the religious state, such as the religious order of the Dominicans, of the Franciscans, and so on); 4) to signify *a distinct moral virtue*. This virtue of religion is defined as: THE MORAL VIRTUE WHICH INCLINES MAN TO GIVE DUE WORSHIP TO GOD AS HIS SUPREME CREATOR.

The remote subject of this virtue is those persons or beings in whom the virtue is found; the *proximate* subject is the faculty of the soul in which the virtue resides.

The remote subject embraces: *a)* men on earth (including Christ Himself); *b)* the souls in purgatory; *c)* the angels in Heaven. On the other hand, the virtue of religion is not to be found in: *a)* animals or in any other irrational creatures; *b)* the devils and the damned; *c)* those who commit the formal sin of irreligion.

The only proximate subject of the virtue is the will.

364. THE NECESSITY OF RELIGION is founded on *a) natural law*, which strictly commands the worship of God, *b) divine positive law*, ordaining the worship of God both in the Old and New Testaments, *c) human law*, commanding the worship of God and punishing the absence of religion.

This necessity of the virtue of religion includes the internal, external, and—sometimes—public worship of God.

ACTS OF THE VIRTUE OF RELIGION

365. The chief acts of religion are: devotion, prayer, adoration, sacrifice, the use of the Sacraments, vows, oaths, adjuration, sanctification of certain days. Sacrifice and the Sacraments will be considered in a special treatise devoted to the Sacraments; for the present we are considering the other acts of religion.

Art. 1. Devotion

366. DEFINITION. Three things are usually designated by the word *devotion*:

1. certain pious exercises, such as devotion toward the Blessed Sacrament;

2. *attention and spiritual consolation in prayer.* Thus, we say: I made my meditation with great devotion;

3. *the primary act of the virtue of religion*, in which sense we define devotion as: A PROMPT WILL (i.e., AN ACT OF THE WILL) OF OFFERING ONESELF TO THE SERVICE OF GOD. This is the definition given by St. Thomas.[230] It is almost identically the same act as that whereby a man determines to do everything for the greater glory of God, but only insofar as such an act proceeds immediately from the virtue of religion and not from charity.

[230] See ST, II-II, q. 81, a. 1, c.

The causes of devotion are either *external*—the grace of God, good example, the moral influence of other devout men—or *internal*—the contemplation of God's kindness or majesty, of Christ's humanity, of our dependence on God as our Creator, Providential Ruler, and Prime Mover.

THE EFFECTS OF DEVOTION are numerous:

1. *spiritual joy*;

2. *accidental or affective devotion* (devotion understood in its second meaning as given above);

3. *a facility and readiness in performing other acts of religion*;

4. *the best possible influence on even external behavior and manner of acting.*[231]

Art. 2. Prayer

§ 1. Definition and Kinds of Prayer

367. DEFINITION. Prayer, understood in its theological sense, may signify:

1. *in its widest sense*, an act of religion—in fact, the entire religious life of man, namely, the life of prayer;

2. *in its wide sense*, any pious movement of the soul toward God; in this sense St. John Damascene defined it as "THE RAISING OF THE MIND TO GOD."[232] Thus, to elicit an act of faith, hope, or charity would be prayer within this meaning of the term;

3. *in its strict sense*, the prayer of petition; and in this sense it is defined by St. John Damascene as "THE ASKING OF SEEMLY THINGS FROM GOD."[233]—It is not man's intention by such prayers of petition to make known to God all his needs since in the divine omniscience He is fully aware of them even before prayer; nor does man desire by such prayers to change the decrees of Providence, since this would be impossible because of God's immutability. The prime intention (in addition to the worship of God) of our prayer of petition is to remove from within ourselves all those obstacles which prevent the fulfillment of our desires, for in prayer we exercise almost all the virtues: humility, faith, hope, charity, and so on.

The *remote* SUBJECT of prayer is the same as that of religion.[234] It is beyond question that the souls in purgatory can pray in the wide sense of the word, and it is also probable that they can offer prayer of petition in the strict sense.—The *proximate* subject of prayer is not the will but the *practical reason*, since prayer is nothing more than a means of speaking with God and of revealing to Him our desires, which are acts of the practical reason.

[231] See MTM, vol. 2, no. 330.
[232] *Exposition of the Orthodox Faith*, bk. 3, chap. 24.
[233] Ibid.
[234] See no. 363.

368. Kinds of prayer.

1. *Mental* (internal) prayer and *vocal* (external prayer). Mental prayer is accomplished by internal acts and is either simple meditation (which consists in a loving and *discursive* consideration of religious truths) or contemplative prayer (which consists in a loving and *intuitive* consideration and admiration of religious truths).[235] Vocal prayer is performed by the mind and external signs.

2. *Public* prayer and *private* prayer. Two things are required for prayer to be public: it must be recited by an official minister, and it must be recited in the name of the Church.[236] A priest while reciting his Office in private is offering public prayer; on the other hand, if he recites his Rosary in private his prayer is not public but private, since he is no longer praying in the name of the Church.

Note. All public prayer must be *vocal*.

§ 2. The Object of Prayer

369. 1. What to pray for. *We are permitted to pray for anything which it is lawful to desire.*[237] *Therefore nothing is excluded from prayer except what is morally evil or sinful.*

2. For whom to pray. *Prayer may be offered for every creature capable of sharing in eternal glory.* Therefore, only the damned in hell are excluded from our prayer. But in consequence of positive ecclesiastical law, excommunicated persons are sometimes excluded from *public* prayer, as will be mentioned in the treatise on censures.

3. To whom to pray. *We must pray to God alone as the only Person Who can give by Himself all that we request, but it is permissible and useful to invoke the saints and the angels in order to ask them to intercede on our behalf with God.*

The Council of Trent defined that the invocation of the saints and angels was lawful and useful;[238] a few theologians[239] have maintained that such prayer was absolutely *necessary.*

It is also permissible to offer private, but not public, prayer to the souls in purgatory and to baptized infants.

---

[235] It is right to distinguish further between ordinary contemplation which can be attained by any person in the state of grace, and extraordinary contemplation which requires an altogether special instinct of the Holy Ghost and is sometimes accompanied by ecstasies and other miraculous events.

[236] See CCL, Can. 1256.

[237] See Augustine, *Letter 130*, chap. 12, no. 22.

[238] See Session 25. See also TCCI 7:392–395.

[239] See Sylvius and Boeckhn.

§ 3. Necessity of Prayer

370. PROPOSITION. *Prayer is not only useful for all adults but also a matter of divine precept; generally speaking, it is a necessary means of salvation also.*

1. That prayer is useful for all adults is evident *a)* from its excellence as an act of religion; *b)* from its power in obtaining such great graces for man.

2. That prayer is necessary for all adults by reason of *divine precept* is evident from many texts of Sacred Scripture—e.g.: "Watch and pray" (Mt 26:41); showing them that they "ought to pray continually and never be discouraged" (Lk 18:1); "Never cease praying" (1 Thes 5:17).

3. That prayer is a *necessary means of salvation*—at least generally speaking and according to ordinary law—is the more common and probable opinion. This absolute necessity of prayer is well expressed in the Commentary on the Rule of St. Benedict: "Just as breathing is always necessary for the continuation of life in the body, so is prayer absolutely essential for spiritual health.... I would more easily believe that a man has no soul than that he could become a perfect religious without prayer." The same conclusion is reached by reason: it is absolutely necessary to worship the majesty of God. But this worship is impossible without a loving movement of soul toward God, which is prayer—at least in the wide sense.

371. FULFILLMENT OF THE OBLIGATION.

In itself this precept obliges us to pray frequently during life, but it is impossible to determine accurately how often we are bound to pray in virtue of *divine law*. It is the common teaching of theologians that the precept in itself binds us to pray; 1) *at the outset of man's moral life*, when man who has attained to the use of reason must first turn himself Godward; 2) *in danger of death*; 3) *frequently during life*.

But *for incidental reasons* the precept obliges us to pray: 1) each time that other precepts cannot be fulfilled without prayer, such as the precept of hearing Mass on Sundays; 2) in moments of temptation to grave sin which cannot be resisted without prayer; 3) in serious disasters, especially of a public nature.

372. NOTE. 1. Since the precept of its very nature obliges us to pray frequently during life, the confessor must ask those penitents who have neither received the Sacraments nor heard Mass for several years, whether during that period they have also neglected prayer, since such negligence is a special sin, at least objectively speaking.

2. Nowhere is there to be found a *general* law commanding morning and night prayers, or grace before and after meals; therefore, their omission is not of itself a sin, neither is it sufficient matter for confession. But in practice, the faithful should be earnestly encouraged not to omit these prayers, since by so doing they are liable to be deprived of many graces which they require for their daily life.

§ 4. The Efficacy of Prayer and Its Conditions

373. *Prayer which fulfills the requisite conditions has three primary effects and many secondary effects.*

a) THE PRIMARY EFFECTS of prayer are: 1) merit, 2) satisfaction, 3) impetration.

1. Prayer merits *de condigno* an increase of grace and glory, provided it is made properly by a man in the state of grace. — The reason is that any good work performed by a person in the state of grace and proceeding from charity merits that twofold increase.

The prayer of the sinner fulfilling all the requisite conditions merits *de congruo* three benefits: *a)* it disposes him for the reception of sanctifying grace; *b)* it obtains temporal goods; *c)* it accustoms him to good works.[240]

2. Prayer is a means of satisfaction seeing that it possesses all the qualities required for satisfaction — it is a work that is good, arduous, and inspired by grace. Therefore, confessors usually impose prayers as salutary penance and satisfaction.

3. Prayer has an impetratory value, *a)* inasmuch as it is a good work, and *b)* insofar as it is a request heard by God.

b) THE SECONDARY EFFECTS of prayer are, e.g., the enlightenment of the intellect, increase of faith, hope, charity, humility and other virtues, spiritual consolation.

374. *Prayer which fulfills the requisite conditions is infallibly heard by God in consequence of His promises.*

This is evident from many texts in Sacred Scripture, as: "Ask, and the gift will come; seek, and you shall find; knock, and the door shall be opened to you. Everyone that asks, will receive; that seeks, will find; that knocks, will have the door opened to him" (Mt 7:7–8). "Believe Me, you have only to make any request of the Father in My name, and He will grant it to you" (Jn 16:23).

The conditions required for the efficacy of prayer relate to its object, its subject, and the person prayed for.

On the part of the object, it is required that it benefit and not hinder man's eternal salvation.

On the part of the subject who prays, there are required the state of grace, humility, confidence, perseverance, attention. What form of attention is required will be discussed below.

On the part of the person prayed for, it is necessary that he be disposed to receive the grace requested or at least that he place no obstacle in the way.

375. THE ATTENTION NECESSARY FOR PRAYER.

Attention is either *external* or *internal*.

[240] See ST, III-Sup., q. 14, a. 4, c.

Since attention is opposed to distraction, external attention is that which excludes external distractions, namely, all those external acts which occupy a person to such an extent that he is no longer able to attend to the meaning of his prayer. Thus, for instance, external attention would be lacking if during his prayer a man reads, or paints, or does some other work which requires keen attention; on the other hand, external attention is present if he prays while he walks or performs some light work which does not require much attention. Such external attention well deserves to be called attention since a person is thus applying himself to prevent his prayer being disturbed by external occupations. For just as a man who takes care that no wild animals wander into his flower garden is said to be attending to his garden, so in the same way a man who turns aside from external occupations is attending to his prayer.

Internal attention excludes all interior distractions or wanderings of the mind to things which have no connection with prayer. Interior attention may be concentrated on any of the following three objects: 1) *the words of the prayer*, so that the words are pronounced correctly (material or superficial attention); 2) *the meaning of the words* (literal or intellectual attention); 3) *the purpose of prayer*, i.e., the worship of God (spiritual or mystical attention).

This third form of attention is more perfect than the others, whereas the second is more perfect than the first. Interior attention may be either actual, virtual, or habitual. *Actual* attention is present when a person *here and now* attends to his prayer; *virtual* attention is present when previous actual attention has never been revoked even though here and now there exists voluntary distraction. *Habitual* attention hardly deserves to be called attention, since in effect no attention exists but only a certain inclination toward it. There are two points of agreement between authors, one point of disagreement.

1. All are agreed that at least some attention (either internal or external) is essential for prayer, because that which is done without any attention is not a human act and, a fortiori, not prayer.

2. It is also agreed that for *mental* prayer some *interior* attention is necessary, since mental prayer is of its nature an act of the mind.

But *the form of attention required for vocal prayer* is a matter of dispute, although its outcome has a practical bearing on the recitation of the Divine Office especially.

Many authors incline to the view that mere external attention is sufficient, e.g., Durandus, Lugo, Silvester Prierias, Tamburinus, Elbel, Noldin, and many recent theologians.

The contrary opinion is proposed by Cajetan, Dom. Soto, Reiffenstuel, Suarez, Billuart. St. Alphonsus regards this opinion as the more probable and common.

1. In practice, seeing that the first opinion is at least extrinsically probable, no one can be accused of not fulfilling the ecclesiastical obligation of reciting the Divine Office or of being obliged to make restitution for the revenue received from his benefice provided he observes external attention and intends to satisfy

his obligation. For it is not certain that the Church intends to demand interior attention for the recitation of the Office. Since anyone obliged to recite the Divine Office prays in the name of the Church, any lack of interior attention can be supplied by her.

2. The essence and, a fortiori, the efficacy of *private* prayer would seem to be lacking in the absence of all interior attention. Prayer is an act of the practical reason or the raising of the mind to God. But to say that the practical reason can at the same time elicit an act directed toward God (prayer) and a contrary act (such as a voluntary impure thought) is a contradiction.

§ 5. The Canonical Hours

376. DIFFERENT NAMES. Various words have been used by the Church for the Canonical Hours: *Collecta; Agenda; Divina Psalmodia; Cursus; Officium Divinum; Officium ecclesiasticum; Opus Dei; Missa; Vespertina; Breviarium; κανών; σύναξις.*

THE COMPOSITION OF THE DIVINE OFFICE. The Divine Office comprises:

1. the seven canonical hours, namely Matins and Lauds, Prime, Terce, Sext, None, Vespers, Compline. Predosa is not a distinct hour but it does form part of the Divine Office;

2. the Office of the Dead to be recited on the Commemoration of All Souls;

3. the Litanies recited on the feast of St. Mark and on the Rogation Days.[241]

NOTE. The *Aperi* and the *Sacrosanctae* prayers are not integral parts of the Office, but they are useful acts of devotion.

Nowadays in the Roman rite there is no obligation to recite: *a)* the Office of Our Lady, *b)* the Office of the Dead (except on the day already mentioned), *c)* the Penitential Psalms, *d)* the Gradual Psalms.[242]

377. WHICH PERSONS ARE UNDER A GRAVE OBLIGATION TO RECITE THE DIVINE OFFICE?

1. All clerics in major Orders[243] who have not been lawfully reduced to the lay state.

2. All beneficiaries, even if they are not in major Orders.[244]

3. All religious of either sex who are solemnly professed, provided they are obliged to sing Office in choir.[245]

All theologians teach that the obligation to recite the Divine Office is grave although it permits of venial transgression. Therefore, anyone who omits a notable part of the Office without excuse commits serious sin. One little Hour or its equivalent is considered a notable part.

[241] See Pius X, Constitution *Divino Afflatu* (Nov. 1, 1911), no. 3. (AAS 3, 646).
[242] See Pius X, Constitution *Divino Afflatu* (Nov. 1, 1911).
[243] See CCL, Can. 135.
[244] See CCL, Can. 1475.
[245] See CCL, Can. 610, § 3.

THE OBLIGATION OF BENEFICIARIES. Beneficed clergy, such as parish priests, bishops, canons, and so on, who *deliberately* omit a notable part of the Divine Office commit grave sin and are bound to make restitution by giving a proportionate amount of their income to church funds or to the diocesan seminary or to the poor.[246] They must hand over all the revenue of their benefice if they possessed a *simple* benefice, but only a half or a quarter if the benefice was conjoined with the care of souls.

The obligation of religious. By common law, religious who are not clerics and lay sisters are not obliged under pain of sin to recite the prayers prescribed by their Rule. The same applies to *religious with simple vows* who are obliged to sing Office in choir; they are not bound to recite the Divine Office *privately* under pain of sin. More recent congregations have no obligation binding under pain of sin to recite the Office of Our Lady. On the other hand, religious of either sex who are solemnly professed and obliged to sing Office in choir have a grave obligation to recite the Divine Office not only in choir but also in private.

378. THE FORM OF THE DIVINE OFFICE IS SERIOUSLY VIOLATED (unless there is a legitimate excuse) in the following ways:

1. if the rite is changed by using any other than the prescribed breviary;[247]

2. if the Office is recited otherwise than in Latin—at least, if one belongs to the Latin Rite;

3. if the Office recited is substantially different both in its quantity and quality from that prescribed. The character of the Office for the day is usually given in a *Calendar* or *Directory*.

Beneficiaries and all clerics attached to a Church are bound at all times and in all places to recite the Office of their own Church. Other secular clerics may follow the Calendar of the diocese in which they are; they are obliged to do so if they have a quasi-domicile in that diocese. Regulars and exempt religious must follow their own Calendar.

When the wrong Office is recited *involuntarily*, i.e., through error, the following rules are to be observed:

1. The accidental substitution of one Office for another satisfies the precept, but if the wrong Office is notably shorter than that prescribed some compensation must be made. The substitution of one Hour for another is not valid, so that, for example, Terce recited twice is no substitute for Sext.

2. When the error is discovered it should be corrected at once. This is a probable opinion. Therefore, a cleric who discovers that he is saying the wrong Office should turn to the corresponding place in the correct office.

---

[246] See CCL, Can. 1475, § 2.
[247] See Sacred Congregation of Rites [hereafter S. R. C.], Jan. 27, 1899.

3. One mistake is not corrected by another. This again is a probable opinion. Thus, if the wrong Office has been recited, exactly the same Office should be repeated on the day for which it is prescribed.

379. THE MANNER OF RECITAL. In order to satisfy the ecclesiastical precept perfectly, the Divine Office should be recited (privately),

1. *in its correct order and in a suitable place and position*, but excuses are easily admitted;

2. *at its correct time*. There is a grave obligation to complete the Divine Office before midnight of the current day. All other directions regarding the time of recitation easily admit of excusing causes. The private recitation of Matins and Lauds may be anticipated from *2 p.m. of the previous day*;[248]

3. *in its entirety*—that is to say, omitting no part or word or syllable of the Office. However, it is permissible to recite the psalms alternately with another, even if the latter is a lay-person;

4. *continuously*, namely, without interruption in any Hour of the Office, but excusing causes are easily admitted;

5. *orally*, and not merely mentally. This obligation is grave, unless one enjoys a contrary privilege;

6. with the requisite attention and intention.[249]

380. REASONS EXCUSING FROM RECITAL are threefold:

1. *physical impossibility*, such as blindness, grave illness;

2. *moral impossibility*, namely, grave inconvenience arising from the recitation of offices, such as the omission of other most pressing duties;

3. *legitimate dispensation* which the local ordinary or religious prelate may grant to their subjects *for a short period*.

Art. 3. Adoration

381. DEFINITION. In its general meaning *adoration is the honor paid to another because of his superior excellence*. There exist three types of excellence: divine, created supernatural, created natural; and, therefore, there are three corresponding forms of adoration: the adoration of God known as *latria*, the worship due to the angels and saints which is called *dulia*, and the worship paid to outstanding men or *civil honor*. In its strict meaning as used today, *adoration is the supreme honor due to the divine excellence alone*.

KINDS. Since adoration is a form of worship it would be useful to mention some of the more usual types of worship.

1. Worship is *absolute* if offered *to persons* because of their internal excellence; it is *relative* if offered *to things* because of their close connection with a person possessing excellence, such as a crucifix or an image.

---

[248] See S.R.C., May 12, 1905.
[249] See no. 375.

2. Worship is *public* if offered in the name of the Church by persons lawfully deputed to do so and by acts prescribed by the Church (liturgical worship); it is *private* if offered in the name of the individual.[250]

3. Worship may be either *latria, hyperdulia, dulia*, or *civil*. Hyperdulia is the worship due to our Lady on account of her unique excellence. The other forms of worship have been explained already.

382. **PRINCIPLE.** 1. *Supreme absolute worship (latria) is due to God alone and to Christ our Lord; supreme relative worship is paid to the Cross and to other instruments of the Passion and also to images of God and of Christ.*

2. *A lesser form of absolute worship—dulia—is due to the angels and saints; relative worship of the same kind is offered to the relics and images of saints and angels.*

3. *A special form of absolute worship—hyperdulia—is due to the Mother of God, and a relative form of this worship is offered to her relics and images.* All the points mentioned in this principle are sufficiently evident from what has been said already regarding the definition and kinds of worship.

Art. 4. Vows

Here will be considered: 1) The Nature and Kinds of Vows; 2) The Subject of Vows; 3) The Matter of Vows; 4) Obligation of Vows; 5) Cessation of Vows through Internal Causes; 6) Cessation of Vows or Their Obligation through External Causes, Namely, through Annulment, Dispensation, Commutation.

§ 1. Nature and Kinds of Vows

383. **DEFINITION.** *A vow is a promise made to God concerning something that is possible, good, and better than its opposite.*[251]

Three things are required to complete the essential nature of a vow:

a) a strict *promise*, so that a mere resolution would not suffice;

b) a promise *made to God* and not to the saints; therefore, a vow is a genuine act of adoration which cannot be offered to the saints. Nevertheless, a vow may be made in honor of the saints in the same way as the Sacrifice of the Mass is offered.

c) a promise relating *to a possible good which is better than its opposite*—that is, to an object which, considering all the circumstances, is not only possible to the person making the vow but is also better than its opposite. Therefore, although it is true that the married state objectively considered is not better than celibacy, nevertheless it may be better for the individual and therefore could be the object of a strict vow.

MORAL USEFULNESS. Vows prudently made for the purpose of worshipping God are morally good and extremely useful to man. This is the Catholic view as opposed to that of many Protestants, Quietists, and liberal theologians. For a vow "is a

---

[250] See CCL, Can. 1256.
[251] See CCL, Can. 1307, § 1.

happy necessity which compels to better things";[252] moreover it invests the acts of other virtues with greater merit, since there is the additional merit flowing from the virtue of religion.

384. KINDS. 1. In respect of their *object* vows are: *a) personal*, if they have as their chief obligation the performance or omission of some action by the individual, such as the vow to pray or to refrain from games; *b) real*, if they are primarily intended to bind a person to devote some object to a specific purpose, such as the vow to give alms; *c) mixed*, if they are partly personal, partly real, such as the vow of making a pilgrimage and of offering a gift.

2. In respect of their *duration*, vows are either *temporary*, if they endure for a stated period of time, or *perpetual*, if one promises to observe them for life.

3. In respect of the *way in which they are made*, vows are either *absolute*, if made with no condition attached, or *conditional*, if they are binding only when a stated condition is verified, such as the vow of going on a pilgrimage if I recover my health. If a person vows to inflict some *punishment* on himself if he commits a specified fault in the future, the vow is said to be *penal*.

4. In respect of their *form*, vows are either *expressed* in a set formula of words, or are *implied* (tacit) in some action freely performed to which a vow is conjoined, such as the so-called tacit religious profession or the reception of the subdiaconate to which the vow of chastity is attached.

5. In respect of their *acceptance by the Church*, vows are either *private*, if made without any intervention on the part of the Church, or *public*, if they are made with the authority and intervention of the Church, such as the normal vows taken in approved religious institutes.

Public vows are further distinguished into *simple* vows which are taken *a)* in all approved religious congregations, and *b)* in religious orders prior to solemn profession; and *solemn* vows which according to the present discipline of the Church are taken *a)* in religious orders after the third year of simple vows, *b)* by certain members of the Society of Jesus, and *c)* by subdeacons of the Latin Rite in respect of the vow of chastity. Authors are not agreed regarding the precise essential difference between solemn and simple vows. The better view would seem to be that proposed by St. Thomas[253] who states that the essence of a solemn vow consists in a certain spiritual *consecration* and surrender of the person making the vow which the Church then accepts in the name of God; simple vows contain nothing more than a spiritual surrender of the individual.

§ 2. Subject of Vows

385. Since the primary purpose of vows is to confirm the will in goodness, no one whose will is already confirmed in good (or even in evil) is a fit subject for vows.

---

[252] Augustine, *Letter 127*, chap. 8.
[253] See ST, II-II, q. 88, a. 9, c.

Therefore, neither Christ nor the angels and saints in Heaven nor the damned in hell make a vow. But all men (including non-Catholics) can make vows provided *a)* they have the perfect use of their reason, *b)* they have the intention of making a vow, *c)* they have sufficient freedom and deliberation, *d)* they are not forbidden by positive law.—This is the prescription of canon law: "All persons having sufficient use of reason in proportion to the object of the vow can make a vow unless forbidden by law."[254]

1. PERFECT USE OF REASON is required by the person making a vow in order that the vow be valid. All who at the moment of making a vow are capable of committing *grave sin* are judged to have perfect use of their reason, seeing that a person who can dedicate himself to the service of the devil through grave sin can certainly attach himself to God through a genuine vow.

2. THE INTENTION OR DESIRE OF MAKING A VOW is essential to its validity, and thus a *fictitious* vow (one made externally without any internal intention) is null and void. The intention need not be actual and explicit; a virtual and implicit intention is quite sufficient, such as is usually present in the reception of the subdiaconate. An interpretative or indirect intention would not be sufficient.

3. THERE MUST BE SUFFICIENT DELIBERATION AND FREEDOM, because without these no person would be considered as imposing on himself such a grave obligation implicit in vows. It is the common teaching of theologians that for the validity of vows there is required that amount of deliberation and knowledge which is necessary for entering upon an onerous contract or any serious undertaking. Deliberation and knowledge are opposed by error, and freedom is either destroyed or diminished by fear.

386. *a) Substantial error* affecting either the substance of what is promised or an essential condition invalidates a vow. The same applies to error regarding the *purpose* of the vow. Thus, if the chief motive for making a vow does not exist, the vow itself ceases to bind; for example, if someone promises to make a pilgrimage for the recovery of his father whom he believes to be ill, whereas at the time the vow is made the father has died, the vow would be invalid.

b) Accidental error relating to accidental conditions does not invalidate a vow but it does enable the vow to be easily dispensed or commuted.

c) There are two instances in which *fear* invalidates a vow: 1) when the fear is so grave that it disturbs the use of reason; 2) when grave fear was unjustly inflicted to force the making of the vow.[255]

Although some authors[256] are of the opinion that any fear—even light fear—invalidates a vow, the truer and more common opinion is that a private vow is not invalidated *a)* by grave fear which results from natural causes or which has been

---

[254] Can. 1307, § 2.
[255] See CCL, Can. 1307, § 3.
[256] See Busembaum and Navarrus.

justly inflicted, such as fear caused by the danger of shipwreck or of illness; *b)* by light fear.[257] — Whenever fear exercised some influence on the making of a vow, the latter is easily dispensed.

387. PROHIBITION OF CERTAIN VOWS BY ECCLESIASTICAL LAW.

a) The Church makes many persons incapable of taking public vows in religious orders and congregations, and therefore she has laid down many conditions for the validity of such vows. These conditions are discussed fully by canonists.[258]

b) Regulars under the vow of obedience are not permitted to make a private vow which is contrary to the will of their superior or to their professed Rule.

c) All private vows made by professed religious can be rendered void by their superiors,[259] with the exception of the vow of entering a stricter order.

d) Private vows made by professed religious and not annulled by their superiors are certainly valid, although normally inadvisable.

§ 3. Matter of Vows

388. The matter or object of vows must be *a)* possible, *b)* morally good, *c)* better than its contrary.

a) The matter of vows must be *possible*, since no one has the power to bind himself to what is impossible.

Thus, a vow made by a poor man to give a large alms is impossible and thus invalid. Similarly, the vow to avoid all sin — even semi-deliberate venial sin — is invalid.

b) The matter of a vow must be *morally good and pleasing to God*, since a vow is an act of worship of God and God is not to be worshipped by acts which are morally evil or even indifferent and useless. Therefore, the vow to give an alms in order to take unjust revenge on one's enemy is invalid.

c) The matter of a vow must be *better than its contrary* — that is to say, the vow must not prevent a person from performing something that is even better than the vow. Not only good acts which are counseled and works of supererogation but also deeds that are already of obligation may form the matter of vows. Thus, a vow made by a person addicted to drink that he will not drink to excess again is valid.

NOTE. It is not required that what is promised by vow should be *absolutely and objectively* better than its omission; it is sufficient if it is *relatively* better for the individual making the vow. Therefore, although, objectively speaking, virginity is better than marriage, nevertheless, in the concrete, marriage may be better for the individual. Such a man could make a vow to marry, as indicated already.[260]

---

[257] See TM, bk. 3, no. 197.
[258] E.g., in MIC, q. 213.
[259] See no. 259ff.
[260] See no. 383.

§ 4. Obligation of Vows

389. 1. The nature of the obligation.

PRINCIPLE. *The obligation of every valid vow is one of religion and binds no one else except the person who makes it.*[261]

Since a valid vow is of the nature of an obligatory promise, it necessarily binds the person who makes it. Furthermore, since it is a personal promise, the obligation does not affect anyone apart from the person who makes it, nor can it be fulfilled by a different person. Thus, for example, if a father makes a vow to fast, his son cannot fulfill the vow for him; if a community vows to fast on a certain day (as, for instance, in Rome on the Vigil of the Purification), their descendants may be bound to fast in virtue of a particular statute or lawful custom, but they are not obliged by the original vow.

Although *real* vows do not impose an obligation in religion on the heirs, nevertheless there are occasions when *justice* requires their fulfillment since they are to some extent burdens forming part of the inheritance. Real vows can be fulfilled by a person other than the one making the vow even during the latter's lifetime. Thus, for instance, a man who vows to give an alms can ask someone else to give it in his place. In such circumstances, the substitute is not fulfilling the vow as such but providing the matter promised.

390. *Is the violation of any vow an act of sacrilege?* Cajetan replies in the affirmative. Others maintain more correctly that only the violation of public vows taken in religion involves sacrilege. Others think that in addition the violation of even a private vow of *chastity* partakes of the malice of sacrilege. The discrepancy between these views is one of terminology. Every serious violation of a vow in grave matter is a mortal sin against the virtue of religion.

391. 2. The gravity of the obligation.

PRINCIPLE. *The gravity of the obligation of a vow depends on a) the gravity of the matter, and b) the intention.*

A vow is, in a certain sense, a private law. Now the extent of a law's obligation depends on the gravity of what is commanded and also on the intention of the legislator who has the power to command grave matter under a light obligation but not light matter under a grave obligation—such a procedure being irrational.—*Public* vows taken in religious institutes and in the reception of the subdiaconate relate to matters which are grave in themselves, and these cannot be vowed under a light obligation since grave harm would be caused to ecclesiastical discipline.

The determination of grave matter. The matter of a vow is regarded as grave if it would have been imposed as grave by the Church.

[261] See CCL, Can. 1310, § 1.

It depends very much on the purpose and circumstances of the law as to what constitutes grave matter in ecclesiastical law. A person is considered to have undertaken a serious matter if, for instance, he vows to say the Rosary or to fast on one day.

In *real* vows, grave matter is considered by some authors to be that which would be grave in cases of injustice. However, this rule cannot be applied too rigidly, since it would mean that one would have to distinguish between absolutely grave and relatively grave matter in the violation of a vow, as occurs in the violation of justice, which no one does.

In real vows (but not in personal vows) slight matter can *coalesce* and become grave, so that a person who on several occasions violates a real vow in a trifling matter may at length be guilty of grave sin. For example: if a man vows to give a small alms to the poor each week and then fails to fulfill his vow during an entire year, he would be guilty of grave sin. On the other hand, if a person makes a vow to give a small alms each *Saturday* having as his chief intention the honoring of our Lady and then overlooks the vow for twelve months, it is probable that this matter would not coalesce because the vow may be personal rather than real and attached to a particular day.

392. 3. THE FULFILLMENT OF THE OBLIGATION.

PRINCIPLE. *Vows must be fulfilled in accordance with the intention existing at the time of making the vow. In doubt, the same rules are to be used as for the interpretation of laws.*

A vow resembles a law in which the person making the vow is himself the legislator who is free to determine for himself and to define all the circumstances of the obligation.

Special attention must be given to the time of fulfilling the vow and to the obligation attached to conditional, disjunctive, penal, and doubtful vows.

a) THE TIME OF FULFILLMENT.

1. A negative vow (such as the vow not to frequent public-houses) binds on all occasions in exactly the same way and never ceases to bind, just as a negative law.

2. If the time for fulfilling the vow was specified by the person making the vow, it must be fulfilled at that stated time, but there is no necessity to *anticipate* the time even if it is foreseen that the vow cannot be fulfilled at its proper time; for instance, if a young man promises to make a pilgrimage in October, he is not bound to make it in September even though he knows that he will be prevented in October owing to his military service.

3. Culpable neglect in not fulfilling the vow at the stated time is sinful, but there is no further obligation to fulfill it if the specified time was intended to be *the limit of the obligation*; for example, if a man vows to fast each Saturday in honor of our Lady, he is not obliged to renew the fast on Monday having failed to fulfill it on Saturday. But if the stated time was not intended to terminate the obligation but merely *to urge the fulfillment* of the vow, then the vow must be satisfied at a

later date, and any appreciable delay would be grievously sinful. If the delay in fulfilling a vow results in some *depreciation of its value*—as may happen if one postpones entry into the religious life—then according to St. Alphonsus a delay of six months (*which has no excusing cause*) constitutes grave matter. But if the delay makes little difference to the original vow, then according to many authors any amount of delay in fulfilling the vow never exceeds a venial sin.

4. If no time was stated for fulfilling the vow it should be fulfilled as soon as possible: "If thou makest a vow to the Lord thy God, do not defer payment of it" (Dt 23:21).

393. THE OBLIGATION OF CONDITIONAL, DISJUNCTIVE, PENAL, AND DOUBTFUL VOWS.

A *conditional* vow is binding only if the condition is verified according to the strict meaning of the words used; it is lawful to use any just means (but not unjust means) to prevent the condition being fulfilled.

2. A *disjunctive* vow is not binding unless the alternatives are suitable matter for a vow and are subject to the free choice of the person making the vow. Consequently, if *prior* to the actual choice of one of the alternatives the other has become inculpably impossible, the vow ceases to bind. In such disjunctive vows special attention must be given to the *intention* of the person making the vow; if the intention is clear, the vow must be fulfilled in accord with that intention and not according to the material sense of the words.

3. *Penal* and *doubtful* vows must be interpreted strictly in accordance with the rules set forth in the following paragraph.

394. FOR THE INTERPRETATION OF VOWS the following rules are to be used:

FIRST RULE. A vow must be interpreted in the first place in accordance with the express or rightly presumed intention of the person who makes the vow.

A vow is in the form of a private law which has for its legislator the person making the vow, and the best interpretation of law is that which conforms to the express or rightly presumed intention of the legislator.

SECOND RULE. When the intention is not clear and cannot be prudently presumed, the vow should be interpreted in accordance with the common practice of men or the general usage of the Church.

Thus, a person who makes the Rosary the object of a vow may recite it with a companion, since this is common custom and the practice of the Church; a person who vows to fast for a month need not fast on Sundays.

THIRD RULE. In doubt as to the existence or extent of a vow one may follow the more benign interpretation.

The obligation of a vow cannot be presumed but must be proved and "in obscure matters the least possible should be observed."[262]

---

[262] Regula Juris 30, in *Liber Sextus.*

§ 5. Cessation of Vows through Internal Causes

INTRODUCTORY. A vow may cease *for some internal reason* (as through its matter changing or its principal reason failing), or *through some extrinsic cause*, namely, by annulment, dispensation, or commutation.[263] First to be considered is the cessation of vows through internal causes.

395. GENERAL RULE. A private vow ceases through intrinsic causes when there occurs such a change either in the object promised or in the person himself which would certainly have prevented the making of the vow if it had been present from the beginning.

Thus, for example, a rich man who promises to give an alms each week and then himself falls a victim to poverty, or a man who in good health vows to enter religion and then contracts an incurable disease are no longer bound by their vows.

NOTE. *Public* vows (of religion and of the subdiaconate) never cease through intrinsic causes, otherwise religious institutes and the person making the vow would be subject to much inconvenience.

§ 6. Cessation of Vows through Annulment

396. DEFINITION. *A vow is annulled or suspended by one who has legitimate authority over the will of the person making the vow or at least over the matter of the vow.*[264]

Consequently, the act of annulment is an act of authority and not of jurisdiction. A distinction must be made between: *a) direct* annulment, whereby a vow is annulled by one who has authority *over the will of the person making a vow,* such as the annulment by a father of vows made by his children below the age of puberty; *b) indirect* annulment, which is the suspension of a vow by one who has authority over the *matter of the vow,* such as a master's suspension of the vows made by his subjects which prevent them from rendering their service.

397. FIRST PRINCIPLE. *A sufficient cause is required for the lawful annulment of vows but not for their valid annulment.*

Certain theologians[265] maintain that no sufficient cause is necessary either for the valid or for the lawful annulment of vows, since the superior is always justified in exercising his authority over his subjects because their vows implicitly suppose the superior's consent. Other theologians[266] hold the opinion that at least a slight cause is required for the annulment of vows, otherwise the superior would be unjustly preventing due worship given to God through the fulfillment of the vow and would also be impeding his subject's welfare. This opinion is confirmed in the Code of Canon Law: "One who has legitimate authority over the will of

---

[263] See CCL, Can. 1311.
[264] See CCL, Can. 1312, § 1.
[265] See Antoninus, Cajetan, and Suarez.
[266] See Dom. Soto, Laymann, Lessius.

a person making a vow can validly annul the vows of the latter and for a just reason can lawfully do so."[267]

SECOND PRINCIPLE. *The power of annulling directly the vows of subjects always remains even if the superior had already permitted or approved such vows; this is not true of indirect annulment.*

The reason for the first part of the principle is that a superior always retains complete authority over his subject's will, even though he had previously given his permission or approval. With regard to the second part, it must be remembered that the power of annulling vows indirectly extends only to the subject-matter of a vow which cannot be reclaimed once it has been given to the free disposal of the person making the vow.

398. THE POWER OF DIRECT ANNULMENT.

1. *The pope and any religious superior* may annul directly the *private* vows of their *professed subjects*, with the exception of the vow of entering a more perfect and stricter religious state since each person remains free to choose a more perfect state. Private vows made by a professed religious prior to his profession (whether made while he was in the world or in religion) are suspended as long as the person remains in the religious life.[268]

2. *Parents* (or, in their default, guardians) may annul directly all the vows of their children made *before* the age of puberty. This power may be exercised not only while the child is below the age of puberty but even afterward, provided that the vow has not already been ratified by a *new vow* distinct from the first on attaining the age of puberty.

3. It is disputed whether a *husband* may annul directly the vows made by his wife *during the time of their marriage*. The better opinion would seem to be that the husband has the power of *indirect* annulment only, since no positive argument can be alleged for the contrary view.

399. THE POWER OF INDIRECT ANNULMENT.

1. *The pope* may annul indirectly all vows relating to ecclesiastical property and to other goods over which he has the power of disposal.

2. *Parents* may suspend vows made by children who are not yet emancipated, if they impede the free direction of the family, such as the vow of undertaking a distant pilgrimage.

3. *A religious superior* may annul indirectly the vows of novices which interfere with the discipline of the novitiate.

4. *Husband and wife* can suspend the vows of the other insofar as they are contrary to marital rights.

5. *A master* can annul indirectly vows taken by his servants or subjects if they prevent the rendering of due service.

[267] Can. 1312, § 1.
[268] See CCL, Can. 1315.

§ 7. Cessation of Vows or Their Obligation through Dispensation

400. DEFINITION. *A dispensation is the extinction of a vow's obligation made in the name of God by someone possessing proper jurisdiction.*

This definition reveals several points of difference between dispensation and annulment.

1. A dispensation is given in the name of God, an annulment is granted on the authority of the individual.

2. Dispensation presupposes jurisdiction, annulment authority.

3. Dispensations require a just cause, annulments do not—at least for validity.

4. While dispensations presuppose the consent of the person being dispensed, annulment does not.

401. REQUISITES FOR DISPENSATION. For valid and legitimate dispensation two conditions must be present: a just reason and legitimate power.

1. *Just reasons* for granting dispensations are *a)* the good of the Church; *b)* the necessity or good of the person making the vow, such as the great difficulty which he experiences in keeping the vow or the risk which he runs of breaking it. However, the superior may always dispense where the existence of a just reason is *in doubt.*

2. *Legitimate power* for dispensing from vows certainly resides in the Church which has the power to loosen the bond even of sin itself. The following exercise this power:

a) THE POPE can dispense in all vows (with the exception of a vow made in favor of a third party) and he has reserved for himself the power of dispensing:

1. in all *public* vows (whether perpetual or temporary) taken in institutes approved by the Holy See. Public vows made in *diocesan* institutes can be dispensed by the local ordinary[269] (except the perfect vow of perpetual chastity[270]);

2. *in two private vows,* namely, those of perfect and perpetual chastity and of entry into an approved religious order with solemn vows. These vows are considered to be reserved only if they are perfect both in their *matter* and in their *form.*

Due to imperfect *matter,* the following vows are not reserved to the Holy See: the vow of virginity, the vow not to marry, the vow of temporary chastity, the vow of receiving Holy Orders, the vow of entering into a religious institute possessing only simple vows. All these vows fall short of the vow of perfect chastity and the vow of entering a religious order with solemn vows.

Due to imperfection in their *form,* the following vows are not reserved: *a)* conditional vows, *b)* disjunctive vows, *c)* penal vows, *d)* vows made under the influence of fear (even if slight), *e)* vows intended by their agent to be binding under a slight

[269] See CCL, Can. 638.
[270] See CCL, Can. 1309.

obligation, *f)* vows already commuted by a legitimate superior into some good work, *g)* vows made before the age of eighteen.[271]

402. *b)* BISHOPS and other prelates with equivalent episcopal jurisdiction may dispense for a just reason in all vows not reserved to the Holy See and also in the two private vows already mentioned:

1. when there is *urgent need* and recourse to the Holy See is morally impossible, e.g., when everything is ready for a marriage which is to take place immediately;

2. when they concern a vow of chastity made previous to marriage;

3. when the vows are doubtful;

4. when they possess special delegated powers.

NOTE. Bishops may dispense in the vows of *strangers*.[272]

403. *c)* RELIGIOUS CONFESSORS who have the privileges of mendicants may dispense either inside or outside of the confessional from all vows not reserved to the Holy See, with the exception of vows which were principally intended for the benefit of a third party and accepted by the latter. This is the more common and probable opinion. Concerning the vow of *chastity*, regulars may dispense *a)* in a case of urgent need in preparation for marriage, *b) after* marriage has taken place, in order that one party may demand the marriage debt of the other.

404. *Parish priests and other ordinary confessors* have no power to grant dispensations from vows except by special indult or during the time of a jubilee. When everything is prepared for marriage and the marriage cannot be postponed without probable danger of grave evil until a dispensation has been obtained from the local ordinary, any confessor may dispense in the vow of chastity and in other vows impeding marriage, provided that the matter is occult.[273]

405. IN EXERCISING THE POWER OF DISPENSATION the following points should be noted:

1. It is permissible to use this faculty either inside or outside the confessional unless the contrary is expressly stated. But in normal circumstances it is more fitting that the dispensation be granted inside the confessional.

2. One may use this faculty even for *oneself* since it is an act of voluntary jurisdiction, unless it is expressly prescribed that the dispensation is to be granted in the tribune of confession.

3. Whoever has the power to dispense in vows may dispense in *those to which an oath is attached.*

4. It is rarely expedient to free the person seeking a dispensation from all obligation of his vow; it is better to commute the matter of the vow into something lighter.

[271] See CCL, Can. 1309.
[272] See CCL, Can. 1313.
[273] See CCL, Can. 1045, § 3.

§ 8. Cessation of Vows or Their Obligation through Commutation

406. DEFINITION. *Commutation consists in transferring the obligation of a vow from one work to another*; or, in other words, it is the substitution of another good work for that which was promised by vow under the same obligation. Therefore, commutation is no different from *partial* dispensation of the vow, if a less difficult work is substituted.

A vow may be commuted *a)* into *a better work*, more pleasing to God; *b)* into *something equally good* which affords almost the same difficulty in its fulfillment; *c)* into *something less good* and less difficult.

407. FIRST PRINCIPLE. *Although the person making a vow may commute the vow into something better or equally good on his own authority, this is not advisable in practice.*

He may commute his vow into what is evidently better since God is rightly presumed to consent to any commutation which is of greater benefit to the one who vows and to the worship of God, and a work which is evidently better is certainly of greater benefit to the one who vows and to the worship of God. On the other hand, it is positive law[274] which permits the individual to commute his vow into something equally good. But these forms of commutation are inadvisable in practice since it is often difficult—if not impossible—to decide which work is better or at least equally good, since one must take into consideration not only the nature of the work itself but also all the circumstances affecting the person making the vow.

NOTE. It is not permissible to commute on one's own authority: 1) vows which are reserved to the Holy See (unless commutation is effected by entry into religion); 2) vows made in favor of a third party, once they have been accepted; 3) the vow of entering a stricter religious order.

408. SECOND PRINCIPLE. *Vows cannot be commuted into what is certainly and substantially less good, unless a) one has special power and b) there exists a sufficient reason.*

Such commutation represents a partial dispensation from the original vow and it has been stated already that special faculties and a sufficient reason are necessary for valid and legitimate dispensation from vows. Whoever has the power of dispensing has the power of commutation. But it is self-evident that for commutation a less good reason is required than for complete dispensation.

FIRST COROLLARY. After commutation (even if repeated) it is permissible to return to the original vow, since commutation is a favor which no one is obliged to use, ordinarily speaking.

SECOND COROLLARY. If the substituted work has become impossible (even if through the fault of the person making the vow) he is not obliged to return to the original vow, provided that the substitution was made by a confessor or legitimate ecclesiastical superior, since the original obligation has been totally destroyed by the legitimate superior's commutation. Some theologians

---

[274] See CCL, Can. 1314.

think it probable that there never exists any obligation of returning to the original vow even when the substitution was performed by the person making the vow, since the original vow or obligation is destroyed by all forms of legitimate commutation.

Art. 5. Oaths

§ 1. Definition and Kinds of Oaths

409. DEFINITION. *An oath is an invocation of God's name to bear witness to the truth.*[275]

From this definition it is clear that an oath in itself is not only morally good (which is denied by Anabaptists, Mennonites, and Quakers) but also an act of religion. Man being conscious of his own fallibility protests by his oath that God is omniscient and the omnipotent avenger of falsehood.

KINDS. 1. In an *assertory* oath God is invoked as witness to the truth of a past or present event—e.g., I swear that I did not commit that crime; in a *promissory* oath God is invoked to bear witness not only to a future act but also to man's present intention of doing or omitting something—e.g., I promise I will faithfully fulfill the office I am now undertaking.

2. An *invocatory* oath simply invokes God as witness to truth; an *imprecatory* oath invokes God not only as witness to the truth but also, expressly, as the avenger of falsehood. In the Old Testament these imprecatory oaths were quite frequent: "The Lord do so to me and more also"; and the oath is now used in the formula: "So help me God."

3. A *solemn* (judicial) oath is taken with a certain external solemnity, such as with lighted candles, or before the crucifix, or touching the Bible; a *simple* oath is taken privately without any solemnity.

§ 2. Conditions Required for Validity and Lawfulness

410. Two conditions are required for an oath to be *valid*: the intention of taking the oath and a specific formula. For an oath to be *lawful* there are also required truth, justice, and right judgment. These three latter conditions are known as the *attendant circumstances of an oath (comites jurisjurandi)*.

1. AN ACTUAL OR VIRTUAL INTENTION of taking an oath is absolutely essential for the validity of the oath; consequently, the mere external use of the formula of an oath makes the oath fictitious and is usually a grave sin since it is an idle invocation of God's witness. I say: *usually*—because if it is easy to gather from the circumstances that the speaker has no intention of taking an oath, no grave sin is committed. Thus, sayings in common use are not genuine oaths: this is as certain as the existence of God, may I die if this is not so.

[275] CCL, Can. 1316, § 1.

2. A SPECIFIC FORMULA is necessary for an oath to be valid, in which God is invoked either explicitly or implicitly. This is evident from the very definition of an oath. In ecclesiastical law the formula usually employed is: "So help me God and these holy Gospels." In civil courts set formulas are usually prescribed but the oaths are not religious oaths if they contain no invocation of God. Thus, for instance, the form used by the Mennonites—I swear by the truth of man—is not a religious oath.

3. THE TRUTH of an oath means that the person taking the oath is not lying. If truth is lacking, then a grievous sin of perjury is committed. Truth not only excludes lying but demands moral certainty of the facts asserted. Thus, an oath may not be made while there is doubt or mere probability regarding the truth. Similarly, it is never permissible to take an oath which is accompanied by *strict* mental reservation; mental reservation in the *wide* sense of the term is also excluded, unless there is grave cause.

4. JUSTICE, as the second accompaniment of an oath, requires that nothing unlawful be either asserted or promised. For example, justice is lacking in any oath which concerns calumny, detraction, fornication, and so on. Oaths which offend against justice are sinful, and indeed grievously sinful if *a)* the injustice committed or about to be committed is itself grave, and *b)* the intention of the person taking the oath was grievously sinful. It is disputed whether it is grievously sinful when the object of the oath is *venially* wrong, e.g., when it concerns a lie or slight deception. In practice, oaths which concern venial sin in the future are rarely oaths in the strict sense, since there is usually lacking the intention of taking an oath.

5. RIGHT JUDGMENT, as the third accompaniment of a lawful oath, demands due discretion so that there may be present *a)* a sufficient cause, and *b)* fitting reverence. Absence of this condition will ordinarily be a venial sin since vain use is made of God's name; it may become grievously sinful through accidental circumstances, if, for instance, it gives rise to grave scandal or the danger of perjury.

§ 3. Obligation of Oaths

411. INTRODUCTORY. We are chiefly concerned with the obligation of promissory oaths, since assertory oaths in themselves do not bind a person to anything else than to speak the truth. However, if an assertory oath offend against truth or justice, there arises the additional obligation of making reparation for the damage caused, as in any other unjust action.

412. PRINCIPLE. *A promissory oath which fulfills all the necessary conditions causes a grave or light obligation according as the object promised is grave or light.*

a) It is self-evident that a genuine obligation is the outcome of an oath due to the fact that if the promise is broken, contempt is shown for God, Who was invoked as surety for the promise. Thus, God commands: "Thou shalt perform what thou hast sworn in the sight of the Lord" (Mt 5:33).

b) Some authors[276] regard every violation of a promissory oath as grievously sinful, inasmuch as it involves perjury; the more common and true opinion is that the violation of a promissory oath admits of slight matter since the obligation arising from such oaths is less than the obligation of vows which certainly admit of slight matter.

CONDITIONS REQUIRED FOR THE EXISTENCE OF AN OBLIGATION.

The object of the promise must be possible and morally good. Therefore, any such oath which relates to something impossible, morally evil, or even vain and useless is invalid. The same applies to an oath of fidelity or obedience which is sometimes imposed on subjects and which does not bind if the superior commands something unlawful.

On the part of the person taking the oath there are required: *a)* the intention to take an oath; *b)* sufficient deliberation and freedom; *c)* absence of substantial error. Fear which is both grave and unjust does not make an oath invalid but makes it capable of rescission.[277]

413. INTERPRETATION OF OATHS.

FIRST RULE. A promissory oath must be interpreted strictly in accordance with the rights and intention of the person who takes it; if deceit is used, the oath must be interpreted according to the intention of him in whose favor it was taken.

SECOND RULE. Certain limitations are always understood to exist in every promissory oath:

a) if the fulfillment of the promise does not become morally impossible,

b) if my superior permits,

c) unless another remits my obligation by yielding his right to its fulfillment,

d) unless the matter undergoes a notable change,

e) if another person stands by his promises.

THIRD RULE. Generally, a promissory oath follows the nature and conditions of the act to which it has been added.

414. THE OBLIGATION OF A PROMISSORY OATH MAY CEASE either from internal or external causes. It ceases to be binding from *internal* causes in almost the same way as a vow—that is, if the object promised changes substantially or if the principal motive ceases to exist.

Extrinsic causes which result in a promissory oath ceasing to bind are:

1. *condonation* by him in whose favor the promise was made;

2. *annulment by a lawful superior,* in the same way as the annulment of vows;

3. *dispensation and commutation,* as in vows;[278]

---

[276] See Cajetan, Lessius, and Concina.

[277] See CCL, Can. 1317, § 2.

[278] See CCL, Can. 1320.

4. *relaxation* which differs from dispensation to the extent that a dispensation is granted as a favor to the *person who took the oath*, whereas a relaxation is imposed normally for grave reasons by the person in whose favor the oath was made. It is similar to annulment except that it can be granted by the pope alone *a)* if the common good requires it, *b)* as a punishment for the commission of a crime.

§ 4. Perjury: The Violation of an Oath

415. DEFINITION. Understood in its widest sense, perjury is identical with any *unlawful* oath, that is, one that lacks any of the three conditions mentioned above. In its strict sense, perjury is a (moral) *lie confirmed by oath*. But the sin of perjury is not committed by one who under oath asserts something false which he invincibly considers to be the truth.

PRINCIPLE. *1) Perjury in its strict sense is a mortal sin which admits of no slight matter; 2) perjury understood in a wide sense is a venial sin if it lacks only the element of right judgment; 3) if, however, it violates justice, it is a grave sin which admits of parvity of matter.*

Perjury in its strict sense is a grave sin allowing of no slight matter since it implies a most serious contempt of God Who can neither deceive nor be deceived. Therefore, Innocent XI condemned this proposition: "To call upon God as a witness to a slight lie is not a great irreverence, because of which God wishes or can condemn man."[279] Those who commit perjury are visited with various punishments by the Church,[280] and suffer imprisonment at the hands of the civil law.

Perjury in its wide sense is venially sinful if it does not violate justice, because the irreverence shown to God in this way does not seem sufficient to constitute mortal sin, since there is no direct violation of any of God's attributes. But it may happen *incidentally* that an oath which lacks the element of right judgment becomes grievously sinful, e.g., through the scandal which ensues.

If the virtue of justice is violated, perjury is a mortal sin, since any violation of that virtue (understood even in its widest sense) is a grave sin which admits of slight matter.

Art. 6. Adjuration

416. DEFINITION. *Adjuration is the use one makes of the reverence, fear, or love which another has for the name of God or a holy thing to induce him to do or omit something.*

In adjuration, therefore, one person tries to obtain something from another in virtue of the latter's reverence or fear of God. All who know God may be adjured—that is to say, God Himself, Christ, our Lady, the saints, men on earth, the devils.

Adjuration is *solemn* if made with the ceremonies prescribed by the Church; otherwise, it is *simple*. It is *precatory* if made in the form of a request; it is *comminatory* (imperative) if accompanied by commands.

[279] DZ 1174.
[280] See CCL, Can. 2323.

PRINCIPLE. *Adjuration which fulfills the requisite conditions is an act of religion and therefore lawful and morally good.*

By such an act recognition is made of God's majesty. Furthermore, it is an act which has often been used by the Church.

The requisite conditions for lawful adjuration are the same as those for a lawful oath; namely truth, justice, right judgment.

Truth demands that the agent should not deceive the individual who is adjured.

Justice demands that he intend something that is lawful.

Right judgment demands that adjuration should be accompanied by due reverence.

417. EXORCISM. In its strict sense, exorcism is the expulsion of the devil from one possessed; in its wide sense, it includes the nullifying of the devil's influence in any creature. In a solemn exorcism, understood in its strict sense, the directions of the Church must be scrupulously observed. It is of prime importance to obtain the ordinary's permission since it is his function to decide whether it is a genuine case of diabolical possession and whether it is fitting to perform the exorcism solemnly.[281] Private exorcism may be performed by anyone, but its influence is greater if exercised by one who has received the Order of exorcist.

Art. 7. Sanctification of Sundays and Feasts

This article is divided into three paragraphs: 1) Nature, Origin, and Utility of This Worship; 2) The Precept of Hearing Mass—the first part of this worship; 3) Prohibition of Servile Work—the second part of this worship. In this article will be included everything prescribed by the first of the Ten Commandments and by the first commandment of the Church.

§ 1. Nature, Origin, and Utility of Sanctifying Feast Days

418. NATURE AND ORIGIN. The precept of sanctifying Sundays and holy days is partly natural law, partly divine positive law, and partly ecclesiastical law.

a) It belongs to *natural law* insofar as it commands a specific time to be devoted to the public worship of God.

b) The divine positive law commands rest from all forms of servile work one day each week for the purpose of giving praise to the Creator; this is a probable opinion.

c) The precept is part of *ecclesiastical law* insofar as the Church alone has decided on which days and in what way God is to be worshipped.

---

[281] See CCL, Can. 1151ff.

419. THE EXTENT OF THE PRECEPT.

1. *Who are obliged by the precept?* All baptized persons who have reached the age of seven and have the use of reason.[282] Even heretics are bound to observe this precept, but transgressors are frequently excused from formal sin through ignorance.

2. *Which days are to be kept holy?* By common law and according to present discipline, all Sundays and the following ten feasts are days of obligation: the Nativity of Our Lord, the Circumcision, the Epiphany, the Ascension, Corpus Christi, the Immaculate Conception, the Assumption of Our Blessed Lady, the feast of St. Joseph her Spouse, the feast of Sts. Peter and Paul, the feast of All Saints.[283]

By local law, some of these feasts are excluded and others have been added, e.g., the feast of St. James in Spain.[284]

3. *What does ecclesiastical law require on Sundays and holy days?* Two things: the hearing of Mass and resting from servile and public work.[285]

420. UTILITY OF THE PRECEPT.

1. Man's natural powers are rested;

2. valuable help is given to man's spiritual and religious life;

3. family life is fostered;

4. social worship and universal religion are encouraged.

§ 2. The Precept of Hearing Mass

421. 1. GRAVITY AND EXTENT OF THIS PRECEPT.

All baptized persons who have reached the age of seven and have the use of reason are obliged under penalty of serious sin to hear Mass on Sundays and holy days. Thus, imbeciles and children who have not yet attained the use of reason are excluded from the precept. Children who attain the use of reason before the age of seven years are not strictly bound to assist at Mass, since ecclesiastical law does not bind them.[286] — A priest who celebrates Mass (even in a private oratory) satisfies this precept.

For the perfect fulfillment of the precept, four things are required: bodily presence, the entire Mass, devout assistance, a proper place.

---

[282] See CCL, Can. 12.

[283] See CCL, Can. 1247.

[284] In England, but not in Scotland, the feasts of the Immaculate Conception and of St. Joseph are not observed as holy days of obligation.

[285] See CCL, Can. 1248.

[286] See CCL, Can. 12.

422. *a) Bodily presence* is considered sufficient if the person hearing Mass is morally united to the celebrant.

Therefore, the following satisfy their obligation: *a)* all who are *in the church* itself, even if they are in a side-chapel and cannot see the celebrant, provided that by the sound of the bell or by adverting to the actions of others they realize to some extent what is being done by the celebrant; *b)* even those who stand *outside the church* close to the door (even if it is shut) or who are in some neighboring building, provided that they have some view of the ceremonies and unite themselves with the celebrant.

b) The entire Mass must be heard from the beginning of Mass up to and including the priest's blessing.

On those days when the priest celebrates three Masses (Christmas Day and the Commemoration of All Souls) the faithful are not obliged to hear more than one Mass. — Whoever omits a notable part of the Mass does not satisfy the precept and thereby commits grave sin. What constitutes a *notable* part is not easily determined. Two points are agreed: *a)* what constitutes a notable part is to be decided not merely from the length of time but more especially from the dignity of the omitted parts; thus, a person who is absent for the Consecration and the Communion, even though he may be present for the rest of the Mass, does not fulfill the precept; *b)* a third part of the Mass constitutes a notable part and is regarded as grave matter. The following are looked upon as *slight omissions*: everything from the beginning of Mass until the Offertory *exclusively*; all that follows the Communion; everything from the beginning until the Epistle together with all that follows the Communion.

423. *c) A devout and not merely physical assistance* is necessary during Mass. Thus, there are required: *a) a right intention* of worshipping God; therefore, a man who comes to church *merely* to listen to the music or to meet some girl does not satisfy the precept; *b) proper attention*. It is disputed whether internal attention is required in addition to external attention.[287] The necessary attention would seem to be lacking if a person were to be in the confessional for the whole of Mass or during a *notable part*. Therefore, unless genuine need excuses them, such penitents would be obliged to hear another Mass. Often, however, there does exist such a need, as, for example, in the case of domestic servants or of those who cannot go to confession at any other time.

424. *d) The proper place* for hearing Mass is normally a church, or a public or semipublic oratory.[288]

A *public* oratory is a place permanently set aside by authority of the ordinary for public worship and which has been blessed or even consecrated. Furthermore,

---

[287] See no. 375.

[288] "The precept of hearing Mass is fulfilled by a person who assists at the Sacrifice celebrated in any Catholic rite in the open or in any church, or oratory (public or semi-public), and in private cemetery chapels but not in other oratories unless this privilege has been granted by the Holy See" (CCL, Can. 1249).

it is required that any of the faithful should be able to enter it, at least during the time of Mass.[289]

A *semipublic* oratory is one which although erected in a somewhat private place or at least not absolutely public is intended to serve the convenience not of some private individual but of some community or gathering; e.g., chapels in seminaries, ecclesiastical colleges, institutes with simple vows, colleges, hospitals, prisons, houses of bishops and cardinals, and so on.

A *private* oratory is one erected by indult of the Holy See in a private house for the convenience of some individual or family. In such an oratory any of the faithful may receive Holy Communion, but only those to whom special permission has been granted can fulfill the precept of hearing Mass. Usually there are many clauses contained in the indult, all of which must be carefully observed. Ordinarily, those who are *guests* of the person to whom such an indult has been granted have permission to fulfill their obligation of hearing Mass in such an oratory, and by the term *guests* are understood even those who have been invited to dinner only.

For a just and reasonable cause, the bishop can allow Mass to be said and heard in any suitable place and even in the open, but such a concession can only be granted for a specific case.[290]

425. 2. CAUSES WHICH EXCUSE a person from fulfilling his obligation of hearing Mass may be reduced to physical or moral impossibility. Others say that necessity, charity, and duty excuse from the obligation. St. Alphonsus rightly declares: "Any cause which is moderately grave excuses from the precept—that is, any reason which involves some notable inconvenience or harm to mind or body either of oneself or of another."[291]

§ 3. Prohibition of Servile Work

426. DISTINCTIONS. There are four types of work:

1. *Servile work* is that which a) requires mainly bodily activity, b) has as its immediate purpose the welfare of the body, c) was formerly done by slaves; e.g., farm work, such as digging or ploughing, mechanical work, like sewing or making shoes.

N.B. The character of servile work is not determined by the worker's intention or by the fatigue involved, or by the fact that wages are received, and so on, but solely *by the nature of the work itself* which remains servile even if done out of charity or for the sake of recreation.

2. *Cultural work* is that which a) is the product chiefly of the mental faculties, b) is immediately directed toward the development of the mind, c) used to be

[289] See CCL, Can. 1188, § 2.
[290] See CCL, Can. 1194.
[291] MTM, bk. 3, no. 324.

performed by persons who were not slaves, such as reading, writing, singing, playing the organ. These acts remain cultural even if energy is lost in their performance and wages received.

3. *Ordinary (natural) work* is that which is done indiscriminately by all classes and is chiefly intended for *the daily sustenance of the body*, such as eating, hunting, travelling, cooking.

4. *Judicial and commercial work* is that which is transacted in the courts or in the course of public trading, such as sitting in court, defending criminals, buying, selling, leasing, and so on.

NOTE. There are forms of work whose exact nature remains in doubt. In order to solve such doubts, one should be guided by *the common opinion of men*. Thus, for example, rowing is servile work, but common opinion regards it as lawful on Sundays if done for the sake of recreation.

427. PRINCIPLE. *All servile, judicial, and commercial work is forbidden on Sundays and holy days, but cultural and ordinary work is allowed.*[292] *Any form of servile, judicial, or commercial work prevents man from giving sufficient attention to the worship of God, since it absorbs the attention of the mind and tires his body. Other forms of work do not have the same effect. A more lenient attitude toward commercial work* is at present in existence, since markets are allowed for the sale of small articles such as flowers or fruit, and private contracts of buying or selling are also permitted.

The prohibition of servile and judicial work is grave but allows of parvity of matter. It is thought that servile work lasting for *more than two hours* (either continuously or with intervals) without any excusing cause constitutes grave matter and is therefore grievously sinful. But if the work is light in character rather than servile, *a space of three hours* is considered necessary before grave matter exists.

428. CAUSES WHICH EXCUSE from this precept can be reduced to three types: 1) personal need or that of another; 2) legitimate custom; 3) legitimate dispensation.

Personal *need* or that of another sometimes excuses from this precept, as, for example, farmers during harvest-time, the poor, domestic servants, workers responsible for the maintenance of machines in factories. Some necessity is thought to exist if there is danger of sinning as the result of idleness.

Custom in certain places excuses hair-dressers, drivers of public vehicles, hunters, fishers, those who sell small articles.

A *dispensation* in this law may be granted by the Holy See and also in particular cases by bishops, religious prelates, parish priests for their own parishioners.[293] A confessor has no power to dispense in this matter, but in doubtful cases he may interpret the law and allow his penitents to undertake necessary work.

[292] See CCL, Can. 1248.
[293] See CCL, Can. 1245.

VICES CONTRARY TO THE VIRTUE OF RELIGION

429. INTRODUCTORY. The virtue of religion is violated either by defect, i.e., *irreverence*, or by excess, i.e., *superstition*. The following chapter is divided into ten articles, the first six being devoted to superstition, and the remaining four to irreverence: 1) Superstition in General; 2) Idolatry; 3) Divination; 4) Vain Observance; 5) Magic and Sorcery; 6) Magnetism, Hypnotism, Spiritism; 7) Tempting God; 8) Blasphemy; 9) Sacrilege; 10) Simony.

Art. 1. Superstition in General

430. DEFINITION. *Superstition is the vice inclining man to render divine worship either to a creature who does not deserve it or in a way contrary to its nature.*[294] This definition will be understood more clearly by considering the various forms of superstition.

There are two SPECIFIC FORMS of superstition, each of which admits of further subdivisions.

1. The first form of superstition consists *in worshipping God in an improper manner* either by false and pernicious honor or by superfluous honor.

False worship of the true God is offered in various ways, such as desiring to worship God according to Jewish ritual which supposes that Christ is yet to come. Such superstition is essentially a grave sin.

Superfluous worship of God is that which is not suited to the purpose of religion, such as demanding a certain number, arrangement, and color of candles in order to pray. This form of superstition is usually a venial sin.—All modes of worshipping God approved by the Church are free from any suspicion of superstition, e.g., novenas, Gregorian Masses, and so on.

2. The second form of superstition consists in *worshipping false gods*, or offering to creatures—especially the devil—honor due to God alone. This is the form of superstition exemplified by idolatry, divination, vain observance, and so on.

Art. 2. Idolatry

431. DEFINITION. *Idolatry is the worship of idols.*

This worship is offered not to the idol or statue itself but to the person or thing represented by the statue, namely, a creature or the devil.

KINDS. 1. Idolatry is *material* (simulated, external) if honor is paid to the idol externally only and in a fictitious manner; it is *formal* (internal) when the honor is internal and genuine.

2. Formal idolatry is either *perfect* or *imperfect*; it is perfect when the divine worship is offered to a creature by one who regards him as truly divine; it is imperfect when the worshipper is fully aware that the idol is not divine and yet offers it worship

---

[294] See ST, II-II, q. 92, a. 1, c.

through some evil desire, such as hatred of God or desire to obtain something through the devil.

MORAL EVIL OF IDOLATRY. All forms of idolatry, whether material or formal, perfect or imperfect, are grievous sins unless they proceed from invincible ignorance.

Idolatry is most strictly forbidden by the first of the Ten Commandments: "Thou shalt not have strange gods before Me" (Ex 20:3), and it is an act of open rebellion against the true God.

Art. 3. Divination

432. DEFINITION. *Divination is the prediction of future events through the use of disproportionate means, that is to say, means not instituted by God Himself.*

Since no knowledge of future events can be gained by man's natural powers or from God, the angels, or the saints, it must be that divination derives its inspiration from the devil. Thus, it would be fitting to define divination as a form of superstition in which the devil is invoked explicitly or implicitly to aid man to discover the occult. Therefore, in all forms of divination there is an explicit or implicit invocation of the devil. There are several different forms: that in which the devil appears in sensible form; *dream-omens, necromancy* (modern spiritualism) in which the devil is asked to raise from the dead someone who will reveal the occult; *pythonism*, whereby the devil reveals the occult through living persons who are possessed; *geomancy* in which the devil instructs men through figures or signs appearing in some earthly body. Rotating tables may be regarded as a type of geomancy when the influence of the devil is actually present in such phenomena, although this appears to be rare. Casting lots is regarded as another form of divination if a person presumes to foretell the future from arbitrary signs, such as the throw of dice, cards, and so on. However, one may cast lots in order to divide things or duties, and so on.

The use of the *divining rod* usually cut from the hazel or willow-tree is permitted for the discovery of underground water or metals but not for the investigation of the occult, since it is possible that there may be a natural explanation for the influence of water and metals on this rod.

433. MORAL EVIL OF DIVINATION. Divination undertaken with an explicit invocation of the devil is essentially a grievous sin; that which is accompanied by an implicit invocation of the devil is a grave sin which admits of slight matter.

The reason for the first part of the statement is that by such divination worship due to God alone is being offered to the devil, the implacable foe of God. Moreover, there is imminent danger of apostasy and other grave sins. The reason for the second part is that in such forms of divination, although divine worship is not offered to the devil, intercourse with him is encouraged. — This form of divination is a venial sin if it is done a) through ignorance or stupidity, b) for fun or pleasure, c) without firm conviction. No specific distinction is made between the various forms of divination—whether accompanied by explicit or implicit invocation of the devil—since they are all reducible to worship of a false deity. Nevertheless, in confession it should be stated whether the invocation of the devil was explicit or implicit, 1) since the confessor is then able to decide more easily the gravity of the sin committed, 2) since many other sins usually accompany divination accompanied by explicit invocation of the devil, such as blasphemy, sacrilege, abuse of sacred things.

Art. 4. Vain Observance

434. DEFINITION AND KINDS. *Vain observance is a form of superstition which in order to obtain some favor uses means not suited to that purpose either by nature or by the prescription of God or His Church.*

There is only an *accidental* difference between divination and vain observance; in the former, one invokes the aid of the devil in order to obtain *knowledge* of the future or of the occult, whereas in the latter, other external favors are sought, such as good health.

Older theologians distinguished three types of vain observance:

1. that which was concerned with obtaining *knowledge* quickly and without labor by using totally unsuitable means (*ars notoria*). St. Thomas[295] is at pains to point out the futility of such practices, since the devil is unable to communicate knowledge quickly;

2. that which was concerned with curing sickness through unsuitable means (*ars sanitatum*), such as wearing an amulet or other charms;

3. that which was concerned with the observation of chance events in order to forecast something propitious or unpropitious and thus adjust one's behavior accordingly (*observantia eventuum*), as practiced, for instance, by a person who firmly believes that some evil is to befall him as the result of sitting at table with thirteen guests.

THE MORAL EVIL OF VAIN OBSERVANCE is of the same species as divination since both of them violate the virtue of religion in the same way.

Art. 5. Magic and Sorcery

435. DEFINITION. In its general sense, *magic is the art of producing surprising results through the use of occult means.*

White magic makes use of natural means, *black* magic resorts to the aid of the devil. Magic used in order to harm persons is termed *sorcery* and, according to the ancients' use, was made either of a philter (a love-potion) in order to arouse feelings of intense love or hatred toward a person, or of actions which inflicted bodily hurt on a person through the aid of the devil.

---

[295] See ST, II-II, q. 96, a. 1.

MORAL EVIL. *a)* White magic is perfectly lawful in itself; *b)* black magic is a grave sin of superstition which differs only accidentally from divination and vain observance; *c)* sorcery violates charity and justice in addition to being an act of superstition.—All these statements should be evident from what has been said previously.

Art. 6. Magnetism, Hypnotism, Spiritism

436. 1. MAGNETISM is either terrestrial or animal. The former is a physical force very similar to electricity. The latter (and this is the only type considered here) is a force probably residing in the nerves of man capable of curing sickness and producing other physical effects by the use of external attraction only. This power is frequently used nowadays by mesmerists, and *objectively* considered it does not contain anything unlawful in itself. It is nothing more than one of the many ways of curing diseases, like electropathy, homeopathy, and so on. But it is often unlawful for incidental reasons, when, for example, it is practiced by men without the requisite knowledge or who are lacking in moral principles, or who use the power for wrong purposes.

Many of the phenomena associated with "rotating tables" may perhaps be explained by means of this magnetic force.[296]

437. 2. HYPNOTISM. Although some authors are inclined to regard hypnotism as merely a higher form of magnetism, nevertheless there is a real distinction to be made between them. Magnetism makes use of purely corporal attraction, hypnotism may resort to the use of many other means, such as looking fixedly at a bright object, or the art of suggestion, and so on. Usually, hypnotism produces artificial sleep in which the patient is subject to the will of the hypnotist. Waking suggestion is to be considered one form of hypnotism in which the patient carries out necessarily the commands of the agent without the use of true hypnosis. The effects of hypnotism are indeed amazing, e.g., catalepsy, lethargy, double personality which can even result in a girl regarding herself as a male, and so on. Although some of the phenomena of hypnotism are difficult to explain, there is no need to attribute them to the intervention of the devil.

PRINCIPLE. *a) In itself hypnotism is not forbidden, b) but it is often unlawful through abuse.*

This is the more common opinion held today. It is evident from what has been said that neither the means used nor the purpose of hypnotism are in themselves unlawful. Neither can the objection be made that it is forbidden to deprive oneself of the use of reason by force or to subject one's will to the free choice of another, since for a reasonable cause there is nothing to prevent one relinquishing the use of one's reason and will for a time, as happens, for instance, in natural sleep and in sleep induced by drugs.

However, hypnotism is often unlawful because of abuse since it is still shrouded in uncertainty, beset with dangers, open to abuse, and is often of little value.

[296] See MTM, vol. 2, no. 521.

438. 3. SPIRITUALISM—understood in its strict sense—*is unlawful communication with the spirits of another world.* On rare occasions this communication is attempted by means of hypnotism, resulting in phenomena peculiar to hypnotism and spiritualism. In spiritualism strictly so-called it is claimed that communication is established with spirits of another world—that is to say with spirits of the known dead. These spirits sometimes produce what is called materialization, when they appear in a sensible and visible form so that they can even be photographed. Mediums are usually employed—persons who have a special power of communicating with these spirits which they materialize by falling into an artificial sleep (a trance). On more than one occasion it has been proved that some of the most sensational mediums were impostors who exercised great skill in producing amazing effects but with purely natural powers. Therefore, some authors are inclined to regard all spiritualistic phenomena as frauds and inventions.

MORALITY. *Spiritualism strictly so-called, namely, unnatural and useless communication with the spirits of another world, is forbidden.*

The phenomena of spiritualism, whether genuine or not, always remain forbidden. For if the phenomena are genuine and the spirits of another world do appear, they are certainly not good spirits, who would never produce such frivolous and often irreligious and immoral effects. Therefore, they proceed from the devil and thus spiritualism is merely one form of forbidden communication with the devil. If the phenomena of spiritualism are not genuine, spiritualism is still forbidden as giving rise to scandal, misconceptions, nothing useful, and dangers to religion. Therefore, it is forbidden to be present at a séance and a fortiori to act as a medium.[297]

So long as there is no scandal, cooperation, or approval, it might be permissible for a trustworthy person to attend spiritualistic séances *for the sole purpose of discovering the exact nature of spiritualism,* which is frequently little more than a series of deceptions practiced by skilled persons.

Art. 7. Tempting God

439. DEFINITION. *Tempting God consists in any word or deed whereby a person tries to discover whether God possesses or exercises a certain perfection,* such as knowledge, power. Therefore, to tempt God is the same as to hope for an unusual manifestation of God.

KINDS. Tempting God is *formal* (explicit, express) when there is an explicit intention to put one of God's perfections to the test; it is *virtual* (interpretative) when the intention is implicit in some action or omission.

440. MORALITY. Formal tempting of God is a grave sin which does not admit of slight matter; implicit tempting of God may be a venial sin.

Explicit tempting of God implies two sins—one against faith, and the other against religion, for it implies at least some doubt regarding one of the divine

---

[297] See Holy Office, Apr. 17, 1917.

attributes. Virtual tempting of God is contrary to the virtue of religion and frequently is caused by excessive self-confidence. Sometimes the gravity of the sin has to be judged by the accompanying violation of other virtues. Thus, for example, a priest commits grave sin if he neglects to prepare for preaching, hoping to receive special help from God. Not only is he tempting God but also giving grave scandal.

Art. 8. Blasphemy

441. DEFINITION. *Blasphemy is contumely against God.*

It is primarily *a sin of the tongue* since blasphemy in its proper and strict sense is committed by words alone, but generally speaking other forms of contumely are included under blasphemy so that some authors speak of blasphemy of the *heart* (blasphemous thoughts), blasphemy of the *tongue* (blasphemous words) and blasphemy in *action* (such as spitting toward Heaven).

KINDS. 1. *Heretical* blasphemy contains formal heresy, *non-heretical* blasphemy contains material heresy. Heretical blasphemy colors the Calvinistic assertion that God is the cause of sin.

2. Non-heretical blasphemy is *simple* when there is derision of God; it is *imprecatory* when it contains a desire that evil should befall Him, e.g., may God perish. The former type of blasphemy was committed by the Jews when they said to Christ: "Come now, Thou Who wouldst destroy the Temple and build it up in three days, rescue Thyself" (Mt 27:40).

3. Blasphemy is *immediate* when it is directed against God Himself, *mediate* when it is directed primarily against sacred things or persons related to God.

442. ITS MORALITY. *Blasphemy is of its nature a grievous sin and only an imperfection in the act itself can render it venially sinful.*

All blasphemy is a grave violation of charity toward God, frequently even of faith itself. The enormity of this sin can be realized by studying the serious punishments *a)* inflicted by God in the Old Testament (the punishment of death), *b)* inflicted by the Church,[298] *c)* inflicted by many civil laws (imprisonment). Frequently, blasphemy is a venial sin—especially in the uneducated—because of imperfection in the act, that is to say, through want of sufficient advertence and consent.

PRACTICAL RULES for deciding in particular cases whether blasphemy is grievously sinful. There are three chief points to be considered:

1. the intention of the person committing the blasphemy;

2. the natural meaning of the words;

3. the common opinion of the district.

Remedies. 1. The blasphemer should be earnestly advised to consider the gravity of the sin of blasphemy and the folly of directing contumely against the supreme God.

---

[298] See CCL, Can. 2323.

2. In order to overcome his habit it is most useful to impose on himself small acts of ordinary penance or ejaculatory prayers to be used each time that he inadvertently resorts to blasphemy.

One should carefully distinguish from blasphemy, cursing, and taking the name of God in vain.

443. *To curse is to invoke evil on someone.* Imprecations of evil may be made against God or holy things or persons, against rational creatures, against irrational creatures, and against the devil.

a) To curse God or holy things or persons is a form of blasphemy, as already stated.

b) To curse rational creatures is normally contrary to charity or justice.

c) To curse irrational creatures, such as the winds or horses, is generally a venial sin of impatience. If these imprecations are uttered for a morally good purpose (e.g., in the course of exorcism) they are not sinful.

d) To curse the devil as the enemy of God and men is lawful. But *exclamations* which in themselves are not sinful may become unlawful for incidental reasons, such as the danger of scandal.

444. *Taking the name of God or sacred things in vain* is in itself venially sinful, since it does not cause grave irreverence toward God.

Art. 9. Sacrilege

445. DEFINITION AND KINDS. *Sacrilege is the violation of sacred things.* Sacred things include also sacred persons and places—anything set aside publicly and by the Church's authority for the worship of God. Thus, we distinguish between *personal* sacrilege, which is the violation of a sacred person, *local* sacrilege, which is the violation of a sacred place, and *real* sacrilege, which is the violation of a sacred thing.

It is important to notice that sacrilege in the strict sense of the word is only committed when there is a *grave* violation of the sacred thing *precisely in its sacred character.* Thus, for example, a man who violates in secret the person of a priest commits sacrilege, but not if he violates his good name or his possessions, and so on. Slight injury to sacred things, such as talking in a sacred place, are not usually considered acts of sacrilege.

MORALITY. *Sacrilege is a grievous sin against the virtue of religion which admits of slight matter.* This is evident from the very meaning of sacrilege. Personal, local, and real sacrilege are three distinct species of sacrilege and must be clearly stated as such in confession.

446. 1. PERSONAL SACRILEGE may be committed in any of the four following ways:

a) by violating the *privilegium canonis*—that is to say, by laying violent hands on clerics or religious of either sex at the instigation of the devil. It is necessary that the acts of violence should be *in deed* (and not merely in word) and that they be *grievously sinful* (not done merely in playfulness, or in the course of just correction or defense);

b) by violating the *privilegium fori*—that is to say, by unlawful citation of clerics and religious before secular courts. For it is forbidden to bring clerics and religious before such courts without first obtaining the permission of the ecclesiastical superior which is granted in some countries in virtue of a concordat, in other countries each time that it is required;

c) by violating the privilege of *personal immunity*—that is to say, by unlawfully demanding from clerics or religious taxes or military service. Many civil governments no longer recognize such immunity and the Church does not always press her claims for fear of causing greater evils;

d) by violating the *public vow of chastity*—that is to say, by the commission of an act of impurity either by or with a person bound by this *public* vow. Therefore, the sin of sacrilege is committed not only by the cleric or religious sinning against chastity but also by the accomplice.

447. 2. LOCAL SACRILEGE which is the violation of a sacred place—a place permanently consecrated or blessed by authority of the Church for the worship of God[299]—may be committed in three ways:

a) by *defilement of a sacred place*, such as by the serious and unjust shedding of human blood, homicide even without the shedding of blood (strangulation), putting the church to impious or unseemly use (e.g., using it for markets or secular trading), the burial of an infidel or sentenced excommunicate.[300] These actions must be certain, notorious, and committed in the church itself. Therefore, the church has not been defiled if the acts were performed in the porch or tower, and so on. The sinful wasting of human seed in a sacred place is no longer considered an act of defilement requiring an act of reconciliation since the Code of Canon Law is silent on this point, but it still seems that local sacrilege is thereby committed. The same applies to all other external acts of impurity which are grievously sinful, since all such acts show grave irreverence for a sacred place;

b) by *grave theft* in a sacred place. Thus, it is laid down in the Decretals of Gratian: "Sacrilege is committed either by removing something sacred from a sacred place, or by removing something that is not sacred from a sacred place, or by removing something sacred from a place that is not sacred."[301] Many authors are of the opinion that theft in a sacred place is a grave act of sacrilege only if the stolen property belongs to the sacred place or has been committed to its keeping. St. Alphonsus regards that opinion as being more probable which maintains that every grave theft committed in a sacred place is grave sacrilege;

[299] See CCL, Can. 1154.
[300] See CCL, Can. 1172.
[301] Pt. 2, Cause 17, q. 4, Can. 21.

c) by *violating the immunity of a place*—a privilege granted to *religious* as well as to sacred places providing the right of sanctuary and preventing many forms of profane actions. Religious places are those in which works of piety and mercy are habitually and by appointment performed and which have been erected with the authority or express permission of the bishop, such as monasteries, religious hospitals, clerical seminaries, a bishop's residence, and so on.

448. NOTE. The actions listed under *a*) and *b*) are not sacrilegious unless they are committed strictly *within* the sacred place itself, namely, within the perimeter of the sacred place, or—so far as churches are concerned—within the space enclosed by walls, floor, and ceiling. Thus, sacrilege is not committed when, for example, human blood is shed in the sacristy or in the porch. On the other hand, actions included under *c*) are sacrilegious even when committed in the immediate precincts of a sacred place. However, this violation of the immunity of such places is not of great importance today owing to contrary customs.

449. 3. REAL SACRILEGE is the use of something sacred for an unworthy purpose. Such sacred things can be reduced to three categories:

1) the Sacraments and the sacramentals, 2) sacred vessels and church decorations, 3) ecclesiastical property.

1. The abuse of the Sacraments is the chief form of real sacrilege, such as the invalid reception of the Sacraments, the commission of grave irreverence toward the Blessed Eucharist, and so on.

2. It is gravely sacrilegious to use consecrated sacred vessels for any profane purpose unless there is most serious need. If there exists a reasonable cause, it is permitted to use such things for a profane purpose provided that their form has first been completely destroyed, for then it is not the things themselves but rather the material out of which they are made which is being put to secular use. Thus, for example, it is not forbidden when there is reasonable cause to melt down consecrated chalices and use the molten metal for other purposes.

3. Unlawful seizure of sacred things and Church property is everywhere regarded in canon law as a form of sacrilege, which will be considered further in the treatise on censures.

Art. 10. Simony

450. DEFINITION. *Simony is the express will of buying or selling (for some temporal price) that which is spiritual or annexed to something spiritual.*

1. *the express will*, that is, a deliberate intention, because the sin of simony is already committed in intent, even if it is not practiced externally.

2. *of buying and selling*: and this includes not only the contract of buying and selling but also any form of *onerous* contract, such as that of lease or hire. Accordingly, a gratuitous contract does not of itself lead to simony. — To determine still further the nature of simony some authors add the words *for*

some temporal price, under which are included: *i*) money and anything which can be valued in money (*munus a manu*); *ii*) patronage, praise, commendation, intercession, defense, and in general any form of patronage which is agreed to as a reward for obtaining some spiritual benefit (*munus a lingua*); *iii*) any temporal service rendered in return for the acquisition of something spiritual, as happens when a cleric instructs the child of his patron on the understanding that he will be appointed to a parish (*munus ab obsequio*).

3. *something spiritual or what is annexed to that which is spiritual*; this represents the subject-matter of simony. A spiritual thing is that which of its very nature or by ordinance of the Church is set aside for the supernatural welfare of the soul, such as grace, the Sacraments, the power of Orders or of jurisdiction, and so on. What is temporal may be annexed to something spiritual in one of three ways: *a*) *antecedently*, when what is spiritual is added to some temporal article already in existence; thus, for example, a chalice first exists as a temporal article before receiving its spiritual consecration; *b*) *concomitantly*, when the temporal and the spiritual exist, so to speak, side by side, such as the effort expended in saying Mass; *c*) *consequently*, when what is temporal is added to something spiritual already in existence; e.g., the revenue of a benefice which is of a temporal character presupposes the existence of that which is spiritual, namely, the parochial care of souls.

COROLLARY. It follows that simony consists essentially in establishing an equality between the temporal and the spiritual. Therefore, simony is not committed when one spiritual thing is exchanged for another of the same nature.

451. KINDS. 1. Simony *against divine law* (sometimes called simony against natural law) is such as already described; simony *against ecclesiastical law* is committed by exchanging ecclesiastical goods in a way contrary to the grave prohibitions of the Church, as, for instance, when one benefice is exchanged for another. Therefore, this form of simony is nothing more than a contract made concerning something spiritual or that which is annexed to something spiritual to which the Church has attached a grave prohibition out of reverence for religion.[302]

2. Simony is either mental, contractual, or real.

Simony is *mental* when the agreement is purely mental and not revealed externally; for instance, a cleric serves his patron for a small or practically no salary with the secret intent that his patron will confer a parish on him in return for services rendered. Such simony is a grave sin but insofar as it is merely internal, it does not incur any ecclesiastical penalty.

Simony is *contractual* when a contract has been entered into by both parties but *not yet executed* of exchanging something temporal for what is spiritual or for what is annexed to something spiritual.

[302] See CCL, Can. 727, § 2.

Simony is *real* when the contract has been executed at least partially by both parties.

3. Simony is *confidential* when it concerns ecclesiastical benefices; it consists in obtaining, conferring, or accepting an ecclesiastical benefice with some confidential reservation which may take one of the following forms: *a)* one person may confer a benefice on another on condition that the benefice will be handed back to the former or to someone else as soon as he becomes capable of holding the benefice which at present he is not (e.g., by reason of lack of age), so that the benefice remains open for himself; *b)* when the beneficed cleric *before* taking possession of his benefice offers it to another on the understanding that once he has handed it over in one way or another he may be allowed to enter his former possession; *c)* when one cleric resigns his benefice which he *already possesses* in favor of another on condition that afterward either he himself or a third party may return to it; *d)* when one person obtains a benefice for another on the understanding that he himself or a third party will receive part of the revenue.

452. SINFULNESS OF SIMONY. *a) Simony against divine law is always a grave sin against religion; b) simony against ecclesiastical law is ordinarily a grave sin but may be venial.*

All forms of simony against divine law, even in small matters, imply grave contempt for sacred things and therefore for God Himself. The gravity of this sin can be estimated from the punishment inflicted upon Simon Magus and which is still inflicted by the Church on those guilty of the sin. — Simony against ecclesiastical law is a transgression of an ecclesiastical precept which although objectively speaking is grave, yet does allow of parvity of matter. When simony is contrary both to divine and ecclesiastical law it is always grievously sinful and does not admit of slight matter, as is evident.

453. PRINCIPLE. *Simony against divine law is committed by selling or buying temporal things intrinsically annexed to something spiritual either consequently or concomitantly, but not by buying or selling temporal things which are annexed only extrinsically to something spiritual either antecedently or concomitantly.*

Temporal things intrinsically annexed to something spiritual either consequently or concomitantly are inseparably joined to the spiritual and thus are regarded as possessing the same character and therefore are incapable of being sold. Although such things cannot be bought or sold, it is permissible to use them as an occasion for giving and accepting an alms or stipend; thus, for instance, it is not forbidden to give a stipend for the upkeep of the priest offering Mass.

Temporal things extrinsically annexed to something spiritual either antecedently or concomitantly are separable from the spiritual and thus can be bought or sold. Therefore, for example, it is not forbidden to receive something even in the form of a genuine price for any special labor attached to the saying of Mass.

454. SIMONY AGAINST ECCLESIASTICAL LAW may be committed in various ways of which the following are the more noteworthy:

1. by giving or taking even when spontaneously offered the smallest thing on the occasion of an examination for the obtaining of a *parochial* benefice;[303]

2. by accepting even spontaneous offerings for the conferment of Orders and the clerical tonsure, for dismissorial or testimonial letters,[304] for testimonial letters of those desiring to enter the religious state;[305]

3. by selling ecclesiastical burial.[306] However one may demand some money if a person wishes to be buried in a particular place;[307]

4. by selling oil that has been blessed or sacred chrism, even in respect of its mere physical value;[308]

5. by accepting money for the erection, institution, or amalgamation of confraternities, and the acts themselves are thereby rendered invalid;[309]

6. by selling rosaries, medals, or anything else blessed and enriched with indulgences; if such articles are sold they lose all their indulgences.[310] Consequently, such articles must be bought or sold before they are blessed. It is likewise sinful to sell relics;[311]

7. by practicing any form of sale or exchange of Mass stipends, whether it be genuine or disguised;[312]

8. by selling the right of patronage.[313] It is not forbidden to sell something, such as a castle, to which the right of patronage is attached, provided that the selling price is not increased because of the additional right.

455. PENALTIES FOR SIMONY.

1. No penalty is incurred by mental simony since this is internal.

2. The following penalties are attached by law to real simony:

a) The simoniacal contract is null and void and therefore even before judicial sentence the thing given and received must be restored if this is possible and if restitution is not contrary to the reverence due to a spiritual thing. Similarly,

---

[303] See Council of Trent, Council of Trent, Session 24, "Decree on Reformation," chap. 18.

[304] See Council of Trent, Session 21, "Decree on Reformation," chap. 1.

[305] See CCL, Can. 545.

[306] See Gregory IX, *Liber Extra*, bk. 3, tit. 28, chap. 13.

[307] See CCL, Can. 1209, § 1.

[308] See Benedict XIV, Constitution *Apostolica* (Feb. 17 1742).

[309] See Clement VIII, Constitution *Quaecumque* (Dec. 8, 1604).

[310] See Sacred Congregation for Indulgences and Sacred Relics [hereafter S. C. Indulgences], July 10, 1896; see also CCL, Can. 924, § 2.

[311] See CCL, Can. 1289.

[312] See CCL, Can. 827 and 2324.

[313] See CCL, Can. 1470, § 1, no. 6.

the revenue obtained from any benefice or office so accepted must be restored; however, the judge or ordinary may condone wholly or in part the fruits received *in good faith.*[314]

b) Those who are guilty of simony in any ecclesiastical office, benefice, or dignity incur excommunication reserved simply to the Holy See; moreover, they are ipso facto deprived of the right of election, presentation, nomination (if they possessed such rights), and, if they are clerics, they are suspended;[315]

c) All persons (even of episcopal dignity) who have knowingly promoted others simoniacally to Orders or themselves been so promoted or have thus administered or received the other Sacraments are suspect of heresy; in addition, clerics incur suspension reserved to the Holy See.[316]

d) Those who traffic in indulgences incur ipso facto excommunication reserved simply to the Holy See.[317]

e) Those who act contrary to the statutes regarding Mass stipends and Church taxes incur certain penalties ferendae sententiae.[318]

QUESTION II
THE VIRTUES OF PIETY, REVERENCE, AND OBEDIENCE—THE FOURTH COMMANDMENT

PIETY

456. DEFINITION. The Latin word *pietas* is used in three different senses: 1) for *religion or divine worship*, in which sense it is found used in 1 Tm 4:8: "Holiness (*pietas*) is all-availing, since it promises well both for this life and for the next"; 2) for *kindness and mercy*, so that God and the saints are referred to as *pii*: "A gracious and a merciful God" (Ecclus 2:13); 3) for that *moral virtue* whereby man honors his parents and his country as the principles of his existence. It is in this sense that piety is defined by St. Thomas: "*Piety consists in a profession of charity for parents and country.*"[319] There are two acts proceeding from the virtue: *loyalty and reverence* toward parents and country as joint principles of our existence. Consequently, the basis and motive of piety is the close union existing between those united by blood or country.—Piety is a distinct virtue since it possesses its own object and motive, as is evident from previous remarks.

457. SINS opposed to piety are specifically distinct sins from those which offend against charity or justice. Therefore, they must be given distinct mention in confession;

---

[314] See CCL, Can. 729.
[315] See CCL, Can. 2392.
[316] See CCL, Can. 2371.
[317] See CCL, Can. 2327.
[318] See CCL, Can. 2324 and 2408.
[319] ST, II-II, q. 101, a. 3, rep. 1.

thus, for example, to strike one's own father and to strike another man are specifically distinct sins. Any offense contrary to piety between those who are *distantly related* to each other, such as hatred or blows, is an aggravating circumstance which does not change the moral species of the sin.

Piety *toward one's country* can be violated both by excess and by defect. Excess is shown in this virtue by those who cultivate excessive nationalism in word and deed with consequent injury to other nations; the virtue is violated by defect by those who boast that their attitude is cosmopolitan and adopt as their motto the old pagan saying: *ubi bene, ibi patria.*

NOTE. The virtue of piety is violated only when parents or children are injured in their *personal* possessions—for instance, in their body, honor, good name—but not in those goods which depend on chance; such sins are not so serious as similar ones committed against those who are not related, since goods which depend on chance are to some extent the common property of relatives.

REVERENCE

458. DEFINITION. *Reverence is the virtue which inclines man to show worship and honor for persons who enjoy some dignity.* There are three forms of reverence depending on three forms of dignity: *a) civil* reverence displayed toward civil dignitaries, such as the king or a commander or national hero; *b) religious* reverence due to ecclesiastical dignitaries, such as the pope, a bishop, or a priest; *c) supernatural* reverence reserved for the saints on account of their supernatural virtues *(dulia).* Reverence is a distinct virtue having its own specific object and motive; the acts which proceed from this virtue are *reverence* and *obedience.*

SINS contrary to reverence are disobedience and lack of reverence toward those deserving of reverence. Such sins are less serious than those against piety which is the source of a more compelling union and obligation.

OBEDIENCE

459. DEFINITION. *Obedience is the moral virtue which inclines the will to comply with the will of another who commands.* Such is the definition given by St. Thomas.[320] There are two types of obedience: *material* obedience, which is the mere physical fulfillment of a commanded act, and *formal* obedience, which consists in doing some act precisely *because it is commanded by a superior.*

The extent of obedience is as wide as the authority of the person commanding. Thus, obedience to God knows no limit, whereas obedience to men is limited *a)* by higher law which must not be transgressed by commands issued by superiors to their subjects, and *b)* by the limited competency of superiors.

Obedience is a noble virtue since it sacrifices to God a noble good, namely, the will of the individual.

[320] See ST, II-II, q. 104, a. 2.

460. SINS contrary to obedience are, *a)* by *excess*: servility or indiscriminate obedience, which is prepared to obey even in unlawful matters; *b)* by *defect*: disobedience, which is either *material*—the violation of any virtue—or *formal*—formal contempt for the command or for the person commanding. Formal contempt of the command is a grave sin which admits of slight matter, but formal contempt of the person commanding is always and in all circumstances a grave sin since it involves grave harm not only to the superior but also to God in Whose place the superior stands.

PIETY, REVERENCE, AND OBEDIENCE AS PRACTICED BY PARENTS, CHILDREN, AND OTHERS

461. 1. THE OBLIGATION OF CHILDREN TOWARD THEIR PARENTS. Children are bound to show *a)* love, *b)* reverence, *c)* obedience toward their parents. This threefold obligation is of its nature serious.

The *love* which is due must be both *affective* and *effective*.

Reverence must be evident in word, deed, and sign.

Obedience must be shown to parents in everything which is part of their care. It is difficult to determine what constitutes grave matter in the violation of due obedience. However, if the act of disobedience is the cause of notable harm to parents or to child, the sin is certainly grave. There are two limits to be placed to the obedience due to parents even in lawful matters: 1) one of *duration*, insofar as the duty ceases once the child after attaining his majority or emancipation begins to live away from the parental home; *b) in the choice of a state of life*, and therefore even minors are free to choose in this matter, and parents commit sin by compelling their children to embrace any particular state of life.

462. 2. DUTIES OF PARENTS TOWARD THEIR CHILDREN.

Parents are obliged to love their children and to provide for their physical and spiritual education.[321]

The *love* that they are bound to show must be both affective and effective so that parents must not only avoid all hatred and ill-will but also wish their children well, act well in their regard, and help them in their need.

The *physical education* of children requires that parents should sedulously protect their bodily welfare from the moment of their conception. Thus, a pregnant mother should avoid everything which threatens to harm the foetus; parents commit sin if they do not provide for their children sufficient food, clothing, shelter, or who neglect their medical care when they are ill, who do not trouble whether their children obtain a suitable state in life.

---

[321] "Parents are bound by a most serious obligation to provide for the religious and moral as well as the physical and civil education of their children and to care for their temporal welfare" (CCL, Can. 1113).

The *spiritual* education of children is most necessary as the means of fostering their eternal salvation. Thus, they must take especial care that their children are baptized without delay, that they grow accustomed to works of religion and piety not only by words of encouragement but more especially by the example of their parents, that they are sent to good schools.

463. DUTIES OF THE MARRIED.

There are certain duties which are *mutual* and others which are *peculiar* to husband or wife.

a) The following *obligations are mutual: i)* mutual love both affective and effective; *ii)* the rendering of the marriage debt; *iii)* life in common (mutual companionship).

b) The husband is obliged i) as head of the family to guide his wife, children, and servants; *ii)* to provide for his wife and family sufficient food, clothing, and maintenance; *iii)* to administer family property wisely.

c) The wife is obliged: i) to show due obedience to her husband; *ii)* to pay careful attention to the home and to the education of her children.

464. SCHOLIUM. THE EMANCIPATION OF WOMEN. Although this question does not fall within the province of the virtue of piety, however since it affects relationships between husband and wife, it may be useful to mention a few points which moral theologians ought to keep in mind regarding this question which is agitating the minds of men and States today.

1. So far as their souls, supernatural grace, and destiny are concerned, men and women are equal.

2. Although in general woman is weaker than man in her physical and intellectual powers, nevertheless there are many women who can do exactly the same work as men. Therefore, there is nothing in the work itself to prevent such works and duties being given to capable women, such as the office of doctor, teacher, and so on.

3. God created woman as man's helper and formed her from Adam's rib; furthermore, He has excluded her from the priesthood. All this would seem to indicate clearly that it was never God's intention for *complete* equality to exist between man and woman. Therefore, the radical emancipation of women and their complete equality with men seem to be alien to the Creator's intention.

4. A woman's chief duty is care for the home and therefore any form of emancipation which disrupts family life must be rejected.

5. So far as Catholicism is concerned, there is nothing to prevent (at least in itself) capable women from possessing *the right to vote* even in political matters. But it is an entirely different question whether any useful purpose is served either in respect of the State or Church by granting women the right to vote in any particular district.

465. 4. DUTIES OF MASTERS AND SERVANTS.

a) Masters and employers are obliged *i)* to treat their servants and employees with kindness; *ii)* to instruct and correct them and to induce them to fulfill their religious duties; *iii)* to pay them a just wage.

b) Servants and employees are bound to render to their masters and employers, *i)* due obedience, *ii)* due reverence, *iii)* faithful service.

466. 5. DUTIES OF TEACHERS AND PUPILS.

a) Teachers occupy the place of parents in matters relating to the spiritual education of children and therefore they have the same obligations in this matter as parents. Therefore, they are bound to provide by word and example suitable knowledge and good behavior for their pupils.

b) Pupils in their turn are bound to love, reverence, and obey their teachers in all matters relating to their studies and behavior.

467. 6. DUTIES OF RULERS AND THEIR SUBJECTS.

a) Rulers must strenuously pursue legal, distributive, and vindictive justice.

b) Their *subjects* are bound *i)* to show reverence, obedience, and loyalty toward their rulers; *ii)* to elect good representatives; *iii)* to pay just taxes; *iv)* in certain circumstances to render military service. Subjects must obey their rulers in all lawful matters in which their rulers have the right to command. It is always forbidden to rebel against a lawful ruler, even if he is a tyrant. However *passive resistance* is permitted in certain circumstances, when his demands are unjust. In itself it is a grave sin against legal justice to elect bad representatives for government, since the voters themselves must be held responsible in part for the harm caused to the State by such representatives. But there may be excusing causes which permit the choice of such persons. Thus, for instance, a worker would be justified in voting for a bad representative if otherwise he would lose his post and be unable to find another. It is also permitted to elect a bad representative in preference to one who is worse, which may frequently occur in so-called second ballots. The reason which permits a person to cast his vote for this evil candidate is that such a vote is no more than material cooperation in another's sin.

QUESTION III
VIRTUES RELATED TO JUSTICE: GRATITUDE, REVENGE, POLITENESS, GENEROSITY, EPIKEIA

Since enough has been said previously[322] regarding lies and other acts contrary to the virtue of *truth*, there is no necessity to devote a special treatise to this virtue *"which inclines man to display in his life and words the sort of man that he is."*[323] The following will suffice as a brief summary: three duties proceed from this noble

---

[322] See no. 261ff.
[323] ST, II-II, q. 109, a. 3, rep. 3.

virtue—1) the duty of loving truth in everything said or done; 2) the duty of preventing oneself from saying or signifying anything contrary to one's own mind; 3) the duty of revealing sincerely the judgment of the mind in words or in other signs, unless there is need to preserve a secret or conceal the truth.

GRATITUDE

468. DEFINITION. *Gratitude is the virtue which inclines man to acknowledge (mentally and in words) gifts received and to make at least some return for the gift.*

EXPLANATION. The duty of gratitude arises from the acceptance of a gift which represents a voluntary and useful payment freely made to a person through the feeling of benevolence. If the gift is given by a superior, e.g., by God or one's parents, the act of gratitude to which it gives rise belongs to other virtues also, such as religion, piety, and so on. Gratitude consists in an internal state—that is, in a grateful heart—rather than in any external effect, i.e., a real return for the gift. Therefore everyone, including the poor, is capable of gratitude.

There are three *duties of gratitude*: 1) to acknowledge the receipt of the gift; 2) to express gratitude in words, such as by praising the benefactor, by expressing thankfulness to him; 3) to make some return in deed for the gift, insofar as that is possible.

The *qualities* of gratitude. Gratitude must be: 1) *prompt*—that is to say, it must be shown as soon as possible after receiving the gift; 2) *internal* and not merely external—that is, it must proceed from the heart and not be expressed merely in words devoid of all feeling; 3) *humble*, with an acknowledgment that the gift is something useful; 4) *free from all covetousness*—that is to say, that gratitude must not be expressed with the principal purpose of receiving further gifts from the benefactor.

The *vice opposed to gratitude* is ingratitude which is either *formal* (contempt of the benefactor or his gift), or *material*—the omission of due thanks without any implication of contempt.

REVENGE

469. DEFINITION. *Revenge consists in inflicting punishment on a private person for the evil which he has voluntarily committed, in order to make reparation for the injury committed and obtain satisfaction for the injured party.*

Since man of his nature is only too ready to take revenge for injuries received, some virtue is necessary to prevent excess in this matter. Punishment inflicted by a superior for the good of society is an act of legal justice, not of revenge. If any private individual takes due vengeance in order to *correct* his brother who has sinned, this is an act of charity; if he does it in order to make reparation for the violated honor of God, it is an act of religion.—In practice, it is often advisable for a private individual to refrain from seeking or taking revenge because under the pretext of obtaining justice there may lurk excessive love of self or even hatred of the neighbor.

VICES CONTRARY to revenge are: 1) *by excess,* cruelty or savagery; 2) *by defect,* excessive laxity in punishment.

POLITENESS

470. DEFINITION. *Politeness* (courteousness, affability, friendliness) *is the virtue whereby each man in consequence of the duty of living in society conducts himself agreeably and fittingly in his companionship with others.*

The chief *acts of this virtue* are: 1) to be a courteous listener to all and to converse with them willingly and cheerfully; 2) to show signs of courtesy befitting each person's station and the custom of the country; 3) to have internal and external charity for one's neighbor and to subdue excessive love of self.

There are two VICES OPPOSED to politeness: one *by excess,* namely, *flattery,* which inclines man to display excessive and inordinate zeal in word and deed in pleasing another for the sake of obtaining some favor, the other *by defect,* namely, *quarrelling* or *peevishness,* which makes a man difficult in society, rarely agreeing with anyone, and frequently contradicting what is said by another with the intention of hurting him or at least of not pleasing him.

GENEROSITY

471. DEFINITION. *Generosity or liberality is the virtue which regulates love of money and makes man ready to distribute his money according to the dictates of right reason.*

Accordingly, the proximate and immediate object of this virtue is not the money itself but the *desire* for money which must be controlled. Therefore, even the poor without money can possess this virtue if they moderate their love of money in accordance with right reason.

There are two VICES OPPOSED to generosity: one by *excess,* namely, extravagance, which is found in the man who gives his money away unnecessarily and without reason; the other by *defect,* namely, avarice, about which we have already spoken, no. 173.

EPIKEIA

472. DEFINITION. *Epikeia or equity is the reasonable moderation of a strict right.* It may be an act of *legal justice,* when it consists in a benign interpretation not of the law itself but of the mind of the legislator. This form of equity has been discussed already in the section on law, no. 105. But it may also be the act of a *distinct virtue* which some authors prefer to call natural justice and which St. Cyprian describes as *justice tempered with the sweetness of mercy.*[324] This virtue of epikeia

---

[324] Hostiensis, *Summa Aurea,* bk. 5, "De Dispensationibus," no. 1.

is exercised, for instance, by a creditor who allows his debtor to postpone the payment of his debt. The violation of this virtue, since it imposes so slight an obligation, is a venial sin.

This virtue resides in the will and is nothing more than the exercise of the virtue of *gnome*, which is part of prudence, residing in the practical reason.

TREATISE XII
THE VIRTUE OF FORTITUDE
AND CONTRARY VICES

This treatise is divided into four chapters: 1) Definition of Fortitude; 2) Acts of Fortitude; 3) Integral and Potential Parts of Fortitude; 4) Vices Contrary to Fortitude.

DEFINITION OF FORTITUDE

473. DEFINITION. *Fortitude is that cardinal virtue which strengthens the irascible appetite (and will) enabling it to continue its pursuit of difficult good even in the face of the greatest dangers to bodily life.*

EXPLANATION. Fortitude *resides* in the irascible appetite to the extent that it is subject to the control of the will, since it strengthens this appetite to curb the passions of fear and recklessness easily and promptly at the approach of supreme danger.

The *matter* of fortitude includes those most severe dangers which ought to be withstood reasonably, namely, the expulsion of excessive fear and the curbing of excessive recklessness.

THE GIFT OF FORTITUDE goes further than the corresponding virtue inasmuch as it begets a firm confidence of riding all dangers.

ACTS OF FORTITUDE

There are two acts of fortitude: the suppression of fear and the curbing of recklessness. These acts reach their peak in martyrdom.

474. *Martyrdom is the endurance of death in witness to the truth of Christianity.* Therefore, three conditions must be verified for martyrdom: *a)* actual death; *b)* the infliction of death by an enemy out of hatred for Christianity; therefore, the following are precluded from genuine martyrdom: those who die by contracting disease in their care of lepers, those who suffer death in defense of natural truths or for heresy, those who commit suicide in order to safeguard their chastity; *c)* the voluntary acceptance of death.

The *effects* of martyrdom are: *a)* the remission of all sin and punishment, since martyrdom is an act of perfect charity; *b)* the martyr's aureole which is a privileged reward corresponding to this privileged victory.

THE INTEGRAL AND POTENTIAL PARTS OF FORTITUDE

475. Since fortitude is a most individual virtue it allows of no further species or subjective parts. But its potential and integral parts are four in number: magnanimity, munificence, patience, perseverance; these virtues are looked upon as integral parts of fortitude inasmuch as they help the latter to bring to perfection the acts mentioned in the preceding chapter; they are potential parts to the extent that they concern less difficult matters.

476. MAGNANIMITY *is a virtue inclining man to perform great works in every virtue—works deserving of high honors.*

The *object*, therefore, of this virtue is the due acquisition of high honors which cannot be obtained except through the exercise of difficult Christian virtues. To seek honors merely in order to obtain wealth or other material possessions is not a sign of magnanimity since such things are not truly great and are not of themselves deserving of honor.

Magnanimity is a distinct virtue in a true sense of the word since it has its own exalted object, in that it impels man to obtain great honors through noble deeds. It is in no way opposed to humility since these two virtues are founded on two different considerations: magnanimity tends toward great works insofar as they can be performed with the help of God's grace; humility considers man's own defects and leads him to despise himself and prefer others to himself.

The *characteristics of this virtue* are well portrayed by St. Thomas following the teaching of Aristotle:[325] the magnanimous man *a)* takes a restrained delight in even the greatest honors offered to him, *b)* remains unruffled both by prosperity and adversity, *c)* willingly helps others although he himself asks hardly anyone to help him, *d)* does not fawn upon important personages neither does he allow his liberty to be restricted by their authority, *e)* is not ambitious, *f)* expresses his opinions boldly when necessary for he has no fear of man, *g)* forgets injuries received, *h)* moves slowly in the external acts of his body.

477. MUNIFICENCE *is the virtue which moderates the love of money so that man is ready to incur great expense in necessary external works.*

Consequently, munificence differs from magnanimity as a species from the genus; magnanimity strives for greatness in every sphere and in all the virtues, munificence inspires a man to greatness *in the construction of external things.* The matter or object of this latter virtue is the incurring of heavy expenses for external works. Since this is something special and difficult, munificence is a distinct virtue to be practiced by rulers and the wealthy who are able to undertake such works. This virtue differs also from liberality inasmuch as the latter concerns itself with moderate sums of money, the former with large amounts.

---

[325] See Aristotle, *Nichomachean Ethics*, bk. 4; and ST, II-II, q. 129.

478. PATIENCE *is the virtue which inclines man to endure present evils so that he may not be unreasonably sorrowful.*

If patience is exercised to control sorrow at the approach of death, it is an *integral* part of fortitude; if the sorrow is caused by minor evils, patience then becomes a *potential* part of fortitude. Patience is indeed a necessary virtue and Christ Himself states: "It is by endurance that you will secure possession of your souls" (Lk 21:19).

The means to be used in the attainment of this virtue are: *a)* the careful consideration of God's patience in bearing with sinners, *b)* Christ's patience in life and in death, *c)* the patience of the saints in enduring all forms of evil, *d)* the results of patience which are satisfaction for past sins and eternal happiness, *e)* evils caused by impatience.

479. PERSEVERANCE *is the virtue which inclines man to continue in the exercise of the virtues in accordance with right reason notwithstanding the irksomeness which results from protracted action.*

It is true that every virtue is constant and sees its act through to the end, but perseverance supplies this constancy for a special motive, that is, for the moral goodness to be found in completing a work in spite of its attendant difficulties.

VICES CONTRARY TO FORTITUDE

480. There are three vices opposed to fortitude, four opposed to magnanimity, two opposed to munificence, two opposed to patience, and two opposed to perseverance.

1. Opposed to FORTITUDE are: *a)* cowardice or timidity, *b)* fearlessness, and *c)* recklessness.

a) Timidity is the inordinate fear of temporal ills and especially of death; it is an *excess of fear and a lack of daring.* That defect in daring is usually known as *cowardice.*

b) Fearlessness is a vice which lacks sufficient fear of danger.

c) Recklessness is a vice which leads a man to excess in meeting danger.

481. 2. Opposed to MAGNANIMITY are: *a)* presumption, *b)* ambition, *c)* vainglory, *d)* pusillanimity.

a) Presumption is a vice which urges man to undertake works exceeding his strength. Consequently, this vice is not to be confused with another form of presumption opposed to the theological virtue of hope, which trusts in obtaining eternal happiness through means not intended by God.

b) Ambition is a vice which gives man an inordinate longing for honor. Such an inordinate desire for honor very often has just the opposite effect to that desired, since it leads a man into derision and contempt.

c) Vainglory is an inordinate desire for vain glory; see what has been said already on this subject in no. 172.

d) Pusillanimity is a vice which inclines man to refuse to undertake or do some-thing as being too much for him and beyond his strength when in fact it is not.

482. 3. Opposed to MUNIFICENCE are: unreasonable expenditure and niggardliness.

a) Unreasonable expenditure is the vice which inclines man to incur expenses which are entirely unreasonable.

b) Niggardliness is the vice which inclines man to refuse unreasonably to incur great expenses even when necessary.

483. 4. Opposed to PATIENCE by defect is insensibility, by excess impatience.

a) Insensibility or lack of feeling is the vice which leaves a man unmoved by his own or other people's ills. This represents a lack of sorrow and an excess of en-durance and has the appearance of coarse brutality.

b) Impatience is the vice which inclines man to excessive sadness and draws him away from good because of his sadness or sorrow. Therefore, the man who is impatient suffers from an excess of sadness and lacks endurance.

484. 5. Opposed to PERSEVERANCE are two vices, one by defect, namely, *inconstancy*, the other by excess, namely, *pertinacity*.

a) Inconstancy is the vice which makes a man only too ready to cease from some work which he has begun because of the difficulties involved in its continuance. Inconstancy is a form of irresolution which finds itself unable to resist the diffi-culties that arise.

b) Pertinacity is the vice which inclines man to continue in some act beyond that which is reasonable.

TREATISE XIII
THE VIRTUE OF TEMPERANCE
AND CONTRARY VICES

This treatise is divided into four chapters: 1) The Nature of Temperance; 2) The Parts of Temperance in General; 3) The Subjective Parts of Temperance and Their Contrary Vices; 4) The Potential Parts of Temperance and Their Contrary Vices.

THE NATURE OF TEMPERANCE

485. DEFINITION. *Temperance is the virtue which regulates the sensitive appetite in the pleasures of touch, namely, in the pleasures of food and sex.*

EXPLANATION. It is customary to distinguish four forms of pleasure:

1. *purely spiritual* pleasure arising from intellectual activity and concerned with spiritual objects, such as the Beatific Vision, or the joy experienced in the posses-sion of theological knowledge;

2. pleasure which is *spiritual only in the wide sense* of the term inasmuch as it arises from intellectual activity regarding material objects, such as the pleasure of the miser in his money;

3. *sense pleasures* of the body arising from the sense perception of some pleasing object, such the pleasure resulting from hearing a pleasant melody, or the pleasure given to the eye by beautiful colors;

4. *carnal or sensual pleasures* caused by an intimate physical union of an object with the special nerves of the organs of taste and procreation, namely, the pleasures derived from food and sex.

Temperance may be understood *a)* in its *widest sense* to mean moderation in any action or passion; *b)* in its *wide sense* to mean moderation in spiritual and sense pleasures; *c)* in its *strict sense* to mean moderation in sensual or carnal pleasures, namely, in food and sexual matters.

The proximate *subject* of the virtue of temperance understood in its strict sense is the concupiscible appetite as subject to the reason and will of man.

The *object* of this virtue is moderation in the pleasures of touch, namely, in food and sex. Other sense and intellectual pleasures are regulated incidentally by temperance, insofar as they affect the pleasures which derive from food and sex.

Natural temperance acquired by natural effort and guided by natural reason alone has no other purpose in view than man's *health*, and therefore it differs specifically from supernatural temperance which is under the direction of *faith* and has as its chief effect man's spiritual welfare. Indeed, supernatural temperance sometimes advises fasting, virginity, and so on which are abhorrent to natural temperance.

THE PARTS OF TEMPERANCE IN GENERAL

486. 1. There are two *integral parts* of temperance: the sense of shame and a love of propriety *(honestas)*. The *sense of shame* is a fear of anything disgraceful; it is not a virtue in the strict sense of the word but rather a praiseworthy feeling which makes men blush as soon as anything shameful touches them. These two—the feeling of shame and the love of what is fitting—are vigilant *protectors* of chastity and temperance and therefore to be highly cherished from one's youngest days.

2. St. Thomas[326] gives four *subjective parts* of the virtue of temperance: *abstinence*, which is temperance in food; *sobriety*, which is temperance in drink—especially in the use of intoxicants; *chastity*, which is temperance in the chief pleasure of the sexual act; *purity*, which is concerned with the attendant circumstances of the act, such as the pleasure arising from kissing or touching, and so on.

3. The *potential parts* of temperance are: continence, meekness, clemency, modesty, which moderate man's appetite in things less difficult than the pleasures of touch. Included under modesty are humility and other virtues. We shall discuss these various parts of temperance later.

[326] See ST, II-II, q. 143, a. 1, c.

THE SUBJECTIVE PARTS OF TEMPERANCE AND THEIR CONTRARY VICES

INTRODUCTION. In this chapter we shall consider: 1) Abstinence and Fasting; 2) The Vice Opposed to Abstinence, Namely, Gluttony; 3) Sobriety and Its Contrary Vice; 4) Chastity and Virginity; 5) The Vice Opposed to Chastity, Namely, Impurity.

Art. 1. Abstinence and Fasting

§ 1. Definition and Obligation of Abstinence and Fasting

487. DEFINITION. *Abstinence is the moral virtue which inclines man to the moderate use of food as dictated by right reason (or by faith) for his own moral good.*

The acts which proceed from this virtue are fasting and abstinence strictly so-called, namely, from definite kinds of food, such as meat.

Fasting is either *a) complete*, i.e., total abstinence from all food and drink, such as precedes the reception of Holy Communion; or *b)* natural *(jejunium philosophicum)*, i.e., a partial abstinence from food and drink such as is demanded for reasons of health or for some other natural purpose; or *c) ecclesiastical* (or arbitrary), which is commanded by laws of the Church. It is this latter type of fasting which we intend to consider here.

488. *The essence of ecclesiastical fasting consists in taking only one full meal.* It was the common opinion amongst older authors that the essence of the ecclesiastical fast was composed of three elements: one full meal, a definite hour for taking this meal, and abstinence from certain foods such as flesh meat, eggs, and milk-foods. Today, the second and third conditions are no longer regarded essential to the ecclesiastical fast but simply add to its *perfection*. Therefore, even if flesh meat or eggs or milk-foods are taken the fast is not broken. If the essence of the fast did consist of these three elements taken together, then today fasting as such would have disappeared, which is certainly untrue. In these days the Church allows one full meal, an evening collation, and some food at breakfast.

489. THE FULL MEAL ON DAYS OF FASTING ONLY.

a) According to modern discipline the *hour* when this one full meal is taken is left to the choice of the individual, and therefore, he is free to interchange the times of the evening collation and the full meal.[327] However, this meal must have a moral *continuity* and not be *unduly protracted*, for if there is a notable interruption (e.g., an interruption of half an hour) it would develop into two distinct meals. Authors are sufficiently agreed that on fast days the meal cannot lawfully be extended beyond two hours.

---

[327] See CCL, Can. 1251, § 2.

490. *b)* The *quality* of the food to be taken was formerly laid down by law, but now on days of fasting *which are not also days of abstinence* any kind of food is allowed by general ecclesiastical law (although particular laws may determine otherwise); it is even permitted to eat both meat and fish at the same meal.[328]

491. THE EVENING COLLATION.

The *hour* of this evening meal is left to the choice of the individual. The *quantity* of food permitted nowadays is commonly put at eight ounces or about half a pound, and the food itself must not be exceedingly nutritious.

The *quality* of the food permitted at the evening meal is determined by custom and local law.

492. BREAKFAST.

There has now grown up the legitimate custom of taking in the morning a small amount of bread or other light food to the extent of two ounces.[329]

The Code of Canon Law expressly permits the taking of some food, morning and evening.[330]

493. DAYS OF FASTING. The days of fasting prescribed by common law are:

a) the days of Lent, except Sundays, until noon on Holy Saturday;[331]

b) Wednesday, Friday, and Saturday in the Ember Weeks;

c) the vigils of Pentecost, the Assumption, All Saints, and Christmas;

d) on the day previous to the consecration of a church, both the bishop and the people who ask for the church to be consecrated must fast. This is laid down in the Roman Pontifical.

494. SUBJECTS OF THE LAW OF FASTING are all baptized persons from the completion of their twenty-first year until the beginning of their sixtieth year.[332]

Although strictly speaking, Protestants and all baptized non-Catholics are obliged by the law of fasting inasmuch as they are subject to the laws of the Church, the Church does not seem to urge this obligation; consequently, these non-Catholics are not to be accused, generally speaking, of grave sin caused by the violation of the ecclesiastical fasts or abstinence.

495. NATURE OF THE OBLIGATION. 1. The law of fasting binds under pain of grave sin but admits of slight matter.

Thus, the following proposition was condemned by Alexander VII: "He who breaks a fast of the Church to which he is bound, does not sin mortally, unless

---

[328] Ibid.

[329] In England, two or three ounces of bread with a little butter may be taken by virtue of a papal indult (June, 1923).

[330] See CCL, Can. 1251.

[331] See CCL, Can. 1252.

[332] See CCL, Can. 1254.

he does this out of contempt and disobedience, e.g., because he does not wish to subject himself to a precept."[333] However, the precept does admit of parvity of matter which seems to exist when the quantity of extra food eaten does not amount to another full meal.

2. It is the common opinion that the precept of abstinence from flesh meat is a negative precept, whereas the law of fasting is an affirmative precept.

Therefore, anyone who eats meat several times on forbidden days commits as many mortal sins as the number of occasions on which the meat is eaten; on the other hand, a man who has broken his fast by taking two full meals, whether through his own fault or not, does not commit a new sin by taking a third or fourth meal—at least according to the common opinion.

496. SCHOLIUM. LIQUIDS. There is a common saying that drinks do not break the fast, but only those things are to be classified as liquids which normally *aid the digestion of food*: therefore, any drink which has a notable nutritive value cannot be regarded as a pure liquid, such as milk, chocolate made with milk. But wine, beer, coffee, and tea are all permissible. Sweets are not forbidden so long as they are taken in small quantity.

497. THE LAW OF ABSTINENCE FROM FLESH MEAT.

1. The law of abstinence forbids the eating of flesh meat and meal soup, but not of eggs, milk foods, and condiments made from animal fats.[334]

By *flesh meat* is meant *a)* the flesh of animals which live and breathe on land and possess warm blood; *b)* blood, lard, broth, suet, the marrow of bones, brains, kidneys. In case of doubt whether something is meat or not, one is permitted to eat it since the law does not bind when doubt exists.

Under *fish* are included all animals whose blood is cold, such as reptiles and amphibians; e.g., frogs, tortoises, oysters, crabs, lobsters, roe. In some regions at least even such animals as otters, beavers, and water-fowl are regarded as fish.

2. The law of abstinence must be observed on all Fridays throughout the year, except those which are holy days of obligation outside Lent.[335]

The law of abstinence and fasting binds on:[336]

a) Ash Wednesday;

b) Fridays and Saturdays of Lent;

c) Wednesdays, Fridays, and Saturdays in the Ember Weeks;

---

[333] DZ 1123.
[334] See CCL, Can. 1250.
[335] See CCL, Can. 1252, § 4.
[336] The law of fasting and abstinence was reduced to Ash Wednesday, Good Friday, and the vigils of the Assumption and Christmas; see Sacred Congregation of the Council, Jan. 28, 1949.

d) the four vigils of Pentecost, the Assumption, All Saints, and Christmas.[337] If these vigils fall on a Sunday the law of abstinence and fasting is dispensed and they are not to be anticipated.

3. All persons under seven years of age and those who have never come to the use of reason are excused from the law of abstinence from meat. The obligation to abstain binds under pain of grievous sin but it admits of slight matter—equal to the size of a *walnut*=about four grammes.

§ 2. Causes Excusing from Fasting and Abstinence

498. All causes which excuse from fasting and abstinence can be reduced to two: dispensation, and moral or physical impossibility.

a) A *dispensation* in the ecclesiastical law of fasting and abstinence can be granted by the pope for the universal Church; local Ordinaries can dispense the *entire diocese* or any part of it for the special reason of a great gathering of people or for reasons of public health. Not only bishops but also parish priests can *in individual cases* and for a just cause dispense their subjects severally and individual families (and that even outside their territory) and also strangers within their territory.

Superiors in a clerical exempt order can dispense all their subjects in the same way as a parish priest can dispense his parishioners.[338] By common law confessors have no power to dispense but provided they are lawfully delegated they can dispense in the law of fasting and abstinence even outside the confessional, unless this is expressly forbidden.—All who possess prudent judgment, such as superiors of nuns, priests, or in fact anyone at all, can *state* in a particular case that the law of fasting and abstinence does not bind owing to grave obstacles.

b) Impossibility exempts from the law whenever there would result considerable harm from the observance of the law of fasting or abstinence.

Thus, exemption extends to the sick and the convalescent, to the poor who lack sufficient food, those engaged on heavy work incompatible with fasting. Generally speaking, reasons are more easily found for the law of fasting than for the law of abstinence rendering it incapable of observance. Consequently, persons of sixty years of age are excused from fasting, but are not normally excused from abstaining from flesh meat. Similarly, the law of fasting ceases to bind those who must undertake heavy and tiring mental work, such as students who apply themselves to their studies earnestly, confessors who sit for six or eight hours in the confessional with consequent fatigue.

499. NOTE. 1. A confessor should not be excessively rigorous in granting dispensations from fasting since in these days there are not so many of the faithful who can keep the fast perfectly for one reason or another, e.g., shortage of food, feeble health,

---

[337] See CCL, Can. 1252, § 1–2.
[338] See CCL, Can. 1245.

strenuous work. However, the faithful should be encouraged to undertake special works of mortification or spirituality during times of fasting.

2. Anyone who avails himself of a dispensation granted by mandate of the bishop is *bound* to recite the prescribed prayer or give the prescribed alms; however, the obligation is not *grave* since the dispensation was granted unconditionally, and the bishop is not presumed to impose a grave obligation unless he expressly says so.

Art. 2. The Vice Contrary to the Virtue of Abstinence—Gluttony

500. DEFINITION. *Gluttony is the inordinate indulgence in food or drink.* This lack of moderation may be due to eating or drinking too soon, too expensively, too much, voraciously, or too daintily.

Moral evil of gluttony. Since gluttony consists in an excessive use of something in itself perfectly lawful, it is of its nature a venial sin; but for incidental reasons it may become grievously sinful, e.g., because of ensuing scandal or other evil effects.

The effects of gluttony are given by St. Thomas[339] as five: unreasonable hilarity, loquacity, dullness of mind, buffoonery, uncleanness.

Art. 3. Sobriety and Its Contrary Vice—Drunkenness

501. SOBRIETY *is the virtue regulating man's desire for and his use of intoxicating drink.* It is a distinct virtue since it has its own object which is most necessary for an upright moral life, namely, the moderate use of alcoholic drink. The need for this virtue becomes even more evident from the consideration of its contrary vice, drunkenness.

502. DRUNKENNESS *is a deliberate excess in the use of intoxicating drink or drugs to the point of forcibly depriving oneself of the use of reason for the sake of gratifying an inordinate desire for such drink and not for the sake of promoting health.*

EXPLANATION. 1. *A deliberate excess in the use of such drinks or drugs,* for if it is not voluntary, it is not a human act; there must also be an *excessive use* of the drink or drug which is harmful to health. God intended drink to minister to bodily health and therefore a man commits sin by using it to such an excess as to cause harm to his health and to deprive himself of the use of his reason. This excess may be practiced not merely in the use of intoxicating drinks but also in the use of other things with similar effects. Therefore, the excessive use of morphia, or opium, and so on, to the point of forcibly depriving oneself of the use of reason is included under the sin of drunkenness.

2. *To the point of forcibly depriving man of the use of his reason.* If one does not forcibly deprive oneself of the use of reason, the sin of drunkenness is not committed. Thus, natural sleep deprives man of the use of reason in a natural manner. The signs of perfect intoxication are: acts totally contrary to normal behavior,

---

[339] See ST, II-II, q. 148, a. 6.

incapability of distinguishing between good and evil, forgetfulness on the morrow of everything done in the state of drunkenness, and so on.

3. *For the sake of gratifying man's inordinate desire for alcoholic drink.* It is not necessary that the drink be taken with great satisfaction, so that a man who drinks to excess when he is goaded by others commits the sin of drunkenness; all that is required is that the drink or drug is not intended for the restoration of health. Thus, for example, anyone who drinks large quantities of Cognac in order to avoid typhoid fever which is already imminent does not commit the sin of drunkenness, even though he may lose the use of his reason for a while.

503. THE MORAL EVIL OF DRUNKENNESS. 1. *Complete drunkenness is a grave sin which admits of slight matter.*

This is the most common opinion today. The reason given is that it is seriously contrary to right reason, *a)* for a man to deprive himself knowingly and willingly of the use of his reason for the sake of gratifying his desire for intoxicants for no sufficient reasons of health; *b)* for a man to expose himself to a grave danger of sin through his manner of acting; *c)* for a man to expose himself to many other dangers as the result of drunkenness, such as ill-health, domestic troubles, damage to his property.

2. *Any state short of complete drunkenness is of itself venially sinful.*

If there is a sufficient cause, such as the desire to rid oneself of the feeling of depression, there is no sin provided that it does not give rise to scandal or to other evils.

NOTE. A man is responsible for the sins committed in a state of complete intoxication to the extent that he could and ought to have foreseen them.

504. THE USE OF MORPHIA AND OTHER REMEDIAL DRUGS. It is not permissible to use such remedies unless there exists sufficient reason conducive to bodily health. Unless such remedies are used with great care, they can cause grave harm to one's health and very often they lead to evil moral effects, as is evident in those addicted to the use of morphia.

Art. 4. Chastity and Virginity

505. DEFINITIONS. 1. *Chastity is the virtue which moderates the desire for venereal pleasure in accordance with the dictates of right reason.* Whereas the chastity of married persons moderates the desire, the chastity of widows and virgins excludes the desire entirely. *Modesty is a special aspect of chastity,* for it concerns itself with external behavior, such as suggestive looks, words, touches, and so on.

Chastity is a distinct virtue since it has its own object — and a difficult one at that — namely, the moderation of venereal pleasure.

506. 2. *Virginity is a firm resolution of abstaining from all venereal pleasure made by one who has never been a partner to the sexual act.*

Virginity is sometimes understood as referring to bodily integrity which is lost in men by voluntary pollution, in women by the lustful rupture of the virginal hymen or vagina; sometimes the word is used for the state of celibacy. But insofar as virginity is a distinct moral virtue, bodily integrity is only accidental to it. Therefore, if a person loses this integrity through a surgical operation or by involuntary attack, the virtue of virginity remains intact, unless the act is accompanied by voluntary and lustful pollution. For the virtue of virginity in its proper sense, voluntary integrity is insufficient; otherwise, we must assert that all young persons living chaste lives, even though they intend to enter upon marriage at the proper time, possess the virtue of virginity as distinct from the virtue of chastity, which seems unlikely to be true. Therefore, it is the teaching of theologians that there is also required a *firm resolve* of preserving chastity always through reverence for God, since the virginity of the Vestal virgins and of others for non-religious motives is not a distinct virtue. According to St. Thomas[340] and other theologians, virginity is not to be considered a distinct virtue unless confirmed *by vow*.

THE EXCELLENCE of the state and virtue of virginity is extolled in Sacred Scripture (see 1 Cor 7:25ff; and Apoc 14:4), by the Fathers of the Church, and by reason herself. For virgins refrain from all venereal pleasure with the express intention of devoting themselves more freely and perfectly to the service of God, which is not only lawful but exceedingly praiseworthy. The objections raised against virginity on the grounds that it is unnatural and injurious to bodily health are of no value.

Art. 5. The Vice Contrary to Chastity — Impurity

This article is divided into five paragraphs: 1) Impurity in General; 2) Internal Sins of Impurity; 3) Unconsummated Sins of Impurity; 4) Natural Consummated Sins of Impurity; 5) Unnatural Consummated Sins of Impurity.

§ 1. Impurity in General

507. DEFINITION. *Impurity is an inordinate desire for venereal pleasure.* Venereal pleasure arises from the movement of those organs and secretions which aid the act of procreation, and reaches its summit in a healthy man in the pleasure accompanying the emission of seed, or, in women and youths below the age of puberty, in the diffusion of some secretion from the sexual glands.

PRINCIPLE. *Directly voluntary sexual pleasure outside marriage is grievously sinful and never admits of slight matter; indirectly voluntary sexual pleasure may be either a mortal or venial sin or no sin at all.*

The first part of this principle is admitted by everyone, since all venereal pleasure is in some way related to the act of procreation which for the highest reasons has been forbidden by God outside the state of marriage. Accordingly, He has issued a grave prohibition against any form of venereal pleasure that is directly voluntary, and not merely the highest pleasure accompanying the act of pollution. And indeed, anyone who directly wills even the slightest degree of

---

[340] See ST, II-II, q. 152, a. 3, rep. 4.

venereal pleasure is in proximate danger of proceeding further, and it is always grievously sinful to expose oneself without sufficient reason to the proximate danger of falling into sin.

The second part of the principle follows from what has been said already regarding acts that are indirectly voluntary. Venereal pleasure that is voluntary in its cause implies that the pleasure is not sought in itself but is the accompaniment of some other action performed by the agent; for instance, a young person reading a book may foresee that sexual pleasure will be caused by such reading. In this form of pleasure there is not always present a proximate danger of consenting to the complete act, and thus it is not always grievously sinful. — To judge in practice whether venereal pleasure that is voluntary in its cause is grievously sinful or not, one must consider to what extent the action tends *of its very nature* toward producing such pleasure and whether there exists a proportionately grave reason for doing the act. Practical examples will be considered below when discussing looks, touches, and so on.

§ 2. Internal Sins of Impurity

There are three internal sins of impurity: taking pleasure in immodest imaginations, taking pleasure in previous sins of impurity, unchaste desires.

508. 1. *Taking pleasure in imaginative representations* of impure actions is grievously sinful since it represents a deliberate desire for the impure action itself, even though this is not performed externally. Unless these impure thoughts are accompanied by evil desires they receive their specific character from the object alone, not from the circumstances. At least this is the opinion to be followed in practice. Therefore, it is quite sufficient for the penitent to accuse himself of taking pleasure in so many impure thoughts, without giving an accurate description of the objects of such thoughts.

509. 2. *Deliberate complacency in previous sins of impurity*, such as an act of adultery, receives its specific character both from the object *and* from the differentiating circumstances of the sinful object; consequently, it would not be sufficient for the penitent to accuse himself of taking pleasure in previous sinful acts of impurity; he must state what those acts were. Such complacency manifests approval of the previous act and thus possesses the same specific morality as the act itself.

510. 3. *Unchaste desires* are acts of complacency in the performance of some future sinful act of impurity. They are of two types: *efficacious* desires present in one who genuinely intends to commit the evil contemplated; *inefficacious* desires which represent a mere wish to do the act. Such desires receive their specific sinfulness both from their object *and* the differentiating circumstances of the object; therefore, in the confessional the penitent should state the object of his evil desires, at least if this is morally possible.

§ 3. Unconsummated External Sins of Impurity

Unconsummated sins of impurity are those which fall short of the full sexual act; they include *a)* sexual motions, and *b)* acts of immodesty.

511. *a) Sexual* or venereal *motions* are disturbances of the genital organs and the fluids in these organs; they are usually accompanied by some slight external *distillation*.

Moral nature of such motions. 1) If they are directly willed, they are grievously sinful since they are a form of venereal pleasure directly willed. 2) If they are completely involuntary, no sin is committed. 3) If they are voluntary in their cause, their sinfulness must be judged from the principles governing acts that are indirectly voluntary.—Such sexual movements are generally controlled easily and effectively if their cause is removed, so far as that is possible, and the mind turns to other matters.

512. *b) External acts of immodesty* are those which normally have some close connection with or some influence on sexual pleasure, such as immodest looks, touches, and so on.

Such acts are not immodest in themselves and therefore are permissible for a sufficient and reasonable cause, such as when they are performed by doctors or midwives, and so on. But it follows with certainty from what has been said previously that such acts are evil when done for the sake of exciting sexual pleasure. However, the further question arises whether such acts are sinful when performed not for the sake of exciting unlawful pleasure nor for any just reason but solely from curiosity, or playfulness, and so on.

Moral theologians usually distinguish between those parts of the body which are *becoming* and which are exposed to the sight of all, such as the face and hands; parts of the body which are *less becoming* and usually covered by clothing, such as the breast and arms; and those parts of the body which are *indecent*, namely, the organs of generation and adjacent parts.

513. GENERAL RULE. *All acts of immodesty which are done without sufficient reason and with evil intent are sinful to the extent that they cause a proximate danger of venereal pleasure.*

The gravity of this danger must be determined *a)* from the nature of the act, *b)* from the disposition of the agent.—The following points should be borne in mind regarding particular types of acts:

514. 1. Normal KISSING which follows the custom of the country is lawful; abnormal or ardent kissing usually gives rise to grave danger of sexual pleasure and is therefore gravely unlawful.

515. 2. TOUCHING the *indecent* parts of another adult for an evil purpose and without necessity is gravely forbidden; *casually* touching the same parts of one's own body or the less becoming parts of another's body would seem to be venially sinful, since the danger of unlawful venereal pleasure is not grave—at least in normal circumstances. If these touches are inspired by an evil intention, then these acts

are impure and therefore grievously sinful.—Touching animals indecently must be judged according to the intention and disposition of the agent.

The immodest touching of another is determined in its moral aspect by the character of the person who is touched immodestly with the evil intention of incest, or of adultery, and so on; this is not true of immodest looks, unless accompanied by the evil desire of touching the person.

516. 3. LOOKS are less likely to cause danger of venereal pleasure than touching. Nevertheless, to look at the indecent parts of an adult of the opposite sex with evil intent is grievously sinful. One can be less severe in one's judgment of looking at statues or pictures of the nude, since artificial things do not usually excite a person so much as natural objects. However, it is self-evident that even such looks can often give rise to severe temptations and therefore are to be avoided unless there exists sufficient reason. It does not seem grievously sinful to look at the indecent parts of oneself or at those of a person of the same sex without sufficient reason, provided there is no impure desire.

517. 4. IMMODEST CONVERSATION regarding obscene matters with the intention of exciting to lust or with the danger of grave scandal is grievously sinful. However, it is often difficult to decide whether such bad conversation is grievously sinful or not, since the danger of sexual pleasure arising depends so much on the varied circumstances both of the speaker and of his audience.—The same applies to reading bad books, attending the theatre or opera, and so on.

SCHOLIUM. FAMILIARITY BETWEEN PERSONS OF DIFFERENT SEX. Such behavior is common between persons contemplating marriage and is frequently the source of sexual pleasure. The confessor should keep the following general rules before him.

1. If sexual pleasure is intended, such behavior is grievously sinful and therefore to be forbidden. This is clear from what has been said already.

2. If venereal pleasure is not merely not intended but also strenuously avoided, mutual signs of affection are permissible, such as kissing, embracing, words of affection, and so on.

3. If this familiar behavior is occasionally but not always a proximate occasion of sin, it should not be forbidden immediately under pain of denying absolution, but the confessor should first inquire whether such acts are morally necessary. In these circumstances the confessor should warn the penitent to refrain from anything which is the proximate cause of lust and to take the necessary precautions. If such behavior which gives rise to occasional sin is neither necessary nor really useful, the confessor should strictly forbid it.

§ 4. Natural Consummated Sins of Impurity

It is normal to list six natural consummated sins of impurity: fornication, rape, abduction, incest, adultery, sacrilege.

518. 1. *Fornication is voluntary sexual intercourse between an unmarried man and woman who is no longer virgo intacta.* The act is intrinsically evil, as is evident from the proposition condemned by Innocent XI: "Thus it seems clear that fornication by its nature involves no malice, and that it is evil only because it is forbidden, so that the contrary seems entirely in disagreement with reason."[341] The internal reason for the sinfulness of fornication is that of itself it causes grave injury to the welfare of the child and to the welfare of society, notwithstanding that sometimes for accidental reasons such injuries do not arise.

Under fornication are included concubinage and prostitution as adding aggravating circumstances to the sin.

519. 2. *Rape* is understood in three different senses: 1) for the unlawful ravishing of a virgin *with her consent*; 2) for the ravishing of a virgin *contrary to her will*; 3) for the complete sexual act with any woman *contrary to her will*. It is in this latter sense that the word is used in civil codes of law.

Rape understood in its first meaning is an aggravating circumstance added to the sin of fornication but ordinarily speaking it does not involve the commission of an additional mortal sin which must be mentioned in confession, as was the opinion of former theologians. Rape understood in the second and third meanings of the word listed above includes in addition to the evil of fornication a grievous sin of injustice, since it is an act of unjust violence.

520. 3. *Abduction is the forcible removal of a person for the purpose of committing a sin against chastity.* Abduction is a grave sin both against justice (because of the unjust force used) and against chastity. Those who commit this act are punished both by civil and by canonical law.[342]

521. 4. *Incest is sexual intercourse between persons related to each other who are unable to enter into marriage.* There are four ways in which persons may be related to each other: relationship by blood, spiritual relationship, legal relationship, affinity. Incest committed between persons related to each other in the first or second degrees involves the commission of two grave sins, both of which must be confessed: one against chastity, another against piety. Incest committed between persons related to each other in more distant degrees adds an aggravating circumstance.

522. 5. *Carnal sacrilege is the violation of a sacred person, place, or thing by an act contrary to chastity.*

Sufficient explanation has been given already of personal sacrilege, local sacrilege, and real sacrilege.[343] An example of real sacrilege committed by an unchaste act

---

[341] DZ 1198.
[342] See CCL, Can. 2353–2354.
[343] See no. 446ff.

is solicitation in the confessional. Carnal sacrilege is grievously sinful on two counts; it is a serious sin against chastity and a serious sin against religion.

523. 6. *Adultery is sexual intercourse between two persons at least one of whom is married.* Two serious sins are committed—one against chastity and the other against justice, since the adulterer seriously injures the right of his spouse. The specific sinfulness of adultery is to be found also in the acts of a married person who touches another immodestly, who acts unnaturally with that person, or who has evil desires toward that person.

§ 5. Unnatural Consummated Sins of Impurity

The unnatural consummated sins against purity are: pollution, sodomy, and bestiality. These are regarded as unnatural acts since they are contrary to the natural purpose of the sexual act, namely, the procreation of children. Therefore, as sins of impurity they are more serious than others.

524. 1. *Sexual pollution* (also termed by doctors onanism, masturbation—*manu stupratio*) *is the emission of seed or its equivalent outside sexual intercourse.*

We say—the emission of seed or its equivalent. Pollution strictly so-called is to be found only in men who have reached the age of puberty, since these alone are capable of secreting seed in the proper sense of the word. But in its wider meaning pollution is a word applied to the emission of what is equivalent to seed, i.e., the emission of any fluid which is accompanied by venereal pleasure and which may occur in women, eunuchs, or those who have not yet reached the age of puberty.—The moral evil of either form of pollution seems almost the same. However, in pollution strictly so-called there is the additional evil of a useless emission of seed contrary to the natural order.

a) *Pollution which is directly willed is always grievously sinful.* Why? Because it is the direct willing of sexual pleasure. The way in which it is procured has little bearing on its moral character, provided that there is no desire for sodomy, bestiality, cooperation, or any other means which is of its nature forbidden.

b) *The sinfulness of pollution which is voluntary in its cause must be judged according to the principles which apply to acts that are indirectly voluntary.* Therefore, one has to consider 1) whether the action resulting in pollution is in itself morally good, such as washing, swimming, riding; 2) whether the purpose of this action is morally good; 3) whether there is sufficient reason for performing the action.

c) *Pollution which occurs during sleep is not sinful unless it is willed in some way.* In practice, men of upright life need not be disturbed by these nocturnal emissions, even if they occur when they are half-awake.

SCHOLIUM. REMEDIES FOR POLLUTION. It is evident from experience that the sin of pollution is widespread amongst young persons of both sexes and cannot be easily checked. It is of supreme importance that the confessor save from despondency anyone who habitually falls into this sin; he must be encouraged to persevere in the firm conviction that victory is possible and to remain faithful to all the means suggested by the confessor. Such remedies are *a*) supernatural and moral; *b*) natural and hygienic.

a) The *supernatural and moral* remedies are frequent reception of the Sacraments, daily exercises of piety, avoidance of the occasions of sin and idleness, horror and loathing of this vice.

b) *Natural and hygienic* remedies are: bodily exercise causing moderate physical fatigue, cold baths, a hard bed which is not too warm, sleep on one's right side with the hands resting on the breast, prompt rising in the morning at the stated hour, the avoidance of any food or drink which is too rich or stimulating, the use of medicines which quieten the nerves. If pollution is frequent as the result of bodily unhealthiness, a doctor should be consulted who is known to be a man of upright conscience.

525. 2. *Sodomy* (sometimes called paederasty or the unnatural vice) *is unnatural carnal intercourse between a male and another person* (*immissio penis in vas posterum alterius personae*). If this other person is a male, sodomy is said to be *perfect*; if the person is a female, it is *imperfect* sodomy. Sodomy is a sin which cries to Heaven for vengeance; see the following section on sexual perversion.

526. 3. *Bestiality is sexual intercourse with an animal*. It is the most grievous of all the sins against chastity. The sin is not committed if, while touching an animal, pollution takes place without performing or willing the full sexual act.

SCHOLIUM. SEXUAL PERVERSION. In practice, the confessor should acquaint himself with the teaching of recent authors on sexual perversion which consists in unnatural acts against chastity and easily becomes almost a pathological condition which is not easily remedied. The more important forms of sexual perversion are:

a) *sadism* (so called from the pervert Count de Sade), which consists in the infliction of cruelty on another in order to excite in oneself venereal pleasure; it may consist in striking, wounding, or killing another, and so on;

b) *masochism* (so called from the seductive novelist Sacher-Masoch), which is the voluntary infliction of cruelty on oneself by another in order to arouse sexual pleasure; for instance, a woman may ask another to beat her so that her sex passions may be aroused;

c) *fetishism* (from the Spanish word *feitico*), which consists in the lustful affection for some thing, such as exciting sexual pleasure by touching a woman's dress, or shoes, or hair. This form of perversion is frequently a pathological state;

d) homosexuality, which is a strong sexual inclination toward persons of the same sex, namely, the attraction of one man for another, or one female for another. Such perversion when existing in females used to be called the lesbian vice, or sapphism, or tribadism.

In some instances, sexual perversion seems almost innate, in others it is acquired by acts of gross impurity, in others it is the cause of a genuine pathological condition. However, it is most rare that such perversion completely disturbs the balance of the mind, and thus the agent must be regarded as responsible for the consequent acts of impurity. The confessor must show great patience and prudence in the guidance of such persons if they desire to escape from their evil habit.

THE POTENTIAL PARTS OF TEMPERANCE

527. 1. *Continence* is a disposition of the will inclining it to resist evil desires concerned with touch. It affords valuable assistance to the virtue of temperance.

2. *Meekness* is the moral virtue which moderates anger in accord with right reason. Humility and fortitude are extremely useful for acquiring meekness.

3. *Clemency* is a moral virtue inclining superiors to moderate or even to remit due punishment insofar as this is reasonable. The contrary vice is *cruelty* which demands and inflicts excessive punishment.

4. *Modesty* is the virtue which moderates all the internal and external movements and appearance of a person within the bounds and limits proper to his state in life, intellectual ability, and wealth. There are four virtues included under modesty: humility, studiousness, modesty in external behavior, modesty in dress.

a) Humility is the virtue which curbs man's inordinate desire for personal excellence and inclines him to recognize his own worth in its true light. Consequently, this virtue has two functions: 1) to restrain the inordinate desire for personal excellence; 2) to subject man to God by the recognition that all the good he possesses comes from his Creator. This second function of humility is its chief, although not always sufficiently recognized as such by ascetical writers.—Humility is a most necessary virtue since it removes the poison of pride which obstructs the effectiveness of divine grace.

Its contraries are inordinate self-depreciation by *excess* and pride by *defect*.

b) Studiousness is the virtue which moderates the desire and pursuit of truth in accordance with the principles of right reason. Its contrary vices are *curiosity*, which is an excessive desire for knowledge, and *negligence*, which is the voluntary omission of knowledge essential to one's state and condition in life.

c) Modesty in external behavior is the virtue inclining man to observe reasonable decorum in externals, which include: 1) his bodily movements, 2) recreation, 3) dress and adornments.

Modesty in bodily behavior is most essential for the preservation of pleasant intercourse amongst men, and thus St. Augustine in his Rule for the servants of God gives the following advice: "In all your movements let nothing be evident which would offend the eyes of another." Modesty in recreation or the right use of recreation is called *eutrapely.* Modesty in dress and bodily adornments inclines a person to avoid not merely everything that is offensive and insufficient but also everything unnecessary. By excess, the virtue is violated especially by women through excessive or even indecent adornment. Women who are gravely indecent in dress or make-up should be turned away from receiving Holy Communion, but in this matter careful consideration must be given to local custom and great prudence must be exercised.

PART TWO

The Sacraments in General and in Particular

TREATISE I
THE SACRAMENTS IN GENERAL

"Since all the Sacraments of the New Law instituted by Christ our Lord are the principal means of sanctification and salvation, the greatest care and reverence should be observed in administering and receiving them fittingly and in accord with the prescribed rites."[344]

This treatise on the Sacraments in general is divided into six chapters: 1) Nature and Existence of the Sacraments; 2) Their Number and Kinds; 3) Their Efficacy and Effects; 4) The Institution of the Sacraments; 5) Minister of the Sacraments; 6) The Recipient of the Sacraments.—In an appendix at the end of this treatise we shall consider the sacramentals.

NATURE AND EXISTENCE OF THE SACRAMENTS

528. DEFINITION. "*A Sacrament is a sensible sign instituted by God to signify and cause justification and sanctification.*"[345] This definition is applicable only to the Sacraments of the New Law, for which three things are necessary: 1) an external sign, 2) productive of interior grace, 3) instituted by Christ.

The external sensible SIGN in the Sacraments is composed of two elements—the matter and the form. The *matter* of the Sacraments is either things or actions; the *form* is the words which give a precise significance and efficacy to the things or actions used. The matter and form compose the essence of each Sacrament, as stated by the Council of Trent.[346]

The matter of the Sacraments is either remote or proximate; the concrete thing used in the Sacraments, such as water in Baptism, chrism in Confirmation, is called the *remote* matter; the actual application of this sensible thing or remote matter, such as the washing with water in Baptism, is called the *proximate* matter.

529. CONDITIONS REGARDING THE MATTER AND THE FORM.

1. The matter and the form are absolutely *essential* to the validity of the Sacraments and they cannot be changed even accidentally without grave reason; any *substantial* change of either would render the entire Sacrament invalid. There is considered to be substantial change if in the ordinary and prudent estimation of men the matter has become a different thing from that instituted by Christ or the form has assumed an entirely different sense.

2. The matter and the form must be morally united *at one and the same time*. For just as in physical substances the matter and the form together constitute one body, so it is essential for a similar *moral* union to exist at the same time between

---

[344] CCL, Can. 731, § 1.
[345] Cf. TCCI 7:173.
[346] See Session 14, "Doctrine on the Sacrament of Penance," chap. 2. See also TCCI 7:180.

the matter and form in order to constitute one Sacrament. Thus, for instance, Baptism is invalid if after pouring the water some interval is allowed to intervene before pronouncing the words of the form.

3. Since the validity of the Sacrament depends on the matter and the form, the minister must be *certain* of their existence. Therefore, it is not permissible to follow any opinion regarding them which is no more than probable, and outside the case of urgent necessity it is grievously sinful to use matter or form which is not certainly valid.

4. Ordinarily speaking, the matter and the form must be applied *by one and the same minister*. There are some exceptions, as, for example, in the Sacrament of Penance where the penitent supplies the proximate matter and the priest pronounces the form.

5. If doubts arise, the matter and form must be repeated in order that the Sacrament be certainly valid.[347] If it proves impossible to decide whether everything essential for the Sacrament is present or not, the form should be used *conditionally*. In such cases, the general rule to be followed is this: *it is always permissible to confer the Sacrament conditionally when there is the danger of the Sacrament being invalid if it is administered absolutely, or when a person would be deprived of great good or eternal salvation imperiled if the Sacraments were denied unconditionally.* Thus, for instance, it is lawful to grant conditional absolution to a dying person who is unconscious when there is grave doubt concerning his previous life and present dispositions. Infants who have been abandoned by parents and found must be baptized conditionally, unless, after diligent inquiry, it is known for certain that they have been baptized.[348]

530. EXISTENCE OF THE SACRAMENTS. In the Old Law there were to be found four types of Sacraments which signified grace through faith in Christ Who was to come: 1) circumcision; 2) various forms of purification; 3) eating the paschal lamb; 4) consecration of Levites and priests. The Councils of Florence and of Trent have defined the existence of Sacraments in the New Testament which not only signify but also cause grace.

NUMBER AND KINDS OF THE SACRAMENTS

531. NUMBER. It is defined that there exist seven Sacraments in the New Testament: Baptism, Confirmation, Eucharist, Penance, Extreme Unction, Orders, Matrimony.[349]

532. KINDS.

1. By reason of their *necessity* there are certain Sacraments which are *necessary for each and every individual* (the first five Sacraments), while others are necessary only for *Christian society* as a whole (the two final Sacraments).

---

[347] See CCL, Can. 732, § 2.
[348] See CCL, Can. 749.
[349] See Council of Florence, Session 8, "Bull of Union with the Armenians"; Council of Trent, Session 7, "On the Sacraments in General," Can. 1; TCCI 7:182, 244.

2. By reason of their *subject*, Sacraments are either Sacraments of the *living* or Sacraments of the *dead*. The former can be received only by those who are spiritually alive, i.e., by those who are in the state of sanctifying grace; these are Confirmation, Eucharist, Extreme Unction, Orders, Matrimony. The Sacraments of the dead are those which were *specifically* instituted to confer spiritual life, namely, sanctifying grace, on those who are spiritually dead (sinners). It may happen that *accidentally* the Sacraments of the dead do not confer but intensify grace when the recipient is already in the state of grace; similarly, the Sacraments of the living may accidentally confer grace without increasing it, when the recipient approaches the Sacrament in a state of inculpable ignorance regarding grievous sin.

3. By reason of their *effect*, Sacraments are divided into those which imprint a *character* (Baptism, Confirmation, Orders) and those which do not. The former cannot be repeated, whereas the latter may be.

4. By reason of the *dispositions of the subject*, Sacraments are either *fruitful* if they produce all the effects proper to them, or *unfruitful* if they confer no grace due to an obstacle interposed by the recipient. A Sacrament which is unfruitful must not be confused with one that is invalid and lacks something essential. If the recipient was aware of the obstacle which rendered the Sacrament unfruitful, then his action is also *sacrilegious*, but not otherwise. A Sacrament received sacrilegiously is known as *formally* unfruitful; where the Sacrament is received without knowledge of the obstacle it is said to be *materially* unfruitful.

THE EFFICACY AND EFFECTS
OF THE SACRAMENTS

533. 1. EFFICACY. All the Sacraments of the New Law produce their grace by reason of the sacred rite itself (*ex opere operato*). This is defined by the Council of Trent.[350]

The expression *ex opere operato* which is frequently used in this context means that the effects of the Sacrament follow from the actual valid administration of the Sacrament, provided that the recipient interposes no obstacle. Therefore, the Sacraments do not produce their grace *ex opere operantis*, i.e., because of the merits and dispositions of minister or recipient.

534. 2. The EFFECTS of the Sacraments are:

a) sanctifying grace which is either given for the first time or increased. The Sacraments of the dead normally give the first grace, whereas the Sacraments of the living normally increase sanctifying grace already existing in the soul;[351]

b) sacramental grace—i.e., some special help proper to each of the Sacraments;

c) an indelible character received in three Sacraments (Baptism, Confirmation, Orders) which consequently cannot be repeated.

---

[350] See Session 7, "Sacraments in General," Can. 8. See also TCCI 7:186ff, 606.
[351] See no. 432.

Although there is no universal agreement regarding the nature of the sacramental character, the following points seem to be certain:

1. the character sets a seal on the soul and distinguishes it from others;

2. the character gives the soul a disposition for offering to God a special form of worship;

3. the character gives the soul a share in Christ's priesthood.

535. The REVIVISCENCE of the Sacraments is the process whereby a Sacrament that was formerly unfruitful, later becomes fruitful. The transition is effected by the removal of the obstacle which existed when the Sacrament was received. According to the more probable opinion, there are five Sacraments whose grace may subsequently revive: Baptism, Confirmation, Extreme Unction, Orders, Matrimony. The same disposition which was required and sufficed for the reception of grace at the time of conferring the Sacrament is also necessary and sufficient for these Sacraments to produce their grace afterward.[352]

THE INSTITUTION OF THE SACRAMENTS

536. *All the Sacraments of the New Law were instituted immediately by Christ prior to His Ascension.* This is theologically certain, although a few theologians before the Council of Trent thought that some Sacraments were instituted by the Church through the authority committed to it by God.

Not only did Christ institute immediately all the Sacraments of the New Law, but He also determined specifically the matter and form of each of the Sacraments so that no substantial change in either of these elements is permissible.

All modern theologians agree that Christ did determine in some way the matter and form of the Sacraments, but they are not agreed to what extent He determined them, for He could have done so either *in detail*, or *generically*, or *specifically*. It is certain that Christ did not institute the matter and the form of the Sacraments *in detail* down to their accidental features, since these have changed in the course of time both in the Latin and in the Greek Churches. Thus, for instance, Christ did not determine whether the bread to be used in the consecration of the Eucharist should be leavened or unleavened. A *generic* institution requires that Christ should have determined the efficacy of each Sacrament but left to His Church the power of choosing the matter and form. A *specific* institution demands in addition that Christ should have determined in detail the *essential* matter and form of each Sacrament. The opinion which maintains that Christ instituted the Sacraments specifically seems preferable, since if Christ determined the matter and the form generically the Church would still retain the power of changing the matter and form, which has been expressly denied by the Council of Trent.

---

[352] See MTM, vol. 3, no. 43.

THE MINISTER OF THE SACRAMENTS

This chapter consists of four articles: 1) The Minister Himself—His Faith and state of Grace; 2) His Attention and Intention; 3) The Obligation of Administering and Refusing the Sacraments; 4) Simulation and Pretense.

Art. 1. The Minister Himself—His Faith and State of Grace

537. 1. THE PERSON OF THE MINISTER. Only men on earth who are legitimately delegated or consecrated are ministers of the Sacraments. Therefore, neither the angels nor the souls in purgatory have the power of administering the Sacraments; further-more, for the administration of certain Sacraments there is required a special consecration and delegation.

a) A minister is said to be *consecrated* for the administration of the Sacraments if he requires to be deputed by a special act of consecration; otherwise, he is *not so consecrated*, as, for instance, the minister in Baptism and Matrimony.

b) The *ordinary* minister of the Sacraments is one who administers them by vir-tue of his office; the *extraordinary minister* is anyone who administers them in a case of necessity in virtue of a special delegation. Thus, the ordinary minister of Confirmation is a bishop, the extraordinary minister a priest properly delegated.

538. 2. FAITH AND THE STATE OF GRACE IN THE MINISTER. a) For the *valid* administration of the Sacraments neither faith nor the state of grace is required in the minister, seeing that the Sacraments operate by God's power.

b) For the *lawful* administration of the Sacraments there is required under pain of mortal sin the state of sanctifying grace—at least when a consecrated minister administers the Sacraments solemnly outside the case of necessity.

In such circumstances, the minister who is consecrated for the worthy admin-istration of the Sacraments is guilty of grave irreverence if, while in a state of mortal sin and in the power of the devil, he wills to confer grace on others in the Person of the most holy Christ, although he himself considers such grace of little worth. A minister who confers a Sacrament while in the state of mortal sin is excused from grievous sin, 1) if he is not a consecrated minister, such as a lay person conferring Baptism in a case of necessity; 2) if there exists urgent need and there is no time to be restored to a state of grace, even through an act of contrition.

A consecrated minister who administers the Sacraments (outside cases of urgent need) while in a state of mortal sin commits sin as often as he performs this un-lawful act. This is the more probable opinion. It is uncertain whether a priest or deacon commits grave sin by administering *Holy Communion* while in the state of mortal sin, seeing that he is not the instrumental cause of grace which comes from the act of receiving and not from the act of giving the sacred host. It is probable that a deacon in mortal sin does not sin grievously by touching or carrying the Eucharist or by assisting the priest during Solemn Mass.

Art. 2. The Attention and Intention of the Minister of the Sacraments

539. 1. ATTENTION. For the *valid* administration of the Sacraments *external* attention is necessary and also sufficient; for their *lawful* administration there is required *internal* intention which excludes all voluntary distraction. Consequently, the minister who confers a Sacrament while willingly yielding to distraction does so validly but unlawfully. The sin is usually venial, but according to St. Alphonsus a priest who allows himself to be distracted during the Consecration in Mass is guilty of such grave irreverence that he commits grave sin — this is not admitted by all theologians.

540. 2. INTENTION is the reasoned direction of the will to some end through the use of certain means. So far as the Sacraments are concerned, the intention ensures that the minister wills through means of the sacramental sign to do that which the Church does.

KINDS OF INTENTION.

a) From the *subject's* point of view the intention is either actual, virtual, habitual, or interpretative. An *actual* intention is one which is elicited here and now while the act is in progress. A *virtual* intention is one made on a previous occasion, never retracted, and still exerting its influence on the present human act of the minister. A *habitual* intention is one which although formed on a previous occasion and never retracted, yet has no positive influence on the act as a human act. An *interpretative* intention is one which never has existed, does not exist at present, but is presumed to exist from clear indications; e.g., a dying Protestant who is unconscious and is known to have been in good faith and to have led an upright life is considered to possess an interpretative intention of receiving absolution and therefore may be absolved conditionally.

b) From the *object's* point of view, the intention may be either *confused* or *clear* according as the object intended is confusedly or clearly present to the mind; it is *definite* if his will is directed toward an object which is precise in every respect, it is *indefinite* if the object is only vaguely indicated; his intention is furthermore either *explicit* or *implicit* depending on whether the object which is clearly recognized is intended in itself or in something else to which it is conjoined. Finally, his intention is *absolute* or *conditional* according to whether the object is intended with or without conditions attached.

541. THE NECESSITY OF AN INTENTION. *a) For the valid administration of the Sacraments, the minister must have at least the intention of doing that which the Church does.*

This is defined as being of faith in the Council of Trent.[353] But theologians are not agreed regarding the exact meaning of that phrase — the intention of doing that which the Church does. Some are of the opinion that the only intention required in the minister is that he should have a serious will to apply the matter

---

[353] Session 7, "Sacraments in General," Can. 11. See also TCCI 7:185, 203.

and the form (an external intention); others state as being the more correct opinion that such an intention is insufficient and that there is also required in the minister the will to perform the rite *insofar as it is considered a sacred rite by the true Church* (an internal intention), since the minister is bound to act as the *minister of Christ*. Therefore, he must intend to perform a rite which is considered sacred by the Church of Christ. But it is not necessary that the minister himself believe the rite to be sacred. Similarly, it is not required that he will to do that which the *Catholic* Church does, provided that he intends to do what the true Church of Christ does.

b) Neither an interpretative intention nor a habitual intention is sufficient; an actual intention is not demanded; a virtual intention is sufficient and must be present.

Art. 3. The Obligation of Administering and Refusing the Sacraments

542. FIRST PRINCIPLE. *Those who have the care of souls in virtue of their office are bound in justice to administer the Sacraments to those who reasonably request them; other ministers have an obligation in charity.*

With regard to the first part of the principle, priests who accept the care of souls enter into a contract whereby they oblige themselves to provide for their subjects all that is necessary and useful for their salvation. Undoubtedly the reception of the Sacraments is a necessary or extremely useful means of salvation and therefore any pastor refusing a reasonable request for the Sacraments violates his contract and accordingly offends against justice. *Even at the risk of his own life* a pastor must administer the Sacraments to those of his subjects who are in extreme spiritual need; thus, he is bound to confer the Sacrament of Penance on the dying during time of plague or any other contagious disease.

The reason for the second part of the principle is that other priests, in refusing a reasonable request for the Sacraments, do not thereby violate any contract, but they offend against charity in depriving their neighbor of the valuable gift of sacramental grace. Moreover, there is frequently danger of scandal if the priest refuses to administer a Sacrament without having sufficient reason for refusal.

543. SECOND PRINCIPLE. *a) The Sacraments must always be refused to those who are NOT CAPABLE of receiving them, who would receive them not only unlawfully but also invalidly; b) one may not administer the Sacraments to those who although capable of receiving them are UNWORTHY to do so, unless there is a very grave cause.*

To administer the Sacraments to those incapable of receiving them would be a grave act of sacrilege directly procured by the minister himself. Thus, for instance, a bishop could never confer Orders on a woman, even to escape death. The administration of the Sacraments to those unworthy to receive them is valid and represents no more than material cooperation in another's sin. If there exists sufficient reason, material cooperation in another's sin is allowed. This is confirmed by Christ's own example in probably administering the Sacraments to

Judas Iscariot, even though he was most unworthy to receive them. *Reasons* which would permit the administration of the Sacraments in such circumstances are:

1. in order to prevent the violation of the seal of Confession;

2. lest the person who although unworthy asks for the Sacrament should fall into grave disrepute through the revelation of some secret sin;

3. lest grave scandal ensue.

PRACTICAL RULES. 1. With the exception of Matrimony, the Sacraments should be denied *a)* to any public sinner when one is not sufficiently certain of his emendation; *b)* to occult sinners if they ask for them privately.

2. The Sacraments are not to be refused to occult sinners if they ask for them publicly, if such refusal would lead to scandal or disrepute.

The Code of Canon Law applies these rules to the Eucharist: "Those who are publicly unworthy, such as the excommunicated, the interdicted, and those who are manifestly infamous, must be excluded from the reception of the Eucharist until after their repentance and amendment are certain and satisfaction has been made for public scandal. The minister must also exclude occult sinners who approach the Sacrament privately and are known by the minister to be unrepentant; however, if they approach publicly and the priest cannot pass them over without causing scandal, he may give them Holy Communion."[354]

Art. 4. Simulation and Pretense in Conferring the Sacraments

544. DEFINITION. *The simulation of a Sacrament consists in the minister changing secretly and unlawfully either the matter or the form or the necessary intention so that the Sacrament becomes invalid and the recipient is led into error.*

Therefore, simulation may be practiced in one of three ways: 1) the minister may use invalid matter, e.g., by pouring into the chalice some other liquid in place of wine; 2) he may secretly change the substantial form; 3) he may withhold internally his intention of administering the Sacraments. — One must distinguish carefully between simulation and *pretense*; in the latter, neither the matter nor the form of the Sacrament is used, so that, although the recipient himself is not led into error, *others* are; for instance, a confessor who has to deny absolution to his penitent expressly informs him of the fact, then recites some prayers and gives a blessing so that the bystanders will not realize that absolution has been denied.

545. PRINCIPLE. *Although it is sometimes permitted to pretend to administer a Sacrament for a sufficiently grave cause, simulation of the Sacraments is never lawful.*

To pretend to administer the Sacraments is sometimes lawful, since one has a sufficient reason for permitting others who have no right to the truth to fall into harmless error.

[354] Can. 855.

Simulation is never permitted, because it is an extremely dangerous lie and a detestable sacrilege. Consequently, Innocent XI condemned the following proposition: "A grave, pressing fear is a just cause for pretending the administration of sacraments."[355]

THE RECIPIENT OF THE SACRAMENTS

1. For the VALID reception of the Sacraments, the conditions required vary in each of the Sacraments. However, the following principles are generally true.

546. *a*) *Faith and a state of grace* are not required in the recipient, with the exception of the Sacrament of Penance; in order that this Sacrament be received validly, contrition (attrition) is necessary and this is impossible without faith and the state of grace (in its initial stages).

b) Neither internal nor external *attention* is necessary for the *validity* of the Sacraments so that even an unconscious person may be validly absolved, provided that he has a virtual or at least interpretative intention of receiving the Sacrament.

c) The *valid reception of Baptism* is required before the other Sacraments may be received validly.

d) No (personal) *intention* of receiving those Sacraments of which they are capable is required in infants and in those who are permanently deprived of the use of reason. In such circumstances, the intention is supplied by the Church. Infants may receive *validly* Baptism, Confirmation, Eucharist, and Orders. But in the present discipline of the Church, only the Sacrament of Baptism is administered to infants and those permanently deprived of the use of reason; in some countries the Sacrament of Confirmation is also administered.

e) In order that those enjoying the use of reason may receive the Sacraments validly (with the exception of the Eucharist), some *intention* is necessary which varies with the different Sacraments, as will be indicated when each Sacrament is considered in detail. *An exception is made of the Eucharist* since this consists in something permanent, namely, the consecrated species, and therefore does not depend for its validity on any intention either of the minister or of the recipient.

2. For the LAWFUL reception of the Sacraments, special conditions are required for each of them, as will be noted below. But the following general rules should be noted:

a) Those who enjoy the use of reason cannot lawfully receive *i*) the Sacraments of the *dead* without at least attrition; *ii*) the Sacraments of the *living* without the state of sanctifying grace.

b) Unless there is a grave cause it is forbidden to receive any Sacrament from a minister who is known to be unworthy. Only in danger of death may the faithful

[355] DZ 1179.

ask for sacramental absolution and, if no other priest is available, for the other Sacraments and sacramentals from excommunicates who are to be shunned and from other excommunicates after they have been explicitly condemned or declared excommunicate.[356]

APPENDIX: THE SACRAMENTALS

547. DEFINITION. *Sacramentals* (in the strict sense) *are objects or actions which the Church uses in the semblance of Sacraments in order to obtain spiritual favors principally through her intercession.*[357]

These sacramentals were sometimes called by older theologians the *minor Sacraments* because of their resemblance to the Sacraments, but there are many differences between them.

a) They differ in their *origin*, since the Sacraments were instituted by Christ, the sacramentals by the Church. According to present discipline, the Holy See can institute new sacramentals, and abolish, interpret, or change those already in existence.[358]

b) They differ in their *effect*: the Sacraments cause and increase sanctifying grace by virtue of the sacred rite itself, but the sacramentals of themselves produce only actual graces and other spiritual and temporal favors.

c) They differ in the *way in which they act*: the Sacraments cause grace in virtue of the rite itself, the sacramentals produce their effects in dependence on the dispositions of the recipient, and the Church through her powerful intercession confers on the sacramentals most fruitful effects—namely, *i)* actual graces, *ii)* remission of venial sin, *iii)* victory over the wiles of Satan, *iv)* temporal benefits.

d) They differ in their *number*: there are seven Sacraments, but the number of sacramentals is indeterminate and variable.

548. RULES. The sacramentals are either *permanent* (*objects*) or *transitory* (*actions*).

The former include certain blessed and consecrated articles by the use of which the faithful acquire various aids toward salvation. Such sacramentals are holy water, scapulars, medals, and so on. Transitory sacramentals include those actions to which the Church has attached special graces, such as blessings, exorcism, and so on.

BLESSINGS are today the chief form of sacramentals. Certain blessings are reserved to the pope, such as the blessing of the "Agnus Dei" or the pallium, and so on; some blessings belong to bishops, such as the blessing of chrism; other blessings are reserved to certain religious institutes, such as the blessing of rosaries, or scapulars, and so on; other blessings are reserved to the parish priest, as the blessing of

[356] See CCL, Can. 2261, § 3.
[357] CCL, Can 1144.
[358] See CCL, Can. 1145.

houses on Holy Saturday (but not on any other day), the nuptial blessing; many blessings may be given by any priest. Blessings are invalid if the form prescribed by the Church is not used.[359] If a deacon obtains permission from his bishop to administer Viaticum, he may bless the sick person with the Blessed Sacrament; similarly, he may bless the grave at a burial.—Lay persons have no power to confer any liturgical blessing or sacramental.

549. THE SUBJECT OF SACRAMENTALS. Sacramentals (and especially blessings) are to be administered primarily to Catholics; they may also be given to catechumens and even to non-Catholics, provided this is not expressly forbidden by the Church, in order that they may receive the light of faith and at the same time recover bodily health.[360] Thus, for instance, it is not forbidden to give a blessed medal to a non-Catholic who will not abuse it.

The Church forbids that sacramentals be given *a)* to excommunicates after declaratory or condemnatory sentence;[361] *b)* to those under personal interdict;[362] *c)* to Catholics who have dared to contract a mixed marriage without the necessary dispensation from the Church.[363] The first two instances are unlikely to occur in these days, but the third case is fairly frequent.

TREATISE II
BAPTISM

This treatise is divided into seven chapters: 1) Nature, Institution, Kinds of Baptism; 2) Matter and Form of Baptism; 3) Effects of Baptism; 4) Necessity of Baptism; 5) Minister of Baptism; 6) Subject of Baptism; 7) Ceremonies of Baptism.

NATURE, INSTITUTION, KINDS OF BAPTISM

550. 1. DEFINITION. Baptism is defined by the *Roman Catechism* as: *the Sacrament of regeneration through water in words.*[364] This definition denotes: *a)* the effect of Baptism—rebirth, since we are born of Adam children of wrath, but we are reborn of God through Baptism children of mercy; *b)* the matter and form of Baptism, i.e., water and words.

2. Baptism was certainly INSTITUTED by Christ, although theologians are not agreed on the exact moment of its institution. Some find the institution of Baptism in Christ's baptism in the Jordan; others look for its institution in Christ's words to Nicodemus: "No man can enter into the kingdom of God unless birth comes to him from water, and from the Holy Spirit" (Jn 3:5); others think it was instituted when before His Passion He sent His disciples to baptize; and yet another group

---

[359] See CCL, Can. 1148, § 2.
[360] See CCL, Can. 1149.
[361] See CCL, Can. 2260, § 1.
[362] See CCL, Can. 2275, no. 2.
[363] See CCL, Can. 2375.
[364] TCCI 7:193.

see the institution of this Sacrament in Christ's words after His Resurrection: "You, therefore, must go out, making disciples of all nations, and baptizing them ..." (Mt 28:19). The first view—that of St. Thomas[365]—seems the best.

551. 3. KINDS. Although there is only one Sacrament of Baptism, yet the *principal* effect of this Sacrament—the remission of original sin and the reception of sanctifying grace—can be obtained in three ways, and these are spoken of as three baptisms:

a) Baptism by *water,* that is, the Sacrament instituted by Christ;

b) baptism of *desire,* which is a perfect act of charity that includes at least implicitly the desire for Baptism by water;

c) baptism of *blood,* which signifies martyrdom endured for Christ prior to the reception of Baptism by water.

Solemn Baptism is the administration of the Sacrament with the full rites and ceremonies laid down in the rituals; otherwise, it is *private.*[366]

THE MATTER AND FORM OF BAPTISM

552. 1. The *remote valid* MATTER is natural water.[367] In judging what is water we are to be guided by the common estimation of men rather than by chemical analysis.

2. The *remote* matter for the *lawful* administration of *solemn* Baptism is baptismal water blessed for that purpose, which is reasonably clean.[368] In *necessity* and in *private* Baptisms baptismal water is to be preferred, but any reason is easily admitted to permit the use of even natural water or of water that has been blessed.

In extreme necessity it is lawful to use doubtful matter, seeing that the Sacraments were instituted for man's salvation. The use of water other than baptismal water in solemn Baptism outside a case of need, or the use of putrid water or water mixed with foreign matter is grievously sinful due to the grave act of irreverence against the Sacrament. If a child is baptized in the womb of the mother, it is lawful to add to the water "one part corrosive sublimate to a thousand parts of water" where there exists a danger of infection.[369]

3. The *proximate* matter of Baptism is the use of the water by a *genuine* minister in such a way that in the common estimation of men an *ablution* has been performed. This ablution can take place in one of three ways: by immersion, sprinkling, or pouring.

In the latter form of Baptism, *a)* the water must be poured three times, *b)* over the head of the person being baptized[370] (except in cases of extreme need); *c)* the

---

[365] See ST, III, q. 66, a. 2, c.
[366] See CCL, Can. 737, § 2.
[367] See CCL, Can. 737, § 1.
[368] See CCL, Can. 757.
[369] Holy Office, Aug. 21, 1901.
[370] If the water was poured on some other part of the child, Baptism should be

water must *flow* directly on the skin; *d)* the same minister must pronounce the form and pour the water.

553. The FORM of Baptism in the Latin Church is: "N. ego te baptizo in nomine Patris et Filii et Spiritus Sancti"; the Greek form is: "Baptizetur (baptizatur) servus Christi N. in nomine Patris et Filii et Spiritus Sancti."

At least two things must be found in the essential form: *a) the action of baptizing* performed by the minister; *b) the authority of the three Persons of the Blessed Trinity* in Whose name Baptism is conferred. In order to express the act of baptizing three things must be mentioned: the baptizer, the subject, and the actual act itself. It is absolutely essential to make explicit reference to the three Persons of the Blessed Trinity.—It is disputed whether the apostles conferred Baptism in the name of Christ alone.

From what has been said it would be easy to recognize which forms would be invalid and which valid. No useful purpose would be served by quoting examples. If Baptism is repeated conditionally, the minister should use the words: "Si non es baptizatus (-a), ego te baptizo in nomine Patris et Filii et Spiritus Sancti."[371]

THE EFFECTS OF BAPTISM

554. INTRODUCTION. Regarding the effects of baptism of desire and baptism by blood, these brief remarks will suffice: 1) neither imprint a character, since they are not Sacraments; 2) both cause sanctifying grace; 3) baptism by blood usually remits all venial sin and temporal punishment; this is not true of baptism by desire, unless it is conjoined with an intensely fervent act of charity.

Now we shall consider the effects of Baptism by water of which there are six in virtue of divine law, and one from ecclesiastical law.

By Divine law the effects of Baptism are:

1. the bestowal of the baptismal character (even if the Sacrament is unlawfully administered or received);

2. the remission of all sin;

3. the remission of all punishment;

4. the bestowal of grace, virtues, and the gifts;

5. the bestowal of sacramental grace;

6. incorporation in the Church.

By ECCLESIASTICAL LAW Baptism results in a spiritual relationship between the baptized on the one hand, and both the minister and sponsor on the other. This will be more fully discussed in the treatise on Marriage.

repeated conditionally afterwards, if this is possible.

[371] *Rituale Romanum*, tit. 2, chap. 4, no. 40.

NECESSITY OF BAPTISM

555. PRINCIPLE. *a) Baptism is a necessary means of salvation; b) so far as its principal effect, i.e., sanctifying grace, is concerned Baptism by water can be supplied in children by baptism by blood, and in adults by baptism of desire.*

This should be sufficiently evident from our previous statements.

THE MINISTER OF BAPTISM

556. IN NECESSITY THE MINISTER of Baptism is anyone who has sufficient use of reason and is willing and able to apply correctly the form to the matter.

The Council of Florence has defined: "In a case of necessity not only a priest or a deacon but also a lay man or woman and even a pagan or a heretic have the power to baptize, provided that they observe the form prescribed by the Church and have the intention of doing what the Church does."[372] Such a case of necessity is the danger of death, and it is not necessary that the person be on the actual point of death. Thus, for example, in the absence of a priest in missionary regions catechists usually baptize children recently born who although at the moment are in reasonably good health may easily die before the priest arrives.

557. THE ORDINARY MINISTER OF SOLEMN BAPTISM is the parish priest (or ordinary); in other words, the right to baptize solemnly is an *exclusive right of parish priests.*

Therefore, the solemn administration of Baptism without the expressed or justly presumed permission of the parish priest or ordinary is a grave violation of that person's right. This right of the parish priest is *territorial*, not personal. Therefore, this Sacrament may not be administered solemnly by a priest, even to his own subjects, in the district of another without due permission.[373] This is the prescription of common law, but there may also exist particular laws regarding this matter. The parish priest may baptize anyone, including strangers in his own territory; but strangers should be baptized by their own parish priests in their own parish where this can be done easily and without delay.[374]

The solemn Baptism of adults, such as Jews who are converted, should be administered by the bishop for the sake of greater solemnity, where this can be done conveniently.[375]

558. THE DELEGATED MINISTER FOR THE ADMINISTRATION OF SOLEMN BAPTISM is any priest or deacon, provided they are free from censure.

It is permissible to delegate any worthy priest to administer Baptism even when there is no reason for such delegation, but since a deacon is only an *extraordinary* minister of the Sacrament, he cannot lawfully administer solemn Baptism

[372] Session 8, "Bull of Union with the Armenians."
[373] See CCL, Can. 739.
[374] See CCL, Can. 738, § 2.
[375] See CCL, Can. 744.

unless 1) there is a moderate necessity, and 2) he has the permission (at least presumed) of the local ordinary or parish priest. If in unexpected necessity a deacon is called upon to baptize, he may presume lawful permission and administer solemn Baptism.[376] The moderate necessity which justifies a parish priest in granting delegation to a deacon would arise if, for example, the parish priest were absent or engaged in hearing confessions or otherwise occupied. When a deacon administers solemn Baptism he must not bless the salt or water, but must use what has been blessed already by a priest.

Private Baptism which is conferred either absolutely or conditionally and without any ceremonies when heretics are received into the Church does not seem to belong to the right of the parish priest.

559. THE ORDER OF PRECEDENCE TO BE OBSERVED IN THE ADMINISTRATION OF BAPTISM IN CASES OF NECESSITY is given by the Roman Ritual as follows: "A priest is to be preferred to a deacon, a deacon to a sub-deacon, a cleric to a lay person, a male to a female unless for decency's sake it is more fitting for a woman to baptize a child before actual birth or unless the woman is better acquainted with the form and manner of Baptism." Parents are not allowed to baptize their own children except in danger of death when no one else is available.[377] — The parish priest should take care to teach the faithful, especially midwives, doctors, and surgeons, the correct manner of baptizing in cases of necessity.

THE SUBJECT OF BAPTISM

THE SUBJECT of Baptism is every human being who is still a wayfarer and not yet baptized.[378]

560. DISPOSITIONS OF THE SUBJECT. 1. *Infants* and those who are perpetually insane do not require any previous disposition in order to be validly and lawfully baptized.

2. *Adults*, i.e., those with sufficient use of reason, must possess *a)* the intention of receiving the Sacrament, *b)* faith, and *c)* repentance. The *intention* is required for the very validity of the Sacrament. *Faith*—a knowledge of the chief articles of faith—and *repentance* (i.e., at least attrition) are required for the lawful and fruitful reception of Baptism. An adult who is certainly not baptized may for the sake of *devotion* confess those sins previously committed, but he is under no obligation to do so. A *heretic* whose previous Baptism was doubtfully valid and who must therefore be baptized again conditionally is bound to confess his previous sins and receive conditional absolution. The contrary opinion held by a few theologians is neither probable nor safe in practice.[379]

If an adult is in danger of death and there is no time to instruct him in the chief mysteries of the Faith he may be baptized, provided that in some way he makes

---

[376] See CCL, Can. 741.
[377] See CCL, Can. 742, § 3.
[378] CCL, Can. 745, § 1.
[379] See MTM, vol. 3, no. 138.

known his assent to those mysteries and seriously promises to observe the commandments of the Christian religion. If he is unable to ask for Baptism, e.g., if he is unconscious, he should be baptized conditionally, provided that in some probably valid manner he has manifested a desire to receive Baptism. But should he recover and if there persists some doubt regarding the validity of his Baptism, the Sacrament should be repeated conditionally.[380]

561. **CHILDREN OF CATHOLIC PARENTS** should be baptized *at the earliest possible moment.* Leo XIII fiercely condemned the custom of postponing the Baptism of children.—Theologians are not agreed what length of delay constitutes matter for grave sin but nothing can be said for certain. In some districts salutary precepts have been promulgated on this subject.

562. **CHILDREN WHOSE BOTH PARENTS ARE HERETICS** (whether schismatics or apostates) are to be baptized by a Catholic minister, if *a) there is extreme necessity*—that is to say, if the death of the child is prudently judged likely before it reaches the use of reason; *b) if there exists a well-founded hope of the child's Catholic education.* Hope is regarded as well-founded when at least *one* of the parents promises to do all in his or her power to provide a Catholic education for their children, or when they have no parents or guardians, or their parents or guardians are unwilling or unable to exercise their right to educate them.

THE CHILDREN OF PAGAN PARENTS cannot (outside the danger of death) be baptized without the knowledge or consent of their parents.[381] When the parents give their consent or if the children are removed from the control of their parents, they may be baptized provided there is a hope of educating them in the Catholic religion.[382]

563. **ABANDONED INFANTS** are normally to be baptized conditionally since it is very rare that one can be certain that they have received valid Baptism.[383]

564. **INFANTS COMPLETELY ENCLOSED IN THEIR MOTHER'S WOMB** can and must be baptized if there is no reasonable hope of administering Baptism after birth. If the child is subsequently delivered alive, Baptism must be repeated conditionally since the previous Baptism may not have been valid.

The Code of Canon Law states: "If the head of the child has been delivered and there is danger of death, Baptism should be given on the head and is not repeated conditionally if the child is subsequently delivered alive."[384] But this is only valid if there is moral certainty that the person administering Baptism on the head used all that was necessary for the validity of Baptism: "If some other part of the child has been delivered and there is danger of death, the child should be

---

[380] See CCL, Can. 752, § 3.
[381] See Benedict XIV, Constitution *Postremo Mense* (Feb. 28, 1747); see also CCL, Can. 750.
[382] See CCL, Can. 750.
[383] See CCL, Can. 749.
[384] Can. 746.

baptized conditionally on that part; if the child is subsequently delivered alive, Baptism must be repeated conditionally. If a mother dies in pregnancy, the fetus must be baptized absolutely by those who extract it if it is certainly living; if there is any doubt whether it is living, Baptism should be administered conditionally."

565. MISCARRIAGES AND MONSTROUS FORMS OF FETUS should be baptized conditionally if there exists any doubt about their life. Every miscarriage which is certainly alive must be baptized absolutely.[385]

THE APPROVED WAY OF BAPTIZING AN EMBRYO which is delivered while still enclosed in its afterbirths is to dip the mass into tepid (not cold) water and tear open its membranes so that the amniotic fluid may escape and the water be able to touch the fetus itself. At the same time the following words should be said immediately: "If thou art alive, I baptize thee ..." and then the fetus should be extracted from the water. The reason for this procedure is that Baptism on the membrane would seem to be invalid. If the membrane were broken out of water, there is danger of the fetus dying at once through contact with the air. But if the membrane is torn open in the water, there is a greater chance of the water reaching the fetus before it dies.

566. SCHOLIUM. CAESAREAN SECTION performed while the mother is alive or after her death.

While the mother is alive Caesarean section *a)* should be advised if there exists a well-founded hope that both the mother and the child will be saved by the operation whereas without it they would die, *b)* need not be performed if there is little hope of saving either the mother or the child, since no one is obliged to undergo such a serious operation without a well-founded hope of success. It is morally certain that a child may be validly baptized in the womb of the mother without Caesarean section.

After the mother's death there is a grave obligation of *charity* to perform a Caesarean section both in order to save the life of the child and in order to baptize it. Therefore, doctors and surgeons have a duty of performing the operation as soon as possible after the death of the mother. If, however, it is morally certain that the fetus has already died either before or at the same time as the mother herself (as frequently happens), or if there is no one present who can perform the operation, then it may be omitted. A priest is never allowed to perform the section himself,[386] but he should use all prudent means to persuade the midwife or doctor to use an instrument to baptize the child which may be still living in the mother's womb.

THE CEREMONIES OF BAPTISM

567. Under this heading we include not only the actions performed by the minister but also everything which the Church has prescribed concerning the place and

[385] See CCL, Can. 747 and 748.
[386] See Holy Office, Dec. 13, 1899.

time of Baptism, with special reference to the sponsors who "have always been considered in the Church of Christ as though they were the chief ceremonies."

OBLIGATION. Baptism must be administered solemnly with all the ceremonies prescribed in the Ritual, except in the case of grave necessity, i.e., in imminent danger of death. Therefore, a priest commits grievous sin by omitting a notable part of the ceremonies. The local ordinary may grant permission for the ceremonies to be omitted when a heretic returns to the fold of the Church, whether Baptism is administered conditionally or absolutely. Similarly, the ceremonies may be omitted in conditional Baptism when they were performed in the previous Baptism,[387] but this is extremely rare.—When Baptism has been administered in danger of death without the ceremonies, they are to be supplied afterward.[388]

568. PLACE AND TIME. 1. The *place* for the solemn administration of Baptism is normally the parish church where there is a baptismal font. But for the convenience of the faithful the local ordinary can permit or even order that the baptismal font for solemn Baptism be erected in another church or public oratory within the parish boundaries.[389] It is permissible to administer Baptism in the sacristy for a reasonable cause approved by the bishop, such as danger to the child's life from the severe cold. Solemn Baptism may not be administered in private houses except *a)* to the sons and grandsons of those who actually exercise the supreme rule over their people or have the right of succession to the throne; *b)* if the local ordinary for a just and reasonable cause grants permission *in some extraordinary case*.[390] Private Baptism, such as the Baptism of converts, and Baptism in cases of necessity may be administered in any suitable place.[391]

2. The *time* for the administration of even solemn Baptism is any day (with the exception of Good Friday). But, if conveniently possible, it is fitting that the Baptism of adults be conferred on the vigils of Easter Sunday and Pentecost.[392]—Children should be baptized as soon as possible,[393] as stated already.

The NAME given in Baptism should be a Christian name. If the parish priest cannot induce the parents to do so, he should add the name of some saint to that suggested by the parents and enter both in the baptismal register.[394]

569. Only one SPONSOR, who may be of a different sex from the child, need be present, or at most two—namely, one man and one woman;[395] this prescription holds

---

[387] See CCL, Can. 760.
[388] See CCL, Can. 759.
[389] See CCL, Can. 774, § 2.
[390] See CCL, Can. 776.
[391] See CCL, Can. 771.
[392] See CCL, Can. 772.
[393] See CCL, Can. 770.
[394] See CCL, Can. 761.
[395] See CCL, Can. 764.

even for *private* Baptism, whenever this is easily possible.[396] If no godparent was present, e.g., during a Baptism in case of necessity, one should be present when the ceremonies are supplied, but in this case the godparent does not contract any spiritual relationship.[397] In conditional Baptism no sponsor is required, but if one is present neither he nor the godparent who may have been present at the previous Baptism contract spiritual relationship, unless the godparent was the same at both.[398]

NECESSARY QUALIFICATIONS.

570. *a)* For *valid* sponsorship five conditions must be fulfilled.

1. The godparent must be baptized and have the intention of acting as sponsor.

2. He (or she) must not belong to any heretical or schismatic sect nor be excommunicated by condemnatory or declaratory sentence nor infamous by law nor excluded from legitimate acts, nor be a deposed or degraded cleric.

3. The sponsor may not be the father or mother or consort of the baptized.

4. The sponsor must have been assigned by the person to be baptized or his (or her) parents, or guardians, or—in default of these—by the minister himself.

5. During the act of baptizing the godparent(s) must personally or by proxy physically touch or immediately raise or receive from the font or hands of the minister the person baptized.[399]

571. *b)* For *lawful* sponsorship the following conditions are necessary.[400]

1. The godparent must have attained the fourteenth year of age, unless the minister has a just reason for acting otherwise; the priest may therefore dispense from this condition for a lawful reason.

2. He must not be excommunicated because of some notorious crime (e.g., a partner to a mixed marriage which is gravely unlawful) nor excluded from legitimate acts nor infamous by law, even though no sentence would have taken place, nor be publicly under interdict nor a public criminal nor infamous in fact.

3. The sponsor must know the rudiments of Faith.

4. The sponsor may not be a novice nor a professed religious in any institute, unless there is urgent need and the express permission of at least the local superior is granted.

5. The sponsor must not be in sacred Orders unless he has the express permission of his own ordinary.

[396] See CCL, Can. 762, § 2.
[397] Ibid.
[398] See CCL, Can. 763.
[399] See CCL, Can. 765.
[400] See CCL, Can. 766.

THE EFFECTS OF SPONSORSHIP. A valid godparent contracts the impediment of spiritual relationship with the baptized[401] and has the obligation of taking the utmost care to see that the baptized fulfills all through his life the promises made on his behalf by the godparent at the time of Baptism.[402]

572. NOTE. 1. The parish priest must exercise the greatest prudence in refusing to allow as sponsor one whom he considers unworthy, lest he should offend others or cause harm to the good of religion. In order to avoid greater evils which would certainly ensue, it seems that the parish priest could in certain cases admit one who is unworthy, provided that there is no danger of scandal. When he is in doubt whether to admit some person as a valid or lawful sponsor, he must consult the ordinary if time permits.[403]

2. After Baptism the parish priest should enter in the baptismal register the names of the baptized, minister, parents, and godparents; he must also note the place and date of Baptism.[404] In the case of illegitimate children the child's name should be entered as the child of unknown father or unknown parents. The mother's name and even the father's name should be entered if they are known as the parents by some public document, or if expressly and of their own accord they request in writing or before two witnesses that their names be entered.[405]

3. Catholic mothers of legitimate children should be encouraged to receive the blessing after childbirth from some priest. This blessing is not a strict right of the parish priest.[406]

TREATISE III
CONFIRMATION

This treatise is divided into four chapters: 1) Definition and Effects of Confirmation; 2) Matter and Form of Confirmation; 3) The Minister and the Subject of Confirmation; 4) The Ceremonies of Confirmation.

DEFINITION AND EFFECTS OF CONFIRMATION

573. DEFINITION. *Confirmation is a Sacrament instituted by Christ whereby the Holy Ghost is given to those baptized by the imposition of hands, the anointing with chrism, and a set form of words, in order that they may boldly profess their Faith in word and deed.*

The EFFECTS of this Sacrament. By divine law this Sacrament has three effects (namely, a character, an increase of sanctifying grace, and sacramental grace), by ecclesiastical law one effect (namely, spiritual relationship, which is no longer

---

[401] See no. 918.
[402] See CCL, Can. 769.
[403] See CCL, Can. 767.
[404] See CCL, Can. 777, § 1.
[405] See CCL, Can. 777, § 2.
[406] See S. R. C., Nov. 21, 1893, *Decreta Authentica*, no. 3813.

treated as an impediment to marriage). Consequently, by divine law the Sacrament of Confirmation produces:

1. an *indelible character*, which establishes and marks out the recipient as a good soldier ready to fight courageously in dangers to Faith, and to lead a life in accordance with the precepts of Faith;

2. an *increase of sanctifying grace* and, especially, of the gifts of the Holy Ghost;

3. *sacramental grace* given for the exercise of special courage against the internal and external foes of the Faith.

574. Although it is certain that the Sacrament was INSTITUTED by Christ, the exact moment is uncertain. Some think that He instituted it at the Last Supper after the institution of the Eucharist, others think that it was instituted after His Resurrection.

THE MATTER AND FORM OF CONFIRMATION

575. The REMOTE MATTER of Confirmation is *sacred chrism*, i.e., an unguent made from olive oil and balsam and specially blessed by the bishop for the purpose of Confirmation.

A *special* blessing is required, and therefore the use of the oil of the sick or the oil of catechumens, although blessed by the bishop, would probably render the Sacrament invalid.

576. The PROXIMATE MATTER of Confirmation is the *anointing* with this chrism performed on the forehead of the recipient in the form of a cross which is done by the direct use of the hands (and not through the means of some instrument). This is the rite observed in the Latin Church; there are some differences in the rite followed in the Greek Churches, but these are purely accidental.

577. The FORM used in Confirmation in the Latin Church consists in these words: "Signo te signo crucis et confirmo te chrismate salutis in nomine Patris et Filii et Spiritus Sancti." The form used in the Greek Church is: "Signaculum doni Spiritus Sancti."

THE MINISTER AND THE SUBJECT OF CONFIRMATION

578. 1. *The ordinary* MINISTER *of Confirmation is the bishop; the extraordinary minister is a priest properly delegated either by common law or by special apostolic indult.*[407]

The *bishop* may administer the Sacrament of Confirmation in his own territory even to persons who are not his subjects; in the diocese of another bishop

---

[407] CCL, Can. 782. Parish priests are empowered as from January 1, 1947, to administer the Sacrament of Confirmation in certain circumstances to those in danger of death from grave sickness (see Sacred Congregation of the Sacraments, Sept. 14, 1946).

he may not confirm without at least the reasonably presumed permission of that bishop, unless he confirms his own subjects privately and without using crozier or mitre.[408]—The bishop is under a grave obligation to provide an opportunity for his subjects to receive Confirmation at least within every five years;[409] but he has no strict obligation to administer the Sacrament to a dying person who asks to receive it, since the Sacrament is not absolutely necessary for that person.

A *priest* has no power to confer the Sacrament without delegation from the Holy See which may be granted in the form of a special indult (as, for instance, when the local ordinary is infirm) or by common law. By common law the power of confirming belongs to Cardinals, abbots and prelates nullius, vicars and prefects apostolic,[410] but these may only administer the Sacrament *validly* within the confines of their own territory and during the term of their office. All priests of the Oriental Rite have a tacit and habitual delegation to administer the Sacrament but only to the faithful of their own rite. Each time that a priest of the Latin Rite administers this Sacrament, he must expressly point out in the vernacular beforehand that he is the minister of the Sacrament in virtue of a special delegation. A new instruction was issued by the Sacred Congregation of the Sacraments on the feast of Pentecost, 1934, regarding the ceremonies to be observed by priests administering Confirmation.[411]

579. 2. The SUBJECT of Confirmation is any baptized person who has not yet been confirmed. With the exception of certain countries like Spain and Latin America, it is not customary at present to administer Confirmation to children until about the seventh year of age.

Nevertheless the Sacrament can be conferred even before this age if the child is in danger of death or if the minister considers it expedient for just and *grave* reasons.[412] Adults must have the intention of receiving the Sacrament and also the state of grace, since Confirmation is a Sacrament of the living. It is recommended that the person to be confirmed should be fasting and receive Holy Communion.

580. *Confirmation is not a necessary means of salvation* and it is probable that there is no grave precept commanding its reception. Therefore, no grievous sin is committed if a person does not receive the Sacrament, provided there is no scandal, no contempt, and no special danger to salvation. Parish priests are urged to see that the faithful approach the Sacrament at a suitable time and with a fitting preparation.[413]

[408] See CCL, Can. 783.
[409] See CCL, Can. 785.
[410] See CCL, Can. 782, § 3.
[411] AAS 27, 2ff.
[412] See CCL, Can. 788.
[413] See CCL, Can. 787.

THE CEREMONIES OF CONFIRMATION

581. The ceremonies prescribed in the Pontifical must be observed; this is a grave obligation so far as those ceremonies are concerned which relate either certainly or probably to the validity of Confirmation, such as the anointing on the forehead in the form of a cross.

Normally speaking, the Sacrament should be administered with all the solemn rites prescribed in the Pontifical, but for a reasonable cause the bishop may confer the Sacrament vested in a stole alone in any becoming place at any time. Neither the *striking* with the hand nor holding the candle are of grave obligation. The recipient may, but need not, assume a new name.

582. SPONSORS. There is a grave obligation enjoining the presence of a sponsor, as at Baptism—at least if this is possible. The same sponsor should present only one or two subjects, but for a just reason the minister can allow one sponsor to present several to be confirmed.[414]

For *valid* sponsorship the same five conditions are required as for the sponsors at Baptism.[415] Moreover, he himself must have been confirmed.[416]

For *lawful* sponsorship the same five conditions are necessary as for the sponsors at Baptism (*mutatis mutandis*). Moreover, the sponsor should be other than the sponsor at Baptism unless the minister for a reasonable cause judge otherwise, or unless Confirmation is legitimately conferred immediately after Baptism; in addition, the sponsor should be of the same sex as the subject presented, unless for a reasonable cause the minister permits otherwise.[417] Spiritual relationship ensues from Confirmation between subject and sponsor, whereby the sponsor must see to the Christian education of the godchild and must have a perpetual care for him, but this relationship is no longer an impediment to marriage.[418]

583. RECORDS. *The administration of Confirmation* must be entered in a special register as in the case of Baptism; moreover, it must be entered into the baptismal register.[419] If the proper parish priest of the subject confirmed was not present at the Confirmation, he must be notified as soon as possible.[420] Thus, for example, if Confirmation was administered in a boys' college, the minister of Confirmation must ordain that the respective parish priests be notified of the Confirmation of the boys.

---

[414] See CCL, Can. 794.
[415] See no. 570.
[416] See CCL, Can. 795.
[417] See CCL, Can. 796.
[418] See CCL, Can. 797, 1079, and 1335.
[419] See CCL, Can. 798.
[420] See CCL, Can. 799.

TREATISE IV
THE HOLY EUCHARIST

INTRODUCTORY. The Holy Eucharist whose dignity surpasses all other Sacraments may be considered from two different aspects—as a Sacrament, and as a sacrifice. Accordingly, it is usual to divide the treatise on the Eucharist into two sections: The Eucharist as a Sacrament, and, The Eucharist as a Sacrifice.

SECTION I
THE HOLY EUCHARIST AS A SACRAMENT

This section is divided into five chapters: 1) Definition and Institution of the Holy Eucharist; 2) The Matter and Form of the Eucharist; 3) The Effects of the Holy Eucharist; 4) The Recipient of the Eucharist; 5) The Minister of the Holy Eucharist.

DEFINITION AND INSTITUTION
OF THE HOLY EUCHARIST

584. DEFINITIONS. The Holy Eucharist is known under several different names; e.g., Synaxis, the Lord's Supper, Viaticum, the Sacrament of the Altar, the Body of Christ, and so on, and it may be considered in three ways—either in its preparation, or in its completed state, or in its reception.

1. IN ITS PREPARATION (*in fieri*) *the Eucharist consists in the changing of bread and wine into the Body and Blood of Christ, while the species remain, in order to provide nourishment for the soul; more briefly, it is the act of transubstantiation.*

2. IN ITS COMPLETED STATE (*in facto esse*) *the Eucharist is the Sacrament of the Body and Blood of our Lord Jesus Christ under the species of bread and wine instituted by Christ for the nourishment of the soul.*

3. IN ITS RECEPTION *the Eucharist is the receiving of the Body of Christ under the eucharistic species.*

Just as each Sacrament has its own special significance, so the Eucharist signifies three things: 1) *the Passion of Christ*; 2) *grace to nourish and support the soul*; 3) *a pledge of future glory.* The Eucharist increases sanctifying grace in the act of reception or eating—that is to say, when the eucharistic species pass from the mouth into the stomach. Therefore, a person who retains the sacred species in the mouth until they are dissolved or a dying person unable to swallow do not receive the effects of this Sacrament. On the other hand, a person who vomits after receiving the sacred species into the stomach has truly received the Eucharist and therefore the gift of grace.

585. The INSTITUTION of the Eucharist was performed by Christ at the Last Supper—on this point there is universal agreement.

THE MATTER AND FORM OF THE EUCHARIST

Art. 1. The Matter of the Eucharist

586. THE REMOTE MATTER of the Eucharist is wheat bread and wine made from grapes. This is stated by the Council of Florence.

For the VALIDITY of the Sacrament of the Eucharist it is necessary:

1. that the bread be made from pure *wheaten* flour, not from barley, rye, oats, and so on. Any form of wheat is sufficient, so long as it remains pure wheat in the common estimation of men;

2. that the flour be mixed with *natural water* and then baked by fire, so that it is true bread. Therefore, if any other liquid (such as milk or oil) is mixed with it in a notable quantity, or if it remains unbaked and in the form of dumpling or dough, the matter is invalid;

3. that the wine be natural wine *from the grape*, and therefore any other liquid is invalid, such as beer, apple wine, wine that has gone sour or has undergone substantial corruption in some other way, wine from which all alcohol has been extracted, artificial wine.

For LAWFUL consecration it is further required:

1. that priests of the Latin Rite use *unleavened* bread, priests of the Greek Rite leavened bread;

2. that the host be clean, entire, recently made, and circular;

3. that the wine has begun to ferment, so that fresh wine or juice recently pressed from ripe grapes are not permitted;

4. that the wine be pure and clear and not mixed with any other liquid—except with the small amount of water which is added to the wine at the Offertory. The Holy Office, Aug. 5, 1896, granted permission for the addition of some *wine alcohol* to weak wine up to a combined total of 18 percent alcohol;

5. that the wine should not have begun to turn sour.

587. THE PROXIMATE MATTER of the Eucharist is the use of the bread and wine in the act of consecration.

Some authors regard the eucharistic species as the proximate matter inasmuch as they contain the Body and Blood of Christ.

For *valid* consecration two conditions must be verified: *a)* the matter to be consecrated must be physically present; *b)* it must be specifically determined.

The matter is said to be *physically present* when in the common estimation of men the words *hic* and *hoc* used in the act of consecration retain their proper significance. Therefore, hosts contained in a ciborium (even if closed) are validly consecrated. Whether hosts contained in a ciborium which has been placed inadvertently at the corner of the altar outside the corporal are validly consecrated or not cannot be decided from their physical presence alone (since this ciborium is certainly more present to the celebrant than is the host to the newly-ordained priest in the ordination Mass). One must therefore consider the virtual intention of the celebrant. It is recommended that each priest form an intention once and for all of consecrating any matter on the altar which he willed to consecrate at the beginning of the Sacrifice.

The matter must be *specifically determined* by an actual or at least virtual intention of the priest, and this is essential to the validity of the Sacrament; therefore, if a host is placed on the altar without the knowledge of the priest it remains unconsecrated.

588. For *lawful* consecration it is necessary that the matter to be consecrated should be:

a) placed on a consecrated or portable altar,

b) within the corporal,

c) and held in the hands of the priest or placed in an open vessel on the corporal.

d) It is further required that the matter be consecrated during Mass and placed on the altar at least before the Offertory. Some consider any act of consecration attempted outside of Mass as not only gravely unlawful but also invalid. The Code of Canon Law states: "It is forbidden, even in cases of extreme necessity, to consecrate one species without the other or even both together outside Mass."[421]

Art. 2. The Form of the Eucharist

589. The form to be used in the consecration of the bread is: "Hoc est enim corpus meum." With the exception of *enim* all these words are essential.

The form to be used in the consecration of the wine is: "Hic est enim calix sanguinis mei, novi et aeterni testamenti, mysterium fidei, qui pro vobis et pro multis effundetur in remissionem peccatorum." The words *hic est calix sanguinis mei* or *hic est sanguis meus* are certainly essential.

If anyone through negligence or bad habit pronounces the words incorrectly "oc, ic, es, copus, calis, sanguis" he commits sin but the consecration remains valid, since these are mere accidental changes.—In practice, all the words of each form should be pronounced distinctly, reverently, continuously, without interruption or repetition. Scrupulous priests are easily excused from sin if they indulge in this forbidden repetition. Such irreverence is involuntary.

THE EFFECTS OF THE HOLY EUCHARIST

590. 1. The Holy Eucharist produces perfect union between man and Christ, both God and man, and therefore is correctly termed Holy Communion.

2. As the food of the soul, the Eucharist *a)* sustains man's spiritual life, *b)* increases grace and the virtues, *c)* remits venial faults and temporal

---

[421] Can. 817.

punishments, *d)* causes spiritual joy, for it is the Bread of Heaven containing within itself all sweetness.

3. As the special sign of Christ's Passion, it provides a pledge of future glory and a powerful protection against the temptations of the devil. The Holy Eucharist produces these effects at the moment when it is actually received or eaten. Consequently, it is probable that these effects are produced even when Holy Communion is administered artificially through a tube inserted in the stomach. However, the Holy Office[422] forbade such artificial administration of Holy Communion.

THE RECIPIENT OF THE HOLY EUCHARIST

This chapter is divided into four articles: 1) The Person of the Recipient; 2) The Necessary Disposition; 3) The Obligation of Receiving Holy Communion; 4) Frequent Communion.

Art. 1. The Person of the Recipient

591. PRINCIPLE. *Every baptized person is capable of receiving fruitfully the Holy Eucharist provided no obstacle is offered to grace through the commission of mortal sin.*

At present it is not customary to give Holy Communion to *children below the age of discretion.* But once a person has attained the use of reason he can and indeed ought to receive Holy Communion. The amount of religious knowledge required so that a child may make a suitable preparation for First Communion is the knowledge, according to its capacity, of the mysteries of the Faith necessary to salvation, and the knowledge that distinguishes the eucharistic bread from common and material bread.[423] It belongs to the parents or to those who occupy their place and to the confessor to decide whether a particular child is sufficiently prepared for receiving the First Communion. It is the duty of the parish priest to see that children do not approach the Sacrament without sufficient dispositions.[424] In danger of death he has the power and the duty of administering Holy Communion to children, provided they can distinguish the Body of Christ from common bread and are able to adore it reverently. Holy Communion should not be given to *lunatics* except as Viaticum when they can receive it without danger of irreverence. In the same category are the dying who are unconscious, who can and must receive Viaticum if this is possible. In order to discover whether it is possible or not it would help to give them first a small unconsecrated particle.

Those who are not completely mental defectives, old persons who have grown childish, those who are deaf and dumb, and so on, may and must receive the Holy Eucharist provided there is no danger of irreverence. The same applies to those who suffer from intermittent coughing or vomiting.

---

[422] Jan. 27, 1886.
[423] See Sacred Congregation of the Sacraments, Aug. 8, 1910.
[424] See CCL, Can. 854.

Art. 2. Dispositions for the Reception of Holy Communion

592. The Holy Eucharist may be received either *spiritually* or *sacramentally*. A spiritual communion is the desire for receiving the Eucharist sacramentally when there are obstacles making this impossible. All ascetical writers strongly recommend the exercise of spiritual communion as productive of many fruits from the act of charity inspiring it. In the following paragraphs we shall speak only of the dispositions required for the sacramental reception of the Holy Eucharist.

593. NECESSARY DISPOSITIONS OF SOUL.

1. *Freedom from excommunication and personal interdict*—this will be discussed more fully in the treatise on censures.

2. *Freedom from mortal sin*; this is absolutely necessary since the Holy Eucharist is a Sacrament of the living and spiritual food should not be given to a spiritual corpse—to a sinner who is spiritually dead.

If anyone is conscious of mortal sin, he is bound to go to Confession before receiving Holy Communion; an act of contrition is insufficient unless a confessor is unavailable and there is urgent need to receive the Sacrament.[425] A confessor is considered not available when the penitent cannot confess without some grave harm *extrinsic to confession itself*, as, for instance, when scandal would be given to the people, or the name of the accomplice would become known, or if the present confessor could not understand, and so on. No inconvenience *intrinsic* to the confession—such as a great feeling of shame—would excuse from the obligation of confession. A priest who celebrates Mass after making an act of contrition when a confessor is not available and there is need to celebrate is bound to go to confession as soon as possible, i.e., *within three days*. This precept still holds even though the priest does not celebrate Mass again within these three days or even within a longer period.[426]

3. *Actual devotion*, because of the reverence due to this noble Sacrament. Therefore, a careful preparation and a fervent thanksgiving are necessary.

594. NECESSARY BODILY DISPOSITIONS.

1. *Suitable dress*, out of respect for the Sacrament; one may offend in this matter either by defect (e.g., by wearing dirty clothes) or by inordinate excess (e.g., immodest dress of females).

2. *External cleanliness*, lacking in one who is dirty or suffering from visible and repulsive sores or in one who has suffered involuntary pollution or in women during their menstrual period.

All visible dirt should be removed before receiving Holy Communion. Ailments which cause serious disfigurement do not prevent the reception of the Holy

---

[425] See Council of Trent, Session 13, "Decree Concerning the Most Holy Sacrament of the Eucharist," chap. 7. See also TCCI 7:273, and CCL, Can. 856.

[426] See CCL, Can. 807.

Eucharist unless they cause revulsion to the other communicants. Involuntary pollution and the menstrual period do not render the body so unclean as to prevent the receiving of Holy Communion, when there exists even a light reason for approaching the Sacrament.

595. 3. *The eucharistic fast,* i.e., abstinence from all food and drink from midnight immediately preceding reception.[427] This is a universal and most ancient custom which has been confirmed by many councils and in the Code of Canon Law.[428]

This law of fasting admits of no parvity of matter either in the quantity of food and drink taken or in time. Three conditions are required in order that what is taken have the character of food or drink: *a)* it must be *digestible,* and accordingly such things as small bones, human nails, or human hair do not violate the fast; *b)* it must be taken *exteriorly,* because what is taken interiorly is not eaten or drunk in the proper sense of the word. Thus, it is not a violation of the fast to swallow saliva or blood from the teeth or nasal cavities; *c)* it must be taken *by the action of eating or drinking.* Therefore, the fast is not violated by anything received into the stomach *a)* mixed with *saliva,* such as a few drops of water swallowed while cleaning the teeth, *b)* through the action of *breathing,* e.g., when a man smokes or inhales tobacco smoke, *c)* through the *injection of a nutritive substance.*

Midnight may be computed in accordance with solar or legal time (whether this be regional or otherwise).[429]

596. *Exemption from this eucharistic fast is granted in six cases:*

1. in order to complete the Sacrifice of the Mass (after the consecration of at least the bread or the wine);

2. in order to preserve the Blessed Sacrament from irreverence;

3. in order to avoid public scandal (when, for instance, ill-repute would be incurred if the priest did not celebrate Mass);

4. in order to receive Viaticum;

5. in order that Holy Communion may be given to the sick who have been confined to bed for a month without any certain hope of speedy recovery. These may receive Holy Communion twice a week though they have taken medicine or liquid food.[430] The words *liquid food* include anything that is drunk, even though it be nutritive food, such as raw eggs (but not cooked eggs);

6. in order that catechumens may receive Holy Communion after tasting salt during their Baptism.

[427] See Appendix II.
[428] Can. 808 and 858.
[429] See CCL, Can. 33, § 1.
[430] See CCL, Can. 858, § 2.

NOTE. No one has the power to absolve from this law of the eucharistic fast except the pope; the dispensation is granted through the Holy Office for priests, through the Sacred Congregation of the Sacraments for lay persons.

Art. 3. Obligation of Receiving Holy Communion

597. PRINCIPLE. *a) Only the desire to receive Holy Communion is a necessary means of salvation; b) all who have the use of reason are bound by divine and ecclesiastical precept to receive Holy Communion.*

Sanctifying grace alone and everything inseparable from it are necessary means of salvation. Now sanctifying grace can be obtained without the actual reception of Holy Communion, e.g., through Baptism. Nevertheless, an explicit or at least implicit *desire* for Holy Communion would seem to be necessary, since the Holy Eucharist is the end of all the Sacraments inasmuch as they tend toward union with Christ which is principally achieved in the Sacrament of the Eucharist.[431] There is clearly a *divine* precept expressed in many of Christ's words, such as: "You can have no life in yourselves, unless you eat the flesh of the Son of Man and drink His blood" (Jn 6:54).

The *ecclesiastical* precept is to be found expressed in the Fourth Council of the Lateran and in the Council of Trent and is also contained in the Code of Canon Law.[432]

N. B. The obligation of the precept of Communion binding children falls principally on those who must take care of them, namely, parents, guardians, confessors, teachers, parish priest.[433]

The divine precept commands the reception of the Eucharist several times during life and probably at the hour of death; the ecclesiastical precept has laid down that all who have reached the age of discretion must receive Holy Communion at least during Paschal time.

Obligation of receiving Viaticum. "In danger of death, no matter from what cause the danger arises, the faithful are bound by precept to receive Holy Communion."[434] This obligation is certainly serious if a man has none or little hope of escaping death and has not received Holy Communion during the preceding week.

"The administration of Holy Viaticum to the sick should not be long deferred, and those who have the care of souls should carefully see to it that sick people receive it while they are in full possession of their senses."[435] It is advisable that Viaticum be given to the sick *a)* who are in only probable danger of death even

---

[431] See ST, III, q. 65, a. 3.

[432] See Can. 859.

[433] See CCL, Can. 860. Once the individual attains the age of discretion, he must make his First Holy Communion. See MTM, vol. 3, no. 211.

[434] CCL, Can. 864, § 1.

[435] CCL, Can. 865.

though there is a probable hope of their recovery; *b)* who have already received Holy Communion early on the same day before the danger had arisen; *c)* repeatedly (even on one day) while the same danger of death continues.[436]

Paschal time runs from Palm Sunday to Low Sunday, but local ordinaries have the power of extending the period from the Fourth Sunday of Lent until Trinity Sunday inclusively.[437] By particular law Paschal time sometimes extends from Ash Wednesday until Trinity Sunday. — Since the Paschal period has been determined in order to stress the obligation and not to terminate it, the duty of fulfilling the precept still continues if it has not been fulfilled within the stated time.[438]

All the faithful are allowed to receive Holy Communion in leavened or unleavened bread even if they wish to do so merely for the sake of devotion, but they should be counseled to receive the Paschal Communion in their own rite whereas they are obliged to receive Holy Viaticum in their own rite, unless there is grave need to the contrary.[439]

598. The faithful are to be recommended (but not commanded) to satisfy their Easter duty in their own respective parishes, but if it is fulfilled in some other parish, their own parish priest should be informed.[440] There is frequently no strict obligation to give this notification, and certainly the following persons are exempt:

1. all priests who satisfy the Paschal precept anywhere by the celebration of Mass;

2. religious of either sex and their domestic staff who can communicate in their own chapels. The same applies to religious sisters, but not to their domestics;

3. soldiers, convicts, students living in college, and others who by particular law or lawful custom may fulfill the Paschal precept in their own chapels;

4. strangers, who may receive their Paschal Communion anywhere.

Art. 4. Frequent Communion

599. By frequent Communion is understood the reception of the Sacrament several times during the week or even daily. Therefore, weekly or fortnightly Communion would not be considered frequent Communion.

The directions given by older theologians regarding the necessary dispositions for the frequent reception of Holy Communion are no longer valid and have been superseded by the Decree of the Congregation of the Council, Dec. 16, 1905, of which the following are the chief points to be noted:

RULES: 1. "Frequent and daily Communion as a thing most earnestly desired by Christ our Lord and by the Catholic Church should be available for all the

---

[436] See CCL, Can. 864, § 1–2.
[437] See CCL, Can. 859, § 2.
[438] See CCL, Can. 859, § 4.
[439] See CCL, Can. 866.
[440] See CCL, Can. 859, § 3.

faithful, of whatever rank and condition of life, so that no one who is in the state of grace and who approaches the Holy Table with a right and devout intention can be lawfully hindered from it." Therefore, all that is required for frequent or daily Communion is the state of grace—and a right and devout intention.

2. "Right intention consists in this: that he who approaches the Holy Table should do so, not out of routine or vainglory or human respect, but in order to please God, to be more closely united to Him, and to seek this divine remedy for his weaknesses and defects."

3. "Frequent and daily Communion is to be promoted especially in religious orders and Congregations of all kinds …; as also in ecclesiastical seminaries and in all Christian establishments of whatever kind for the training of youth."

4. "After the promulgation of this decree, all ecclesiastical writers are to cease from contentious controversy concerning the dispositions required for frequent and daily Communion."

THE MINISTER OF THE HOLY EUCHARIST

This chapter is divided into two articles: 1) The Consecration and Administration of the Holy Eucharist; 2) The Reservation of the Blessed Sacrament.

Art. 1. The Consecration and Administration of the Holy Eucharist

600. 1. *Priests alone have the power of consecrating the Eucharist validly.*[441]

For lawful consecration further conditions are required which will be discussed below.

2. The *ordinary* minister of Holy Communion is a priest; the *extraordinary* minister is a deacon properly delegated. This delegation may be granted by the bishop or parish priest or religious superior for a grave reason.[442]

When there exists grave need to administer Viaticum to a dying person, this delegation is not required; in such circumstances not only a deacon but any cleric is empowered to administer Viaticum. Noldin and others maintain correctly, "if special skill is required in administering Holy Communion to the sick, the priest may allow a woman, such as a Daughter of Charity who may be nursing the sick, to give Viaticum on a spoon." No one can administer the Holy Eucharist to himself except in two cases: 1) a priest during his own Mass; 2) in a case of extreme necessity. It is probable that in the absence of any other priest or a deacon a priest may administer Holy Communion to himself *for the sake of devotion.*

601. CONDITIONS REQUIRED FOR THE LAWFUL ADMINISTRATION of the Eucharist are: 1) proper jurisdiction, 2) proper time, 3) proper place, 4) proper rite.

602. 1. DUE JURISDICTION is necessary, since the duty of feeding the faithful with the eucharistic food is one which belongs to a pastor of souls. According to present

---

[441] See Fourth Lateran Council, Const. 1.
[442] See CCL, Can. 845.

discipline *any priest wheresoever he legitimately celebrates Mass may also legitimately distribute Holy Communion to all persons rightly disposed, unless the local ordinary forbids this in special cases for just reasons.* — Even outside the time of Mass any priest enjoys the same faculty by reason of at least the presumed permission of the rector of the Church, if he does not belong to it.[443]

The administration of *Holy Viaticum*. This ordinarily belongs to the parish priest and his delegate, but the following are exceptions.

a) In *cases of necessity* when the parish priest is not available, any priest or deacon may administer Viaticum.

b) The administration of Viaticum to a diocesan bishop belongs to a dignitary or canon of the chapter.[444]

c) In all *clerical religious* houses, it is the right and duty of superiors to administer themselves or through their delegate Viaticum (and Extreme Unction) not only to their professed subjects but also to novices and to others living in the religious house night and day whether for domestic work or for education or for shelter or for health reasons.[445]

d) In houses of *nuns* the ordinary confessor or anyone taking his place has the same right and duty.[446]

e) In other *lay* congregations and orders this right and duty belongs to the local parish priest or to the chaplain to whom the ordinary has given full parochial powers.[447]

NOTE. Any priest may *privately* bring Holy Communion to the sick who desire to receive it for the sake of devotion; this does not apply to the reception of Viaticum.[448]

603. 2. TIME. Holy Communion may be administered on any day and at any hour when the Sacrifice of the Mass can be offered. This is the general rule. Only Viaticum can be administered on Good Friday.[449] On Holy Saturday, Holy Communion cannot be given to the faithful except during the Mass of the day or immediately afterward.[450] If there is reasonable cause, Holy Communion may be administered even after midday and at other times when it is not permissible to celebrate Mass.[451]

604. 3. PLACE. Holy Communion may be administered wherever Mass is allowed to be said; Viaticum may be given in any suitable place. The celebrant is not allowed

---

[443] See CCL, Can. 846.
[444] See CCL, Can. 397, no. 3.
[445] See CCL, Can. 514, § 1.
[446] See CCL, Can. 514, § 2.
[447] See CCL, Can. 514, § 3.
[448] See CCL, Can. 849, § 1.
[449] See CCL, Can. 867, § 2.
[450] See CCL, Can. 867, § 3.
[451] See CCL, Can. 867, § 4.

to give Holy Communion during the Mass to people who are so far away from the altar that the priest must go out of sight of the altar.[452]

605. 4. THE PROPER RITE. The rite to be used is that prescribed by the Roman Ritual or by any other approved Ritual. In the Latin Rite it is never permissible—not even for Holy Viaticum—to administer Holy Communion under the species of wine; however, permission has now been granted for all the faithful—even for the sake of devotion—to receive Holy Communion in a rite other than their own from a priest belonging to that rite.[453]

606. The following are the chief *rubrics* to be observed in administering Holy Communion:

a) The priest should administer Holy Communion with the index finger and thumb of the right hand. If any lingering disease affects these fingers permission to say Mass and distribute Holy Communion must be sought from the Sacred Congregation; if, however, the priest is unable to use these fingers for only a short period but is able to use his other fingers quite well, it seems that for a just reason he may celebrate Mass and distribute Holy Communion, since it is the entire hand of the priest that has been consecrated.

b) Unless grave necessity requires otherwise, the priest should administer Holy Communion with two or at least one lighted candle, and clothed in sacred vestments, such as (outside Mass) the cotta and white stole (or a stole corresponding to the color of the day). On All Souls' Day the stole may be white or purple.[454] Before Holy Communion the Confiteor must be recited; afterward (outside the time of Mass) the priest should recite the prayer O *Sacrum Convivium* with its versicles and prayer with the *long conclusion*.[455]

c) If while administering Holy Communion a host falls to the ground, the place should be covered and afterward cleansed (this is a slight obligation); if the host falls on to the clothing of a woman and it cannot be recovered by the priest easily and without scandal, the woman should be taken to the sacristy and she herself take up the host and then wash her fingers; the ablution should be poured down the sacrarium.

d) In taking Holy Communion to the sick, the statutes legitimately approved by the local ordinary are to be followed.

Art. 2. The Reservation of the Blessed Sacrament

607. THE PLACE OF RESERVATION. By common law the Blessed Sacrament *must* be reserved:

1. in the cathedral church, in the principal church of an abbey or prelature nullius, of a vicariate or prefecture apostolic;

---

[452] See CCL, Can. 868.
[453] See no. 597.
[454] See S.R.C., Apr. 19, 1912.
[455] See *Rituale Romanum*, tit. 4, chap. 2, editio typica.

2. in all parochial and quasi-parochial churches;

3. in a church attached to an exempt institute whether of men or of women.

The Blessed Sacrament may be reserved — with the permission of the local ordinary —

1. in collegiate churches,

2. in the *principal* oratory, public or semipublic, of a pious or religious house, and in the principal oratory of an ecclesiastical college which is governed by secular priests or religious.

For the reservation of the Blessed Sacrament in any other church or public oratory the permission of the Holy See is required, but the local ordinary may grant permission for reservation in other churches and public oratories, but only for a good reason and as a temporary concession.

Wherever the Blessed Sacrament is reserved it is required that a priest should celebrate Mass there at least once a week.[456] For a grave reason, approved by the local ordinary, such as the danger of sacrilegious theft, the Blessed Sacrament may be kept at night on a corporal in a becoming place with a light burning before it.[457]

608. THE MANNER OF RESERVATION. The Blessed Sacrament must be reserved:

1. *in a suitable tabernacle* which has been blessed and placed in an immovable position at the center of the altar.[458]

There is a grave obligation for a lamp to be kept burning before the tabernacle; the flame must be fed with olive oil. When it is difficult to obtain such oil, any other oil is suitable, particularly vegetable oil or beeswax; in the last resort an electric light may be used according to the prudent judgment of the ordinary.[459]

2. *in a ciborium* made of solid and decent material; the ciborium must be clean, blessed, and covered with a white silk veil, and the lid should fit tightly.[460] The ciborium need not be made of silver but the interior should be gilded in the same way as a chalice.

3. Consecrated hosts should be frequently *renewed* to prevent any danger of corruption. It is the duty of the local ordinary to issue instructions regarding their renewal and these must be observed by all priests (including those who are exempt). Grave sin is committed by a priest who defers the renewal of the consecrated particles for so long that there is certain danger of corruption. What constitutes such a period is to be determined relatively to the danger of corruption. But it is not permissible to keep hosts which are *three months old.*[461]

---

[456] See CCL, Can. 1265.
[457] See CCL, Can. 1269, § 3.
[458] See CCL, Can. 1269, § 1.
[459] See S.R.C., Feb. 23, 1916.
[460] See CCL, Can. 1270.
[461] See Sacred Congregation of the Sacraments, Dec. 7, 1918.

609. SCHOLIUM. *Exposition of the Blessed Sacrament.* Exposition is said to be *private* when the door of the tabernacle is opened; it is *public* when the Blessed Sacrament is placed in a monstrance on a throne. Private exposition is allowed for any just reason without the ordinary's permission, and after exposition the priest may give the blessing with the ciborium.[462] Public exposition is permissible by common law on the feast of Corpus Christi and during its Octave during Solemn High Mass and Vespers; on all other days the previous permission of the local ordinary is required by all priests (even by those who are exempt).

SECTION II
THE HOLY EUCHARIST AS A SACRIFICE

This section contains three chapters: 1) Nature and Effects of the Sacrifice of the Mass; 2) The Obligation of Celebrating Mass; 3) Liturgical Requisites for the Celebration of Mass.

NATURE AND EFFECTS OF THE SACRIFICE OF THE MASS

This chapter is divided into three articles: 1) The Nature of the Sacrifice of the Mass; 2) The Value, Effects, and Fruits of the Mass; 3) The Application of the Mass.

Art. 1. The Nature of the Sacrifice of the Mass

610. THE MEANING OF SACRIFICE. Sacrifice (in its strict sense) is the offering of a sensible gift by a legitimate minister, whereby through the destruction—either physical or moral—of what is offered man professes the supreme excellence of God and His complete dominion over the life and death of all creatures.

Therefore, four things are required for a true sacrifice:

1. on the part of the *matter*—some sensible gift;

2. on the part of the *form*—some form of destruction of this offering;

3. on the part of the *minister*—a priest;

4. on the part of its *purpose*—worship of God.

611. *The Mass is a) a true sacrifice, and b) a representation in an unbloody manner of the bloody sacrifice of the Cross.*

The Mass is a true sacrifice since it verifies the four conditions required for sacrifice.

It is a dogma of Catholic Faith that the Mass represents the sacrifice of Calvary.

THE ESSENCE OF THE SACRIFICE OF THE MASS probably consists in the consecration of both species with a view to their reception in Holy Communion as an integral part of the Sacrifice.

---

[462] See S.R.C., Nov. 30, 1895.

1. It is not permissible to apply the Mass or even to change its application once the consecration of both species is complete, since the essence of the Mass has been perfected already.

2. Consecrated hosts in the ciborium must remain on the altar until after the priest's Communion, since this is an integral part of the Mass.

Art. 2. The Value, Effects, and Fruits of the Mass

612. 1. The VALUE of the Mass embraces two points: its dignity and its efficacy. Now its *dignity* is infinite because of the infinite dignity of both the principal Offerer (Christ) and the Victim (Christ). The *efficacy* of the Mass is infinite a) in relation to its sufficiency, b) in relation to its effects of worship, thanksgiving, and propitiation, c) in relation to its so-called special fruits.[463]

All these principles follow from the fact that the Sacrifice of the Mass has the same efficacy as the sacrifice of the Cross. What these effects and fruits are will be considered in the following paragraph.

613. 2. The EFFECTS of the Mass include everything actually produced by the Mass in reference to God and in reference to the world. Five such effects are normally given:

a) *worship* (or *latria*);

b) *thanksgiving*;

c) *impetration for grace*;

d) *propitiation* for the sins of the world;

e) *satisfaction* for the punishment due to sin.

All these effects result from the very nature of the Mass itself (*ex opere operato*) but are in part due to the holiness of the Church, the dispositions of the priest and faithful who offer the Sacrifice. However, these effects—with the exception of worship and thanksgiving—are not produced *infallibly*.

614. 3. The FRUITS of the Mass. Some authors regard the fruits of the Mass as identical with its effects, but it would be preferable to restrict the term to those effects which result from the Mass *for men* (and not for God), since we use the term *fruits* for products which we ourselves can enjoy (*fruor*). Therefore, the fruits of the Mass are to be restricted to the *propitiatory*, *impetratory*, and *satisfactory* effects.

The fruits of the Mass actually produced are certainly *limited*, and the limitation is caused partly by the dispositions of men who receive the fruits and partly by the free will of Christ Himself.

All theologians agree that the fruits of the Mass mentioned above are in fact limited—otherwise one Mass would be sufficient for the salvation of the entire world and for the release of all souls from purgatory, neither would it be permissible to offer several Masses for one and the same departed soul. But it is disputed

[463] See no. 614.

how the limitation arises. Some theologians[464] maintain that the fruits are limited *merely by the will* of Christ; others[465] think that the limitation is caused primarily by the *dispositions of the offerer or of the person receiving the fruits*. It is impossible to reach any certain conclusion on this question.

The fruits of the Mass are usually divided in reference to the *persons* whom they benefit:

a) the *general* fruit which benefits all the faithful, living and dead;

b) a *special* fruit received by the faithful who assist at Mass;

c) the *personal* fruit received by the priest offering the Sacrifice;

d) the *ministerial* fruit which benefits those for whom the Mass is offered.

Art. 3. The Application of the Mass

615. DEFINITION. *The application of Mass consists in the priest's intention or desire to apply the ministerial fruit for a particular purpose.*

This application must be made by the priest for each and every Mass, otherwise the fruit remains in the treasury of the Church. When the priest forgets to determine the application, the ministerial fruit probably passes *to the priest himself*. If the priest has received a stipend to offer Mass for a dead person who is already in Heaven or in hell, it is probable that the fruit goes to the person giving the stipend.

616. THE MANNER OF APPLICATION. It is necessary that the ministerial fruit be applied:

1. *for a particular purpose;*

It is not essential nor is it advisable that the determination of this purpose be too strict and precise. It is sufficient that the Mass be offered for the intention of the person who gave the stipend. It is never allowed to offer Mass for the intention of a person whom the priest foresees will offer a stipend and ask for the application of a Mass — although he has not yet done so — and then retain the stipend given for the Mass already offered.[466]

2. *before the second consecration at least.*

The second consecration would seem to complete the essence of the Mass, and therefore the priest is no longer free to dispose of its fruits. In practice, it is recommended that the application be made *before* Mass.

617. PERSONS FOR WHOM MASS MAY BE OFFERED. This depends on ecclesiastical law, since by divine law Mass may be offered for anyone to whom it may be of benefit; Christ offered the sacrifice of Calvary for all and it is the fruits of that sacrifice which are applied in the Mass. By ecclesiastical law Mass may be said for the living and the souls in purgatory. If offered for an *excommunicate* — e.g., a heretic — the

---

[464] See Noldin, Pesch, Lehmkuhl, Genicot, and so on.

[465] See St. Thomas, St. Alphonsus, Holzmann, Marc, and Aertnys.

[466] See CCL, Can. 825, no. 1.

Mass must be said in private and without giving scandal; if the excommunicate is *vitandus*, it may be said for his conversion only.[467]

THE OBLIGATION OF CELEBRATING MASS

The obligation of celebrating Mass may arise from one of six sources: 1) From the Priesthood; 2) From the Pastoral Office; 3) From a Benefice; 4) From the Acceptance of a Stipend; 5) From a Promise; 6) From Obedience.

618. 1. OBLIGATION ARISING FROM THE PRIESTHOOD.

All priests are bound to celebrate Mass several times each year unless they are legitimately prevented.[468] The bishop or religious superior must see that the priests subject to them celebrate Mass at least on Sundays and on other days of obligation.[469]

a) There cannot be any reasonable doubt that such an obligation *exists*, since everyone is bound to make use of the grace given them when opportunity arises, and certainly the power to celebrate Mass is an outstanding grace conferred by God on priests.

b) Regarding the *gravity* of this obligation, nearly all theologians—at least modern theologians—agree that every priest has a *grave* obligation to celebrate Mass on certain occasions, unless legitimately excused. St. Alphonsus thinks that every priest is under a grave obligation to celebrate Mass at least three or four times a year on the more solemn feast days, unless legitimately prevented.

c) Regarding the *source* of this obligation there is some discussion whether it arises from ecclesiastical or from divine law. It would be contrary to Catholic dogma to deny that Christ has imposed a command *on the Order of priests* to celebrate Mass, but it is not certain that this divine precept affects priests *individually*. The more probable opinion would seem to be that priests are not bound individually by the divine precept seeing that the Church does sometimes grant permission for a priest to be reduced to the lay state when he no longer celebrates Mass. If every priest were bound by divine precept to celebrate Mass it would not be easy to explain such an indult.

619. 2. OBLIGATION ARISING FROM THE PASTORAL OFFICE.

PRINCIPLE. *All who exercise the pastoral office are bound by divine law to offer Mass for their flock several times; ecclesiastical law determines certain days on which such Masses must be said.*

EXPLANATION. 1. *All who exercise the pastoral office*: that is, all those who have the care of souls in virtue of their *office*, such as: the Holy Father, residential bishops, abbots nullius, religious superiors, diocesan administrators

---

[467] See CCL, Can. 809.
[468] See CCL, Can. 805.
[469] Ibid.

(excluding the vicar general), vicars and prefects apostolic, parish priests and quasi-parish priests.[470]

2. Are bound by divine law to offer Mass several times. Consequently, the Council of Trent states: "Since by divine precept all who have the care of souls are commanded to know their flock and *to offer sacrifice for them.*"[471]

If Mass is never applied on behalf of their flock, it seems difficult to assert that the care of souls is being exercised sufficiently.

3. Ecclesiastical law determines certain days on which such Masses must be said. a) This obligation is *grave*, and no contrary custom nor sickness nor poverty can be urged as excuses; *b)* the obligation is *personal* and consequently a pastor cannot fulfill his obligation through a substitute, unless he is legitimately prevented from offering the Mass; *c)* the obligation is binding *on certain specified days*, i.e., on all Sundays and thirty-six feast days indicated in the Directory. Vicars and prefects apostolic and quasi-parish priests are to offer the Sacrifice for their people on eleven days only.[472] *d)* The obligation affects *certain persons*, namely, residential bishops, abbots nullius, parish priests, quasi-parish priests, vicars, and prefects apostolic.

NOTE. On the feast of Christmas and when a holy day of obligation falls on a Sunday it is sufficient for one Mass to be applied for the people.[473] If a feast day is transferred with *all* its obligations, parish priests must offer Mass for them on the day substituted; otherwise, he must apply the Mass on the proper feast day.[474] For a just reason (such as a funeral) the ordinary can allow the pastor to apply Mass for the people on a day other than that specified in law.[475] A bishop who rules or administers two or more dioceses, or a parish priest who rules or administers two or more parishes, satisfies the obligation by offering one Mass for all the people under his care.[476]

620. 3. OBLIGATION ARISING FROM BENEFICE. *A benefice* (or chaplaincy, of which we are now speaking) *is a pious foundation properly made and accepted by a legitimate ecclesiastical superior to which is attached the perpetual obligation of saying Masses (at a specified church, altar, day or hour, and so on).* Such an obligation is permanent. Although in the present discipline of the Church so-called foundation Masses cannot be properly called benefices, the following rules apply equally well to them.

FIRST RULE. The terms of the original contract accepted by legitimate ecclesiastical authority must be clearly stated and faithfully observed, since the foundation of a benefice is a genuine bilateral contract.[477]

---

[470] See CCL, Can. 306, 315, 339, 440, 466, 475, and 476.
[471] Session 23, "Decree on Reformation," chap. 1.
[472] See CCL, Can. 306 and 466.
[473] See CCL, Can. 339, § 2.
[474] See CCL, Can. 339, § 3.
[475] See CCL, Can. 466, § 3.
[476] See CCL, Can. 339, § 5, Can. 466 § 2.
[477] This rule is explained more fully in MTM, vol. 3, no. 260.

SECOND RULE. It is permissible for the ordinary (the diocesan bishop or major superior of any clerical exempt religious institute) to interpret or even dispense from conditions attached to a foundation in matters of less importance, if the obligations prove impossible of fulfillment through no fault of the administrators, but recourse must be had to the Sacred Congregation of the Council when it is desired to *reduce or condone the Masses to be said.*[478]

621. 4. OBLIGATION ARISING FROM STIPEND RECEIVED.

a) Meaning, Origin, and Lawfulness of Accepting Stipends. Stipends offered for the celebration of Mass are not given as a price for the Sacrifice—which would be a gross form of simony—but as an alms for the proper maintenance of the priest himself. Those who serve the altar may also live by the altar. The origin of offering Mass stipends is to be found in the offerings made by the early Christians during the Sacrifice of the Mass; later these offerings were made even outside Mass. *Any* priest (not merely one who is poor) who celebrates and applies Mass may receive a stipend.[479] A priest who celebrates Mass which he would not otherwise have celebrated if a stipend had not been given does not commit sin, provided that he puts the money to good use. But the Church has issued a grave prohibition against receiving several stipends for one and the same Mass, even though the priest applies the personal fruit of the Mass,[480] and also against receiving several stipends for several Masses celebrated on the same day[481] (with the exception of Christmas Day and any particular indult).

622. *b)* THE OBLIGATION IN GENERAL. When a priest accepts a stipend, he incurs a grave obligation in justice to apply the Mass by virtue of a gratuitous contract *do ut facias*, and he is bound to apply the Mass according to the conditions imposed and accepted.

Thus, a priest who accepts a stipend and fails to fulfill his promise to offer Mass not only sins gravely but is also bound to restitution.

A stipend given to a priest for the offering of Mass passes *immediately* into his ownership so that if it is lost he and not the donor is the loser; accordingly he is bound to say the Mass after accepting the stipend even though it is stolen from him.[482] When a sum of money is offered for Masses and the donor does not indicate the number of Masses desired, that number should be determined in accordance with the custom of the place *in which the donor is staying*, unless the priest can legitimately presume that the donor's intention was otherwise.[483]

---

[478] See CCL, Can. 1517, § 2.
[479] See CCL, Can. 824, § 1.
[480] See DZ 1110.
[481] There is nothing to prevent a priest who binates from accepting a stipend for one of his Masses or offering it for the people; he may use his second Mass to satisfy any obligation he has incurred by fidelity, vow, precept, statutes, and so on.
[482] See CCL, Can. 829.
[483] See CCL, Can. 830.

623. *c)* THE OBLIGATION WITH REGARD TO CIRCUMSTANCES. The obligation arising from the acceptance of a stipend extends not only to the Mass itself but also to all the circumstances tacitly or expressly stated, such as circumstances of time or place, privileged altar, votive character of Mass, Gregorian Masses, and so on.

i) With regard to the TIME OF CELEBRATION the Mass should be said within the time agreed upon by the priest and offerer. If no particular time was specified, then Masses to be celebrated for some urgent need (such as the recovery of health) must be offered as soon as possible within the useful time[484] in other cases, Masses are to be celebrated within a short time relative to their greater or smaller number.[485] No one is allowed to undertake to say *personally* more Masses than it is possible to say within one year.[486]

ii) With regard to Masses which are to be said AT A PRIVILEGED ALTAR (whether personal or local) this circumstance must be observed if it is expressly stipulated, and it may not be fulfilled by any other form of plenary indulgence.

iii) If stipends are accepted for thirty GREGORIAN MASSES, this obligation must be fulfilled; if the series is interrupted *through no fault* of the celebrant himself, it does not seem necessary to commence the series again, especially if some of the Masses are then said at a privileged altar. Such a burden would appear excessive for a priest; furthermore, it is not certain that such an interruption would cause serious loss to the soul of the dead person for whom the Gregorian Masses are being offered—at least if some of the Masses are said at a privileged altar.[487]

624. THE AMOUNT OF THE STIPEND for manual Masses is determined by the *diocesan standard* which must be observed by all, including exempt religious. Nevertheless, it is permissible to accept a larger stipend if this is offered *spontaneously*, and

---

[484] Useful time is that which is assigned for the exercise or establishment of a right, so that it is said not to run against a person if he is ignorant of the obligation or is prevented from acting (see CCL, Can. 35). Thus, for example, if a priest receives a stipend for a Mass for a person who is seriously ill, he must say the Mass as quickly as possible since the need is urgent. Should the priest be unable to say this Mass owing to his own unexpected illness for several weeks, the useful time does not run against him and he may satisfy his obligation afterward.

[485] See CCL, Can. 834.

[486] See CCL, Can. 835. In a Decree of the Congregation of the Council, May 11, 1904, it was laid down that the time allowed for one Mass is one month, the time for twenty Masses accepted at the same time is two months, the time for forty Masses three months, and the time for one hundred Masses six months. Since this has not been incorporated in the new Code it no longer enjoys the force of an obligation but is merely directive. The Code gives the following useful advice: in churches where on account of the special piety of the faithful alms are so abundant for Masses that they cannot all be celebrated in the church at the proper time, the faithful should be advised by a notice placed in an open and evident position that the Masses will be celebrated there as soon as conveniently possible. Whoever receives Masses for distribution to others must do so as soon as possible, but the legitimate time for their celebration begins to run from the day on which the priest who is to celebrate Masses has received them, unless some other obligation is, evident (see Can. 836 and 837).

[487] See MTM, vol. 3, no. 269; see also Arregui, *Summarium Theologiae Moralis*, no. 561.

even to demand a larger one if there are special duties attached to the Mass, such as the late hour at which it is to be celebrated or the appointment of a definite place. The amount of the stipend for *foundation* Masses is fixed by the ordinary—that is to say, by a bishop for all his priests not exempt from his jurisdiction or by a major superior for exempt religious.[488]

625. THE TRANSMISSION OF MASS STIPENDS. Anyone who has a number of Masses which he is allowed to give to others may transmit them to priests of his choice, provided he is certain that they are absolutely trustworthy or are recommended by the testimony of their own ordinary.[489] Consequently, the stricter injunctions previously in force are no longer binding. Whoever transmits Mass stipends to another remains bound by the obligation to offer Mass until he has received notice that the obligation has been accepted and the stipend received.[490]—The bishop or even a provincial council cannot forbid the clergy to send out of the diocese *manual* stipends to priests whom they know well.[491]

The following distinctions are usually made: *a) foundation* Masses are those which must be said in a specified place or by a particular priest; *b)* Masses which are *equivalently manual* Masses (*ad instar manualium*) are foundation Masses which may be celebrated elsewhere; *c) manual* Masses are those which may be said by any priest.[492] In transmitting Mass stipends, every semblance of trading or barter must be avoided,[493] but there are no longer any penalties inflicted ipso facto on those who transmit Mass stipends to booksellers or who make temporal profit from them.

The whole stipend as received must be sent to those to whom it is transmitted. But it is permissible to send less than the whole stipend *a)* if the donor expressly allows some portion of it to be retained, or if it is quite certain that the excess above the diocesan standard was given out of regard for the person;[494] *b)* if the stipends are quasi-manual, when one is allowed to keep the excess if the larger stipend takes the place of a partial endowment of the benefice or pious foundation;[495] *c)* if there exists a special indult of the Holy See; *d)* if the celebrant to whom the stipend is transmitted freely forgoes part of the stipend without being requested to do so.

626. NOTES. 1) Manual Masses which cannot be said by the priest to whom they are originally given must be sent to others within a year from the day of their acceptance; 2) quasi-manual Masses are to be transmitted to others before December 31 of the year in which they should have been said.

---

[488] See CCL, Can. 1550.
[489] See CCL, Can. 838.
[490] See CCL, Can. 839.
[491] See Sacred Congregation of the Council, Feb. 19, 1921 (AAS 13, 230).
[492] See CCL, Can. 826.
[493] See CCL, Can. 827.
[494] See CCL, Can. 840, § 1.
[495] See CCL, Can. 840, § 2.

All priests must keep an accurate account in some book of the Masses which they undertake and which they have fulfilled—otherwise serious inconvenience may easily ensue.

627. 5. OBLIGATION ARISING FROM PROMISE.

RULE. If the promise begets an *obligation of justice* to apply the Mass, then the priest has a grave obligation to fulfill the promise; if the obligation is one of *fidelity*, it is slight.

628. 6. OBLIGATION ARISING FROM OBEDIENCE.

Prelates whether secular or religious have the power of imposing on their subjects an obligation of applying Mass when there exists a just cause. This is by far the more common opinion and the one to be followed in practice insofar as it affects priests bound by the religious vow of obedience.[496]

LITURGICAL REQUISITES FOR THE CELEBRATION OF MASS

By ecclesiastical law four things are required for the lawful celebration of Mass: 1) legitimate time; 2) a suitable place; 3) sacred utensils; 4) observance of the prescribed rite.

Art. 1. The Time of Celebration

629. Both the day and the hour when Mass may be celebrated have been specified.

1. A priest may celebrate Mass on ANY DAY, but special statutes must be observed during the last three days of Holy Week.[497]

2. A priest is allowed (but not obliged) to celebrate three Masses on Christmas Day and on All Souls' Day, November 2nd. Blind priests who have been granted an indult to say a votive Mass each day may say this Mass three times on the days just mentioned.[498]

3. Two Masses may be said on Sundays and on holy days of obligation by those priests who have the *faculty of duplicating* granted either by common law or by an indult of the ordinary.

630. By *common law* (but in dependence on the ordinary who has the right of passing judgment in these matters) bination is not only permitted but also commanded in two cases: *a)* when a parish priest has two parishes or two parts of his flock so far distant from each other that one part cannot be present on holy days of obligation at the Mass of their parish priest owing to the distance to be travelled; *b)* when there is only one church which is too small to accommodate all the congregation at the same time.[499] Such cases are frequent in rural districts.

---

[496] See Sacred Congregation for Religious, May 3, 1914.

[497] See MTM, vol. 3, no. 281ff.

[498] See S. R. C., January 26, 1920 and January 12, 1921 (AAS 12, 122 and 13, 155).

[499] See Instruction of the Sacred Congregation for the Propagation of the Faith, May 24, 1870.

By special indult of the ordinary bination is sometimes allowed owing to the shortage of priests, even in churches where more than two Masses are said.

A priest is not allowed to accept a stipend for the second Mass nor fulfill any obligation of *justice*, unless the Holy See grants him special permission.[500]

631. 4. Mass may be offered at any hour from an hour before dawn until an hour after midday.[501] This ecclesiastical law forbidding the celebration of Mass at an hour notably before or after the stated period is binding under pain of grave sin; however, there are certain occasions when Mass may begin earlier or later than the stated times:

a) when a host has to be consecrated for the administration of Viaticum;

b) Midnight Mass at Christmas;

c) when there exists a reasonable custom;

d) when a bishop or religious superior grants permission;

e) when the Holy See grants such a privilege, as she has done to several religious institutes.

632. DURATION OF MASS. In normal circumstances a private Mass should not be longer than half an hour nor shorter than twenty minutes. Some theologians of repute consider that a priest who says his Mass in quarter of an hour commits a grave sin of irreverence and sometimes a grave sin of scandal.

Art. 2. The Place of Celebration

The place where Mass may be celebrated includes both the space within which Mass may be offered and the altar on which it is offered.

633. FIRST PRINCIPLE. *By common law Mass may be celebrated only in churches or oratories which have not been violated or desecrated and which are free from interdict.*

The principle refers to *common law* only, for by privilege some priests may celebrate Mass in any suitable place, e.g., cardinals, bishops, missionaries, and so on. In extraordinary circumstances and only occasionally the local ordinary (or major superior in the case of an exempt religious house) may grant permission for Mass to be celebrated in a becoming place, but not in a bedroom. — The violation of churches and oratories has been discussed already in the treatise on the virtue of religion, no. 447. Local interdict will be considered in the treatise on censures. A church is desecrated when it is changed to such an extent that it can no longer be regarded as the same church, as, for instance, if it were totally destroyed or the greater part of it destroyed—even though it may have been rebuilt—or if it has been converted to secular purposes.[502] A church is not

---

[500] See no. 621, note.
[501] See CCL, Can. 821, § 1; see also Appendix II, regarding evening Masses.
[502] See CCL, Can. 1170.

considered to have been destroyed by the plaster falling off or being removed from the walls on which were arranged the crosses of consecration.

634. SECOND PRINCIPLE. *Mass must always be celebrated on a consecrated altar whether fixed or portable.*

What is required prior to the consecration of a fixed or portable altar is discussed in liturgical law.[503]

MASS MAY NOT BE CELEBRATED:

a) in a heretical or schismatic church, even though it was originally duly consecrated or blessed: Can. 823, § 1. This canon is not considered as revoking special indults relating to churches used by Catholics and non-Catholics in turn;

b) on an altar belonging to another Catholic rite. But if there is no altar of the priest's own rite, he may celebrate Mass on an altar consecrated by another Catholic rite, following his own rite in the celebration of Mass;[504]

c) on the Greek *antimensia*, unless a priest has a special indult;

d) on a papal altar without an apostolic indult.[505]

Art. 3. Sacred Utensils

The sacred utensils for the celebration of Mass include 1) the altar furnishings; 2) the priest's vestments; 3) the sacred vessels.

635. THE ALTAR FURNISHINGS include:

a) three cloths made of linen or hemp, and blessed;

b) a Missal resting on a cushion or small stand;

c) two lighted candles made from wax;

d) a crucifix.

It is considered a grave sin to celebrate Mass with no altar cloth or lighted candle.

636. THE PRIEST'S VESTMENTS for Mass are the amice, alb, girdle, maniple, stole, chasuble. All these vestments must be blessed by a bishop or someone possessing the requisite faculties.[506]

It is grievously sinful to celebrate Mass with no sacred vestments or even without a chasuble and alb. The color of vestments prescribed for the different offices and feasts must be used; this is a light obligation.

---

[503] We have considered these questions at greater length in our *Manuale Juris Ecclesiastici*, q. 358ff and 366ff.

[504] See CCL, Can. 823, § 2.

[505] See CCL, Can. 823, § 3.

[506] The Code of Canon Law states in Can. 1304: "The following persons enjoy the power to bless those sacred utensils which must be blessed before they are used for their proper purpose:

1. *all cardinals and bishops (for all churches and oratories)*;

637. THE SACRED VESSELS required for Mass are the chalice and paten, cruets for wine and water, corporal, pall, purificator, chalice veil, and burse.

The paten and cup of the chalice must be of gold, or if silver, tin, or aluminium, must be gilted. The chalice and paten must be consecrated, and they lose this consecration once they lose their original form, as, for instance, through breakage, but not if they are regilt.[507] There is a grave obligation to use a blessed corporal for Mass.

The purificator and pall are not blessed.

The first washing of corporals and purificators must be performed by a subdeacon, or by a cleric in major Orders.[508] This may not be done by another cleric except in a case of necessity, although the contrary opinion was maintained by several theologians prior to the new Code.

Art. 4. The Rubrics of the Mass

638. PRINCIPLE. *All the rubrics of the Missal are binding in conscience in varying degrees.* This is evident from the Constitution of Pius V and from the Decree of the Congregation of Rites to be found at the beginning of the Missal. The Code gives the following rule: "The priest when celebrating Mass must observe accurately and with devotion the rubrics of his liturgical books and guard against adding prayers or ceremonies of his own choice; all contrary customs are disapproved."[509]

The gravity of this obligation must be determined from the nature of what is prescribed and from the common opinion of learned men. Thus, for example, there is a grave obligation to have a server for Mass unless the celebrant has been granted an apostolic indult;[510] any notable change in the Canon is gravely

2. *local ordinaries who do not possess the episcopal character,* for churches and oratories within their territory;

3. *parish priests* for the churches and oratories situated within the confines of their own parish, and *rectors* of churches for their own churches;

4. *priests delegated by the local ordinary* within the limits of their delegation and the jurisdiction of the person delegating;

5. *superiors of religious institutes* (even those which are not exempt) and *priests of the same order whom they delegate,* for their own churches and oratories and for the churches of the nuns subject to them."

[507] See CCL, Can. 1305, § 2.

[508] See CCL, Can. 1306, § 2.

[509] Can. 818.

[510] "A priest may not celebrate Mass without someone to serve him and make the answers. A female server may be used only if no male person is available and there exists a just cause. In no case may the woman serve at the altar but she must answer the prayers at a distance" (CCL, Can. 813). Therefore, a priest is allowed to celebrate Mass for devotion with a woman as server if there is no man present capable of serving. It would be a grave sin for a woman to serve immediately at the altar, for example, by offering the cruets to the priest (see TM, bk. 6, no. 392).

forbidden, likewise the omission of those integral parts outside the Canon which must be said *at every Mass*, such as the Gospel. The remainder does not seem to be binding under any serious obligation.

639. BRIEF INTERRUPTIONS during Mass are permissible if there is a just cause. Thus, for example, a sermon may be preached or the banns of marriage published after the Gospel; after the celebrant's Communion an interruption may be made to give a short exhortation to those about to make their First Communion or to those who have taken religious vows. But only an extremely grave reason would permit the interruption of the Mass between the commencement of the Canon and the priest's Communion—such as the need to administer Viaticum to a dying person or the celebrant's temporary indisposition.

To DISCONTINUE the Mass *before* the Consecration is only permitted for a grave cause;[511] it is never permitted to discontinue Mass *after* the Consecration except in imminent danger of death or to preserve the Holy Eucharist from profanation. If Mass is interrupted after the Consecration, it must be resumed either by the celebrant himself or another priest even if not fasting—otherwise sacrilege will result.[512] If, however, the interval is longer than an hour, there would seem to be no moral union between the two parts of the Mass, and thus it is probable that there no longer exists any strict obligation of completing the Mass; however, it is not forbidden to resume a Mass even several hours after its interruption.[513]

TREATISE V
PENANCE

This treatise is divided into three chapters: 1) The Nature of Penance; 2) The Subject of Penance; 3) The Minister of Penance.

THE NATURE OF PENANCE

The word *penance* is used by theologians in three different senses, either 1) for the moral virtue of penance; or 2) for the Sacrament of Penance; or 3) for that part of the Sacrament of Penance which is known also as satisfaction. We shall consider 1) The virtue of penance; 2) the Sacrament of Penance both in its essence and in its effects.

Art. 1. The Virtue of Penance

640. DEFINITION. *The virtue of penance is a supernatural habit infused by God whereby man readily inclines both to sorrow for sins committed inasmuch as they offend God and to a firm purpose of amendment.*[514]

---

[511] See ST, III, q. 83, a. 6, rep. 1.
[512] Ibid.
[513] See TM, bk. 6, no. 355.
[514] See ST, III, q. 85, a. 3, c.

1. Penance is a *supernatural habit* because although it is true that one may grieve over the commission of sin with one's natural powers and for purely natural reasons, such penance is not a perfect virtue nor does it remove the stain of sin.

2. The virtue *readily inclines man to prompt sorrow for sin inasmuch as it is an offense against God*. Therefore, not every form of sorrow for sin (e.g., sorrow because of the natural distressing consequences of sin) is an act of the virtue of penance, but only when sin is hated precisely as an offense against God.

3. This sorrow must be *accompanied by a purpose of amendment*, since true sorrow must always include such resolution.—It follows from what has been said that there are three elicited acts of the virtue of penance: 1) sorrow for sin committed; 2) detestation of sin; 3) resolution not to sin again.

641. The proximate SUBJECT of the virtue of penance is the will. Therefore, the faithful are not to be worried because they lack any sensible feeling of sorrow for sin. The remote subject of the virtue is any man guilty of sin or at least capable of sin.

642. The material OBJECT of the virtue is any personal sin (not original sin); the formal object is the offense against God which must be expiated, or the injured rights of God for which reparation must be made through satisfaction.

643. The virtue of penance is a NECESSARY MEANS OF SALVATION for all sinners and is also commanded. The Council of Trent has defined: "Penance has been necessary at all times for all men who have stained themselves with mortal sin, in order to obtain grace and justification."[515] And Christ Himself said: "You will all perish as they did, if you do not repent" (Lk 13:5). Ecclesiastical law also commands the virtue of penance by enjoining confession once a year.

Theologians are not agreed concerning *the time when the precept of penance is of obligation*, but the following seems to be generally admitted.

The precept binds *incidentally* when some other obligation must be fulfilled which of its nature presupposes penance—for example, when a priest in the state of mortal sin must administer some Sacrament. *Of its very nature* the precept is of obligation at the hour of death or in grave danger of death, but there exists no strict obligation to elicit an act of penance immediately after the commission of sin. Nevertheless, a notable delay (e.g., more than a year) in eliciting such an act would be a special grave sin.

Art. 2. The Sacrament of Penance: Its Nature and Its Effects

644. DEFINITION. *The Sacrament of Penance is a Sacrament of the New Law instituted by Christ in the form of a judgment for the remission through sacramental absolution of sins committed after Baptism, granted to a contrite person confessing those sins.*

Christ seems to have INSTITUTED this Sacrament after His Resurrection when He breathed on His apostles and said: "Receive the Holy Spirit; when you forgive

---

[515] Session 14, "Doctrine on the Sacrament of Penance," chap. 1. See also TCCI 7:286.

men's sins they are forgiven, when you hold them bound, they are held bound" (Jn 20:22–23).

The Sacrament has been instituted *in the form of a judgment*[516] in which the penitent is at once the accused, the witness, and the accuser, while the priest is the judge who generally absolves and does not condemn the guilty sinner.

Only sins committed *after* Baptism are forgiven in this Sacrament and these therefore constitute the remote matter of the Sacrament.

By the words *granted to a contrite person confessing sin* is indicated the proximate matter, while the form of the Sacrament is signified by the words *through sacramental absolution.*

Special consideration must be given to: 1) The Remote Matter of the Sacrament; 2) The Proximate Matter; 3) The Form; 4) The Effects.

§ 1. The Remote Matter of the Sacrament

645. The remote matter—or, more correctly, the matter to be removed—are all sins committed after Baptism, and such matter is: 1) either necessary or free; 2) either certain or doubtful; 3) either sufficient or insufficient.

NECESSARY MATTER *for the Sacrament of Penance is all mortal sins committed since Baptism and not yet revealed in confession nor directly remitted by sacramental absolution.* All such sins must be confessed.

FREE MATTER *for the Sacrament comprises: a) venial sins committed since Baptism; b) all mortal and venial sins already remitted since Baptism by sacramental absolution.* Therefore, these sins may be confessed but there is no obligation to do so.

CERTAIN MATTER is every genuine and certain sin whether mortal or venial.

DOUBTFUL MATTER includes all doubtful sins, i.e., sins which probably were not committed.

SUFFICIENT MATTER is that which suffices for the valid reception of sacramental absolution, i.e., certain matter whether necessary or free.

INSUFFICIENT MATTER is doubtful matter or anything which is not genuinely sinful, such as so-called imperfections.

646. SCHOLIUM. *Generic confession.* The essence of the Sacrament of Penance consists in the fact that it is a judgment, as we have stated already. But a judge is unable to pass judgment unless he has knowledge of the crimes committed by the criminal. Since in the judicial court of Penance God Himself—the searcher of hearts—is the principal Judge, and the purpose of this judgment is to reconcile and *free* the sinner, it is not necessary that the confessor himself be *perfectly* aware of the sins of the penitent. Therefore, in a case of extreme necessity either a generic accusation or no accusation whatsoever is sufficient for receiving absolution. Apart

---

[516] See CCL, Can. 870.

from such cases of extreme need, generic confession is never permissible; if the matter is *necessary* both the species and number of sins must be confessed, and if the matter is *free* it is both necessary and sufficient that the accusation mentions the virtue or commandment violated.[517]

§ 2. The Proximate Matter of the Sacrament

647. *The proximate matter of the Sacrament of Penance comprises the three acts of the penitent, namely, contrition, confession, satisfaction.*

This is the most common opinion, denied by a few theologians who regard the act of absolution as the proximate matter of the Sacrament insofar as it is an *external ceremony*, whereas the same act considered as a sign is considered to be the form of the Sacrament.

Contrition must be present either actually or at least virtually. Sometimes it is sufficient for the validity of the Sacrament if only the *desire* for confession and satisfaction is present, since these are then considered to be included implicitly in the act of contrition. We shall return later to a detailed consideration of each of these three acts of the penitent.

§ 3. The Form of the Sacrament

648. *The essential form* of the Sacrament of Confession is the words: "Deinde ego te absolvo a peccatis tuis in nomine Patris et Filii et Spiritus Sancti. Amen." Everyone admits that the priest validly absolves if he uses these words only: "Absolvo te a peccatis tuis." The following forms are likewise probably valid: "Absolvo te" and "absolvo a peccatis tuis." But it is not lawful to use such forms, and no reasonable excuse ever exists for permitting the use of forms which are no more than probably valid. In cases of necessity, as in a shipwreck, it would be quite valid and lawful to give absolution to several persons at the same time, using this form: "Ego vos absolvo a peccatis vestris in nomine Patris ..." and so on.

The rubrical form of absolution is to be found in the Roman Ritual or in any approved Ritual.

649. *Obligation of using the prescribed ceremonies. a)* The raising of the priest's hand from the beginning of the prayer *Indulgentiam* until the signing with the cross during the act of absolution is not of strict obligation but it is most praiseworthy. *b)* The prayers *Misereatur, Indulgentiam, Passio* are not to be omitted except for a just cause,[518] such as a great number of penitents. *c)* It would not be grievously sinful to omit the absolution from censures if the confessor were morally certain that the penitent had not incurred any censure. *d)* External ceremonies, such as the place to be used for hearing the confessions of women, must be carefully observed.

---

[517] See MTM, vol. 3, no. 325.
[518] See CCL, Can. 885.

650. MANNER OF GIVING ABSOLUTION.

1. Absolution must be given *orally*, and therefore written absolution handed to a penitent is invalid.[519]

2. Absolution must be given by the priest *while the penitent is morally present*. Since absolution must be given orally it cannot be given to any penitent who is unable to hear the words or to whom the priest is unable to speak. In cases of extreme necessity this presence is to be interpreted widely, so that everyone—even those far distant from the priest—can be absolved, provided that in some sense of the word they can be perceived. However, it seems probable that absolution is invalid if given over the telephone or by other forms of long-distance communication. In real necessity absolution could be given in this way conditionally.

651. PRACTICAL DIRECTIONS. If the penitent leaves the confessional before receiving absolution, the following procedure is to be adopted:

a) if they can be recalled easily, the priest should do so;

b) if they cannot be recalled without causing inconvenience or surprise, the priest should pronounce the essential words of absolution before the penitent has departed more than twenty paces from the confessional; it is not necessary that the confessor be able to hear or see the penitent, provided that the latter is in close proximity to the confessional;

c) if the penitent has gone some distance and cannot be recalled and will not return to the same confessor, there is nothing to be done except to commend him to the mercy of God;

d) if the penitent returns later to the same confessor he should be informed of the previous lack of absolution and then absolved.

652. Absolution must be given *absolutely, not conditionally nor in the form of a wish*. The act of absolution is a judicial sentence which cannot be conditional nor expressed in the form of a wish. Absolution given in the latter way—unless the wish is equivalently an indication of the priest's judgment—is not only unlawful but also probably invalid.—Conditional absolution in which the condition regards the *future*, such as: I absolve you if you make restitution: is certainly invalid; absolution given conditionally on some *present* event is valid and lawful as often as the Sacrament might be invalid if given absolutely, or some notable spiritual harm would ensue to the penitent if absolution were refused.

The chief causes permitting conditional absolution are:

1. doubt whether the penitent is alive or dead;

2. doubt whether the penitent has sufficient use of reason;

3. doubt whether absolution was given correctly;

4. doubt whether the penitent is morally present;

5. doubt concerning the jurisdiction of the confessor;

---

[519] See the Decrees of Clement VIII, June, 1602 and of Paul V, July 13, 1605.

6. doubt whether the penitent has sufficient sorrow and purpose of amendment and there is danger of greater harm resulting from any postponement of absolution.

653. SCHOLIUM. REPETITION OF ABSOLUTION. If the penitent has already received absolution and then mentions some serious sin which he had forgotten or some grave circumstance affecting his sins or the number of times when grave sin was committed differing substantially from that mentioned previously, the confessor must repeat absolution; otherwise, the penitent would be obliged to confess those sins again in his next confession.

§ 4. The Effects of the Sacrament

654. The Sacrament of Penance duly received has the following effects: 1) the remission of all sin and eternal punishment; 2) the infusion (or increase) of sanctifying grace, the virtues, and the gifts of the Holy Ghost; 3) the revival of all merits previously acquired in the state of grace. — Theologians are not agreed regarding the manner and extent of this revival of merit.[520]

THE SUBJECT OF THE SACRAMENT OF PENANCE

655. The subject capable of receiving the Sacrament of Penance is every baptized person who after Baptism commits personal (and at least venial) sin and is able to elicit these three acts of contrition, confession, and satisfaction. Each of these acts will be considered separately.

Art. 1. Contrition

This article is divided into four paragraphs: 1) The Nature, Kinds, and Effects of Contrition in General; 2) Attrition; 3) Qualities of Contrition and Attrition; 4) The Purpose of Amendment.

§ 1. Nature, Kinds, and Effects of Contrition in General

656. DEFINITION. *Contrition* (understood in its wide meaning) *is sorrow and hatred for sin committed, together with the determination not to sin again.* This is the definition given by the Council of Trent.[521] Three integral acts are necessary for contrition: *a)* sorrow, *b)* detestation, *c)* resolution.[522]

KINDS. Contrition understood in its wide sense is either *perfect contrition* if sorrow is elicited from the motive of love of God, or *attrition* if sorrow arises not from the motive of charity but from some other supernatural motive, such as fear of eternal or temporal punishment due to sin. *Natural motives*, such as the natural evil of sin or its natural evil effects, are not sufficient for genuine attrition.

---

[520] See MTM, vol. 3, no. 337.
[521] Session 14, "Doctrine on the Sacrament of Penance," chap. 4. See also TCCI 7:298.
[522] See MTM, vol. 3, no. 339.

THE EFFECT of perfect contrition is the remission of all sins, provided that there is present also a desire to receive the Sacrament of Penance; attrition never remits sin (at least, mortal sin) unless it is actually conjoined with the Sacrament of Penance. The *necessity* of contrition in general has been noted when discussing the necessity of penance, no. 643.

§ 2. Attrition

657. THE VALUE OF ATTRITION. Although attrition of itself is not sufficient for the remission of mortal sin, yet it does *suffice* for obtaining justification in the Sacrament of Penance.

This statement is certain and now admitted by everyone, so that it would be rash to hold the contrary opinion proposed by several theologians prior to the Council of Trent. Attrition based on nothing more than the fear of hell is a *morally good act*, since in such attrition there are to be found three elements which are all good in themselves:

a) the motive inducing attrition, namely, fear of hell;

b) the means for avoiding hell, namely, detestation of sin;

c) the direction of this detestation toward the avoidance of hell.

Luther, the Jansenists, and others falsely maintained that attrition founded solely on fear of hell was evil and made man a hypocrite.

Whether this form of attrition based on the fear of hell is sufficient for the Sacrament of Penance without any initial love of God is fiercely disputed, but the controversy seems to be one of words rather than of fact, since every act of attrition elicited *from some supernatural motive* is in some way referred to God and therefore includes love and subjection.

§ 3. Qualities of Contrition and Attrition

658. Contrition or attrition necessary for the Sacrament of Penance must possess four qualities.

1. It must be *true and formal* contrition for sins committed, not merely external and fictitious or imagined or implicit.

2. Contrition must be *supernatural, a)* in its *principle*, insofar as it must be elicited with the aid of supernatural grace and not merely through man's natural powers; *b)* in its *motive*, insofar as it results not from natural motives but from motives known through the light of faith.

3. Contrition must be *supreme*; this does not mean that the penitent must experience an *intense* feeling of sorrow for sin but rather that he must look on sin as a *greater evil* than any other, so that he would be prepared to endure all other evils rather than commit sin.

4. Contrition must be *universal*, inasmuch as contrition or attrition must embrace all mortal sins committed by the penitent.

659. COROLLARIES. Since contrition is part of the proximate matter of the Sacrament of Penance and absolution is its form, the following conclusions can be made:

a) Contrition or attrition must be expressed *in some external sign*, and therefore merely internal contrition or attrition does not suffice; however, it is not necessary that it be expressed in words.

b) Contrition must be elicited *prior to absolution and exist together with the act of absolution*, for the Sacrament is constituted by the union of its matter and form; in practice, however, contrition should be elicited before confession.

c) Contrition must have *some reference to the absolution*, for the same reason.

d) However, contrition need not be repeated when the penitent immediately after receiving absolution confesses a mortal sin which he had forgotten and is then absolved again. The previous act of contrition continues virtually.

§ 4. The Purpose of Amendment

660. DEFINITION. *The purpose of amendment is a resolution not to sin again.* Therefore, a mere wish is insufficient, but it is not strictly necessary that the resolution be in the form of a promise or a vow of avoiding all sin.

The purpose of amendment may be explicit and formal when it is a special act distinct from the act of contrition, or implicit and virtual such as is contained in every act of sincere contrition which of its very nature implies not merely detestation of past sin but also determination to avoid future sins.

NECESSITY. *At least an implicit purpose of amendment is required for the validity of the Sacrament of Penance*, since the implicit resolve to avoid sin which is inseparably united with contrition is just as necessary as contrition itself.

In practice, the penitent should elicit not only an implicit purpose of amendment but also one that is explicit and centered on some special sin, since this will be more effective for the amendment of his life.

661. THE CHARACTERISTICS of the purpose of amendment should be three in number.

1. It must *be firm*, at least insofar as it affects the present determination of the will, although it may be weak in relation to the future. Thus, a firm determination is not the same as a constant determination, and so it is not necessary that the penitent be firmly persuaded that he will not sin again.

2. It must be *efficacious* to the extent that *a)* the penitent must use all the means necessary to avoid sin, such as prayer and vigilance; *b)* the penitent must avoid voluntary proximate occasions of sin; *c)* he must do all in his power to repair any damage caused by his sins.

3. It must be *universal*, so that the penitent resolves to avoid all mortal sins.

Even if the penitent confesses only venial sins or free matter for absolution, a genuine purpose of amendment is no less essential for the validity of the Sacrament than sincere contrition, and it must extend either:

a) to the avoidance of all venial sins, or

b) to the avoidance of one specific venial sin, or

c) to the correction of one type of sin, such as sins of the tongue, or

d) to the avoidance of all deliberate venial sins, or at least

e) to the less frequent commission of venial sins.

Art. 2. Confession

This article is divided into three paragraphs: 1) The Nature and Necessity of Confession; 2) The Qualities of Confession; 3) The Repetition of Confession.

§ 1. The Nature and Necessity of Confession

662. DEFINITION. *Confession is an accusation of personal sins committed since Baptism, which is made to a competent priest for the purpose of obtaining absolution.*

If only one of these elements is lacking from an individual confession, there is no sacramental confession and the *seal* of Confession has no place; e.g., if sins are confessed for the sake of obtaining advice or seducing the priest.

The NECESSITY of sacramental confession for all sinners arises both from divine and from ecclesiastical precept.

Divine law instituted the Sacrament of Penance in the form of a *judgment,* since Christ gave to His apostles and their successors the power either to retain or to forgive sin. But no confessor is able to pass judgment unless he is first acquainted with the sins of the penitent, and such knowledge can be gained only through the penitent's accusation. Therefore, confession of sin is required by divine institution in the Sacrament of Penance.[523]

Ecclesiastical law requires the following, according to Can. 906: "Every one of the faithful of either sex on attaining the age of discretion, i.e., the use of reason, is bound to confess sincerely all sins at least once a year." This precept is not satisfied by a sacrilegious or invalid confession;[524] but all the faithful may make their confession to any approved confessor even of another rite.[525]

663. THE TIME OF THE OBLIGATION. 1. *Of its very nature the divine precept* enjoining confession of sin is binding on sinners *a)* in actual or probable danger of death; *b)* several times during life. The same precept is binding *for incidental reasons, a)* when the sinner wishes to receive Holy Communion; *b)* when a state of grace is necessary

---

[523] See cf. Council of Trent, Ssession. 14, "Doctrine on the Sacrament of Penance," chap. 5. See also TCCI 7:310–311.

[524] See CCL, Can. 907.

[525] See CCL, Can. 905.

and the sinner cannot be morally certain of eliciting an act of perfect contrition; c) when it is impossible to overcome some serious temptation, especially an evil habit, without the aid of confession.

2. *The ecclesiastical precept* regarding confession is binding only once in the year and probably affects only those who are guilty of mortal sin. Theologians do not agree how the year is to be reckoned. In practice, it is sufficient that the year be reckoned from one Easter until the next.

§ 2. Qualities of Confession

664. There are certain necessary qualities which the confession must possess, others which are useful. St. Thomas together with other older theologians used to give sixteen:

"Sit simplex, humilis confessio, pura, fidelis,
tque frequens, nuda, discreta, libens, verecunda,
Integra, secreta, lacrimabilis, accelerata,
Fortis et accusans et sit parere parata."

1. The confession must be *simple, unadorned, sincere, humble*—that is to say, free from all superfluous words and commentary; it should be made humbly both in word and deed and therefore the penitent should kneel, unless he is excused by some infirmity or other reason; it should be sincere, i.e., made with the right intention.

665. 2. The confession should be *truthful*, i.e., free from all lies. To lie in confession concerning a grave matter which ought to be revealed is a grave sacrilege and renders the confession invalid; to lie concerning some matter which is not necessary for confession is sinful but does not invalidate the confession, unless the gravity of the matter makes it gravely sinful. Thus, for instance, confession is invalid if the lie affects a circumstance of the sin which changes its species, or if in the course of the confession grave calumny is spoken against one's neighbor; if the penitent denies having committed some venial sin or a mortal sin which had been forgiven in a previous confession, his confession is not invalid, although venially sinful. Nevertheless, such a sin which, objectively speaking, is venial does introduce a circumstance which greatly aggravates the sin because to commit sin at the same time as one is seeking remission of sin shows want of reverence for the Sacrament.

3. The confession should be *discreet and modest*, i.e., the penitent should not reveal the sins of others, nor should he use obscene words or extremely coarse language to confess sins against the sixth commandment.

4. Confession should be *oral*, i.e., expressed in words and not merely by nodding or by word or in writing, unless there is a just cause, such as an inability to speak.

5. Confession must be *secret*, i.e., not public, and therefore no one is obliged to make use of the services of an interpreter.[526]

[526] See CCL, Can. 903.

The most important quality of confession is its integrity to which we must now devote more careful attention.

THE INTEGRITY OF CONFESSION.

666. DEFINITIONS. Confession is *formally* integral when it includes all those mortal sins which, taking everything into consideration, the penitent can and must confess here and now; confession is *materially* integral when it includes all mortal sins committed after Baptism and not yet directly remitted.

THE NEED FOR INTEGRITY. *1) Formal integrity is absolutely essential for the validity and lawfulness of confession; 2) legitimate excuses can be found for the absence of material integrity.*

The first part of this statement is evident from the Council of Trent[527] where it is stated that divine law requires the confession of each and every mortal sin (remembered after due and careful consideration), even those which are hidden and contrary to the last two commandments of the Decalogue, and the circumstances which affect the species of the sin.

The second part of the statement is evident from the fact that sometimes material integrity is impossible, and Christ, although commanding that confession be complete, does not bind anyone to the impossible.

667. THE EXTENT OF INTEGRITY. It is certain that the penitent must reveal in confession:

a) the *ultimate* moral species of mortal sins;[528]

b) the *number* of mortal sins, insofar as this is morally possible;[529]

c) circumstances which *change the species* of sin.

It is not so certain that the penitent is bound to confess those circumstances which *notably aggravate* a sinful act. A strict obligation to confess such circumstances cannot be proved, yet it is better to confess them, and it may be necessary to do so for *incidental* reasons—*a)* because of the reservation attached to those circumstances, *b)* because of an occasion or habit of sinning, *c)* because of the satisfaction and other things which must be performed after confession.[530]

---

[527] See Session 14, "Doctrine on the Sacrament of Penance," chap. 5. See also TCCI 7:309.

[528] The specific difference of sins has been discussed already in the treatise on sin; see no. 158ff.

[529] A penitent who finds it impossible to remember the exact number of his sins should approximate to it as near as possible *a)* by using the word *about;* consequently, about ten times might mean either eight or twelve times; *b)* by mentioning how long the habit has existed and how many times each day or week the sin was committed.
Note. The confessor should not worry penitents unduly—especially the uneducated—regarding the number of their sins, since it is often impossible to obtain even a roughly accurate estimate. It is sufficient that the confessor be able to determine the state of the penitent's soul.

[530] See MTM, vol. 3, no. 370ff.

d) the external act of sinning. Thus, it would not suffice for a person who has committed fornication to say: I intended to commit fornication; he is bound to admit that he committed the act of fornication;

e) any external evil effect which was foreseen as following from this sin. This is at least the general rule. Thus, for example, a man who foresees pollution resulting from his reading of an obscene book must confess not only the reading of the book but also the pollution which actually followed.

Doubtful sins need not be confessed when the doubt is entirely *negative*; if the doubt is well-founded and *positive*, then according to the probabilists there is no strict obligation to confess such sins, whether the doubt relates to their actual commission or to their gravity or to their remission on a previous occasion; in their view a doubtful law does not bind. However, in practice it is to be highly recommended that such doubtful mortal sins be confessed, unless the penitent is excessively scrupulous.[531]

668. REASONS WHICH EXCUSE FROM MATERIAL INTEGRITY are physical and moral impossibility.

a) PHYSICAL IMPOSSIBILITY is considered to exist in the following and similar cases:

1. *extreme sickness*;

2. *defect of speech*, e.g., in those who are dumb or whose language cannot be understood by the confessor;

3. *lack of time because of imminent danger of death, as in shipwreck*;

4. *invincible ignorance or forgetfulness.*

b) MORAL IMPOSSIBILITY is considered to exist when material integrity would result in some grave moral inconvenience *extrinsic* to confession and only *accidentally* conjoined with the confession which has to be made here and now. Any inconvenience which is *intrinsic* to confession, such as a feeling of shame or the loss of good repute in the eyes of the confessor, would not be sufficient to excuse from material integrity.

Examples of moral impossibility are:

1. *imminent danger to life* resulting from confession either for the penitent, confessor, or a third person, such as during a time of plague;

2. *the danger of scandal or sin* on the part of the penitent or confessor — a case which is quite rare;

3. *risk of violating the sacramental seal* — e.g., if a person hard of hearing were to confess while others were close at hand;

4. *danger of loss of repute*, especially that of a third party; for instance, when a sin cannot be confessed without the confessor becoming aware of the accomplice, for the name of the accomplice is to be withheld as often as

---

[531] See MTM, vol. 3, no. 375.

this can be done without grave inconvenience. The confessor would commit grave sin by asking directly for the name of the accomplice, but he is allowed to inquire about the circumstances of the sinful act which have to be revealed, even though at the same time the name of the accomplice will be made known indirectly.

669. THE MEANS to be used for obtaining integrity in confession is a careful examination of conscience.[532]

§ 3. The Repetition of Confession

670. A confession may be invalid or only incomplete through lack of integrity; it is invalid if *formal* integrity is lacking, incomplete when *material* integrity is wanting.

An incomplete confession should be completed by the accusation of the sin inculpably omitted in the previous confession; an invalid confession must be repeated in its entirety, for sin is not remitted by invalid confession.

671. GENERAL CONFESSION. A *general confession* is the repetition of some or all the previous confessions of one's life.

a) A general confession is *necessary* when it is morally certain that some of the previous confessions were invalid.

b) A general confession is *harmful* when it would cause additional anxieties (for scrupulous souls) or other inconveniences, e.g., temptations.

c) A general confession is *useful* when the penitent would be roused to a more efficacious sorrow and amendment of life.

Art. 3. The Sacramental Penance

§ 1. Definition and Necessity of Penance

672. DEFINITION. *The sacramental penance is the means whereby the sinner compensates for the temporal punishment due to sin by willingly accepting good acts of a penal character imposed by the confessor.*

According to the mind of the Council of Trent,[533] this penance has a fourfold purpose:

1. it is an effective means of bringing home to the sinner that sin is a grave evil deserving dire punishment;

2. it makes the sinner more careful and vigilant not to fall into the same sin again;

3. it acts as a remedy for the infirmity resulting from sin and destroys evil habits;

---

[532] The way in which it should be made and the care to be used are discussed in MTM, vol. 3, no. 383ff.

[533] See Session 14, "Doctrine on the Sacrament of Penance," chap. 8. See also TCCI 7:323–325.

4. it makes the penitent like to Christ inasmuch as He Himself made satisfaction for sin.

673. THE NECESSITY OF PENANCE. *The confessor possesses not only the power but also, in normal circumstances, the obligation under pain of grievous sin of imposing a penance on the penitent.*

The confessor has the power of imposing penances since he must act in a similar way to God Himself Whose minister he is. But God, although He remits the debt of eternal punishment, continues to require temporal satisfaction.

The confessor has an obligation of imposing a penance in accordance with the precept of the Council of Trent: "The priests of the Lord should impose salutary and suitable penances, relative to the kind of sins confessed and the condition of the penitent, insofar as the Holy Spirit and prudence suggest as proper, lest they themselves should share in the sins of others by imposing light penances for the most serious sins and thus connive at sin and deal too gently with their penitents."[534]—In *normal* circumstances the priest is bound to impose a penance, for there are occasions when the obligation ceases: *a)* if the penitent is unable to perform the penance, as at the hour of death; *b)* if the penitent has already received absolution and then confesses some necessary matter and again receives absolution. However, in this second case it would be much better if the confessor imposes a new penance (even if light), or at least imposes the penance already given for a new reason.

Normally the priest has a *grave obligation* to impose a suitable penance, and this is admitted by all in those cases where the penitent submits grave matter; if the penitent confesses only free matter, some authors[535] think that the priest's obligation is only slight; however the contrary opinion would seem preferable, because by the voluntary omission of the penance the confessor is not fulfilling the duties of his office: he is depriving the Sacrament of an integral part and inflicting harm on his penitent.

674. THE AMOUNT AND NATURE *of the penance must be determined by the kind of sins confessed and by the condition of the penitent.* Such is the instruction given in the passage previously quoted from the Council of Trent and in the Code of Canon Law, Can. 887. Therefore, a grave penance should be imposed for a grave sin. A penance is considered *grave* if it is equivalent to some work which the Church would enjoin under grave sin, such as fasting, the hearing of Mass, five decades of the Rosary, one of the canonical hours; a *light* penance would be, for instance, the recitation of the *De Profundis*, five Our Fathers, and so on. A confessor who neglects to impose a grave penance for grave sin *without just cause* certainly commits sin. But there are just causes permitting the imposition of a smaller penance than usual:

[534] Ibid. See also CCL, Can. 887.
[535] See Lugo and Noldin.

1. the penitent's *physical infirmity*;

2. his *spiritual weakness*—when there is good reason to fear that a more severe penance is likely to harm rather than benefit the penitent due to his weakness in faith and religious fervor;

3. *deep and unusual contrition*;

4. *the occasion of a jubilee or plenary indulgence*;

5. *when the confessor himself performs part of the penitent's penance.*

The kind of penance to be imposed should conform to the state and correction of the penitent, for it is meant to be not only a punishment but also a cure. Generally speaking, all good works may be given as penances, but especially works of piety, charity, mortification, and prayers endowed with indulgences.[536]

In themselves there is nothing to prevent the following works being given as penances: *a)* internal acts, such as meditation, although they should be conjoined in some way to external works; *b)* works to be offered for the dead; *c)* a work which is already obligatory. A confessor should never impose unsuitable penances.[537]

§ 2. Acceptance, Fulfillment, and Commutation of the Penance

675. ACCEPTANCE AND FULFILLMENT. *The penitent is bound not only to accept but also to fulfill any reasonable penance imposed by his confessor.*

The penitent is so obliged, seeing that the penance is an integral part of the Sacrament of Penance. Therefore, anyone who wishes to receive the Sacrament must complete its integral parts. This obligation is considered to be grave when the penitent confesses mortal sins not previously remitted or a grave penance is imposed.—The penitent is bound to accept and fulfill a *reasonable* penance, for if the confessor imposes an unreasonable penance the penitent is not bound to accept it or he could seek commutation of the penance from another confessor.

If the penitent has *forgotten* his penance it becomes impossible to fulfill, unless he can conveniently return to the same confessor; if the confessor does not recall the penance he imposed nor the sins which were confessed, he is not obliged to ask the penitent to repeat his confession (at least, not in its entirety); it is sufficient for him to make a general estimate of the state of the penitent before imposing a new sacramental penance. The penance must be fulfilled by the *penitent himself* and not by a substitute. Since it was the penitent who committed and confessed his sins, so he himself must fulfill the penance imposed for those sins.

Regarding the *time* and *manner* of fulfilling the penance, the following points should be borne in mind.

1. If a time limit has been imposed by the confessor it must be observed; if not, the penance should be fulfilled as soon as morally possible. There is no obligation to

---

[536] See CCL, Can. 932.
[537] See TM, bk. 6, no. 513.

fulfill it *before receiving Holy Communion*, although normally speaking this is most fitting. If the penance is deferred so long that it is not fulfilled until the penitent again relapses into mortal sin, the command of the confessor is probably fulfilled, but it is difficult to understand how such a penitent can then remove the temporal punishment due to his former sins. Accordingly, penitents are to be encouraged to fulfill at least part of their penance as soon as possible.

2. The penance should be fulfilled according to the command and intention of the confessor.

676. COMMUTATION. It is easy to commute a penance already imposed *prior* to giving absolution, since the sacramental judgment is still incomplete; *after* absolution has been conferred and the penance accepted, commutation may be requested for a just reason either from the confessor who imposed the penance or from another confessor; the *penitent himself* has no power to commute his own penance, neither has any other person who lacks the necessary jurisdiction for hearing confessions. Commutation may always be granted provided there exists a *moral* continuity with the previous absolution. Therefore, it would not be possible to commute a penance long after absolution was granted.[538] Another confessor has no power to commute a penance except by granting a new absolution; thus, for instance, he could not commute a penance imposed for reserved sins unless he himself has power to absolve from such sins. This is the more probable opinion.

THE MINISTER OF THE SACRAMENT OF PENANCE

This chapter is divided into four articles: 1) The Power of the Minister; 2) The Duty and the Obligations of the Minister; 3) Various Classes of Penitents; 4) Misuse of the Sacrament.

Art. 1. The Power of the Minister

In this article will be considered: 1) The Sacred Orders of the Minister and His Jurisdiction in General; 2) Jurisdiction of Religious and for Confessions of Religious; 3) Restriction of Jurisdiction; 4) Absolution from Reserved Cases.

§ 1. The Sacred Orders of the Minister and His Jurisdiction in General

677. In order to administer the Sacrament of Penance validly and lawfully there is required in the minister sacred Orders and jurisdiction. Thus, the Code directs in Can. 872: "For valid absolution of sin there is required in the minister not only the power of Orders but also the power of jurisdiction—ordinary or delegated—over the penitent."

1. THE SACRED ORDER OF THE PRIESTHOOD is required by divine law for the valid administration of the Sacrament of Penance. This is defined by the Council of

---

[538] On the other hand, some authors—Lugo, Ballerini, Arreuig—maintain that commutation may be granted by the confessor who imposed the penance originally, even a long time after confession and outside the Sacrament.

Trent.[539] Therefore no deacon—still less a lay person—has the power of absolving validly from sin.

678. 2. ECCLESIASTICAL JURISDICTION in general is the power of ruling, judging, and coercing baptized persons in matters affecting their spiritual welfare and supernatural happiness. Sacramental jurisdiction is conferred by a legitimate superior who designates an approved priest to absolve or retain the sins of a determined number of subjects. Approval and jurisdiction are at present granted together by the same superior. Prior to the new Code a different ruling existed.

679. THE NECESSITY OF JURISDICTION. Jurisdiction is demanded by both ecclesiastical and divine law for the valid absolution of sin in the Sacrament of Penance. This is laid down by the Council of Trent[540] and follows from Christ's institution of the Sacrament in the form of a judgment. Now no one has power to give authentic judgment except in reference to his own subjects over whom he receives authority through the conferring of jurisdiction.

Ecclesiastical law demands that the necessary jurisdiction be *expressly* granted in writing or orally, and *no payment* can be demanded for the grant of jurisdiction.[541]

KINDS. 1. Jurisdiction may regard either the *external regimen* of the Church (*fori fori*) which guides the *external social* relations of the faithful toward the Church, or the *internal regimen* (*fori poli*) by guiding the *internal moral* relations of the faithful with God. The latter form of jurisdiction is *sacramental* when exercised only in the Sacrament of Penance, or *extra-sacramental* when it guides and binds the faithful in conscience only, even outside the Sacrament.

2. *Ordinary jurisdiction* is that which is annexed to some ecclesiastical office duly obtained, such as the episcopal office; *delegated jurisdiction* is conferred either by law or by an individual without any accompanying ecclesiastical office.

680. ORDINARY JURISDICTION for hearing confessions.

1. *The pope and the cardinals* possess ordinary jurisdiction over all members of the Church, including all members of religious orders.[542] The pope has the power of limiting the jurisdiction of everyone else.

2. *Local ordinaries* (such as the residential bishop, the vicar capitular, and the vicar general) have jurisdiction within the confines of their respective territories over all the faithful who are in those territories; they also exercise jurisdiction over their own subjects outside their territory.

---

[539] See Session 14, "On the Most Holy Sacrament of Penance," Can. 10. See also TCCI 7:315–317.

[540] See Session 14, "Doctrine on the Sacrament of Penance," chap. 7. See also TCCI 7:315.

[541] See CCL, Can. 879.

[542] See CCL, Can. c. 239, § 1, no. 1.

3. *The canon penitentiary of cathedral and collegiate churches* possesses ordinary jurisdiction over all those in the diocese, and may absolve the members of their diocese outside their territory.[543]

4. *Parish priests and all who occupy their place* have ordinary jurisdiction over their parishioners both within and outside their parishes.[544]

5. *Exempt religious superiors* have ordinary jurisdiction over their subjects in accord with their religious Constitutions.[545] Subjects include not only those who are professed but also novices, postulants, and those continually residing in the house, such as servants or students in the college.

NOTE. All who possess ordinary jurisdiction may hear the confession of their subjects anywhere at all and do not require the approval of the local ordinary. Cardinals, canons penitentiary, and parish priests cannot delegate their jurisdiction.[546]

681. DELEGATED JURISDICTION is derived either from law or from an individual.

1. Jurisdiction is delegated *by law*:

a) if the penitent is in grave danger of death. In such circumstances any priest may validly and lawfully absolve any penitent (rightly disposed) from all sins and censures, even though another approved priest be present.[547] However, if the dying person recovers, he is sometimes obliged to have recourse to certain authorities, as will be explained later. Soldiers who are mobilized or called up for war are considered to be in such a danger of death.[548]

b) to priests on a sea voyage, provided they have received the faculty of hearing confessions from their own ordinary[549] or from the ordinary of any port of call; they may hear the confessions of any of the faithful not only on board but also in any port at which the ship calls and absolve them even from sins reserved to the ordinary;[550]

c) for the absolution of persons from another diocese or parish or those of no fixed abode or Catholics of any Oriental Rite;[551]

d) to those priests whom cardinals and bishops choose to be their confessors.[552]

---

[543] See CCL, Can. 401; 873, § 2.
[544] See CCL, Can. 873, § 1.
[545] See CCL, Can. 873, § 2.
[546] See Pontifical Commission [hereafter Pont. Comm.], Oct. 16, 1919.
[547] See CCL, Can. 882.
[548] See Sacred Apostolic Penitentiary [hereafter S. Penitentiary], Mar. 12, 1912.
[549] Even if the confessor is a religious this ordinary is the local ordinary and not the religious ordinary, as stated by the Pont. Comm., July 30, 1934 (AAS 26, 494).
[550] See CCL, Can. 883.
[551] See CCL, Can. 881, § 1.
[552] See CCL, Can. 349.

2. Jurisdiction delegated *by an individual* must be given expressly and freely in writing or orally.[553] Nothing may be demanded for the grant of jurisdiction.[554] Ordinaries should not grant jurisdiction except to those who have been found on examination to be suitable; in the case of priests known by the ordinary to possess sufficient theological learning, such an examination would be superfluous and therefore should be omitted. But if after granting jurisdiction the ordinary has a prudent doubt regarding the continued fitness of a priest of whom he previously approved he should submit him to another examination, even if he is a parish priest or canon penitentiary.[555]

682. JURISDICTION SUPPLIED.

1. The Church supplies jurisdiction *in common error*—that is, if nearly all or the majority of the faithful in one place think that a priest hearing confessions has the necessary faculties, even though in fact he has not. No longer is there required what was known as a *titulus coloratus*, for the Code states simply and without restriction: "In common error ... the Church supplies jurisdiction both in the internal and in the external forum."[556] The reason for this law is the common good which would otherwise suffer grave harm. The Church does not supply jurisdiction in individual error, i.e., when one person or a few are in error.

2. The Church supplies jurisdiction *in probable and positive doubt* whether of fact or of law.[557] Thus, for example, a confessor absolves validly if he has positive reason to think that a sin is not reserved or that his temporary faculties have not expired. Thus, it is expressly stated in Can. 207, § 2: "If a priest who has received faculties for the internal forum *inadvertently* grants absolution even though he has completed the cases for which the faculties were granted or the time of his jurisdiction has finished, his absolution is valid."

3. The Church supplies jurisdiction *when a priest absolves from censures in ignorance of their reservation*, except in the case of censures imposed by a precept of a superior or of censures most specially reserved to the Holy See.[558]

683. JURISDICTION CEASES:

1. when it is *revoked* by a legitimate superior, although only a grave reason permits the revocation or suspension of jurisdiction.[559] This is self-evident since such revocation or suspension is extremely distasteful. Without consulting the Holy See a bishop has no power to revoke *at one and the same time* the faculties of all the confessors of so-called formed religious houses;[560]

---

[553] See CCL, Can. 879, § 1.
[554] See CCL, Can. 879, § 2.
[555] See CCL, Can. 877.
[556] Can. 209.
[557] Ibid.
[558] See CCL, Can. 2247, § 3.
[559] See CCL, Can. 880, § 1.
[560] See CCL, Can. 880, § 3.

2. *when the stated time comes to an end*; however, if absolution is inadvertently given after the expiry of the stated time or when the number of cases for which faculties were granted has been completed, the absolution is valid;[561]

3. *when the delegated person incurs certain censures;*[562]

4. *when the office ceases* to which jurisdiction was annexed.[563] NOTE. —Jurisdiction does not cease by the removal from office of the grantor (as, for instance, when a bishop dies or is transferred to another see), unless the contrary is evident from the accompanying clauses.[564]

§ 2. Jurisdiction of Religious and for Confessions of Religious

Special precepts exist regarding the jurisdiction of confessors belonging to clerical religious institutes and for the confessions of those who live in the religious state.

684. CONFESSORS BELONGING TO CLERICAL EXEMPT RELIGIOUS ORDERS may receive jurisdiction either *a) from the local ordinary* in order to hear the confessions of any person, including religious; but, ordinarily speaking, they should not use this faculty without at least the presumed permission of their superior.[565] Local ordinaries should not grant such habitual faculties except to religious who have been presented by their own superior; to those presented by their superior they should not deny this faculty without a serious reason.[566] Therefore religious no longer receive jurisdiction immediately from the Holy See as many theologians used to think;

or *b) from their proper religious superior* in accordance with the constitutions, but only in order to hear the confessions of the professed, the novices, and others who live day and night in the religious house either as servants or for the purpose of education or as guests or for convalescence.[567] This jurisdiction may also be given by the same religious superiors to secular priests and priests of another order or congregation.

Religious superiors may hear the confessions of those of their subjects who of their own free will ask to be heard, but without a grave reason this should not be done *habitually.*[568] The same applies to the master of novices and his associate,[569] unless there exists a privilege to the contrary.

685. *a)* MALE RELIGIOUS (whether professed or novices) according to existing discipline may be lawfully and validly absolved (even from cases reserved in their own

---

[561] See CCL, Can. 207, § 2.
[562] This is evident from Can. 873.
[563] See CCL, Can. 873, § 3.
[564] See CCL, Can. 183, § 2; 207, § 1.
[565] See CCL, Can. 874, § 1.
[566] See CCL, Can. 874, § 2.
[567] See CCL, Can. 875, § 1.
[568] See CCL, Can. 518, § 2.
[569] See CCL, Can. 891.

order) by any confessor approved by the local ordinary.[570] In every religious house of all clerical religious, several confessors lawfully approved must be appointed in proportion to the number of religious; if the religious are exempt, they must be granted jurisdiction over cases reserved in the institute.[571] But at present the reservation of cases in religious institutes seems almost useless and ineffective, since in a particular case any confessor may absolve from these reserved cases, as has been noted already.—In a *lay* religious institute, such as that of the Alexian brothers, there must be appointed an ordinary and extraordinary confessor, but any religious must be free to ask for any other confessor.[572]

b) CONFESSIONS OF NUNS. Special jurisdiction granted by the local ordinary is needed for hearing the confessions of a *community* of female religious. Cardinals alone have faculties to absolve any person, including religious of either sex, as we have noted already.[573]

In ordinary circumstances one *ordinary confessor* is to be appointed for each house who—unless a dispensation is granted—

i) must be at least forty years of age;[574]

ii) should not exercise his office for more than three years (and in no circumstances may he be reappointed beyond a third term);[575]

iii) has no jurisdiction in the external forum over the sisters;[576]

iv) should not in any way interfere in the internal or external rule of the community.[577]

In addition to the ordinary confessor, an *extraordinary* confessor is to be assigned to each religious house; all the sisters must present themselves to him four times each year, at least to receive his blessing, if they are unwilling to make their confession to him.[578] *Supplementary* confessors also are to be appointed by the local ordinary for each religious community who may be called upon easily to hear the confessions of sisters in particular cases.[579]

In addition to these confessors any female religious may a) ask for a special confessor or director for peace of soul or greater progress in her spiritual life;[580] b) approach any other confessor approved for hearing women's confessions.[581]

[570] See CCL, Can. 519.
[571] See CCL, Can. 518, § 1.
[572] See CCL, Can. 528.
[573] See CCL, Can. 876.
[574] See CCL, Can. 524.
[575] See CCL, Can. 526.
[576] See CCL, Can. 524.
[577] See CCL, Can. 524, § 3.
[578] See CCL, Can. 521.
[579] See CCL, Can. 521, § 2.
[580] See CCL, Can. 520, § 2.
[581] See CCL, Can. 522. A fuller discussion of this question concerning the hearing of the confessions of religious is to be found in the author's *Manuale Juris Ecclesiastici*, q. 188ff.

§ 3. The Restriction of Jurisdiction

INTRODUCTION. Jurisdiction may be restricted in various ways:

a) as to *persons*, if certain individuals, such as nuns, are excluded from the confessor's jurisdiction;

b) as to *place*, if jurisdiction is restricted to a specified district;

c) as to *time*, e.g., to three years;

d) as to certain *sins*, if the confessor has no power to absolve from more grievous sins. This form of restriction is more usually known as the *reservation of sin*, and this alone is considered here.

686. DEFINITION. *Reservation is the withdrawal of a case (a sin or a censure) to a special tribunal so that the only persons who may grant absolution are the individual who made the reservation, his successor, superior, or delegate.*[582]

There are two forms of reservation: a sin may be reserved as a *sin (ratione peccati),* or because the *censure* annexed to it is reserved *(ratione censurae);* consequently, we distinguish between reserved censures and reserved sins. Furthermore, these cases are either papal or non-papal reserved cases depending on whether they are reserved to the pope or to another superior.

The PURPOSE of reservation is to preserve ecclesiastical discipline and to inflict a more effective deterrent on the penitent.[583] It is for this reason that more serious and dangerous sins are reserved to judges endowed with greater prudence and experience; and penitents laboring under these reserved sins receive a beneficial medicinal punishment since they themselves incur the burden of having recourse to higher authority and, normally speaking, of receiving a more severe penance. Nevertheless, although reservation is so praiseworthy in itself, in modern conditions it is to be used most sparingly since penitents are apt to have little regard for it and in consequence the confessor himself incurs a heavy burden. Therefore, local ordinaries should not reserve sins to their own tribunal except after discussing the matter in diocesan synod, or, failing that, unless they have taken the advice of the cathedral chapter and of some of the more prudent and approved parish priests of the diocese, so that the real necessity or benefit of reservation may be evident.[584] The reservation should not remain in force longer than necessary for the extirpation of some inveterate public vice or for the restoration of weakened Christian discipline.[585]

687. THE POWER OF RESERVATION OF SIN.

a) The pope has reserved many censures to his own tribunal and one sin,[586] as will be noted more fully below.

[582] See CCL, Can. 893.
[583] See CCL, Can. 897; 2246, § 1.
[584] See CCL, Can. 895.
[585] See CCL, Can. 897.
[586] See CCL, Can. 894.

b) The local ordinary may reserve cases in his own diocese; however, a bishop should reserve only a few cases (i.e., three or four) which are not already reserved to the Holy See and on which the law has not already inflicted some censure, even though it is not reserved to anyone. One medicinal penalty is sufficient. The vicar capitular and vicar general have no power to reserve cases to themselves except by special mandate, even when they are local ordinaries.

c) The superiors of an exempt religious order may reserve sins for their own subjects. Amongst such superiors the superior general of an exempt clerical religious order and abbots in monasteries with independent jurisdiction can reserve sins of their own subjects, but in both cases after consultation with their council.[587] At present this power of reservation is almost of no practical value since any confessor approved by the bishop has the power to absolve in particular cases from such reserved cases in a religious order, as previously noted, no. 685.

688. CONDITIONS REQUIRED FOR THE RESERVATION OF CASES. No sin can be reserved so far as its absolution is concerned, unless:

a) the sin is *mortal* (both objectively and subjectively). This is evident, since the reservation of venial sin is useless;

b) it is *external*, even if occult. Although the Church has the power to reserve even internal sin, in practice she does not;[588]

c) it is *consummated in point of fact*; that is to say, it is necessary that the words of the reservation be verified in their strict sense; if even the smallest detail is lacking, the reservation is not incurred;

d) it is *certain* and not doubtful (whether the doubt be one of law or of fact or relating to its gravity).

689. IGNORANCE of the reservation excuses from the reservation in all *censures* reserved to the Holy See or to a bishop by common law.[589] But ignorance does not excuse *a)* from the reservation attached to the sin of false accusation of an innocent confessor; *b)* from the reservation of *sins* reserved to the bishop, unless he states otherwise. This is the probable opinion. Reservation is akin to incapacitating laws which do not admit ignorance as an excuse.[590]

§ 4. Absolution from Reserved Cases

690. 1. AT THE HOUR OF DEATH OR IN DANGER OF DEATH *reservation of sin ceases to operate, so that any priest (even if another is present with the necessary faculties[591]) may absolve*

---

[587] See CCL, Can. 896.
[588] See CCL, Can. 897.
[589] However, see no. 742.
[590] See CCL, Can. 16, § 1.
[591] A priest validly but illicitly absolves his own accomplice when that person is in danger of death, if another priest is present (see CCL, Can. 884).

from any sin and censure. This is the prescription of the Council of Trent[592] and of the Code of Canon Law.[593]

If such a person recovers from their illness, recourse must be made to the lawful superior or his delegate, if absolution was granted:

a) from a censure *most specially* reserved to the Holy See;[594]

b) from *public* and notorious censures, at least if reparation must be made for scandal given;

c) from a censure inflicted *by an individual.*[595]

Recourse is not necessary in any other case.

691. 2. Outside the danger of death the following rules are to be observed:

1) *Absolution from papal cases may be granted:*

a) by cardinals who may absolve any penitent from any sin or censure, with the exception of censures most specially reserved to the Holy See and those incurred by revealing secrets of the Congregation of the Holy Office;[596]

b) by ordinaries (i.e. bishops, and so on, major superiors of a clerical exempt religious order) who by virtue of Can. 2237 may absolve their own subjects *in the internal forum* either personally or through their delegate from all occult censures, provided that they are not reserved to the pope either most specially or specially. *In the external forum* bishops may grant absolution from the censure incurred because of heresy; the penitent thus absolved may then seek absolution in the internal forum from any confessor.[597] Sometimes bishops enjoy wider powers of dispensation in virtue of special faculties;

c) by any confessor in urgent cases when absolution cannot be delayed without grave inconvenience to the penitent. Although *direct* absolution is then granted, nevertheless if it is morally possible the penitent should have recourse either personally or through the confessor within one month to the Sacred Penitentiary or to a bishop having special faculties, or else he should seek absolution again from another confessor having the power to absolve from papal cases; if the penitent neglects these duties he falls again into the same censure.[598]

The case is considered urgent not only when there is danger of grave scandal or infamy arising from delay in granting absolution, but also when it is burdensome for the penitent to remain in the state of grievous sin during the period necessary for the competent superior to make provision. If the penitent has no earnest desire

[592] See Session 14, "Doctrine on the Sacrament of Penance," chap. 7. See also TCCI 7:316.
[593] See Can. 882.
[594] See CCL, Can. 2252.
[595] Ibid.
[596] See CCL, Can. 239, § 1, no. 1.
[597] See Holy Office, Feb. 19, 1916; see also CCL, Can. 2314, § 2.
[598] See CCL, Can. 2254, § 1.

to be absolved as quickly as possible, the confessor may legitimately urge him to that desire and then absolve him.—In such urgent cases any confessor may absolve even from cases *most specially* reserved to the Holy See; thus, for example, he may absolve a priest who presumed to absolve his accomplice in a sin against chastity. But, outside the danger of death, it is never possible to absolve validly one's own accomplice.

If it is *morally impossible* to fulfill the obligation of recourse—such as when the penitent is unable to return to the same confessor and he himself is unable to write to the Sacred Penitentiary, then the confessor can give absolution without imposing any obligation of recourse (except in the case of a priest who has illegitimately absolved his accomplice in sin), but he must:

a) enjoin whatever is required by law, such as the reparation of scandal or damage caused;

b) impose a fitting penance and satisfaction for the censure incurred, so that the penitent would relapse into the same censure unless he fulfilled the penance and made the satisfaction within the suitable period to be determined by the confessor.[599] Accordingly, a penitent who incurs excommunication through reading heretical works may be absolved in an urgent case by any confessor who happens to be staying for a short time in a place, but the confessor must say to such a person: you must surrender or burn those heretical books; moreover you must recite the Rosary twice within a month, otherwise you relapse into the same censure.

692. 2) *Absolution from episcopal cases* may be granted in the same way as absolution from papal cases, provided that the cases are reserved to the bishop *by law* (namely, the six or nine excommunications reserved by law to him).[600]

Religious confessors with the privileges of mendicants probably have the power to absolve from these cases reserved to the bishop *by common law*.

Cases which the bishop has reserved *in his own name* to his tribunal (whether a censure has been attached or not) and which should never number more than three or four may be absolved by any confessor *outside the territory of the bishop*, even if the penitent goes outside the diocese for no other purpose than to receive absolution.[601] Furthermore, they may be absolved *within the territory of the bishop reserving the cases*:

a) by an *ordinary confessor*,

i) whenever (in the prudent judgment of the confessor) faculty to absolve cannot be sought from the legitimate superior without grave inconvenience to the penitent or the danger of the violation of the sacramental seal;[602]

[599] See CCL, Can. 2254, § 3.
[600] See MIC, q. 680.
[601] See CCL, Can. 900, no. 3.
[602] See CCL, Can. 900, no. 2.

ii) whenever the legitimate superior refuses to grant faculty to absolve for a specific case;[603]

iii) in cases of the sick who cannot leave their house and of those who confess with a view to marriage;[604]

b) by missioners when they are conducting a mission given to the people.[605] This seems to hold true for spiritual exercises given to clerics and laypeople;

c) by parish priests (and by those who are in law called parish priests) during the time set apart for the fulfillment of the Paschal precept;

d) by the canon penitentiary and vicars forane. The canon penitentiary receives his faculty to absolve these reserved sins from common law; vicars forane receive their faculty from the bishop who should grant them power to subdelegate this faculty in their own district for a specific case.[606]

693. NOTE. 1. When a confessor possessing no special faculty absolves from a reserved censure either *through inadvertence or ignorance* the absolution is valid, provided that the censure was not imposed by an individual or reserved most specially to the Holy See.[607] Therefore, in this case the Church supplies jurisdiction—as previously mentioned—so that the penitent may not suffer any harm; this is even more true when the confessor acts through ignorance.

2. Priests without special faculties who *knowingly and without necessity* absolve from reserved sins commit grave sin themselves and are ipso facto suspended from hearing confessions;[608] those who presume to absolve without due faculty from cases either most specially or specially reserved to the Holy See incur excommunication simply reserved to the Holy See.[609]

3. *Travelers* and persons of no fixed abode may be absolved in exactly the same way as inhabitants. Although the contrary opinion was formerly proposed by many authors, it is no longer tenable in view of the clear decision of the Pontifical Commission, November 24, 1920.[610]

Art. 2. Duties and Obligations of the Confessor

694. The confessor enjoys a fourfold office—that of *judge, doctor, physician* and *father.* His chief office is that of *judge,* since the Sacrament of Penance was instituted by Christ in the form of a judgment.

[603] Ibid.

[604] See CCL, Can. 900, no. 1.

[605] See CCL, Can. 899, § 3.

[606] See CCL, Can. 899, § 2. The author discusses in MTM, vol. 3, no. 426ff how the confessor must proceed in practice if the penitent confesses a reserved sin and especially how the necessary recourse must be made.

[607] See CCL, Can. 2247, § 3.

[608] See CCL, Can. 2366.

[609] See CCL, Can. 2338, § 1.

[610] AAS 12, 575.

We shall consider the duties and obligation of the confessor: 1) Before Confession; 2) In the Act of Confession; 3) After Confession.

1. Before Confession

695. The confessor must prepare himself for hearing confessions by acquiring sufficient knowledge, the necessary prudence, and the Christian virtues.

a) *Sufficient knowledge* exists in a confessor who knows how to solve cases which generally occur and how to exercise prudent doubt in more difficult cases. Such knowledge is acquired by careful study and preserved by constant revision.

b) *Prudence is of prime importance* to the confessor in asking questions, passing judgment, suggesting remedies, giving advice, and imposing suitable penances.

c) *The Christian virtues* most necessary for the confessor are an ardent zeal for souls, untiring patience, fortitude, outstanding piety.

2. In the Act of Confession

696. During the actual confession,

1. the confessor must *judge correctly* the sins confessed and whether he is to grant or refuse absolution. Therefore, he must strive to obtain by suitable questions sufficient knowledge of the penitent's state of soul. In the words of the Roman Ritual: "If the penitent has not expressed as he ought the number, species and circumstances of his sins, the priest must question him prudently."[611] This interrogation must be:

a) *moderate, discreet, prudent.* Accordingly, the following instruction is given in the Code of Canon Law: "The confessor must never ask the name of the penitent's accomplice nor should he ask curious and useless questions, especially in regard to the sixth commandment, and especially must he refrain from putting imprudent questions to the young concerning matters of which they are ignorant."[612] If the confessor were to ask directly *the name of the accomplice* this would be a grave abuse of the Sacrament of Penance. Nevertheless, he is not forbidden to ask questions necessary to the integrity of the confession, even though these may reveal incidentally the name of the accomplice.

b) *opportune.* Generally speaking, it is not advisable to ask questions of the penitent *before* he has completed his confession, otherwise he is easily disconcerted and forgets the sins which he had to confess.—If the penitent conceals some grave sin which the confessor knows from other sources that he has committed, he must be careful to propose his questions in such a way as not to violate any secret, especially a confessional secret. Thus, for example, if the husband has openly confessed many sins committed with his wife and she in her turn fails to mention them, the confessor is not permitted to ask her questions different from those which he would put to any other married woman. If the wife persists in

[611] Tit. 3, chap. 1, no. 15.
[612] Can. 888, § 2.

concealing her sins, it is better to absolve conditionally (if nothing else is wanting) rather than to simulate absolution.

2. The confessor must *instruct and warn the penitent*, if this is advisable or necessary.

The confessor must *instruct* an ignorant penitent not only in the truths which are necessary for salvation but also in all that necessarily relates to contrition, purpose of amendment, confession, satisfaction, and so on. Sometimes the confessor is bound to instruct him in the duties of his state of life, such as the duties of the married state. Furthermore, if the penitent erroneously judges something to be sinful which in fact is not, or to be grievously sinful when it is venially sinful, the error must be corrected as harmful to him. But if as the result of an erroneous conscience a penitent is firmly convinced that something is lawful or valid which in fact is either unlawful or invalid, the penitent is to be corrected only if the admonition is likely to be profitable. Should the confessor prudently judge that such instruction would more likely lead to greater evils, the penitent can and should be left in good faith so as to prevent his material sins from becoming formal sins. — If the confessor has *grave doubts* whether the instruction will be of benefit to the penitent or not, it should be omitted.

The confessor must *warn* the penitent of the obligations which he must fulfill, such as the duty of making restitution, avoiding the proximate occasion of some sin, and so on.

697. 3. The confessor must *dispose his penitent to a sincere act of contrition and purpose of amendment*.

The Roman Ritual[613] contains the following instruction: "The confessor should use persuasive words to strive to lead the penitent to sorrow and contrition and to persuade him to amend his life and live better for the future; he should also suggest suitable remedies for his sins." If the confessor judges that the penitent is well disposed, he has no further obligation than to give absolution, but it is almost always useful for everyone (even for the learned and the pious) to suggest some motive of contrition and good resolution for the future. — If the confessor *doubts* whether the penitent is sufficiently disposed, he cannot absolve until the individual is rightly disposed.

There are many signs which indicate that the penitent is *sufficiently disposed*; e.g., *spontaneous* confession made willingly in order to fulfill some precept or to acquire the state of grace; on the other hand, if the penitent comes *merely* because he was so ordered by his parents or superiors or from force of habit, his dispositions would be regarded insufficient. Other signs of sufficient contrition would be the penitent's own sincere expression of sorrow, his sincere promise to amend his life, a special reason for approaching the confessional—such as the death of his father, a special sermon, and so on.

---

[613] Tit. 3, chap. 1, no. 17.

4. The confessor must *grant, deny, or postpone absolution.* Absolution must be granted to any penitent rightly disposed and confessing his sins and seeking absolution here and now,[614] but absolution must be refused to anyone who is certainly unworthy and incapable of receiving it. Absolution *must* be deferred if there exists a genuine doubt regarding the penitent's present dispositions and if there is no urgent reason for granting conditional absolution; it *may* be deferred for a short period even if the penitent is rightly disposed, when the confessor considers such postponement beneficial to the correction of the penitent, who must consent to this delay.

If there is no doubt regarding the due dispositions of the penitent and the latter seeks absolution here and now, the confessor can neither refuse nor postpone absolution. This is the express ruling of the canon.[615] The reason for this is that the penitent who is rightly disposed and has accused himself of his sins seems to have a strict right to the immediate reception of absolution. This is at least the existing discipline of the Church.[616]

3. After Confession

698. After confession the confessor has two chief duties—one incidental, the other essential. The essential duty flowing from the nature of the Sacrament is to observe most carefully the seal of the Sacrament; the incidental duty consists in correcting any defects which may have occurred in the course of the confession.

The Obligation of Correcting Errors

Errors may occur:

1. *concerning the validity of the Sacrament,* as, for instance, if the confessor omits the absolution or some words essential to it;

2. *concerning the integrity of the Sacrament,* as when the confessor refrains from asking about the specific character of sins confessed or circumstances which affect their specific character, or if he neglects to impose a penance.

3. *concerning the obligations of the penitent,* e.g., in the matter of restitution.

1. Errors Affecting the Validity of the Sacrament

699. Any error in respect of the validity of the Sacrament must be corrected.

Not only parish priests and other pastors of souls but also all confessors have an obligation *in justice* to administer validly the Sacrament of Penance, although the obligation varies in degree. For once the confessor has heard the penitent's accusation of sin he is bound to administer the Sacrament validly as a result of the quasi-contract between them, and therefore the obligation is based on justice. Consequently, if he neglects this obligation, he is responsible for unjust damage,

[614] See CCL, Can. 886.
[615] Ibid.
[616] See MTM, vol. 3, no. 438.

which is at least *materially* unjust if there is no blame attached to his action (which is rarely the case in practice); if the Sacrament is invalid through the confessor's fault, he commits a *formal* sin of unjust damage. In either case he is bound to restitution for the damage caused.

The gravity of the obligation must be determined

a) from the gravity of the harm which ensues to the penitent,

b) from the gravity of the blame or neglect incurred by the confessor in administering the Sacrament invalidly.

This principle will be more evident from examples: 1. A confessor who forgets to absolve a dying person who has confessed grave sin has a grave obligation to correct his error, if this is possible, since it would be a most serious injury to the penitent to die without receiving absolution. Moreover, it would hardly be possible for a confessor to omit absolution in such circumstances except through culpable negligence.

2. A confessor who forgets to absolve any other penitent who has duly confessed his sins has a serious obligation to correct his omission, but not if this would cause him grave inconvenience, because in normal circumstances such a penitent would not incur such great harm from not receiving absolution, since he obtains the state of grace—if he does not already possess it—probably in his next Holy Communion, certainly in his next confession.[617]

2. Errors Affecting the Integrity of the Sacrament

700. There are two errors which the confessor may commit with regard to the integrity of confession; *negatively*, he may fail to discover the species and number of grave sins committed or to impose a penance; *positively*, he may state expressly that it is unnecessary to confess all mortal sins.

a) A *negative* error must be corrected in the next confession if this is possible without serious inconvenience; there is no obligation to correct the error *outside confession.*

b) A *positive* error must be corrected even outside confession, but in such circumstances he must first obtain permission from the penitent to speak about confessional matters. The obligation arises from the culpability of the confessor in leading the penitent into dangerous error.

3. Errors Affecting the Duties of the Penitent

701. Again, there are two errors which the confessor may commit in this respect—*negatively*, he may neglect to warn the penitent of some obligation, such as that of making restitution or reparation for scandal; *positively*, he may expressly induce error in the penitent by excusing him from necessary restitution or obliging him to make unnecessary reparation.

---

[617] See MTM, vol. 3, no. 440.

a) There is a slight obligation in charity to correct a *negative* error, but not if this would cause grave inconvenience since the confessor is not the culpable cause of serious harm. Therefore, if the confessor fails to warn his penitent of the obligation of making restitution, he is not himself bound to make restitution to the person to whom such restitution is due, because he has no obligation in justice of seeing that reparation is made for injury caused to a third party.[618] The case would be different if his omission amounted to positive liberation of his penitent from further obligation, for then the following rule would apply.

b) A *positive* error affecting a penitent's obligation must be corrected, if it involves personal injury. Such a confessor is the cause of unjust damage by advising something which is harmful. Therefore, when he is seriously to blame for inducing a penitent to make unnecessary restitution or for error in excusing him from such obligation, he has a grave duty to correct this error. If he neglects this correction, the confessor himself is obliged to make restitution either to the penitent whom he falsely persuaded to make restitution or to a third party if the penitent was wrongly excused from making restitution.

4. The Sacramental Seal

702. DEFINITION. *The seal of Confession or the sacramental seal is the strict obligation of maintaining silence regarding any matter disclosed by a penitent with a view to sacramental absolution, when such disclosure would render the Sacrament burdensome or odious.*

This definition will become clearer from a consideration of the subject, object, obligation, and violation of the seal.

THE SUBJECT bound by the sacramental seal is primarily the confessor, secondarily all those who (whether intentionally or unintentionally, lawfully or unlawfully) have knowledge of confessional matter, but the penitent himself is not bound by the seal.[619]

Consequently, the following persons are bound by the seal:

a) the *confessor,* even when consulted outside the confessional regarding sins of which the penitent accuses himself in the Sacrament. The same obligation affects anyone who pretends to be a priest and hears confession;[620]

b) one who acts as *interpreter* in confession;[621]

c) any *superior* approached by a confessor or penitent for faculties to absolve from a reserved case;

d) any *theologian consulted* by the confessor with the express permission of the penitent;

---

[618] See TM, bk. 6, no. 621.
[619] See CCL, Can. 889.
[620] See Aquinas, *Commentary on the Sentences,* Sent. 4, d. 21, q. 3, a. 1, sol. 3.
[621] See CCL, Can. 889.

e) those who *read* the written confession of another, at least when it is found in the hands of the confessor or in the confessional, that is, in a place where the confessor sits to hear confessions;

f) all who intentionally or unintentionally *overhear* what the penitent says in confession, unless the penitent confesses in a loud voice without due cause and without troubling about the bystanders.

NOTE.—Although the penitent himself is not bound by the sacramental seal seeing that it was introduced for his protection, nevertheless he is under an obligation to preserve as a *natural* and *committed* secret whatever the confessor has said to him, at least when the manifestation of his words would be detrimental to the confessor—as is usually the case.

703. THE OBJECT of the sacramental seal.

a) All mortal sins confessed either generically or in detail and all venial sins confessed in detail (not those confessed generically), unless the confessor obtains knowledge of these sins apart from confession.

b) Everything which is known only from confession and which, if disclosed, would give rise to hatred for the Sacrament and would prove distasteful to the penitent.

Therefore: 1. the confessor is bound by the seal of Confession even though he has had to refuse absolution, since the obligation arises not from the act of absolution but from the act of confession.

2. The seal includes also the penance imposed on the penitent—*at least when it is grave*—since it would be possible for a man to deduce the gravity of sins confessed from the nature of the penance. Similarly, the name of the penitent's accomplice and the refusal of absolution are included under the seal, but not the granting of absolution. However, in practice, a confessor should never declare in word or writing that a penitent has been absolved but only that he has made his confession, provided that the request for such information is legitimate.

3. *Natural defects* of the penitent, such as his scrupulosity, illegitimate birth, his lack of education, and so on, are subject to the seal when the knowledge of such defects is gained solely through confession and the penitent endeavors to conceal them outside confession.

4. A confessor who has heard the confession of a notorious thief is certainly permitted to speak about his universally known thefts of which the priest has gained knowledge from other sources, but he is not entitled to state that this notorious thief has confessed his crimes.

5. It is not directly contrary to the seal for the priest to state that his penitent has lived such an innocent life that he has confessed hardly any venial sins, since every man is liable to commit such sins, but it is better to avoid such statements and the discussion of a penitent's virtues and gifts since penitents find such disclosures embarrassing. Therefore, the Code justly states in reference to the process

of canonization: "Priests are to be debarred (from giving witness) in all matters which they have learned from sacramental confession, even though they have been freed from the obligation of the seal."[622]

6. A confessor is not bound by the seal if the penitent approaches him not for the sake of confessing his sins but for some other reason, e.g., to tempt the priest or to seek his advice. This follows from the fact that only *sacramental confession* is the foundation of the obligation of the seal.

NOTE. — *Outside the confessional* the priest is not allowed to discuss even with the penitent himself any sins already confessed, unless the penitent freely grants permission to do so. *In the course of the Sacrament* the confessor is perfectly free to speak about sins confessed in some previous confession. — If the penitent has availed himself of two confessors they are not allowed to discuss such sins between themselves without the penitent's explicit permission.

704. THE OBLIGATION of the seal is most serious so that its violation (at least if direct) does not admit of parvity of matter nor of any exception. The obligation springs from three sources.

1. It has a foundation in *natural law*, since the penitent confesses his sins only on condition of secrecy. Therefore, a quasi-contract is established between priest and penitent so that its violation is contrary to natural law and results in grave harm to the penitent.

2. *Divine positive law* (implicitly, although not explicitly) demands the sacramental seal, since it was Christ Who instituted the Sacrament in the form of a judgment in which the faithful would be obliged to confess their sins, and thereby He implicitly established the need for the seal since without such a safeguard the accusation of sin would seem to be morally impossible.

3. *Ecclesiastical law* has commanded on several occasions the observance of the seal.[623] The Code of Canon Law contains the following instruction: "The sacramental seal must not be violated; consequently the confessor must exercise the greatest care not to betray the sinner by word or sign or in any other way for any reason whatsoever."[624]

The obligation of the seal is so strict that:

a) no one has the power to dispense from it;

b) no one may use epikeia;

c) no one may use a probable opinion (whether it concerns a law or fact).

Permission of the penitent excuses from the obligation of preserving the seal, provided that the permission is given freely; *presumed* or *involuntary* permission is

---

[622] Can. 1757, § 3, no. 2.
[623] See Gratian, *Decretum*, pt. 2, Cause 33, q. 3, dist. 6, Can. 2; see also Fourth Lateran Council.
[624] Can. 889, § 1.

insufficient. The confessor should seek this permission only on rare occasions and for a grave reason; if the penitent refuses his permission the obligation of the seal persists, even though he may be forced to refuse absolution.

705. Although the obligation of the seal does not prevent the use of all knowledge gained in the confessional, nevertheless the use of such sacramental knowledge is normally gravely forbidden. Therefore, it is laid down in Can. 890: "A confessor is absolutely forbidden to make use of knowledge derived from confession *in any manner disagreeable to the penitent*, even though there be no danger of revelation. Actual superiors and confessors who are made superiors afterward cannot use in any way the knowledge they have gained from confessions for the purpose of external government." Moreover, in order to safeguard any danger of misusing such knowledge the master of novices and his associate, the superior of a seminary or college are forbidden by common law to hear the confessions of their pupils living with them in the same house, except in particular cases when the students spontaneously ask them to do so for grave and urgent reasons.[625]

706. Therefore, IT IS FORBIDDEN TO USE KNOWLEDGE DERIVED FROM HEARING CONFESSIONS:

1. *even for the greatest spiritual or temporal good.* Thus, for example, a confessor is prevented from confessing his own sin, when its revelation would violate the seal; he cannot take to flight or omit to say Mass if he knows from confession alone that his life is threatened or the wine is poisoned; he cannot dismiss a servant whom he knows from confession to be a thief or to be with child;

2. *for the public good.* Consequently, a priest is not allowed to disclose the name of a penitent whom he knows from confession is about to betray his country or to murder some innocent person;

3. *for the good of religion.* Consequently, a priest cannot expose a penitent whom he knows from confession will receive Holy Communion unworthily; he is obliged even to administer Holy Communion to such a person if the latter asks for it.

IT IS LAWFUL FOR THE CONFESSOR TO USE KNOWLEDGE DERIVED FROM THE SACRAMENT in order to improve his own spiritual state, to pray for the penitent, to study moral theology better, to consult learned men. But in the latter instance he must take special care to avoid any danger of violating the seal.

707. THE VIOLATION OF THE SACRAMENTAL SEAL may be either direct or indirect.

1. The seal is violated *directly* if anything subject to the seal is revealed as having been confessed by a particular penitent, e.g., when the confessor states: Peter has confessed the sin of adultery to me.

Such direct violations of the seal admit of no slight matter and are always grievously sinful both against justice and against religion. Therefore, any confessor

[625] See CCL, Can. 891.

who presumes to violate the seal directly incurs the most serious ecclesiastical punishment, i.e., excommunication most specially reserved to the Holy See.[626]

2. The seal is violated *indirectly* when there arises a *proximate danger* of recognizing the penitent's sin or of rendering the Sacrament distasteful through the confessor's manner of speaking or acting.

Accordingly, to violate the seal indirectly it is not required that the penitent and his sin be revealed; it is sufficient that there be a probable danger of this happening, and therefore the violation of the seal will be slight if such danger is slight. If a confessor violates the seal indirectly *through his own grievous fault* he is to be punished no less severely than a priest guilty of solicitation; that is to say, he is to be suspended from the celebration of Mass and the hearing of confessions, and if the gravity of his guilt demands it, he is to be declared incapable of hearing confessions, he is to be deprived of every benefice, office, dignity, active and passive vote, and declared incapable of ever acquiring these. In more serious cases he is to be degraded.[627] — Other persons (distinct from the confessor) who rashly violate the sacramental seal are to be punished in proportion to the gravity of their fault by salutary penalties, even, if need be, by excommunication.[628]

708. **WAYS IN WHICH THE SEAL MAY BE VIOLATED INDIRECTLY.**

a) A confessor on the basis of his knowledge gained solely from hearing confessions declares that in some college, convent, or small village sins of impurity are committed frequently; if the community is large (numbering at least three thousand persons) such a statement would not violate the seal, although it might often be imprudent.

b) A confessor in describing something from confession mentions certain circumstances which might probably lead to the recognition of the penitent.

c) A confessor advises the parents to maintain special watch over their daughter whom he knows from confession is going out at night.

d) A confessor declines to hear a penitent's confession merely because he knows from previous confessions that he is scrupulous or has contracted some sinful habit.

e) A confessor refuses to sign a form testifying that the penitent has made his confession (where such forms are in use) after refusing to grant him absolution.

PRACTICAL WARNING. The Holy Office, June 9, 1915, issued an instruction on the inviolable sanctity of the sacramental seal to all local ordinaries and moderators of religious congregations, in which a grave warning is given that confessors "are not to mention confessional matter under any form or pretext, not even incidentally, neither directly nor indirectly" in public or private sermons, even though there may be no direct or indirect violation of the seal. Such references sometimes

---

[626] See CCL, Can. 2369, § 1.
[627] Ibid.
[628] See CCL, Can. 2369, § 2.

prove a source of scandal to the faithful. Therefore, in one word, *confessors should never mention matters declared in confession except in their prayer to God on behalf of their penitents.*

Art. 3. Various Classes of Penitents

§ 1. Penitents Who Are in the Occasions of Sin

709. **DEFINITIONS.** *Penitents are said to be in the occasion of sin (occasionarii)* when they are in a proximate occasion of sin. An occasion of sin is any *extrinsic* circumstance (person, thing, book, play, and so on) which offers a strong incitement to sin and a suitable opportunity.

Therefore,

a) an occasion of sin differs from *the danger of sinning,* as any species from its genus, for every occasion of sin is a danger but not vice-versa, seeing that the danger of sinning may be internal, arising from passion or evil habit, and so on;

b) an occasion of sin differs from *scandal* (although sometimes the difference is slight), which entices to sin but does not always provide a suitable opportunity.

710. **KINDS OF OCCASIONS.**

A *remote* occasion of sin is one which offers a slight danger of sin in which a person rarely commits sin. A *proximate* occasion is a grave external danger of sinning either for all men or only for certain types. The gravity of the danger depends on *a) general experience* (such as the reading of an extremely obscene book), *b) the frequency of relapse* into the same sin (e.g., an inn for a habitual drunkard), *c) the character of the penitent* (e.g., a girl for an unchaste youth).

The occasion is said to be *absolutely proximate* if some external circumstance causes a serious danger of sinning for all men (such as the reading of extremely obscene literature); it is *relatively proximate* if it is dangerous for a certain individual (such as an inn for a habitual drunkard).

A proximate occasion is either *free* or *necessary.* It is free if it can be avoided easily (e.g., an inn); it is necessary if it cannot be avoided (e.g., a minor's parental home).

A proximate occasion may be *continually present* (*in esse seu praesens*) if a person remains in the occasion always and continually (e.g., keeping a mistress in the house); it is *not continually present* (*non in esse, non praesens*) if a person is in the occasion only at certain times (e.g., an inn for the inebriate).

ABSOLUTION OF PENITENTS WHO ARE IN THE OCCASION OF SIN.

711. **FIRST RULE.** *a) A penitent in a remote occasion of sin may be absolved; b) penitents in necessary proximate occasions of sin may also be absolved if they are truly contrite and seriously resolve to use all the means necessary for avoiding sin.*

Penitents in remote occasions of sin may be absolved, since such occasions are common to everyone and cannot be avoided.

The reason for the second part of the rule is that if the penitent seriously proposes to use the means necessary for avoiding sin, he will conquer his temptations with the help of God, "Who will not allow you to be tempted beyond your powers" (1 Cor 10:13). The chief means to be used for converting a proximate occasion of sin into a remote occasion are fervent prayer, frequent confession, avoidance of all familiarity and private conversation with an accomplice. —If a penitent promises to take these means and then neglects them, falling again into similar sins, he must be regarded as a recidivist.[629]

SECOND RULE. *Absolution must be denied to any penitent refusing to relinquish a free proximate occasion of sin.*

Such a penitent is considered to lack a sincere desire of avoiding sin. Thus, Innocent XI, March 2, 1679, condemned the following proposition: "He can sometimes be absolved, who remains in a proximate occasion of sinning, which he can and does not wish to omit, but rather directly and professedly seeks or enters into."[630]

NOTE. Generally speaking, one should *defer* the absolution of a penitent in a free proximate occasion of sin which is *continually* present until the penitent has *actually* removed this occasion, at least if he is a recidivist. Thus, for example, a man who keeps a mistress in his house should not be absolved in normal circumstances until he has dismissed her, especially if he promises to do this in a previous confession and has failed to keep his promise. But notice— *in normal circumstances,* because there are exceptions when absolution may be given immediately, provided that the penitent seriously promises to leave the free proximate occasion.[631]

§ 2. Penitents Who Have Contracted Habits of Sin

712. DEFINITION. *A penitent is said to have contracted the habit of some sin when by frequent repetition of acts of that vice he has contracted an inclination to commit it.* If the sin has been confessed over and over again and nevertheless the penitent continues to commit it, he has not only contracted a habit of sin but he is also a recidivist.[632]

It cannot be determined with precision *how many acts* are required before an evil habit is acquired, since this depends *a) on the weakness of the will in failing to resist the sin, b) on the nature and manner of the sin, c) on the interval between the individual sins.* According to St. Alphonsus[633] a person must be thought to have contracted a sinful habit if he commits an *external* sin five times a month. With regard to *internal* sins (such as evil desires) a far greater number is required—perhaps five times a week. The sinful habit may arise from an external circumstance when the penitent is also in an occasion of sin, or from a diabolical temptation or

---

[629] See no. 714ff.
[630] DZ 1211; see also 1212–1213.
[631] See MTM, vol. 3, no. 451.
[632] See no. 714ff.
[633] See *Praxis Confessarii,* chap. 5, no. 70.

inordinate passion when the penitent is a habitual sinner in the proper sense of the word, to whom the following rule applies.

713. ABSOLUTION. *A penitent who has contracted a habit of sin can and must be absolved whenever he is truly attrite and sincerely promises to use all the means necessary for overcoming his evil habit.*

An evil habit does not of itself prove that the penitent is not rightly disposed. In accordance with the principle that the penitent is to be believed when he speaks in his own favor just as much as when he speaks against himself, the penitent who firmly avows his sorrow and resolves to use all the necessary means to rid himself of his evil habit is deserving of belief and is capable of receiving absolution. The 60th proposition condemned by Innocent XI[634] is not contrary to this teaching.

§ 3. The Recidivist

714. DEFINITION. In the strict and formal meaning of the term, *a recidivist is one who after repeated confession (on three or four occasions) frequently falls into the same sin with the result that there exist just reasons for doubting the good will of the penitent.*

In the *wide* sense of the term, everyone must be considered a recidivist, since man falls again into the same sins after his confession. But it is not of such recidivists that we speak here. What we might call the characteristic sign of a formal recidivist seems to be that after repeated confession (on three or four occasions) the penitent commits the same sin in similar circumstances of time and place, so that one may prudently infer the continuance of an evil will in the penitent.[635]

A formal recidivist differs from a person who has contracted a sinful habit, as noted already; however, earlier theologians often made no such distinction and therefore their remarks must be read with care. The following rule applies to formal recidivists.

715. ABSOLUTION. *In normal circumstances the recidivist cannot be absolved unless he shows special signs of sincerity such as to destroy the presumption against him of lack of suitable dispositions.*

I say *in normal circumstances*, since in a case of necessity the Sacrament may be administered even to one who is doubtfully disposed to receive it. The reason for the above rule is that the penitent's frequent relapses into the same sin with no sign of amendment create a strong presumption that he lacks sincere attrition and firm purpose of amendment. For it is hardly possible that a man genuinely sorry for his sins and firmly proposing to use the means necessary to avoid falling into sin should then commit the same sins *in exactly the same way*. Consequently, this presumption of lack of suitable dispositions must first be destroyed before absolution may be granted, and a simple avowal to this effect on the part of the penitent is insufficient. The penitent has already asserted his willingness on several

---

[634] See MTM, vol. 3, no. 452.
[635] See CCL, Can. 2208, § 1.

occasions to make amends and yet no amendment is evident, so that his present declaration deserves little credence. Therefore, his assertion must be strengthened by *special signs* of contrition and firm purpose of amendment.

716. SPECIAL SIGNS of contrition and purpose of amendment are, e.g., the voluntary avoidance of a proximate occasion of sin, the permanence of the penitent's resolution for at least some time after his confession, spontaneous confession especially at an unusual time, a pious pilgrimage undertaken in order to make his confession, spiritual exercises, and so on. The general rule to be followed is that *taking all circumstances into consideration the confessor must possess sufficient certainty that the penitent here and now sincerely repents of his sins and firmly resolves not to sin again.* It is not the confessor's chief concern to consider what will happen *after* confession but only what are the penitent's present dispositions. — If *doubt persists regarding the penitent's dispositions* after a suitable exhortation has been given, absolution should be deferred for *a short while* but in cases of necessity it may be granted conditionally. It is self-evident that in speaking to these penitents the confessor must use gentleness and avoid all harsh words. Let him bear in mind the old saying: "fortiter in re, suaviter in modo." Because of the weakness of faith so characteristic today of the majority of recidivists, absolution should rarely be deferred, since this delay is often more harmful than useful to the penitent.

Art. 4. Misuse of the Sacrament

There are three ways in which the minister may misuse this Sacrament, 1) by inquiring the name of the penitent's accomplice, 2) by absolving his own accomplice, 3) by solicitation.

§ 1. Inquiring the Name of an Accomplice

717. FIRST PRINCIPLE. *Ordinarily speaking, a confessor commits an objectively grave sin if he directly asks his penitent for the name of the latter's accomplice.*

Such a question usually makes the Sacrament extremely distasteful. Accordingly, it has been laid down in the Code of Canon Law, Can. 888, § 2: "The confessor must take care not to inquire the name of the penitent's accomplice." The penalties formerly inflicted by the Church on those who taught the legality of asking for the name of the penitent's accomplice have not been renewed in the Code and therefore are abrogated.

To prevent serious harm to the common good or to a third party a penitent may be required under pain of being denied absolution to denounce an accomplice; e.g., if a boy in a college confesses that he has committed a sexual act with one of his companions who is seducing other boys, he may be compelled by the confessor to denounce this seducer. But it is far preferable for the denunciation to be made to the competent superior rather than to the confessor himself (whether inside or outside the confessional).

718. SECOND PRINCIPLE. *The confessor may lawfully inquire about such circumstances of a sin which have to be confessed and any proximate occasion of sin, and so on, even though he may thus learn indirectly the name of the penitent's accomplice.*

The reason is that the confessor is bound to do all in his power to ensure the integrity of the confession. Thus, for example, if a youth known to the confessor reveals that he has committed fornication, the confessor can and must ask whether the youth is living in a free or necessary proximate occasion of sin and whether the occasion is continually present or not, even though such questions will immediately reveal the female accomplice.

§ 2. Absolution of an Accomplice

719. PRESENT DISCIPLINE. *a)* "A priest's absolution of his own accomplice in a sin of impurity is invalid, except in danger of death; *b)* and even in danger of death such absolution is unlawful except in case of necessity, according to the rules of the Apostolic Constitutions, especially the Constitution of Benedict XIV *Sacramentum Paenitentiae*, June 1, 1741."[636] Later we shall return to a discussion of the penalties incurred by a priest absolving his accomplice.

In order to explain this prohibition more fully, it must be carefully noted what is understood by absolution, an accomplice, and a sin of impurity.

720. ABSOLUTION. The existing prohibition forbids under pain of excommunication *both genuine* and *pretended* absolution. Thus, the penalty is not incurred:

a) if the confessor hears the confession of his accomplice but does not absolve the penitent, or probably if he absolves the penitent from the other sins confessed but states expressly that he does not intend to absolve the sin in which the priest himself was an accomplice;

b) if the accomplice omits to confess the sin without the confessor being responsible in any way for such an omission. If the confessor directly or indirectly induces the penitent to conceal his sin, he incurs excommunication by absolving or pretending to absolve the accomplice.[637] *Direct* inducement would consist in urging the penitent not to confess that sin here and now; *indirect* inducement would be given by persuading the penitent that the act was not grievously sinful or that it need not be confessed, since the priest himself is already aware of the sin. The absolution of any accomplice in a sin of impurity is *invalid*, since the confessor does not possess jurisdiction in ordinary circumstances for absolving directly such penitents; according to the opinion of many theologians he is deprived of all jurisdiction over his accomplice until the sin has been directly remitted. However, there are certain *exceptions*:

THE ABSOLUTION OF ONE'S ACCOMPLICE IS VALID:

1. in *danger of death*. However, when another priest is present, even though not approved for hearing confessions, to whom the dying penitent can and is willing

---

[636] CCL, Can. 884.
[637] See S. Penitentiary, Feb. 19, 1896.

to confess, the priest may validly absolve his accomplice, but the absolution is gravely unlawful and incurs the penalty of excommunication.

2. According to many authors of repute[638] the absolution of an accomplice is valid and lawful even outside the danger of death when the *circumstances are so extraordinary* as to constitute a case of extreme necessity; that is to say, in places where parishes are widely separated from each other so that it is impossible to find any other priest apart from the accomplice, and the penitent is unable to undertake a long journey to find another confessor. In such circumstances the priest by using *epikeia* may validly and lawfully absolve his accomplice. However, in such instances the absolution would be *indirect* and therefore the penitent would be obliged to confess the same sin again to another confessor as soon as possible. That which justifies the use of epikeia in such cases is the conflict between two laws. The divine law prescribes that on certain occasions (at least once a year) Holy Communion must be received worthily, and at the same time ecclesiastical law forbids a penitent to make his confession to his accomplice. Therefore, if it is impossible to find another confessor, the divine law would seem to take precedence.

3. If the confessor absolves his accomplice in good faith, i.e., without adverting to the sin of complicity, it is probable that the absolution is valid and that the sin is remitted *indirectly* as in the preceding instance quoted; the priest would not incur excommunication in this instance.

4. Similarly the sin is *validly*, though *indirectly*, absolved when the penitent of his own free choice and in good faith omits to confess the sin. Similarly in most urgent cases when the confessor expressly states before granting absolution that he has no intention of absolving from the sin in which he was an accomplice but only from the penitent's other sin. However, in both these instances the confessor would be acting unlawfully.[639]

5. If the sin was not *formally* sinful. What is required for the formal sin of complicity will be explained immediately.

721. AN ACCOMPLICE (or companion in a sin against the sixth commandment) may be any person capable of committing grave sin; even a person with whom the priest committed sin prior to receiving the priesthood remains his accomplice until that sin has been remitted directly. It does not seem necessary that the complicity be *immediate*—that is to say, it is not necessary that the priest and his accomplice commit the act of impurity together; it would be sufficient for both parties to commit the same serious sin against chastity both internally and externally. Thus, for example, a husband becomes a priest's accomplice by cooperating externally in making it possible for the priest to commit adultery with his wife. However, many theologians, e.g., Noldin, Arregui, and so on, regard a person as an accomplice only when he participates *immediately* in the sinful act.

[638] See Lehmkuhl, Tanquery, Bucceroni, D'Annibale, Noldin, and so on.
[639] See MTM, vol. 3, no. 458.

Certainly, *formal complicity* is required both at the time when the sin is committed and at the time of absolution. When the *sin* is committed, such formal complicity will be lacking if the priest commits sin with a woman who does not recognize him as a priest, or if he commits sin with a woman who is unwilling to cooperate, or with one who is completely drunk, mad, or asleep. Formal complicity is lacking at the time of *absolution* if the confessor is not aware that the penitent is his accomplice or seriously doubts this fact. He is certainly not allowed to ask the penitent: Did you commit this sin with me?—If formal complicity is lacking, there is no question of the misuse of confession which the Church is so anxious to avoid.

The object of the act of complicity is a sin of impurity.

722. A SIN OF IMPURITY is any sin against the virtue of chastity, provided that it is *a)* grave (both objectively and subjectively), *b)* external, *c)* certain, *d)* not yet directly remitted.

Therefore, we must exclude

a) sins contrary to other virtues, such as theft or murder. Accordingly, a priest may absolve his accomplice in theft, although it is evident to all how unsuitable his act would be;

b) sins contrary to chastity which are slight either because of some imperfection in the act or because of an erroneous conscience. Thus, a woman who erroneously thinks that it is not grievously sinful to touch a priest immodestly could be absolved by that priest, who would not incur excommunication;

c) internal sins, such as impure pleasure or desires;

d) sins already directly remitted on a previous occasion. Thus, if a penitent confesses an impure act committed with a priest to another confessor and receives absolution, the same sin may be confessed again as free matter to the priest who was the accomplice, but in ordinary circumstances such a confession is not recommended.

723. PENALTIES. A priest incurs excommunication *most specially* reserved in the Holy See "who absolves or pretends to absolve his accomplice to a sin of impurity. Even in danger of death the priest cannot without incurring excommunication absolve his accomplice so long as another priest can be had (even though not approved for confession) without great danger of defamation or scandal, except in the case when the sick person refuses to confess to another priest. The excommunication is incurred also when the penitent does not mention the sin of complicity from which he has not yet been absolved, if the guilty confessor directly or indirectly induced the penitent not to confess the sin."[640]

Since all penalties are subject to strict interpretation *this excommunication is not incurred;*

a) in those cases already noted in no. 720 when absolution has been granted validly and licitly;

---

[640] CCL, Can. 2367.

b) if the accomplice without being induced directly or indirectly by the confessor fails to mention this particular sin. But in such circumstances the confessor would commit grave sin in misusing the Sacrament.

724. ABSOLUTION FROM THIS EXCOMMUNICATION may be granted in an urgent case by any confessor, but recourse within a month to the Sacred Penitentiary is always of obligation from which severe penances are usually received. If the priest absolves his accomplice on three or more occasions, the Holy See ordinarily demands that the priest lay aside forever his office as confessor. In the petition to the Sacred Penitentiary, it is necessary to state the number of occasions on which the priest has absolved his accomplice (or accomplices).

§ 3. Solicitation

725. EXISTING DISCIPLINE. "According to the Apostolic Constitutions, especially that of Benedict XIV, *Sacramentum Paenitentiae,* June 1, 1741, a penitent is bound to denounce to the ordinary or the Sacred Congregation of the Holy Office within one month any priest who is guilty of solicitation in confession; the confessor has a duty under pain of mortal sin to advise the penitent of this obligation."[641]

726. 1. THE CONDITIONS REQUIRED for this sin of solicitation and the consequent obligation of denunciation are almost capable of being deduced from the very nature of the sin itself. *The sin of solicitation consists in this, that a priest abuses genuine or feigned sacramental confession in order to provoke the penitent to commit a grave sin against chastity.*

Accordingly, the following conditions must be fulfilled:

a) there must exist provocation to a grave sin contrary to chastity.

Therefore, that form of solicitation which merits ecclesiastical punishment does not exist if the penitent is encouraged to commit some other sin, such as theft, or some other evil act which is not *certainly and objectively* a grave sin, such as a casual kiss. However, in order to incur the penalties it is not required that the solicitation succeed in its purpose of inducing the penitent to commit actual sin nor that the penitent be induced to sin with the priest himself. Therefore, the sin of solicitation seems to be committed if, for example, a confessor urges a youth to commit sin with a girl.

b) the confessor must solicit the penitent in his formal capacity as confessor; in other words, there must exist a genuine misuse of the Sacrament.

Thus, solicitation does not exist if a cleric or lay person pretends to be a priest and a confessor and then attempts to provoke another to commit some sin against chastity.

There are four occasions when the priest is considered to be acting as confessor, if his attempt to seduce a penitent takes place:

[641] CCL, Can. 904.

1. *in the act of sacramental confession*—that is to say, from the beginning of confession until the absolution; this is immediately evident;

2. *immediately before or after confession*, when no other external acts occur between the confession and the act of solicitation;

3. *under pretext of confession*, when confession is used by the priest as an opportunity or mask for committing a sin against chastity;

4. *even outside the occasion of hearing confessions in a confessional or other place set apart or chosen for hearing confessions, provided that there is simulation of hearing confession in that place.* The essential words in such circumstances are: provided that there is simulation of hearing confessions. It is necessary to recall the distinction already made[642] between simulation and pretense in administering the Sacrament. Simulation is used in order to deceive the penitent himself, whereas pretense is used to deceive others and this is not sufficient for the sin of solicitation.

727. 2. THE OBLIGATION TO DENOUNCE ANY PRIEST GUILTY OF SOLICITATION arises both from *natural* and *ecclesiastical* law.

Natural law demands reparation for the grievous scandal given by the confessor guilty of solicitation, and such reparation seems hardly possible except by denunciation to the priest's legitimate superior.

Ecclesiastical law punishes with instant excommunication not reserved to anyone those who neglect or culpably omit to denounce within a month those confessors or priests guilty of solicitation in confession.[643]—Any confessor has power to absolve from this excommunication provided that the prescribed denunciation has been carried through or at least seriously promised.[644]

CAUSES WHICH EXCUSE FROM THE DUTY OF DENUNCIATION are:

a) the death of the priest guilty of solicitation;

b) grave danger either to life, reputation, or livelihood which is incidentally attached to the act of denunciation;

c) dispensation granted by the Holy Office or Sacred Penitentiary—a dispensation which can be obtained only with difficulty;

d) lack of complete certainty regarding the verification of all the conditions required for the sin of solicitation.

728. 3. METHOD OF DENUNCIATION.

a) Denunciation must be made *personally* and not by letter—especially of an anonymous nature—to the bishop or Holy Office. However, if it proves impossible for the penitent to approach the bishop or Holy Office in person, he must write asking for further instructions.

[642] See no. 544.
[643] See CCL, Can. 2368, § 2.
[644] Ibid.

b) The competent bishop in such circumstances is primarily the bishop of the priest guilty of solicitation, then the bishop of the territory in which the solicitation occurred, and finally the bishop of the penitent.

c) In these cases, the bishop acts as the delegate of the Holy Office and consequently has jurisdiction over exempt religious guilty of this crime.

729. 4. ALL THE PENALTIES FOR SOLICITATION are *ferendae* sententiae and normally are not inflicted until the third denunciation,[645] but in themselves they are extremely grave. "Priests who commit the crime of solicitation in confession are to be suspended from the celebration of Holy Mass and the hearing of confession, and, if the gravity of the guilt demands it, they shall be declared incapable of hearing confessions; they are to be deprived of every benefice, office, dignity, active and passive vote and declared incapable of ever acquiring these. In more serious cases they shall be degraded."[646]

NOTE. 1. The sin of solicitation is not reserved (at least not by common law) and therefore the unfortunate priest guilty of such a sin may be absolved by any confessor, provided that he is rightly disposed.

2. *Anyone who falsely accuses* a priest of solicitation commits a grave sin reserved of its nature to the Holy See. All those who participate in such false denunciation are similarly guilty of this reserved sin, such as those persons who command or advise the act. However, this sin is not reserved if the denunciation is made privately and not in the *juridically* prescribed form. Furthermore, it is stated in the Code of Canon Law, Can. 2363: "If anyone either in person or through others wrongfully denounce a confessor to a superior as guilty of solicitation, he incurs ipso facto excommunication specially reserved to the Holy See, from which he cannot be absolved unless the false denunciation is formally retracted and reparation made as far as is possible for any damage caused; a severe and prolonged penance must be imposed." According to present discipline, therefore, a penitent guilty of false denunciation made in *juridical* form (and not merely by private letter sent to the bishop):

a) always commits a grave sin reserved to the Holy See and does not seem to be excused by ignorance of the reservation;

b) and incurs excommunication specially reserved to the Holy See, provided he is not ignorant of the censure.

The penitent cannot be absolved from his sin or from the censure *in any circumstances*, unless the false denunciation is formally retracted and reparation made for the harm caused. Furthermore, the confessor is bound to impose a special penance.

PRACTICAL DIRECTIONS. The confessor should proceed cautiously if his penitent mentions genuine or imagined solicitation. In the first place, he must decide

---

[645] See the instruction of the Holy Office given at the end of this book.
[646] CCL, Can. 2368, § 1.

whether the person is *worthy of belief*, for it frequently happens that hysterical women discuss matters which are either entirely false or very different from the original. Then the priest should inquire diligently whether all the conditions required for solicitation were verified or not. If it is certain that even one condition is lacking or that one of the points remains doubtful, he must not impose the duty of denunciation on his penitent. However, if there cannot be any doubt regarding the fact of solicitation, the confessor should endeavor to persuade the penitent to undertake the act of juridical denunciation. If for sufficient reason the penitent refuses to denounce the confessor, the bishop or Sacred Penitentiary should be consulted regarding further action.

TREATISE VI
ECCLESIASTICAL PUNISHMENT

This treatise is divided into three chapters: 1) Ecclesiastical Penalties in General; 2) Censures in General; 3) Particular Censures. For the sake of brevity only one vindictive punishment will be discussed in no. 759.

ECCLESIASTICAL PENALTIES IN GENERAL

730. DEFINITION. *An ecclesiastical penalty is a painful evil contrary to the will of the sufferer inflicted by the Church in punishment of some delinquency*, or, in the words of the Code: "An ecclesiastical penalty is the privation of some good, inflicted by legitimate authority on the delinquent for his correction and for punishment of the offense."[647]

Ecclesiastical law understands delinquency (*delictum*) as an *external* and morally sinful violation of a law to which is attached at least an indeterminate canonical sanction.[648] Although it might be possible for the Church to punish even internal acts, in fact she never does so but leaves the punishment of such acts to the justice of God.—Ecclesiastical punishment has a twofold *purpose*, the good of society and the good of the individual, or, in other words, the reparation of the harm caused to the social order and the correction of the delinquent.

731. KINDS. 1. By reason of their *purpose*, ecclesiastical penalties are either *vindictive* or *medicinal*, or *penal remedies*, or *canonical penances*.

A penalty is vindictive when its primary purpose is the expiation of delinquency and reparation of the harm caused to the social order, e.g., deposition, deprivation of benefice.

A penalty is medicinal when it has as its chief purpose the emendation of the delinquent, e.g., censures.

Penal remedies (which are four in number—admonition, reproof, precept, vigilance) are *preventive* medicinal penalties since they are intended to act as a

---

[647] CCL, Can. 2215.
[648] See CCL, Can. 2195, § 1.

safeguard against all delinquency or a particular form of delinquency which would be punished by censure or vindictive penalties.

Canonical penances are inflicted in order that a delinquent may either escape punishment or obtain absolution or dispensation from a penalty which he has contracted already.[649]

2. By reason of their *author*, penalties are inflicted either *by law* or *by an individual*, according as they are imposed by the law itself or by a legitimate superior.[650]

3. By reason of their *object*, penalties are either purely *spiritual* when they deprive a person of a spiritual benefit, such as the prayers of the Church, or *temporal* when they subject the delinquent to some temporal evil, such as prison or a fine.

4. By reason of their *form*, a penalty is *latae* sententiae if it is incurred by the very fact of transgressing the law without the necessity of any condemnatory sentence by a judge; a penalty *ferendae* sententiae is one which is incurred *after* such a sentence.

732. REVIEW OF ECCLESIASTICAL PENALTIES IN FORCE AT PRESENT. All penalties inflicted by the Church can be reduced to the following four types:

1. *censures*, or medicinal penalties: excommunication, suspension, interdict;

2. *vindictive penalties: a)* twelve affect clerics or religious only, such as deprivation of benefice or ecclesiastical office, loss of active and passive vote, deposition, degradation, and so on; *b)* twelve affect both clerics and lay persons, e.g., infamy of law, deprivation of ecclesiastical burial, removal from legitimate acts, fines, and so on;

3. *penal remedies*: admonition, reproof, precept, vigilance;

4. *canonical penances*, e.g., the recitation of certain prayers, the performance of spiritual exercises, giving a stated alms.

733. THE AUTHOR OF PENALTIES. *The general rule is that those who have the power of enacting laws or imposing precepts possess the power also of attaching penalties to those laws or precepts. Persons who possess juridical power only can do no more than apply the penalties legally prescribed in the manner demanded by law.*[651]

Thus, the following have the power of imposing penalties:

a) the pope for the whole Church;

b) bishops, superiors of clerical exempt religious orders for their own subjects; a vicar general has no power to do so without a special mandate.[652] The rules to be observed in inflicting penalties, especially so far as judges are concerned, are discussed by canonists.[653]

---

[649] See CCL, Can. 2312.
[650] See CCL, Can. 2217, § 1, no. 3.
[651] See CCL, Can. 2220.
[652] See CCL, Can. 2220, § 2.
[653] See for instance, MIC, q. 554.

734. THOSE SUBJECT TO PENALTIES. *The general rule is that persons subject to a law or precept are subject likewise to any penalty attached thereto, unless they are explicitly excepted.*[654]

Therefore, in order to incur such penalties a person must be:

a) subject to the person inflicting the penalty. Consequently, the pope alone has the power of inflicting penalties *i)* on those who hold the supreme power in a State, their sons and daughters, those who have the right of immediate succession, *ii)* on cardinals, *iii)* on legates of the Holy See and all bishops (even titulars);[655]

b) above the canonical age of puberty. Children who have not attained this age are excused from penalties latae sententiae, and they should be punished with disciplinary chastisement rather than by censures or other more serious punitive penalties;[656]

c) able to observe the penalty without loss of good repute, so far as penalties latae sententiae are concerned;[657]

d) aware of the law and the penalty attached. Affected ignorance does not excuse from any penalty latae sententiae,[658] and therefore the contrary opinion held formerly must now be rejected; however if the law contains the words *shall have presumed, or dared, or acted knowingly, temerariously, of set purpose* and the like which demand full knowledge and consent, any diminution of responsibility either on the part of the intellect (ignorance—but not affected ignorance—inadvertence) or on the part of the will (fear) exempts from penalties latae sententiae.[659] Thus drunkenness, omission of due care, debility of mind, impulse of passion, exempt from incurring such penalties precisely because they diminish responsibility, even though sometimes they may not excuse from the guilt of grave sin. The same holds true when these offenses are committed by minors, i.e., by those who have not completed their twenty-first year.[660] Thus, for instance, a minor reading a heretical book does not seem to incur excommunication.

If the law does not contain the terms already mentioned, *crass* or *supine* ignorance of the law or of the penalty only does not excuse from any ecclesiastical penalty, but if the ignorance was other than crass or supine it does exempt from medicinal penalties (censures, but not from other penalties).

735. THE REMISSION of penalties (whether by *absolution* in the case of censures or by *dispensation* in the case of vindictive penalties) can be granted only by the person who inflicted the penalties, or his competent superior, or successor, or a person

[654] See CCL, Can. 2226.
[655] See CCL, Can. 2227.
[656] See CCL, Can. 2230.
[657] See CCL, Can. 2232.
[658] See CCL, Can. 2229, § 1.
[659] See CCL, Can. 2229, § 2.
[660] See CCL, Can. 2204.

with delegated faculty. Consequently, anyone with the power to grant exemption from the law has the power to remit the penalty attached to the law, but a judge who in virtue of his office applies a penalty determined by the superior cannot pardon from the penalty once he has imposed it.[661]

Penalties can be remitted either in writing or by word of mouth, whether the person so pardoned is present or absent.

All ordinaries (i.e., all local ordinaries and major superiors of clerical exempt religious orders) have ample powers of remitting penalties inflicted on their subjects, namely:

1. *In public cases* the ordinary can remit all penalties latae sententiae of the common law with the exception of:

a) cases brought to court for trial;

b) censures reserved to the Holy See;

c) penalties which render a person incapable of holding benefices, offices, dignities, positions in the Church, an active or passive vote, penalties which deprive persons of such favors, perpetual suspension, infamy of law, privation of the right of patronage and of a privilege or favor granted by the Holy See.[662]

2. *In occult cases*, even if they are not urgent, the ordinary may himself or through someone delegated by him remit penalties latae sententiae of the common law, with the exception of censures *most specially* or *specially* reserved to the Holy See.[663] When considering *urgent* occult cases, the ordinary possesses the same faculties granted to all confessors in such circumstances.[664]

ECCLESIASTICAL CENSURES IN GENERAL

This chapter is divided into six articles: 1) Definition and Kinds of Censures; 2) Their Author; 3) Those Subject to Censures; 4) The Cause of Censures; 5) Reasons Which Excuse from Censures; 6) Absolution from Censures.

Art. 1. Definition and Kinds of Censure

736. DEFINITION. *A censure is a medicinal ecclesiastical penalty by which a baptized person is deprived of certain benefits whether spiritual or connected with matters spiritual, because of obstinate violation of some law of the Church, until such time as he repents and obtains absolution.*[665]

This definition will gain in clarity from later discussion regarding the subject and cause of censures.

---

[661] See CCL, Can. 2236.
[662] See CCL, Can. 2237, § 1.
[663] See CCL, Can. 2237, § 2.
[664] See no. 691.
[665] See CCL, Can. 2241.

The more important KINDS of censure are the following.

1. By reason of their *specific nature*, censures take the form of excommunication, suspension, or interdict.

2. By reason of their *efficient cause*, censures are said to be inflicted either by law or by an individual.

3. By reason of the *way* in which they are inflicted, censures are either latae sententiae or ferendae sententiae.

4. By reason of the *power of absolution*, certain censures are reserved, others are not reserved.

Art. 2. The Author of Censures

737. 1. *It is of faith that the Church possesses the power to inflict censures.*[666] In the *ordinary way* this power resides only in all ecclesiastical prelates who exercise jurisdiction in the external forum;[667] the power may be *delegated*, but only to clerics.[668]

The ordinary power to inflict censures resides in:

a) the Supreme Pontiff and an ecumenical council in regard to all members of the Church, legates a latere in the territory of their delegation,

b) bishops in regard to their own subjects, but not a vicar general unless he possess a special mandate,[669]

c) the vicar capitular while a See is vacant,

d) prelates possessing quasi-episcopal jurisdiction in the external forum, provincial councils, and chapters of religious orders.

The delegated power of inflicting censures is not granted to lay persons nor, a fortiori, to women.

738. 2. The following *conditions* must be fulfilled in order that censures be inflicted validly and lawfully.

a) He who inflicts the censure must be of sound mind; he must also intend to inflict a genuine censure, and he should proceed with prudence and circumspection.

b) He must act freely and not under violence.

c) He must possess jurisdiction which he is not prevented from using.

d) He should first reprimand and admonish the delinquent in the prescribed legal or canonical form, since he must be certain that the delinquent remains obstinate.[670]

---

[666] See Council of Constance.
[667] See CCL, Can. 2220, § 1.
[668] See CCL, Can. 118.
[669] See CCL, Can. 2220, § 1.
[670] See CCL, Can. 2233, § 2.

Art. 3. The Subject of Censures

739. Those subject to censures are all persons on whom a censure can be inflicted. The following conditions must be verified:

a) the person must be *baptized,* } The Church has no jurisdiction over
b) *alive,* } those who are unbaptized or dead.

c) *possess the use of his reason and be capable of a grave deliberate transgression of the law.*

These conditions must be fulfilled since censures presuppose delinquency and obstinacy. Furthermore, habitual aments, even though they have rational intervals, are incapable of delinquency and therefore do not incur censures.[671] Although persons who have reached the canonical age of puberty have the use of their reason and are capable of grave transgression of the law, nevertheless according to existing discipline they do not incur censures latae sententiae.[672] Such persons are better corrected by corporal punishment than by censures.

d) He must be a *subject* of the person inflicting the censure, since it is an act of jurisdiction which can be exercised only over one's subjects.

740. COROLLARIES. 1. No superior incurs any censure which he himself has determined.

2. By privilege, cardinals (unless they are mentioned expressly) are not subject to any penal law, nor are bishops subject to ipso facto suspension or interdict.[673]

3. Since those who hold supreme power in a State, their sons and daughters, and their successors, cannot be judged by anyone except the Supreme Pontiff himself, it would seem that they do not incur censures reserved to a bishop (whether they be inflicted by law or by a superior).

4. Members of exempt religious orders cannot be visited with episcopal censures, unless this is specifically stated in the law.

5. *Territorial* censures are not binding on strangers nor on those who are absent from that territory.[674]

6. *Moral* persons (communities) are liable to interdict and suspension but not to excommunication.[675]

One and the same person may incur SEVERAL CENSURES (either of the same or a different character):

a) if he has committed a delinquency to which a censure has been attached by different superiors (which is rare nowadays);

---

[671] See CCL, Can. 2201, § 2.
[672] See CCL, Can. 2230.
[673] See CCL, Can. 2227.
[674] This is not true of censures inflicted by means of a special precept (see CCL, Can. 1566, § 1).
[675] See CCL, Can. 2255.

b) if he has committed different offenses or the same offense on different occasions.[676] Thus, for example, a person who contracts a marriage before a non-Catholic minister and agrees that his children should be brought up in heresy, has them baptized by a non-Catholic minister, and reads heretical books on seven occasions, incurs ten excommunications. As a general rule, there are as many penalties incurred as there are delinquencies committed.[677]

Art. 4. The Cause of Censures

741. The cause of censures — sometimes called the object or subject-matter of censures — is the delinquency on account of which the punishment is inflicted. But according to present discipline[678] no delinquency is punished by censure unless it is:

a) grave, both objectively and subjectively; therefore, anything which excuses from the grave imputability of an offense excuses also from censure;[679]

b) external (whether it is public or occult). Consequently, internal sins, such as heresy which is completely internal, is not punishable by censure;

c) actual (and not merely attempted, unless even attempted delinquency is subject to punishment)—that is to say, the censure is not incurred unless the delinquency fulfills all the conditions mentioned in the pronouncement of censure, since censures are not to be interpreted strictly; accordingly, e.g., no censure is incurred by a person who causes an explosion to occur close by a cleric without he himself actually touching the cleric;

d) accompanied by obstinacy, i.e., by at least virtual contempt for the censure.

This contempt—and, in consequence, the censure also—is not present when the sinner is not aware of the law forbidding the act or of the special punishment inflicted on those transgressing the law. This holds for the internal forum at least, since in the external forum sometimes *presumed* obstinacy is sufficient. For when a law is sufficiently promulgated the subjects are presumed to be aware of that law so that if they transgress it, they must incur in the external forum all the penalties and censures attached.

Art. 5. Causes that Excuse from Censures

742. The following causes excuse from censures:

1. *lack of jurisdiction* which prevents the censure being incurred;

2. *some defect in the offense itself* which does not fulfill all the conditions mentioned in the preceding article;

---

[676] See CCL, Can. 2244.
[677] See CCL, Can. 2224, § 1.
[678] See CCL, Can. 2242.
[679] See CCL, Can. 2218, § 2.

3. *grave fear*, as often as it is sufficient to excuse from the observance of ecclesiastical law; in such circumstances contempt is absent. Certain exceptions are to be found listed in Can. 2229, § 3, no. 3;

4. *ignorance of the censure. a) Crass* or supine ignorance, but not *affected* ignorance excuses from censures directed against those who act "knowingly, of set purpose, temerariously," and so on; *b)* ignorance that is only slightly culpable excuses from all other censures.

NOTE. Since a censure obliges in exactly the same way as any ecclesiastical law, whatever excuses a person from fulfilling such laws will excuse also from the observance of censures. Thus, for example, a priest under occult excommunication is not obliged to abide by that censure if he is liable to incur public, grave disrepute in consequence.

Art. 6. Absolution from Censures

743. FIRST PRINCIPLE. *Once a censure (in the strict sense of the word) has been incurred, it is only removed by legitimate absolution.*

Therefore, censures do not cease on the death of the superior inflicting the censure, or of the individual punished by censure, nor are they removed by the guilty party making amends or satisfaction. Consequently, an excommunicate who elicits an act of perfect contrition recovers the state of grace but does not cease to be excommunicated and separated from communion with the Church. However, absolution cannot be refused, once the delinquent has ceased from his obstinacy.[680]

Absolution from censure may be granted either for the external forum or for the internal forum; it may be granted *ad cautelam*, or on condition that the censure will be incurred again if certain conditions are not fulfilled.[681]

744. SECOND PRINCIPLE. *a) Any confessor may give absolution in the internal forum from unreserved censures; b) no one may absolve from reserved censures unless he has the required ordinary or delegated jurisdiction; c) the following censures are reserved: i) all censures imposed by a special judgment; ii) all censures expressly declared in the law to be reserved.*

All these statements would seem to be evident. However, the following should be noted regarding delegated jurisdiction for the absolution of censures. Delegation is granted either *by an individual superior*, when everything stated in the document whereby jurisdiction is granted must be observed, or else *by the law itself*. The faculty to absolve from reserved censures is delegated by law:

745. 1. *in danger of death*, when every *priest* (even if another is present with the requisite faculties) may absolve from all censures. But there are two instances when the person in danger of death must have recourse to the competent superior, if he

---

[680] See CCL, Can. 2248, § 2.
[681] See MTM, vol. 3, no. 491.

recovers his health within a month (presuming that such recourse is morally possible), that is, when absolution was given: *a)* from censures most specially reserved to the Holy See; *b)* from censures imposed by sentence in an ecclesiastical court.[682]

2. *in urgent cases*[683] when any *confessor* may absolve directly from all censures inflicted by law (but not from those inflicted by an individual) with the proviso that a person so absolved is bound under pain of relapse into the same censure to have recourse within a month to the Sacred Penitentiary or to seek a fresh absolution from one who has the requisite faculties. When such recourse is morally impossible it may be omitted.[684]

3. *Cardinals* can absolve any penitent from all censures, with the exception of those most specially reserved to the Holy See and the censure attached to the revelation of secrets of the Holy Office.[685]

4. *Ordinaries* have the power in virtue of Can. 2237, § 2 to absolve their subjects in all occult cases from censures simply reserved to the Holy See. Similarly, they may absolve in the *external* forum from the censure incurred through heresy.[686]

5. Religious confessors may absolve from censures reserved by law to the local ordinary, since the new Code does not seem to have revoked this privilege which was existing prior to the Code.[687]

746. NOTE. 1. In granting absolution from censures the confessor must demand: *a)* that the penitent repair any scandal or harm he may have caused; and *b)* that he receive a special penance distinct from the sacramental penance.

2. Absolution for the *external* forum may be given in any way, but it is better that the rite should be determined by a competent superior or follow the form set forth in the Roman Ritual;[688] for the *internal* forum the customary form used in the granting of any absolution should be followed.[689]

3. Absolution given for the *external* forum is valid for the internal forum also, but if a penitent is absolved in the internal forum he may act in the external forum as a person absolved, provided he does not give scandal; but unless the absolution is proved in the external forum or at least lawfully presumed, the superior may still demand a special absolution in the external forum.[690]

---

[682] See CCL, Can. 2252.

[683] A case is considered urgent if a censure incurred ipso facto cannot be observed externally without danger of grave scandal or defamation, or if it is burdensome to remain in the state of a grievous sin during the time necessary for the superior to make provision for granting absolution (see CCL, Can. 2254, § 1).

[684] See CCL, Can. 2254.

[685] See CCL, Can. 239, § 1.

[686] See CCL, Can. 2314, § 2.

[687] See Noldin, *de Poenis* 12, no. 95.

[688] See tit. 3, chap. 3.

[689] See CCL, Can. 2250, § 3.

[690] See CCL, Can. 2251.

4. If a person has incurred several censures, he may be absolved from one while the others remain. But such a case is extremely rare. If, however, a *general* absolution from censures was granted legitimately, it is valid also for those cases which were concealed *in good faith*, with the exception of four censures most specially reserved to the Holy See, but it does not avail for those concealed in bad faith.[691]

5. Absolution obtained by violence or grave fear is invalid by law.[692]

PARTICULAR CENSURES

INTRODUCTION. We shall consider briefly only those matters with which the confessor is liable to be confronted in practice.[693]—Since there are three kinds of censures, as already mentioned, we divide this chapter into three articles: 1) Excommunication; 2) Interdict; 3) Suspension.

Art. 1. Excommunication

747. DEFINITION. *Excommunication is a censure by which a person is deprived of communion with the faithful of the Church.*[694]

If a person is completely excluded from this communion, he is to be *shunned* (i.e., if he has laid violent hands on the person of the pope, or if he has been excommunicated by the Holy See by name and publicly denounced as one to be shunned); otherwise, he is *tolerated.* Consequently, according to present discipline, only the Holy See has the power to declare that an excommunicate is to be shunned.

748. THE EFFECTS of excommunication. Exclusion from communion with the Church resulting from excommunication has the following eight effects:

1. WITH REGARD TO SACRED THINGS, i.e., the Sacraments, whose administration and reception are partially forbidden to excommunicates:

a) the excommunicate who is to be *shunned*, since he lacks ecclesiastical jurisdiction, may not validly administer any Sacrament for which genuine jurisdiction is necessary. An exception is made in danger of death;

b) the excommunicate who is tolerated may *validly administer* the Sacraments and also *lawfully* administer them, if explicitly requested to do so by the faithful;[695]

c) no excommunicate may *lawfully receive* the Sacraments, unless he be excused by ignorance or fear of great loss. An excommunicate after declaratory or condemnatory sentence cannot receive even sacramentals.[696]

[691] See CCL, Can. 2249.
[692] See CCL, Can. 2238.
[693] Those who require a fuller treatment may refer to MTM or to the canonists.
[694] See CCL, Can. 2257.
[695] See CCL, Can. 2261.
[696] See CCL, Can. 2260, § 1.

2. EXCLUSION FROM RITES, i.e., *from divine liturgical offices* (but not from sermons). However, according to the present discipline of the Church, tolerated excommunicates may assist at these liturgical offices (but not excommunicates who have to be shunned).

This is the ruling given in the Code, Can. 2259, § 2: "If a tolerated excommunicate assists *passively* at a religious service he is not to be expelled, but an excommunicate who has to be shunned must be expelled, or if this is not possible, the service must be discontinued if possible without grave inconvenience; not only excommunicates who are to be shunned but also those who are declared such after declaratory or condemnatory sentence or who are otherwise notoriously excommunicated are debarred from all *active* assistance (which implies some participation) in the celebration of the Divine Offices." It is evident that the Church today does not so severely exclude Protestants from Catholic Divine Offices.

3. EXCLUSION FROM THE COMMON SUFFRAGES OF THE CHURCH AND FROM INDULGENCES, which however are sometimes allowed to tolerated excommunicates. A priest may offer Mass privately and apart from scandal for a tolerated excommunicate, such as a Protestant.[697]

4. EXCLUSION FROM ECCLESIASTICAL BURIAL, but only after declaratory or condemnatory sentence.[698]

5. EXCLUSION FROM POWER, which includes:

a) ecclesiastical *jurisdiction* both in the external and in the internal fora, which cannot be exercised *validly* by excommunicates after declaratory or condemnatory sentence (except in cases of danger of death); such jurisdiction cannot be even *lawfully* exercised by any excommunicate, unless the faithful solicit him to do so for a good reason;[699]

b) *the right of election, nomination, or presentation;*[700]

c) *the power to obtain ecclesiastical offices or to receive orders;*[701]

d) *the power to exercise legitimate acts,* which are: the office of administrator of church property; acting as judge, auditor, and relator, defender of the bond of marriage, promoter of justice and the Faith, notary and chancellor, courier and beadle, lawyer and procurator in ecclesiastical cases; godparents at the Sacraments of Baptism and Confirmation; voting in ecclesiastical elections; exercising the right of patronage.[702]

6. EXCLUSION FROM ECCLESIASTICAL INCOME. After declaratory or condemnatory sentence an excommunicate is deprived of the revenue from dignities, offices,

---

[697] See CCL, Can. 2262.
[698] On this question, see MIC, q. 372ff.
[699] See CCL, Can. 2261.
[700] See CCL, Can. 2265, § 1, no. 1.
[701] See CCL, Can. 2265, § 1, nos. 2 and 3.
[702] See CCL, Can. 2256, no. 2.

benefices, pensions, positions, if he possessed any of these in the Church; an excommunicate who must be shunned is also deprived of dignities, offices, benefices, and pensions.[703]

7. EXCLUSION FROM PARTICIPATION IN CIVIL OR ECCLESIASTICAL COURTS. But present discipline is less severe.

8. EXCLUSION FROM CERTAIN CIVIL RIGHTS. Present discipline has been modified even in respect of excommunicates who have to be shunned.[704]

749. NOTE. 1. An excommunicated cleric (or one under any other censure) incurs irregularity by exercising voluntarily any act proper to sacred Orders.[705]

2. Anyone who continues obstinately in the censure of excommunication for *one year* incurs suspicion of heresy.[706]

Art. 2. Interdict

750. DEFINITION. *Interdict is a censure whereby the faithful while remaining in communion with the Church are forbidden the use of certain Sacraments and other sacred things.*[707]

Although interdict is termed a censure, frequently it is also a vindictive penalty or merely a prohibition which causes suffering even to the innocent. However, since an interdict does not sever communion with the Church, it is normally a less severe form of punishment than excommunication.

KINDS. 1. A *local* interdict is one which affects a place immediately and only indirectly the persons living in that place, including externs and those who are exempt; a *personal* interdict is one which affects the individual directly and accompanies him wherever he goes. — No mention is made in the new Code of a form of interdict which affects both place and individual in the same way.

2. An interdict is *general*, if it affects either a whole territory (a general local interdict) or all the individuals in one place (a general personal interdict); otherwise, it is *particular*, when it affects either one place (such as a church or monastery) or certain individuals.

3. An *interdict forbidding entrance into a church* is a partial interdict forbidding a person to celebrate the Divine Offices in any church or to assist at such offices or to receive ecclesiastical burial; however, if he should assist at these offices he need not be expelled, and if he is given ecclesiastical burial his body need not be removed.[708]

751. AUTHOR. A general interdict affecting an entire diocese or realm or exempt places or the persons in a diocese or realm can be inflicted by the Holy See only; a general

[703] See CCL, Can. 2266.
[704] See CCL, Can. 2267.
[705] See CCL, Can. 985, no. 7.
[706] See CCL, Can. 2340, § 1.
[707] See CCL, Can. 2268, § 1.
[708] See CCL, Can. 2277.

interdict affecting a parish or the people of a parish, and certain particular interdicts can be issued by the bishop.[709]

752. THE EFFECTS of an interdict and its extent are usually determined in each specific case by the legitimate superior. But in general, the following rules apply.

1. A *local interdict*

a) forbids the celebration of Divine Offices and the administration of sacred rites in the place under interdict, except on five feast days (Christmas Day, Easter, Pentecost, Corpus Christi, the Assumption of Our Lady) when the interdict is suspended to allow all sacred rites, with the exception of the conferring of Orders and the solemn blessing of marriage;[710]

b) does not forbid:

i) the private administration of the Sacraments and the sacramentals *to the dying* nor the burial of the faithful in a cemetery but without any ecclesiastical rite;[711]

ii) the celebration *in private* and in a subdued voice of all the divine services and sacred functions in any church or oratory with the doors closed and without ringing of church bells, if the local interdict is *general* and nothing to the contrary is expressly stated in the decree;[712]

iii) the celebration of one Mass each day, reservation of the Blessed Sacrament, the administration of Baptism, of Holy Eucharist, Penance, marriage without the nuptial blessing, funerals without any solemnity, blessing of the baptismal water and holy oils, preaching of the Word of God, in the cathedral and in parochial churches and in any church which is the only one in the town. In all these functions singing, display in sacred utensils and vestments, ringing of church bells, playing of the organ and of other musical instruments are forbidden.[713]

From this it is evident that a *local* interdict is not such a serious punishment, at least for those who are innocent.

2. A *personal interdict* forbids those under interdict:

a) to celebrate or assist at Divine Offices, with the exception of sermons. *Passive* assistance at these services is not so strictly forbidden; but if the interdict was imposed by a condemnatory or declaratory sentence, or is otherwise notorious, they must be repelled from any *active* assistance which implies participation in the celebration of Divine Offices;[714]

b) to consecrate, administer, or receive the Sacraments and sacramentals, with the exceptions mentioned above in no. 748 relating to excommunicates. Those

---

[709] See CCL, Can. 2269, § 1.
[710] See CCL, Can. 2270, § 2.
[711] See CCL, Can. 2270, § 1; 2272, § 2.
[712] See CCL, Can. 2271, no. 1.
[713] See CCL, Can. 2271, no. 2.
[714] See CCL, Can. 2275.

under personal interdict are subject to the same restrictions as excommunicates in respect of their rights of voting, presentation, nomination, in respect also of their obtaining dignities, offices, benefices, pensions, positions in the Church, papal favors, and likewise of their reception of sacred Orders;[715]

c) to receive ecclesiastical burial.[716]

753. An interdict CEASES in the same way as other *vindictive* penalties, i.e., by legitimate dispensation or lapse of the stated period, if it was inflicted in the form of a vindictive punishment. If the interdict was imposed in the form of a *censure* (as is usually the case), what has been said already regarding the absolution of censures applies also to the cessation of interdict.

Art. 3. Suspension

754. DEFINITION. *Suspension is a censure whereby a cleric is restrained from the use of his office or benefice or both, either in part or completely.*[717]

EXPLANATION. 1. It is a *censure* since it is normally a medicinal punishment, although on occasions it is a vindictive penalty and thus resembles an interdict. When doubt arises whether suspension is a censure or a vindictive penalty, it is presumed to be a censure.[718]

2. Suspension is inflicted on *clerics only*, while excommunication and interdict can be inflicted on lay persons.

755. KINDS. 1. Suspension is either *general* or *restricted*, according as the cleric is forbidden either *all use* of his sacred Orders, office, and benefice, or the use of one of these three. A suspension inflicted without any further qualification is considered to be general.

2. Suspension *from office* is either *general* or *restricted*; it is general if it forbids the exercise of the power of Orders and jurisdiction and also of mere administration proper to an office (with the exception only of the administration of the goods of one's own benefice[719]); it is restricted if it forbids only certain acts attached to his office. — General suspension from office (and this applies also to general suspension from benefice) affects *all* offices (or benefices) which the suspended cleric holds in the diocese of the superior who issues the suspension.[720] The local ordinary cannot suspend a cleric from a specified office or benefice which he holds in another diocese, since he has no jurisdiction in that diocese. But a suspension latae sententiae inflicted by the common

---

[715] See no. 748.
[716] See CCL, Can. 2275, no. 4.
[717] See CCL, Can. 2278.
[718] See CCL, Can. 2255, § 2.
[719] See CCL, Can. 2279, § 1.
[720] See CCL, Can. 2281.

law affects all offices or benefices no matter in which diocese they are held.[721] Thus, for example, a cleric who knowingly receives sacred Orders through simony is suspended from all offices and benefices, even though he holds them in different dioceses.

3. There are nine restricted forms of suspension.[722]

a) *Suspension from jurisdiction in general* forbids every act of the power of jurisdiction in either forum.

b) *Suspension from the divine ministry* forbids every act of the power of Orders even if possessed by privilege, such as the power of Confirmation delegated to a simple priest.

c) *Suspension from Orders* forbids the exercise of any act of the power of Orders received by ordination.

d) *Suspension from sacred Orders* forbids the exercise of the powers of major Orders.

e) *Suspension from the exercise of a certain definite Order* forbids not only the exercise and reception of that Order but also the reception of any higher Order and its exercise, if received.

f) *Suspension from conferring a certain specified Order* forbids the conferring of the Order specified, not however of a higher or lower Order.

g) *Suspension from a specified ministry*, such as the hearing of confessions, or *from a specified office*, such as that of the care of souls. It forbids every act of that ministry or office.

h) *Suspension from the pontifical Order* forbids the exercise of every act of the power belonging to the Order of bishops.

i) *Suspension from pontificals* forbids the exercise of episcopal functions in which the liturgy requires the use of the mitre and crozier.

756. EFFECTS OF SUSPENSION.

1. A suspended cleric commits grave sin by exercising any act forbidden to him (but there is the possibility of parvity of matter in such cases), unless there exist excusing causes which are the same as those that justify the non-observance of censures in general.[723]

2. A cleric suspended from a sacred Order who violates that suspension by exercising an act proper to that Order incurs irregularity;[724]

3. Suspension *from benefice* deprives the cleric of the revenues of the benefice (with the exception of dwelling in the residence belonging to the benefice) but not of the right of administering the goods of the benefice. This is the normal rule. If the

---

[721] See CCL, Can. 2282.
[722] See CCL, Can. 2279.
[723] See no. 742.
[724] See CCL, Can. 985, no. 7.

beneficiary in spite of the suspension does receive the revenue of the benefice, he is bound to restitution.[725]

4. Generally speaking, suspension has the same effects as excommunication.[726]

757. Suspension CEASES in the same way as other penalties whether vindictive (if the suspension is a vindictive punishment) or medicinal (if the suspension is in the form of a censure).

758. SCHOLIUM. SUSPENSION EX INFORMATA CONSCIENTIA. This suspension is an extremely grave punishment and an extraordinary remedy. It may be inflicted by the ordinary or by the major superior of an exempt religious order of clerics. It applies to *offices* only (either to all or to some), Can. 2186, § 1, and not to benefices.[727]

The conditions required for the valid and lawful infliction of this penalty are:

a) that the ordinary cannot without grave inconvenience proceed against his subject in the ordinary course of law;[728]

b) that the decree of suspension be given *in writing* (unless circumstances demand otherwise) with the day, month, and year clearly stated; moreover, it must be stated explicitly that the suspension is inflicted *ex informata conscientia* and for how long the penalty is valid. — The reason is twofold: firstly, to prevent the ordinary having recourse to this extraordinary measure in a sudden fit of anger, and secondly, to allow the subject to exercise his right of recourse more easily. If the suspension is inflicted as *a censure*, the ordinary must inform the cleric of the reason for this punishment; otherwise, he is under no strict obligation to do so, although it is fitting that he should. If the cleric appeals against the suspension, the ordinary must forward to the Holy See the proofs from which it is certain that the cleric actually committed the offense which deserves this extraordinary penalty;[729]

c) that the delinquency punished in this severe manner should be *certain, occult* and *sufficiently grave* to be punished in this way.[730] In extraordinary circumstances a *public* delinquency may be punished by this suspension, but a *notorious* delinquency never.[731]

Art. 4. Other Ecclesiastical Penalties

INTRODUCTION. In no. 732 we have already given a summary of those ecclesiastical penalties in existence at present. Since it does not belong to the province of moral theology but to that of ecclesiastical law to discuss vindictive penalties, canonical

---

[725] See CCL, Can. 2280.

[726] See no. 748.

[727] The manner and time of instituting an appeal against this severe penalty is described in MIC, q. 556.

[728] See CCL, Can. 2186, § 2.

[729] See CCL, Can. 2194.

[730] See CCL, Can. 2190–91.

[731] See CCL, Can. 2191–92.

penances, and penal remedies, we must refer the indulgent reader to the author's *Manuale Iuris Canonici*. Furthermore, these penalties do not occur frequently and when such a case does arise a superficial knowledge—the only type possible in this brief *vade mecum*—would be insufficient. However, it may be useful to outline what one ought to know regarding one form of vindictive penalty with which the confessor is sometimes confronted in practice, i.e., infamy.

Infamy

759. **DEFINITION.** *Infamy consists in the loss or at least diminution of a person's good repute or honor* (reputation, character).

We are here considering only canonical or ecclesiastical infamy, and not its civil counterpart. There used to exist some authors who thought that a person declared infamous by a civil judge incurred infamy also in ecclesiastical law, but at least according to present discipline this opinion is not true, as will become clear from what follows. It is not denied that a person declared infamous by civil law incurs canonical infamy also, but he does so not because of the civil judgment but for another reason.

760. **KINDS.** There are two forms of infamy—of law, and of fact. Infamy *of law* is that which is specified in certain cases *by common law*.[732] Infamy *of fact* is incurred when a person loses his good reputation amongst good and reliable Catholics as the result of evil conduct or the commission of some crime, the judgment of which belongs to the ordinary. One offense is sufficient, provided that it is so grave and notorious that in the judgment of the ordinary (to the exclusion of any other man) it destroys the person's good reputation with upright and seriously-minded Catholics.

NOTE. In the old law infamy was sometimes incurred by the discharge of certain offices regarded as evil, such as those of executioner or actor. According to present discipline, infamy is incurred *for delinquency only*, and this is to be understood personally. Consequently, infamy does not affect the person's blood relations or relations by marriage.[733] But it is possible to incur irregularity from defect by exercising the office of executioner, for example.

761. There are SEVEN INSTANCES IN WHICH INFAMY OF LAW IS INCURRED ipso facto, and two instances where it is incurred after judicial sentence. *The following are infamous ipso facto:*

1. those who formally join a non-Catholic sect or who publicly adhere to one;[734]

2. those who throw away the consecrated species or remove or retain them for an evil purpose;[735]

---

[732] See CCL, Can. 2293, § 2.
[733] See CCL, Can. 2293, § 4.
[734] See CCL, Can. 2314, § 1, no. 3.
[735] See CCL, Can. 2320.

3. those who have violated the bodies or graves of the dead by theft or other crimes;[736]

4. those who lay violent hands on the person of the pope, cardinals, or legates;[737]

5. those who fight a duel, and their seconds;[738]

6. those who commit bigamy;[739]

7. lay people lawfully condemned for crimes of impurity with minors under sixteen years of age, or for rape, sodomy, incest, bawdry.[740]

The following are to be declared infamous:

1. apostates, heretics, schismatics, unless they return to the Faith after they have been admonished;[741]

2. clerics who commit similar sins of impurity as previously mentioned in respect of lay persons, likewise those who commit sins of adultery, bestiality, incest of the first degree.[742]

762. THE EFFECTS *of infamy of law are:*

1. irregularity by defect;[743]

2. inability to obtain benefices, pensions, offices, ecclesiastical dignities;[744]

3. inability to exercise legal ecclesiastical actions;[745]

4. inability to exercise ecclesiastical right or office;[746]

5. a prohibition to exercise the ministry in sacred functions.[747]

The effects of infamy of fact are:

1. exclusion from receiving orders, dignities, benefices, ecclesiastical offices;[748]

2. exclusion from exercising the sacred ministry and legitimate acts.

763. *Infamy of law* CEASES by dispensation only, granted by the Holy See; infamy *of fact* ceases when the individual recovers his good reputation with good and reliable Catholics, provided that all the circumstances are taken into consideration and especially the amendment of the guilty party made long ago. The ordinary is to

[736] See CCL, Can. 2328.
[737] See CCL, Can. 2343.
[738] See CCL, Can. 2351, § 2.
[739] See CCL, Can. 2356.
[740] See CCL, Can. 2357.
[741] See CCL, Can. 2314, § 1, no. 2.
[742] See CCL, Can. 2359, § 2.
[743] See CCL, Can. 984, no. 5.
[744] See CCL, Can. 2294, § 1.
[745] Ibid.
[746] Ibid.
[747] Ibid.
[748] See CCL, Can. 2294, § 2.

judge concerning the recovery of this reputation. What constitutes an amendment made *long ago*—whether, for example, the period of three years proposed by older authors is sufficient—is to be left to the prudent judgment of the ordinary.

CENSURES OF THE PRESENT DAY

INTRODUCTION. The following general direction is given in the Code, Can. 6, no. 5: "All former ecclesiastical punishments, whether spiritual or temporal, corrective or punitive, latae or ferendae sententiae, of which the Code makes no mention, are held to be abolished." Therefore, by common law only those punishments found in the Code are at present in existence.—For hearing confessions, it is extremely useful to possess a brief summary of the censures which are still in existence. Other forms of ecclesiastical punishment are not so frequently encountered in the confessional. Therefore, we intend to treat briefly of censures of the present day: 1) Excommunications; 2) Interdicts; 3) Suspensions.

Art. 1. Excommunications of the Present Day

There are five categories of excommunication incurred ipso facto, according to the manner in which their absolution is reserved; 1) Most Specially to the Holy See; 2) Specially to the Holy See; 3) Simply to the Holy See; 4) To Ordinaries; 5) To No One.

1. Sins which Incur Excommunication Most Specially Reserved to the Holy See

Excommunications most specially reserved to the Holy See are four in number (in addition to those which are incurred for the violation of a secret of the Holy Office or Sacred Congregation or of a Consistory in electing a bishop).

764. The following persons incur this excommunication:

1. those who throw away the consecrated species or carry them off or retain them for an evil purpose.

Thus, for instance, thieves who sacrilegiously break open the tabernacle and scatter the hosts incur this excommunication.—Anyone guilty of this offense is also suspected of heresy and incurs infamy ipso facto. If he is a cleric he must be deposed.[749]

2. those who lay violent hands on the person of the pope.[750]

Moreover, the delinquent is to be shunned ipso facto and incurs infamy of law; if he is a cleric he must be deposed.

3. Those who absolve or pretend to absolve their accomplice in a sin against chastity;[751]

---

[749] See CCL, Can. 2320.
[750] See CCL, Can. 2343.
[751] See CCL, Can. 2367; see also no. 723.

4. a confessor who presumes to violate the seal of Confession directly. The manner in which the seal is violated directly has been explained in no. 707. As a result of the words used in the Code, Can. 2369, § 1—"excommunication most specially reserved to the Holy See awaits a confessor who presumes to violate directly the sacramental seal"—some authors (because of the use of the verb *awaits* with the accusative) regard this censure as being ferendae sententiae and not latae sententiae, but the contrary opinion is more probable and common.

2. Sins which Incur Excommunication
Specially Reserved to the Holy See

There are eleven such excommunications, in addition to those which may be incurred because of abuses in papal elections.

765. The following persons incur this excommunication:

1. apostates from the Christian Faith, heretics, and schismatics;[752]

It has been explained already, no. 201, what is meant by an apostate, a heretic, and a schismatic. Anyone suspected of heresy who shows no sign of amendment within six months after contracting the penalty is considered to be a heretic and therefore is liable to penalties inflicted on heretics.[753]—If the sin of heresy or apostasy or schism has been brought to the external forum of the local ordinary, no matter in what way (even by voluntary confession), the local ordinary (but not the vicar general, unless he enjoys a special mandate) may absolve in the external forum in virtue of his ordinary authority, but he must previously obtain an abjuration of heresy and observe all that is prescribed by law; a person so absolved may then seek absolution in the internal forum from any confessor.[754] This statute is of practical importance when converts are received into the Church. Other penalties mentioned in Can. 2314 are incurred by apostates, heretics, and schismatics.

766. 2. those who publish books of apostates, heretics, or schismatics, which defend apostasy, heresy, or schism, those who defend such books or other books specifically condemned by apostolic letters, and those who knowingly read or keep such books without due permission;[755]

This censure, originally contained in the Bull *Apostolicae Sedis*, has undergone some modification. By way of explanation, we will indicate briefly which books and which actions come within the prohibition. The books to which this canon refers (excluding manuscripts and pamphlets, but including periodicals that are bound in the form of a volume[756]) are:

[752] See CCL, Can. 2314, § 1.
[753] See CCL, Can. 2315.
[754] See CCL, Can. 2314, § 2.
[755] See CCL, Can. 2318, § 1.
[756] See Holy Office, Jan. 13, 1892.

a) those which of set purpose defend (and which do not merely contain) apostasy, heresy, or schism. According to some authors such books would not be prohibited under pain of excommunication if, while defending heresy, they were written anonymously or by a Catholic or by a non-baptized person, since such authors could not be regarded as heretics, and so on in the strict sense of the word; but such an opinion seems to be extremely formalistic and against the spirit of the law which seeks to protect the faithful against the serious dangers caused by any work which expressly defends apostasy, and so on.

b) those which are forbidden specifically (i.e., under their own particular title, and not under the general heading: all the works of such an author) by apostolic letters, e.g., a brief or an encyclical (but not a decree of the Holy Office) under pain of excommunication. Such books are very few in number and in the new Index of prohibited books are indicated by the sign † .

FOUR ACTIONS are prohibited under pain of excommunication:

a) the effective publication of the work by the author, printer, editor, but this probably excludes all other persons who cooperate in the publication;

b) the reading of such works: this refers to those persons who read the book with their own eyes and understand at least to some extent what they are reading, and thus it does not include a person who listens to such books being read or one who does not understand what he reads or who reads such a small portion of the book that there is no danger of perversion. It is further required that they *knowingly* read such books; hence any form of ignorance (excepting affected ignorance) excuses from the censure;

c) the defending of such books—that is to say, defending a book not because of its fine style or other good qualities, but precisely because it defends apostasy, and so on;

d) retaining such works—that is to say, retaining these books in one's own name without real necessity. Consequently, those employed in libraries and bookbinders are not subject to this excommunication.

NOTE. 1. In addition to this excommunication there is another (reserved to no one) which is inflicted on those who print the Sacred Scriptures without due permission, see below.

2. In addition to those books which are forbidden *under pain of censure* there are many other prohibited books;[757]

3. those who, not being priests, simulate the celebration of Mass or hear sacramental confessions;[758]

---

[757] See MIC, q. 417ff.
[758] See CCL, Can. 2322.

4. those who appeal from the mandates of the pope to a general council;[759]

5. those who have recourse to the secular power in order to impede the letters or other documents of the Holy See;[760]

767. 6. those who publish laws, orders, or decrees against the liberty or rights of the Church, as also those who directly or indirectly impede the exercise of ecclesiastical jurisdiction of either the internal or external forum by having recourse for such purpose to any lay authority;[761]

This excommunication could be frequently incurred in those countries where many evil laws are passed by members of parliaments or senators, but in practice the censure is avoided through ignorance of the censure or as the result of an existing concordat. However, any private individual who has recourse to the civil authorities in order to impede the exercise of ecclesiastical jurisdiction does not deserve such an excuse.

7. those who dare without due permission from the Holy See to cite before a lay judge a cardinal, papal legate, or major official of the Roman Curia on matters arising from their office, or their own ordinary;[762]

The Holy See sometimes grants general permission in a concordat to allow clerics to be cited before the civil courts, as happens in many Latin American countries. To cite a cleric before the civil court seems to mean compelling a cleric to appear as a *defendant* and not merely as a *witness* before the court.

768. 8. those who lay violent hands on a cardinal, papal legate, archbishop, or bishop, even though merely titular;[763]

To lay violent hands on such persons means some grave violation of the *privilegium canonis*, such as striking or imprisoning these persons. A similar injury inflicted on other clerics is punished by other censures;[764]

9. those who usurp or retain property belonging to the *See of Rome*;[765]

10. those who falsify letters or decrees of the Holy See or knowingly use such letters;[766]

11. those who falsely denounce a confessor for the crime of solicitation.[767]

[759] See CCL, Can. 2332.
[760] See CCL, Can. 2333.
[761] See CCL, Can. 2334.
[762] See CCL, Can. 2341.
[763] See CCL, Can. 2343.
[764] See nos. 764.2, 773.6.
[765] See CCL, Can. 2345.
[766] See CCL, Can. 2360, § 1.
[767] See CCL, Can. 2363. See no. 729, where it was emphasized that such false denunciation is always a sin reserved to the Holy See even if the censure is not incurred, as happens when the individual is ignorant of the penalty.

3. Sins which Incur Excommunication
Simply Reserved to the Holy See

769. The following persons incur excommunication simply reserved to the Holy See:

1. those who make profit from indulgences;[768]

This seems to include all persons who deliberately seek gain from indulgences, whether they use the profit for themselves or not.

770. 2. those who join the sect of the Masons or other societies which plot against the Church or the lawful civil authority;[769]

The Holy Office, May 10, 1884, made a distinction between those societies *which simply fall under condemnation*, and societies *which are condemned and whose members are excommunicated*. Under the first class are included all societies which exist for some evil purpose, e.g., cremation, and those which make use of evil means to achieve their purpose, as also those which exact the strictest secrecy and absolute obedience from their members. Societies whose members incur excommunication include the sect of the Masons and all societies which of set purpose plot against the Church or legitimate civil authority, such as the Communists, Bolsheviks, Nihilists. It is doubtful whether all socialists fall under this censure.

771. 3. those who without due faculties presume to absolve from an excommunication reserved either most specially or specially to the Holy See;[770]

Any form of ignorance (excepting affected ignorance) excuses from this excommunication, since it is issued against those who presume to absolve.

4. those who aid or abet anyone in a crime for which he was declared an excommunicate to be shunned by all; similarly, clerics who knowingly and willingly hold communion with such excommunicates *in divinis* and admit them to divine services;[771]

Since excommunicates who have to be shunned are today extremely rare, no further explanation is required here.[772]

5. those who without due permission dare to cite before a civil court a bishop (not of their own diocese), or an abbot, a prelate nullius, or any of the major superiors of religious institutes approved by Rome;[773]

This excommunication is incurred by those who violate the *privilegium fori* in respect of certain prelates. Regarding other excommunications incurred as the result of violating this privilege, see no. 767.7, where the highest prelates are concerned, and no. 777 in respect of other ecclesiastical persons.

[768] See CCL, Can. 2327.
[769] See CCL, Can. 2335.
[770] See CCL, Can. 2338, § 1.
[771] See CCL, Can. 2338, § 2.
[772] See MTM, vol. 3, no. 519.
[773] See CCL, Can. 2341.

6. those who violate the enclosure of nuns, and women who enter the enclosure of religious men, likewise those who admit or introduce such persons; furthermore, nuns who leave their enclosure without due permission;[774]

The enclosure to which this canon refers is the so-called *papal* enclosure which is normally found only in houses of religious with solemn vows. Therefore, those who violate any other form of enclosure do not incur this excommunication. Regarding the circumstances which permit entry into or departure from the enclosure.[775]

7. those who convert to their own use ecclesiastical property or who hinder those who have a right to the income from Church goods;[776]

Those who commit such an offense incur other penalties mentioned in the same canon. Ordinary thieves and robbers would not seem to incur this censure:[777] similarly, a mayor and his advisers who retain Church property not for their own use but for the benefit of the city;[778] also those who freely undertake the administration of such stolen property.[779] But the excommunication is inflicted on those who have bought or hired *for their own use* Church property, i.e., property belonging to a *moral* ecclesiastical person, as also on intruding parish priests and beneficed clerics. Absolution from the censure cannot be granted until the ill-gotten goods have been restored. In some countries, e.g., France and Italy, bishops have special faculties to grant or facilitate this absolution.[780]

8. those who fight a duel, or who make or accept a challenge to a duel, or who permit it, as also those who purposely go to see the duel or who give any aid to it, or favor it.[781]

772. 9. clerics in major Orders or regulars or nuns who have taken the solemn vow of chastity who presume to contract marriage—even civil marriage—and also all persons who attempt to contract it with them.[782]

Prior to the new Code this excommunication was reserved to the ordinary, to whom is now reserved a somewhat similar excommunication inflicted on those who having taken simple vows presume to contract marriage.[783] If clerics or religious live in concubinage without attempting (at least apparent) marriage, they do not incur this excommunication.

---

[774] See CCL, Can. 2342.
[775] See MIC, q. 228.
[776] See CCL, Can. 2346.
[777] See Holy Office, Mar. 9, 1870.
[778] See S. Penitentiary, January 3 and Mar. 8, 1906.
[779] See S. Penitentiary, Sept. 17, 1906.
[780] See S. Penitentiary, Aug. 5, 1907.
[781] See CCL, Can. 2351. See also what has been said previously on this subject, no. 279.
[782] See CCL, Can. 2388, § 1.
[783] See no. 773.9.

10. those who are guilty of simony in any office, benefice, or ecclesiastical dignity;[784]

Those who are guilty of simony incur other penalties, as is evident from Can. 2392, but the excommunications inflicted prior to the new Code on those who committed simony in entering religion or in collecting Mass stipends appear to have been abolished.

11. those who steal, destroy, conceal, or substantially alter any document belonging to the episcopal curia.[785]

4. Sins which Incur Excommunication Reserved to the Ordinary

773. The following persons incur excommunication reserved to the ordinary:

1. those who marry before a non-Catholic minister[786] acting as such and not as a mere civil authority. This excommunication is incurred in the external forum even by those who are ignorant of the censure.[787] It is customary for bishops to determine the way in which reconciliation may be effected:

2. those who contract marriage on the understanding that their offspring shall be educated outside the Catholic Church;[788]

3. those who knowingly present their children to non-Catholic ministers for Baptism;[789]

4. parents, or those who take the place of parents, who knowingly hand over their children to be educated or brought up in a non-Catholic religion;[790]

5. those who manufacture or knowingly sell, distribute, or expose for public veneration false relics;[791]

6. those who lay violent hands on a cleric (below the status of prelates, already mentioned in I, 2 and II, 8) or a religious of either sex;[792]

7. those who effectually procure an abortion, not excepting the mother;[793]

8. religious who apostatize from the religious life. This excommunication is reserved to the major superiors of the respective order or, if the institute is lay or not exempt, to the local ordinary of the place in which they live;[794]

---

[784] See CCL, Can. 2392.
[785] See CCL, Can. 2405.
[786] See CCL, Can. 2319.
[787] See Holy Office, May 17, 1892.
[788] See CCL, Can. 2319.
[789] Ibid.
[790] Ibid.
[791] See CCL, Can. 2326.
[792] See CCL, Can. 2343, § 4.
[793] See CCL, Can. 2350.
[794] See CCL, Can. 2385.

9. professed religious of simple perpetual vows (whether in an order or congregation) who attempt to contract marriage, even a civil marriage, and those persons with whom they contract marriage.[795]

NOTE. Regular confessors may absolve from any of these nine censures, unless the ordinary has specially reserved one to himself. In danger of death any confessor has the requisite faculty to absolve from such censures, and there is no obligation to approach the bishop if the absolved person recovers.

5. Sins which Incur Excommunication Not Reserved

774. The following persons incur excommunication which is reserved to no one:

1. authors and publishers who without due permission publish books of the Bible, or annotations or commentaries on the same;[796]

2. those who dare to command or compel the Church to give ecclesiastical burial to infidels, apostates, heretics, schismatics, or other excommunicated or interdicted persons enumerated in Can. 1240, § 1;[797]

In addition to those mentioned, the following persons are excluded from ecclesiastical burial: 1) suicides; 2) duelists killed in a duel or dying from some wound received in it; 3) cremationists; other public sinners.—If any sign of repentance was given prior to death, these persons may be granted ecclesiastical burial.

3. those who in any way are guilty of unlawful alienation of Church property without the necessary permission of the Holy See;[798]

4. those who use any force to compel another to enter the clerical life or a religious community;[799]

5. those who knowingly neglect to denounce within a month a confessor guilty of solicitation.[800]

Art. 2. Forms of Interdict of the Present Day

775. 1. Universities, colleges, chapters, and other *moral persons* of whatsoever kind, who appeal from the laws, decrees, and mandates of the reigning pope to a general council, incur an interdict specially reserved to the Holy See.[801]

Physical persons guilty of this offense are suspected of heresy and incur excommunication specially reserved to the Holy See, as stated already, II, 3. The interdict inflicted on moral persons is specially reserved to the Holy See.

[795] See CCL, Can. 2388, § 2; see also nos. 771.3 and 772.
[796] See CCL, Can. 2318, § 2.
[797] See CCL, Can. 2339.
[798] See CCL, Can. 2347, no. 3.
[799] See CCL, Can. 2352.
[800] See CCL, Can. 2368, § 2.
[801] See CCL, Can. 2332.

2. Those who knowingly celebrate or cause to be celebrated Divine Offices in places under interdict or who allow clerics under excommunication, interdict, or suspension to celebrate after condemnatory or declaratory sentence such Divine Offices as are forbidden by censure incur an *interdict forbidding entrance into a church*, until they have made fitting satisfaction according to the discretion of the superior whose sentence they ignored.[802]

3. Those who are the cause of a local interdict, or of an interdict on a college or community incur a personal interdict.[803]

This interdict does not seem to be reserved.

4. Those who *of their own accord* grant ecclesiastical burial to infidels, apostates, heretics, schismatics, excommunicates, or those under interdict, incur an *interdict forbidding entrance into a church* and this penalty is *reserved to the ordinary.*[804]

5. Catholics who without due permission have dared to contract a mixed marriage (even though valid) are ipso facto excluded from legitimate acts and *sacramentals*, until they have obtained the requisite dispensation from the ordinary.[805]

Art. 3. Forms of Suspension of the Present Day

Certain suspensions are reserved to the Holy See, others to the ordinary, others to religious superiors, while some are not reserved. Amongst these suspensions there are some which are vindictive penalties rather than censures.

1. Suspension Reserved to the Holy See

776. 1. Those who confer or receive episcopal consecration without leave from the Holy See are ipso facto suspended, until such time as the Holy See dispenses them.[806]

2. All clerics (including bishops) who administer or receive Orders or any other Sacrament through simony incur suspension.[807]

3. Those who *presume* to receive Orders from one who is excommunicated, suspended, or under interdict (after condemnatory or declaratory sentence) or from a notorious apostate, heretic, or schismatic incur suspension from the divine ministry. Those who are ordained in this manner *in good faith* are forbidden to exercise any Order thus received until they are dispensed.[808]

[802] See CCL, Can. 2338, § 3.
[803] See CCL, Can. 2338, § 4.
[804] See CCL, Can. 2339.
[805] See CCL, Can. 2375.
[806] See CCL, Can. 2370.
[807] See CCL, Can. 2371.
[808] See CCL, Can. 2372.

4. Suspension from conferring orders for a year is incurred ipso facto by those who confer Orders *a)* without the necessary testimonial or dimissorial letters; *b)* before the canonical age; *c)* on religious without the requisite permissions.[809]

5. An abbot or a prelate nullius who in spite of no existing impediment delays his consecration for over three months after receiving the papal letters is suspended ipso facto from exercising the power of jurisdiction.[810]

There is some doubt whether this suspension is reserved, since the Code makes no mention of any such reservation.

6. A religious in major Orders whose profession has been declared null and void on account of deceit on his part is suspended until the Holy See dispenses him.[811]

7. A professed religious in major Orders who having taken perpetual vows is dismissed because of some minor offense (enumerated in Can. 670) is suspended ipso facto.[812]

8. Priests who without the necessary letters required by the Sacred Congregation of the Consistory[813] rashly and arrogantly emigrate from Europe or territories bordering on the Mediterranean to America or the Philippines remain ipso facto suspended from the divine ministry; if in spite of this prohibition they exercise some act of the ministry (which God forbid) they incur irregularity, and only the Sacred Congregation of the Consistory can absolve them from these penalties.[814]

2. Suspension Reserved to the Ordinary

777. A cleric who without due permission from the local ordinary dares to sue in a civil court any ecclesiastical person who is neither a cardinal, bishop, nor major prelate, incurs *suspension from office*.[815]

3. Suspension Reserved to the Major Superior of a Religious Order

778. Religious in major Orders who become fugitives are suspended.[816]

Not only religious in the strict sense of the term but also brothers without vows living the common life in a community of men incur the same penalty if they become fugitives from their religious institute.[817]

---

[809] See CCL, Can. 2373.
[810] See CCL, Can. 2402.
[811] See CCL, Can. 2387.
[812] See CCL, Can. 671.
[813] Dec. 30, 1918.
[814] See AAS 11, 43.
[815] See CCL, Can. 2341.
[816] See CCL, Can. 2386.
[817] See Pont. Comm., June 3, 1918.

4. Suspension Not Reserved

779. 1. Priests who presume to hear sacramental confessions without proper jurisdiction are ipso facto suspended from the divine ministry; those who presume to absolve from reserved sins are ipso facto suspended from the hearing of confessions.[818]

2. Clerics who *maliciously* receive Orders without dimissorial letters or with false ones or before the canonical age or without observing the prescribed sequence of Orders are ipso facto suspended from the Orders thus received.[819]

3. Clerics who *presumptuously* resign an office, benefice, or ecclesiastical dignity into the hands of lay persons incur *suspension ipso facto from the divine ministry.*[820]

4. A vicar capitular who grants dimissorial letters unlawfully is ipso facto *suspended from the divine ministry.*[821]

5. Religious superiors who in violation of the law have *presumed* to send their subjects for ordination to a bishop of another place are ipso facto suspended for one month *from the celebration of Mass.*[822]

This suspension is likewise incurred by superiors of clerical congregations which do not take vows, if they have the privilege of granting dimissorial letters for their own subjects.[823]

TREATISE VII
INDULGENCES

This treatise is divided into three chapters: 1) Indulgences in General; 2) Conditions Required for Gaining Indulgences; 3) Individual Indulgences.

INDULGENCES IN GENERAL

780. DEFINITION. *An indulgence is a remission in the sight of God of that temporal punishment due for sins whose guilt has been forgiven, granted outside the Sacrament of Penance by ecclesiastical authority from the treasury of the Church: if given to the living it is granted in the form of absolution, if given for the faithful departed it is applied in the form of suffrage.*[824]

EXPLANATION. 1. An indulgence is *a remission in the sight of God of temporal punishment,* for indulgences do not remit either mortal or venial sin, as the Protestant calumny would have men believe. Once the guilt of sin has been forgiven in other ways, indulgences remit the remaining temporal punishment, not merely in the ecclesiastical forum but also in the tribunal of God, and therefore temporal

---

[818] See CCL, Can. 2366.
[819] See CCL, Can. 2374.
[820] See CCL, Can. 2400.
[821] See CCL, Can. 2409.
[822] See CCL, Can. 2410.
[823] See Pont. Comm., June 2–3, 1918 (AAS 10, 347).
[824] CCL, Can. 911.

punishment remitted in this way does not have to be endured again either in this world or in purgatory.

2. Indulgences are *granted outside the Sacrament of Penance by ecclesiastical authority from the treasury of the Church*. Temporal punishment remaining after the forgiveness of sin can be remitted in many ways: by the sacramental penance, by deeds of mortification undertaken voluntarily, and by the patient endurance of the trials of this life. Indulgences likewise remit this temporal punishment inasmuch as the Church offers from her treasury—i.e., from the accumulation of the satisfactory merits of Christ and the saints—the satisfaction that is due. Therefore, indulgences are founded on two doctrines: the treasury of the Church, and vicarious satisfaction.[825]

3. Indulgences are *given for the living by way of absolution, for the dead by way of suffrage*. Since the Church possesses the power to absolve the faithful from anything which might prevent them entering Heaven in virtue of her jurisdiction over the living, she absolves them from temporal punishment by means of indulgences; on the other hand, since she lacks jurisdiction over the dead, she can only offer from her treasury satisfaction or indulgences for the dead by way of suffrage.

781. **Kinds.** 1. By virtue of their *effect*, indulgences are either *plenary* or *partial* depending on whether they remit all or only part of the punishment.

A *plenary* indulgence is to be considered granted in such manner that if it cannot be gained fully, it may be gained partially according to the disposition of the subject.[826] A plenary indulgence attached to some prescribed work can be gained once a day only, even though the work is performed repeatedly, unless the contrary is expressly stated.[827]—It is impossible to determine with any degree of certainty how much punishment is remitted by a *partial* indulgence. It is most commonly held by authors that a partial indulgence of seven years and seven quarantines, for example, remits as much temporal punishment as a penance of similar length in the original discipline of the Church. Unless any restriction is expressed, partial indulgences may be gained repeatedly on the same day by repetition of the prescribed good work.[828]

2. By virtue of their *subject*, indulgences may be gained for either *the living* or *the dead* according to whether they are applied for the living or for the dead.

All indulgences conceded by the pope are applicable to the souls in purgatory unless the contrary is stated.[829] All indulgences gained by those who make the heroic act are applicable to the souls in purgatory.[830]

---

[825] See MTM, vol. 3, no. 541.
[826] See CCL, Can. 926.
[827] See CCL, Can. 928.
[828] Ibid.
[829] See CCL, Can. 930.
[830] See *Raccolta*, no. 531.

3. By virtue of the *way* in which they are granted, indulgences are either *personal*, *real*, or *local*: they are personal if granted to specified persons, e.g., to the members of some confraternity; they are real, if attached to some object, e.g., a rosary; they are local, if attached to a place, e.g., a church.

782. THE FOLLOWING PERSONS MAY GRANT INDULGENCES:

a) the pope (whose power is unlimited);

b) cardinals, up to 200 days' indulgence;[831]

c) archbishops for their entire province, up to 100 days' indulgence;[832]

d) residential bishops in their own diocese, up to 50 days' indulgence;[833] but they are permitted to grant greater indulgences when consecrating a church or an altar;[834]

e) vicars and prefects apostolic within the limits of their own territory and during the period of their office, up to 50 days' indulgence.[835]

NOTE. Those inferior to the Roman Pontiff cannot:

a) give to others the faculty to grant indulgences;

b) grant indulgences applicable to the souls in purgatory;

c) attach an indulgence to an object, pious work, or association to which the Holy See or another authority has already attached an indulgence, unless they prescribe additional conditions for gaining the indulgence;[836]

f) nuncios, legates a latere, the major Penitentiary of Rome and others may likewise grant indulgences.

CONDITIONS FOR GAINING INDULGENCES

Three things are required for the gaining of indulgences: 1) the right intention, 2) the state of grace and perfect union with the Church, and 3) the fulfillment of the prescribed good work.[837]

783. 1. Any virtual *intention*, and even a habitual intention which has been made once and never retracted, is sufficient for the gaining of indulgences, since an indulgence is an act of kindness which a person is presumed willing to accept unless he positively refuses. But if a person desires to apply some indulgence to a particular soul, there is required an explicit intention (which must be virtual at least).

---

[831] See CCL, Can. 239, § 1, no. 24.
[832] See CCL, Can. 274, no. 2.
[833] See CCL, Can. 349, § 2, no. 2.
[834] See CCL, Can. 1166. Bishops are empowered to grant indulgences to exempt religious, even in their own churches; see Pont. Comm., Dec. 6, 1930 (AAS 23, 25).
[835] See CCL, Can. 294, § 2.
[836] See CCL, Can. 913.
[837] See CCL, Can. 925.

784. 2. *A state of grace and perfect union with the Church are necessary for gaining indulgences.* Consequently, the following persons are debarred from indulgences:

a) unbaptized or excommunicated persons;

b) those in the state of mortal sin. Even venial sin prevents the remission of *all* temporal punishment. In such cases the punishment due to those sins whose guilt has been forgiven is remitted, but not the punishment due to those venial sins not yet forgiven. — There are a few authors who maintain that indulgences may be gained for the souls in purgatory even by one who is in the state of mortal sin, but such an opinion is hardly probable and is clearly opposed to the teaching of St. Thomas.[838] It is sufficient that the state of grace be present at least *at the end* of the prescribed work.[839]

785. 3. *The good work prescribed* for the gaining of an indulgence must be carried out faithfully, and any substantial change of the work prevents the indulgence being gained.

The prescribed work:

a) must be performed *personally*, with the exception of almsgiving which may be performed by proxy. Accordingly, in the present discipline of the Church it is impossible to gain an indulgence for other *living* persons;[840]

b) cannot be fulfilled by doing some other work *already obligatory under pain of sin* (unless the contrary is expressly stated in the indult); thus, when a visit to a church is prescribed, this is not fulfilled by hearing Mass on Sunday. However, a person who receives as his penance in sacramental confession some good work which happens to be enriched with an indulgence may by one and the same act fulfill his penance and gain the indulgence.[841]

Similarly, indulgences may normally be gained through the Paschal Communion.[842]

NOTE. 1. Unless the contrary is stated or expressed, or unless the good work prescribed is Confession or Holy Communion, several indulgences cannot be gained by performing one and the same work to which many indulgences are annexed by various titles.[843] Thus, for example, if anyone recites his Rosary on beads which have been properly blessed, he gains at the same time the Crosier and Dominican indulgences.[844]

2. Confessors can commute the pious works prescribed for the gaining of indulgences for people who on account of some legitimate impediment cannot perform

---

[838] See ST, III-Sup., q. 27, a. 1.
[839] See CCL, Can. 925, § 1.
[840] See CCL, Can. 930.
[841] See CCL, Can. 932.
[842] See S. C. Indulgences, *Decreta Authentica*, no. 327.
[843] See CCL, Can. 933.
[844] See Pius X, June 12, 1907; Beringer-Hilgers, *Die Ablässe*, vol. 1, p. 113.

these works.[845] Since this faculty has been granted generally and has no restriction attached to it, the confessor may avail himself of it even outside confession and even as far as Holy Communion is concerned.

Individual works which are normally prescribed for the gaining of indulgences are confession, Holy Communion, visit to a church, certain prayers.

786. a) *Confession*, if prescribed, must be made even by those who have committed only venial sin. It may be made within *eight days* before or after the day to which the indulgence is attached, and this confession suffices for gaining all indulgences during these periods.[846] An indult is granted to some dioceses enabling the faithful to gain all indulgences, provided they go to confession within fifteen days either before or after the day to which the indulgence is attached. The faithful who are in the habit of going to confession at least twice a month unless legitimately impeded, or who receive Holy Communion daily (even though they may abstain from receiving once or twice a week), can gain all indulgences without actual confession which would otherwise be necessary for gaining the indulgences (with the exception of the indulgences of a jubilee).[847] Thus, for example, a priest who is in the habit of saying Mass daily may gain all indulgences, even though he cannot go to confession more frequently than once in six weeks.

787. b) *Holy Communion* received once (and this includes the Easter Communion) suffices for gaining several indulgences on the same day, each of which requires the reception of Holy Communion. If the indulgence is attached to a specified day, one may receive Communion on the eve of that day or within its octave. If as the result of a long illness or some other physical impediment a person is unable to receive the prescribed Holy Communion, the confessor may substitute some other pious work. Confessors may use the same power of commuting for *children* who have not yet made their first Holy Communion.

788. c) *The visit to a church* sometimes prescribed for the gaining of indulgences must be made in the church which is so specified. If, on the other hand, the visit to a church is left in general terms, it suffices to visit any church or even a public oratory, but not a semipublic or private oratory. However, those who for the sake of religious perfection, or study and education, or for the sake of health lead a community life in houses approved by the ordinary but lacking a church, or public oratory, and all other persons living there to do service, may visit their own semipublic chapel in order to fulfill the prescribed visit to a church which is *not specifically named*.[848]

---

[845] See CCL, Can. 935.
[846] See CCL, Can. 931, § 1.
[847] See CCL, Can. 931, § 3.
[848] See CCL, Can. 929.

A *plenary* indulgence granted either *daily and perpetually* or *for some time* to those who visit a specified church or public oratory is to be understood in such a way that it can be gained any day but *only once a year* by any of the faithful, unless the contrary is stated expressly in the indult.[849]

In order to gain an indulgence *attached to a certain day* for which a visit to some church or oratory is prescribed, the visit can be made from *noon* on the preceding day until midnight of the day appointed for the indulgence.[850] Thus, for example, the time for gaining a *toties quoties* indulgence is now longer than it was before the new Code.

789. *d) The prescribed prayers* must be vocal, and therefore mental prayer is not sufficient, unless the contrary is expressly stated. Prayers prescribed *in general terms* for the pope's intentions may be any oral prayers, such as the *Pater Noster* or a litany, and so on.[851] But if *special* prayers are prescribed, these may be recited in any language, but any addition, subtraction, or interpolation destroys the indulgence.[852] This statute seems sufficiently severe, and therefore, for instance, indulgences granted for the recitation of the Rosary do not cease if after each decade, or after each Hail Mary, a pause is made for meditation on the mystery, as is stated by the Sacred Penitentiary, Jan. 22, 1921.[853]—If the prayers are recited *with a companion* it is sufficient that they be recited *alternately* or else followed *mentally* while they are recited by another.[854]

MUTES can gain indulgences if, being in the same place as those who are reciting the prayers, they raise their mind and affections to God. If the prayers prescribed are private prayers, it is sufficient that they say them mentally or by signs or by scanning them with their eyes.[855]

790. THE CESSATION of indulgences is clearly indicated in the new Code. 1. *Local in-dulgences* cease if the church or oratory to which they are attached is completely destroyed; they revive if the church is rebuilt within fifty years in the same place or almost the same place and under the same title.[856]

---

[849] See CCL, Can. 921, § 3.

[850] See CCL, Can. 923.

[851] If no set prayers have been prescribed for the intentions of the Holy Father, it is sufficient to recite one *Pater*, one *Ave*, and one *Gloria*, or any other prayer (see S. Peniten-tiary, Sept. 20, 1933: AAS 25, 446). The *Pater, Ave,* and *Gloria* must be recited six times for *toties quoties* indulgences (see S. Penitentiary, July 10, 1924: AAS 16, 347; Jan. 13, 1930: AAS 22, 43; July 5, 1930: AAS 22, 363). See also "Preces et pia opera in favorem Omnium Christi fidelium vel quorundam Coetuum Personarum indulgentiis ditata et opportune recognita" (Typis Polyglottis Vaticanis, 1938, p. xv, Adnot. la and b).

[852] See CCL, Can. 934, § 2.

[853] AAS 13, 164.

[854] See CCL, Can. 934, § 3.

[855] See CCL, Can. 936.

[856] See CCL, Can. 924, § 1.

2. *Real* indulgences cease in only two ways: *a)* if the object itself is completely destroyed, or *b)* if the object is sold.[857]

Thus, indulgences do not cease if the object to which an indulgence is attached, such as a rosary, is *given* or *lent* to another, even if the original owner has used it to gain the indulgences; neither does the indulgence cease if the object undergoes *repeated* minor repairs so that eventually the original object has been completely changed. On the other hand, the indulgence does seem to cease if the chain of rosary beads is so badly broken that one possesses nothing more than a handful of beads.

SOME PARTICULAR INDULGENCES

We shall now consider a few indulgences in detail, especially those with which the priest is more likely to be concerned in the course of his apostolate: 1) the plenary indulgence at death, 2) the indulgence attached to the papal blessing, 3) the indulgences attached to a general absolution, 4) the indulgence of a privileged altar, 5) indulgences annexed to rosaries, 6) the indulgence of the Stations of the Cross.

1. Plenary Indulgence at Death

791. ITS NATURE. *The plenary indulgence at the hour of death is one which the pope himself either personally or by proxy grants to the dying in the form of a blessing or absolution.* This indulgence should not be confused with others which the faithful can gain at the hour of death, e.g., by kissing the crucifix, or by holding certain medals, or by virtue of their membership of some confraternity. For whereas it is the individual who is responsible for applying such indulgences to himself, the indulgence attached to the papal blessing cannot be gained except by means of the blessing of a priest who is authorized by the pope to give it. This indulgence does not attain its effect until *the very moment at which the soul is separated from the body* and about to appear before the supreme Judge; furthermore, it seems impossible to apply the indulgence to any other dead person, even if the heroic act has been made. When the Sacred Congregation for Indulgences was questioned on this matter, it replied, Jan. 23, 1901, "no decision is to be given."

ITS SUBJECT. The blessing at the hour of death to which a plenary indulgence is attached may be received by all who are in grave danger of death and who are capable of receiving sacramental absolution and have not so far received the blessing during the same danger of death.

EXPLANATION. 1. *All who are in grave danger of death*—or, all who may receive Viaticum, as soldiers before battle, prisoners condemned to death, and so on.

2. *and who are capable of receiving sacramental absolution.* Therefore, even those who are unconscious, and children who are capable of committing sin (even though they have not yet received their First Holy Communion) are included.

[857] See CCL, Can. 924, § 2.

3. *and have not yet received the blessing during the same danger of death.* Since this blessing attains its effect at the final moment of a person's life, it cannot be repeated during the same danger of death. This rule must be followed even if the individual received the blessing while in a state of mortal sin or relapsed into mortal sin after receiving it. If the sick person recovers and then falls into a new danger of death, the papal blessing can be repeated, but this is not necessary.

792. NECESSARY CONDITIONS.

a) On the part of the priest giving the blessing, no special faculty is required, since it is stated in the Code, Can. 468, § 2: "The parish priest and any other priest assisting the dying has the faculty to give the apostolic blessing with a plenary indulgence for the moment of death according to the formula prescribed in the approved liturgical books, and he should not neglect to give this blessing."

The formula prescribed by Benedict XV and contained in the Roman Ritual is to be used even by those religious who have a special rite of their own. If the blessing is given after the administration of Viaticum and Extreme Unction (as is the custom), the Confiteor must be repeated, so that it will then be said three times.[858]

b) The recipient:

i) must not be under excommunication or evidently lacking in contrition;

ii) must willingly accept death as coming from the hand of God;

iii) must invoke the Holy Name of Jesus with his lips or, if this is impossible, in his heart.

Therefore, the priest must warn the sick person to invoke the Holy Name.

2. Indulgence Attached to the Papal Blessing

793. DEFINITION. *The papal or apostolic blessing is a blessing granted on more solemn occasions by the pope or his delegate to which a plenary indulgence is attached.*

THE FOLLOWING CONDITIONS ARE REQUIRED OF THE PERSON GRANTING THE INDULGENCE.

a) He must possess *a special faculty,* which is granted *by common law* to the following persons:

i) to bishops in their respective territories twice a year—on Easter Sunday and one other solemn feast of their own choosing;

ii) to abbots and prelates nullius, vicars and prefects apostolic (even though not bishops), in their own territory on *one* of the more solemn feasts of the year.[859] Many secular and religious priests possess the same faculty in virtue of a special delegation.

b) Bishops and other secular prelates must use *the formula* given in the appendix of the Roman Pontifical: prelates who are religious must follow that given in the

---

[858] See S. C. Indulgences, *Decreta Authentica,* no. 286, no. 6.
[859] See CCL, Can. 914.

Roman Ritual, tit. VIII, chap. 32, and this must likewise be observed by preachers, normally speaking. However, if no specific formula is prescribed, a single blessing with a crucifix is sufficient, while saying the words: "Benedictio Dei omnipotentis Patris et Filii et Spiritus Sancti descendat super vos et maneat semper. R. Amen."[860]

3. Indulgence Attached to a General Absolution

794. DEFINITION. *A general absolution is one granted to regulars, nuns, and tertiaries of certain orders by special privilege on stated days; a specified formula must be used, and to the absolution is attached a plenary indulgence and the remission of censures and transgressions of the Rule.*

THE FOLLOWING CONDITIONS ARE REQUIRED ON THE PART OF THE PRIEST GIVING THE ABSOLUTION.

1. A *special faculty* is necessary if the absolution is given *publicly*. This faculty is possessed by the proper superior and his delegate for their subjects, by the confessor to a monastery or any other priest delegated by the ordinary for monks and sisters leading a community life, and also by the director or any confessor for secular tertiaries.

2. A *special formula* must be used, which is to be found in the appendix of the Roman Ritual. The absolution may be given privately in the confessional by any priest using the shorter form: "Auctoritate apostolica mihi concessa plenariam omnium peccatorum tuorum indulgentiam tibi impertior. In nomine Patris et Filii et Spiritus Sancti. Amen."[861]

ON THE PART OF THE RECIPIENT, all that is required is the state of grace and legitimate membership of the sodality to which has been granted the privilege of this general absolution.

4. Indulgence of a Privileged Altar

795. DEFINITION AND KINDS. *A privileged altar is nothing other than a plenary indulgence attached to the saying of Mass either on a specified altar or by a certain priest.*

KINDS. 1. An altar is privileged *for the living and the dead* if a plenary indulgence may be gained both for the living and the dead; otherwise, it is restricted *to the dead.* The former type is today extremely rare.

2. The privilege is *local* if the plenary indulgence is attached to a specified altar for all who celebrate Mass there, or *personal* if it is granted to an individual priest wherever he celebrates Mass, or *mixed* if it is attached to an altar for certain priests.

All altars are privileged in a church where the devotion of the Forty Hours is being held; similarly, all altars on All Souls' Day.[862] — Certain prelates have the faculty of designating a privileged altar in each church.[863]

---

[860] S.R.C., May 11, 1911; see also Beringer, *Die Ablässe,* vol. 2, p. 456.

[861] Beringer, *Die Ablässe,* vol. 2, p. 455.

[862] See CCL, Can. 917.

[863] See CCL, Can. 916.

A *personal* privilege is granted to every priest making the heroic act.[864]

THE REQUISITE CONDITIONS ARE:

1. that the altar be fixed, in order that it may be privileged; this is not necessary when the privilege is personal;

2. that the Mass and the indulgence be applied to one and the same soul, but it is not necessary to celebrate a Requiem Mass.[865]

5. Indulgence Attached to Rosaries

796. Many rosaries have indulgences attached to them, such as the Dominican Rosary, the Rosary of St. Bridget, the Rosary of the Canons Regular of the Holy Cross, the Rosary of the Servites or of the Seven Dolors, and so on. The nature of the indulgences and the conditions under which they may be gained are discussed in those books which treat specifically of this subject, e.g., Beringer, *Die Ablässe*. For the present it is only necessary to note that several indulgences may be attached to the same rosary beads, but only the indulgences for the Dominican Rosary and the Rosary of the Canons Regular of the Holy Cross may be gained by the *one* recital.[866]

6. Indulgence of the Stations of the Cross

797. Many plenary and partial indulgences are attached to the Stations of the Cross and all are applicable to the souls in purgatory. However, it is forbidden to give any catalogue of these indulgences.

THE FOLLOWING CONDITIONS must be fulfilled in order that the indulgences may be gained.

1. A short *meditation*—no matter how brief—must be made at each Station *on the Passion of Christ*, at least in a general manner. *Vocal* prayers are not necessary, but their use is praiseworthy.

2. One must *move* from one Station to the next, if this is possible. When the Stations are made in common, it is sufficient for the congregation to rise and genuflect for each Station, provided that at least one person passes from one Station to the next.

3. *No notable interruption* should occur in the exercise, although a short interruption in order to approach confession or Holy Communion would not destroy the continuity.

NOTE. Any of the faithful who are reasonably *prevented* from visiting each Station may hold a crucifix in their hands which has been specially blessed for this purpose, and recite twenty times the *Pater*, *Ave*, and *Gloria*—that is to say, once for each Station to which is added some meditation on the Passion of Christ, five

---

[864] See S. C. Indulgences, Aug. 25, 1897.
[865] See Holy Office, Feb. 20, 1913.
[866] See S. C. Indulgences, June 12, 1907.

times in memory of the wounds of Christ, and once for the intentions of the Holy Father. They will thus gain all the indulgences attached to the exercise.

ERECTION OF THE STATIONS. Only a priest possessing special faculties may now erect the Stations. The manner of their erection is set forth in the Roman Ritual.

Fourteen wooden crosses (without the figure of Christ) are required, which must be blessed, attached to the wall, and placed at some distance from each other. Pictorial or sculptured representations of the Passion are recommended but are not essential.

The indulgences cease: a) if the crosses are moved from one church to another, but not if they are moved from one place to another in the same church; b) if all or the majority of the crosses are destroyed, but if less than seven are destroyed they may be replaced by new crosses even if the latter are not blessed.

TREATISE VIII
EXTREME UNCTION

This treatise is divided into three chapters: 1) The Nature of the Sacrament of Extreme Unction; 2) Its Effects; 3) The Subject and Minister of the Sacrament.

THE NATURE OF EXTREME UNCTION

798. DEFINITION. *Extreme Unction is a Sacrament of the New Law through which by means of anointing with blessed oil and the prayer of the priest spiritual health and sometimes bodily health are conferred on a man who is seriously ill and capable of grave sin.*

This definition will be clarified in the course of further discussion on the matter, form, effects, subject, and minister of the Sacrament.

THE REMOTE MATTER required for the *validity* of the Sacrament is olive oil (*Oleum Infirmorum*, O.I.) specially blessed; the ordinary minister for the blessing of this oil is a bishop, the extraordinary minister any priest delegated by the Supreme Pontiff.[867] In the Greek Church all priests possess this delegation tacitly.

The remote matter required for *lawfulness* in ordinary cases is oil which has been blessed a) in the same year in which it is used, b) by the bishop of the diocese (or, if the see is vacant, by the bishop of a neighboring diocese).

Old oil should not be used except in cases of necessity. "When the holy oils are about to fail, other olive oil that has not been blessed may be added, even repeatedly, but always in smaller quantity than the holy oils."[868] The oil of catechumens and chrism are *doubtful* matter.

799. THE PROXIMATE MATTER consists in the use of the remote matter, that is, the anointing of the sick person with the holy oil. In case of necessity a single anointing of one of the senses, preferably however of the forehead, is sufficient for *validity*

[867] See CCL, Can. 945.
[868] CCL, Can. 734, § 2.

together with the prescribed shorter form, but the obligation remains to supply the other anointings when the danger ceases and the person lives.[869] For the *lawful* administration of this Sacrament outside the case of necessity, it is required that the anointings be performed, *a)* with the thumb of the right hand, *b)* in the form of a cross, *c)* on each of the organs (where these exist), beginning with the sight, *d)* in the order of anointing the senses prescribed in the Ritual, and at the same time observing the other rubrics.

If the sick person lacks any organ (e.g., a hand), the anointing is to be performed on the adjoining part, provided this is possible. Thus, for instance, if he lacks both feet and legs, he is not to be anointed on the hip.

When there exists a danger of contagion, the priest may use a brush or small stick. The anointing of the loins is always to be omitted. The anointing of the feet may be omitted for any good reason.[870] *The ordinary* FORM (in the Latin Church) is: "Per istam sanctam unctionem et suam piissimam misericordiam indulgeat tibi Dominus, quidquid per visum (auditum, odoratum, gustum, locutionem, tactum, gressum) deliquisti. Amen."

The form to be used *in a case of necessity* when only a single anointing on the forehead is possible is: "Per istam sanctam unctionem indulgeat tibi Dominus, quidquid deliquisti. Amen."[871] If only one anointing is possible and this form is used, once the danger passes, all the anointings are to be supplied together with their respective forms. Although the Sacrament was validly administered in the first instance by a single anointing and one form of words, nevertheless, while there remains a moral union it is necessary to supply everything required for the integrity of the Sacrament.

800. NOTE. If the Sacrament is conferred conditionally, the condition to be expressed is not "si dispositus es," but "si es capax." For if the Sacrament were administered under the first condition and the recipient did not possess the requisite dispositions, there would be no Sacrament and it could not revive; on the other hand, if the second condition is used, once the impediment ceases the Sacrament revives.

Extreme Unction must be administered conditionally in four cases: when there is a doubt *a)* whether the invalid has attained the use of reason; *b)* whether the danger of death is really present; *c)* whether the person is dead; *d)* whether the person stubbornly perseveres in mortal sin without repentance.[872]

THE EFFECTS OF EXTREME UNCTION

Some effects are regarded as the primary effects of the Sacrament, others as its secondary effects.

---

[869] See CCL, Can. 947, § 1.
[870] See CCL, Can. 947, § 2 and 3.
[871] Holy Office, Apr. 25, 1906.
[872] See CCL, Can. 941–942.

801. THE PRIMARY effects are:

1. *an increase of sanctifying grace*, which of its nature destroys the remnants of sin and consequently sin itself.

The Sacrament of Extreme Unction is primarily and of its nature a Sacrament *of the living* and therefore prior to its reception the individual should be in a state of sanctifying grace, either by receiving absolution or by an act of contrition which is at least *considered* to be perfect. But secondarily, and as a consequence, Extreme Unction is a Sacrament *of the dead* causing the first grace and the remission of sins, as is evident from the words of St. James: "If he is guilty of sin, they will be pardoned" (Jas 5:15) and also from the form used: "Indulgeat tibi Dominus, quidquid deliquisti," as also from the Council of Trent.[873]—Extreme Unction can be regarded as a more certain cause of the first grace than sacramental absolution given to an unconscious dying person, since the absolution cannot have effect unless there is a genuine act of attrition manifested externally, whereas for Extreme Unction nothing more is required than habitual attrition which need not be manifested externally. Therefore, all care must be used to see that Extreme Unction is administered to one who is unconscious.

2. *sacramental grace* causing strength of soul against all evils, past, present, and to come, and the remission of venial sin and the remnants of sin.

THE SECONDARY EFFECTS of this Sacrament are: 1) bodily health, if this is expedient for spiritual salvation; 2) remission of mortal sin, if the invalid being attrite inculpably omits both confession and perfect contrition.

THE SUBJECT AND THE MINISTER OF EXTREME UNCTION

802. THE SUBJECT of Extreme Unction is any baptized person, capable of serious sin, who is in probable danger of death from sickness or old age.[874]

For the *valid* reception of this Sacrament it is necessary that the recipient be *a)* baptized (with water); *b)* capable of personal sins, and therefore children before the age of reason and those who are permanent lunatics cannot receive this Sacrament; *c)* in probable danger of death from sickness or old age. St. James states expressly: "Is one of you sick (ἀσθενεῖ)?" (Jas 5:14). Therefore, Extreme Unction cannot be administered to soldiers prior to battle, nor to prisoners about to be executed, nor to women before a dangerous delivery. Since old age itself is a sickness, it is lawful to administer the Sacrament to an aged person who is ailing; *d)* habitually intending to receive this Sacrament.

For the *lawful* reception of the Sacrament there is required the state of grace, or contrition, or confession accompanied by attrition, or at least attrition, if confession or contrition is impossible.

---

[873] See Session 14, "Of the Sacrament of Extreme Unction," Can. 2.
[874] See CCL, Can. 940, § 1.

NOTE. Extreme Unction should not be delayed until there is extreme danger of death but should be administered as soon as possible in a dangerous illness. Since it is not certain when the soul actually departs from the body the Sacrament may be administered conditionally up to half an hour after apparent death.

803. THE OBLIGATION to receive Extreme Unction is not considered grave, provided that there is no scandal and no contempt for the Sacrament.

No precept to this effect can be found either in Sacred Scripture or in Tradition or in ecclesiastical law, and therefore during the period of an interdict this Sacrament cannot be administered except to those unable to receive the Sacraments of Holy Eucharist and Penance. Although, generally speaking, there is only a slight obligation to receive this Sacrament, no one is allowed to neglect it and all care should be taken that the sick receive it while they are fully conscious.[875]

804. THE MINISTER for the *valid* administration of the Sacrament is any priest and no one other than a priest, as is evident from the words of St. James: "Let him send for the presbyters of the Church" (Jas 5:14) and also from the definition of the Council of Trent.[876]

The minister for the *lawful* administration of the Sacrament in ordinary cases is the pastor of souls, that is: *a)* the parish priest of the place in which the sick person happens to be, or another priest with the permission at least presumed of the parish priest;[877] *b)* a religious superior for his professed subjects, novices, domestics, and those who continually reside with him; *c)* a confessor to nuns. What has been said previously regarding the administration of Viaticum, no. 602, applies also to the administration of Extreme Unction. Religious who presume to administer Extreme Unction to lay persons are no longer subject to the excommunication formerly inflicted.—Pastors of souls have a grave obligation to administer this Sacrament to those of their subjects who reasonably request it; other priests are under an obligation of charity.[878]

In one and the same illness this Sacrament cannot be *repeated*, unless the sick person recovered from his illness after receiving the anointing and again relapsed into another danger of death.[879]

The reason for this prohibition is that the efficacy of this Sacrament endures as long as the sick person is in danger of death from this illness or until he dies. The danger of death is considered to have ceased if the sick person makes some improvement over a notable period, e.g., a month, during the same long illness.

[875] See CCL, Can. 944.
[876] See Session 14, "Of the Sacrament of Extreme Unction," Can. 4.
[877] See CCL, Can. 938.
[878] See CCL, Can. 939.
[879] See CCL, Can. 940, § 2.

TREATISE IX
HOLY ORDERS

This treatise is divided into four chapters: 1) The Nature of Orders; 2) The Minister of Holy Orders; 3) The Subject of Holy Orders; 4) Irregularities and Impediments. By this method we shall treat of these questions in such a way that sufficient matter will be at hand for the examinations prior to the reception of Orders.

THE NATURE OF HOLY ORDERS

Art. 1. Definition and Effects of Holy Orders

805. DEFINITION. *The Sacrament of Holy Orders is a Sacrament of the New Law wherein certain spiritual powers are conferred together with the grace to perform ecclesiastical duties worthily.*

EXPLANATION. In a general sense, Orders are defined by St. Thomas (following the definition proposed by Peter Abelard): "*A seal of the Church whereby spiritual power is granted to the ordinand.*"[880]—Orders may be understood in an *active* sense to refer to ordination, to the action which confers a spiritual power and institutes a hierarchy of different grades; it may also be understood in a *passive* sense to refer to the actual power itself conferred in ordination and to the resultant hierarchy.

Orders understood in its active sense is a true Sacrament, and accordingly it has been defined by the Council of Trent: "If anyone shall say that Orders or sacred Ordination is not truly and properly a Sacrament instituted by Christ ... *anathema sit.*"[881]

NUMBER. In the Latin Church there are seven Orders in addition to the episcopate: four minor Orders of doorkeeper, lector, exorcist, and acolyte; three major Orders of subdiaconate, diaconate, and priesthood. In the Oriental Church only four Orders are expressly admitted: the Orders of lector, subdiaconate, diaconate, and priesthood; but the three Orders omitted seem to be conferred with the others—that is to say, the offices of lector and acolyte with the subdiaconate, the office of exorcist with the diaconate.—The clerical tonsure whereby a lay person is raised to the office of cleric is neither an Order nor a Sacrament, but a sacramental.

806. Three CONTROVERSIAL points should be noted briefly:

1. *Do the four minor Orders and the subdiaconate have the character of a true Sacrament?* The older theologians, e.g., St. Albert the Great, St. Thomas, St. Bonaventure, Paludanus, Scotus, replied in the affirmative; recent theologians commonly reply in the negative. Neither opinion is certain.

[880] ST, III-Sup., q. 34, a. 2.
[881] Session 23, Can. 3. See also TCCI 7:345.

2. Is the episcopate an Order essentially distinct from the priesthood or merely its fulfillment? While the older theologians were inclined to regard the episcopate as the fulfillment of the priesthood, recent theologians tend to regard it as a distinct Order. Again, neither opinion is certain.

3. Is the episcopate received validly by one whose priesthood was invalid? The negative opinion seems preferable and is the one to be followed in practice.

807. THE GENERAL EFFECTS OF THE SACRAMENT OF HOLY ORDERS are four in number. Orders (at least major Orders):

1. produce *an increase of sanctifying grace and their proper sacramental grace*;

2. imprint an indelible *character*;

3. confer *a spiritual power* which is related in varying degrees to the Holy Eucharist;

4. cause the ecclesiastical *hierarchy* to continue.

808. THE EFFECTS OF THE INDIVIDUAL ORDERS.

1. The office of *doorkeeper* confers the power *ex officio* of opening and closing the doors of the church, admitting the worthy and excluding the unworthy.

2. The office of *lector* confers the power *ex officio* of reading the Psalms and lessons in the church, catechizing and instructing the people in the rudiments of the Faith, blessing bread and the new fruits.

3. The office of *exorcist* confers the power *ex officio* of expelling the devils from those possessed. However, according to the present discipline of the Church this power is not to be exercised (at least publicly) without the explicit permission of the ordinary.[882]

4. The office of *acolyte* confers the power *ex officio* of assisting the subdeacon at a Solemn Mass, carrying the cruets to the altar, and lighting the candles.

5. The *subdiaconate* confers the power of preparing the matter for consecration in their sacred vessels, serving at a solemn Mass, singing the Epistle, washing corporals, purificators, and palls after they have been used.

6. The *diaconate* confers the power of assisting the priest immediately at a solemn Mass, singing the Gospel, and preaching with the permission of the local ordinary. The conditions required in order that a deacon may administer solemn Baptism and distribute Holy Communion have been set forth already in nos. 580 and 600.

7. The *priesthood* confers the power of consecrating the Body and Blood of Jesus Christ, the power to remit sins, to nourish his subjects by deed and doctrine, to administer the other Sacraments which do not demand the episcopal character.

8. The *episcopate* confers the power of administering the Sacraments of Confirmation and Holy Orders, performing many sacramentals, e.g., consecration, ruling those persons legitimately subject to him.

[882] See CCL, Can. 1151.

SCHOLIUM. EFFECTS OF THE FIRST TONSURE. Although the first clerical tonsure is not an Order, as we have noted already, it disposes a person for the reception of Order and enjoys the following effects:

1. it transfers the recipient into the clerical state and incardinates him into a diocese;[883]

2. it confers on him the so-called clerical privileges: *privilegia fori, canonis, immunitatis, competentiae;*[884]

3. it makes the recipient fitted for the reception of Orders, ecclesiastical benefices, and pensions, and also for the exercise of the power of jurisdiction.

Art. 2. The Matter and Form of Holy Orders

809. MATTER AND FORM OF THE MINOR ORDERS.

The remote matter are the symbols proper to each of the Orders, namely: for the office of *doorkeeper*, the keys; for the office of *lector*, the book of lessons (Missal or breviary or Bible); for the office of *exorcist*, the book of exorcisms (Ritual, Pontifical, Missal); for the office of *acolyte*, a candlestick with unlighted candle, and empty cruets.

The proximate matter consists in handing over these symbols. The *form* comprises those words spoken by the bishop as he hands over the various instruments to the ordinands; for the Order of *doorkeeper*: "Sic agite, quasi reddituri Deo rationem pro iis rebus, quae his clavibus recluduntur"; for the Order of *lector*: "Accipite et estote verbi Dei relatores, habituri, si fideliter et utiliter impleveritis officium vestrum, partem cum iis, qui verbum Dei bene administraverunt ab initio"; for the Order of *exorcist*: "Accipite et commendate memoriae et habete potestatem imponendi manus super energumenos sive baptizatos sive catechumenos"; for the Order of *acolyte*: "Accipite ceroferarium cum cereo, et sciatis vos ad accedenda ecclesiae luminaria mancipari in nomine Domini. R. Amen," and (in handing over the cruets): "Accipite urceolum ad suggerendum vinum et aquam in eucharistiam sanguinis Christi in nomine Domini. R. Amen."

810. MATTER AND FORM OF THE MAJOR ORDERS.[885]

In the *subdiaconate* there is a twofold remote and proximate matter, similarly a double form: 1) the handing of the empty chalice with a paten placed upon it, which each of the ordinands must touch with their right hand, while the bishop pronounces the form: "Videte, cujus ministerium vobis traditur; ideo vos admoneo, ut ita vos exhibeatis, ut Deo placere possitis"; 2) the handing of the book of the Epistles (Missal, or Bible) which each of the ordinands must touch, while the bishop pronounces the form: "Accipite librum epistolarum, et habete potestatem

---

[883] See CCL, Can. 108 and 111, § 2.

[884] See CCL, Can. 120–21.

[885] Editor's Note: Pope Pius XII ruled definitively on certain disputed theological questions raised in this section; see *Sacramentum Ordinis* (1947).

legendi eas in Ecclesia sancta Dei, tam pro vivis quam pro defunctis, in nomine Patris et Filii et Spiritus Sancti. R. Amen."

In the *diaconate* the remote and proximate matter, as also the form, are twofold:

1) the imposition of hands by the bishop while he recites the words: "Accipe Spiritum Sanctum ad robur et ad resistendum diabolo et tentationibus ejus: in nomine Domini"; 2) the handing of the book of the Gospels (Missal, Bible) which each of the ordinands must touch with their right hands, while the bishop recites the form: "Accipite potestatem legendi evangelium in Ecclesia Dei tam pro vivis quam pro defunctis, in nomine Domini. R. Amen."

Regarding the essential matter and form of the *priesthood*, theologians are divided into six schools of thought.[886] But as the result of various decisions from the Holy Office[887] the following is certain: the entire ceremony must be repeated if anything was omitted from the following matter and form—the *first* imposition of the hands accompanied by the prayer, *Exaudi Nos* and so on, and the handing of the chalice containing wine and the paten on which rests a host while the bishop recites the words: "Accipe potestatem offerre sacrificium Deo, Missasque celebrare tam pro vivis quam pro defunctis, in nomine Domini."

For the *episcopate* the matter seems to be the imposition of hands by the consecrating bishop, and the form is the prayer which accompanies this imposition.

811. SCHOLIUM. SUPPLYING DEFECTS WHICH OCCUR DURING ORDINATION. If any defect occurred in the conferring of an Order (even of a minor Order) which was *certainly* not accidental, the entire ordination must be repeated at least conditionally. In practice, recourse should be made to the Holy Office when there is doubt whether some essential part of the rite has been omitted.

THE MINISTER OF HOLY ORDERS

Art. 1. The Minister of Valid Ordination

812. *a)* The *ordinary* minister is every consecrated bishop and no one else.[888] Therefore, even a schismatic bishop or one who has been degraded or one who has been declared irregular, and so on may ordain validly, provided that his own consecration was valid and that he uses the essential matter and form.

b) The *extraordinary* minister for conferring the tonsure and minor Orders is a priest who, although not possessing episcopal consecration, has received either by law or by a special indult of the Holy See the power to confer these Orders.[889]

---

[886] See MTM, vol. 3, no. 594.
[887] See, e.g., July 6, 1898; Jan. 11, 1899; Jan. 17, 1900.
[888] See Council of Trent, Session 23, Can. 7. See also TCCI 7:356.
[889] See CCL, Can. 951.

By law this power has been conferred on:

a) cardinals;[890]

b) vicars and prefects apostolic, abbots and prelates nullius, but only during their term of office and within their own territory;[891]

c) the regular abbot in charge of a monastery, even without a territory nullius, to confer tonsure and minor Orders on those candidates who are his subjects by virtue of at least simple profession.[892]

Art. 2. The Minister of Lawful Ordination

813. *a) Episcopal consecration* is reserved to the Roman Pontiff or a bishop with a special mandate from the pope.[893]

b) For the lawful administration of other Orders the minister is the proper bishop or his delegate, but the extraordinary ministers of Orders already mentioned may confer the first tonsure and minor Orders without delegation from the bishop.

814. A bishop is regarded as being the PROPER bishop of the ordinand from one of the following titles (*tituli competentiae*)—the former titles of benefice and familiarity are no longer valid.

1. The title of *domicile and place of birth* exists when the candidate has a genuine domicile and place of birth in the diocese of the ordaining bishop.

2. The title of *domicile alone* suffices, but in such a case the candidate must take an oath to remain permanently in the diocese, except in three cases: when the cleric has already been incardinated into the diocese by the first tonsure, or when the candidate is destined for another diocese, or when the ordinand is a religious.[894]

Religious are considered to possess a domicile in that diocese in which their religious house is situated of which the ordinand is a member; consequently, it is the bishop of that diocese who is their proper bishop for the purposes of ordination, and it is to him that the religious superior must send the dimissorial letters.[895]

---

[890] See CCL, Can. 239, § 1, no. 22.
[891] See CCL, Can. 957, § 2.
[892] See CCL, Can. 964, no. 1.
[893] See CCL, Can. 953.
[894] See CCL, Can. 956. The proper bishop for ordination is also: 3. the bishop of the diocese into which the cleric is incardinated by the first tonsure. If a lay-person receives the tonsure from his own bishop for service elsewhere with the permission of the bishop of the latter diocese, he is incardinated into this diocese, according to Can. 111, § 2. The bishop of the diocese for service in which the cleric received the first tonsure from his own bishop has the power and exclusive right of conferring Orders or granting dimissorial letters in accordance with Can. 955, § 1, even though the cleric has not yet acquired a domicile in that diocese (see Pontifical Commission for the Authentic Interpretation of the Canons of the *Codex Juris Canonici* [hereafter P.C.C.J.], July 24, 1939: AAS 13, 321).
[895] See CCL, Can. 965.

There are only five cases when the superior may send the ordinands and the dimissorial letters to another bishop: 1) if the bishop of the diocese gives permission; 2) if the bishop should be of a different rite from that of the religious; 3) if he is absent; 4) if the bishop will not hold ordinations on the next ordination days; 5) if the see is vacant and the person in charge has no episcopal consecration. But it is essential that in each of the cases mentioned the ordaining bishop must have an authentic statement from the episcopal curia giving the reason why the religious may be ordained outside the diocese.

Religious superiors are forbidden to send their candidates for ordination to another house of their institute, thus *defrauding* the bishop of the diocese of his right, or to defer intentionally the sending of dimissorial letters until such time when the bishop will be absent or will confer no ordination.[896]

815. A bishop is lawfully DELEGATED to confer Orders if the *dimissorial letters* have been sent to him. The following persons are empowered to grant such letters:

a) for seculars and religious who are not exempt: the proper bishop after he has taken lawful possession of his diocese, even though not yet consecrated; the vicar general, by special mandate of the bishop; the vicar capitular with the consent of the chapter and after the see has been vacant for one year; the vicar capitular even during the first year of the see's vacancy for those clerics who are styled "arctati"; vicars apostolic, prefects apostolic, abbots, and prelates nullius;[897]

b) for exempt religious: the major religious superior who must also give dimissorial letters to his subjects who are to be ordained by the proper bishop, in accordance with what has been said above; but to those subjects who have not yet made their perpetual profession he cannot grant such letters except for the reception of the first tonsure and the minor Orders.[898]

In addition to these dimissorial letters there are further required testimonial letters, of which we shall speak below, no. 817.

THE SUBJECT OF HOLY ORDERS

INTRODUCTION. On the part of the candidate to be ordained certain conditions are required for *valid* ordination, others for *lawful* ordination. For *valid* ordination the ordinand must be a baptized male person, with at least the habitual intention to receive Orders. Nothing further need be said regarding these conditions, since they are sufficiently clear in themselves. For *lawful* ordination *divine law* requires a vocation by God, a right intention, the state of grace, and probity of life; *ecclesiastical* law demands the fulfillment of other conditions, each of which will be considered below.[899]

---

[896] See CCL, Can. 967.
[897] See CCL, Can. 958.
[898] See CCL, Can. 964, nos. 3 and 4.
[899] See CCL, Can. 968, § 1.

Art. 1. Conditions Required by Divine Law

816. 1. A *divine vocation* is absolutely necessary for the lawful reception of Orders. St. Paul says when speaking of the priesthood: "His vocation comes from God as Aaron's did; nobody can take on himself such a privilege as this" (Heb 5:4).

Such a vocation is necessary since a priest is the mediator between God and man and the dispenser of God's mysteries. But no one can lawfully assume the office of mediator or dispenser unless asked to do so by the parties concerned.

THE SIGNS OF A VOCATION are: *a) a right intention,* whereby one does not look for temporal advancement through the priesthood, but simply for God's honor and the salvation of one's own and the neighbor's soul; *b) ability to undertake ecclesiastical tasks,* which demand knowledge, good health, and so on; *c) well-tried virtue and perseverance in grace,* and therefore it is not sufficient that the ordinand be absolved from grave sins after expressing sincere contrition, but he must give proof of long practice of virtue so as to provide moral certainty that his future life will pursue the same course of virtue; *d) vocation by the legitimate ecclesiastical superior,* and therefore the *Roman Catechism* states aptly: "those are said to be called by God who are called by the legitimate ministers of the Church."[900]

2. The *right intention* which is demanded must center on the honor of God and the spiritual welfare of men, as stated already.

3. A *state of grace and probity of life* are required under pain of grave sin. The Sacrament of Holy Orders is a Sacrament of the living, and the Council of Trent issues this warning: "Bishops must realize that they should not raise anyone ... to these Orders, but only those who are worthy and whose upright life has been in evidence for some time."[901]

Art. 2. Conditions Required by Ecclesiastical Law

By ecclesiastical law, it is required that the ordinand: 1) possess testimonial letters; 2) be of canonical age; 3) possess the requisite knowledge; 4) undergo an examination; 5) make a retreat; 6) observe the intervals between successive Orders; 7) possess a canonical title, for the reception of major Orders; 8) be free from all irregularity and impediment.

817. 1. TESTIMONIAL LETTERS.

1) Those ordained for the *secular* priesthood (and also religious who are not exempt) must provide the following documents:[902]

---

[900] Cf. TCCI 7:341. See also CCL, Can. 970, and Lahitton, *La Vocation Sacerdotale.*

[901] Session 23, "Decree on Reformation," chap. 12. A new instruction of the highest importance was issued by the Sacred Congregation of the Sacraments (Dec. 27, 1930) to local ordinaries regarding the examination of candidates before they are promoted to Orders. A similar instruction was issued by the Sacred Congregation of Religious (Dec. 1, 1931) to superiors of clerical religious institutes and societies (AAS 23, 120ff and 24, 74ff).

[902] See CCL, Can. 993–994.

a) a certificate of their last ordination, or, if they are to receive the first tonsure, their baptismal and Confirmation certificates;

b) the certificate of the studies required for the various Orders;

c) a testimonial to their good moral character from the rector of the seminary or of the priest in charge of those who do not board in the seminary;

d) testimonials from every ordinary in whose diocese the ordinand has resided for such a length of time that he could contract a canonical impediment. This period is considered to be three months in the case of soldiers, six months after puberty in other cases, unless for the sake of prudence the ordaining bishop should decide on a shorter period in an individual case. If the candidate has spent some time in several dioceses so that it would be almost impossible or at least extremely difficult to obtain testimonial letters from all, or if the candidate is not sufficiently well known to the local ordinary to enable him to testify that the ordinand has not contracted any canonical impediment, the ordinary may take the testimony of the candidate on oath regarding his freedom.

2) *Exempt religious* who are to be ordained must bring a testimonial letter from their own major superior in which he testifies that the candidate has made his religious profession and is a member of the community in the diocese, that he has completed the necessary studies and has satisfied everything else required by law.[903]

818. 2. THE CANONICAL AGE.

For the reception of the tonsure and the minor Orders the law does not state any exact age, but since they cannot be received before the student has commenced his theological course,[904] in practice these Orders will not be conferred in normal circumstances before the age of 18. *For the subdiaconate* the candidate must have completed his twenty-first year, *for the diaconate* his twenty-second year, and *the priesthood* his twenty-fourth year.[905]

The episcopate may not be conferred on anyone until he has completed his thirtieth year of age.[906]

819. 3. THE REQUISITE KNOWLEDGE.

No one may receive *the first tonsure or minor Orders* before completing his course of philosophy and commencing his theological course. *The subdiaconate* is not to be conferred until almost the end of the third year of the candidate's theological course.

---

[903] See CCL, Can. 995, § 1. An example of these testimonial letters can be found in the appendix of MIC.
[904] See CCL, Can. 976.
[905] Cf. CCL, Can. 975, requiring "completion of the twenty-fifth year."
[906] See CCL, Can. 331, § 1.

The diaconate is not to be conferred until the fourth year is commenced.

The priesthood may not be conferred until after the first half of the fourth year of the theological course.

The theological course must be followed in schools properly constituted for this purpose and not in private.[907]

The episcopate may not be conferred on anyone who does not possess a doctorate or is not at least well-versed in theology or canon law.[908]

820. 4. THE EXAMINATION FOR ORDERS.

Candidates for the secular priesthood, and also religious, must undergo prior to the reception of Orders a careful examination *regarding the Order which they are about to receive.* Those who are to receive *major* Orders must also be examined in some treatise of theology. The bishop has the right to determine the method of examination, the examiners themselves, and the subject-matter in which all candidates (even exempt religious) are to be examined.[909] However, he may — without being under any obligation — accept the testimony given that the candidate has already undergone a suitable examination elsewhere. Not only the testimonial letters mentioned above but also the *publication* of the names of the candidates for Orders relate in some way to the examination of these candidates. The names of the candidates for major Orders, with the exception of religious who have taken perpetual vows, should be publicly announced in the parishes to which the candidates belong; but the ordinary may for good reasons dispense with the publication, or he may demand that their names be published also in other churches, or that in place of such an announcement the names be posted at the door of the church for several days, including at least one Sunday or holy day of obligation. All the faithful are obliged to reveal to the ordinary or parish priest any impediment they may know of concerning the candidate.[910]

821. 5. SPIRITUAL EXERCISES.

Every candidate for Orders must make a retreat prior to ordination in some religious or pious house specified by the ordinary, and they must present to the ordaining bishop a statement that they have duly completed the exercises. If after the end of the retreat ordination is delayed for any reason *for more than six months,* the retreat must be made again; in shorter delays the ordinary shall decide whether it should be repeated or not.[911]

Candidates for the first tonsure and for minor Orders shall make *at least three full days of retreat.*

907 See CCL, Can. 976.
908 See CCL, Can. 331, § 1,. no. 5.
909 See CCL, Can. 996.
910 See CCL, Can. 998ff.
911 See CCL, Can. 1001.

Candidates for major Orders are to spend *at least six full days* in retreat. If a candidate receives several major Orders within six months, the bishop or major religious superior can reduce the days of retreat *for the diaconate* to not less than three days.[912]

822. 6. INTERVALS BETWEEN SUCCESSIVE ORDERS.

The "interstices" are the intervals which must exist between the reception of successive Orders to allow time for the ordinand to exercise the Order received and to prepare himself fittingly for the higher Order. The Code of Canon Law modified former practice and has laid down the following in Can. 978.

a) The interval between the first tonsure and the first minor Order, as well as the intervals between the various minor Orders, are left to the prudent judgment of the bishop, but he may not confer the tonsure and the first minor Order, or all minor Orders, on the same day. However, the immemorial custom existing in some countries of conferring the tonsure and the minor Orders on the same day may be continued if there is a reasonable cause.

b) Between the last minor Order and the subdiaconate there must be an interval of one year.

c) Between the various major Orders there must be an interval of three months. A bishop may dispense from these canonical intervals, if necessity or the utility of the Church require it, but he is not permitted to confer the minor Orders and the subdiaconate, or two major Orders, on the same day.

Major superiors of religious orders (and all who share their privileges) may likewise dispense their subjects from these intervals.[913]

823. 7. CANONICAL TITLES.

Since every cleric in major Orders must devote all his services to the Church and is not permitted to engage in any secular business, it is necessary that lawful provision be made for his sufficient and suitable support during his lifetime (the so-called *titulus sustentationis*). In the present discipline of the Church common law admits the following canonical titles.

1) *For secular clerics* (and religious who are not exempt or who do not possess perpetual vows):

a) the title of benefice, which is the peaceful possession of a sufficient ecclesiastical benefice. Since this title is frequently lacking, there is also permitted:

b) the title of a patrimony, which consists in the possession of personal goods by which the cleric may live fittingly. The amount of such goods which would be considered sufficient must be determined by the ordinary;

[912] Ibid.
[913] See Leo XII, Constitution *Plura Inter* (July 11, 1826).

c) the title of a pension, which is in the nature of a gift (from the Church or State). If the cleric possesses neither the title of a patrimony nor that of a pension, there is allowed:

d) the title of service of the diocese (or, in territories subject to the Propaganda, *the title of service of the mission*). In such cases the candidate must promise under oath to serve the diocese or the mission forever. The ordinary must give to one so ordained a benefice or office sufficient to provide suitable maintenance.[914]

If a cleric in major Orders loses his title, he must procure another for himself, unless in the judgment of the bishop adequate provision can be made for his maintenance in some other way. A bishop who (apart from an apostolic indult) knowingly ordains or allows to be ordained to major Orders one of his subjects without a canonical title must assume obligation for himself and for his successors to provide the needy cleric with his essential sustenance, until other provision is made for his adequate maintenance; if the bishop ordains such a person on the understanding that the one ordained will not ask him for support, such an agreement is null and void.[915]

2) *For regulars who are solemnly professed the canonical title is that of poverty or solemn religious profession;*

3) *For religious with perpetual simple vows the title is that of common board or congregation, or a similar one, according to their constitutions.*

8. FREEDOM FROM IRREGULARITIES AND IMPEDIMENTS is required in the candidate for ordination; this will be discussed in the following chapter.

IRREGULARITIES AND IMPEDIMENTS

Since this chapter covers a wide field, we shall consider: 1) Irregularities in General; 2) Individual Irregularities; 3) Impediments to Ordination.

Art. 1. Irregularities in General

824. DEFINITION. *An irregularity is an impediment of its nature perpetual, constituted by the law of the Church, which prevents primarily the reception of Orders, secondarily their exercise.*

EXPLANATION. 1. *An impediment of its nature perpetual:* because irregularity is not a punishment or a censure but a form of unworthiness which does not make him incapable of receiving or exercising orders but renders him permanently unsuitable. Irregularities are therefore distinct from temporary impediments.

2. *Constituted by the law of the Church:* thus, irregularity is not inflicted *by a superior,* and it cannot be contracted unless it is expressly contained in the new Code.[916]

[914] See CCL, Can. 981.
[915] See CCL, Can. 980.
[916] See CCL, Can. 983.

3. *Which prevents primarily the reception of Orders, secondarily their exercise*: these are the effects of irregularity, which does not invalidate but *prevents* the reception of an Order (even the first tonsure) and the exercise of any Orders already received.[917]

KINDS. 1. Irregularity may arise *from defect* or *from delinquency*. The former takes its origin in the lack of some quality of which the candidate is ignorant; the latter arises from a grave personal delinquency which is external and completed and committed since Baptism.

2. Irregularity is either *total* or *partial*, depending on whether it prevents the reception and exercise of all Orders, or *a)* advancement to a higher Order, or *b)* the partial exercise of a specified Order. Thus, for example, a priest who possesses only one hand contracts an irregularity which prevents the celebration of Mass but not the hearing of confessions.

825. CONDITIONS REQUIRED FOR CONTRACTING IRREGULARITY. It is necessary that the action responsible for irregularity be:

a) certain. A doubtful irregularity is no irregularity; however, if there is some doubt regarding the existence of a physical defect, such as epilepsy, it is the duty of the ordinary to resolve the doubt and then dispense.[918]

b) a grievous, external sin, complete, committed since Baptism; otherwise, it is impossible to contract an irregularity from delinquency. Therefore, anything which excuses from grave sin, e.g., parvity of matter, lack of advertence, good faith, excuses likewise from irregularity. If an adult allows himself to be baptized by a non-Catholic when there was no extreme necessity, the delinquency is committed both prior to and during the administration of Baptism, but nevertheless he incurs irregularity.[919]

NOTE. 1. *Ignorance* of irregularities (whether from defect or from delinquency) and impediments is not admitted as an excuse.[920] Consequently, the more lenient opinion of many authors must now be rejected.

2. Every irregularity is incurred ipso facto and thus no declaratory judgment is required.

3. Irregularities and impediments are multiplied if their sources are *different*, but not by a repetition of the same cause, except in the case of irregularity arising from voluntary homicide.[921] Thus, for example, an excommunicated priest who celebrates Mass five times incurs irregularity once only; but anyone procuring five abortions incurs irregularity five times, and an excommunicated priest who celebrates Mass on several occasions and hears several confessions and procures one abortion incurs two irregularities—one from abuse of the Sacrament, and the second from murder.

[917] See CCL, Can. 968, § 2.
[918] See CCL, Can. 15.
[919] See no. 831.2.
[920] See CCL, Can. 988.
[921] See CCL, Can. 989.

826. DISPENSATION. Lawful dispensation is normally the only way in which an irregularity can be removed (however, see what is said below regarding irregularity arising from illegitimacy and from physical defect).

The following persons enjoy the power to dispense from irregularity.

1. *The pope* is able to dispense in all irregularities; these are dispensed in the external forum by the Congregation of the Sacraments, in the internal forum by the Sacred Penitentiary.

2. The *ordinary* (the bishop or major religious superior of an exempt clerical order) may dispense his subjects either personally or through his delegate *a)* in all irregularities from which the Holy See usually dispenses, if there is some *doubt* regarding their existence;[922] *b)* in irregularities arising *from occult delinquency*, except those incurred by deliberate homicide or effective abortions, and other crimes brought before the ecclesiastical court.[923]

3. Any *confessor* may dispense from irregularities which prevent the *exercise* of Orders already received (but not from those which prevent the reception of Orders) in those cases in which the ordinary has the power to dispense, provided that it is a *more urgent* occult case when recourse to the ordinary is impossible and there is imminent danger of great harm or infamy.[924] Although the confessor has no power to dispense in the irregularity arising from effective abortion, nevertheless if the penitent would suffer grave defamation if he ceased to exercise the Order already received, there is nothing to prevent the confessor making use of epikeia, but a dispensation must be obtained afterward. No positive law is binding when there is grave inconvenience.

827. NOTE. 1. Privileges granted to certain religious superiors and confessors have not been revoked.[925]

2. In the petition for dispensation from irregularities (or impediments) all irregularities and impediments must be specified; otherwise, a *general* dispensation will be valid for irregularities concealed *in good faith* (except those irregularities previously mentioned from which neither the ordinary nor the confessor have power to absolve), but it will not be valid for those concealed *in bad faith*.[926]

3. If there is a question of voluntary homicide the number of crimes must be stated under pain of invalidity.[927]

4. A *general* dispensation for the reception of Orders is valid also for major Orders, and the person dispensed can obtain non-consistorial benefices, even those to which the care of souls is attached (e.g., a parish), but without a new

---

[922] See CCL, Can. 15.
[923] See CCL, Can. 990, § 1.
[924] See CCL, Can. 990, § 2.
[925] See MIC, q. 245.
[926] See CCL, Can. 991, § 1.
[927] See CCL, Can. 991, § 2.

dispensation he cannot be made a cardinal, bishop, abbot, or prelate nullius, nor major superior in a clerical exempt order.[928]

5. A dispensation given in the internal, extra-sacramental forum must be given in writing, and note of it must be made in the secret records of the curia.[929]

Art. 2. Particular Kinds of Irregularity

§ 1. Irregularities Due to Defect

828. *Irregularities due to defect* are seven in number:

1. *Illegitimacy,* whether public or occult, unless the illegitimate has been legitimized or has made solemn profession.[930] Illegitimacy is considered a bar to the clerical state, since such persons bear the stigma of their parents and in many cases they imitate their unchaste conduct. Legitimate children are those *conceived or born in true or at least putative wedlock,* unless at the time of conception the parents were forbidden the use of marriage previously contracted by reason of solemn profession or reception of major Orders.[931] Children who are born at least six months after the date of marriage or within ten months from the dissolution of conjugal life are presumed legitimate.[932] Similarly, in accordance with the principle: "The father of a child is considered he who appears to be such by lawful marriage": children born during wedlock are presumed legitimate, even though they may be born of an adulterous union, unless there are *evident* signs to the contrary.[933]

This irregularity *ceases a)* by legitimate dispensation, *b)* by legitimization through a subsequent marriage,[934] but only natural children of the parents may be legitimized in this way; *c)* by solemn religious profession.

829. 2. *Bodily defects* which prevent the ministry of the altar being exercised either safely because of weakness or fittingly because of deformity.[935] A more serious defect is necessary to prevent the exercise of an Order already received lawfully, nor would any defect be an obstacle to the exercise of those acts which can be performed properly.

Such defects would be:

a) mutilation, such as the loss of a foot or a hand or a thumb or a forefinger or anything which would prevent a person from breaking the host properly with the thumb and forefinger.

[928] See CCL, Can. 991, § 3.
[929] See CCL, Can. 991, § 4.
[930] See CCL, Can. 984, no. 1.
[931] See CCL, Can. 1114.
[932] See CCL, Can. 1115, § 2.
[933] See CCL, Can. 1115, § 1.
[934] See CCL, Can. 1116–1117.
[935] See CCL, Can. 984, no. 2.

b) weakness, such as blindness, dumbness, excessive stammering, lameness which prevents a person standing at the altar without the aid of a stick, paralysis.

c) deformity, which causes a person to suffer from a form of external affliction which can be seen easily and gives rise to ridicule or abhorrence, e.g., those who have no nose, those who are genuine dwarfs or giants, those who are excessively hunchbacked. If the deformity is not serious, irregularity is not incurred, e.g., if a person is blind in one eye, or squints, or is slightly lame, and so on. It is the duty of the ordinary to pass judgment in such cases.[936]

830. 3. *Mental defects*, such as epilepsy, insanity, diabolical possession, whether past or present. If these defects were contracted after the reception of Orders and are now known beyond doubt to have disappeared, the ordinary may again allow his subjects the exercise of the Orders already received.[937]

4. *Bigamy*, by which the present law understands persons who have contracted successively two or more valid marriages.[938] Thus, interpretative bigamy is no longer included; analogous bigamy is the cause of an irregularity arising from delinquency.

5. *Infamy of law.*[939]

6 and 7. A judge (and probably jury under oath) who has pronounced sentence of death, those who have held the office of executioner, and those who *voluntarily* undertook the office of *immediate* assistants in the execution, incur an irregularity arising from what was known as *defectus lenitatis*.[940]—This irregularity is not incurred by soldiers fighting in a just war.

§ 2. Irregularities Due to Delinquency

831. There are seven *irregularities due to delinquency*, and these are incurred by:

1. apostates from the Faith, heretics, schismatics,[941]

2. men who, outside the case of extreme necessity, allow themselves in any way to be baptized by non-Catholics;[942]

This is an abuse of the Sacrament of *Baptism*.

3. men who dared to attempt to contract marriage or to go through the civil formalities of marriage *a)* while they themselves were married or in major Orders or professed religious, whether with simple, perpetual, or temporary vows, or

---

[936] See no. 826.2.
[937] See CCL, Can. 984, no. 3.
[938] See CCL, Can. 984, no. 4.
[939] See no. 761.
[940] See CCL, Can. 984, nos. 6 and 7.
[941] See CCL, Can. 985, no. 1. To the same class belong such persons who are or were members of any atheistic sect (see P.C.C.J., July 30, 1934: AAS 26, 494).
[942] See CCL, Can. 985, no. 2.

b) with a validly married woman or with a sister bound by either perpetual or temporary vows;[943]

This is an abuse of the Sacrament of *Marriage*, and the irregularity is nothing more than an extension of what was formerly called analogous bigamy (*bigamia similitudinaria*).

4. men who exercise an act of Orders reserved to clerics in major Orders, whether they themselves have not received these Orders or have been forbidden to exercise them by canonical penalty, either personal or local, corrective or vindictive;[944]

This is an abuse of the Sacrament of *Orders*. In the present discipline of the Church, a simple cleric is allowed to exercise the office of subdeacon at a Solemn Mass, with certain restrictions.

5. voluntary murderers, and those who have procured an abortion, if effective, and all cooperators;[945]

This irregularity is incurred, for example, by doctors who procure an abortion or craniotomy, by soldiers who *willingly* (and not under compulsion) take part in a war which is manifestly unjust, by judges, lawyers, witnesses in an unjust capital trial. If the trial is just, the judges nevertheless incur irregularity from the so-called *defectus lenitatis*.

6. men who have mutilated themselves or others, and those who have attempted suicide;[946]

Mutilation here refers to the *removal of an important member* of the body, such as an eye, a hand, or a foot. To understand the exact nature of this irregularity and of the preceding one, it must be borne in mind that no irregularity is incurred by any delinquency which is not a grave external sin. Thus, for example, if a man kills or mutilates another either in the course of self-defense when he does no more than is absolutely necessary to ensure self-protection or through inculpable ignorance, he does not incur these irregularities.

7. clerics who practice medicine or surgery forbidden to them, if thereby the death of their patient is caused;[947]

It is evident that when a cleric is justified in practicing medicine, e.g., on the missions, he does not incur this irregularity.

Art. 3. Impediments to Ordination

832. The new Code[948] includes seven *temporary* impediments to ordination in addition to the irregularities already mentioned. These impediments cease either through

---

[943] See CCL, Can. 985, no. 3.
[944] See CCL, Can. 985, no. 7.
[945] See CCL, Can. 985, no. 4.
[946] See CCL, Can. 985, no. 5.
[947] See CCL, Can. 985, no. 6.
[948] See Can. 987.

lapse of time or by legitimate dispensation which, it seems, only the *Holy See* can grant. — They can be reduced to three, to what were formerly called lack of faith, lack of freedom, and lack of good repute.

The following persons are simply forbidden to be ordained:

1. the sons of non-Catholics, as long as their parents persist in their error;

The Pontifical Commission, Oct. 16, 1919,[949] stated that this impediment existed even if only one of the parents was a non-Catholic, but in a subsequent reply, July 14, 1922,[950] the Commission decided that this impediment affects only children *in the paternal line* to the first degree. The impediment probably ceases on the death of the non-Catholic partner.

2. married men;

Therefore, even if the husband obtains the consent of his wife he may not receive major Orders without the permission of the Holy See.

3. officials and administrators holding an office forbidden to clerics and of which they have to give an account, until they have resigned the office or administration, rendered their account, and become free.

4. slaves, strictly so-called, before they have been freed.

5. those bound to common military service by civil law, until they have fulfilled their period of service;

The Pontifical Commission when asked to give an authentic interpretation of this canon replied, June 2 and 3, 1918, that this impediment preventing the reception of any Order affects even those who will probably be so called to serve, though not yet called, owing to age or because they have been declared temporarily unfit as a result of their examination.[951] Common military service seems to refer to armed service, not to ambulance work, nor to chaplains, and so on.

6. neophytes (i.e., adult converts from Judaism, paganism, or similar sects, who have been but recently baptized) until in the judgment of the ordinary they have been sufficiently tested;

7. those who are infamous in fact so long as, in the judgment of the ordinary, their ill-repute continues. The character of this form of infamy has been explained already, no. 760.

---

[949] AAS 11, 478.
[950] AAS 14, 528.
[951] See AAS 10, 345.

APPENDIX: INCIDENTAL REQUIREMENTS FOR THE RECEPTION OF ORDERS

833. 1. Candidates for the secular priesthood must reside prior to their ordination in a seminary properly constituted for the purpose.[952]

2. With regard to the actual ordination itself, careful attention must be given to the detailed instructions regarding the rite to be used and time and place of ordination.

a) THE PROPER RITE to be used includes many things; for, a higher Order cannot be conferred until the lower has been received.[953] If this prescription is ignored the Order received is valid, unless the episcopate is conferred on one who is not yet a priest. The Mass of ordination must be celebrated by the ordaining bishop, and during that Mass at least those who have received major Orders must receive Holy Communion.[954] No one may be ordained by a minister of a different rite.

Those who have received the subdiaconate or the diaconate are commanded by the bishop to recite one Nocturn to be determined by himself. If he uses no more than the words of the Pontifical, he must be understood to refer to a ferial Nocturn, or to the first Nocturn of a feast or a Sunday, depending on whether the ordination itself took place on a feria, a feast day, or a Sunday. It is not necessary to recite the *Invitatorium*, the hymn, or the lessons.[955] — Newly-ordained priests may receive a stipend for each of the three Masses which are imposed upon them by the bishop and apply them for the intention of the donor of the stipend.

834. *b)* THE TIME OF ORDINATION. The consecration of a bishop must take place during Mass on a Sunday or on the feast day of an apostle. Major Orders are to be conferred during Mass on the Saturdays in Ember Weeks, or on the Saturday before Passion Sunday, or on Holy Saturday. For a grave reason the bishop is allowed to ordain on any Sunday or holy day of obligation.[956]

The first tonsure can be given on any day and at any hour; minor Orders on all Sundays and feasts of the rank of doubles, but only in the forenoon.

Contrary customs are disapproved and abolished.[957] There are, however, certain privileges in existence. Whenever an ordination has to be repeated or some ceremonies are to be supplied, whether absolutely or conditionally, this may take place privately and outside the prescribed ordination days.[958]

---

[952] See the author's discussion of seminaries in MIC, q. 408ff.

[953] See CCL, Can. 977.

[954] See CCL, Can. 1003 and 1005.

[955] See S. R. C., June 27, 1899 and July 10, 1903.

[956] The term *festo de praecepto* does not include feasts suppressed in the universal Church by the Code (see P. C. C. J., May 15, 1936: AAS 28, 210).

[957] See CCL, Can. 1006.

[958] See CCL, Can. 1007.

c) THE PLACE OF ORDINATION. *General* ordinations are to be held publicly in the cathedral church or some other church, if these ordinations take place outside the episcopal see. But the bishop is not forbidden when occasion demands to have *special* ordinations even in other churches, or in the chapel of the episcopal residence, in the seminary, or in a religious house. The first tonsure and the minor Orders may be conferred in private oratories also.[959]

835. NOTIFICATION AND RECORD OF ORDINATION.

After ordination, the names of those ordained and of the ordaining minister, also the place and date of ordination, shall be recorded in a special register to be preserved carefully in the curia of the place of ordination, and all the documents required in the various ordinations shall be preserved.[960] Furthermore, the ordinary in the case of seculars, the major superior in the case of religious subject to him, must send notification to the parish priest of the place where those were baptized who have been ordained *subdeacons*, so that the ordination may be entered in the baptismal register.[961]

To each of the ordained clerics must be given an authentic certificate of the orders received which, if they were ordained by a strange bishop with dimissorials from their own, they shall present to their ordinary so that record of the ordination may be kept in the episcopal curia.[962]

TREATISE X
MARRIAGE

This treatise is divided into nine chapters: 1) Nature and Kinds of Marriage; 2) Marriage as a Sacrament; 3) The Properties of Marriage; 4) The Benefits of Marriage; 5) The Obligations of Marriage; 6) Preparation for Marriage—Betrothal, Preliminary Investigation, Publication of the Banns; 7) The External Celebration of Marriage; 8) Impediments to Marriage; 9) Civil Marriage.

NATURE AND KINDS OF MARRIAGE

836. DEFINITION. *Marriage is the conjugal union of a man and woman who are free from impediments, which binds them to a life lived in common and together.*

Such a union between baptized persons is a sacramental contract because of the institution of Christ; between unbaptized persons this union is not a Sacrament, but it is nevertheless "from its very nature and meaning something holy."[963]

---

[959] See CCL, Can. 1009.
[960] See CCL, Can. 1010, § 1.
[961] See CCL, Can. 1011.
[962] See CCL, Can. 1010, § 2.
[963] Leo XIII, Constitution *Arcanum* (Feb. 10, 1880).

EXPLANATION OF THE DEFINITION. 1. *Union*: this word, if taken in its *active* meaning, i.e., for the transitory act of internal and external consent by which the man and woman promise conjugal fidelity to each other, refers to the marriage *actually being made (in fieri)* and is the Sacrament of Marriage (between Christians); if understood in its *passive* meaning, i.e., for the effect produced or the state of life resulting from the consent, it refers to *the state of marriage (in facto esse)* and is the actual *bond of marriage*. Therefore, the essence of the contract (which is the Sacrament) of marriage consists in the mutual consent of both parties, and not in the act of sexual intercourse, as some authors have taught.

2. *a conjugal union*, whereby is signified the special purpose of this union. Man and woman join together to lead a lawful conjugal life and not for lust or business purposes.

3. a conjugal union of *one man and one woman*, and not of several men and women, in order to signify monogamy and exclude polygamy.

4. *who are free from impediments*, so that not every person may enter into the contract of marriage, but only those who are not prevented by some impediment.

5. which binds them to *a life in common and together*, in order to signify primarily the indissolubility of marriage, but secondarily *a)* their united domestic life; *b)* their spiritual union in charity and desire to act in unison; *c)* at least some sharing of temporal goods.

837. KINDS OF MARRIAGE. 1. A marriage is either *legitimate, ratified*, or *consummated*.

A *legitimate* marriage is a valid matrimonial contract between two persons, at least one of whom is *not baptized*—that is to say, it is a valid marriage which is not a Sacrament; and it makes no difference whether sexual intercourse has taken place or not.

A *ratified* marriage is a valid matrimonial contract between two *Christians* which has not yet been completed by conjugal intercourse.

A *consummated* marriage is one in which the contract has been followed by sexual intercourse directed to the procreation of children. Therefore, a marriage is not regarded as consummated by any sexual intercourse which may have occurred prior to a valid marriage. Once the marriage contract is concluded, consummation of the marriage is *presumed* in law if the parties have lived together, until the contrary is proved.[964]

2. A marriage is either *public, clandestine*, or *secret*.

A *public* marriage is one which is celebrated in the face of the Church or in some other public way recognized by the Church as valid.

A *clandestine* marriage is one which is contracted without the presence of the parish priest and two witnesses. According to the present discipline of the Church,

[964] See CCL, Can. 1015, § 2.

clandestine marriages are invalid (apart from cases of grave necessity), except such marriages between non-Catholics.

A *secret* marriage (or *marriage of conscience*) is that which is contracted before the parish priest and two witnesses but secretly, for a very grave reason. Such marriages are not to be entered in the ordinary registers of marriage, but are to be kept in the secret archives of the curia.[965] Special permission is required from the bishop for the celebration of such marriages.[966]

3. A marriage is *valid* (or true) when there exists no annulling impediment between the two parties.

Marriage is *invalid* (null and void) when there exists such a diriment impediment; if the two parties being conscious of such an impediment contracted marriage in bad faith, the marriage is said to be *attempted*. Marriage is *putative* when it is invalid because of the presence of an annulling impediment and yet was contracted in good faith by at least *one* of the parties. When both parties become certain of the invalidity of their marriage, it is no longer a putative marriage.[967] Such a marriage is not recognized by the Church unless it was contracted publicly and without her disapproval. Children born of a putative marriage are considered legitimate, as was stated above, no. 828.

A *presumed* marriage is no longer recognized, except when sexual intercourse has taken place willingly after a marriage which was contracted conditionally.

MARRIAGE AS A SACRAMENT

838. PRINCIPLE. *Any marriage lawfully celebrated between two Christians is a genuine Sacrament (in the proper sense of the term) of the New Law instituted by Christ.*

This has been defined in the Council of Trent,[968] and may be proved both from Sacred Scripture (see Eph 5:22–32) and from Tradition.[969]

Theologians are not agreed on the exact time when Christ INSTITUTED this Sacrament. Some authors incline to the view that He raised the contract of marriage to the dignity of a Sacrament at the marriage feast of Cana; others, that the Sacrament was instituted when He abrogated the writ of separation; others include the institution of this Sacrament amongst the various instructions on the kingdom of God which Christ gave to His apostles after His Resurrection.

Amongst baptized people, the contract and the Sacrament are inseparable, so that if either is invalid, both are invalid, and whenever there exists a valid contract, there also is the Sacrament.[970]

---

[965] See CCL, Can. 1107.
[966] See CCL, Can. 1104.
[967] See CCL, Can. 1015, § 4.
[968] See Session 24, Can. 1. See also TCCI 7:361.
[969] See MTM, vol. 3, no. 643.
[970] See CCL, Can. 1012.

COROLLARIES. 1. *Only the Church has the right to determine and to pass judgment on everything which affects the essence of Christian marriage,* since it is the duty of the Church only and not of the civil authority to regulate the Sacraments.

839. 2. *The civil authority has no power to establish annulling or prohibitory impediments for Christian marriages; likewise, she possesses no power to pronounce complete divorce or to allow Christians to remarry after obtaining a divorce.*

All such matters affect the essence and sacramental character of marriage, over which the civil authority has no power.

3. *The civil power can and must on its own authority regulate the civil consequences of the marriage contract.*[971]

It is in the best interests of civil society that even the temporal side of marriage should be duly controlled, such as the sharing of property and its administration, questions relating to succession and inheritance, and so on which do not come within the direct jurisdiction of the ecclesiastical courts. On all such matters civil authority can and should make just laws which are binding in conscience.

840. 4. *A marriage between two unbaptized persons, or between one baptized and one unbaptized person, is not a Sacrament.*

The first part of this statement is certain and is now admitted by all, since without Baptism (which is the gateway to all the other Sacraments) no Sacrament can be received validly.

The second part is denied by many theologians,[972] but nevertheless it would seem to be true. For if a marriage is invalid in respect of one party, then it must be invalid in respect of the other; marriage cannot exist in one person only, and certainly the unbaptized party does not receive the Sacrament, even though contracting a valid marriage. So neither does the other party, although baptized, receive the Sacrament.

What has just been said regarding marriages between Catholics and pagans applies similarly to those marriages in which one of the two pagans later receives Baptism. Such a marriage does not assume a sacramental character for the person receiving Baptism. However, a marriage contracted between two pagans does become a Sacrament if both are later baptized, so long as their marriage consent persists.

841. 5. *A legitimate marriage between pagans is not subject to the laws of the Church, but is subject to all the just laws and impediments instituted by the State.*

This corollary is the subject of fierce discussion, but the principle as proposed seems not merely probable but also at present more common and more in conformity with the practice of the Roman Curia.[973]

[971] See CCL, Can. 1016.
[972] Dom. Soto, Christ. Pesch, and Scherer.
[973] For a fuller discussion of this question the student is referred to MTM, vol. 3, no. 651ff.

842. THE REMOTE MATTER OF THE SACRAMENT is to be found in the bodies of the two parties, or, as some authors desire, in the right over the body of each other for the purpose of sexual intercourse.

THE PROXIMATE MATTER consists in the application of the remote matter, namely, the signs or words used to express the *transference of that right*.

THE FORM of the Sacrament is the *mutual acceptance of this transference expressed externally*. Consequently, the opinion proposed by Melchior Canus and a few others that the blessing by the priest constitutes the form is false; this is also evident from what remains to be said regarding the minister of this Sacrament.

It follows from the principles proposed regarding the matter and form that it is the marital consent of the two parties which, considered from different aspects, constitutes the matter, form, and efficient cause of this Sacrament. Therefore, there can be no Sacrament of marriage without the consent.

843. THE CONSENT of the two parties must be:

1. *genuine*; and therefore, a fictitious consent does not suffice;

2. *free and deliberate*; consequently, grave fear and substantial error prevent certain essential conditions;

3. *present*; therefore, any consent relating to the future is not sufficient;

4. *mutual and simultaneous*, since marriage is a bilateral contract;

5. *externally and legitimately expressed*, since the matter and form of the Sacraments constitute the external sign;

6. *absolute and unconditional*. It is rare that a condition attached to the marriage contract does not affect its lawfulness, and sometimes a condition which is genuinely suspensive destroys the *validity* of the marriage. The following points are worthy of note:

a) A marriage contracted with a condition attached *relating to the present or to the past* is valid or invalid according as the condition is verified or not.

b) If a condition is added which refers *to the future* and it is a lawful condition, the validity of the marriage is suspended until the condition is fulfilled; once the condition is fulfilled the marriage immediately becomes valid and there is no strict necessity for the consent to be renewed. If the marriage was contracted with the following condition added: "if the pope grants a dispensation": once the dispensation is obtained the consent must be renewed in accordance with the form specified by law, since the parties prior to obtaining this dispensation were incapable of giving an effective consent.

c) If a condition attached is *contrary to the essence of marriage*, the marriage is void.

The essence of marriage consists in the three benefits of offspring, conjugal fidelity, and the Sacrament. For a discussion of these benefits, see no. 858.

d) If a condition *refers to the future and is an immoral condition, although not contrary to the essence of marriage,* the marriage is valid since such conditions are considered as not having been present.

844. THE MINISTERS of the Sacrament are the two contracting parties. This is now the most common opinion and it is morally certain, for there are occasions when the Sacrament of marriage may be celebrated *when a priest is not present,* as will be noted later on. Therefore, it is abundantly clear that the priest cannot be the minister of the Sacrament, and there is no foundation whatsoever for regarding the priest as the ordinary minister and the contracting parties as the extraordinary minister.

845. THE SUBJECT capable of receiving the *valid* Sacrament of marriage is any baptized person who is free from any *annulling* impediment. In order to receive the Sacrament worthily and fruitfully it is necessary that the parties be in a state of sanctifying grace and free from all *prohibitory* impediments.

There is no prescription of the common law enjoining the reception of the Sacraments of Penance and Holy Eucharist prior to marriage, provided that the two parties are in the state of sanctifying grace, but all will realize how fitting it is that these Sacraments should be received prior to marriage.

THE PROPERTIES OF MARRIAGE

The essential properties of marriage are its unity and its indissolubility. We shall consider these properties in general, and then treat in detail of divorce which is contrary to the indissolubility of marriage.

Art. 1. The Unity and Indissolubility of Marriage

846. THE UNITY of marriage (monogamy) is the bond of marriage existing between one man and one woman. This properly excludes *simultaneous* polyandry and polygamy.

Simultaneous polyandry, which consists in a marital union between one woman and two or more men, is forbidden by the natural law.

Simultaneous polygamy, which consists in a conjugal union between one man and two or more women, existed before the time of Christ not only amongst the gentile nations but also amongst the Jews, with *the permission of God.* But since the era of the New Dispensation, polygamy has been forbidden to *everyone,* to Christian and pagan alike. Christ restored marriage to its original unity and regarded as adulterous anyone who married another after sending away his first lawful wife. Therefore, a fortiori, a person commits adultery by marrying another while retaining his first lawful wife.

Successive polygamy is lawful and therefore constitutes a true Sacrament when both parties are Christians.[974] Some of the older Fathers held stricter views on this form of polygamy.

---

[974] See CCL, Can. 1142.

847. THE INDISSOLUBILITY of marriage was once more instituted by Christ, and therefore the valid marriage of *Christians*, consummated by the conjugal act, cannot be dissolved by any human authority for any reason.[975] Neither can the following text from Scripture be urged as an objection: "He who puts away his wife, not for any unfaithfulness of hers, and so marries another, commits adultery" (Mt 19:9). For God certainly allows a separation from the wife in the event of her unfaithfulness, as will be explained more fully below, but in those circumstances neither of the parties is permitted to contract a new marriage.

Art. 2. Divorce

Divorce is contrary to the indissolubility of marriage; it is *perfect* or absolute if it affects the bond of marriage itself, it is *imperfect* if it consists in the mere discontinuance of married life while the bond of marriage persists.

1. Perfect or Absolute Divorce

848. PRINCIPLE. *Perfect divorce occurs in three cases: a) through the Pauline privilege; b) through papal dispensation; c) through solemn religious profession. But the two latter affect only ratified marriages which have not been consummated.*

849. *a)* THE PAULINE PRIVILEGE permits the complete dissolution of a legitimate marriage, even if consummated, provided the following conditions are verified:

1. *one of the parties (not both) is validly baptized.*

It is therefore supposed that *since* contracting a legitimate and valid marriage one of the parties has been validly baptized. Therefore, the Pauline privilege cannot be invoked in a marriage between a Catholic and an unbaptized person if contracted with the dispensation from the disparity of cult.[976]

But the privilege may be used even if the convert after receiving Baptism renews married life with the unbaptized party, if the latter refuses to live peacefully and without offense to God with the converted Catholic or separates from him (or her) without just cause.[977] Notice that the canon adds: *without just cause*, for if the baptized party *after receiving Baptism* gives just cause for separation, e.g., by adultery, he cannot contract a new marriage.[978]

2. *that the unbaptized party either a) departs or refuses to live peacefully with the baptized partner, or b) refuses to live with the other without offense to God.*

In order to make certain of the existence of these conditions it is necessary in ordinary circumstances, i.e., unless the Holy See declares otherwise, to *ask* the unbaptized party two questions: *a)* whether he wishes to be converted to the

---

[975] See CCL, Can. 1118.
[976] See CCL, Can. 1120, § 2.
[977] See CCL, Can. 1124.
[978] See CCL, Can. 1123.

Faith; *b)* whether he or she is willing to live in marriage peacefully and without offense to God.[979]

Offense is given to God if the unbaptized partner tries to persuade the other to commit grievous sin or blasphemes the name of God or refuses to dismiss his mistresses.

These interpellations should normally be made by the bishop or ordinary of the converted party; however, it is sufficient if they are made in some other way and even privately, provided that there is written proof or the testimony of two witnesses that they were in fact made.[980] No one has the power to dispense on his own authority from these interpellations, with the exception of the Holy See which sometimes delegates the faculty to vicars apostolic.

NOTES 1. The bond of the first marriage contracted in infidelity is dissolved not when one of the parties is baptized but when the convert actually contracts a new and valid marriage.[981]

2. The Code of Canon Law states, Can. 1125: "The Constitutions of Pope Paul III *Altitudo*, June 1, 1537; of Pope St. Pius V, *Romani Pontifices*, Aug. 2, 1571; of Pope Gregory XIII, *Populis*, Jan. 25, 1585, given to individual countries, are, as far as marriage is concerned, extended to all other countries in the same circumstances."

Paul III allowed the husband who before receiving Baptism possessed several wives to retain the wife whom he first married, or, if he could not remember which was the first one he married, to take any one of them and contract marriage with her.

St. Pius V allowed these same polygamous husbands (even in those cases where they could remember which was their first wife) to continue to live in marriage with the wife who received Baptism with him.

Gregory XIII granted faculties to local ordinaries, parish priests, and priests of the Society of Jesus to dispense from the customary interpellations, provided that it was certain (even in summary and extrajudicial form) that the absent pagan party could not be legitimately questioned or, if interpellated, did not reply within the time fixed for the answers. If the convert then contracts a new and legitimate marriage it is to be considered firm and valid, even though afterward it becomes known that the unbaptized party had no chance to reply to the interpellation or that he had become a Catholic by the time the second marriage took place.

These three constitutions are to be found at the end of the Code of Canon Law.

3. When there is any doubt whether all the conditions required for the Pauline privilege are verified or not, the privilege enjoys the favor of law—that is to say, judgment is to be given in favor of the freedom of the baptized party.[982]

---

[979] See CCL, Can. 1121, § 1.
[980] See CCL, Can. 1122.
[981] See CCL, Can. 1126.
[982] See CCL, Can. 1127.

850. *b)* A DISPENSATION OF THE HOLY SEE can dissolve a ratified marriage between Christians which has not yet been consummated. This is the constant practice of the Roman Curia, so that at present no one could lawfully question this power to dispense. But it is necessary that the request for the dispensation should come not from a third party but from the married partners themselves or from one of the parties even though the other objects.[983]

851. *c)* SOLEMN RELIGIOUS PROFESSION dissolves a non-consummated Christian marriage. This is defined by the Council of Trent: "If anyone declares that a ratified non-consummated marriage is not dissolved by the solemn religious profession of one of the parties, *anathema sit.*"[984] Neither simple profession nor the solemn vow of chastity made during the reception of the subdiaconate dissolves a previous marriage.

Formerly, if one of the parties considered entering a religious order within the first two months of the marriage, he or she could refuse the marriage debt, but the Code of Canon Law states, Can. 1111, that *from the moment the contract has been concluded* both parties must render the debt if requested. Accordingly, the ancient privilege has been withdrawn.

2. Imperfect Divorce

852. Married partners are obliged to live together by reason of the very nature of marriage which is an undivided partnership, and from the words of Christ Himself: "A man therefore, will leave his father and mother and will cling to his wife" (Mt 19:5). This obligation includes *a)* living under the same roof, and *b)* sharing the same bed, i.e., the use of marriage. Neither partner may live apart from the other for a long time contrary to the wish of the other, unless there are grave reasons.[985]

Imperfect divorce may be *a)* permanent or temporary; *b)* undertaken on private or public authority; *c)* limited to *conjugal relations,* or extended also to *cohabitation* if both parties refuse to live together in the same dwelling.[986]

CAUSES which permit imperfect divorce, or divorce in the restricted sense of the word, are: 1) carnal adultery; 2) spiritual adultery, i.e., heresy or apostasy; 3) grave danger to soul or body; 4) mutual consent.

853. 1. CARNAL ADULTERY committed by either of the parties gives the right to the innocent party to discontinue conjugal life.

The innocent person who, either upon sentence of the judge, or by his or her own authority, leaves the guilty party, has *no longer any obligation* to admit the

[983] See CCL, Can. 1119.
[984] Session 24, Ccan. 6.
[985] See CCL, Can. 1128.
[986] Separation effected by public authority is to be decreed in administrative form, unless the ordinary decides otherwise *ex officio* or at the instance of the parties (see P. C. C. J., June 25, 1932: AAS 24).

adulterer again to conjugal life; however, the innocent partner has the right to admit the guilty person and even to oblige him or her to return, unless the latter has in the meantime, with the consent of the former, embraced a state of life contrary to marriage.[987] If, therefore, the guilty party has embraced the religious life with the consent of the other person, he or she cannot be obliged to return later on. Although it is highly desirable that the consent of the ordinary should be obtained before the parties cease living together because of adultery or for other reasons to be mentioned later, since this would obviate much inconvenience, nevertheless the innocent party may separate from the guilty person on his or her private authority if there is *certainly* and without any doubt a sufficient reason for separation and there is danger in delay.[988]

The innocent party cannot separate from the other, unless the adultery is:

a) morally certain;

b) formal, blameworthy, freely committed;

c) not condoned: tacit condonation *i)* exists when the innocent party, after having become certain of the crime, nevertheless continues to live with the other in marital relations; *ii)* is presumed to exist, if the innocent party has not protested against the guilty party within six months;[989]

d) not mutual or committed by common consent.[990]

NOTE. 1. The innocent party is *permitted* to sever conjugal life because of the adultery of his or her partner, but it is very rare that there is any obligation to do so. Generally speaking, it is preferable for the two parties to attempt a reconciliation.

2. The innocent party may enter a religious order or receive major Orders, even contrary to the will of the guilty partner.

854. 2. SPIRITUAL ADULTERY, i.e., heresy or apostasy (occurring *after* marriage), committed by one of the married parties who formally adheres to a non-Catholic sect or educates the children in heresy, is a sufficient reason for separation.

After such a crime there usually exists a serious danger of perversion either of the innocent party or of the children. But it is rarely lawful to effect a separation on *private* authority for such a reason; however, if this is done, the innocent party is bound to return to the other if the latter ceases to be a heretic.[991]

855. 3. GRAVE DANGER TO SOUL OR BODY is a sufficient reason for divorce in this restricted sense. There is considered to be grave spiritual danger if one of the parties constantly solicits the other to commit grave sin, e.g., theft, onanism, prostitution, or to transgress the laws of the Church, and so on, so that separation becomes the

---

[987] See CCL, Can. 1130.
[988] See CCL, Can. 1131, § 1.
[989] See CCL, Can. 1129, § 2.
[990] See CCL, Can. 1129, § 1.
[991] See CCL, Can. 1131, § 2.

only remedy for avoiding grave sin. It is rarely advisable to resort to separation for this reason since there are nearly always other remedies which may be used against this constant inducement to sin.

Grave physical danger arises *a)* from *serious cruelty* inflicted by one of the parties in word or deed;

b) from an *intolerable life under the same roof,* caused by the criminal and base life of the guilty party, or by strife, quarrels, habitual drunkenness, wanton neglect of the home, waste of money, and so on;

c) from *serious contagious disease* which has been contracted *as the result of grave sin* by one of the parties. Such a disease would be syphilis which is usually contracted through adultery.

856. 4. MUTUAL CONSENT freely and lawfully given is a sufficient reason for severing *conjugal relations* even *permanently.*

For although the married may indulge in sexual intercourse they remain at liberty to observe continence by mutual consent. In order that the married cease by mutual consent *to live together* either permanently or for a time, not only must there be a sufficient reason but it is likewise necessary to avoid scandal, harm to the offspring, any danger of incontinence, and so on.

857. NOTES. 1. RESUMPTION OF CONJUGAL LIFE. If the separation was due to adultery there is never any strict obligation on the innocent party to resume conjugal life, as noted already; in all other cases the common life must be restored when the reason for the separation ceases: if, however, the separation was pronounced by the bishop either for a time or indefinitely, the innocent party is not obliged to return except when the time specified has elapsed or the bishop gives orders to return.[992]

2. THE DUTIES OF THE SEPARATED PARTIES. After the separation, the children are to be placed in charge of the innocent party; if one of the parties is a non-Catholic, the Catholic party is to have charge of them. However, the ordinary is always free to decide otherwise for the sake of the welfare of the children, always safeguarding their Catholic education.[993] The amount of *support* to be provided, if any, is usually determined by the civil court.

THE BENEFITS OF MARRIAGE

858. The *Roman Catechism* sets forth the following instruction: "The faithful are to be taught that marriage has three benefits: offspring, conjugal fidelity, and the Sacrament; by these three means are alleviated those troubles mentioned by the apostle: 'those who do so will meet with outward distress' (1 Cor 7:28); and thus it comes about that the physical union which is rightly condemned when practiced

---

[992] See CCL, Can. 1131.
[993] See CCL, Can. 1132.

outside the state of marriage is regarded as morally good."[994] — Any action which seriously violates one or other of these benefits is a mortal sin.

1. *The benefit of offspring* consists in the acceptance and education of children for the worship of God, and thus it is necessary that the parents should care for the physical and spiritual welfare of their children. Therefore, parents who procure an abortion or who neglect the feeding and proper education of their offspring commit grave sin.[995]

2. *Conjugal fidelity*, to which must be conjoined the right to sexual intercourse — to be discussed in the following chapter — is another benefit of marriage. Such fidelity is an immense blessing proper to the married state, and the more carefully it is preserved, the greater the happiness existing between the married partners. It is violated by adultery and by all similar acts, even by solitary pollution.

3. *The benefit of the Sacrament* refers to the indissolubility of the bond of marriage and to the union of love existing between the partners. This marital union is violated not only by improper divorce but also by any neglect of those duties which belong to husband and wife. These duties were discussed in the treatise on the fourth commandment, no. 462ff.

THE OBLIGATIONS OF MARRIAGE

INTRODUCTION. There are many obligations flowing from the benefits of marriage enumerated in the preceding chapter. Here we shall consider no more than the obligation arising from the benefit of conjugal fidelity, namely, the marital dues.

859. 1. THE LAWFULNESS OF THE CONJUGAL ACT.

PRINCIPLE. *The conjugal act is lawful and even meritorious as often as it is not opposed to the benefit of offspring and conjugal fidelity.*

St. Paul writes: "Let every man give his wife what is her due, and every woman do the same by her husband" (1 Cor 7:3). — The intrinsic reason for this is that the conjugal act is necessary not only for the propagation of the human race but also for the fostering of married love. As often as one of these purposes is desired, the conjugal act is lawful, provided that no other ills or inconveniences ensue. Consequently, the partners in marriage are not obliged to exercise sexual intercourse simply for the sake of procreation. Therefore, this act is lawful even if both parties are sterile, also during the time of lactation or pregnancy, on Sundays and on feast days; but it is forbidden to exercise the sexual function by means of onanism or with serious danger to health or at the same time causing scandal to others, and so on.

CIRCUMSTANCES OF THE CONJUGAL ACT. Not only the conjugal act itself but also touches and looks and all other acts are lawful between the married, provided that there is no *proximate* danger of pollution and the sole intention is not mere

---

[994] Cf. TCCI 7:373.
[995] See CCL, Can. 1113.

sexual pleasure. Therefore, in ordinary circumstances the confessor should not interrogate married persons about these accompanying acts.

860. 2. THE OBLIGATION TO RENDER THE MARRIAGE DUES.

FIRST PRINCIPLE. *As often as one of the parties asks reasonably and seriously for the rendering of the marriage dues, the other is bound in justice to accede to the request; otherwise, grave sin is committed.*

EXPLANATION. *The request must be reasonable and serious.*

The request is unreasonable if made in a state of drunkenness, or when one of the parties is seriously ill, or if the request is too frequent or causes scandal to others, or if the act is accompanied by the practice of onanism.—The request is not considered serious if made in the form of a desire rather than a definite will.—But if the request is reasonable and serious, then the other party is obliged in justice to render the marriage debt under pain of grievous sin, as is evident *a)* from the words of St. Paul quoted above, and *b)* from the nature of the marriage contract in which the right to sexual intercourse is handed over from one party to the other. This obligation of rendering the marriage dues, although of its nature serious since it is concerned with a grave matter stipulated in a just contract, does admit of parvity of matter. Thus, if the wife were to refuse marital relations once or twice, awaiting a time more suitable to herself, she would not be guilty of grave sin—at least, if the husband is not thereby placed in proximate danger of incontinence or provoked to excessive anger.

It is self-evident that there is no obligation to render these dues if one of the parties has forfeited the right to ask for them by reason of his or her adultery or as the result of severance of conjugal relations having been legitimately obtained.

861. SECOND PRINCIPLE. *a) In itself there is no obligation to ask for the act proper to the married state, and therefore it is permissible for both parties by mutual free consent to abstain from the act either permanently or for a time; b) but incidentally, by reason of charity, there does exist on occasions such an obligation.*

The reason justifying the first part of the principle is that both parties are free to renounce their right to sexual intercourse. Thus, our Lady and St. Joseph, although truly married, freely renounced their right of asking for the marriage dues, and at least temporary continence is usually beneficial in promoting the spiritual life of husband and wife.

The reason for the second part of the principle is that the withholding of marital relations can be the cause of many evils, e.g., danger to chastity, a weakening of married love.

862. 3. SINS OF THE MARRIED.

PRINCIPLE. *a) Whatsoever is directly and seriously opposed to the benefits of offspring and conjugal fidelity is a grave sin against chastity; b) anything that is done for mere sexual pleasure is a slight sin, provided it is not directly contrary to the offspring or to conjugal fidelity; c) whatever is useful for or necessary to the perfect fulfillment of the conjugal act and the fostering of marital love is not sinful.*

EXPLANATION. The second and third parts of this principle are sufficiently evident from what has been said in no. 859 regarding the use of the conjugal act for mere sexual pleasure and the circumstances accompanying the use of the act.

Serious harm is caused to the offspring and conjugal fidelity by:

a) sins of impurity committed with others either in deed or desire;

b) solitary pollution;

c) the practice of onanism. Enough has been said already in no. 518ff in the treatise on chastity regarding sins belonging to the first and second categories. We must now consider the sin of onanism.

863. Onanism is of two kinds; solitary onanism, which is the same as pollution or self-abuse, and conjugal onanism which is practiced either *a)* by breaking off the conjugal act before semination,[996] or *b)* by the use of various instruments (e.g., a pessary) which prevent the seed of the male reaching its proper place. Here we shall speak of conjugal onanism only.

MORAL CHARACTER. *Conjugal onanism, no matter in what way it is freely practiced, is always grievously sinful.*

Such is the teaching of right reason and of the Church. Right reason testifies clearly that onanism is directly contrary to the procreation of children and to conjugal fidelity and is merely a form of pollution. Furthermore, this practice usually has disastrous consequences; the bodily health of both parties is often seriously affected, the birth of children is prevented, families and states are underpopulated, the feelings are exposed to every form of lust. — The Holy Office, May 21, 1851, declared as "scandalous, erroneous, and contrary to the natural law of marriage" the following proposition: "For morally good reasons married people may use marriage in the manner proposed by Onan." The Sacred Penitentiary, Nov. 13, 1901, replied: "It is not permissible to absolve any penitent who refuses to desist from a way of acting which is plainly onanism."

864. *Formal cooperation* in the practice of onanism is never lawful; *material* cooperation in onanism which is practiced by withdrawal is sometimes lawful, provided there is a proportionately grave reason. The reason for the prohibition against formal cooperation is that it is never permitted to cooperate formally in the sin of another.[997] Material cooperation is sometimes permitted

---

[996] It is gravely unlawful to wash out the vagina immediately after sexual intercourse with the express intention of expelling the seed or destroying the spermatozoa (by means of a liquid specially prepared for the purpose) so as to prevent conception. However, such washing is lawful if undertaken for hygienic reasons and not immediately after sexual intercourse, for it is certain that in those circumstances conception is not rendered impossible.

[997] See no. 234.

because the action of the person who cooperates materially is objectively good, and its evil character arises from the misuse of the act by the other person. Accordingly, we must apply here the rules concerning evil actions which are indirectly voluntary. Reasons which are sufficiently grave to permit one of the parties to cooperate materially in the practice of onanism would be, e.g., a well-grounded fear of strife and quarrelling, or of adultery, and so on. Furthermore, it is required: *a)* that the innocent party is purely *passive* in the act of withdrawal; *b)* that he or she should try to persuade the other to refrain from the evil practice; *c)* that all internal pleasure in the evil act is withheld. If all these conditions are verified, either party may not only render but also request the marital duties from the other who practices onanism. However, the innocent party is quite justified in refusing intercourse, since the other has no right to the conjugal act as the result of the desire to abuse marriage in that way. Material cooperation in that form of onanism which is practiced by the use of mechanical contrivances can only be permitted when there is fear of very grave harm, so that the innocent party is obliged to offer positive resistance to any act which of its nature and from its commencement is unlawful. Some authors maintain that the wife should then behave in almost the same way *as a virgin* would if attacked by a man.

865. No other known remedies against onanism exist at present which are both effective and lawful, apart from *virtuous continence* and firm *trust in God*. There are known to exist many *physical* means of preventing conception but they are all either unlawful or not certainly effective. To make use of the so-called *safe period* (i.e., to refrain from the conjugal act for fifteen days before and four days after menstruation) has been declared lawful by the Sacred Penitentiary, but it is not a certain means of preventing conception, since there is no infallible way of determining the safe period.

PREPARATION FOR MARRIAGE

INTRODUCTION. There are three acts performed prior to marriage: 1) Betrothal; 2) The Investigation of the Betrothed; 3) The Publication of the Banns.

Art. 1. Betrothal

866. DEFINITION. *Betrothal is a mutual promise of marriage in the future made in legal form between two persons capable of being betrothed.*

EXPLANATION. 1. *a mutual promise of marriage in the future*: consequently, betrothal is essentially a promise relating to the future and not to the present. Such a promise must be:

1) *free*, i.e., free *a)* from error; *b)* from fear. Substantial error, inasmuch as it invalidates any contract, also renders betrothal null and void; a serious accidental error enables the contract of betrothal to be rescinded. Grave fear *justly* induced by some natural cause or even by a free agent neither

invalidates betrothal nor renders it voidable. Slight fear *unjustly induced* does render the contract voidable, at least if the fear was not merely concomitant but was the cause of the contract being made; grave fear *unjustly induced* certainly renders betrothal voidable.[998]

2) *deliberate.* Since betrothal is an onerous contract having most serious consequences, that amount of deliberation is required which is generally necessary for entering into valid and lawful onerous contracts.

3) *mutual,* and therefore a one-sided promise is insufficient, since betrothal must be a bilateral and reciprocal agreement.

2. *between persons capable of betrothal.* Persons are incapable of being betrothed either by nature or by law. They are *naturally* incapable of betrothal if they lack sufficient use of reason to undertake so onerous a contract of such importance, e.g., lunatics, the perfectly intoxicated, persons under hypnotism, infants. Persons are *legally* incapable of being betrothed *a)* if they do not observe the form prescribed in canon law;[999] *b)* if they labor under some impediment prohibiting or annulling marriage. They are certainly incapable if the impediment is one which is not normally dispensed, since in such circumstances the act of betrothal would be a promise regarding something unlawful. But if it is easy to obtain a dispensation in the impediment which exists, it is not so certain whether in those circumstances the betrothal would not be conditionally valid. The case is most likely to arise when the parties are *of mixed religion.* In practice, any betrothal between two persons who require a dispensation in order to contract marriage because of some prohibitory or annulling impediment can be regarded as invalid. Accordingly, the parish priest will not sanction such a betrothal to be made before the requisite dispensation has been obtained; *c) those below the age of puberty,* who nevertheless may be validly betrothed after attaining the use of their reason but the contract is spontaneously voidable *within three days* after attaining the age of puberty or after learning of this privilege.

3. *made in legal form.* Unless the following conditions set forth in Can. 1017, § 1 are fulfilled, the contract is null and void: *a)* the promise must be made *in writing* with the day, month, and year indicated; *b)* it must be *signed* by the parties and by the parish priest (or ordinary), or at least two witnesses. If one or both parties are unable to write (whether because they do not know how to write or because of some physical infirmity), this should be expressly stated in the document and an extra witness employed to sign this addition. If both parties to the contract are *non-Catholics,* whether baptized or not, they are not bound by these instructions.

No obligation is contracted in either forum by a betrothal, if it is not made according to the legally prescribed form. However, if any *deceit* was practiced in such a contract which does not observe the canonical form, there exists an obligation of making reparation for any ensuing damage.

---

[998] See CCL, Can. 103, § 2.
[999] See no. 866.3.

867. **THE EFFECTS OF BETROTHAL** are twofold: 1) a grave obligation to contract marriage at a suitable and legitimate time; 2) an impediment prohibiting any other marriage.

By reason of the first effect, grave sin is committed by anyone who withdraws from a contract of betrothal without sufficient reason, or who contrary to the will of the other party postpones the marriage unduly. By reason of the second effect, all other betrothals are rendered invalid and other marriages unlawful, unless the first betrothal has been legitimately dissolved.

NOTE. The engagement to marry, although it be valid and there is no just reason to refuse to fulfill it, does not in law admit of action in the ecclesiastical court to force the other party to marry; action for possible injury caused by the breaking of the engagement is admitted.[1000] This action for damages is more effectively undertaken in the civil courts, and may be undertaken even by Catholics, since it is a matter which belongs to either forum.[1001]

868. **THE DISSOLUTION OF BETROTHAL.** Betrothal can be rescinded: 1) by mutual consent; 2) by a notable change of circumstances; 3) by a violation of the fidelity proper to the betrothed; 4) by the adoption of a more perfect state of life; 5) by a dispensation granted by the Holy See.

1. *Mutual consent given freely* and not obtained by fear or deceit dissolves the contract of betrothal, even if it was sanctioned by oath, since the contract was arbitrary.

2. *A notable change of circumstances* occurring *after* the contract has been made dissolves the betrothal. A change of circumstances is considered notable if it would have prevented one or both of the parties entering upon the betrothal, had it been known previously. Such a change could occur: *a)* in *bodily* gifts, e.g., if one of the parties suffers blindness or lameness; *b)* in personal *wealth*, as when one of the parties loses a large part of his or her possessions; *c)* in *spiritual or mental* gifts, e.g., if one of the betrothed is discovered to be a drunkard, or a spendthrift, or subject to evil habits; *d)* in *external circumstances*, e.g., if great enmity arises between the families of both parties, or if the parents fall into serious disagreement.

3. *The fidelity which is proper to the betrothed may be violated* in three ways: *a)* by fornication or other serious acts of impurity committed with another person; *b)* by marriage with a third party; *c)* by undue postponement of marriage.

4. *The choice of a more perfect state of life*, such as the religious state (even if only simple vows are taken) or the clerical state, dissolves a previous contract of betrothal, which is made with the implicit condition—"unless I choose a more perfect state." There are some authors who maintain that the contract may be rescinded by embracing *the state of virginity* through a private vow of perpetual chastity.

[1000] See CCL, Can. 1017, § 3.
[1001] See AAS 10, 345.

5. *A papal dispensation* can dissolve a betrothal. If the pope has the power of dissolving a ratified marriage, a fortiori he has the power to dissolve a betrothal. Although the contract has the effect of giving to each of the betrothed a strict right preventing the other from withdrawing from the fulfillment of the promise, nevertheless one must bear in mind the lamentable consequences which ensue both for the parties themselves and for the Church from marriages contracted under duress. The pope has the right of safeguarding the Church from harm and consequently he may restrict the right of the individual in virtue of *his supreme power*. Sometimes the pope in the course of dissolving a valid betrothal imposes damages to be paid by the party which has withdrawn unjustly from the contract; in other cases, he leaves the question to be decided by the civil authorities.

THE MANNER OF DISSOLUTION is not prescribed in law, and therefore betrothal may be rescinded for a just cause, even spontaneously, provided that scandal is avoided and there is no diocesan law to the contrary.

Art. 2. The Preliminary Investigation and Publication of the Banns of Marriage

Before marriage is celebrated it must be established with certainty that there are no obstacles to its valid and lawful celebration.[1002] To ensure this it is necessary to hold a preliminary interrogation of the parties to be married and to publish the banns of marriage. But in danger of death, if other proofs are not available and there are no indications to the contrary, the sworn affirmation of the parties that they are baptized and that there is no impediment to their marriage suffices.[1003]

869. 1. THE INTERROGATION OF BOTH PARTIES must take place in the presence of their parish priest or his delegate—that is to say, in the presence of the parish priest whose right it is to assist at the marriage. Who this parish priest is will be indicated when the celebration of marriage is discussed. This parish priest:

a) must ask for the *baptismal certificate* of both parties (unless the Sacrament was conferred in his own parish) or of the Catholic party only, if the parties are to be married with a dispensation from disparity of cult.[1004] If the marriage is mixed, the priest must inquire about the validity of the Baptism of the heretic, since there may exist an impediment of disparity of cult;

b) must ask for the *certificate of Confirmation*. Catholics who have not yet received Confirmation should first receive that Sacrament, if they can do so without great inconvenience;[1005]

c) should prudently *question* both the man and the woman separately whether they are under any impediment, whether they freely consent to the marriage,

---

1002 See CCL, Can. 1019, § 1.
1003 See CCL, Can. 1019, § 2.
1004 See CCL, Can. 1021, § 1.
1005 See CCL, Can. 1021, § 2.

and whether they are sufficiently instructed in Christian doctrine, unless he knows from some other source that they are well instructed in their religion. The local ordinary usually prescribes special regulations for this examination into the freedom of the parties to marry.[1006] If the parish priest discovers that the parties are ignorant on matters of Christian doctrine, he should give them at least the essential elements, but he should not deter them from marriage;[1007]

d) should *instruct* both parties regarding the sanctity of marriage, their mutual obligations, the duties of parents toward their offspring. He should also admonish them to make a good confession prior to marriage and to receive Holy Communion devoutly.[1008] The parish priest must earnestly warn *young people* not to contract marriage against the reasonable objections of their parents or without their knowledge; if they nevertheless persist, he must not assist at their marriage without first consulting the local ordinary.[1009]

870. 2. THE PUBLICATION OF THE BANNS OF MARRIAGE consists in a public announcement prior to the celebration of marriage in order to ensure that possible impediments can be discovered with greater ease and certainty.

OBLIGATION. The law of the Church imposes a grave obligation to publish the banns of marriage. This is the common opinion, and the obligation follows from the serious purpose of the banns. The law does not cease to bind in an individual case, even when it is certain that there is no impediment to a future marriage. The omission of one of the three publications and even, perhaps, of two of them is a *slight* sin.

The banns are *omitted a)* in a case of urgent necessity; *b)* when a dispensation is obtained from the proper ordinary; [1010] *c)* in mixed marriages or those contracted with a dispensation of disparity of worship. However, the local ordinary may order the publication of the banns even for those marriages, but then no mention must be made of the religion of the non-Catholic party.

871. TIME of publication. "The publication of the banns is to be made in church on three successive Sundays or holy days of obligation during the Mass or at other services (e.g., Vespers) to which the people come in large numbers."[1011] If marriage is delayed for six months after the announcement of the banns they must be repeated, unless the local ordinary decides otherwise.[1012]

[1006] See CCL, Can. 1020, § 2 and 3.
[1007] See AAS 10, 345.
[1008] See CCL, Can. 1033.
[1009] See CCL, Can. 1034.
[1010] If the parties belong to two different dioceses, the bishop in whose diocese the marriage is to take place has the right to dispense. If the marriage is to be contracted outside either of the two dioceses, either bishop is competent to dispense.
[1011] CCL, Can. 1024.
[1012] See CCL, Can. 1030, § 2.

FORM. The banns are to be announced in the vernacular in the form given in the Roman Ritual[1013] or according to any other approved diocesan formula, mentioning *a)* the Christian name, surname, place of residence, and parents of both parties; *b)* the precise number of the publication; *c)* the obligation incumbent on the faithful of revealing any impediment to the parish priest or ordinary. No reference is to be made to anything odious or likely to cause embarrassment, e.g., the fact that one of the parties is a non-Catholic, or illegitimate, or the age of either party, and so on.

The ordinary may also substitute in his diocese another form of publishing the banns, by posting the names of the parties at the church doors and leaving them there for at least eight days, during which there must be two Sundays or holy days of obligation.[1014]

872. PLACE. The banns of marriage are to be announced by the *proper* parish priest of each of the parties,[1015] where the parties have a domicile or quasi-domicile. Therefore, objectively speaking, the banns should be published in all places where the parties have possessed a domicile since attaining the age of puberty, but since this may sometimes lead to grave inconvenience, if either of the parties has lived in some other place for six months after the age of puberty, the parish priest should refer the matter to the bishop who may either have the banns announced in that place or otherwise order investigations to be made regarding the freedom of the parties to marry.[1016] If the banns are published in several places, all the parish priests concerned should inform the priest who is to assist at the marriage by sending some authentic document.[1017] However, in each diocese it is usual to find certain statutes determining the places in which the banns are to be published.

THE REVEALING OF IMPEDIMENTS. Since the primary purpose of the publication of the banns is to discover the possible existence of any impediments to marriage, it follows that all the faithful are under a serious obligation to reveal any impediments of which they are aware to the parish priest or local ordinary prior to the celebration of marriage.[1018]

Causes which would excuse them from revealing such impediments are:

a) grave danger to themselves or to others;

b) when the disclosure would be useless—that is to say, if the impediment is already known to the parish priest;

c) the seal of Confession or a professional secret. Thus, for example, a confessor or doctor or nurse cannot reveal anything which they have learned in the course

[1013] Tit. 7, chap. 1, no. 13.
[1014] See CCL, Can. 1025.
[1015] See CCL, Can. 1023, § 1.
[1016] See CCL, Can. 1023, § 2.
[1017] See CCL, Can. 1029.
[1018] See CCL, Can. 1027.

of discharging their office; however, they must admonish both parties, so far as this may be possible, to disclose the impediment themselves.

873. **WHAT IS TO BE DONE AFTER THE PARTIES HAVE BEEN QUESTIONED AND THE BANNS PUB-LISHED.** There are three possible alternatives; once the investigation is complete and all the essential documents received, 1) *no* impediment has been discovered: then the parish priest should assist at the marriage, but normally not before the lapse of three days,[1019] and in the case of a marriage between persons with no fixed abode, not before obtaining the permission of the ordinary; 2) a *doubtful* impediment has been disclosed; the doubt must then be removed by a more thorough inquiry; if the doubt cannot be removed, the local ordinary is to be consulted;[1020] 3) a *certain* impediment has been disclosed: a dispensation must then be sought from this impediment.[1021]

THE EXTERNAL CELEBRATION OF MARRIAGE

874. **INTRODUCTION.** To the external form of marriage as *demanded by the canons* are *obliged* under pain of their marriage being invalid;[1022] "all persons baptized in the Catholic (Latin) Church and converts to the Church from heresy or schism, even though the first mentioned as well as the latter should have subsequently fallen away," if:

a) they contract marriage *among themselves*, i.e., they contract a *purely* Catholic *marriage*;

b) they contract *a mixed marriage with non-Catholics* (whether baptized or unbaptized, even after they have obtained a dispensation from disparity of cult or mixed religion). Indults previously granted to Germany and Hungary in this matter are no longer valid;

c) they marry Catholics or non-Catholics *belonging to Oriental Rites*.

THE FOLLOWING PERSONS ARE NOT OBLIGED TO OBSERVE THIS FORM:

a) non-Catholics (whether baptized or unbaptized) when they contract marriages amongst themselves and thus contract *a non-Catholic marriage*;

b) *children of non-Catholics* (even though they were baptized in the Catholic Church) who have been reared from their infancy in heresy or schism or infidelity or without any religion, if they marry non-Catholics.[1023]

[1019] See CCL, Can. 1030, § 1.
[1020] See CCL, Can. 1031.
[1021] See no. 932.
[1022] CCL, Can. 1099.
[1023] The phrase *those born of non-Catholics* includes those born of parents only one of whom is a non-Catholic, even if the guarantees had been given prior to a mixed marriage (see CCL, Can. 1061 and 1071; see also P.C.C.J., July 20, 1929: AAS 21, 573). This interpretation is declaratory and does not extend the original (see P.C.C.J., July 25, 1931: AAS 23, 388). The same phrase includes also children of apostate parents (see P.C.C.J., Feb. 17, 1930).

c) those belonging to Oriental Rites when they contract marriage among themselves. This is the ruling given by common law, but by local law members of the Ruthenian Church are obliged to the same form as Latin Catholics.

In order to give a clearer explanation of what is required for the celebration of marriage, the following chapter is divided into three articles: 1) what is required for the valid and lawful external celebration of marriage in normal cases; 2) what is required in extraordinary cases, namely, in danger of death, or when no priest is present with the proper delegation; 3) the rite to be observed and the registration of marriage.

Art. 1. The Valid and Lawful Celebration of Marriage in Ordinary Cases

875. REQUISITES FOR VALID EXTERNAL CELEBRATION.

THE LAW: "Only those marriages are valid which are contracted either before the parish priest or the ordinary of the place or a priest delegated by either, and at least two witnesses."[1024]

Consequently, under pain of the marriage being invalid there is required for the external celebration of marriage the presence of:

either the local ordinary
or the parish priest of the place   }   and two witnesses.
or a priest properly delegated

THE TERM *PARISH PRIEST* includes:

1. all parish priests strictly so-called;

2. all who are equivalently parish priests, that is, *a)* the administrator of a vacant parish; *b)* a quasi-parish priest who exercises the care of souls in a specified territory which has not been raised to the dignity of a parish; *c)* a permanent or temporary vicar of a parish ruled in conjunction with others; *d)* chaplains or rectors of pious establishments of any type exempt from parochial jurisdiction; *e)* personal parish priests, e.g., military chaplains.

THE TERM *ORDINARY* includes: diocesan bishops, administrators, vicars apostolic, prelates or prefects exercising the power of jurisdiction in a separate territory of their own, and their vicars general in spiritual matters, and, while the see is vacant, the vicar capitular or legitimate diocesan administrator.[1025]—The senior forces chaplain is the ordinary for all persons belonging to the army by virtue of civil law.

THE TERM *DELEGATED PRIEST* includes any priest who receives the faculties to assist validly at a marriage either from the local parish priest or ordinary. The delegation must be granted for each individual marriage—that is to say, to a specified

---

[1024] CCL, Can. 1094.
[1025] See CCL, Can. 198, § 2.

priest for a specified marriage, all general delegation being excluded. Such general delegation cannot be given except to regularly appointed assistants (curates), for the parish to which they are appointed.[1026] The delegation need not be granted explicitly; it is sufficient that it be tacitly given, that it can be clearly deduced from actions which presume that delegation has been granted; but delegation may not be presumed nor is it retrospective. — Any priest *with general delegation* to assist at all marriages, e.g., an assistant priest, may subdelegate for particular marriages; a priest who is delegated for a specified marriage cannot subdelegate, unless such a power has been given expressly.[1027]

Delegation ceases a) when it is revoked, *b)* when the stated period has elapsed, but not by the death or passing out of office of the one delegating.[1028] Therefore, for example, if a parish priest dies suddenly, his assistant may continue to assist validly and lawfully at marriages in the parish.

876. THREE CONDITIONS must be fulfilled by the parish priest and local ordinary in order that their assistances at marriage may be valid:

1. *They must have taken canonical possession of their benefice or office and not be excommunicated, interdicted, or suspended from office by a condemnatory or declaratory sentence of the ecclesiastical court.*[1029]

A parish priest takes canonical possession of his parish by induction;[1030] the local ordinary, i.e., the bishop, by presentation of the apostolic letters.[1031] — Even a putative parish priest may validly assist at marriages, since the Church supplies jurisdiction in a case of common error.[1032]

2. *They must assist at marriages within the limits of their own territory.*[1033]

Therefore, it does not matter — so far as the validity of the marriage is concerned — whether the parties married are members of his parish or not, provided that the priest is assisting at the marriage within the limits of his own parish. Parish priests with *personal* faculties may assist at the marriage of their subjects anywhere.

3. *They must not ask for nor receive the consent of the contracting parties under stress of violence or grave fear.*[1034]

Therefore, any assistance under duress or extorted by fear is no longer considered sufficient; the priest must freely ask for and freely accept the consent of the parties.

[1026] See CCL, Can. 1096, § 1.
[1027] See CCL, Can. 199, § 4.
[1028] See CCL, Can. 207.
[1029] See CCL, Can. 1095, § 1, no. 1.
[1030] See CCL, Can. 1444, § 1.
[1031] See CCL, Can. 334, § 3.
[1032] See CCL, Can. 209.
[1033] See CCL, Can. 1095, § 1, no. 2.
[1034] See CCL, Can. 1095, § 1, no. 3.

Even when the parish priest is a mere *passive* spectator, he must ask for and receive that consent. The circumstances in which such passive assistance is lawful will be discussed later in no. 894 in the treatise on mixed marriages.

877. TWO WITNESSES in addition to the parish priest or another priest must assist at the celebration of marriage. Nothing further is required of these two witnesses than that they should be able to testify to the celebration of the marriage. Therefore, lunatics, the perfectly intoxicated, those who are both deaf and blind cannot be witnesses. It is fitting that the witnesses be persons of upright life; heretics may be tolerated for a just cause, provided that there is no danger of scandal.[1035]

878. LAWFUL CELEBRATION OF MARRIAGES.

1. *There must be moral certainty of the freedom of the contracting parties, according to the regulations of the Code.*[1036]

The free state of the parties means their freedom from all prohibiting and annulling impediments. Moral certainty of their freedom may be obtained: *a)* through interrogation of the parties themselves; *b)* through publication of the banns; *c)* in certain circumstances, through the testimony of the parties themselves to their freedom given on oath.

2. *The priest must be sure that one or other of the parties has a domicile or quasi-domicile in the place of marriage or has lived there at least a month.*[1037]

What constitutes a domicile or quasi-domicile has been discussed already in the treatise on law, no. 84. Those who have but a *diocesan* domicile or quasi-domicile have for their parish priest the one in whose territory they are actually staying;[1038] therefore, such a priest may assist validly and lawfully at their marriage. Consequently, a domicile in the parish is no longer necessary.—The month's residence is not interrupted if the parties were absent from the place for one or two days during the thirty preceding marriage; such a short absence is counted as none at all.

3. *Marriage is to be celebrated by the parish priest of the bride, unless some just reason excuses.*[1039]

This obligation does not appear to be grave, and an excusing cause can be discovered easily. However, the diocesan statutes on this matter must be observed, if such exist. When Catholics of different rites marry (e.g., Catholics of the Latin and Oriental Rites) marriage shall be contracted in the presence of the parish priest of the husband's rite, unless a particular law rules otherwise.

[1035] See Holy Office, Aug. 19, 1891.
[1036] See CCL, Can. 1097, § 1, no. 1.
[1037] See CCL, Can. 1097, § 1, no. 2.
[1038] See CCL, Can. 94, § 3.
[1039] See CCL, Can. 1097, § 2.

4. *The permission of the ordinary (or of a priest delegated by him) of the place where the marriage is to be celebrated must be sought (in normal circumstances) in order to assist at the marriages of persons who have no fixed abode.*[1040] In this context, persons of no fixed abode refer to all those who at the time of their marriage have no parish priest or proper ordinary through lack of a domicile or quasi-domicile or at least a month's residence. In a case of necessity, e.g., if there is danger of a civil marriage being contracted or if these persons are actually travelling,[1041] the parish priest may lawfully assist at their marriage without the previous permission of the ordinary.

5. *Permission must be obtained from the parish priest or ordinary where one of the parties has a domicile or quasi-domicile or one month's residence, unless there is grave necessity which excuses from obtaining permission.*
A parish priest celebrating marriages *in his own territory* where he always assists validly does not require the *delegation* of any other parish priest or ordinary, but he does require their permission unless at least one of the parties has a domicile or quasi-domicile or a month's residence in his territory. If a parish priest assists at a marriage without the requisite permission, he cannot retain the stole fee for himself but must forward it to the proper parish priest of the contracting parties, namely, the parish priest of the bride.[1042] The stole fee is the tax due by diocesan law to the priest who assists at the marriage; it does not include the stipend received for the nuptial Mass or any other gifts which may be presented.

Art. 2. The Valid and Lawful Celebration of Marriage in Extraordinary Cases

The two extraordinary cases to be considered are: 1) marriage in danger of death; 2) marriage when the legitimate priest cannot be obtained.

879. THE CELEBRATION OF MARRIAGE IN DANGER OF DEATH.

If the parish priest or ordinary or priest delegated by either cannot be present or the parties cannot go to him without great inconvenience in order that he should assist at their marriage in danger of death, marriage contracted in the presence of two witnesses is both valid and lawful; but if some other priest (who is not delegated) can be present, he should be summoned and together with the witnesses assist at the marriage, but only the two witnesses are necessary for validity.[1043]

EXPLANATION. 1. *in danger of death*, i.e., of either party. It makes no difference whether the danger is caused by illness or by something else, e.g., war, shipwreck, and so on.

[1040] See CCL, Can. 1032.
[1041] See CCL, Can. 1097, § 1, no. 3.
[1042] See CCL, Can. 1097, § 3.
[1043] See CCL, Can. 1098.

2. if the priest cannot be present or the parties cannot go to him without great inconvenience ... For since the celebration of marriage without the assistance of the legitimate priest is most unfitting and could give rise to great inconvenience, there is required a grave excusing cause, which is easily to be found in danger of death when there is insufficient time to summon the parish priest or another delegated priest.

3. if another priest can be present, he should be summoned ... The case frequently arises where a confessor discovers that a dying person is not validly married; in such circumstances the putative husband and wife may give their conjugal consent in the presence of the confessor and two witnesses. Since the confessor has the faculty to dispense from the canonical form of marriage and from all ecclesiastical impediments (with the exception of the two mentioned in Can. 1043), the two parties may for a just cause be dispensed from the obligation of summoning witnesses and give their consent in the presence of the confessor alone; however they are under an obligation to dispel any scandal which may already exist and to give the usual promises, if either of the parties is under the impediment of mixed religion or disparity of worship.

880. The celebration of marriage in the absence of a competent priest

Even apart from the danger of death, marriage celebrated in the presence of two witnesses is valid and lawful if the parish priest or ordinary or a priest delegated by either cannot be had or the parties cannot go to him without grave inconvenience, provided that it is prudently foreseen that this state of affairs will continue for a month. If there is another priest not delegated who can be present, he should be summoned and together with the two witnesses assist at the marriage, but without prejudice to the validity of the marriage in the presence of the witnesses only.[1044]

Such cases are most likely to arise in missionary countries. If the parties desire to contract marriage, and neither now nor within the space of a month can they obtain or visit a properly delegated priest without grave inconvenience, they may validly and lawfully contract marriage in the presence of two witnesses only. It is to be recommended that they should follow the procedure set forth in the instruction of the Sacred Congregation of Propaganda, June 23, 1830:

> In such circumstances the parents shall select two witnesses; these, together with the contracting parties and their relatives, should proceed to church, and kneeling down recite together the customary acts of faith, hope, charity, and contrition, and thus the parties will prepare themselves fittingly for the contract of marriage. When these prayers are concluded, the bride and bridegroom will express their mutual consent in the presence of the two witnesses, making use of any formula of words which express a present consent; afterward having given thanks to God they

[1044] See CCL, Can. 1098.

shall return home. If it is impossible to go to a church, the procedure outlined already may be observed in a private house.

It is immediately evident that the two parties should take care to be free from mortal sin and from all impediments to marriage. The procedure to be adopted for absolution from these impediments if a simple priest happens to be present will be discussed in no. 927, where special attention will be given to marriage impediments.

After the celebration of such marriages, the witnesses and the contracting parties are severally responsible for seeing that the marriage is entered without delay in the marriage and baptismal registers of their own church or of the neighboring church, if they have no church of their own.[1045]

Art. 3. The Rite of Celebration and the Registration of Marriage

881. THE RITE OF CELEBRATION. "Outside the case of necessity marriage is to be celebrated in accordance with the sacred rites prescribed in the liturgical books approved by the Church or sanctioned by laudable customs."[1046]

Among these rites the *nuptial blessing* holds pride of place; it may be either simple, as set forth in the Roman Ritual,[1047] or solemn, as found in the Missal for the Nuptial Mass.

a) The *solemn nuptial blessing* consists of three prayers, two of which are recited after the *Pater Noster*, the third after *Ite Missa Est* or *Benedicamus Domino*. The parish priest should see to it that the married receive the solemn blessing, and this may be given them even after they have lived together in marriage for a long time but it can be pronounced only during a Nuptial Mass with the observance of the special rubric, and on all days with the exception of the days specified in Can. 1108.[1048] No one but the priest who can validly and lawfully assist at the marriage or his delegate can give this solemn blessing,[1049] since the blessing is, so to speak, the fulfillment of the priest's assistance at marriage. It is not required that the Mass in which the blessing is given should be the votive Mass for bride and bridegroom[1050] nor is it necessary that it be applied for the parties themselves;

[1045] See CCL, Can. 1103, § 3.
[1046] CCL, Can. 1100.
[1047] Ttit. 7, chap. 2.
[1048] See CCL, Can. 1101, § 1.
[1049] See CCL, Can. 1101, § 2.
[1050] The votive Nuptial Mass is forbidden on those days which exclude the celebration of doubles of the second class, namely Sundays, holy days of obligation of the first and second order, privileged octaves of the first and second order (namely, those of Easter, Pentecost, Epiphany, Corpus Christi), privileged ferias (namely, Ash Wednesday, Holy Week), the Vigil of Christmas. On these days the Mass of the day may be said with the prayer added *pro sponsis* either under one conclusion with the first prayer on those feasts which exclude all commemorations, e.g., Christmas Day, Easter Sunday, and so on, or under two separate conclusions on other days and feasts (see S.R.C., June 14, 1918: AAS 10, 332).

but the blessing must not be given: 1) outside the time of Mass (unless there exists a special privilege to the contrary); 2) during the closed times (namely, from the First Sunday of Advent until Christmas Day inclusive, and from Ash Wednesday until Easter Sunday inclusive), except with the sanction of the ordinary;[1051] 3) in mixed marriages; 4) if the woman has already received the blessing in a previous marriage.[1052] — The bride and bridegroom are to be encouraged to receive Holy Communion during the Nuptial Mass.

b) The *simple blessing*, as set forth in the Ritual, may be given outside the time of Mass in a church or public or semipublic oratory, but not in a private dwelling, unless the local ordinary grants permission in an extraordinary case.

882. c) *The time and place of celebration of marriage.* Marriage (together with the simple blessing) may be contracted *any time of the year*, but the *solemn* nuptial blessing of marriage is forbidden during the closed times (as already noted), unless the local ordinary grants his permission for a good reason.[1053]

The *place* in which marriage is to be celebrated in normal circumstances is the parish church, but the parish priest can give permission for marriage to be contracted in another church or in a public or semipublic oratory; the local ordinary may permit marriage to be celebrated in a private oratory or in some other fitting place. Ordinaries cannot permit the celebration of marriage in the churches or chapels of seminaries or of religious women, except in urgent necessity and with due precautions.[1054]

Mixed marriages shall be contracted outside the church, unless the local ordinary permits otherwise, but the Nuptial Mass may never be allowed.[1055]

883. THE REGISTRATION OF MARRIAGE. After the celebration of marriage, the parish priest or he who takes his place must as soon as possible enter in the marriage register the names of the married couple and of the witnesses, the place and date, and other items prescribed in the rituals and by the local ordinary; the entry shall be made even though another priest, delegated either by himself or by the ordinary, assisted at the marriage.[1056]

Moreover, the parish priest must note in the baptismal record that the parties contracted marriage in his parish on a specified day. If one or both parties were baptized in another parish, the priest in whose parish the marriage was celebrated must send notice of the fact either directly or through the episcopal curia to the parish priest where the parties were baptized, so that the marriage may be recorded in the baptismal register.[1057]

[1051] See CCL, Can. 1108, § 3.
[1052] See CCL, Can. 1143.
[1053] See CCL, Can. 1108.
[1054] See CCL, Can. 1109, § 2.
[1055] See CCL, Can. 1109, § 3.
[1056] See CCL, Can. 1103, § 1.
[1057] See CCL, Can. 1103, § 2.

Whenever marriage was contracted in danger of death or in other extraordinary circumstances without the assistance of the parish priest or his delegate,[1058] then any other priest who was present, and otherwise the witnesses, are severally obliged together with the contracting parties to see to it that the marriage is entered in the registers of marriages and Baptisms as soon as possible.[1059]

The obligation to make these entries is *grave*, since their purpose—the recording of the state of the parties—is grave. The entries must be made without delay, i.e., within at least three days; otherwise, omissions or inaccuracies may occur through forgetfulness.

A marriage of conscience must not be entered in the ordinary register of marriages and Baptisms, but in a special register kept in the episcopal curia.[1060]

IMPEDIMENTS TO MARRIAGE

This chapter is divided into four articles: 1) Definition and Kinds of Impediments; 2) The Prohibiting Impediments; 3) The Annulling Impediments; 4) Dispensation from Impediments.

Art. 1. Definition and Kinds of Impediment

884. DEFINITION. *An impediment to marriage is any circumstance which prevents the marriage contract between two persons being valid or at least lawful.*

Although the impediment may exist in only one of the parties, e.g., insufficient age, marriage is either illicit or invalid for both.[1061] "Matrimonium nequit claudicare."

Impediments *of the natural and divine laws* are binding on all men; impediments *of ecclesiastical law* affect the baptized only (whether Catholic or non-Catholic). Unbaptized persons are indirectly obliged by these impediments when they wish to contract marriage with a baptized person, because of the same principle quoted already: "Matrimonium nequit claudicare." —*Annulling impediments of the civil law* are not obligatory unless both parties are unbaptized.

885. KINDS.

1. *By reason of their effects*, impediments are either *annulling* (diriment) if they seriously forbid and invalidate an attempted marriage, or *prohibiting* if they seriously forbid but do not invalidate the marriage;[1062]

2. *By reason of their origin*, impediments arise either *from the natural law* (e.g., impotency), or *from the divine positive law* (e.g., the bond of a previous marriage), or *from the ecclesiastical law* (e.g., affinity);

[1058] See no. 879ff.
[1059] See CCL, Can. 1103, § 3.
[1060] See CCL, Can. 1107.
[1061] See CCL, Can. 1036, § 3.
[1062] See CCL, Can. 1036.

3. *By reason of their scope*, impediments are either *absolute* if they prevent marriage being contracted with any person (e.g., the bond of an existing marriage), or *relative* if they forbid marriage with a particular person (e.g., consanguinity);

4. *By reason of the way in which they are known*, impediments are either *public* or *occult*, depending on whether they can be proved in the external forum or not;[1063]

5. *By reason of their liability to dispensation*, some impediments are *capable of being dispensed*, others are not. The former are further distinguished, according as they can be dispensed with greater or less ease and according to the manner of their dispensation, into:

minor and *major* impediments. There are five *minor* impediments:[1064]

a) consanguinity in the third collateral degree;

b) affinity in the second collateral degree;

c) public propriety in the second degree;

d) spiritual relationship;

e) crime arising from adultery with either promise to marry or attempted civil marriage.

All other impediments are *major*.

886. **AUTHOR.** The Holy See alone has the right to state authoritatively in what circumstances the divine law prohibits or annuls marriage. This is self-evident, since no one apart from the Holy See has the right to give an *authentic* interpretation of divine law. Furthermore, she possesses the *privative* right (i.e., to the exclusion of all other authorities) of declaring in the form of a general or particular law other annulling or prohibiting impediments which will be binding on the baptized.[1065] Regarding the unbaptized, the State seems to possess the power of establishing annulling impediments. Special consideration will be given below to the prohibition of particular marriages—the so-called prohibition of the Church.

Custom is no longer able to introduce or abrogate any impediment.[1066]

The *cessation* of impediments will be discussed in no. 921.

Art. 2. The Prohibitory Impediments

INTRODUCTION. For a long time, the prohibiting impediments have been numbered differently, some authors giving nine, others eight, others six, and others five. In the new Code three only are given: the impediment of simple vow; that of legal relationship; and the impediment of difference of religion. In order to

---

[1063] See CCL, Can. 1037. In order for an impediment to become public it is sufficient for the fact giving rise to the impediment to be public (see P.C.C.J., June 25, 1932: AAS 24, 284).

[1064] See CCL, Can. 1042.

[1065] See CCL, Can. 1038.

[1066] See CCL, Can. 1041.

avoid confusion, it has been thought better to follow the old verse which lists five prohibitory impediments:

Ecclesiae vetitum, tempus, sponsalia, votum,
Cultusque impediunt mixtus, sed facta valebunt.

887. I. THE PROHIBITION OF THE CHURCH is a *particular precept* (not a law) by which the Holy See or local ordinary forbids a particular marriage for a just cause.

1. *The Holy See* usually attaches such a prohibition: *a) to the dispensation from a public and perpetual vow of chastity* granted to allow the individual to contract a specific marriage: "if he or she outlives the other party, he (or she) must abstain forever from any further marriage"; *b) to a dispensation from a ratified marriage granted because of impotency*: "the man (or woman) is forbidden to contract any other marriage without first consulting the Holy See"; *c) to a dispensation granted from the impediment of abduction*: "if the man mentioned in the dispensation outlives the woman, he must abstain from any further marriage."

The Holy See alone can attach to its prohibition the pain of invalidity, so that the prohibition then assumes the form of an annulling impediment.[1067]

2. A *local ordinary* can forbid anyone actually staying in his diocese (including, therefore, travelers and those with no fixed abode), and his subjects also while they are outside his diocese, to contract marriage, if there is some special reason, and only *for the time* that the reason lasts,[1068] e.g., when there is suspected some hidden impediment or when there is fear of grave harm—especially spiritual harm—resulting from the marriage.

Obligation and cessation. This prohibition of the Church binds under grave sin both the contracting parties and the priest invited to assist at the marriage. But it is always permissible to have recourse to legitimate ecclesiastical authority. The prohibition ceases when it is revoked by the ecclesiastical superior concerned.

888. II. THE FORBIDDEN OR CLOSED TIMES are those periods when the solemn blessing of marriage is forbidden. But according to common law, marriage itself may be contracted any time of the year.[1069] "The solemn nuptial blessing of marriage is forbidden from the First Sunday in Advent to Christmas Day inclusive, and from Ash Wednesday to Easter Sunday inclusive. But the local ordinary may permit marriage during these periods for a good reason, without prejudice to liturgical laws, but the parties must be warned to refrain from excessive pomp."[1070]

Therefore, present discipline on this matter is much less severe.

889. III. BETROTHAL legitimately contracted constitutes a prohibitory impediment in respect of any other marriage, since it is an onerous promise which cannot be

---

[1067] See CCL, Can. 1039, § 2.
[1068] See CCL, Can. 1039, § 1.
[1069] See CCL, Can. 1108, § 1.
[1070] CCL, Can. 1108, § 2 and 3.

broken except by permission of the other party or by legitimate dissolution of the betrothal or by dispensation.[1071]

890. IV. THE VOW which constitutes a prohibiting impediment to marriage is not a *solemn* vow (which not merely prohibits but also annuls marriage) but a *simple* vow which is the cause of obligations incompatible with the married state. There are five such vows.[1072]

1. *The vow of virginity* has for its object the preservation of bodily integrity, and therefore anyone bound by this vow commits grave sin by contracting marriage, unless in a very exceptional case there was moral certainty that this vow would not be violated, e.g., if the other party agreed to respect the vow. Once virginity has been lost through sexual intercourse, the vow has become impossible of observance and consequently is no longer binding.

2. *The vow of perfect chastity* has for its object the observance of complete chastity, externally and internally. Therefore, any person under such a vow commits grave sin by contracting marriage, unless in a very exceptional case there exists moral certainty that this vow will not be violated by marriage; if, nevertheless, marriage is contracted contrary to the law, the person bound by vow cannot ask for the marriage dues first, but he (or she) is bound to render them when legitimately asked, since the other party has a right to them.

3. *The vow of celibacy* has for its object the exclusion of marriage, and therefore anyone bound by this vow commits grave sin by contracting marriage, but if marriage is contracted such a person can lawfully give and request the marriage dues.

4. *The vow of receiving sacred Orders* renders the contract of marriage gravely unlawful, since it makes the fulfillment of the vow morally impossible. However, if marriage is contracted, the person under the vow may lawfully request and render the marriage dues. If he is subsequently freed from the bond of marriage, he must abide by his original vow, that is still possible.

5. *The vow of entering the religious life* obliges and ceases in the same way as the vow of receiving sacred Orders.

NOTE. Confessors with the privileges of mendicants cannot dispense from *public* vows, but may dispense from all *private* vows with the exception of the vows of perfect chastity and of entering a religious order with solemn vows, if such vows have been made unconditionally after the age of eighteen. Not only in danger of death but also in other cases when all preparations for marriage have been made and the marriage cannot be postponed without the probable danger of grave harm until the dispensation is obtained from the competent superior, a parish priest or confessor may dispense from any of these five vows.[1073]

[1071] See no. 867.
[1072] See CCL, Can. 1058, § 1.
[1073] See no. 927ff.

891. V. The impediment of MIXED RELIGION exists between two persons, one of whom is a Catholic and the other a member of a non-Catholic or schismatic sect. The Code of Canon Law, Can. 1060, gives the following instruction: "The Church forbids most severely and in all countries marriage between two baptized persons, one of whom is a Catholic and the other a member of a heretical or schismatic sect; if there is danger of perversion for the Catholic party and the offspring, such marriages are forbidden also by divine law."

THE DUTY OF THE ORDINARY AND OTHER PASTORS OF SOULS IN THE AVOIDANCE OF MIXED MARRIAGES.[1074]

1. Priests must use all their energy and power of persuasion and even rebukes to deter the faithful from mixed marriages. This purpose is more readily achieved if in each country all pastors of souls would *unite together in a common plan.*

2. If they cannot prevent these marriages, they should endeavor by all means possible to see to it that they are not contracted against the laws of God and those of the Church, i.e., they must ensure that the promises are given, as will be discussed later.

3. After any mixed marriage in their own or in another parish, they must carefully see to it that those who contracted such a marriage live up to their promises.

892. The DISPENSATION required for the lawful celebration of a mixed marriage is reserved to the Holy See, namely, the Holy Office. In what way the local ordinary, or parish priest, or confessor, may grant a dispensation from this impediment in danger of death and in any other urgent case is indicated below, in the section devoted to dispensation from all impediments, no. 924ff.

CONDITIONS REQUIRED FOR GRANTING A DISPENSATION FROM THE IMPEDIMENT OF DIF-FERENCE OF RELIGION.

The Church does not grant such a dispensation, unless:

1. *there are good and serious reasons*, e.g., a grave danger of contracting a purely civil marriage or marriage in the presence of a non-Catholic minister;

2. *the non-Catholic party promises to remove all danger of perversion of the Catholic party, and both parties promise that all their children shall be baptized and brought up as Catholics: such promises are normally to be made in writing;*[1075]

3. *there is moral certainty that the promises will be kept.*[1076]

893. DUTIES OF THE CONTRACTING PARTIES.

1. The Catholic party must prudently endeavor to convert the non-Catholic partner,[1077] e.g., by prayer, by the good example of a Christian life, by exhortation, and so on.

[1074] See CCL, Can. 1064.
[1075] See Instruction of the Holy Office, Jan. 14, 1932 (AAS 24, 25).
[1076] See CCL, Can. 1061.
[1077] See CCL, Can. 1062.

THE SACRAMENTS IN GENERAL AND IN PARTICULAR

2. The parties to a mixed marriage are not allowed either before or after their Catholic wedding to approach either in person or through proxies a non-Catholic minister *as such* to give or renew their consent. If the parish priest knows that the parties will certainly violate this law, he shall not assist at their marriage unless there are *very* serious reasons and provided that all scandal has been removed and the ordinary has been consulted. But the Church does not censure those parties who are forced by civil law to appear before a non-Catholic minister, *acting as an official of the government*—but their intention must be merely to comply with the requirements of law for the sake of securing the civil effects of marriage.[1078]

THE EXTERNAL RITE FOR THE CELEBRATION OF MIXED MARRIAGES. By common law, all sacred rites are forbidden in mixed marriages, and therefore the parish priest must ask for and receive the matrimonial consent of the parties in a suitable place without wearing any sacred vestments. But if greater evils are foreseen to follow from this prohibition, the local ordinary may allow some of the usual church ceremonies, with the exception of the celebration of Mass.[1079]

894. PASSIVE ASSISTANCE at mixed marriages whereby the parish priest merely fulfills the role of a qualified witness *without using any sacred rite* (i.e., without sacred vestments and outside a sacred place) and afterward records the consent of the parties in the register of marriages, is not at present recognized by common law as being either valid or lawful.[1080] In some countries, however, (e.g., in Chile, Austria, Hungary, and in certain dioceses of Germany) in order to avoid greater evils the Holy See has permitted passive assistance at mixed marriages when the parties stubbornly refuse to give the necessary guarantees.[1081] But these indults seem to have been revoked by the decree of the Holy Office already quoted.

895. PENALTIES inflicted on those who contract a mixed marriage contrary to the law.

1. Catholics who have dared to contract such a marriage, even though validly, without a dispensation from the Church are by that very fact excluded from legitimate ecclesiastical acts and from the use of the sacramentals, until a dispensation is obtained from the ordinary.[1082] Unlawful but valid mixed marriages cannot be contracted in present circumstances, except *a)* where passive assistance is both valid and lawful; *b)* in danger of death and in those cases when marriage can be contracted validly before two witnesses only.[1083]

2. Those who contract marriage in the presence of a non-Catholic minister incur excommunication reserved to the ordinary.[1084] Such marriages are always invalid.

[1078] See CCL, Can. 1063.
[1079] See CCL, Can. 1102, § 2.
[1080] See Holy Office, Nov. 26, 1919.
[1081] See MIC, q. 334.
[1082] See CCL, Can. 2375.
[1083] See no. 879ff.
[1084] See CCL, Can. 2319, § 1, no. 1.

896. SCHOLIUM. MARRIAGE OF A PUBLIC SINNER. Because of the grave dangers which will ensue, the faithful are to be discouraged from contracting marriage with notorious apostates from the Faith, even though they have not joined a non-Catholic sect, and with notorious members of any sect condemned by the Church, e.g., the society of Freemasons. The parish priest shall not assist at such marriages without first consulting the ordinary who may permit him to assist at such a marriage, provided there are serious reasons, if a) sufficient safeguard is made for the Catholic education of the children, and b) all danger of perversion of the Catholic party is removed.[1085]

If a public sinner or a person known to be under censure, e.g., a formal socialist or anarchist, refuses to go to confession and be reconciled with the Church prior to marriage, the parish priest shall not assist at the marriage unless there is grave and urgent reason, concerning which he should consult the ordinary, if it is possible.[1086]

Art. 3. The Diriment (or Annulling) Impediments

897. INTRODUCTION. The Church displays such great wisdom in instituting these impediments that her directions are frequently adopted even by the civil authorities for civil marriages.

All these impediments have as their primary effect the *invalidating* of attempted marriages; the element of *punishment* to be found in some of them, e.g., in the impediments of crime and public propriety, is quite secondary, and consequently ignorance never excuses from these impediments.

The *purpose* which the Church intends by these diriment impediments is a) the public good; b) the good of the contracting parties; c) the good of religion.

The *number* of annulling impediments is variously reckoned, still more so now because in the new Code the impediments of error, violence, and fear are included in the chapter "On Matrimonial Consent," and the impediment of clandestinity in the chapter "On the Form of Celebration of Marriage." We shall discuss the following fourteen impediments:

1) error (and servile condition); 2) duress and fear; 3) abduction; 4) impotency; 5) existing marriage bond; 6) insufficient age; 7) disparity of worship; 8) major Orders and religious profession; 9) crime; 10) consanguinity; 11) affinity; 12) public propriety; 13) spiritual relationship; 14) legal relationship.

1. The Impediments of Error and of Servile Condition

898. DEFINITIONS. Error and servile condition are sometimes considered as two distinct impediments, although in effect they are one, having a twofold material object. Error affects either the actual person and the qualities of that person, or the servile condition or status of one of the parties. In the first case there exists the impediment of error, in the second case the impediment of servile condition.[1087]

[1085] See CCL, Can. 1065.
[1086] See CCL, Can. 1066.
[1087] For the various kinds of error, see MTM, vol. 3, no. 787.

FIRST PRINCIPLE. *By natural law, only substantial error is an annulling impediment to marriage.*

The reason is that only substantial error renders a genuine marital consent, and therefore marriage itself, impossible.

Substantial error exists in three cases:

1. if a *mistake is made regarding the actual person with whom marriage is contracted.* Such an error (as existed in the marriage of Jacob with Leah) is hardly possible in modern conditions, at least when the marriage is not contracted by proxy.

2. if a *mistake is made concerning a certain quality of one of the parties which amounts to an error regarding the person.*[1088]

This type of error is never recognized in the external forum as a diriment impediment unless the quality was expressly mentioned as a condition sine qua non. Consequently, the same rules apply in this case as for any marriage contracted conditionally. The Code states concerning such a condition: "If the condition is either of the past or the present, the marriage is valid if the condition is verified, but invalid if it is not verified."[1089]

3. if a mistake is made *regarding the three benefits of marriage*; namely, offspring, conjugal fidelity, and the Sacrament.

Thus, for example, a virgin who does not know that marriage is a permanent union for the procreation of children cannot contract a valid marriage.[1090] The mere error concerning the unity and indissolubility or sacramental dignity of marriage does not annul the matrimonial consent, even if the error was the cause of the consent.[1091] But a different situation arises if some explicit condition is made contrary to the unity or indissolubility of marriage: "If either one or both parties *by a positive act of the will* exclude the contract itself or all right to the conjugal act or any of the essential qualities of marriage, the marriage is null and void."[1092]

The error is accidental and not substantial if one of the parties was gravely mistaken or deceived about the wealth, health, or moral character of the other; such marriages are valid.

899. SECOND PRINCIPLE. *By ecclesiastical law, error regarding the servile condition of one of the parties is a diriment impediment to marriage.*

Such is the teaching of the Code, Can. 1083: "Error concerning some quality of the person renders a marriage invalid, if a free person contracts with another believed to be free when he, or she, is in fact a slave properly so-called." Slavery in the strict sense of the word is today almost universally unknown, since it

---

[1088] See CCL, Can. 1083, § 2.
[1089] Can. 1092, no. 4.
[1090] See CCL, Can. 1082.
[1091] See CCL, Can. 1084.
[1092] CCL, Can. 1086, § 2.

only exists when a master possesses a servant in such a way that he can sell or exchange him as though he were a thing.

The impediment does not exist: 1) if a free person *knowingly* marries a slave; 2) if one slave marries another; 3) if a slave marries someone whom he supposes to be free but who is in fact a slave.

A DISPENSATION from the impediment caused by *substantial* error can be granted by no one but the Holy See, since it is an impediment of the natural law. Therefore, such marriages can be rendered valid only by the person who erred renewing his, or her, consent.

2. The Impediments of Duress and Fear

The DEFINITIONS of duress and fear have been given already in no. 26ff.

900. FIRST PRINCIPLE. *By natural law marriage is null and void if contracted under the influence of physical violence or of that form of fear which completely disturbs the use of reason.*

This is agreed by all, since in such circumstances there is no genuine matrimonial consent and therefore no marriage.

SECOND PRINCIPLE. *By ecclesiastical law, and probably by natural law also, marriage is null and void if contracted under the influence of fear which is a) grave (absolutely or relatively considered); b) unjustly inflicted by an outside free agency; c) of such a nature that a person is forced to choose marriage.*

The Code states: "Marriage is invalid if contracted by grave fear or force unjustly inflicted by an outside agency, and by which a person was forced to choose marriage as a means to free himself from the force or threats. No other fear, even if it is the cause of the contract, renders marriage null and void."[1093]

There are many learned authors who maintain that even *by the natural law* marriage is null and void if entered upon through grave fear, e.g., St. Raymond de Pennafort, St. Thomas, Reiffenstuel, Wernz, and so on, because while such fear exists, although it is true that other human acts are possible, the contract of marriage which of its nature is incapable of being rescinded cannot be made fittingly. — It follows from this that not only Christian marriages but also pagan marriages are rendered invalid if contracted under such fear. This must be carefully considered in practice, since marriages between pagans are frequently contracted under the influence of grave fear inflicted unjustly.

CASES. 1. A person living in concubinage who contracts marriage in danger of death through a vivid fear of hell contracts a valid marriage, since the fear is not inflicted unjustly. Similarly, marriage is valid if entered upon by a youth who has seduced a virgin and whose father now compels him through grave fear either to marry her or to make reparation for the harm caused.

2. A marriage laboring under the impediment of fear is not only contracted invalidly but also remains invalid so long as the party under the influence of fear does

---

[1093] CCL, Can. 1087.

not give a free consent in the recognized form. Consequently, the right remains of asking for a marriage contracted through fear to be declared invalid even after several years of married life and the birth of children.

A DISPENSATION from this impediment is not granted by the Church; consequently, in order to convalidate a marriage contracted under the influence of fear, it is necessary that the matrimonial consent be given freely in the presence of the parish priest and two witnesses, if the impediment is *well known*; otherwise, it is sufficient for the party suffering from grave fear to give his or her consent privately in some external sign, so long as the consent of the other party persists at least virtually.

3. The Impediment of Abduction

901. DEFINITION. *The impediment is caused by the forcible abduction of a woman from a safe place to one which is not safe with a view to contracting marriage with her.*

EXPLANATION. In order that abduction constitute an annulling impediment, distinct from the impediments of duress and fear, there is required:

1. *the forcible abduction of a woman from a safe place to one which is not safe*: that is to say, the woman must be removed from a place in which she was safe to another place physically and morally distinct from the first, in which she is no longer safe, e.g., from one city to another city; the removal must be *forced*, i.e., *contrary to the will of the woman*. The force may be either *physical* (*raptus violentiae*), or *moral* (*raptus seductionis*) which is exercised through grave fear, deceit, guile, hypnotic suggestion. If the woman willingly consents to her abduction, then it is an elopement rather than an abduction, and no impediment ensues.

2. *the abduction of a woman*; therefore, the impediment does not arise if a man is forcibly abducted;

3. *with a view to contracting marriage with her*. Therefore, the purpose of abduction must not be the satisfaction of lust, or a desire for revenge;

4. The *forcible detention* of a woman is equivalent to forcible abduction, as, when the man forcibly detains a woman with the intention of marrying her in the place where she lives, or to which she came of her own free will. This is stated in the Code, Can. 1074, § 3, thus bringing to an end the controversy which existed on this point.

CESSATION of the impediment. This impediment ceases not by dispensation but through the release of the woman. "If the abducted woman, after having been separated from the man and attained complete freedom consents to marry him, the impediment ceases."[1094] However, in danger of death the confessor or parish priest may dispense from this impediment, even though the woman has not been placed at full liberty, provided that her consent is perfectly free.

PENALTIES for abduction. "Those men who with a view to marriage or for the satisfaction of lust have abducted a woman against her will through force or

[1094] CCL, Can. 1074, § 2.

deceit, or who elope with a girl of minor age without the knowledge or consent of her parents, even though she herself is willing, are ipso facto deprived of the right to legal ecclesiastical actions and shall incur other penalties according to the gravity of the offense."[1095] Other punishments inflicted by ancient law are now revoked. — Even civil law usually punishes with severity men guilty of rape.

4. The Impediment of Impotency

902. DEFINITION. *The impediment of impotency arises from the impossibility of sexual intercourse, or, from some defect of mind or body or of both which prevents a person from exercising the act with another in the normal way.*

EXPLANATION. Impotency is not the same as sterility which neither prohibits nor annuls marriage.[1096] Sexual intercourse is regarded as impossible when the true and natural conjugal act cannot be performed. Sexual intercourse is rightly defined by Cardinal Gasparri: "the insertion of the male organ into the vagina of the woman with the emission of the seed."[1097] Therefore, if conjugal intercourse is possible, even though the procreation of children is impossible, e.g., in the case of a woman from whom both ovaries and the womb have been removed, the impediment of impotency does not exist. The *causes* which make sexual intercourse impossible are either *physical* or *mental*. Due to some physical defect the following persons suffer from this impediment: *a) men* who are eunuchs or who have been castrated, that is, who lack both testicles; similarly, those who lack the male organ or whose organ is so deformed that intercourse is impossible, e.g., in some cases of hypospadia and epispadia; *b) women* who possess no vagina or whose vagina is so small that intercourse is impossible, or who suffer from some incurable disease of the vagina. Due to mental defects men who are afflicted with complete sexual anaesthesia or with certain mental diseases suffer from this impediment.

It is probable that the impediment likewise arises from *vasectomy*, i.e., from the excision of the vas deferens. This surgical operation is performed frequently in these days.

KINDS. 1. Impotency is *antecedent* if it exists prior to marriage, *consequent* if it ensues after marriage.

2. Impotency is *permanent* if it will never cease; otherwise, it is *temporary*.

3. Impotency is *absolute* if it prevents sexual intercourse with all persons; it is *relative* if it prevents intercourse with some individual.

903. PRINCIPLE. "*Antecedent and permanent impotency, whether on the part of the man or the woman, whether known to the other or not, and whether absolute or relative, annuls marriage by the very law of nature. If the impediment is doubtful, either as to fact or as to law, marriage is not to be forbidden.*"[1098]

[1095] CCL, Can. 2353.
[1096] See CCL, Can. 1068, § 3.
[1097] *De Matrimonio*, vol. 1, no. 571.
[1098] CCL, Can. 1068.

There were some of the older theologians who maintained that impotency was not an impediment to marriage if it were known to both parties, but this opinion cannot now be held.

DUTY OF THE PARISH PRIEST AND CONFESSOR. If the confessor or parish priest is in any doubt whether a penitent about to contract marriage or already married is impotent or not, he must act with the greatest prudence.

a) If the doubt arises *before* marriage, the truth should be discovered by a skilled and trustworthy doctor. If the doubt persists, marriage is not to be forbidden, provided there exists a grave reason for marriage and both parties are aware of the doubtful impediment.

b) If the doubt should arise *after* marriage, the services of a skilled and trustworthy doctor should be used; if he *affirms* the existence of impotency, the two parties may be left in good faith for a grave reason. But if they are in bad faith, i.e., they know of the impediment, they can and must separate spontaneously from each other so far as conjugal relations are concerned, but complete separation (of the bond and of life together) is impossible without permission of the Holy See. — If the existence of impotency still remains in doubt even after serious inquiry, the parties are permitted the use of marriage, even though carnal intercourse cannot be performed perfectly.

5. The Impediment of an Existing Bond

904. DEFINITION. *The impediment of an existing bond consists in the incapability of contracting a new marriage while the bond of a previous marriage, whether ratified or consummated, still endures.*

This impediment is founded on natural law and on divine positive law. We have discussed already[1099] how a ratified marriage may be dissolved by solemn religious profession and by papal dispensation, and how a legitimate marriage may be dissolved by the Pauline privilege. But even though the first marriage be, for some reason, invalid or dissolved, it is not lawful for Catholics to contract another marriage until legal proof of the invalidity or dissolution of the previous marriage is obtained.[1100] Consequently, especially when the death of a former spouse is in doubt, a *death certificate* must be obtained not only from the civil authority but also from ecclesiastical authority.[1101]

PENALTIES INFLICTED ON THOSE IGNORING THIS IMPEDIMENT.

1. If a person contracts a new marriage *in good faith* while still bound by the tie of a former marriage, he incurs no ecclesiastical penalty, but the two parties must separate immediately from each other, once the truth is discovered.

[1099] See no. 849ff.
[1100] See CCL, Can. 1069, § 2.
[1101] The manner in which such a document may be obtained is discussed in MTM, vol. 3, no. 806.

2. Anyone who *knowingly* attempts a second marriage while bound by a former one incurs ipso facto:

a) the impediment of crime;[1102]

b) irregularity through bigamy;[1103]

c) infamy of law.[1104]

If the person continues to live in unlawful union after ignoring the admonition given by the local ordinary, he incurs excommunication or personal interdict according to the gravity of the offense.[1105]

6. The Impediment of Age

905. DEFINITION. *The impediment of age arises from the absence of the age required by ecclesiastical law for a valid marriage.*

It is stated in the Code, Can. 1067: "A male before his sixteenth year of age completed and a female before her fourteenth year of age completed cannot contract a valid marriage. Although marriage is valid when these years are completed, pastors of souls should dissuade young people from marriage at an earlier age than is commonly the custom in their respective countries."

Since this impediment is instituted by ecclesiastical law, it does not affect the unbaptized and therefore marriages contracted by pagans before the canonical ages are valid.

7. The Impediment of Disparity of Worship

906. DEFINITION. *"The impediment of disparity of worship annuls marriage contracted between a person not baptized and another baptized in the Catholic Church, or received into the Church from heresy or schism."*[1106]

EXPLANATION. This impediment is founded on ecclesiastical law and therefore (according to present discipline) does not bind Protestants or others baptized outside the Catholic Church. Accordingly, if a Protestant contracts marriage with a Jewish girl, he is not bound by this impediment. So far as marriage is concerned, doubtful Baptism is regarded as being valid. If a person at the time of the marriage was commonly held to have been baptized, or if the Baptism was doubtful, the validity of such marriage must be upheld, until it is proved with certainty that one party was baptized and the other was not.[1107] But when it is known for *certain* that a doubtful Baptism was in fact invalid, the marriage cannot be rescinded *on private authority* on the grounds that there existed an impediment of disparity

---

[1102] See no. 908.
[1103] See CCL, Can. 984, no. 4.
[1104] See CCL, Can. 2356.
[1105] Ibid.
[1106] CCL, Can. 1070, § 1.
[1107] See CCL, Can. 1070, § 2.

of worship, but the authority of the local ordinary must be invoked who, after having summoned the parties and having given the *defensor vinculi* opportunity to examine into the case, may declare the nullity of the marriage.[1108]

CESSATION of the impediment.

1. The impediment ceases if the unbaptized party *receives valid Baptism* and the consent of both parties is renewed legitimately.

2. The impediment also ceases *if a dispensation is granted by the Holy See* (i.e., the Holy Office). In granting such a dispensation which in danger of death or in other urgent cases may be given by the local ordinary, parish priest, or confessor, all the promises must be obtained, such as were required for a dispensation from the impediment of mixed religion.[1109]

8. The Impediments of Sacred Orders and of Religious Profession

907. PRESENT DISCIPLINE. Marriage is invalid if attempted by:

1. clerics in major Orders;[1110]

2. religious who have taken solemn vows or whose simple vows have by a special law of the Holy See the power to annul marriage.[1111]

EXPLANATION. THE IMPEDIMENT OF MAJOR ORDERS. In the *Oriental* Church, only bishops, priests, and deacons are forbidden to marry, but in the *Latin* Church the prohibition extends to subdeacons. It is necessary that the major Order should have been received validly and freely, without grave fear having been unjustly inflicted, and with sufficient knowledge of the obligation of celibacy. Otherwise, the impediment will not exist, unless after the fear was removed he ratified his ordination at least tacitly by the exercise of the Order received with the intention of subjecting himself to the obligations of the major Orders.[1112]

CESSATION of the impediment. It is most difficult for a cleric to be freed from this impediment. The extent of a confessor's faculties in danger of death will be discussed below, no. 927.

THE IMPEDIMENT OF RELIGIOUS PROFESSION. The vows which render marriage impossible are:

1. *solemn* vows taken in religious orders strictly so-called;

2. *simple* vows taken by Jesuits.[1113]

CESSATION of the impediment. It is easier to be freed from this impediment than from the former.

[1108] See CCL, Can. 1990.
[1109] See no. 892; see also CCL, Can. 1071.
[1110] See CCL, Can. 1072.
[1111] See CCL, Can. 1073.
[1112] See CCL, Can. 214.
[1113] See Gregory XIII, Constitution *Ascendente Domino* (May 25, 1584).

PENALTIES inflicted on clerics and religious solemnly professed who attempt marriage, are:

1. *excommunication* simply reserved to the Holy See;[1114]

2. *irregularity arising from crime* (from analogous bigamy);[1115]

3. *dismissal from their order*.[1116] Religious who attempt or contract even civil marriage are by that very fact considered as having been legitimately dismissed;

4. *those punishments inflicted on clerics leading a life of concubinage*.[1117]

9. The Impediment of Crime

908. DEFINITION. *The impediment of crime is the law of the Church which denies valid marriage to those who have committed either adultery or murder of the consort with varying degrees of malice.*

EXPLANATION. There are three degrees of malice with which adultery may be committed: 1) with an added promise of subsequent marriage; 2) with attempted marriage; 3) with murder of the consort. The malice of conjugicide is increased when it is committed by mutual cooperation. Therefore, there are four cases in which the impediment of crime exists:

1. *adultery with an added promise of marriage;*

2. *adultery accompanied by attempted marriage;*

3. *adultery accompanied by murder of the consort committed by one of the adulterous parties;*

4. *murder of the consort committed by mutual cooperation.*

The older authors used to distinguish three different cases in which the impediment arose by these words: by *joint* commission of murder—the fourth case; by *individual* commission of murder—the third case; by *neither* committing murder—the first and second cases.

909. I. ADULTERY WITH AN ADDED PROMISE OF MARRIAGE.

In order that the impediment of crime be contracted in this way, it is necessary:

THAT THE ADULTERY BE:

1. *true* adultery, so that a genuine, valid marriage is violated;

2. *formal in both parties*, i.e., both parties must realize that they are causing injury to one and the same marriage (or to two marriages)—in other words, each must realize that one of them is married, and it is not sufficient if each is only aware of his own married state;

[1114] See CCL, Can. 2388.
[1115] See CCL, Can. 985, no. 3.
[1116] See CCL, Can. 646, § 1, no. 3.
[1117] See CCL, Can. 2359.

3. *consummated*, i.e., by complete sexual intercourse which of its nature is directed to the procreation of children. Therefore, sexual intercourse accompanied by onanism would not be sufficient.

THAT THE PROMISE BE:

1. *genuine and serious*. Therefore, a fictitious promise is insufficient, so also would be a mere desire or proposal of marriage;

2. *free*, and not obtained through grave fear;

3. *mutual*. The Code[1118] requires that each party give to the other a promise of subsequent marriage;

4. *absolute*, or at least, if made conditionally, that the condition be verified;

5. *made in the course of the same marriage*, i.e., both the adultery and the promise must take place during the same legitimate marriage. Therefore, for example, the impediment would not arise if Peter promised to marry Bertha, then marries Anne, and during this latter marriage commits adultery with Bertha.

910. II. ADULTERY COMBINED WITH ATTEMPTED MARRIAGE.

1. The act of *adultery* must fulfill the conditions given already for the first case.

2. An *attempt at marriage* exists when a man and woman being aware of the impediment of an existing bond of marriage truly and seriously give their consent to each other in words referring to the present, whether publicly or secretly. Such attempts at marriage are today frequent in *civil* marriages contracted by one of the parties after obtaining a civil divorce from a previous valid marriage. The impediment of crime would not exist if both parties intended no more than to live in concubinage, or if one party were unaware of the bond of a previous marriage.

911. III. ADULTERY COMBINED WITH MURDER OF CONSORT COMMITTED BY ONE OF THE PARTIES.

1. The act of *adultery* must fulfill the conditions previously given.

2. *The act of murder*:

a) must *result in actual death* caused by the physical or moral action of one of the parties;

b) must *have as its motive marriage with the accomplice* in the act of adultery.

Therefore, if murder is committed for some other reason, e.g., out of hatred, the impediment does not arise.

912. IV. MURDER OF CONSORT COMMITTED BY MUTUAL COOPERATION. In this instance adultery is not required, although in practice it is usually present. The murder must be:

1. *true*, i.e., murder of a true consort (and not of a putative one);

2. *committed by mutual cooperation*, i.e., there must exist a mutual plan directed toward the murder of a consort. Therefore, each must exercise a genuine influence on the death of the consort; subsequent approval of the act would not be sufficient;

[1118] See Can. 1075, no. 1.

3. *committed with the intention of marrying the accomplice.*

913. THIS IMPEDIMENT MAY BE MULTIPLE:

1. if two or more marriages are injured;

2. if *different* crimes are committed in respect of the same marriage, but not if the same crime is repeated, e.g., when during the same marriage two accomplices commit several acts of adultery and make several promises of marriage.

CESSATION of the impediment. This impediment is removed by legitimate dispensation, which is not normally granted if the murder of the consort is publicly known. When the impediment arises from adultery accompanied by promise of marriage or attempted marriage, it is considered to be a minor impediment, as stated already.

NOTE. Although this impediment possesses also a penal character, ignorance of it is not admitted as an excuse.

10. The Impediment of Consanguinity

914. DEFINITION. *The impediment of consanguinity or natural relationship is the intimate union existing between persons belonging to the same stock through carnal descent, which invalidates marriage within certain degrees.*

EXPLANATION. In order to determine and measure consanguinity correctly, three points must be borne in mind: the stock, the line, and the various degrees of relationship.

1. The *stock* (root, trunk) of the descendants is that person (male or female) from whom the parties about to be married are descended by birth as from a common source. Thus, for example, a grandfather is the common stock of all his grandchildren.

2. The *line* is the natural *series of persons* springing from the same stock. The line is *direct* if we consider either the descent of individuals from each other (direct descent: grandfather, father, son) or their ascent to a common stock (direct ascending line: son, father, grandfather); the line is *collateral* in the case of several individuals having one and the same stock, but not being descended *from each other*, e.g., brother and sister do not stem from each other but from the same stock, that is, their father.—If those about to marry are equidistant from a common stock, as in the example of brother and sister, the collateral line is said to be *equal*; otherwise, it is *unequal*.

3. The *degree* of relationship is the measure of the distance from a common ancestor, and the following rules are used:

a) In the direct line, the number of degrees is the same as the number of generations, or (which comes to the same thing), *the number of degrees is the same as the number of persons, omitting the ancestor*; e.g., between grandfather and grandson there are two degrees because there are two generations, the grandfather giving birth to the father, and the father to the son — or, to put it in another way, there are three persons counting the ancestor, namely, grandfather, father, and son.

b) In the collateral line, when direct degrees are equal, the number of degrees is the same as the number of generations (or persons omitting the common stock) *in either line of descent*; e.g., between cousins there are two degrees collateral, because there are two generations from a common stock in either line of descent.

c) In the collateral line, when the direct degrees are not equal, there are as many degrees as there are generations in the longer line of descent;[1119] and thus the less remote degree has to be adjusted to the more remote degree; e.g., if there are three generations in one line of descent and two in the other, it is customary to say that the parties about to be married are related to each other in the third degree touching the second.

In order to discover and count the degrees of consanguinity more easily, the text of the old canon law carried a so-called tree of consanguinity; this we reproduce below with the changes made necessary by the new law.

Fig. 1

[1119] See CCL, Can. 96.

915. KINDS OF CONSANGUINITY.

a) Consanguinity is *legitimate* if the act of generation took place in legitimate marriage; it is *illegitimate* if the birth occurred outside of marriage. Illegitimate children can be legitimated, as will be shown later, no. 942.

b) Consanguinity is *complete* (perfect) if the persons related to each other are descended from the same *two* parents; it is *less complete* (imperfect) if they are descended from the same father or from the same mother. — Brothers having the same father but not the same mother are known as "half-brothers" *(consanguinei)*; those having the same mother but not the same father are called "brothers uterine"; those having the same mother and the same father are known as "brothers german."

c) Consanguinity may exist either *on the father's side* or *on the mother's side.*

d) Consanguinity is *simple* if two persons related to each other are descendants of one and the same ancestor; it is *multiple* if their common stock is multiple. This is the explanation adopted in the present discipline of the Church.[1120] Previously there were other instances of multiple consanguinity.

Since in practice difficulties often occur in discovering the existence of multiple consanguinity, it is advisable to give a somewhat fuller explanation of two cases of such relationship.

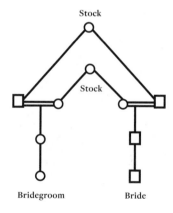

Fig. 2
First Case

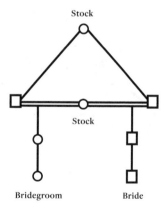

Fig. 3
Second Case

[1120] See CCL, Can. 1076, § 2.

MULTIPLE CONSANGUINITY. *First case.* In tracing back the line of two persons intending to marry it is discovered that the members of one family have intermarried with members of the other; e.g., two brothers of one family married two sisters of another. In this case there are two common stocks, as is evident from Fig. 2. The grandparents of the bridegroom and those of the bride were brothers and sisters. Therefore, the parties to be married are related to each other doubly in the third degree. As is immediately evident, it is possible to think of similar examples.

Second case. It is discovered that the ancestors of the parties intending to contract marriage were related to each other by blood, and one of them married successively two sisters, as indicated in the third figure. In this case there are two common stocks, and the parties are related to each other both in the second and in the third degree.

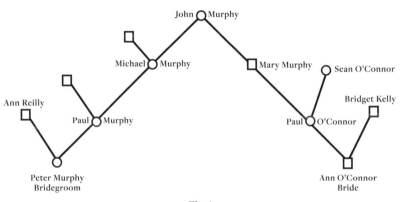

Fig. 4

NOTE. In applying for a dispensation from the impediment of consanguinity it must be stated whether the consanguinity is simple or multiple, whether it is perfect or imperfect, whether it exists in the direct or in the collateral lines. It is useful to include in the petition *a scheme* showing the relationship, such as is given in Fig. 4; in some dioceses such a scheme is expressly demanded in petitions from this impediment.

METHOD OF DISCOVERING THE DEGREE OF CONSANGUINITY. There are many methods suggested, but the following seems to be easier, clearer, and safer than any other. If the parish priest is in any doubt regarding the blood relationship of the parties presenting themselves for marriage, the names of both parties should be written on a large piece of paper, then above the name of the bridegroom insert the names of his ancestors, and above the name of the bride her ancestors. One then proceeds to count the number of intervening generations until one arrives at a common stock. The number of these generations between the common stock and the bridegroom gives the degree of consanguinity existing on his side; the number of generations between the common stock and the bride gives the degrees existing on her side. If, for example, there are found to be three generations on both sides, the parties are related to each other in the third degree collateral; see Fig. 4. If there are four generations on the side of the bridegroom from the common stock, and three on the side of the bride, the parties will be related to each other in the fourth degree collateral touching the third. In this latter case, a dispensation will not be required because, according to the principle already given, *the less remote degree must be adjusted to the more remote degree* and a dispensation is only required if the parties are related to each other in any degree up to the third inclusive. If the consanguinity is multiple, the degrees are to be reckoned from each of the common stocks, or according to the different lines in which it is possible to rise to a common stock.

916. EXTENT of this impediment.

a) In the *direct* line marriage is invalid between any two persons related by blood, whether they are legitimate or natural offspring.

b) In the *collateral* line the impediment extends to all who are related to each other in any degree up to the third inclusive.[1121]

An easy rule to give to the people and to use in practice in order to discover whether there exists an impediment of consanguinity in the collateral line is this: *no impediment exists unless the grandparents were brothers or sisters.*

CESSATION of this impediment. The impediment ceases to exist by lawful dispensation only, which is never granted in the direct line nor in the first degree collateral.[1122] Consanguinity in the third degree collateral is a minor impediment.[1123]

11. The Impediment of Affinity

917. DEFINITION. *Affinity is relationship by marriage whether consummated or not between a man and certain blood relations of his wife, and vice versa between a woman and certain blood relations of her husband.*[1124]

EXPLANATION. Prior to the new Code affinity arose from sexual intercourse whether licit (up to the fourth degree) or illicit (to the second degree collateral); but now it arises from Christian marriage only, and carnal intercourse is not essential. Consequent affinity which was admitted in the old law is no longer recognized.

NUMBERING OF THE DEGREES. The degrees of affinity are counted in such a way that *the blood relations of the husband are related by affinity to his wife in the same line*

[1121] See CCL, Can. 1076.
[1122] See CCL, Can. 1076, § 3.
[1123] See CCL, Can. 1042, § 2, no. 1.
[1124] See CCL, Can. 97, § 1 and 2.

and degree as they are related by consanguinity to him, and vice versa;[1125] or, in other words, there are as many degrees of affinity on one side as there are degrees of consanguinity on the other.

EXTENT OF THE IMPEDIMENT. The impediment extends indefinitely in the direct line and to the second degree inclusive in the collateral line. Therefore, the extent of the impediment has been greatly reduced. The following principle should be noted: *affinity does not cause affinity.* Therefore, no affinity exists between the blood relations of the husband and the blood relations of the wife; consequently, e.g., there is nothing to prevent two brothers marrying two sisters, or a father and son marrying a mother and daughter, or a son marrying a mother and his father marrying the daughter of that mother.

MULTIPLE AFFINITY. Affinity is multiple in two cases only;[1126]

1. where the consanguinity from which affinity arises is itself multiple;

2. by successive marriage with the blood relations of a deceased consort. Thus, e.g., if Peter marries two sisters, he has a double affinity with any third sister.

CESSATION OF THIS IMPEDIMENT. The impediment is removed by lawful dispensation which is *never* granted (not even in danger of death) in the direct line, if the affinity arises from consummated marriage. Affinity in the second degree collateral is included among the minor impediments, as previously indicated.

12. The Impediment of Public Propriety

918. DEFINITION. *The impediment of public propriety* (which is also known as quasi-affinity) *is the relationship between two persons arising from a) an invalid marriage, whether consummated or not; or b) from public or notorious concubinage.*[1127]

EXPLANATION. This impediment was introduced or at least expressed in this form by the new Code. The impediment known as that of public propriety existing previously was something entirely different, arising from betrothal (extending to the first degree) or from a ratified marriage (extending to the fourth degree inclusive). The new impediment resembles the former impediment of affinity which arose from illicit intercourse, but it goes much further insofar as it arises from any invalid marriage, even when the putative married parties are in good faith. If the impediment is caused by concubinage, the latter must be *public* or *notorious*; therefore, secret concubinage is not sufficient. A *civil* marriage contracted by a Catholic is regarded as public or notorious concubinage.[1128]

[1125] See CCL, Can. 97, § 3.
[1126] See CCL, Can. 1077, § 2.
[1127] See CCL, Can. 1078.
[1128] The impediment of public propriety does not arise from a civil act only, independently of cohabitation (see P.C.C.J., Mar. 12, 1929: AAS 21, 170).

EXTENT OF THE IMPEDIMENT. The impediment extends to the first and second degree of the direct line between a man and the blood relations of the woman, and vice versa.[1129] Since it is an ecclesiastical impediment, it does not affect unbaptized persons, at least directly. Indirectly, when an unbaptized person desires to marry one who is baptized and who is affected by this impediment, he himself is likewise affected.

CESSATION of the impediment. This impediment is removed by lawful dispensation. But it is disputed amongst authors whether this impediment becomes an impediment of genuine affinity, so that it ceases if the invalid marriage is subsequently convalidated when the two parties living in concubinage marry each other, or whether in similar circumstances it continues. Both opinions are probable. In practice, it is safer to state clearly in the petition for a dispensation the exact nature of the case under consideration. — The impediment of public propriety in the second degree is a minor impediment, as stated already.

13. The Impediment of Spiritual Relationship

919. DEFINITION. The impediment of spiritual relationship is the relationship incurred by the conferment and reception of Baptism.

EXPLANATION. Although spiritual relationship is likewise incurred by the conferment and reception of Confirmation,[1130] it is no longer regarded as an impediment to marriage. In order that the impediment may arise from Baptism, the following conditions must be verified.

1. Genuine Baptism whether private or solemn must have been administered validly. Consequently, the impediment does not arise from the ceremonies which may be supplied afterward, nor from the conditional repetition of the Sacrament, unless the same sponsor was present at both Baptisms.[1131]

2. The minister of the Sacrament and the sponsor must be baptized. Since the impediment is ecclesiastical, it does not bind those who are unbaptized.

3. The sponsor must exercise his office knowingly and freely, and fulfill all that is required by law for the validity of his action. These legal requisites have been indicated already, no. 570. Thus, for example, no Protestant may be admitted as a valid sponsor; therefore, if such a person exercises that office he does not contract the impediment of spiritual relationship.

THE EXTENT of the impediment has been much restricted in the new Code. The impediment exists only a) between the minister of the Sacrament and the recipient; b) between the sponsor and the baptized.[1132]

CESSATION of the impediment. It is a minor impediment and is removed by lawful dispensation.

[1129] See CCL, Can. 1078.
[1130] See CCL, Can. 797.
[1131] See CCL, Can. 763, § 2.
[1132] See CCL, Can. 1079.

14. The Impediment of Legal Relationship

920. DEFINITION. *The impediment of legal relationship is the relationship arising from legal adoption.*

EXPLANATION. Ecclesiastical law prior to the new Code followed the ancient civil law of Rome, but now it adapts itself to the civil code of each country. "In those countries where by civil law marriage is forbidden on account of legal adoption, marriage is likewise illicit by canon law."[1133] "Those who are declared by civil law to be *incapable* of contracting marriage on account of legal adoption cannot under canon law enter into valid marriage."[1134] It is not abundantly clear in which countries legal adoption is a *prohibitory* impediment, and in which countries it is an *annulling* impediment. It seems to be regarded as *annulling* marriage in Spain,[1135] Italy,[1136] Switzerland,[1137] in certain Latin American countries, e.g., Bolivia,[1138] Brazil,[1139] Costa Rica,[1140] Peru.[1141] On the other hand, legal adoption seems to *prohibit* marriage in Germany,[1142] France,[1143] Belgium.[1144]

Legal adoption seems to offer *no obstacle to marriage* in England, Holland, Austria, Portugal, Argentina, Chile, Mexico, and other American countries.[1145]

CESSATION of the impediment. The impediment is removed not only by a lawful dispensation granted by the Church but also by *civil* enactments. Since canon law follows the various civil codes on this question, when the latter cease to regard legal adoption as an impediment to marriage, so likewise does the Church.

Art. 4. Dispensation from Impediments

921. INTRODUCTION. Impediments to marriage may cease in three ways:

1. *through lapse of time*, e.g., closed times, or the bond of an existing marriage by the death of the consort;

2. *through legitimate consent of both parties*, e.g., the impediments of error, violence, fear;

[1133] CCL, Can. 1059.
[1134] CCL, Can. 1080.
[1135] See art. 84.
[1136] See a. 60 and 104.
[1137] See a. 100.
[1138] See a. 108.
[1139] See a. 183.
[1140] See a. 140.
[1141] See a. 143. See also Ferreres, *Compendium Theologiæ Moralis*, vol. 2, no. 1051ff.
[1142] See § 1311 and 1741.
[1143] See a. 348.
[1144] See a. 348.
[1145] See De Smet, *De Sponsalibus et Matrimonio*, no. 499.

3. *through legitimate dispensation*. This will now be given special consideration under the following headings: *a)* Definitions and Kinds of Dispensation; *b)* Author of Dispensations; *c)* Causes for Dispensation; *d)* The Petition Itself; *e)* The Grant of Dispensations.

§ 1. Definition and Kinds of Matrimonial Dispensations

922. DEFINITION. *Dispensation from a matrimonial impediment is the relaxation of a law annulling or prohibiting marriage granted in a particular case by legitimate ecclesiastical authority.*

KINDS.

1. A dispensation may be granted either for the *internal* forum or for the *external* forum. It is necessary to remember that *a dispensation granted in the external forum is valid also in conscience, but not vice versa*; at least, that is the usual procedure.

2. A dispensation is granted either for *contracting* marriage or for *convalidating* a marriage previously invalid.

3. A dispensation is granted *in forma gratiosa*, if it is granted directly and immediately by the Roman Curia; it is granted *in forma commissoria*, if it is transmitted to a bishop or priest so that the latter may dispense in the name of the Holy See. Nowadays, dispensations are normally given *in forma commissoria*.

§ 2. The Power of Dispensation

923. PRINCIPLE. *"The Roman Pontiff alone can abolish or modify ecclesiastical impediments (whether prohibitory or annulling); similarly, no one else can dispense in these impediments unless they are given the faculty to do so by common law or special indult of the Holy See."*[1146]

The pope has *no power* to dispense in those impediments which annul marriage owing to natural or divine positive law, as in the impediments arising from lack of consent or from the bond of a consummated marriage.

He *does not dispense* (although possessing the power to do so) in the impediments of consanguinity in the first degree of the collateral line, of affinity in the direct line—at least when the affinity is caused by consummated marriage—of crime arising from notorious murder of consort, of abduction; but he does dispense in other impediments if there exists a proportionate cause.

THE ROMAN PONTIFF usually exercises his power of dispensation:

1. *through the Congregation of the Holy Office* for the impediments of mixed religion and disparity of worship, and also for the omission of the interpellations in the use of the Pauline privilege;[1147]

2. *through the Congregation of the Sacraments* for all other impediments (affecting members of the Latin Rite) so far as the *external* forum is concerned, and also for

---

[1146] CCL, Can. 1040.
[1147] See CCL, Can. 247, § 3.

the dissolution of a ratified marriage. But in the case of the impediment arising from religious profession, the application for a dispensation must be made to the Congregation for Religious;

3. *through the Congregation for the Eastern Church*, regarding marriages of Catholics belonging to that Church, whether they are marrying each other or a Catholic of the Latin Rite or a pagan;[1148]

4. *through the Sacred Penitentiary* for secret impediments and so far as the internal forum alone is concerned.[1149]

924. POWERS OF LOCAL ORDINARIES TO DISPENSE.

For the sake of clarity, we shall consider these powers: 1) in ordinary cases; 2) in urgent cases; 3) in danger of death.

1. IN ORDINARY CASES local ordinaries may dispense:

a) *from impediments concerning which there exists a doubt of fact*, provided that they are impediments in which the pope usually dispenses,[1150] e.g., if there exists some doubt whether in an impediment of crime a genuine promise to marry can be found or not;

b) *from the publication of the banns, from vows not reserved to the Holy See, and from the observance of the closed time.*

925. 2. IN URGENT CASES OF NECESSITY, namely, when an impediment is discovered only after everything has been prepared for the marriage and the ceremony cannot be delayed until dispensation from the Holy See can be obtained without probable danger of great evil, local ordinaries may dispense from all and every ecclesiastical impediment (whether public or secret, and even if multiple), except from the impediments arising from the priesthood or from affinity in the direct line when the marriage has been consummated. Any scandal that may have been caused must be removed, and the usual guarantees must be obtained from both parties when a dispensation is required from difference of worship or mixed religion.[1151]

Local ordinaries may use this power of dispensing a) for their own subjects wherever they may be and for all persons actually staying in their territory, e.g., travelers and persons with no fixed abode;

b) not only for contracting marriage but also for convalidating an invalid marriage.[1152]

926. 3. IN URGENT DANGER OF DEATH local ordinaries enjoy the same power of dispensation which they have in urgent cases of necessity. Moreover, in these circumstances

---

[1148] See CCL, Can. 257.
[1149] See CCL, Can. 258.
[1150] See CCL, Can. 15.
[1151] See CCL, Can. 1045, § 1.
[1152] See CCL, Can. 1045, § 2.

they may dispense from the *canonical form* for the celebration of marriage.[1153] Thus, for example, a bishop may grant a dispensation for a just cause in order to allow a putative spouse in urgent danger of death to contract marriage in the presence of the confessor without the two witnesses, but he cannot convalidate a marriage without the renewal of consent.[1154]

NOTE. By virtue of special faculties, local ordinaries may have the power to grant other dispensations, as will be evident from the appendix at the end of this work.

927. POWERS OF PARISH PRIESTS AND CONFESSORS TO DISPENSE.

1. In ordinary cases, parish priests and confessors have no power to grant dispensations.

2. *In urgent cases of necessity*, as mentioned previously in no. 925, when the local ordinary cannot be approached or only with danger of violating the seal of Confession, the following persons enjoy the same power possessed by local ordinaries: *a)* parish priests; *b)* priests who legitimately assist at a marriage, when the parish priest is not available; *c)* confessors. But this power of dispensation is restricted *to occult cases*.[1155] In *public* impediments, the local ordinary can and must be approached without any great inconvenience.

3. *In urgent danger of death*, as mentioned above in no. 926, and only when there is no time to approach the ordinary, the same faculties as those given to local ordinaries in the same circumstances are granted to: *a)* parish priests, *b)* priests who legitimately assist at a marriage in the absence of the parish priest, *c)* confessors. But the power of the confessor to dispense is restricted to the *internal* forum and may be exercised only in the course of sacramental confession.[1156] Thus, for example, if a confessor while hearing the confession of a dying man discovers that he has contracted an invalid civil marriage and furthermore cannot contract a valid marriage at present owing to the impediment of crime, the priest may dispense both from the latter impediment and from the canonical form of celebrating marriage, provided that there is not sufficient time to have recourse to the ordinary. If both parties know that their marriage is null and void, they should first take care to be in the state of grace and then renew their consent in the presence of the confessor. If the invalidity of the marriage is known to one party only, it is sufficient if that person (being in the state of grace) renews the consent, since the consent of the other party is considered to persevere virtually.[1157]

928. NOTE. 1. The parish priest or other priest who in urgent danger of death granted a dispensation for the external forum from an impediment or the form of marriage must at once inform the local ordinary of this fact and note it in the marriage

[1153] See CCL, Can. 1043.
[1154] See no. 928.4.
[1155] See CCL, Can. 1045, § 3.
[1156] See CCL, Can. 1044.
[1157] See CCL, Can. 1135.

register.[1158] It is obvious that a confessor who has granted a dispensation for the internal forum in the course of sacramental confession cannot and must not say anything to anyone.

2. One who has a *general indult* to dispense can normally (unless the contrary is stated expressly) dispense from one and the same impediment even if it is multiple and from several impediments of various species occurring in one and the same marriage.[1159] This power is known as *facultas cumulandi*.

3. If he who has an indult to dispense from several *public* impediments meets with a case where there is also another impediment from which he cannot dispense, he *cannot* exercise his power of dispensation but must ask the Holy See for dispensation from all the impediments in the case. If, however, the impediments from which he can dispense are discovered only *after* dispensation has been obtained from the Holy See, he may make use of his faculties.[1160]

4. Those who dispense in the cases mentioned above from any diriment impediment in virtue of a *general indult* (and not by reason of a particular rescript), such as bishops, parish priests, confessors, effect ipso facto the legitimation of the offspring, with the exception of adulterous or sacrilegious offspring.[1161]

5. Unless the rescript of the Sacred Penitentiary states otherwise, dispensations from *occult impediments* granted by this tribunal for the internal *sacramental* forum are not valid for the external forum, and therefore a new dispensation is required if the impediment later becomes public; if granted for the internal *extra-sacramental* forum, they are valid for the external forum, even if afterward the impediment becomes public. This latter dispensation granted by the Sacred Penitentiary should be recorded in the secret archives of the episcopal curia.[1162]

929. SCHOLIUM. "CASUS PERPLEXUS." This phrase was used formerly by theologians in reference to a case in which an annulling impediment was discovered immediately prior to the celebration of marriage, so that the marriage could not be postponed without grave inconvenience and yet there was insufficient time to obtain the requisite dispensation. But by reason of the wide indults granted to local ordinaries, parish priests, and confessors, (as noted already) this case is hardly possible in present circumstances, and thus no useful purpose would be served by noting the various procedures proposed by earlier theologians.

§ 3. Causes for Dispensation

930. THE NECESSITY OF A CAUSE. The Council of Trent has stated: "In contracting marriages rarely, if ever, should dispensations be granted; if they are, they must be

---

[1158] See CCL, Can. 1046.
[1159] See CCL, Can. 1049.
[1160] See CCL, Can. 1050.
[1161] See CCL, Can. 1051; see also no. 943.
[1162] See CCL, Can. 1047.

granted for some cause and without payment."[1163] By a concession of the law, and thus incidentally, no cause is required *for the validity* of dispensations granted from the *five minor impediments*. A dispensation from any of these impediments "is not invalidated by any misrepresentation or concealment of facts, even though the only motive reason advanced in the petition be false."[1164]

KINDS. 1. Causes are said to be *final* (or motive) if they are self-sufficient for obtaining the required dispensation; if they are not in themselves sufficient but aid in obtaining a dispensation, they are *impelling* causes.

2. Causes *reflect defamation* (or dishonor) if they arise from delinquency and usually cause infamy (e.g., if the bride is pregnant as the result of fornication), or they are *morally good* if they have no suspicion of delinquency or defamation, e.g., the large family of a widow;

3. Causes are *canonical* if accepted by the Roman courts as final and sufficient; otherwise, they are *uncanonical* (reasonable, certain) which are the same as the impelling causes previously mentioned.

931. CANONICAL CAUSES for dispensation are usually regarded as being sixteen in number:

1. *place of domicile very restricted*, either *absolutely* (containing less than approximately fifteen hundred inhabitants and is more than a mile away from any other place) or *relatively*, if the family of the petitioner is very numerous in the locality;

2. *advancing age of the woman*, i.e., if she is more than twenty-four years old. This cause is not accepted if the woman is a widow;

3. *lack or at least insufficiency of means*;

4. *legal proceedings in respect of inheritance of property*;

5. *poverty of the widow* who has a large family to support;

6. *the benefit of peace*;

7. *excessive, suspected familiarity or cohabitation*;

8. *pregnancy of the woman and therefore legitimation of offspring*;

9. *defamation of the woman as the result of suspected intercourse*;

10. *convalidation of an invalid marriage*, contracted publicly and in good faith;

11. *danger of contracting a mixed marriage even in the presence of a non-Catholic minister*;

12. *danger of incestuous concubinage*;

13. *danger of a civil marriage*;

14. *removal of grave scandal*;

15. *cessation of concubinage known to all*;

16. *excellence of merits*.

[1163] Session 24, "Decree on the Reformation of Marriage," chap. 5.
[1164] CCL, Can. 1054.

932. UNCANONICAL CAUSES ARE NUMEROUS, e.g., *a)* in respect of the *woman*: difficulty of finding another man equally acceptable, sickness and other failings, need of helping parents; *b)* in respect of the *man*: sickness which requires the help of a good wife, care of offspring from a previous marriage; *c)* in respect of *both parties*: the intention to marry already known to many which could not be changed without causing defamation of character, the virtues and good character of both, help to parents.

§ 4. The Petition Itself

933. 1. All requests for matrimonial dispensations are to be made in the name of the contracting parties and therefore must be made in the third person, e.g., John Smith requests. The parties petitioning for the dispensation are known in curial language as: *oratores, orator, oratrix, latores, lator, latrix.*

2. If a dispensation is required for the *external* forum, the petition should be made by the parish priest, normally the parish priest of the bride, through the episcopal curia; if the dispensation is required for the *internal* forum, the petition is made by the confessor either through the episcopal curia, or, if there is danger of violating the seal, directly to the Sacred Penitentiary.

3. If a dispensation is required from a *public impediment*, the petition must contain:

a) the surname and Christian names of the petitioners, the diocese of their origin or of their actual domicile;

b) the nature of the impediment precisely defined; thus, for instance, in a case of consanguinity not merely the degree but also the line must be recorded;

c) the number of the impediments;

d) the various circumstances, e.g., whether the petition refers to a marriage not yet contracted or to one already contracted;

e) the causes for dispensation;

f) the social condition of the petitioners.

4. If a dispensation is sought from an *occult* impediment, fictitious names must be used in the petition, and the confessor must exercise the utmost care not to violate the seal of Confession; however, he is obliged to state clearly the precise nature of the impediment and the causes for dispensation.

5. If a dispensation is required from two or more impediments of which one is public, a dispensation must be obtained from the public impediment, as indicated already in no. 933.3, but no mention is to be made of the occult impediment. In the petition for a dispensation from an occult impediment, mention must be made of any public impediment from which a dispensation has been granted already or at least requested in the proper forum.

§ 5. The Granting of Dispensations

934. GENERAL RULE. According to present discipline, the Roman Curia usually grants all matrimonial dispensations *in forma commissoria*, whereas local ordinaries normally grant them *in forma gratiosa*, at least when the impediments are public. Dispensations from public impediments committed by the Holy See to the ordinary of the petitioners shall be executed by the ordinary who gave letters of recommendation or who forwarded the petition to the Holy See, even if by the time the dispensation arrives the parties have left the former diocese in which they had a domicile or quasi-domicile with the intention not to return; but the ordinary of the place where they wish to contract marriage must be advised of the dispensation having been granted.[1165]

All who grant a dispensation in virtue of delegated powers received from the Holy See must make explicit mention of the papal indult in granting the dispensation,[1166] e.g., by the use of these or similar words: *Auctoritate Apostolica mihi commissa dispense . . .*

935. CONDITIONS. Once the rescript is received, the executor must heed carefully all the clauses or conditions attached to it, since it becomes invalid if he ignores *essential conditions* or does not follow *substantially* the form of procedure indicated. Only those clauses are considered essential which are introduced by the conditional words *if, provided that,* and similar terms.[1167]

The more important conditions expressed are the following:

1. *"If the request is founded on fact."* Normally for the validity of the dispensation it is necessary that at the moment of concession (for dispensations granted without an executor) or execution (for other dispensations) everything stated in the petition should be at least substantially true. Therefore, before the dispensation is executed it is necessary to *verify the petition* by undertaking a new and short inquiry into the actual truth of the statements made in the course of the petition. If an essential mistake is discovered a new dispensation (*Perinde valere*) must be sought. — An exception is made in the case of dispensations granted from *the minor impediments* of marriage[1168] which are never invalidated by either false statements or concealment of facts.

Sometimes a particular method of verifying the truth of the petition is demanded for the *external forum*. All that is required for the *internal* forum is that the confessor should repeat in a summarized form the statements previously made by the penitent.

2. *"A salutary penance being imposed suited to the gravity of the offense and left to your own choice."* This penance is distinct from the sacramental penance, but its omission would not render the dispensation invalid.[1169]

[1165] See CCL, Can. 1055.
[1166] See CCL, Can. 1057.
[1167] See CCL, Can. 39.
[1168] See no. 885.
[1169] See S. Penitentiary, Nov. 12, 1891.

3. "*This document having been destroyed immediately*," i.e., the rescript granted by the Sacred Penitentiary must be destroyed without delay, i.e., within *three days* of the execution of the dispensation. But there is nothing to prevent a confessor making a copy of this rescript for his own guidance and retaining it, so long as there is no danger of violating the seal of Confession.

936. NOTE. For the *external* forum the dispensation must be executed in writing[1170] and the fact recorded in the matrimonial register; for the *internal* forum it is usually required that the dispensation be granted by word of mouth, which may be done in the following or any similar manner: after giving the customary absolution from censures and sins, the confessor should say: "Insuper auctoritate Apostolica mihi specialiter delegata dispenso tecum super impedimento affinitatis (vel criminis), ut eo non obstante matrimonium cum dicta muliere contrahere valeas. Eadem auctoritate prolem susceptam vel suscipiendam legitimam declaro. In nomine Patris et Filii et Spiritus Sancti. Amen. Passio D. N. I. Ch., merita B. M. V.," and so on. For a reasonable cause the dispensation may be granted in the vernacular.

Art. 5. Rectification of Invalid Marriages

937. INTRODUCTION. When a marriage is discovered to have been invalid due to the presence of a diriment impediment the greatest prudence is required. There are four courses open.

1. SEPARATION OF THE TWO PARTIES. Normally speaking, this should be avoided because of the many inconveniences which would ensue; however, if the impediment is one which cannot be dispensed and the putative spouses cannot live together as brother and sister, this is the course of action which must be taken; but before such a separation a declaration is normally required from the local ordinary to the effect that the marriage was invalid.

2. TO LEAVE THE PUTATIVE SPOUSES IN GOOD FAITH; this is not lawful unless there exists an urgent reason.

3. BOTH PARTIES MAY CONTINUE TO LIVE TOGETHER AS BROTHER AND SISTER; this may be permitted *a)* if the invalidity of the marriage is not public, and *b)* if there is no proximate danger of incontinence.

4. RECTIFICATION OF THE INVALID MARRIAGE. This may be done in one of three ways: *a)* by a simple renewal of consent without any dispensation; *b)* by an ordinary dispensation; *c)* by regularizing the original consent (*sanatio in radice*). Each of these methods must be considered in turn.

§ 1. Rectification by Renewal of Consent

938. An invalid marriage may be rectified by a simple renewal of consent in three cases:

1. when the marriage was invalid *solely through defect of true consent* (e.g., when the consent was fictitious or extorted by fear or duress or accompanied by substantial error);

[1170] See CCL, Can. 56.

2. when the marriage was contracted in spite of the existence of an annulling impediment which has now ceased to exist through lapse of time, e.g., when the parties were below the age of puberty, or one of the parties was already married;

3. when the marriage was contracted with an impediment which can be freely removed by the action of one of the parties, e.g., the impediment of disparity of worship which ceases to exist when Baptism is received voluntarily.—The renewal of consent must be a new act of the will for the marriage that is known to have been invalid from the beginning.[1171]

Regarding *the form in which this renewal of consent should be made*, the following points are to be noted:

a) If the invalidity of the marriage is *public*, the consent must be renewed in public in accordance with the form prescribed by law in the celebration of marriage.[1172] Otherwise the scandal would not cease to exist.

b) If it is *occult* but known to *both* parties, it suffices that the consent be renewed privately and secretly by both parties.[1173]

c) If it is *occult* and known to *one party only* and cannot be revealed to the other without great inconvenience, it is sufficient if the party conscious of the impediment renews the consent *privately and secretly*, provided the other party continues to consent.[1174] Therefore, the various methods devised by earlier theologians of inducing the party unaware of the impediment to renew the consent implicitly are no longer of use.

d) If the marriage is null and void on account of the want of the prescribed form, e.g., if a mixed marriage is not contracted before a competent priest, it must be validated by contracting the marriage anew in the form prescribed by law, i.e., in the presence of the parish priest and two witnesses.[1175] No one (outside the danger of death) has power to dispense from this form except the Holy See or someone delegated by her.

§ 2. Rectification by Dispensation

939. *In danger of death*, the marriage of either of the reputed spouses may be convalidated by the ordinary, or parish priest, or indeed by any priest, provided that the impediments are capable of being dispensed and all the requisite conditions are verified, as already explained in no. 926ff.

Outside the danger of death, a simple dispensation may be obtained from *a) a public impediment* in order to rectify an invalid marriage, if both parties are prepared to give a new consent in the form prescribed by law; *b) an occult impediment*, if it

[1171] See CCL, Can. 1134.
[1172] See CCL, Can. 1135, § 1.
[1173] See CCL, Can. 1135, § 2.
[1174] See CCL, Can. 1135, § 3.
[1175] See CCL, Can. 1137.

is possible to renew the consent in the manner described in the preceding paragraph. If there is any difficulty in this respect, one must have recourse to retrospective convalidation.

§ 3. Retrospective Convalidation

940. DEFINITION. *Retrospective convalidation (sanatio in radice) is a dispensation granted by the Holy See which renders an invalid marriage valid, even (by fiction of law) in reference to the canonical effects not merely from the moment of granting this dispensation but also from the beginning of the marriage.*[1176]

The same thing can be stated more briefly thus: by retrospective convalidation, an invalid marriage is rendered just as valid *in regard to the canonical effects* as if there had been no annulling impediment present from the beginning. Accordingly, once the original consent is regularized in this way there is no longer required: *a)* legitimation of natural offspring, *b)* renewal of consent, since this has been healed at its source. By retrospective convalidation, the moral effect of marriage and especially *the sacramental grace* are not extended to the beginning of the marriage but only to the moment of the granting of the dispensation. This is at least the more common opinion. — The *sanatio in radice* can be granted by the Holy See alone.[1177]

941. THE CONDITIONS required for granting this form of convalidation are:

1. that the diriment impediment concerned in the case is *capable of dispensation,* i.e., it is not an impediment of the natural or divine positive law;

Consequently, marriage contracted under an impediment of the natural or divine law (e.g., the impediment of an existing bond) is not validated by the Church by means of retrospective convalidation, even though the impediment should have ceased afterward, not even from the moment of the cessation of the impediment;[1178]

2. that at the inception of marriage there existed a genuine consent; if consent was wanting in the beginning but was given later on, the *sanatio in radice* can be applied from the moment when the consent was given;[1179]

3. that the consent virtually persists and has never been revoked with certainty;[1180]

4. that there exists a grave and urgent reason, e.g., the impossibility of obtaining a renewal of the consent.

942. PETITION FOR RETROSPECTIVE CONVALIDATION AND ITS EXECUTION.

Anyone may petition for a *sanatio in radice,* since it may be obtained and used even *without the knowledge of the putative spouses.*[1181] But normally the confessor or

---

[1176] See CCL, Can. 1138.
[1177] See CCL, Can. 1141.
[1178] See CCL, Can. 1139, § 2.
[1179] See CCL, Can. 1140, § 2.
[1180] See CCL, Can. 1140, § 1.
[1181] See CCL, Can. 1138, § 3.

parish priest will ask for this dispensation; the petition must include the grave reasons prompting the request for a *sanatio*, rather than a simple dispensation.—In executing the convalidation, careful attention must be paid to all the conditions expressed in the rescript. Furthermore, care should be taken to see that the parties are in the state of grace when the convalidation takes place, since they then receive the Sacrament of Marriage.

943. SCHOLIUM. ILLEGITIMATE CHILDREN. Generally speaking, legitimate children are those conceived or born in valid marriage, or in marriage contracted in good faith though invalidly.[1182] All other children are illegitimate, and these are either *natural* if born from *simple fornication*, or *spurious* if born from adultery (adulterous offspring) or sacrilege (sacrilegious offspring) or incest (incestuous offspring).

The LEGITIMATION of illegitimate children is effected in three ways:

1. *by subsequent marriage* of the parents contracted validly or in good faith, or by validation of marriage.[1183] This affects only natural children, not spurious children;[1184]

2. by the children being *solemnly professed* in a religious order or simply professed in certain institutes which possess a special privilege. This method of legitimation is valid for the reception of Orders but not for the acceptance of any dignity;

3. *by a rescript from the Holy See* or by dispensation granted by one who dispenses from an annulling impediment in virtue of a *general indult*,[1185] e.g., in danger of death or in any other urgent case. Legitimation must be recorded in the baptismal register.

CIVIL MARRIAGE AND DIVORCE

This chapter is divided into two articles: 1) Civil Marriage; 2) Civil Divorce.

Art. 1. Civil Marriage

944. DEFINITION. *Civil marriage is the contract of marriage (even of Christians) entered upon in the presence of a civil magistrate.*

EXPLANATION. The term applies to *the contract of marriage* only, i.e., a contract which is concerned not merely with the civil effects of marriage but also with the marital rights.

Civil marriages are today universal, but they vary in kind.

In some countries they are *obligatory* for all, e.g., in France, Germany, Switzerland; in others they are *optional*, insofar as Christians are allowed the alternatives of

---

[1182] See CCL, Can. 1114.
[1183] See CCL, Can. 1116.
[1184] Offspring born of parents between whom there existed the impediment either of age or of disparity of worship is not legitimated by the subsequent marriage of the parents at a time when the impediment had ceased to exist (see P.C.C.J., Dec. 6, 1930: AAS 23, 25).
[1185] See CCL, Can. 1051.

contracting a religious or civil marriage, as in England and North America; in other countries they are *subsidiary* in the sense that they are accepted by the State when the parties are either unable or unwilling to contract a religious marriage, e.g., in Austria and Spain.

945. FIRST PRINCIPLE. *A civil marriage between Christians is not recognized by the Church and is deprived of all canonical effects.*

The chief reasons why the Church has always condemned such civil marriages are the following:

1) they violate the right of the Church which alone has authority over Christian marriages insofar as they are Sacraments; 2) they make marriage a purely secular affair; 3) they are a potent cause of indifference and divorce.

The effects of a civil marriage are negative rather than positive.

a) Civil marriage lacks the force of a true marriage, and since it must be considered a form of public concubinage it gives rise to the impediment of public propriety.

b) Children born of such civil marriages are illegitimate.

c) Persons contracting a civil marriage are regarded as public sinners since they are living in concubinage and therefore they cannot be admitted to the Sacraments nor to ecclesiastical burial and they are likewise debarred from all legitimate acts.

d) A consummated civil marriage contracted after a divorce from a previous legitimate marriage engenders the impediment of crime.

e) Clerics in major Orders and solemnly professed religious who contract a civil marriage incur excommunication reserved to the Holy See and other penalties, previously noted in no. 770.

Religious with *simple profession* incur excommunication reserved to the ordinary.[1186]

NOTE. Although civil marriage *as such* produces no canonical effect, it is *valid marriage*—provided it is contracted with true consent—*a)* between all non-Catholics; *b)* in those cases where marriage may be celebrated without the presence of an assistant priest.[1187]

946. SECOND PRINCIPLE. *For a reasonable cause, Christians contracting marriage are permitted to observe the civil law regarding the celebration of marriage, provided there is no intention of receiving the Sacrament itself in the presence of a civil official.*[1188] Such is the explicit teaching of Leo XIII in his encyclical *Arcanum.*

Is it lawful to assist at a civil marriage as an official or witness?

1. Yes, if the parties to be married intend no more than to gain the civil effects of marriage; likewise, if they intend and actually contract a true and valid marriage.

[1186] See CCL, Can. 2388, § 2.
[1187] See nos. 879–880.
[1188] See CCL, Can. 1063, § 3.

2. Probably, if the parties knowingly and with certainty contract marriage invalidly, provided there exists a grave reason and there is no special ecclesiastical prohibition. Those officials who for a grave reason assist at such civil marriages cooperate merely materially in the sin of the parties. This is the more common opinion.

Art. 2. Civil Divorce

947. DEFINITION. *Civil divorce is the separation of married partners by civil authority.* The separation affects either the bond of marriage or bed and board.

Principle. *Any civil law permitting complete divorce of a valid marriage is evil and deserving of the most severe condemnation.*

Such a law permits an action which is intrinsically evil, that is, the dissolution of the bond of marriage, and produces most evil results.

948. COROLLARIES.

1. For a grave reason THOSE WHO ARE MARRIED may petition the civil authorities for a separation (imperfect divorce), but they are never allowed to seek an absolute divorce of the marriage bond.[1189]

2. A CIVIL JUDGE *a)* must recognize his lack of authority in matters relating to the Sacrament of Marriage, and he is not permitted to pronounce a civil divorce in a country where there exists a special prohibition;

b) may pronounce a civil divorce in a marriage which is certainly invalid, e.g., when two Catholics contract a civil marriage;

c) he cannot grant a decree of absolute divorce in any Christian marriage unless there exists a very grave reason. If this latter condition is verified, it seems that he cannot be forbidden to pronounce the decree if he intends nothing more than the *civil effects* of divorce. This at present is the more common opinion, as opposed to those who think that such a pronouncement is intrinsically evil.

The reason justifying this concession is that by his action the judge intends no more than to protect the parties from *legal punishment* if they subsequently contract a new and valid marriage. In other words, such a pronouncement seems merely *to destroy the previous civil marriage*, and this cannot be regarded as an intrinsically evil act. Furthermore, there can be no grave scandal resulting from his action since all must realize that civil law compels him to act in this way.

949. 3. ADVOCATES rarely have sufficient reason to justify them undertaking a divorce suit, since they are under no compulsion to do so by reason of their office. In practice, a confessor should not cause disquiet to any Catholic advocate who cannot refuse to undertake such cases without very serious inconvenience, provided that there is no scandal and nothing more is intended than the civil effects of divorce.

[1189] See Holy Office, Dec. 19, 1860.

APPENDICES
APPENDIX I

Some recent documents from the Roman Curia are here included for the benefit of the confessor.

On the appearance of the new Code all quinquennial, triennial, and similar faculties were withdrawn, but bishops may now regain such faculties which are listed below.

I
THE SUPREME SACRED CONGREGATION OF THE HOLY OFFICE

THE ADMONITION TO BE GIVEN TO PRIESTS GUILTY OF SOLICITATION

After due consideration beforehand, this Supreme Sacred Congregation usually decides in the majority of cases that those who have been denounced once or twice for the evil crime of solicitation *"should be admonished in the name of the Holy Office without violation of its secret."* Whoever is entrusted with the task of delivering this admonition will summon the priest who has been denounced, while at the same time taking all due precautions; he will then advise him in grave yet friendly terms depending on the circumstances of the case, but speaking in such a general way as not to disclose either directly or indirectly the persons responsible for the denunciation, *"that it has been brought to the notice of the Holy Office that he has not conducted himself in the confessional with the proper prudence and integrity, so that there exist just grounds for the fear that in his indiscretion he has attempted to use the very Sacrament of reconciliation for the ruin of souls; accordingly, it is in his best interests that for the future he take good care not to oblige the Sacred Congregation to take more stringent measures."*

As soon as convenient he will inform the Sacred Congregation of the outcome of the interview, but in every aspect of the case and no matter with whom he deals he must observe the inviolable secret of the Holy Office.

II
THE SACRED CONGREGATION OF THE CONSISTORY

FORMULA II

Quinquennial faculties for the ordinaries of European countries, with the exception of Italy and Russia

In the year when a local ordinary is obliged to make a report on the state of his diocese in accordance with the prescription of Can. 340, § 2 — and even in those cases when a bishop is dispensed from making this report due to the fact that he has but recently taken possession of his See — he may request the following faculties from the proper congregations; however, he will be obliged to observe the various clauses attached to the rescripts regarding the use of such faculties. The first request for these faculties may be made even outside this prescribed time on the understanding that they will be valid only until the time when the ordinary must make his approaching diocesan report. Given at Rome at the Sacred Congregation of the Consistory, March 17, 1922.

C. Card. de Lai Ep. Sab.

Secretary

I. From the Congregation of the Holy Office

1. The faculty to permit priests and lay persons to read for a time forbidden books with the exception of works which deal explicitly and *ex professo* with obscenity, but under certain restrictions which will vary according to the different nature of the individual cases and circumstances.

2. Only for those countries where Catholics and non-Catholics mix freely with each other, with the exception, therefore, of France, Spain, and Portugal, the faculty of dispensing in mixed marriages from the impediment of mixed religion or of disparity of worship, with conditions, restrictions, and instructions added varying with the nature of the different cases and localities.

II. From the Congregation of the Discipline of the Sacraments

Switzerland, France, Spain, Luxembourg, and Belgium are excluded from the grant of the following faculties:

1. of dispensing for a just and reasonable cause in all minor matrimonial impediments mentioned in Can. 1042 and also in the prohibitory impediments mentioned in Can. 1058 but only for the purpose of contracting marriage;

2. of dispensing for a grave and urgent reason, whenever delay is dangerous and the marriage cannot be postponed until dispensation from the Holy See is obtained, from the following major impediments:

a) of consanguinity in the second or third degrees touching the first, provided there is no scandal or surprise;

b) of consanguinity in the second degree of the collateral line;

c) of affinity in the first collateral line even if mixed with the second;

d) of public propriety in the first degree, provided that no doubt exists of the possibility of one of the parties being the offspring of the other;

3. of dispensing at the time and in the act of the Pastoral Visitation or of Missions, and at no other times, from all the matrimonial impediments mentioned above together with those arising from concubinage;

4. of granting retroactive convalidation for a marriage which was invalid because of some minor impediment, if there is great inconvenience entailed in asking the party ignorant of the impediment to renew the consent, provided however that the first consent still persists and there is no danger of divorce, but the party

aware of the impediment must be advised of the effect of this convalidation and the grant of the *sanatio* must be recorded in the matrimonial register.

III. FROM THE SACRED CONGREGATION OF THE COUNCIL

1. The faculty of converting perpetual Mass obligations for five years into an alms for some charity lawfully established in the diocese when the income from funded capital decreases, provided there is no one who is obliged by law and who can be usefully urged to increase this alms and on the understanding that the diocesan curia is legitimately informed each year by the priests concerned that they have celebrated the reduced number of Masses.

2. The faculty of transferring Mass obligations for five years to days, churches, or altars differing from those specified in the original foundation but always within the confines of the diocese, provided that there exists genuine necessity and divine worship is not thereby impaired and the people suffer no inconvenience, always excepting however those bequests which can easily be satisfied in the places designated by increasing the alms, and with the proviso added that each year the diocesan curia is informed by the celebrants that the Masses so transferred have been offered.

3. The faculty of transferring for five years even to places outside the diocese any excess of Masses, with the proviso that the greatest number should be celebrated within the diocese and that the most minute attention must be paid to the prescriptions of the Code of Canon Law regarding the precautions to be observed in transmitting Masses to others.

IV. FROM THE SACRED CONGREGATION OF RELIGIOUS

1. The faculty of dispensing from illegitimacy of birth to permit entry into the religious life to the extent required by the constitutions of the institute concerned, provided that the child is not the offspring of a sacrilegious union, that the superiors request the dispensation, and that those so dispensed are not elected as major superiors in accordance with Can. 504.

2. The faculty of permitting the celebration of three ritual Masses at midnight on Christmas Day in the churches of those religious houses not included in Can. 821, § 3 and of allowing the administration of Communion to the faithful present, but the three Masses must be celebrated by one and the same priest.

3. The faculty of dispensing from any excess over the age required by the constitutions of an institute for entering the religious life, having first obtained in each case the opinion of the general superioress or provincial and their consent and that of their council, provided that the postulants are not older than forty and are endowed with the other necessary qualities.

4. The faculty of dispensing from defect of canonical age for the priesthood, not however beyond … months, even in respect of exempt religious, provided that they have received the necessary dimissorial letters from their superiors and that the candidates satisfy the other qualifications determined by canon law and especially that they have completed their theological course as required by Can. 976, § 2.

5. The faculty of dispensing either completely or partially from lack of a dowry in respect of nuns and sisters, provided that the economy of the institute is not thereby impaired and the postulant is endowed with such qualities as to provide a well-founded hope that she will be of great benefit to the order.

6. The faculty of confirming a confessor in his post for a fourth or even fifth period of three years provided that all the religious are gathered together including those who have no right of casting votes in other matters, that each person casts her vote individually and in secret, and that a majority favor the appointment; however, provision must always be made for those who dissent, if there are any who desire other arrangements.

7. The faculty of permitting the celebration of the Holy Sacrifice of the Mass on Maundy Thursday and the administration of Holy Communion to those who habitually dwell in the community, even in order that they may fulfill their Easter obligation.

8. The faculty of permitting religious sisters to enter the church so that they themselves may clean and adorn it more fittingly, but all other persons must first leave the church including the confessor and those who serve in the convent and those living outside the enclosure; the doors of the church are to be closed, the keys given to the superioress; the nuns must always be in pairs, and the door which gives entry into the church must be closed by two keys, one entrusted to the superioress, the other to one of the nuns designated by the ordinary, and this door must never be unlocked except in the cases specified and with the precautions mentioned.

9. The faculty of allowing nuns to leave their enclosure for the period of time strictly required for a surgical operation, even when there is no imminent danger of death or serious harm, stating clearly the necessary precautions to be observed.

V. FROM THE SACRED CONGREGATION OF RITES

1. The faculty of delegating the vicar general or another priest invested with ecclesiastical dignity to consecrate fixed and portable altars according to the rite and form of the Roman Pontifical.

2. The faculty of delegating priests—if possible, priests invested with an ecclesiastical dignity—to consecrate fixed and portable altars which have been desecrated, using the shorter form B for the cases mentioned in Can. 1200, § 2; this faculty was already granted by the Code for the case mentioned in Can. 1200, § 1 and formula A must be used.

3. The faculty of delegating the vicar general or another priest invested with an ecclesiastical dignity to consecrate chalices and patens in accordance with the rite and form of the Roman Pontifical.

4. On the days in Holy Week when the Passion is read, the faculty of allowing priests who by virtue of a special apostolic indult celebrate two Masses to read in one of their two Masses the last part of the Passion (*Altera autem die*, and so

on) saying beforehand, *Munda cor meum . . .* and so on. — *Sequentia sancti Evangelii secundum (Matthaeum).*

5. The faculty for the bishop or ordinary to bless pious objects with the sign of the cross, observing the rites prescribed by the Church. But on the occasion of a pastoral visitation and when many present several objects of various kinds to be blessed, often having their own special form of blessing, the bishop or ordinary is allowed to use one short formula while making the sign of the cross over the objects: *Benedicat haec omnia Deus Pater, Filius, et Spiritus Sanctus. Amen.*

6. The faculty for the bishop or ordinary to celebrate one Requiem Mass each week in his own oratory.

VI. From the Sacred Penitentiary

1. The faculty of absolving any penitents (with the exception of those who are deliberately spreading heresy among the faithful) from any censures or ecclesiastical penalties incurred by reason of heresy preached whether in the hearing of others or not, whether they heeded the teaching or not, but the penitent must first denounce as required by law those who teach heresy *ex professo* if he knows of such and all clerics and religious who may have been his accomplices; if for just reasons he is unable to make such a denunciation prior to receiving absolution, he should make a serious promise of doing so at his earliest convenience and in the best way possible, after secretly abjuring his heresies before the confessor in each case; the ordinary must impose a grave salutary penance proportionate to his excesses, and also oblige him to receive the Sacraments, and to avoid those persons to whom he made known his heresy, and to make reparation for any scandal given.

2. The faculty of absolving from censures and ecclesiastical penalties those who have defended or those who while knowing of the censure have read or retained without due permission books written by apostates, heretics, or schismatics advancing the cause of apostasy, heresy, or schism, or other books condemned by name by apostolic letters; they must receive a fitting penance and be obliged either to destroy these books prior to absolution so far as possible or else to give them to the ordinary or confessor.

3. The faculty of absolving from censures those who have prevented directly or indirectly the exercise of ecclesiastical jurisdiction whether in the internal or in the external forum, having had recourse for this purpose to some secular authority.

4. The faculty of absolving from the censures and ecclesiastical penalties attached to the crime of dueling, provided that the matter has not been brought before the external forum; a grave penance must be imposed together with the other obligations required by law.

5. The faculty to absolve from censures and ecclesiastical penalties those who have given their allegiance to the Masons or to any other similar society which schemes against the Church or legitimate civil authority, on condition that they separate themselves completely from the sect and abjure it and that in accordance

with Can. 2336, § 2 they denounce those clerics and religious whom they know to be members of the same sect; they must hand over all books, manuscripts, and emblems belonging to the sect or at least destroy them, if there exist just and grave reasons for this alternative; they shall receive a grave penance proportionate to the gravity of their offenses and be obliged to approach the Sacrament of Penance and to make reparation for any scandal given.

6. The faculty of absolving from censures and ecclesiastical penalties those who enter without due permission the enclosure of religious of either sex and also those who introduce or admit them, provided that this was not done for some evil purpose which in some respect was gravely sinful, even if the purpose was not achieved, and the case has not been brought before the court; a salutary penance suited to the offense must be imposed.

7. The faculty to grant a dispensation in order to permit the request for the marital dues from one who has violated a vow of perfect and perpetual chastity privately made after the eighteenth year of age completed to those who contracted marriage while under this vow, but such penitents must be instructed that they are obliged to observe their vow apart from the lawful use of marriage and also if they outlive their partner.

8. The faculty of dispensing from an occult impediment of crime, provided there is no intrigue and the marriage has been contracted already; the parties must be instructed to renew their consent in secret and a grave and lengthy penance must be imposed.

Likewise, the faculty of dispensing from the same occult impediment provided there is no evidence of intrigue, even if the marriage has not been contracted; a grave and lengthy penance must be imposed.

APPENDIX II
THE SUPREME SACRED CONGREGATION
OF THE HOLY OFFICE

INSTRUCTION ON THE DISCIPLINE TO BE OBSERVED
REGARDING THE EUCHARISTIC FAST[1190]

(*Const., no. I.*)

The Apostolic Constitution *Christus Dominus,* given this day by the Supreme Pontiff Pius XII, now happily reigning, grants several faculties and dispensations in regard to the observance of the law of the eucharistic fast, but it also largely confirms in substance the rules of the Code of Canon Law[1191] which bind those priests and faithful who are able to observe this law. However, to these persons also is extended the favorable first rule of the constitution in virtue of which *natural* water (that is, water to which no other element has been added) no longer breaks the eucharistic fast.[1192] Regarding the other concessions, only those priests and faithful may take advantage of them who are placed in the particular conditions laid down in the constitution, or who celebrate or receive Holy Communion at evening Masses authorized by ordinaries within the limits of the new faculties which have been granted to them.

Therefore, in order that uniformity may reign in the observance of the rules relating to these concessions and that all interpretation be avoided which would widen the faculties given, as well as to prevent all abuse in this matter, this Supreme Sacred Congregation of the Holy Office at the bidding and command of the Supreme Pontiff himself has decreed as follows:

REGARDING THE SICK WHETHER LAITY OR PRIESTS

1. The faithful who are sick, even though not confined to bed, may take something non-alcoholic to drink if, on account of their sickness, they are unable to observe the full fast before receiving Holy Communion without grave inconvenience. They may also take something by way of medicine, either liquid (non-alcoholic) or solid, provided it is genuine medicine prescribed by a physician or commonly regarded as such. But it must be noted that any solid taken for nourishment cannot be regarded as medicine.

2. The conditions in which one is justified in taking advantage of this dispensation from the law of fast—for which no time-limit before Communion is prescribed—are to be prudently weighed by the confessor and no one may take advantage of it without his advice. The confessor may give such advice either in the internal sacramental forum or in the internal non-sacramental forum, even once and for all so long as the circumstances of the same sickness persist.

[1190] Holy Office, Jan. 16, 1953: AAS 45, 47–51.
[1191] See Can. 808 and 8589, § 1.
[1192] See Pius XII, Instruction *Christus Dominus* (1953), no. 1.

3. Priests who are sick, even though not confined to bed, may also avail themselves of the dispensation whether they are about to celebrate Mass or to receive the most Holy Eucharist.

REGARDING PRIESTS IN SPECIAL CIRCUMSTANCES

(Const., nos. III and IV.)

4. Priests who are not sick, who are to celebrate Mass *a) at a late hour* (i.e., after 9 a.m.), or *b) after heavy work in the sacred ministry* (e.g., from early morning or for a long time), or *c) after a long journey* (i.e., at least about two kilometers on foot, or proportionately longer according to the type of vehicle used, bearing in mind also the difficulties of the journey or of the person), may take something non-alcoholic to drink.

5. The three cases mentioned above are such that they include all the circumstances in which the legislator intends to grant the above dispensation and therefore any interpretation which would widen the faculties given must be avoided.

6. Priests who are in these circumstances may take something by way of a drink either once or several times, provided they fast for one hour prior to the celebration of Mass.

7. Furthermore, all priests who are to celebrate two or three Masses may in their earlier Masses take the two ablutions prescribed by the rubrics of the Missal, but using water only, which according to the new principle does not break the fast.

But any priest who celebrates three Masses without a break on Christmas Day or on All Souls' Day must observe the rubrics concerning the ablutions.

8. If, however, through inadvertence a priest who has to celebrate two or three Masses takes wine also in the ablution, he is not forbidden to celebrate the second or third Mass.

REGARDING THE FAITHFUL IN SPECIAL CIRCUMSTANCES

(Const., no. V.)

9. The faithful also who cannot observe the eucharistic fast not because of sickness, but *because of some other grave inconvenience*, may take something non-alcoholic to drink, provided they fast for one hour before receiving Holy Communion.

10. Three causes of *grave inconvenience* are set forth and no additions may be made to them.

a) Tiring work undertaken before Holy Communion.

The type of people affected are workers in factories, transport, shipping, or other public utility services who have to work day and night shifts; also, those who whether from duty or charity have to stay up at night (e.g., nurses, night-watchmen, and so on); also, pregnant women and mothers of families who before they can go to church must spend a long time on domestic duties; and so on.

b) The late hour at which Holy Communion is received.

Many of the faithful have to wait until a late hour before they can have a priest amongst them to say Mass; there are many children for whom it is too heavy a burden to go to church, receive Holy Communion, and then return home for breakfast; and so on.

c) *A long journey to be made* in order to reach the church.

As already indicated [no. 4], for present purposes a journey is considered long if it is not less than two kilometers by foot or proportionately longer by vehicle according to the type of vehicle used, taking into account the difficulties of the journey and of the individual.

11. The causes of grave inconvenience are to be considered prudently by the confessor in the internal sacramental or non-sacramental forum, and the faithful who are not fasting cannot receive the most Holy Eucharist without his advice. The confessor may give such advice *once and for all* as long as the same cause of grave inconvenience persists.

REGARDING EVENING MASSES

(Const. no. VI.)

By virtue of the constitution, *local ordinaries*[1193] *have the faculty of permitting the celebration of evening Mass in their own territory when circumstances make this necessary, notwithstanding the rule of Can. 821, § 1. For the common good sometimes requires that Mass be celebrated after midday: for example, for workers in certain industries where shift-work continues even on days of precept; for those categories of workers who are engaged on the mornings of Sundays and holy days, such as dock-workers; also, for those who gather together in one place in large numbers, sometimes coming long distances, to celebrate a religious or social occasion, and so on.*

12. *Nevertheless, such Masses may not be celebrated before four o'clock in the afternoon and only on certain days which are exclusively* defined as follows:

a) existing days of obligation in accordance with Can. 1247, § 1;

b) suppressed feasts, in accordance with the index published by the Sacred Congregation of the Council on Dec. 28, 1919;[1194]

c) the first Friday of the month;

d) other solemnities which are celebrated with a great gathering of people;

e) one day of the week, in addition to those mentioned above, if the good of special classes of people requires it.

13. Priests who celebrate Mass in the evening and the faithful who receive Holy Communion at such Masses may take *with proper moderation*, alcoholic drinks which are customarily taken with meals (e.g., wine, beer, and so on), spirits being excluded. Such drinks may be taken only *during a meal* which must be concluded three hours before the beginning of Mass or Communion. Before or after such

---

[1193] See CCL, Can. 198.
[1194] See AAS 12, 42–43.

meals they may take something in the form of a drink up to one hour before Mass or Communion, but *all alcoholic drinks* are excluded.

14. Priests may not celebrate Mass in the morning and evening of the same day unless they have express permission to say two or three Masses, according to the norm of Can. 806.

Likewise, the faithful cannot receive Holy Communion in the morning and evening of the same day according to the norm of Can. 857.

15. The faithful may receive Holy Communion *during Mass* or *immediately before or after*,[1195] even though they do not belong to the category of persons for whose benefit this Mass has been introduced, but they must observe all the above-mentioned rules relating to the eucharistic fast.

16. In territories where *missionary law* and not *the common law* is in force, ordinaries may allow evening Masses on all days of the week on the same conditions.

Directives Regarding the Execution of These Norms

17. Ordinaries must exercise great care to ensure that every abuse and irreverence toward the most Blessed Sacrament is avoided.

18. They must also take care that the new discipline is uniformly observed by all their subjects, who should be instructed that all faculties and dispensations, whether territorial or personal, heretofore granted by the Holy See, are abrogated.

19. The interpretation of the constitution and this instruction must faithfully follow the text and must not in any way extend the concessions which are already so favorable. With regard to customs which might differ from the new discipline, the clause should be borne in mind: "notwithstanding anything to the contrary, even if worthy of very special mention."

20. Ordinaries and priests who must avail themselves of the faculties granted by the Holy See should earnestly exhort the faithful to go to Mass and receive Holy Communion frequently and should promote with suitable means, especially preaching, that spiritual good in view of which the Supreme Pontiff Pius XII willed that the constitution should be published.

The Supreme Pontiff, in approving this instruction, decreed that it should be promulgated by publication in the *Acta Apostolicae Sedis* together with the Apostolic Constitution *Christus Dominus*.

From the Palace of the Holy Office, January 6, 1953.

+ I. Card. Pizzardo, Secretary.

A. Ottaviani, Assessor.

[1195] See CCL, Can. 846, § 1.

ABBREVIATIONS

The following abbreviations are cited in the text:

AAS   *Acta Apostolicæ Sedis*
CCL   1917 Code of Canon Law
DZ   The Sources of Catholic Dogma (Denzinger)
MIC   *Manuale Iuris Canonici* (Prümmer)
MTM *Manuale Theologiæ Moralis* (Prümmer)
ST   *Summa Theologiæ* (Aquinas)
TCCI Tradivox Catholic Catechism Index
TM   *Theologia Moralis* (Liguori)

INDEX

All references are given for paragraph numbers.

A

Abandoned children, Baptism of, 563

Abbess lacks jurisdiction in strict sense, 75

Abbot, as minister of ordination, 812; suspended if delays consecration, 776

Abduction, 520; an impediment to marriage, 901

Ablution in Baptism, 552

Abortion, 283; penalties for, 284. *See* Craniotomy

Abrogation of customs, 128; of law, 123

Absence of canons from choir, 377

Absolution, of accomplice, 719; from censures, 743; conditional, 652; of habitual sinners, 712; illegitimate, from censures most specially and specially reserved, 772; manner of, 650; of persons in occasion of sin, 711; of recidivists, 715; refusal or postponement of, 697; repetition of, 653; of reserved cases, 692; from sin, 648–653

Abstinence, days of, 497; exemption from, 498; law of, 497; subject and object of, 497; vice contrary to, 500

Abuse of the Sacrament of Penance; absolution of an accomplice, 719; inquiring after name of an accomplice, 717; solicitation, 725

Acceptance of law by subjects, 89

Accession, title to ownership, 257

Accidents in the Holy Eucharist. *See* Species

Accomplice, absolution of, 719; inquiring after name of, 668, 717; revelation of, 668

Accusation, false, of solicitation, 729; general, of sins, 646

Accused persons. *See* Criminals

Acolyte, order of, matter and form of, 808–809

Act, *conjugal. See* Conjugal act

| — | *external*, lacks morality, 57

| — | *heroic*, not subject to positive law, 79

| — | *human*: definition and kinds of, 11; principles of, 12–42; sources of morality of, 45–54

| — | *indifferent*, 55

| — | *internal*, as the object of human law, 78

Action, legal, ensuing from betrothal, 867

Acts, legitimate, of the Church, 748

Adjuration, definition and kinds of, 416; of the devil (*see* Exorcism)

Administration of property belonging to child, 246; belonging to wife, 245

Administration of the Sacraments, 539–545

Admonition, given by confessor, 696; prior to censure, 738

Adoption, legal, 919

Adoration, definition and kinds of, 381; of the cross, 381

Divine Office, anticipation of Matins in, 379; obligation of, 377; order of, 379; reasons excusing from, 380; time of, 379

Divining rod, 432

Divorce, absolute, 848; and advocates, 949; imperfect, request for, 852; judicial declaration of, 948

Docility, part of prudence, 236

Domicile, definition of, 84; for marriage, 878; for ordination, 814; for publication of banns, 872

Doorkeeper, Order of, matter and form in, 808, 809

Double Effect, principle of, 23

Doubt, definition of, 146; kinds of, 146; obligation of doubtful law, 148; possessor in doubtful faith, 308; practical, prevents action, 147; regarding faith, 189; regarding jurisdiction, 682; regarding matrimonial impediments, 923; regarding sins, 667

Dowry, 930; of wife, 245

Drugs, abuse of, 502; addictive, 504

Drunkenness, definition of, 502; sinfulness of, 503

Dueling, definition and sinfulness of, 279; and obligation of restitution, 279; penalties for, 279

Dulia, 381

Duress, an impediment to marriage, 900

E

Easter duties, law relating to, 597; place for fulfillment of, 597

Ecclesiastical property, 248

Education, of children, 462; non-Catholic, punished by excommunication, 773

Effects of sin to be confessed, 667

Eggs, on days of fasting, 488

Election of an evil deputy, 467

Electric light before the Blessed Sacrament, 608

Emancipation, of children, 246; of women, 464

Embryo, Baptism of, 565

Employers, obligations of, 465; vows of servants annulled by, 399

Enclosure, religious, violation of, 770

End, cessation of, annuls law, 124; definition and kinds of, 4; and evil means, 53; God as ultimate end, 6; grace necessary for attainment of ultimate, 8; influence on morality of acts, 52–53

Enemies, love of, 223; reconciliation with, 223

Envy, definition of, 175; effects of, 175; remedies for, 175; sinfulness of, 175

Epikeia, use of, in laws, 105; virtue of, 472

Epileptics incur irregularity, 830

Episcopal law, 75

Episcopal reservation, 687

Episcopate, matter and form of, 808, 810

Equiprobabilism, 153

Equity. *See* Epikeia

F

Faculties, new, granted to bishops. *See* Appendix

Faith, communication with persons not possessing, 205; concealment of, 198; dangers to, 204; definition of, 186; necessity of, 192–198; object of, 188; pretense of, 198; profession of, 196; properties of, 189; subject of, 187; vices opposed to, 199

Faith, good, in possessing another's property, 305; in prescription, 295

Falsehood, in dispensation, 116

Family wage, 355

Fast, *eucharistic*, dispensation from, 596; exemption from law of, 596; matter of, 595; period of, 595; violation of, 595. *See also* Appendix II.

|—| *prior to Confirmation*, 579

Fasting, causes excusing from, 498; ecclesiastical, 487; kinds of, 487; subjects of, 494; time of, 493

Fault, theological and juridical, in unjust damage, 270

Fear, in censures, 738, 742; in contracts, 319; definition of, 28; gift of, 180; an impediment to marriage, 900; influence of, on morality of acts, 30–32; kinds of, 29; passion of, 34; in vows, 386

Fear of hell in attrition, 657

Feasts, Mass for people on, 619; observance of, 418; ordinations on, 834

Fetishism, 526

Fetus, Baptism of, premature, 565; killing of, 283

Fidelity, oath of, 409

Finder of lost property, rights and obligations of, 256

Fish on days of abstinence, 497

Fishing, 253

Fixed altar, 795

Flattery, opposed to the virtue of politeness, 470

Flight, from occasions of sin, 711; passion of, 34

Font, baptismal, 568

Fontes moralitatis, 45–54

Food, petty thefts of, 265

Forbidden books, retaining, 766

Foresight, and aid to prudence, 236

Fori privilegium, 446

Form of the Sacraments, 528; of Baptism, 553; of Confirmation, 577; of the Eucharist, 589; of Marriage, 842; of Orders, 809–810; of Penance, 648; of Extreme Unction, 799; conditional, 529; immutability of, 529; necessity of, 529; repetition of, 529

Form of the virtues, 184

Form, correct, lack of, in betrothals, 866; in contracts, 320; in the Sacraments, 532; in wills, 329

Fornication, definition of, 518; restitution arising from, 285; sinfulness of, 518

Fortitude, gift of, 180; parts of, and vices opposed to, 475, 480; virtue of, 473

Forum, internal and external, for absolution from censures, 746; for matrimonial dispensations, 921

Fraternal correction, conditions for, and manner and obligation of, 228

Freedom, lack of, an impediment to ordination, 832; violation of, 767

Freedom to marry, 869

Nocturn to be recited by ordinands, 833
Non-Catholics. *See* Heretics; Pagans; Schismatics
Non-Catholic schools, 206
Novices, confession of, 684
Number, of matrimonial impediments, 887, 897; of sins to be mentioned in confession, 667
Numerical distinction of sins, 163
Nuns, attempting marriage, 770; confession of, 685; enclosure of, 770
Nuptial blessing, 881

O

Oaths, conditions for valid, 410; in contracts, 322; definition of, 409; dispensation from, 414; interpretation of, 413; kinds of, 409; obligation of, 411; violation of, 415
Obedience, of children, 461; definition of, 459; object of, 459; of servants, 465; vices opposed to, 460; of wife, 463
Object, moral, definition of, 46; specifies sins, 47
Observance, vain, 434
Obstacles to the grace of the Sacraments, 522
Occasions of sin, absolution of persons in, 711; definition of, 709; kinds of, 710
Occasions of unjust damage, 271
Occult compensation, 269
Occult matrimonial impediments, 885, 926–927
Occult sinner, 543
Occupancy, 251
Offspring. *See* Children
Oils for Confirmation, 575; for Extreme Unction, 798
Onanism, 863; cooperation in, 864; duty of confessor toward, 865; remedies for, 865; sinfulness of, 863
Opinion, definition of, 147; of confessor, cannot be imposed on penitent, 156
Opium, use of, 502, 504
Oratory, celebration of Mass and administration of Holy Communion in, 424, 633; hearing Mass in, 424; kinds of, 424
Order, of charity, 224; of fraternal correction, 228; of making restitution, 310
Ordinary, 878
Ordinary jurisdiction, 679–680
Ordination, canonical titles for, 823; minister of, 812–815; prerequisites to, 816–823; record of, 835; rites, time and place of, 833–834
Oriental Rite, and marriage, 874
Ovariotomy, not an impediment to marriage, 902
Ownership, definition of, 240; kinds of, 240; means of acquiring, 250; object of, 241; subject of, 244–249

P

Pagans, communication with, 205; dissolution of marriages of, 849; marriages of, subject to civil authority, 841; Mass for, 617; not subject directly to laws of Church, 80
Pall, 637
Pamphlets, evil, 766

INDEX

BENEDICTUS
BOOKS

Our mission is to publish authentically Catholic books
that are traditional, accessible, and beautiful.

Benedictus Books takes its name from the opening Latin phrase of the Canticle of Zechariah, prayed daily in the Catholic Church since the earliest centuries. Our logo evokes the antiquity of Gregorian chant and the illuminated manuscript tradition, emphasizing continuity with the faith and worship of the past and the continuing relevance of our sacred patrimony today.

Benedictus Books was established in 2021 with the launch of our acclaimed periodical *Benedictus*, the "Traditional Catholic Companion"—a daily devotional drawing on the theological riches and customs of the ancient Roman Rite, and allowing for a deeper experience of the traditional Latin Mass, liturgical calendar, and writings of countless saints and theologians. This periodical reflects the three core values of Benedictus Books:

TRADITIONAL. We are committed to preserving and handing on the Faith of our forefathers without diminution or change, publishing works that are both inspired by and conformable to traditional Catholic doctrine, liturgy, and spirituality. Our primary focus is on republishing reliably orthodox works that help to promote the interior life and sanctification of the domestic church through classical forms of prayer and worship.

ACCESSIBLE. Recognizing that many aspects of Catholic doctrine, liturgy, and custom have become obscured in recent decades, we place an emphasis on texts that explain and assist readers in mining the vast theological wealth that is contained and expressed in the traditional Roman Rite, as well as those writings of saints and scholars that have been profoundly shaped by the same.

BEAUTIFUL. Rooted in the perennial tradition of Western sacred art, we believe that texts treating such exalted subjects deserve a truly beautiful and durable presentation. We invest extensive time and meticulous care to create inspiring new typesettings with rich ornament and illustration, crisp typography, clean layouts, and classic bindings to make every book as pleasing to hold and look at as it is to read.

In order to be worthy of the noble content they contain, all of our books are crafted to the most exacting standards, allowing these priceless treasures from our Catholic tradition to be cherished for years to come.